DISCARD

LIBRARY
UNIVERSITY OF NEW HAVEN

THE YALE EDITION

OF

HORACE WALPOLE'S

CORRESPONDENCE

EDITED BY W. S. LEWIS

VOLUME THIRTY-EIGHT

HORACE WALPOLE'S CORRESPONDENCE

WITH

HENRY SEYMOUR CONWAY
LADY AILESBURY
LORD AND LADY HERTFORD
LORD BEAUCHAMP
HENRIETTA SEYMOUR CONWAY

II

EDITED BY W. S. LEWIS
LARS E. TROIDE
EDWINE M. MARTZ
AND
ROBERT A. SMITH

NEW HAVEN
YALE UNIVERSITY PRESS
LONDON · OXFORD UNIVERSITY PRESS

1974

© 1974 by Yale University

Printed in the United States of America

All rights reserved. This book may not be reproduced, in whole or in part, in any form (except by reviewers for the public press), without written permission from the publishers.

Library of Congress catalog card number: 52-4945

International standard book number: 0-300-01764-2

DA
483
W2
A12
v. 38

TABLE OF CONTENTS

VOLUME II

75. 371. 7

LIST OF ILLUSTRATIONS

VOLUME II

HORACE WALPOLE'S CORRESPONDENCE

To CONWAY, Friday 19 January 1759

Printed from *Works* v. 61–2.

Arlington Street, January 19, 1759.

I HOPE the Treaty of Sluys advances rapidly.[1] Considering that your own court is as new to you as Monsieur de Bareil[2] and his, you cannot be very well entertained: the joys of a Dutch fishing town and the incidents of a cartel will not compose a very agreeable history. In the meantime you do not lose much: though the Parliament is met,[3] no politics are come to town: one may describe the House of Commons like the price of stocks: debates, nothing done. Votes, under par. Patriots, no price. Oratory, book shut. Love and war are as much at a stand: neither the Duchess of Hamilton[4] nor the expeditions are gone off yet.[5] Prince Edward[6] has asked to go to Quebec, and has been refused.[7] If I was sure they would refuse me, I would ask to go thither too. I should not dislike about as much laurel as I could stick in my window at Christmas.

We are next week to have a serenata at the Opera House for the King of Prussia's birthday:[8] it is to begin, *Viva Georgio, e Federigo viva!* It will, I own, divert me to see my Lord Temple whispering *for* this alliance,[9] on the same bench on which I have so often seen

1. Mr Conway was sent to Sluys to settle a cartel for prisoners with the French. Monsieur de Bareil was the person appointed by the French Court for the same business (HW); see *ante* 10 Dec. 1758, n. 1; *post* 21 Jan. 1759, n. 13, 28 Jan. *bis*, n. 6.

2. Louis-Jacques-Charles (ca 1709–73), Marquis du Barail; Brig-Gen. 1744; maréchal de camp, 1748; Gov. of Dunkirk, 1754; Lt-Gen., 18 Dec. 1758 (*Répertoire . . . de la Gazette de France*, ed. de Granges de Surgères, 1902–6, ii. 239; [Ludovic], Comte de Colleville and F. Saint-Christo, *Les Ordres du roi*, [1925], p. 265; *Mercure de France* Feb. 1759, i. 209).

3. On 16 Jan.

4. Elizabeth Gunning, Duchess dowager of Hamilton (HW).

5. The expedition to Quebec did not leave until 13 Feb. (MANN v. 266).

6. Afterwards created Duke of York (HW).

7. HW also mentions this to Mann 9 Feb. (MANN v. 267).

8. 'We hear that there is now in rehearsal, and will soon be exhibited at the King's Theatre in the Haymarket, a grand musical entertainment (with dances, scenes, and other proper decorations) the chief subject of which is to celebrate the glorious alliance between Great Britain and Prussia; and the happy effects which are naturally expected to accrue from thence, to the liberties of Europe' (*Daily Adv.* 18 Jan.). The entertainment, entitled *Il Tempio della Gloria*, by Gioacchino Cocchi (ca 1715–1804), was first performed on 31 Jan. and repeated 20 Feb. (ibid. 31 Jan., 20 Feb.); HW describes it to Chute 1 Feb. (CHUTE 105–6 and n. 8).

9. With Prussia. Temple had long been in opposition, but was Privy Seal in the present administration.

him whisper *against* all Germany. The new opera pleases universally,[10] and I hope will yet hold up its head. Since Vanneschi[11] is cunning enough to make us sing *the roast beef of old Germany*, I am persuaded it will revive: politics are the only hotbed for keeping such a tender plant as Italian music alive in England.

You are so thoughtless about your dress, that I cannot help giving you a little warning against your return. Remember, everybody that comes from abroad is *censé* to come from France, and whatever they wear at their first reappearance immediately grows the fashion. Now if, as is very likely, you should through inadvertence change hats with a master of a Dutch smack, Offley[12] will be upon the watch, will conclude you took your pattern from Monsieur de Bareil, and in a week's time we shall all be equipped like Dutch skippers. You see I speak very disinterestedly; for, as I never wear a hat myself, it is indifferent to me what sort of hat I don't wear. Adieu! I hope nothing in this letter, if it is opened, will affect *the conferences,* nor hasten our rupture with Holland.[13] Lest it should, I send it to Lord Holderness's office;[14] concluding, like Lady Betty Waldegrave,[15] that the government never suspect what they send under their own covers.

Yours ever,

HOR. WALPOLE

10. During the 1758–59 season there were 55 performances of five operas (*London Stage* Pt IV, ii. 681–2).

11. Abbate Vanneschi, an Italian, and director of the opera (HW). Francesco Vaneschi (fl. 1732–59) (MANN i. 141, n. 9, supplemented by this letter). The season 1758–9 is the last in which he is mentioned in connection with the opera in London in the *London Stage*.

12. John Offley (?1717–84), M.P. for Bedford 1747–54, Orford 1754–68, East Retford 1768–74; groom of the Bed-

chamber 1757–62. He was a man of fashion, prominent in gaming circles, and a friend of Lord Lincoln and a close connection of Newcastle (Namier and Brooke iii. 223).

13. For fear of a war with the Dutch at the time, see MANN v. 260 and n. 1, 268 and n. 1. The points in dispute were gradually adjusted during the winter and spring (ibid. v. 285–6 and n. 7, 287–8, n. 4, 290–1 and nn. 7, 8).

14. The Secretary of State's office.

15. See *ante* 1 Aug. 1758, n. 28,

From CONWAY, Sunday 21 January 1759

Printed from the MS now WSL, formerly Rutnam. Previously printed *Fraser's Magazine*, 1850, xli. 433–4.

Sluys, 21 January 1759.

Dear Horry,

I EXPECT to be abused, at least I deserve it, for having let so many days go without writing a line to you, being with new people in a new place and in a new situation. The very truth is that though I have been idle in fact, I have been intentionally the best correspondent in the world and have not writ to anybody literally to nobody but Lady Ailesbury and my letters of business.[1] But it has happened to me as it generally does, I believe, to those in business, that I make bad calculations of my time and the business itself, which is little, appears still less till one sets about it, and then one finds it multiply under one's hands and fill up the time of the post to the last minute.

I landed at Ostend on the 14 in the morning[2] after a most excellent passage of eleven hours, found no difficulty at all at the place, had few questions asked me, and after making my bow to the lieutenant de Roi[3] who commands there, came away for Bruges in less than half an hour with three French officers[4] who were going to join Monsieur du Barail there,[5] having with great regret left my

---

1. To Vct Barrington, Secretary at War. Conway's official correspondence, in the Public Record Office, W.O. 1/863, ff. 487–576, includes letters dated 19 Jan. 1759 (ff. 487–90) enclosing a list of ranks of the army and ransoms (ff. 491–7); 24 Jan. 1759 (ff. 499–502) enclosing a draft of the treaty and convention (ff. 503–28); 31 Jan. 1759 (ff. 535–8) enclosing a copy of Barail's letter of 31 Jan. to Belleisle (f. 539); 4 Feb. 1759 (ff. 541–3); and the cartel 6 Feb. 1759 (ff. 545–76).

2. 'Ostend, Jan. 17. On the 14th instant a vessel arrived from Dover with two English officers [Conway and, mistakenly, Baron Dieskau], in quality of commissioners, who went directly to l'Ecluse in Flanders, to confer with Marquis de Baraile, Governor of Dunkirk, concerning an exchange of French and English prisoners of war' (*Daily Adv.* 27 Jan.; see also Conway to Devonshire Jan. 1759, Chatsworth MSS, 416/59).

3. Louis Guiguer wrote Barrington from Ostend 10 April 1759, 'I have made my visit of ceremony to Monsieur de St Aldegonde, the Lieutenant de Roy, who commands here, during the absence of the Governor Monsieur Le Comte de la Mothe' (W.O. 1/863, f. 601).

4. Not identified.

5. 'Brussels, Jan. 14. The Governor of Dunkirk went yesterday to Sluys, to negotiate the exchange of French and English prisoners, in conjunction with an English officer commissioned for that purpose' (*Daily Adv.* 24 Jan.).

poor *compagnon de voyage* le Baron D'ieskau[6] much out of order there.[7]

My new companions were very agreeable, polite men; and the *rencontre* of Monsieur du Barail at Bruges[8] was a very lucky one, as it abridged or in a manner annihilated all disagreeable ceremony between us. We went to a French play there together and were invited to the same house where we played at cards and supped. We embarked next morning in a Dutch trachschuit[9] together, and landing within less than a little league of this place, got all into a little Dutch wagon covered with oil-cloth, nine of us in a vehicle made for six; and in this curious equipage jumbled through a miserable deep road, and having not so much as sent a servant before us (for I found my cook[10] who set out a week before at Dover), we drove in that genteel equipage immediately to the commandant's[11] door, mistook it, and made a visit to another, but content with that went to look out for an inn, a dinner, etc. We soon pitched upon one, had all our quarters laid out, and from that moment have lived together if not a gay life, which I think even Frenchmen can scarce do in this good town, yet with the greatest ease and familiarity. We keep but one table at which we are nine of our two families besides an accidental Dutch or Swiss officer whom we invite.

We walk and play a little at cards and do our business, and in that way our time passes much better than I could have expected.

Monsieur du Barail is as fair and open a man in business as he is

---

6. Lt-Gen. Baron Ludwig August von Dieskau (1701–67), German officer in the French service, maréchal de camp and commander-in-chief of the French forces in North America, 1755; Lt-Gen., 1762. He had been a prisoner of war since being captured at the first battle of Lake George 8 Sept. 1755 (CHUTE 257 and n. 4a). French sources give his first names as Jean Erdman (*Dictionnaire de biographie française*, 1933– , xi. 312).

7. 'I left the poor Baron Dieskau there by no means well having had a fever all the night on board and his lameness much increased and grown very troublesome with the effect of it. I don't know whether he fell in your Grace's way but he is a sensible, a knowing and in all appearance an exceeding good sort of man' (Conway to Devonshire Jan. 1759, Chatsworth MSS, 416/59).

8. 'Our rencontre at Bruges and the little difficulties we encountered together from the similar awkwardness of our situation, having neither of us a servant before or the least preparation for our reception here, threw us into a state of familiarity which has continued with mutual comfort to us; and with the help of an excellent disposition both in him and those with him made our life much more agreeable than anything else could in such a place' (ibid.).

9. An anglicized form of 'trekschuit,' 'a canal- or river-boat drawn by horses, carrying passengers and goods, as in common use in Holland' (OED *sub* 'trekschuit').

10. Not identified.

11. Not identified.

amiable and polite out of it,[12] and, as far [as] depended upon us, it was soon settled, but we wait and may wait some time for approbations from our Courts[13] and the forms of business still.

He is just made a lieutenant-general,[14] by which, however, I am very glad I don't lose him, as he has orders from his Court at the same time to continue his negotiation with me.

By the last post he had an account of eighteen persons of the first rank and distinction taken up in Portugal with a list of their names;[15] this looks very serious, and shows that the story of the fall in his chamber or stairs[16] had a meaning which they have conducted with great secrecy and policy.

The death of the Princess *Gouvernante*[17] will, I doubt, make

12. Conway wrote of him to Devonshire Jan. 1759 (loc. cit.), 'His character and behaviour have in everything more than answered the best I had heard of him, he is quite a soldier but in all appearance both an honest and polite one, not a smooth outside, courtly politesse, but of that good kind that seems to come from the heart . . . I found such a disposition in Monsieur du Barail as made it quite easy between us so that had we come more authorized and instructed from our Courts it would have been over by this time.' Conway also wrote Barrington 19 Jan. 1759, 'I think I never knew anybody less inclined to make difficulties than Monsieur du Bareil' (W.O. 1/863, f. 488).

13. Conway wrote Barrington 24 Jan. 1759, 'Monsieur du Bareil having last night received a courier from his Court with their answers to the propositions which he had sent there agreeable to what I had the honour before to inform your Lordship, and as that answer contains I think in effect their consent to the several articles mentioned, I take the first opportunity to acquaint your Lordship therewith. . . . And as Monsieur du Bareil has received a full power to make any other little alterations in the treaty that might tend to the perfection of it, and at the same time to conclude and sign it without any other reference to his Court, he has allowed me to send the enclosed copy that in case my powers on the return to my dispatches should not be equally extensive and that it should be

thought necessary to send over a draft of the treaty for approbation as little time as possible may be lost. If my instructions should appear sufficient on their arrival, I shall then proceed to give all proper dispatch to the business agreeable thereto' (W.O. 1/863, ff. 499–500). Barrington's replies of 23 and 30 Jan. were acknowledged by Conway on 31 Jan. and 4 Feb.; see *post* 28 Jan. 1759 *bis*, nn. 2, 6.

14. On 18 Dec. 1758 (*ante* 19 Jan. 1759, n. 2); Conway also mentions this in his letter to Devonshire Jan. 1759.

15. An attempt had been made to assassinate the K. of Portugal 3 Sept. 1758. The exact nature of the attack had been partially concealed at the time and a full 'official' account was not published until 9 Dec. Accounts, presumably similar to those Barail had received, that the conspirators had been arrested, reached London on 15 Jan. (*Daily Adv.* 16 Jan.), and a list of eleven of the conspirators was printed in the *London Gazette* No. 9861, 13–16 Jan. Ten of the accused had already been executed on 13 Jan. For the affair, see MANN v. 250–1 and nn. 2–6, 264–5 and nn. 8–9, 267 and n. 7; MORE 9 and nn. 3–5.

16. The official account given out at the time of the assassination attempt was that the King, in passing through a gallery to go to the Queen's apartments, had fallen and bruised his right arm (ibid. 9, n. 3; MANN v. 265, n. 9).

17. The Princess of Orange (*ante* 24 June 1748 NS) died 12 Jan. She had been *Gouvernante* of the Dutch Republic since

some stir here. It's said an augmentation of 25 ships is already determined.[18] She preserved her senses and courage and did business to her last moments. The King[19] and the Princess Dowager[20] are declared tutors to the young Prince, with the Duke of Wolfembuttle,[21] and the Prince of Nassau Welbourg[22] to marry the Princess.[23] All this probably you know and much more, but one must tell some Dutch news, and Sluys does not abound.

We have had the finest weather in the world and been in the best health without either getting drunk or smoking tobacco, which is astonishing. The wind is now got to the east and the frost just begun which is to preserve us from all evils and pinch our toes off.

Yours most affectionately,

H.S.C.

TO HENRIETTA SEYMOUR CONWAY, Saturday 27 January 1759

Missing; a 'card' mentioned *post* Sept. 1768.

---

her husband's death in 1751, during the minority of her son; see MANN iv. 279; v. 260, n. 5.

18. 'The important resolution of the States of Holland, for equipping twenty-five men of war was carried to the States General last Wednesday [17 Jan.]' (*Daily Adv.* 2 Feb., *sub* The Hague 23 Jan.). The council of state of the Republic did not authorize them until 26 Feb. (MANN v. 269 and n. 2).

19. Her father, George II.

20. Her mother-in-law Marie Luise (1688–1765), of Hesse-Cassel, m. (1709)

Johann Wilhelm Friso, Prince of Orange, 1708 (Isenburg, *Stammtafeln*, ii. taf. 1). She and the King were declared honorary tutor and tutoress (*Daily Adv.* 22 Jan.).

21. Karl I (1713–80), Duke of Brunswick-Wolfenbüttel, 1735 (Isenburg, op. cit. i. taf. 73).

22. Karl Christian (1735–88), Prince of Nassau-Weilburg, 1753 (ibid. i. taf. 113).

23. Wilhelmina Carolina (1743–87), Princess of Orange, m. (1760) Karl Christian, Prince of Nassau-Weilburg. He had been anxious to marry her since 1756 (MONTAGU i. 187).

To Conway, Sunday 28 January 1759

Printed from *Works* v. 63–4.

Arlington Street, January 28, 1759.

YOU and Monsieur de Bareil may give yourselves what airs you please of settling cartels with expedition: you don't exchange prisoners with half so much alacrity as Jack Campbell[1] and the Duchess of Hamilton have exchanged hearts.[2] I had so little observed the negotiation, or suspected any, that, when your brother told me of it yesterday morning, I would not believe a tittle—I beg Mr Pitt's pardon, not an *iota*.[3] It is the prettiest match in the world—since yours—and everybody likes it but the Duke of Bridgwater[4] and Lord C———.[5] What an extraordinary fate is attached to those two women![6] Who could have believed that a Gunning would unite the two great houses of Campbell and Hamilton?[7] For my part, I expect to see my Lady Coventry Queen of Prussia. I would not venture to marry either of them these thirty years, for fear of being shuffled out of the world *prematurely*[8] to make room for the rest of their adventures. The first time Jack carries the Duchess into the Highlands, I am persuaded that some of his second-sighted subjects will see him in a winding-sheet, with a train of kings behind him as long as those in Macbeth.

We had a scrap of a debate on Friday on the Prussian and Hessian treaties.[9] Old Vyner[10] opposed the first, in a pity to that *poor*

1. The present Duke of Argyll (HW). He was Lady Ailesbury's brother.

2. They were married 3 Feb. (*Notes and Queries* 1905, 10th ser., iv. 384–5).

3. Perhaps a habitual expression of Pitt's; HW reports that in a speech of Nov. 1758 Pitt 'protested, that at the peace he would not give up an iota of our Allies for any British consideration' (*Mem. Geo. II* iii. 150).

4. Francis Egerton (1736–1803), 3d D. of Bridgwater. According to Lord Chesterfield, the Duchess of Hamilton had refused him (Chesterfield to his son 2 Feb., *Letters*, ed. Dobrée, 1932, v. 2339).

5. Presumably, as previous editors have assumed, George William Coventry (1722–1809), 6th E. of Coventry, the Duchess's brother-in-law.

6. The Gunning sisters.

7. The rivalry of the two families had

been bitter for generations. HW also comments on the union of the families through this marriage to Chute 1 Feb. (Chute 105) and to Mann 9 Feb. (Mann v. 267–8), and inserted it in his 'Strange Occurrences,' *Works* iv. 366.

8. The 6th D. of Hamilton had died in his 34th year of a cold caught while hunting (gec).

9. On 19 Jan. Pitt presented the convention concluded 7 Dec. 1758 with the K. of Prussia, and the treaty concluded 17 Jan. 1759 with the Landgrave of Hesse-Cassel; they were referred to committee of supply 26 Jan., and voted 29 Jan. The subsidy to the K. of Prussia was £670,000, and to the Landgrave of Hesse £60,000 (*Journals of the House of Commons* xxviii. 362–3, 379, 382; *London Chronicle* 25–7 Jan., v. 93).

10. Robert Vyner (ca 1685–1777), M.P.

woman, as he called her, the Empress Queen.[11] Lord Strange[12] objected to the gratuity of £60,000 to the Landgrave, unless words were inserted to express his receiving that sum in full of all demands.[13] If Hume Campbell had cavilled at this favourite treaty, Mr Pitt could scarce have treated him with more haughtiness;[14] and, what is far more extraordinary, Hume Campbell could scarce have taken it more dutifully. This *long* day was over by half an hour after four.

As you and Monsieur de Bareil are on such amicable terms, you will take care to soften to him a new conquest we have made. Keppel[15] has taken the Island of Gorée.[16] You great ministers know enough of its importance; I need not detail it. Before your letters came we had heard of the death of the Princess Royal:[17] you will find us black and all black. Lady Northumberland and the great ladies put off their assemblies: diversions begin again tomorrow with the mourning.[18]

You perceive, London cannot furnish half so long a letter as the little town of Sluys; at least I have not the art of making one out. In truth, I believe I should not have writ this unless Lady A. had bid me; but she does not care how much trouble it gives me, provided it amuses you for a moment. Good night!

Yours ever,

HOR. WALPOLE

Great Grimsby 1710–13, Lincolnshire 1724–61. He is 'Old' to distinguish him from his son Robert (1717–99), M.P. Okehampton 1754–61, Lincoln 1774–84, Thirsk 1785–96.

11. He had opposed the Prussian subsidy treaty as a monstrous expense, saying 'we should soon be doing the same for the Queen of Hungary,' and 'gave a single negative' to the question (BM Add. MSS 32887, ff. 351, 355, quoted Namier and Brooke iii. 589; Chesterfield, op. cit. v. 2339).

12. James Smith Stanley (1717–71), erroneously styled Lord Strange; M.P. Lancashire 1741–71.

13. When Pitt appealed to him, he moved no amendment to this effect, but voted against the treaty (Namier and Brooke iii. 453).

14. An allusion to the debate of 10 Dec. 1755 when Pitt, then opposing subsidy

treaties with Russia and Hesse, had attacked Hume Campbell, once his friend and ally, but who was then defending the treaties for the government (*Mem. Geo. II* ii. 107, 113–14; Namier and Brooke ii. 653–4; HW to Bentley 17 Dec. 1755, CHUTE 262).

15. Hon. Augustus Keppel (*ante* ca 15 Feb. 1752 OS, n. 18) had been appointed commander of the expedition to Gorée in Sept. 1758.

16. Off Cape Verde on the West African coast, on 29 Dec. The news, which had arrived on the 27th, was published in a *London Gazette Extraordinary* 29 Jan.

17. The Princess of Orange was the eldest dau. of George II. News of her death reached London on the morning of the 20th (*Letters from George III to Lord Bute 1756–1766,* ed. Sedgwick, 1939, p. 22; *Daily Adv.* 22 Jan.).

18. The Lord Chamberlain's orders for

PS. I forgot to tell you that the King has granted my Lord Marischall's[19] pardon, at the request of Monsieur de Knyphausen.[20] I believe the Pretender himself could get his attainder reversed if he would apply to the King of Prussia.

From CONWAY, Sunday 28 January 1759

Printed from the MS now WSL, formerly Rutnam. Previously printed *Fraser's Magazine*, 1850, xli. 434.

Sluys, 28 January 1759.

I DON'T know what art you have of drawing news and entertainment from a dull town but so it is, and your manner of saying you have nothing to say contradicts yourself so ingeniously and agreeably that one does not perceive the imposition. When somebody[1] asked me yesterday, What news from London? I was going to tell 'em a whole cargo of it, and when I hesitated and could not make out a scrap, I cursed my own memory that retains nothing. I don't know in fact any material difference between Sluys and London. London can but have no news and be excessive dull and so is Sluys. It is indeed superlatively dull and of a dullness that to my poor imagination can yield nothing [but] a *caput mortuum*. I don't know what your ingenuity might do, but for me I think the task of extracting fire from a cucumber is easier.

the mourning, to begin 28 Jan., are printed in the *London Gazette* No. 9863, 20–23 Jan.

19. George Keith (1693–1778), 9th E. Marischal, had been attainted for his part in the Jacobite rising of 1715. He also took part in the rising of 1719, but subsequently entered the K. of Prussia's service and had been his ambassador at Paris and Madrid. Pitt informed Andrew Mitchell, the British minister to Prussia, on 26 Jan. that the King had granted the pardon; it was mentioned in the newspapers on 2 Feb.; and Frederick himself notified Marischal of it 11 Feb. and sent his acknowledgments to England on the 12th (*Chatham Corr.* i. 400; *Daily Adv.* 2 Feb.; Frederick II, *Œuvres*, Berlin, 1846–57, xx. 278; idem, *Politische Correspondenz*, Berlin, 1879–1939, xviii. 70). The

pardon did not pass through all the forms until 29 May (GEC; Lord Marischal to Pitt 30 July, *Chatham Corr.* i. 415).

20. Dodo Heinrich (1729–89), Freiherr von Knyphausen; Prussian minister to France 1754–6, to England 1758–63 (MANN v. 258, n. 14; MORE 12, n. 18). Frederick himself had in fact written to George II on 6 Jan. requesting the pardon; however, he had also instructed Knyphausen to press it on the same day, and had discussed it with Mitchell at about the same time, saying that he would consider it 'as a personal favour done to himself' (Frederick II, *Politische Correspondenz*, xviii. 5, 11–12; idem, *Œuvres*, xx. 276, 278–9; *Chatham Corr.* i. 395).

————

1. Written over 'If anybody had.'

You have heard all my history already, how friendly and prettily we live amongst one another, and how rapidly our part of the treaty advanced; and that is all our history—the whole plot and *dénouement,* after which it was fit to come away. But these Dutch winds, not so quick in their operations, have hung sluggishly in one point and prevented any return to my very first letters,[2] and it will be on Monday or Tuesday next a fortnight since I wrote 'em.

As to the rest, we have walked *a-coursing* one day, another day round the ramparts, one day three miles north, and another three miles south upon the same dull, dirty plain. What materials for an history! They won't even squeeze into the French *mémoires* of any of my friends here. Last night we amused ourselves with a curious fellow, servant to one of the company, who fancies himself an actor, and without talking either French or Italian or any other language, acted and sung in both, much to our entertainment, and to the unspeakable astonishment of two Swiss officers who dined with us and thought the actor and the audience equally mad.

Yesterday was a day of events and had like to have been the epoch of a great revolution in the history of Sluys; for Genet,[3] who, you know, is very alert, happening to discover at the end of a fortnight that our landlord charged four guineas a day for our lodging, exclusive of eating, drinking, etc., this discovery caused a general fer-

2. Conway's first letter to Barrington ca 15 Jan. was apparently lost. In the second letter of 19 Jan. Conway wrote, 'We are very unlucky in our situation here in regard to the post which goes out for Flushing but twice a week, and just now not till four days hence so that I again take my chance by Ostend' (W.O. 1/863, f. 489). This letter was returned to Conway, as he wrote in his third letter on 24 Jan., 'I herewith enclose to your Lordship a letter I had the honour to write some days ago and which I thought gone off by Ostend from whence it was last night returned me' (ibid. f. 501). Conway received replies from Barrington dated 23 and 30 Jan., acknowledged in Conway's letters of 31 Jan. and 4 Feb. (ibid. ff. 535, 541).

3. Described by Conway in a letter to Devonshire 26 Oct. 1758 as 'an old, honest, and very faithful servant who has a large and increasing family. I have long promised him my endeavours to assist him

. . . I don't presume to ask for this thing [a vacancy as sergeant at arms] tho' a servant of my brother's had it but if your Grace bestows it otherwise . . . may I hope it will be reasonable to ask for £50 a year for poor old Genet' (Chatsworth MSS, 416/56). Conway wrote again 2 Nov. 1758, 'I thank your Grace for your promises to poor Genet who as I so nobly gave up all claim to the place I had begged I hope you'll think of in a more favourable light than a common solicitor and remember that he is very old, and can only be the better for his place whenever he has it by living to save for his family' (ibid. 416/57). On 26 July 1759 he wrote, 'I am most exceedingly obliged to you for your goodness to Genet; who is as happy and as thankful as possible, and will certainly comply most readily with any settlement your Grace thinks proper in regard to the deputyship on which head he writes to Mr Hans for instructions' (ibid. 416/60).

men[ta]tion, and Monsieur du Barail and I, entering immediately into *conférence,* agreed to change our lodging, nay, we actually sent and agreed for others and were to have moved this very day, when behold, our reasonable host who had ask[ed] five guineas and was a *loser* at four, had the goodness to come down to two. Now I have really mustered my forces and made my greatest effort. With the extraordinary helps I have mentioned, you may judge what Sluys is. Yet if Mr Offley or Sir Rob[ert] Rich[4] or any of our Bedchamber have a mind to a Sluys hat, and will say but half a word, they shall have it; and *sauve votre présence* I think it much better than *none* —I who am not a beau.

I am glad there are no politics in Parliament, and as glad that they are transferred to the Opera. If Mr Pitt would but sing an *ariette* in the House now, our diversions would be much mended, and one should attend Parliament with some pleasure.

Lady Ailesbury has told me a dismal story of poor Kniphausen and the wrath of Lady Mary[5] which would make an history like that of Achilles. She says she frightened him so that it would have made his hair stand on end if it had not been at his utmost pitch before. I doubt it's the only thing an angry lady can make stand on end, which is a truth worth Lady M.'s knowing. Adieu. Nobody ever longed for a *billet-doux* more than I for my Lord Barrington's dispatches,[6] which will decide my fate between Sluys and London and, if one must be in a dull town, I own I should choose the latter.[7]

Yours sincerely,

H.S.C.

4. (1685–1768), 4th Bt; field marshal, 1757. He had been a groom of the Bedchamber to George II (as P. of Wales and as King) since 1718.

5. Lady Mary Coke. No other reference to this incident has been found.

6. Conway wrote Barrington 31 Jan., 'I had the honour of your Lordship's letter of the 23d instant, signifying his Majesty's pleasure, upon some articles of the cartel,' and that he awaited the King's approbation of the draft of the treaty which had 'since been transmitted' (W.O. 1/863, f. 535). On 4 Feb. Conway wrote, 'I had the honour of your Lordship's of the 30th ultimo signifying his Majesty's

approbation of the cartel settled with the Marquis du Barail. . . . If Monsieur du Barail's courier should bring from his Court any letter or approbation equivalent to that his Majesty has been pleased to have writ in his name I shall have them inserted, if not, have agreed with him to put in words at the end expressing the intention or consent of our masters respectively to ratify the convention at the requisition of either party' (ibid. f. 542). The cartel was executed 6 Feb.

7. In his letter of 24 Jan. to Barrington Conway wrote, 'I shall take it as a particular kindness if your Lordship will be so good as to obtain an order for me to have

From CONWAY, Thursday 3 May 1759

Printed for the first time from the MS now WSL, formerly Rutnam.

Park Place, 3 May 1759.

Dear Horry,

LADY A. is in the utmost *embarras* about her party, her engagements and disengagements. She had appointed Monday, Mingotti's benefit,[1] thought herself in honour bound to alter her day, put it off till Wednesday when she herself and probably all her party are *prié* to Lady Bessborough. That's not the worst; she has received a most polite note from the Duchess of Bedford saying she intended to come to her on Monday but shall be gone out of town on Wednesday. Now as Lady Ailesbury had not a good right to put off her own day for Mingotti's and would be vastly sorry to do the least *impolitesse* to the Duchess of Bedford she much wishes that if you see her Grace you will tell her how unhappy Lady A. is about this strange *embarras,* that her concluding the Duchess would be engaged to Mingotti's was one of her reasons for putting off her party, but if the Duchess will either after Mingotti's concert or otherwise come and make a loo party it will extremely oblige Lady A. and she has sent you her list to make it up of any you may happen to meet with and she hopes you'll excuse this trouble and asks a thousand pardons, etc. This is for Monday next, observe.

Adieu. I can scarce afford myself time to finish my letter. The weather is grown so divine and the country such a paradise.

Yours most affectionately,

H. S. C.

---

one of Mr Minkette's boats as a cartel ship sent as before to Ostend' (W.O. 1/ 863, f. 502). On 4 Feb. Conway wrote, 'I am thankful for the leave he ['his Majesty'] is pleased to grant me to return to England, which I propose to defer no longer after I shall have received the list of our posts and ranks with my final orders thereon' (ibid. f. 543). He arrived in London 10 Feb. (*Daily Adv.* 13 Feb.).

1. 'By desire at the King's Theatre in the Haymarket, Monday, the 14th instant, will be performed a concert of vocal and instrumental music for the benefit of Signora Mingotti. Tickets half a guinea. To be had at her house in John Street, Berkeley Square' (*Daily Adv.* 4 May and successive days; *London Stage* Pt IV, ii. 728).

To CONWAY, ca Thursday 14 June 1759

Missing; answered *post* 17 June 1759.

From CONWAY, Sunday 17 June 1759

Printed for the first time from the MS now WSL, formerly Rutnam.

Park Place, 17 June 1759.

I AM much obliged to you for your care of my commission.[1] My patience in not inquiring after them [the orange trees] arose from a very natural cause exclusive of natural nonchalance of my temper, your promise to let me hear what was done about 'em. And I wish you had kept all your promises as well, but instead of letting me hear when you *did not come to Park Place* you promised to let me know when you did. This is rather a greater trial of my patience than the orange trees: but from a man absorbed in fine parties and genteel parties there's nothing to be expected. Of all dull things in the world a visit to relations is the dullest and the most unfashionable, even a voluntary one; there is but one thing more dull or more disagreeable and that is a forced one; so don't think I mean to scold you into it; quite the contrary, even though you passed us like the comet[2] and did not even give us a jog nor a brush with your tail nor bring your friend Mrs Clive[3] to give us a scorch *en passant,* I shall not complain. I desire you never to come till you choose it, and till it is agreeable to you if that can ever be for in thinking ourselves over, I am conscious we are rather stupid here, when we have no company which is the case at present; for I don't call company my old maiden sister,[4] nor my aide-de-camp[5] though the very best people in the world. They were good old times when cousins used to come with bag and baggage and cram for months together.—But now everybody is so fond of their own place they never think of any-

1. About orange trees; see below.
2. Halley's comet, first observed in England 30 April (MANN v. 294, n. 7).
3. Mrs Clive (*ante* 8 Nov. 1752) had occupied HW's cottage Little SH ('Cliveden') since 1754. HW frequently joked about her red complexion (e.g., MONTAGU ii. 97, 224, 245).
4. Hon. Henrietta Seymour Conway (*ante* 29 Aug. 1746 OS, n. 3).
5. Not identified.

body's else; all one's friends come to see one's place once at least, that's of course, and then leave each couple like Adam and Eve in their respective paradises to converse with the beasts and the serpents.

I am going to town tomorrow to endeavour to save my £150 though by the management of the ingenious Mr Crewys[6] I doubt in vain. Lady A. has writ to several friends and relations to contribute who have all refused but one hitherto.

I am very glad Guadalupe is taken[7] and I think the officers employed have done themselves great honour; though I don't find it will immediately contribute largely to the support of the German War;[8] I doubt much if it will suffice to put the militia in motion,[9] who seem as hard to move as any German army.

I think poor Lady Lyttelton's affair[10] is in a manner settled. Rich[11]

---

6. Probably Thomas Augustus Cruwys (d. 1770), clerk (ca 1739–59) to his uncle Henry Cruwys (1689–1760) and successor in his law business; solicitor to the Stamp Office (MANN ix. 440, n. 17). He was a chief collaborator in the drawing up of the colonial stamp tax of 1765 (Bernhard Knollenberg, *Origin of the American Revolution*, New York, 1960, pp. 221, 373).

7. Grande-Terre and Basse-Terre capitulated 1–2 May. The news arrived 13 June and was published in detail in a *London Gazette Extraordinary* 14 June. See also MANN v. 300–1.

8. The war in Germany was at a stalemate at this time (ibid. v. 294, 306 and n. 9).

9. A French invasion had been expected since mid-May, and attempts to assemble the militia on the coasts had been under way since the King's message on 30 May asking that the militia be 'drawn out and embodied' (ibid. v. 293–4 and nn. 2, 3, 296, n. 4, 299–300 and nn. 1–5; MONTAGU i. 238–9).

10. Her separation from her husband. The marriage, never very successful, had been acutely strained since 1756 because of her possible affair with one George Durant, and had reached a crisis in the spring of 1759 when, according to her husband, she 'made herself the talk of the town by writing love letters to Signor Tenduchi [an opera singer] one of which has been shown to several people.' He explained to his brother that, because he had been unable to obtain the letter, he was 'obliged to make it an amicable separation, without assigning any one special cause; but putting it on a general charge of misbehaviour, and an impossibility of my living with her either reputably or in quiet. This being the case, Mr Conway, as a common friend to us both, has been employed to mediate in this affair; and as Lady Ailesbury thinks her own reputation connected with my wife's to a certain degree, because of the intimacy in which they have lived and still live, his mediation has been very favourable to her. In short . . . I found no way to get rid of her without a quarrel with all her friends, but by making her separation maintenance equal to her jointure. . . . Perhaps when we are parted her conduct will permit me not only convincing but convicting proofs [of her misconduct]. Till then I must pay for the folly I committed in trusting to Lady Ailesbury's character of her, and that of some other friends whom you know I consulted about the match' (quoted in Maud Wyndham, *Chronicles of the Eighteenth Century*, 1924, ii. 279–80; see also pp. 266, 271–2).

11. Presumably her brother Robert Rich (*ante* 18 April 1746 OS, n. 23), although possibly her father Sir Robert Rich (*ante* 28 Jan. 1759).

Sir Joshua Reynolds.   G. Skury.

VISCOUNT BEAUCHAMP.

From the original Picture in the possession of the Earl of Carnarvon.

HON. FRANCIS INGRAM-SEYMOUR-CONWAY, LORD BEAUCHAMP, BY SIR JOSHUA REYNOLDS

has, I find, told you pretty near upon what terms,[12] and I am indeed glad as you are they are so good and for your reasons.

I went to Eton yesterday to hear Lord Beauchamp[13] speak, which I did with great pleasure; he has not use enough to be quite master of the thing; it was his second time; but his voice is exceeding good, and his figure advantageous and his manner sensible. One boy there pleased me much by his very lively and sensible elocution.

Lady A. has an account that *her boy*[14] is actually pardoned on the best terms, viz.: to serve on board the fleet.

Yours sincerely,

H. S. C.

I had a letter from Fitzroy[15] yesterday which says our army is at last assembled at *Werle*.[16] I don't know when we shall say so much of our English army, but Mr P[itt] has engaged the French not to come this month at soonest.

From HERTFORD, Saturday 14 July 1759

Printed for the first time from a photostat of BM Add. MSS 23218, f. 5.

London, July 14th 1759.

Dear Horry,

YOUR coming to London seems now so uncertain that I am afraid to trust absolutely to it, though I intend upon business to be in town [the] greatest part of next week myself. If your build-

12. Dean Lyttelton told Gov. Lyttelton on 23 June that he understood 'she is to have £600 per. an. alimony, besides her £200 per. an. pin money, which, in short, is as much as if her husband was dead and she in possession of her jointure' (Wyndham, op. cit. ii. 279).

13. Lord Hertford's eldest son, Francis Seymour-Conway (after 1807 Ingram-Seymour-Conway) (1743–1822), styled Vct Beauchamp 1750–93 and E. of Yarmouth 1793–4; 2d M. of Hertford, 1794. He had been at Eton since 1754; he was apparently speaking at the triennial Etonian festival of Montem (*Leinster Corr.* i. 227).

14. Possibly either George Symons (or Symonds, or Simmonds); or Andrew Grant, both of whom had been sentenced to death at the Old Bailey 28 April, and both of whom were respited 13 June (GM 1759, xxix. 192, 290; *Daily Adv.* 14 June).

15. Charles Fitzroy (*ante* 29 Aug. 1757, n. 6), at this time an aide-de-camp to Prince Ferdinand in Germany.

16. This letter is missing. The *Daily Adv.* 22 June, *sub* The Hague 14 June, reported that Prince Ferdinand's headquarters were at Werl as of the 10th.

ing[1] and press[2] can spare you for a day I shall be glad to meet you in town about the middle of the week and shall hope you will call at Mr Adams's[3] to see the design you fixed on for my saloon, in colours.

In the meantime give me leave to inform you that, from the time fixed upon by the judges for holding the assizes at Warwick,[4] we have been under a necessity of altering the time for the races there, and they stand now fixed and have been advertised for the 14th and 15th of next month. We must therefore beg your company there at that time,[5] a week sooner than you intended coming to us at Ragley.

I saw Mr Selwyn last night and told him what I was going to propose to you. I understand you go to him from my house, and he did not express the least difficulty about the alteration, only wishes when you have fixed the time to be at his house, to know it.

I hear no news, and am, dear Horry,

Always most sincerely yours,

HERTFORD

1. HW was in the process of constructing the 'Holbein Chamber,' the completion of which he announced in September (CHUTE 296; W. S. Lewis, 'Genesis of Strawberry Hill,' *Metropolitan Museum Studies*, 1934, v pt i. 75–6; Thomas Gray, *Correspondence,* ed. Toynbee and Whibley, Oxford, 1935, ii. 641–2).

2. HW was at this time occupied with plans for a new printing-house, while being distracted by a succession of unsatisfactory printers. Robinson, who had left early in March 1759, was succeeded by Williams, who lasted two months, and Lister, who stayed a week. Thomas Farmer, the fourth printer, arrived two days after this letter was written (HW, *Journal of the Printing-Office at Strawberry Hill,* ed. Toynbee, 1923, pp. 8–9). The printing of the SH Lucan had been interrupted (Hazen, *SH Bibl.* 46; CHATTERTON 22, 27).

3. In Lower Grosvenor Street, where he was Hertford's neighbour. Robert Adam (1728–92), the architect, had returned to England in January 1758 after several years of study in Italy. The designs under discussion are probably those for the saloon in Hertford's town house, 10 Grosvenor Street; they have apparently not been preserved (*Court and City Register,* 1759, p. 20; information kindly supplied by Messrs John Fleming, Villa Marchio, Lucca, Italy; John Harris, Royal Institute of British Architects, London; Howard Colvin, Oxford University).

4. The assizes at Warwick, in the Midland circuit, were appointed to be held 20 Aug., the judges being Sir Thomas Parker and Heneage Legge (*London Gazette* No. 9909, 30 June – 3 July; *Court and City Register* 1759, p. 117). The races were apparently usually held around 19 Aug. (*post* 24 July 1760).

5. HW planned to arrive at Ragley on the 12th, but finally did not make the visit nor the one to Selwyn mentioned in the next paragraph (MONTAGU i. 243; SELWYN 155; *post* 14 Aug. 1759).

To HERTFORD, ca Monday 16 July 1759

Missing; implied *post* 18 July 1759.

From HERTFORD, Wednesday 18 July 1759

Printed for the first time from a photostat of BM Add. MSS 23218, f. 6.

London, July 18th 1759.

Dear Horry,

MY Lady Hertford would have been better satisfied with the goodness of your resolution, if she could have brought you to town this week; however I am to inform you that you make us ample amends by coming to Ragley.

I can tell you no news but what you have probably heard, that an account of a battle is daily expected from Prince Ferdinand.[1]

My Lady says that Lady Mary Coke[2] regrets her not being able to put herself at the head of the Rays, Sutherlands and Campbells.[3]

My brother's direction is to the Lines at Chatham.[4] Yours, dear Horry,

Always very sincerely,

HERTFORD

1. Intelligence to this effect from Ferdinand's headquarters at Dissen was printed in the *London Gazette* No. 9913, 14-17 July. The battle, Minden, did not take place until 1 Aug., the news reaching London on the 8th (*London Gazette Extraordinary* 8 Aug.; MANN v. 314-15).

2. Who had developed a great attachment for Lady Hertford the previous year (*ante* 27 Aug., 17 Sept. 1758).

3. As a Campbell, Lady Mary was inevitably an ardent Hanoverian, and the Lords Reay (Mackays) and Sutherland had supported the government in the rebellion of 1745. The heads of these families had been leading the recruiting of the loyal clans for service against France in 1759. Col. John Campbell (who was Lady Mary's cousin as well as Lady Ailesbury's brother) was made colonel of a new bat-

talion or Argyllshire Fencibles in Aug. 1759; and William, 18th E. of Sutherland, was given a commission at the same time as colonel commandant to raise a battalion of Highlanders for foreign service, a regiment which he officered in part with his allies of the '45 the Mackays (GEC; *Scots Peerage* i. 386, vii. 174, viii. 357-9; GM 1759, xxix. 393; *Army Lists* 1760, pp. 152-3).

4. Conway had become colonel of the 1st Regiment of Dragoons in April 1759, was appointed one of the commanders of the special military encampments during July, and finally promoted Lt-Gen. 25 Aug. (apparently antedated 30 March) (MANN v. 286, n. 15; *London Gazette* No. 9924, 21-5 Aug.; *Army Lists*, p. 4; *London Chronicle* 3-5 July 1759, vi. 10; Conway to Devonshire 26 July, Chatsworth MSS,

To HERTFORD, Thursday 26 July 1759

Missing; answered *post* 3 Aug. 1759.

From HERTFORD, Friday 3 August 1759

Printed for the first time from a photostat of BM Add. MSS 23218, f. 7.

Ragley, August 3d 1759.

Dear Horry,

DO not think me idle; I did not receive your letter of the 26th July till today, or I should have informed you sooner that my intention was to carry you to Warwick races on the 14th, where we are to stay that and the next day, and to return to Ragley on the 16th. However if you do not like it, you see I deal fairly with you, and do not mean to draw you into it, but then you are to deal as fairly with me and let us see you after the races; I am to be at the Duke of Devonshire's[1] on the 6th where I expect to be informed when the Duchess of Grafton is to be here. Will you give me leave to acquaint you with her Grace's resolution, and then you shall fix the time yourself for coming to us, for you will be always welcome though I would not bring you into a dull family party.

I take it for granted Mr Phillips[2] my builder in Brook Street must have taken Mr Adams's design, for I know no other person that was empowered to do it; will you send for it there?

Lady Hertford desires her best compliments, and I am, dear Horry,

Always most truly yours,

HERTFORD

416/60). The Lines were a series of fortifications around the dockyards and military installations at Chatham, begun in 1758 but not finished until 1807 (Edward Hasted, *History . . . of Kent*, Canterbury, 1797–1801, iv. 198–9; T. K. Cromwell, *Excursions in . . . Kent*, 1822, p. 145; *Murray's Handbook for Travellers in Kent and Sussex*, 1858, pp. 47–8).

1. At Chatsworth in Derbyshire.
2. John Phillips (fl. 1739–76), King's carpenter and London speculative builder (H. M. Colvin, *A Biographical Dictionary of English Architects 1660–1840*, 1954, p. 453; B. H. Johnson, *Berkeley Square to Bond Street*, 1952, pp. 179, 180; *Court and City Register*, *passim sub* 'Board of Works').

From HERTFORD, Tuesday 7 August 1759

Printed for the first time from a photostat of BM Add. MSS 23218, f. 8.

Chatsworth, August 7th 1759.

Dear Horry,

BY the message I have received from the Duke of Grafton I think his coming to Ragley, and I suppose consequently her Grace's, is very uncertain. He does not seem at present inclined to leave his own house;[1] so I must leave the time of your journey to yourself. I intend making a visit for two or three days to a Warwickshire friend[2] from the 20th, and from the 22d or 23d I do not propose to lie from Ragley till I return towards London.

His Royal Highness[3] is now here with Lord Waldegrave,[4] Lord Besborough, Sir John Moore,[5] the Lord Cavendishes[6] and myself. The Duke of Bridgewater, Lord Rockingham and Lord Gower went away this morning; the Duke goes from hence on Thursday to Trentham[7] in his road to London.[8]

I propose being at home again on Saturday where, if you hear any news, it will be charitable to let me know it. Adieu, dear Horry,

Yours ever,

HERTFORD

---

1. Euston Hall, about 4 miles from Thetford, Suffolk.

2. Not identified.

3. The Duke of Cumberland. 'Last Friday [3 Aug.] his Royal Highness the Duke passed through Leicester in his way to Chatsworth' (London Chronicle 4–7 Aug., vi. 126). Conway wrote Devonshire 26 July from Chatham Lines, 'I suppose his Royal Highness will be with you soon and am particularly mortified I cannot have the honour of being with you on this occasion. I wonder he is; and am amazed the fears of the Ministers will let the only person able to plan or to execute properly what is necessary for our defences remain unsolicited at least, if unemployed' (Chatsworth MSS, 416/60).

4. Lord Waldegrave (ante ca 15 Feb. 1752 OS, n. 36) had married HW's niece Maria (1736–1807), illegitimate daughter of Sir Edward Walpole, on 15 May.

5. (d. 1790), 5th Bt, of Fawley, Berks.

6. The Duke of Devonshire's three brothers: Lord George Augustus (ca 1727–94), Lord Frederick (ante 11 Aug. 1757, n. 5) and Lord John Cavendish (1732–96).

7. Staffordshire, seat of Lord Gower.

8. Cumberland on Sunday 12 Aug., 'came to Kensington from the Duke of Devonshire's seat at Chatsworth in Derbyshire' (London Chronicle 11–14 Aug., vi. 147).

To Conway, Tuesday 14 August 1759

Printed from the MS now wsl; first printed Wright iii. 472–4. For the history of the MS, see *ante* 29 June 1744 OS.
Endorsed: H. W. 14 Aug. 1759.

Arlington Street, Aug. 14, 1759.

I AM here in the most unpleasant way in the world, attending poor Mrs Leneve's deathbed,[1] a spectator of all the horrors of tedious suffering and clear sense, and with no one soul to speak to— but I will not tire you with a description of what has quite worn me out!

Probably by this time you have seen the Duke of Richmond or Fitzroy[2]—but lest you should not, I will tell you all I can learn—and a wonderful history it is. Admiral Byng was not more unpopular than Lord George Sackville.[3] I should scruple repeating his story, if Betty,[4] and the waiters at Arthur's did not talk of it publicly, and thrust *Prince Ferdinand's orders*[5] into one's hand.

You have heard I suppose of the violent animosities that have reigned for the whole campaign between him[6] and Lord Granby[7]— in which some other warm persons have been very warm too.[8] In the heat of the battle the Prince finding 36 squadrons of French[9] coming

1. She died either 17 or 19 Aug. (Mann v. 316, n. 11; *Daily Adv.* 20 Aug.).

2. Richmond and Col. Charles Fitzroy had arrived in London from Germany on 11 Aug., the latter bringing letters and dispatches from the army at Minden (Mann v. 314, n. 5; *Leinster Corr.* i. 247).

3. Who was accused of disobedience and cowardice at the battle of Minden, 1 Aug. Conway wrote Devonshire 30 Aug., 'It's imagined L[ord] G[eorge] is come to town incog. I don't know how truly it's said the spirit against him is very great' (Chatsworth MSS, 416/62).

4. The news-mongering apple-seller (*ante* 11 June 1758 and n. 3).

5. His orders to Lord George to bring up the cavalry; see below.

6. Lord George.

7. There is no particular evidence of ill-will between the two before Minden, although they were temperamentally incompatible and Granby had resented sar-

casm by Lord George in Parliament in 1758. Sackville, however, was on very bad terms with Prince Ferdinand, while Granby was his favourite drinking-companion. See W. E. Manners, *Some Account of the . . . Marquis of Granby*, 1899, pp. 83–4; Alan Valentine, *Lord George Germain*, Oxford, 1962, pp. 44–8; Louis Marlow [i.e., L. U. Wilkinson], *Sackville of Drayton*, 1948, pp. 102–6.

8. Sackville was closely connected with Bute and Leicester House; Granby and Prince Ferdinand were popular with both ministers and 'mob.'

9. The figure is apparently not quite correct; the French centre consisted of 55 squadrons of cavalry in two lines, with a third line of 18 more in reserve; when the Anglo-Hanoverian infantry advanced upon them, eleven squadrons charged, fell back, and after a rally, the second line charged (J. W. Fortescue, *History of the British Army*, 1910–30, ii. 499, 501). It is not clear

down upon our army, sent Legonier[10] to order our 32 squadrons under Lord George to advance.[11] During that transaction, the French appeared to waver, and Prince Ferdinand, willing, as it is supposed, to give the honour to the British Horse of terminating the day, sent Fitzroy to bid Lord George bring up only the British cavalry.[12] Legonier had but just delivered his message, when Fitzroy came with his[13]—Lord George said, 'This can't be so—would he have me break the line? Here is some mistake'—Fitzroy replied, he had not argued upon the orders, but those were the orders—'Well!' said Lord George, 'but I want a guide'—Fitzroy said, he would be his guide—Lord G[eorge]. 'Where is the Prince?' F[itzroy]. 'I left him at the head of the left wing, I don't know where he is now.'[14] Lord George said, he would seek him, and have this explained. Smith[15] then asked

from accounts of the battle at which moment in these events the first aide-de-camp was sent.

10. Edward Ligonier (1740–82), illegitimate son of Vct Ligonier's brother; 2d Vct Ligonier, 1770; cr. (1776) E. Ligonier; at this time a Capt. in Granby's Royal Horse Guards and one of Prince Ferdinand's aides-de-camp. He had arrived in London 9 Aug. with verbal accounts of the battle (MANN v. 314, nn. 2, 5).

11. Lord George was commanding the cavalry on the right wing of the Allied army. According to Fortescue, op. cit. ii. 497, there were 24 squadrons under Lord George, 15 of them British.

12. According to Fitzroy, in his letter to Sackville 3 Aug., when he delivered the orders for the 'British' cavalry to advance towards the left,' he mentioned the 'circumstance, that occasioned the orders' and added ' "That it was a glorious opportunity for the English to distinguish themselves, and that your Lordship, by leading them on, would gain immortal honour" ' (quoted GM 1759, xxix. 418).

13. Fitzroy's letter to Sackville, 3 Aug., and the 'Declaration' of Sackville's aide-de-camp Smith, both state clearly that Ligonier arrived first, but Sackville's letter to Fitzroy, 3 Aug., implies strongly that Fitzroy arrived first, saying that he was advanced near the village of Halen 'and no further when you came to me. Ligonier followed almost instantly' (ibid. 1759, xxix. 417, 418). His letter to Prince Ferdinand,

2 Aug., does not mention the orders from Ligonier at all, but only one from 'M. Malhorti' to advance to Halen, and that by Fitzroy to bring up the British cavalry only (Hist. MSS Comm., Stopford-Sackville MSS, 1904–10, i. 312).

14. HW may have been told of this conversation by Fitzroy himself; it is very close to Fitzroy's account in his letter to Sackville 3 Aug., which had not yet been published: 'You . . . expressed your surprise at the orders, saying it was impossible the Duke could mean to break the line.—My answer was, that I delivered his Serene Highness's orders, word for word, as he gave them.—Upon which you asked which way the cavalry was to march, and who was to be their guide.—I undertook to lead them towards the left round the little wood on their left as they were then drawn up. . . . Your Lordship continued to think my orders neither clear nor exactly delivered; and expressing your desire to see Prince Ferdinand, ordered me to lead you to him; which order I was obeying when we met his Serene Highness' (GM 1759, xxix. 418).

15. John Smith (d. 1804), Lt, 3d Foot Guards and Capt. in the army, 1753; Lord George Sackville's aide-de-camp. He quit the army after Sackville's court martial. He was later (ca 1775–1804) a gentleman usher to Queen Charlotte; the builder of a home at Dover known as 'Smith's Folly'; and the father of Admiral Sir William Sidney Smith (ibid. 1804, lxxiv pt i. 190,

Fitzroy to repeat the orders to him, which being done, Smith went and whispered Lord George,[16] who says, he then bid Smith carry up the cavalry[17]—Smith is come,[18] and says, he is ready to answer anybody any question[19]—Lord George says Prince Ferdinand's behaviour to him has been most infamous,[20] has asked leave to resign his command, and to come over, which is granted.[21] Prince Ferdinand's behaviour is summed up in the enclosed extraordinary paper,[22] which

215; *Army Lists* 1758, p. 45; *Court and City Register, passim;* George Barrow, *Life and Correspondence of Admiral Sir William Sidney Smith,* 1848, i. 3–4; *Mem. Geo. II* iii. 274).

16. Both Smith and Fitzroy agree that this was done, Smith saying that he 'immediately went up to Col. Fitzroy, and made him repeat the orders to me twice. —I thought it so clear and positive for the *British* cavalry only to advance where he should lead, that I took the liberty to say to his Lordship, I did think they were so; and offered to go and fetch them, while he went to the Prince, that no time might be lost.' Lord George argued for a minute and then 'said then do it as fast as you can' (GM 1759, xxix. 418). Fitzroy wrote: 'Capt. Smith, one of your aides-de-camp, once or twice made me repeat the orders I had before delivered to your Lordship. . . . He went up to you, whilst we were going to find the Duke. . . . I heard your Lordship give him some orders. What they were I cannot say—but he immediately rode back towards the cavalry' (ibid.).

17. Sackville had written to Fitzroy, 3 Aug., 'But, that no time might be lost, I sent Smith with orders to bring on the British cavalry . . . and I reckoned, by the time I had seen his Serene Highness, I should find them forming beyond the wood. . . . The Duke then ordered me to leave some squadrons upon the right, which I did, and to advance the rest to support the infantry. This I declare I did, as fast as I imagined it was right in cavalry to march in line.' He then described how he twice ordered Granby to halt to keep the line, then let him proceed until they both halted together to the rear of the infantry, then on further orders extended the line towards the morass; 'and then, instead of finding the enemy's cav-

alry to charge, as I expected, the battle was declared to be gained, and we were told to dismount our men' (ibid. 1759, xxix. 417).

18. He arrived in London on Monday, the 13th (*Daily Adv.* 15 Aug.).

19. His declaration (quoted above, nn. 13, 16) was published before 22 Sept. (*post* 11 Oct. 1759, n. 12). He also started rumours, not wholly unfounded, that Pitt and Leicester House were insistent that Sackville not be condemned unheard (MANN v. 320, n. 14; *Letters from George III to Lord Bute 1756–1766,* ed. Sedgwick, 1939, pp. 29–30; *Stopford-Sackville MSS,* i. 315).

20. Sackville had written ɔ Fitzroy, 'His Serene Highness has been pleased to judge, condemn, and censure me, without hearing me, in the most unprecedented manner; as he never asked me a single question in explanation of any thing he might disapprove, and as he must have formed his opinion upon the report of others, it was still harder he would not give me an opportunity of first speaking to him upon the subject' (GM loc. cit.).

21. Sackville's official letter to Holdernesse of 3 Aug. asking leave to resign had been enclosed in one to Bute, received on the 11th; it was delivered and on the 14th Sackville was informed that he had the King's permission to return to England. He arrived 6 or 7 Sept. (Sedgwick, op. cit. 29; MANN v. 314, n. 5, 316, n. 14, 320, n. 13, 328, n. 10; Pitt to Bute 15 Aug., *Chatham Corr.* i. 417–18; *Stopford-Sackville MSS,* i. 313).

22. Prince Ferdinand's order of the day 2 Aug. which had been brought to England by Fitzroy on the 11th. It was printed in the *Daily Adv.* 15 Aug.; *London Chronicle* 14–16 Aug., vi. 153; GM 1759, xxix. 388.

you will doubt as I did, but which is certainly genuine—I doubted, because in the military, I thought direct disobedience of orders was punished with an immediate arrest, and because the last paragraph[23] seemed to me very foolish. The going out of the way to compliment Lord Granby with what he would have done,[24] seems to take off a little from the compliments paid to those that have done something[25]—but in short, Prince Ferdinand or Lord George, one of them is most outrageously in the wrong, and the latter has much the least chance of being thought in the right.[26]

The particulars I tell you, I collected from the most *accurate* authorities—I make no comments on Lord George; it would look like a little dirty court to you,[27] and the best compliment I can make you, is to think as I do, that you will be the last man to enjoy this revenge.

The Hereditary Prince[28] has demolished another body of 6,000, and has taken Contades's baggage and his *segretaria* with all his papers.[29] The French are posting to the Rhine, and seem quite ruined in those parts.

The *defeated* Russians certainly thrashed the Prussians severely:[30]

23. In the version printed in the *Daily Adv.* there a⁀ᵉ, only two paragraphs, the last very long. HW more likely means the last sentence: 'And his Serene Highness desires and orders the generals of the army, that upon all occasions when orders are brought to them by his aide-de-camp, that they should be obeyed punctually, and without delay.'

24. 'His Serene Highness further orders it to be declared to Lieutenant-General the Marquis of Granby, that he is persuaded, that if he had had the good fortune to have had him at the head of the cavalry of the right wing, his presence would have greatly contributed to make the decision of that day more complete and more brilliant.' Granby had commanded the second line of the Hanoverian-British cavalry, and was twice ordered to halt by Lord George Sackville (MANN v. 315, n. 6, 320, n. 11).

25. Many individuals were mentioned in the order of the day.

26. HW comments on his large number of personal enemies to Mann 29 Aug. (ibid. v. 320-1) and in the *Memoirs* of how his imperious conduct had alienated much of the army (*Mem. Geo. II* iii. 253-4).

27. HW discusses this rivalry in his letter to Mann 3 Feb. 1760 (MANN v. 366-7). Sackville had also been on the committee of inquiry into the Rochefort expedition, and HW presumably believed that he was at least partly responsible for Conway's exclusion from employment during 1758 (ibid. v. 155, n. 18; *ante* 15, 17 Oct. 1758).

28. Karl Wilhelm Ferdinand (1735-1806), Prince (from 1780, Duke) of Brunswick-Wolfenbüttel.

29. According to the *London Gazette* No. 9922, 14-18 Aug., which published the most sensational letter taken, these papers were captured at Detmold on 5 Aug.; see MANN v. 321, nn. 18, 19. However, news of this does not seem to have reached England until 17 Aug. (*London Chronicle* 16-18 Aug., vi. 165), and the other details in this sentence all fit the account of the engagement at 'Coveldt' [Gohfeld], 1 Aug., reported in the *London Gazette* No. 9920, 7-11 Aug. See also R. Waddington, *Guerre de sept ans*, [1899-1914], iii. 71-2.

30. The first reports of the battle of Palzig on 23 July, received in London 5 Aug., had represented it as a Prussian victory, but mails arriving from Holland on the 11th had indicated that, although

the King has joined Wedel,[31] and has taken an advanced post.[32]

You will be sorry for poor Mckinsy[33] and Lady Betty who have lost their only child at Turin.[34] Adieu!

Yours ever,

H. W.

From HENRIETTA SEYMOUR CONWAY, Friday 24 August 1759

Printed for the first time from a photostat of BM Add. MSS 23218, f. 9.

London, August 24, 1759.

Good Mr Walpole,

THE contents of this, I believe, will not a little surprise you. It is to acquaint you that your old friend Mrs Conway is in town, and has been so for these seven weeks. She has made her inquiry often after you, but find you are immovable when at Strawberry Hill. She has had thoughts of surprising you with a visit, for Lady Harrington was so obliging as to offer to bring her; but the weather was so extremely hot, and she not very well, that she could not put her inclination in execution. However her stay here will be a fortnight longer, and if her stars should favour her in bringing Mr Walpole to town in that time, it would make no one more happy to see him than

His humble servant,

H. SEYMOUR CONWAY

I lodge at Mrs Moss's by Oxford Chapel.

inconclusive, the advantage was on the Russian side (SELWYN 156, n. 5; MANN v. 315, n. 7).

31. Karl Heinrich Wedell (1712–82), Prussian Lt-Gen., 1759; the commander at Palzig (ibid.).

32. He was defeated again by the Russians at Kunersdorf on 12 Aug., another defeat first reported as a victory (SELWYN 156 and nn. 2, 4; MANN v. 317, n. 2, 319, n. 4).

33. Hon. James Stuart Mackenzie (?1719–1800), Lord Bute's brother; M.P. Argyllshire 1742–7, Buteshire 1747–54, Ayr burghs 1754–61, Ross-shire 1761–80; envoy extraordinary to Turin 1758–61 (Namier and Brooke iii. 503–4; *Scots Peerage* ii. 300).

34. They had two children, both of whom died young (Namier and Brooke, loc. cit.).

To Hertford, August 1759

Missing; answered *post* 1 Sept. 1759.

From Hertford, Saturday 1 September 1759

Printed for the first time from a photostat of BM Add. MSS 23218, ff. 10–11.
Memoranda (by HW): Saturday. Andover
                              10–3—Cathedral¹—dine—Lord Folkston's²
                              Sunday
                              Wilton³—dine—Stonehenge—return

Ragley, September 1st 1759.

Dear Horry,

AS long as I had any expectation of seeing you here you will excuse me that I did not write; at present that I despair of it for this summer, it may be necessary for me to answer one part of your letter,⁴ wherein you desire me to employ Mr Bevan⁵ in keeping my courts in Suffolk.⁶ Mr Bevan's character I do not know; you seem to think well of it. I have had many applications for the employment, but none whose recommendation comes with the same weight as any friend of yours. I have delayed returning answers to any of the solicitations made me till I had an opportunity of talking to you

1. Salisbury. This proposed jaunt must have occurred 8–9 Sept. since HW mentions returning to London on 11 Sept. after 'rambling about, having been at the Vine, at Salisbury, at Wilton and two or three other places' (HW to Lady Townshend 12 Sept. 1759). See also CHUTE 296 and *post* 13 Sept.

2. Longford Castle, 2½ miles southeast of Salisbury, the seat of Jacob Des Bouverie (1694–1761), cr. (1747) Vct Folkestone. HW does not seem to have been acquainted with Folkestone (whom he describes in his letter to Mann of 26 June 1747 OS, MANN iii. 419, as 'a considerable Jacobite') but he would have been attracted to Longford by the collection of pictures there. Whether he actually visited it, or Stonehenge, at this time is uncertain.

3. Lord Pembroke's seat, 2½ miles northwest of Salisbury. Though HW found the house 'grand, and the place glorious,' he 'was astonished at the heaps of rubbish' and wished to 'shovel three parts of the marbles and pictures into the river' (CHUTE, loc. cit.).

4. Missing.

5. Possibly son of Arthur Bevan (ca 1688–1743), of Laugharne, co. Carmarthen; Middle Temple, 1712; M.P. Carmarthen 1727–41; to whom HW presented a copy of *Ædes Walpolianæ* (Sedgwick i. 461; *London Magazine* 1743, xii. 153). HW also solicited Lord Cardigan (later D. of Montagu) for a similar post for Mr Bevan (HW to Cardigan 20 Nov. ?1759).

6. I.e., the manorial or baronial courts held on Hertford's Suffolk estates; see *post* 27 Sept. 1759, n. 5.

upon it, which I wish to have before I determine; I will then submit the merit of the different candidates to your opinion, and if you desire me after that to employ Mr Bevan, I will do it because you recommend him.

As my sons[7] are to return to Eton we propose leaving Ragley the beginning of next week; I shall be glad to hear from you at Taplow when I may hope to meet you. This morning we have had a letter from a servant at Taplow to acquaint us that Mr Chute[8] of the Vine, your friend, had been there to see it, approved much the situation of the place and desired to be immediately informed upon what terms it was to be let.[9] The lease I took for seven years, two of which were unexpired at Midsummer last; I have with the house about fourteen acres of land for which with the gardens etc. I give one hundred pounds a year; the furniture, consisting chiefly of washing beds,[10] is my own which I bought for that house and propose to remove into Suffolk.[11] There are some few hangings belonging to the house which will of course remain there. I have likewise a clause of renewal for a farther term of seven years if it be agreeable, which is binding upon Lord Inchiquin.[12] I hear Mr Chute likes it for the dryness of the place; whatever may be his reasons I shall under my present circumstances be glad to part with it. May I therefore beg the favour of you to acquaint him with the circumstances of the lease, to make my excuses for not writing myself if you think it necessary, and that I am very willing to submit the terms of my giving up the lease to him to his own opinion. There is a brewhouse and all necessary offices for a family, and some few fixtures.

I propose bringing back with me Mr Adams's design for the saloon, as I am inclined to have some parts of it altered, which I think far from being perfect. Adieu, dear Horry,

Yours always most truly,

HERTFORD

7. Lord Beauchamp (*ante* 17 June 1759, n. 13) and the Hon. (later Lord) Henry Seymour-Conway (1746–1830). Lord Beauchamp left Eton during the year and matriculated at Christ Church, Oxford, 2 Feb. 1760; Henry remained until 1761 (R. A. Austen-Leigh, *Eton College Register 1753–1790*, Eton, 1921, p. 119).

8. John Chute (1701–76) of the Vyne; HW's correspondent.

9. No evidence appears that he took over the lease of Taplow Court.

10. Presumably bedsteads with linen hangings.

11. To Sudbourne Hall, Hertford's seat in Suffolk (*post* 27 Sept. 1759, n. 5).

12. William O'Brien (d. 1777), 4th E. of Inchiquin. He had acquired the property through his wife Anne, Countess of Orkney (*Vict. Co. Hist. Bucks* iii. 242).

To Conway, Thursday 13 September 1759

Printed from the MS now wsl; first printed Wright iii. 480–1. For the history of the MS see *ante* 29 June 1744 OS.
Endorsed: H. W. 13 Sep. 1759.

Arlington Street, Sept. 13, 1759.

I INTENDED to send you the brief chronicle of Lord G[eorge] S[ackville][1] but your brother says he has writ to you this morning. If you want to know minute particulars which neither he nor I should care to detail in a letter, I will tell you them if you will call for a minute at Strawberry on Sunday or Monday, as you go to your camp.[2] I ask this boldly, though I have not been with you; but it was impossible; Geo[rge] Montagu and his brother[3] returned to Strawberry with me from the Vine,[4] and I am expecting Mr Churchill and Lady Mary who sent me word they would come to me as soon as I came back, and I think you will find them with me.

Lady Mary Coke is stripping of[f] all the plumes that she has been wearing for Niagara etc.,[5] and is composing herself into religious melancholy against tomorrow night when she goes to Princess Elizabeth's[6] burial. I passed this whole morning most deliciously at my Lady T[ownshend]'s. Poor Roger,[7] for whom she is not concerned, has given her a hint that her hero George[8] may be mortal too; she scarce spoke unless to improve on some bitter thing that Charles[9]

1. HW in his letter to Mann 13 Sept. describes the developments in Sackville's affair since his return to England on the 6th or 7th (MANN v. 328).

2. At Chatham (*ante* 18 July, *post* 11 Oct. 1759). Conway was apparently in London for his attendance on the King as groom of the Bedchamber; on 30 Aug. he wrote the D. of Devonshire from London, 'I am now attending my fortnight's duty on his M[ajesty]' (Chatsworth MSS, 416/62).

3. Charles Montagu.

4. Chute's house in Hampshire; for HW's excursion see *ante* 1 Sept. 1759, n. 1.

5. Fort Niagara had been taken 25 July, Ticonderoga, 27 July, and Crown Point, 4 Aug. The news had arrived 8 Sept. and was published in a *London Gazette Extraordinary* 10 Sept. News of Boscawen's

naval victory at Lagos, 18–19 Aug., had also arrived shortly before, and was published in a *London Gazette Extraordinary* 7 Sept.

6. Elizabeth (1741–4 Sept. 1759), 2d dau. of Frederick, P. of Wales (MANN v. 327, n. 5). Accounts of the burial 'last night at ten o'clock' in Henry VII's Chapel at Westminster Abbey are in the *Daily Adv.* 15 Sept. and *London Chronicle* 15–18 Sept., vi. 265.

7. Hon. Roger Townshend (ca 1731–59), had been killed at Ticonderoga 25 July; the news arrived ca 8 Sept. (MONTAGU i. 32, n. 6, 248, n. 10; *Daily Adv.* 10 Sept.). See also HW to Lady Townshend 12, 21 Sept. and CHUTE 294–5. HW wrote an epitaph for him which was not used ('Short Notes,' GRAY i. 34 and n. 228).

8. Her eldest son; he was at Quebec.

9. Charles Townshend.

said, who was admirable—he made me all the speeches that Mr Pitt will certainly make next winter, in every one of which, Charles says and I believe, he will talk of *this great campaign* 'memorable to all posterity, with all its imperfections—a campaign, which though obstructed, cramped, maimed—but I will say no more—'

The campaign in Ireland I hear will be very warm;[10] the Primate[11] is again to be the object; Ponsonby,[12] commander against him. Lord George's situation will not help the Primate's.[13] Adieu!

Yours ever,

H. W.

To Conway, after ca 17 September 1759

Missing; mentioned *post* 11 Oct. as of 'a shocking ancient date,' but obviously written after Conway had gone to Chatham about 17 Sept. (*ante* 13 Sept. 1759).

To Hertford, ca Sunday 23 September 1759

Missing; answered *post* 27 Sept. 1759.

10. The three factions in the Irish Parliament were headed by Abp Stone, John Ponsonby, and the E. of Kildare. During the D. of Bedford's absence in England in 1759 Stone, Ponsonby, and the E. of Shannon were left as lords justices (see *Bedford Corr.* ii. 377–8; J. A. Froude, *The English in Ireland in the Eighteenth Century*, 1872–4, i. 617–21; Lord Ilchester, *Henry Fox*, 1920, ii. 82–9).

11. Abp Stone (*ante* 16 Sept. 1755, n. 7) had been allied with John Ponsonby in opposition to the government in 1756–7 and had been appointed a lord justice, along with the E. of Shannon and Ponsonby, in April 1758 (*Mem. Geo. II* iii. 91–2, 96; Froude, loc. cit.).

12. Hon. John Ponsonby (1713–89), M.P. Newtown borough, co. Down, 1739; secretary, 1742–4, and first commissioner, 1744–71, of the revenue board; privy councillor, 1748; Speaker of the Irish House of Commons 1756–71; brother-in-law of the Duke of Devonshire (*ante* 11 Dec. 1755, n. 6).

13. Lord George Sackville had been chief secretary when his father the Duke of Dorset was lord lieutenant 1751–5, and Stone had supported them against the Opposition led by Henry Boyle; see Ilchester, op. cit. ii. 71–2; *post* 17 Nov. 1763, n. 71.

From HERTFORD, Thursday 27 September 1759

Printed for the first time from a photostat of BM Add. MSS 23218, f. 12.

Taplow, September 27th 1759.

Dear Horry,

IF I did not feel that my regard and affection for you were beyond suspicion I should be mortified at what I had done; as they are I am still ashamed. Your reproach is too just: I did recollect your talking of coming to Kensington on Saturday.[1] It was near six o'clock before I left it and I thought it possible you might have been prevented; my engagement which I had inconsiderately made was to go to my sister;[2] all this I do allow is no excuse, and my Lady says I have none to make, though her good memory I do maliciously think sent the message to my sister for that evening. You are good and can forgive and I am all penitence. I came from London today and my sister is come down with us; I intend returning there on Saturday[3] evening to be at Leicester House[4] on Sunday, from whence I propose going to Newmarket for two or three days' shooting in my way to Sudborne,[5] and to be back again some time in the following week.

There is no news in town. I shall be always glad to see and meet you when you can make the time convenient.

Adieu, dear Horry, accept the best compliments of the family and believe me always,

Most truly yours,

HERTFORD

1. 22 Sept.
2. Probably the Hon. Mrs Harris, who lived in London, although his half-sister, the Hon. Henrietta Seymour Conway, who lived in Chichester, was in London in Aug. 1759 (ante 24 Aug. 1759).
3. 29 Sept.
4. The residence of the Princess of Wales and her sons.
5. Sudbourne Hall, Hertford's seat near Orford, Suffolk, was built by Sir Michael Stanhope (d. 1621). Thomas Martin described it ca 1750 as 'a good bricked building, handsomely fitted up and well seated with a fine park and good gardens.' It was rebuilt for Hertford by James Wyatt in 1784, still in a plain style. Sudbourne had always been 'chiefly used as a sporting residence, the park and neighbourhood abounding with game' (John Britton and E. W. Brayley, The Beauties of England and Wales, 1801–16, xiv pt i. 326; W. A. Copinger, The Manors of Suffolk, London and Manchester, 1905–11, v. 178; Country Life 1901, ix. 240–5; John Kirby, The Suffolk Traveller, 1764, p. 127; Antony Dale, James Wyatt, Oxford, 1936, p. 119).

From CONWAY, Thursday 11 October 1759

Printed from the MS now WSL; previously printed Toynbee, *Supp.* ii. 112–14. The MS was bought in, Sotheby's 5 Dec. 1921 (1st Waller Sale, lot 110) along with the MS of *post* 23 Dec. 1790, and sold Christie's 15 Dec. 1947 (2d Waller Sale, lot 6) to Maggs for WSL.

Chatham Lines, 11 Oct. 1759.

I FIND upon looking on your letter[1] a shocking ancient date, but I hope you won't follow my bad example. I make no excuses that I may have the more room for contrition and shall only say I wish you were better acquainted what sort of a place Chatham Camp is.

I did read Lord Chesterfield's letter[2] and read it at the fountain-head, that is in Lord Holdernesse's hands, the political fountain to whom I believe it was sent and who published it; and I did not admire it, I suppose for want of knowing whose it was; now I do I can see something tolerable in it; but too much of it and too much in the pert foreign gazette style; just such as the Cologne and ingenious Brussels Gazettes deal in. Have you heard a sort of epigram on the Duke of Newcastle, which is I think just tolerable, too?

> Oxford in spite of all her factions
> Has gain'd two ample benefactions.
> Ratcliff[3] a library decreed
> Because the Doctor could not read.
> A riding school was left by Hyde[4]
> Because his Lordship could not ride:
> Let Pelham famed for generous actions
> To emulate these benefactions
> On his lov'd Cam's fair margin fix
> A nursery for politics.

1. Missing.
2. Not identified.
3. Dr John Radcliffe (1650–1714), court physician, left the funds with which the Radcliffe Camera was built 1737–47 by James Gibbs.
4. Henry Hyde, styled Vct Cornbury, cr. (1751) Bn Hyde of Hindon, who had died in 1753 as a result of a fall from his horse, had left the papers of his ancestor, the Earl of Clarendon, to Oxford with the provision that the money derived from the sale of any publication of them should be used to begin a fund for supporting a school for riding and other exercises. Although his bequest was disallowed at the time, his sister the Ds of Queensbury gave the papers to Oxford with the same provision in 1759. By 1868 the fund amounted to about £12,000, but instead of building a riding school, the money was used to erect laboratories and lecture rooms and the University Museum for the Professor of Experimental Philos-

But I'll tell you one I heard since which pleases me much better for since vice and insignificance have entitled people to an instalment in Westminster Abbey[5] one Gen. Hargreaves[6] has slipped in among the crowd, and, on his tomb, is represented as rising from the dead[7] —a Westminster boy wrote on the tomb:

> Lie still if you're wise
> You'll be damn'd if you rise.[8]

There's a simplicity and conciseness in it that please me much.

I had heard Charles Townshend's *Earthquake*,[9] and I had heard a furious retort of Mr Pitt's to their memorial,[10] which it seems was never made but on the contrary an answer, mixed with proper caution or at least very decent reserves on the occasion. For indeed as we were I believe certainly aggressors I think too much bullying so weak a foe would not be noble.

I see they have not done with Lord G[eorge] yet; did you read *A Second Letter* to him?[11] It is much the strongest thing that has

ophy (V. J. Watney, *Cornbury and the Forest of Wychwood*, 1910, p. 191 and n.).

5. Burial in the Abbey at this time was largely a matter of fees; see the comments collected in K. A. Esdaile, *Life and Works of Louis-François Roubiliac*, 1928, p. 115.

6. William Hargrave (1672–1751), Col. 31st Foot, 1730; 9th Foot, 1737; 7th Foot, 1739; Governor of Gibraltar, 1739; Lt-Gen., 1743 (*The Marriage, Baptismal, and Burial Registers of the . . . Abbey of . . . Westminster*, ed. J. L. Chester, 1876, p. 380 and n. 1; R. Beatson, *Political Index*, 1806, ii. 131, 166, 208, 210, 229; see also Sir William Musgrave, *Obituary*, ed. Armytage, 1899–1901, iii. 146).

7. His monument by Roubiliac, finished in 1757 (*Daily Adv.* 7 Oct. 1757), is described in Esdaile, op. cit. 114–16 and illustrated from a mezzotint by Philip Dawe, Plate 36.

8. According to Mrs Esdaile (op. cit. 115), who quotes this epigram from this letter, it is also discussed in *Anticipation*, 1781, as fittingly commemorating 'the *famous* or rather *infamous* general officer and governor.'

9. Charles Townshend was very restless and discontented at this time. To pacify him Newcastle was considering him for either secretary at war or chancellor of

the Exchequer if there were a vacancy, and wrote Hardwicke 31 Aug., 'If Charles Townshend had not such a character, I would make him chancellor of the Exchequer at once, but there is no depending upon him, and his character will not go down in the City, nor anywhere else' (BM Add. MSS 32895, f. 76). Although Hardwicke favoured Lord Barrington (ibid. ff. 115–16), Newcastle wrote again 5 Oct., 'I begin to think . . . we must find a new chancellor of the Exchequer:—Will Charles Townshend do less harm in the War Office, or in the Treasury?' (BM Add. MSS 32896, f. 300; Sir Lewis Namier and John Brooke, *Charles Townshend*, 1964, pp. 59–60). The rumour was published in the *London Chronicle* 4–6 Oct. (vi. 334): 'We hear that the Right Hon. Henry Bilson Legge will shortly be created a peer of Great Britain by the title of Lord Stawell; that Lord Viscount Barrington will succeed Mr Legge, as chancellor of the Exchequer; and that the Hon. Charles Townshend will be appointed secretary at war.'

10. Not explained.

11. 'A Second Letter to a Late Noble Commander of the British Forces in Germany. In which the Noble Commander's Address to the Public, his Letter to Colonel

appeared, being founded on the facts in his own letter and Smith's declaration.[12] I don't hear what becomes of the court martial.[13]

I had a letter from poor FitzRoy yesterday who has been very ill with his old complaint; but now recovered and with the army again.[14] He seems to think nothing will be done there as both armies are in strong ground and entrenching.[15]

Our victory over the Army of the Empire[16] is I think a comical one as by our own account we lost some cannon and retired,[17] the Imperialists say sixteen.[18]

I have had a letter from Lord Stormont who is actually married[19] and the happiest creature in the world; I would have him always so

Fitzroy, together with the Colonel's Answer, and Captain Smith's Declaration, are Candidly and Impartially Considered. By the Author of the First Letter. Printed for R. Griffiths, at the Dunciad, opposite Somerset House in the Strand.' It was apparently published 4 Oct. (*Daily Adv.* 4–8 Oct.).

12. Sackville had published a 'Short Address . . . to the Public' on 18 Sept. (ibid. 18 Sept.; reprinted GM 1759, xxix. 416–17). His letter to Fitzroy 3 Aug., Fitzroy's reply of the same date, and Capt. Smith's declaration, had all been published before 22 Sept. in 'Lord George Sackville's Vindication of Himself, In a Letter to Col. Fitzroy,' etc. (Jenkinson to Grenville 22 Sept., *Grenville Papers* i. 327, MS now WSL; BM Cat.). They are all reprinted GM 1759, xxix. 417–18, as having 'been published without his Lordship's knowledge or consent.'

13. Sackville had applied for a court martial immediately on returning to England, but had been told it was impossible until the officers in Germany could return (MANN v. 328 and nn. 11, 12). It was finally held in March–April 1760 (ibid. v. 366–7 and nn. 21–25, 377 and nn. 14–15, 384–5 and nn. 4–5, 387).

14. See *ante* 17 June 1759, n. 15; MANN v. 316, nn. 13, 15. He arrived in London 18 Nov. (*London Chronicle* 17–20 Nov., vi. 486).

15. The *London Gazette* No. 9937, 6–9 Oct. reported by letters from Prince Ferdinand's army of 30 Sept. that 'their camp continued still at Krossdorff' and that 'the principal army of the French remained in their camp behind Giessen.'

Other items in the *Daily Adv.* 10 Oct. reported that the 'two armies are employed in entrenching their camps' and that the French were 'fortifying Giessen.'

16. An engagement at Korbitz, near Dresden, 21 Sept. Various conflicting reports from Berlin, 25 Sept., and Dresden, 25 Sept., had appeared in the *Daily Adv.* 6, 8 Oct.; but the *London Gazette* loc. cit. printed a very long 'Translation of an Authentic Relation of the Defeat of the Army of the Empire at Korbitz near Dresden, Sept. 21.'

17. The 'Authentic Relation' says in one passage: 'The battalion of Kreckwitz's Grenadiers took eleven pieces of cannon, and one pair of colours; and the advantages would have been still more considerable, had not the superiority of the enemy's cavalry made our dragoons give way again, which obliged the battalions of Charles and Kreckwitz to retreat towards a wood, as well with a view to occupy a place of security for the Prussian cavalry to rally in, as to cover the rear of the rest of our infantry. By this incident we were under the necessity of abandoning the eleven pieces of cannon taken from the enemy, with five more of our own, which could not be got out of a hollow way in time.' It continues to describe how the Austrians nevertheless retired from the field during the night.

18. The figure had appeared in an account from the *Amsterdam Gazette* 'by divers letters from the headquarters of the Army of the Empire,' printed in *Daily Adv.* 10 Oct., which described the battle as an Austrian victory.

19. Stormont m. (16 Aug. 1759) in War-

for he is the best. He has been at Prince Czartoriski's[20] country house,[21] who has he says a fine place, literally elegant and in taste, French elegance in *Poland!* but then his life is two good centuries old, with all the nasty hospitality and troublesome state of our fore-fathers. I long to see him and his wife, but a man absorbed in the diplomatic course I look upon as lost to his friends.

Adieu. Lord[22] and [Lady][23] Effingham are away, Lady Ailesbury is at Park Place so that I am reduced to my pack here and having except for the field, dinners, etc. no acquaintance nor *conversables* among them, am in a manner *enterré vis-à-vis de* Mr Stephens.[24] I have just of late been sometimes at Col. Onslow's,[25] the Speaker's[26] heir, who is here with wife.[27] Yesterday I reviewed the militia and as I don't doubt you'll see in the newspapers, how *well they performed* and *what* particular *satisfaction* they gave to me and a *crowd of spectators; and what spirits they are in.*[28] I leave that description to their better pens and am dear Horry,

Most sincerely yours,

H. S. C.

---

saw, Henrietta Frederica (d. 1766), dau. of Henry, Count von Bünau of Saxony, and widow of — de Berargaard.

20. Presumably Aleksander August Czartoryski (1697–1782), palatine of Red Russia. HW and Conway had known his son, who had been in England in 1757 (MANN vi. 248 and nn. 12, 13).

21. Possibly 'Lubnice, maison de campagne située dans le palatinat de Sendomir, appartenant au prince palatin de Russie [Czartoryski]' (Stanislas Augustus Poniatowski, *Mémoires*, St Petersburg, 1914–24, i. 48). He also had a residence at Wolczyn, in the palatinate of Lithuania, where he stayed during the winters of 1759–60 and 1760–1 (ibid. 359, 365).

22. Conway wrote 'Ld &' apparently omitting 'Lady.' The E. of Effingham (*ante* 31 Oct. 1741 OS, n. 28) was at this time Col. of the 34th Foot and a Maj.-Gen.; he was one of the commanders of the special military encampments during the summer (*London Chronicle* 3–5 July 1759, vi. 10).

23. Elizabeth Beckford (1725–91), m. 1 (1745) Thomas Howard, 2d E. of Effing-

ham, 1743; m. 2 (1776) Sir George Howard, K.B.; lady of the Bedchamber to Q. Charlotte 1761–91 (BERRY i. 367, n. 4).

24. Perhaps Philip Stephens (1723–1809), cr. (1795) Bt, M.P. Liskeard 1759–68, Sandwich 1768–1806, who had recently become second secretary to the Admiralty (Namier and Brooke iii. 475).

25. George Onslow (1731–1814), cr. (1776) Bn Cranley; 4th Bn Onslow, 1776; cr. (1801) E. of Onslow. At this time he was Lt-Col. in the Surrey militia (*London Chronicle* 19–21 July, vi. 70; S.P. 36/140, f. 266); he became lord lieutenant of Surrey, 1776, and Col. in the Army, 1794. Conway wrote the D. of Devonshire 1 Aug. that the Surrey militia 'is shortly to encamp here' at Chatham (Chatsworth MSS, 416/61).

26. Arthur Onslow, Speaker of the House of Commons.

27. Henrietta Shelley (1731–1809), m. (1753) George Onslow.

28. Such accounts of reviews of the militia had appeared frequently during the summer, e.g. *London Chronicle* 3 July – 23 Aug., vi. 14, 30–1, 70, *et passim.*

To Conway, Sunday 14 October 1759

Printed in full for the first time from the MS now wsl; first printed, with an omission, Wright iii. 482–3. For the history of the MS see *ante* 29 June 1744 OS; it was marked by HW for inclusion in *Works,* but was not included.

Endorsed: H. W. 14 Oct. 1759.

Strawberry Hill, Oct. 14th 1759.

IF Strawberry Hill was not as barren of events as Chatham, I would have writ to you again; nay if it did not produce the very same events. Your own light horse are here,[1] and commit the only vivacities of the place—two or three of them are in the cage[1a] every day for some mischief or other. Indeed they seem to have been taken from school too soon,[2] and as Rigby said of some others of these new troops, the moment their exercise is over, they all go a-birdnesting. If the French load their flat-bottom boats[3] with rods instead of muskets, I fear all our young heroes will run away. The invasion seems again come into fashion: I wish it would come, that one might hear no more of it—nay I wish it for two or three reasons. If they don't come, we shall still be fatigued with the militia, who will never go to plough again till they see an enemy: if there is a peace before the militia runs away, one shall be robbed every day by a constitutional force. I want the French too to have come that you may be released; but that will not be soon enough for me, who am going to Park Place.[4] I came from Chaffont[5] today, and I cannot let the winter appear without making my Lady Ailesbury a visit. Hitherto my im-

1. Presumably from the 1st Regiment of Dragoons (*ante* 18 July 1759, n. 4; Charles Philip de Ainslie, *Historical Record of the First or the Royal Regiment of Dragoons,* 1887, p. 91). Conway's light troops were among the list of regiments augmented at this time (S.P. 44/191, ff. 250–1). He wrote the D. of Devonshire 1 Aug., 'As your Grace was so good to say you might possibly give me some assistance in completing my dragoons which by the last weekly return want 23 dragoons and 25 light troopers, if it be agreeable to your Grace I would send an officer and party to Derby where they shall receive any directions you are pleased to give them, and without giving yourself much trouble I imagine your name and countenance

alone might be a great help in this time of need' (Chatsworth MSS, 416/61; see also ibid. 416/62).

1a. 'A prison for petty malefactors' (Samuel Johnson, *Dictionary,* 1755).

2. Montagu wrote HW that his first cousin once removed, aged 17 and a major in the Bedfordshire militia, had told him that only two officers in the corps were of age (MONTAGU i. 248).

3. Another invasion attempt was expected at this time (*post* 18 Oct. 1759; MANN v. 336 and n. 7; MONTAGU i. 249–50).

4. HW planned to go on the 22d; he remained for a week (CHUTE 297).

5. Chalfont, Bucks, where Lady Mary Churchill lived. HW and Bentley had gone there on the 12th (MONTAGU i. 249).

pediments may have looked like excuses, though they were nothing less. Lady Lyttelton goes on Wednesday; I propose to follow her on Monday; but I won't announce myself, that I may not be disappointed, and be a little more welcome by the surprise; though I should be very ungrateful, if I affected to think I wanted that.

Your epigrammest epigram[6] is good: I am sorry to say the longer one is not equal to the subject. I can send you one, but it is only a translation; however, it will appear tolerable, by so many bad ones that have preceded it in the newspapers—you saw the original, did not you? *Bateaux plats à vendre,*[7] etc.

> O yes! here are flat-bottom boats to be sold;
> And soldiers to let, rather hungry, than bold;
> Here are ministers richly deserving to swing,
> And commanders whose recompense should be a string.
> O France, still your fate you may lay at _____'s[8] door;
> You was sav'd by a maid,[9] are undone by a whore.[10]

I cannot say I have read the second letter on Lord George; but I have done what will satisfy the booksellers more; I have bought nine or ten pamphlets; my library shall be *au fait* about him,[11] but I have an aversion to paper-wars, and I must be a little more interested than I am about him, before I can attend to them; my head is to be filled with more sacred trash.

The Speaker[12] was here t'other day and told me of the intimacy between his son and you and the militia. He says the lawyers are examining whether Lord George can be tried or not.[13]

I am sorry Lord Stormont is marriediski; he will pass his life un-

6. The one on General Hargrave.

7. The original was printed *Daily Adv.* 3 Oct. and *London Chronicle* 2–4 Oct., vi. 326, *sub* 4 Oct., with a translation. Other versions are ibid. 9–11 Oct., vi. 352 and *Daily Adv.* 4, 5 Oct. The French epigram and a translation are also printed GM 1759, xxix. 496. HW's version, which he sent to Montagu 11 Oct., is his own translation (MONTAGU i. 249 and n. 6).

8. 'Pitt' written in by Mary Berry.

9. Joan of Arc.

10. Mme de Pompadour.

11. None of the pamphlets in this controversy appears in Hazen, *Cat. of HW's Lib.* HW wrote the titles of three of them

on Montagu's letter to him 9 Oct. (MONTAGU i. 247). At least twenty-five titles on the subject are included in a list of books published in September and October in GM 1759, xxix. 499.

12. Arthur Onslow.

13. Sackville's request for a court martial, 7 Sept., had been referred (as would be a later one of 1 Dec.) to the Attorney and Solicitor Generals to decide whether 'an officer may be tried under the Mutiny Act in Great Britain for a military offence committed out of his Majesty's dominions' after being 'dismissed from all his military employments.' They did not report until 12 Jan. 1760 (MANN v. 366, n. 21).

der the North Pole, and whip over to Scotland by the way of Greenland without coming to London.

I dined t'other day at Sion with the Holderness's. Lady Mary Coke was there, and in this great dearth of candidates she permits Haslang[14] to die for her. They were talking in the bow window when a sudden alarm being given that dinner was on table, he expressed great joy and appetite—you can't imagine how she was offended[15] that he was thinking of his own belly instead of hers. Adieu!

Yours ever,

H. W.

PS. Before next winter is over I think you will have occasion to display Campbell-colours. That clan and the Townshends will not fight under the same standard[16]—don't mention this—but I have seen a woman[17] come out of a weather-glass,[18] who portends very foul weather.

From CONWAY, ca Tuesday 16 October 1759

Missing; answered *post* 18 Oct. 1759.

14. Joseph Xaver (ca 1700–83), Freiherr (later Graf) von Haszlang: Bavarian minister to England 1741–83 (MONTAGU i. 185, n. 25).

15. The rest of the sentence has been omitted by previous editors.

16. Probably an allusion to the plans which Charles Townshend had been meditating during the summer and early autumn for succeeding the D. of Argyll as the government manager for Scotland; see

Sir Lewis Namier and John Brooke, *Charles Townshend*, 1964, pp. 57–8, and Namier and Brooke iii. 542. Townshend had lost interest in the project by November.

17. Probably Lady Townshend.

18. 'A kind of thermometer, used to ascertain the temperature of the air, and also to prognosticate changes in the weather' (OED); see MANN i. 467, viii. 379.

To Conway, Thursday 18 October 1759

Printed from *Works* v. 64–6.

Strawberry Hill, Oct. 18, 1759.

I INTENDED my visit to Park Place to show my Lady A. that when I come thither it is not solely on your account, and yet I will not quarrel with my journey thither if I should find you there;[1] but seriously I cannot help begging you to think whether you will go thither or not, just now. My first thought about you has ever been what was proper for you to do; and though you are the man in the world that think of that the most yourself, yet you know I have twenty scruples, which even you sometimes laugh at. I will tell them to you, and then you will judge, as you can best. Sir Edward Hawke and his fleet is dispersed, at least driven back to Plymouth:[2] the French, if one may believe that they have broken a regiment for mutinying against embarking,[3] were actually embarked at that instant. The most sensible people I know, always thought they would postpone their invasion, if ever they intended it, till our great ships could not keep the sea, or were eaten up by the scurvy. Their ports are now free; their situation is desperate: the new account of our taking Quebec[4] leaves them in the most deplorable condition; they will be less able than ever to raise money,[5] we have got ours for next year;[6] and this event would facilitate it, if we had not: they must try

1. Despite HW's advice against it in this letter, Conway did go to Park Place on 20 Oct.; he wrote the D. of Devonshire from there 23 Oct., 'I left Chatham with Lord Ligonier's approbation on Saturday and with leave to pass a little time here before my next waiting, which begins on the 4th of next month' (Chatsworth MSS, 416/63; CHUTE 297).

2. 'Admiral Hawke, we hear, is returned to Plymouth from the Bay, and Commodore Boys has also been obliged to quit his station off Dunkirk and come into the Downs, the last hard gales at S.W. not admitting of their staying longer on those coasts' (*London Chronicle* 13–16 Oct., vi. 366–7).

3. A mutiny of the '9th Regiment of France' against embarking at Havre had

been reported in ibid. 11–13 Oct., vi. 358. HW also mentions it and the storm that drove the English fleet back in his letter to Mann 16 Oct. (MANN v. 336).

4. It had capitulated 17–18 Sept. after a decisive battle on the Plains of Abraham 13 Sept.; the news arrived 16 Oct. and was published in a *London Gazette Extraordinary* 17 Oct. Previous reports, which had arrived on the 14th and were published in a *Gazette Extraordinary* 16 Oct., had been far from optimistic about taking it.

5. France was virtually bankrupt; see MANN v. 349, nn. 7, 8; *Mem. Geo. II* iii. 223–4.

6. Taxes and credits for the year 1759 had been voted 21 and 24 May.

for a peace, they have nothing to go to market with but Minorca. In short, if they cannot strike some desperate blow in this island or Ireland,[7] they are undone: the loss of 20,000 men to do us some mischief, would be cheap. I should even think Madame Pompadour in danger of being torn to pieces, if they did not make some attempt. Madame Maintenon, not half so unpopular, mentions in one of her letters her unwillingness to trust her niece Mlle Aumale[8] on the road, for fear of some such accident.[9] You will smile perhaps at all this reasoning and pedantry; but it tends to this—If desperation should send the French somewhere, and the wind should force them to your coast, which I do not suppose their object, and you should be out of the way, you know what your enemies would say; and, strange as it is, even you have been proved to have enemies. My dear Sir, think of this! Wolfe,[10] as I am convinced, has fallen a sacrifice to his rash blame of you.[11] If I understand anything in the world, his letter that came on Sunday[12] said this: 'Quebec is impregnable; it is flinging away the lives of brave men to attempt it. I am in the situation of Conway at Rochfort; but having blamed him, I must do what I now see he was in the right to see was wrong, and yet what he would have done; and as I am commander, which he was not, I have the melancholy power of doing what he was prevented doing.'[13] Poor

7. HW thought Ireland more likely to be their destination (MANN v. 336).

8. Marie-Jeanne d'Aumale (1683–1756), dau. of Jacques d'Aumale, Seigneur de Mareuil in Picardy; educated at St-Cyr and Madame de Maintenon's secretary and companion 1705–15, although not her 'niece' (Comte d'Haussonville and G. Hanotaux, *Souvenirs sur Madame de Maintenon*, [1902–?1904], i. pp. x–xi, xv, xciii).

9. Mme de Maintenon wrote to Mlle de la Viefville, Abbess of Gomerfontaine, 23 Feb. 1709: 'Vous allez être bien fâchée de n'avoir point Mlle d'Aumale: mais il nous a pris, à elle et à moi, une crainte de quelque aventure désagréable sur le grand chemin: la famine met le peuple dans un mouvement, auquel il ne se faut pas exposer: le mal est à un point à ne pouvoir durer: et j'espère que les soins, que le roi prend pour faire trouver du blé, rameneront la tranquillité' (*Lettres de Madame de Maintenon*, Amsterdam, 1756, iii. 84;

HW's copy, with marginalia throughout, now WSL, is Hazen, *Cat. of HW's Lib.*, No. 1280).

10. James Wolfe (1727 – 13 Sept. 1759), Maj.-Gen., 1759, the hero of Quebec.

11. Wolfe, who had been fiercely critical of the conduct of the Rochefort expedition, had appeared as a witness against Conway and Mordaunt at the inquiry in Nov. 1757 and as a witness for the prosecution in Mordaunt's subsequent court martial (MANN v. 267, n. 5).

12. To Pitt; it was dated 2 Sept.; extracts from it were printed in a *London Gazette Extraordinary* 16 Oct. Several paragraphs were so despondent that they were ordered to be 'omitted in the paper to be published' (Newcastle to Hardwicke 15 Oct., BM Add. MSS 32897, f. 88), and even those printed were pessimistic enough to give the impression that the siege would fail (MANN v. 336).

13. HW's imaginative interpretation of

man! his life has paid the price of his injustice; and as his death has purchased such benefit to his country, I lament him,[14] as I am sure you, who have twenty times more courage and good nature than I have, do too. In short, I, who never did anything right or prudent myself (not, I am afraid, for want of knowing what was so), am content with *your* being perfect, and with suggesting anything to you that may tend to keeping you so:—and (what is not much to the present purpose) if such a pen as mine can effect it, the world hereafter shall know that you was so. In short, I have pulled down my Lord Falkland,[15] and I desire you will take care that I may speak truth when I erect you in his place; for remember, I love truth even better than I love you. I always confess my own faults, and I will not palliate yours.—But, laughing apart, if you think there is no weight in what I say, I shall gladly meet you at Park Place, whither I shall go on Monday, and stay as long as I can, unless I hear from you to the contrary. If you should think I have hinted anything to you of consequence, would not it be handsome, if, after receiving leave, you should write to my Lord Ligonier, that though you had been at home but one week in the whole summer, yet as there might be occasion for your presence in the camp,[16] you should decline the

Wolfe's letter is based on passages at the beginning and end of the printed version. In the second paragraph Wolfe wrote that Quebec was so strongly reinforced that 'I could not flatter myself that I should be able to reduce the place.' In the conclusion he wrote: 'In this situation, there is such a choice of difficulties, that I own myself at a loss how to determine. The affairs of Great Britain, I know, require the most vigorous measures; but then the courage of a handful of brave men should be exerted only, where there is some hope of a favourable event. However, you may be assured, Sir, that the small part of the campaign which remains, shall be employed (as far as I am able) for the honour of his Majesty and the interest of the nation' (*London Gazette Extraordinary* 16 Oct.). HW also comments on Wolfe's letter in *Mem. Geo. II* iii. 217–19.

14. HW gives a graphic and sympathetic account of Wolfe's death, ibid. iii. 221–2.

15. Lucius Carey (1610–43), 2d Vct of Falkland. He was generally much admired for probity and nobility of character, but HW had written of him in the *Royal and Noble Authors*: 'There never was a stronger instance of what the magic of words and the art of an historian can effect, than in the character of this Lord, who seems to have been a virtuous well-meaning man with a moderate understanding, who got knocked on the head early in the Civil War, because it boded ill: and yet by the happy solemnity of my Lord Clarendon's diction, Lord Falkland is the favourite personage of that noble work. . . . Not to descant too long; it is evident to me that this Lord had much debility of mind and a kind of superstitious scruples, that might flow from an excellent heart, but by no means from a solid understanding' (*Works* i. 501–2). HW's character of him was much criticized; see HW to Hume 15 July 1758; MORE 200–1.

16. Mr Conway was encamped in Kent near Canterbury (HW); see *ante* 18 July

permission he had given you?—See what it is to have a wise relation, who preaches a thousand fine things to you which he would be the last man in the world to practise himself. Adieu!

Yours ever,

HOR. WALPOLE

To LADY AILESBURY, Saturday 29 December 1759

Printed from a photostat of the MS, now in the Scottish Record Office. First printed Coke, *Journals,* iii. pp. ix–x; also printed Toynbee iv. 336–8. The MS was among the papers of Charles H. Drummond Moray, of Abercairny, Crieff, Perthshire at the time of his death in 1891 (see MORE xiii–xiv).

Arlington Street, Dec. 29, 1759.

YOU laughed, my Lady, at my telling Prince Edward, that I should marry Lady Mary Coke, as soon as I got a regiment,[1] but the affair was more serious than you imagined. As Mr Pitt lets everybody raise a regiment that desires it, and as there certainly is nothing left for these regiments to do, I intend to offer my services too. The Clan of the Campbells[2] to be sure will flock to my standard, and being of a very huckaback[3] complexion, I shall not be often put to the expense of levy money. I should have chosen to call it the Regiment of Loo, and to have dressed them like Pam,[4] but Lord Pultney[5] has already anticipated the thought of accoutring his men like the knave of clubs; and at present I have no fixed design for any distinction; but

1759, n. 4; *London Chronicle* 6–8 Nov., vi. 442, which implies that Conway's regiment was quartered at 'Brentford, Hounslow, etc.'

———

1. HW writes of this incident to Montagu 23 Dec. 1759 (MONTAGU i. 264 and n. 11). HW's letter to Lady Mary Coke 27 Dec. 1759, enclosing his petition to Pitt, imputes his military zeal to his passion for her; see MORE 14–15 and n. 1.

2. Lady Ailesbury and Lady Mary Coke were Campbells; see CHUTE 297 and n. 9; *ante* 18 July, 14 Oct. 1759.

3. Durable, 'that will stand wear and tear' (OED, which quotes HW to Strafford

30 Oct. 1759 and to Cole 9 March 1765 [CHUTE, loc. cit.; COLE i. 90]).

4. 'The knave of clubs, esp. in the game of five-card loo, in which this card is the highest trump' (OED).

5. Who in July was appointed Lt-Col. of a regiment to be raised in Wales; it became the 85th Foot, Craufurd's Royal Volunteers (MANN v. 311 and nn. 3, 4; *Army Lists* 1760, p. 143). Conway wrote the D. of Devonshire 26 July, 'I hear Lord Pultney is raising a regiment; I can't say I approve of *regiments* or approve of them much the least of all augmentations' (Chatsworth MSS, 416/60).

as Colonel Hale[6] has a death's-head[7] for his pompon, I propose to take a strawberry. In the meantime I have drawn up a petition, but as I am not used to those sort of things, if Mr Frederic[8] is with you, I should be glad if he would correct it, and stick in a few law terms to give it more the air of a formal memorial: here it is;

To Mr Pitt.[9]

To raise a troop a thousand ask;
To please 'em all how hard the task!
For whether they are Whig or Tory,
You've vow'd (a thing unheard in story)
To grant what's ask'd for England's glory.
I too, Sir, on great actions bent,
Propose to raise a regiment;
But as my glowing breast, like yours,
Abhors all martial sinecures,
If but a troop or company,
In the French service let it be;
For you, Engrosser, have no longer
Left Britons anything to conquer.

This, I think, can't fail—but if it should, you know, Madam, I have one or two places, that I can resign, and the worst that can happen is to have them again, with the Garter into the bargain.[10] It is true, I am very lean, and a blue ribband will not become me much, but

6. John Hale (d. 1806), 4th son of Sir Bernard Hale, m. (1763) Mary, dau. of William Chaloner, Esq. of Guisborough, Yorks; Capt., 1752, Maj., 1755, and Lt-Col., 1758 in the 47th Foot. In Oct. 1759 he volunteered to raise a regiment of the footmen and chairmen of London and to lead them against the best household troops of France; in Nov. he became Lt-Col. Commandant of the 18th (later 17th) regiment of Light Dragoons with the badge of 'Death's Head' and the motto 'Or Glory' underneath ([R. Cannon], *Historical Record of the Seventeenth Regiment of Light Dragoons;—Lancers*, 1841, pp. 10–11, 14, 75–7; J. W. Fortescue, *A History of the British Army*, 1910–30, ii. 509–10; *Mem. Geo. II* iii. 234–5; Sir Ber-

nard Burke, *Landed Gentry*, 1925, p. 814; DNB *sub* Sir Bernard Hale; GM 1759, xxix. 95, 496, 607). He was later Gov. of Limerick, 1770, Maj.-Gen., 1772, Lt-Gen., 1777, and Gen., 1793.
7. Described in the *London Chronicle* 17–20 Nov., vi. 486.
8. Lord Frederick Campbell, Lady Ailesbury's brother and a lawyer (Namier and Brooke ii. 182).
9. See *Horace Walpole's Fugitive Verses*, ed. W. S. Lewis, 1931, pp. 128–31.
10. Alluding to Lord Temple's resignation of the Privy Seal and request for the Garter; HW describes this to Mann 16 Nov. 1759 (MANN v. 345–6). For HW's 'places' see MORE 14, n. 3.

when one takes it only to show one's importance, one must bear it as other great and awkward[10a] personages have done.

There is nothing new, for there is nobody in town. I was at Mrs Harris's[11] last night, and I am sure your Ladyship will agree with me in a criticism I made on the house. Mrs Howe[12] said, it would be a very good house, if the rooms did but lie together—I said, I thought there was a much greater fault in it, which is, that the master and mistress do lie together. I should not repeat this, but as I have a great opinion of your Ladyship's taste in architecture.

Lady Stafford, and Lord Farnham[13] and their child,[14] for she is big, were presented on Thursday: They have been married eight or nine months,[15] and she has changed her religion. It is a pity that so much secrecy should be thrown away upon legalities! Adieu! Madam, this is charming weather for planting laurels for everybody but the King of Prussia.[16]

I am your Ladyship's
Most obedient servant

Hor. Walpole

To Beauchamp, February 1760

Missing; answered *post* 3 March 1760.

10a. Lord Temple was generally known as 'Lord Gawkee.'

11. Conway's sister Anne, who in 1759 lived in Pall Mall (*Court and City Register*, 1760, p. 61).

12. Presumably Hon. Caroline Howe, who belonged to Princess Amelia's circle; see Ossory i. 109, Mann i. 209, n. 3, Berry i. 108, n. 7.

13. Robert Maxwell (ca 1720–79), 2d Bn Farnham, 1759, cr. (1760) Vct and (1763) E. of Farnham; M.P.; m. 1 (1759) Henrietta Cantillon, Cts of Stafford (see *ante* 27 Nov. 1755, n. 6).

14. Henrietta (d. 6 March 1852), m. (1780) Rt Hon. Denis Daly (d. 1792), of Dunsandle, co. Galway (Burke's *Peerage*, 1928, p. 915; *Leinster Corr.* iii. 239).

15. They were married '11 Oct. 1759, at St Mary Magdalen's, Old Fish Str., London' (GEC v. 259). Apparently the marriage was not announced until Dec., for the *London Chronicle* (27–9 Dec. 1759, vi. 624) reports *sub* Sat. 29 Dec., 'A few days since the Right Hon. Lord Farnham was married to the Countess Dowager of Stafford, in St James's Square'; see also GM 1760, xxx. 46; *Daily Adv.* 29 Dec. 1759.

16. Who was held responsible for Lt-Gen. Finck's surrender at Maxen on 21 Nov.; see HW to Mann 13 Dec. 1759 (Mann v. 354 and nn. 8, 9).

From BEAUCHAMP, Monday 3 March 1760

Printed for the first time from a photostat of BM Add. MSS 23218, f. 16. Dated '1760' in pencil (probably by J. W. Croker). This and the letter dated 17 March were both evidently written during Beauchamp's first year at Oxford, where he matriculated 2 Feb. 1760, and before HW's visit to Oxford on 15 July.

Ch[rist] Ch[urch] March the 3d.

Dear Sir,

I CAN assure you negligence did not prevent me from acknowledging sooner the receipt of yours, but the inability of answering properly your inquiries. In obedience to your commands, I went to New College (which I suppose you mean by Winchester College)[1] and inquired for the picture of the Founder.[2] It hangs up in the Hall between two other benefactors[3] to the College, which seem to have

1. The legal style of New College is 'the College of St Mary of Winchester in Oxford,' but the better-known name was in use as early as 1400 to distinguish it from the other and older St Mary's College (later part of Oriel College) in Oxford. Nevertheless, the name 'Winchester College' was apparently used occasionally for New College in the eighteenth century, though it was usually confined to Winchester School (Hastings Rashdall and Robert S. Rait, New College, 1901, pp. 30, 33). HW's use of the name probably arose from confusing the location of a portrait of William of Wykeham engraved by Jacob Houbraken (1698–1780) in 1738 'from a picture at Winchester College' and published in The Heads . . . of Illustrious Persons of Great Britain . . . with Their Lives and Characters, by Thomas Birch, 1743–51, with which HW was familiar (Anecdotes of Painting, 1762–71, i. 23; COLE i. 207, n. 14).

2. William of Wykeham (1324–1404), Bp of Winchester and lord chancellor, founded New College in 1379. The portrait discussed, on an oak panel, still hangs in the Hall of New College, and is now attributed to Sampson Strong (ca 1550–1611) who was paid £6 by the College in 1596 for a portrait of the founder (Mrs Reginald Lane Poole, Catalogue of Portraits in the Possession of the Univer-

sity, Colleges, City, and County of Oxford, Oxford, 1912–26 [Oxford Historical Society, Vols 57, 81, 82], ii pp. xi–xiii, 146–7, and plate 20, facing p. 146). Beauchamp, despite mentioning its being on panel, seems to have confused it with a slight variant on canvas then (and still) hanging over the dais in the Hall, which was either executed or extensively repainted in the seventeenth or eighteenth century, possibly by John Taylor (ca 1630–1714) who did a portrait of Wykeham for New College in 1668–9 (ibid. ii pp. xiv, 146; Anthony à Wood, The History and Antiquities of the Colleges and Halls in the University of Oxford, ed. John Gutch, Oxford, 1786, pp. 196–7; Thieme and Becker; post 17 March 1760). HW used the information about the portrait supplied by Beauchamp in this and the following letter in the Anecdotes of Painting, loc. cit., which he had begun to write in Jan. 1760: 'There is a portrait taken from a bust of the same age [of Edward III], the face of which is far from being executed in a contemptible manner. It represents that artist and patron of arts William of Wickham, Bishop of Winchester, and prime minister to Edward III . . .'

3. Probably Henry Chichele (ca 1362–1443), Abp of Canterbury and founder of All Souls, and William Waynflete (?1395–1486), Bp of Winchester, lord chancellor,

been done by the same hand. I am informed that it is little esteemed and not reckoned an original, which is conjectured from the resemblance of the painting (which is upon wood) to the other two which are of a modern date. I own I think the piece is rather well done and curious, though I should suppose it is not an original. There is one of the same person at Winchester[4] which is very much admired, of which I can inquire of a correspondent there any particulars, if you are curious about it. With regard to the picture in dispute, I have wrote to a fellow of New College,[5] who is a great antiquarian, to inform me whether he knows any anecdotes about it: as soon as I receive an answer I shall communicate the contents to you.[6] Let me add, that I take it as the highest compliment, that you entrust me with your literary commands,[7] and as a most agreeable mark of your friendship, though indeed I have received so many proofs of that, that I am already sufficiently convinced of it. I cannot conclude without hoping that at a convenient opportunity you will make Oxford a visit.[8] Your goodness has not yet made me so vain as to imagine that my company is a sufficient inducement, but there are various curiosities here which I know have an attractive power. I am, dear Sir,

Your very sincere friend and humble servant,

BEAUCHAMP

Mr Trail and Holwell[9] desire their respects to you.

---

and founder of Magdalen College, both students of New College. Their portraits, now tentatively attributed to John Taylor (see n. 2), flanked that of William of Wykeham over the dais in 1786 as they still do today (Anthony à Wood, op. cit. 197; Mrs Lane Poole, op. cit. ii. 148–9).

4. Winchester School, where it still hangs in the Hall. It is on panel, very similar to the New College portrait on canvas, and in a similar frame. As it was purchased by the school in 1597 for £4. 12s. 6d., it has also been attributed to Sampson Strong (T. F. Kirby, *Annals of Winchester College*, 1892, p. 43; Mrs Lane Poole, op. cit. ii pp. xii, 146).

5. Not identified.

6. Beauchamp did so, *post* 17 March.

7. Lord Beauchamp's literary pretensions made him unpopular: 'July 11 [1760].—Lord Beauchamp not liked at Oxford, very proud and too fond of the superiority of his abilities in the literary way' (Elizabeth, Duchess of Northumberland, *Diaries of a Duchess*, ed. James Greig, 1926, p. 19).

8. HW did so on 15 July (*Country Seats* 24–5; MONTAGU i. 285, 287; *post* 9 July 1760).

9. William Holwell (1726–98), Lord Beauchamp's tutor; tutor of Christ Church and proctor, 1758; vicar of Thornbury, Glos; chaplain in ordinary to George III. HW met him at Thornbury Castle in 1774 (COLE i. 345).

To BEAUCHAMP, March 1760

Missing; answered *post* 17 March 1760.

From BEAUCHAMP, Monday 17 March 1760

Printed for the first time from a photostat of BM Add. MSS 23218, f. 17. For the dating, see *ante* 3 March 1760.

Christ Church, Monday the 17th.

Dear Sir,

I AM sorry to confess my great ignorance in mistaking a copy for a warranted original. My correspondent informs me that the two pictures[1] in dispute are both undoubtedly copies of a statue or bust at Winchester,[2] which is much admired. Though I have been so unlucky as not to be able to satisfy your inquiries with regard to the present subject, I hope you will not entirely discard me as a virtuoso, though I made so palpable a mistake about the originality of the picture.

You cannot expect anything worth hearing from so retired a town as this: politics retailed from a monthly magazine, the value of fellowships, exhibitions, and studentships, seasoned with a spice of scandal and secret insinuation are the topics of coffee-house disputants, whose ideas naturally gravitate to the alluring power of preferment.

I find myself so entirely free from all interruptions to study, and so entirely master of my own time that I am rather prejudiced in favour of a collegiate life. Each person has his different point of view, each his particular inclination, which he gratifies without troubling his neighbour. Some consider Oxford as a mere place of entertainment, where they must in conformity to custom loiter away the three tedious years from 18 to 21. No great literary improvement is to be expected from them, since learning is not their object. Coffee-houses are the common resort of those who are denominated

1. That at New College and the one at Winchester School mentioned *ante* 3 March.

2. The portrait resembles a bust, supposedly that of William of Wykeham, on a corbel in the muniment room at Winchester School (illustrated in Arthur F. Leach, *A History of Winchester College*, New York, 1899, facing p. 50).

Loungers,³ where (as an Oxford wit would say) they peruse divinity over port, politics over coffee, and the accusations of bad ministers and Lord G. Sackville over custards and syllabubs.⁴

I own I cannot look upon Oxford as a vicious drunken town as it is commonly represented. Some I suppose out of such a number must be very irregular, but they live so entirely among themselves, that unless you seek their company, you seldom see anything of them. This I say of the University in general; as to the behaviour of the Christ⁵ Churchmen, I can assure you that they are as regular as possible. The obligations to study may be superseded, but those to decency and regularity cannot. Our Dean⁶ is a very vigilant active governor, and does everything in his power to raise emulation among the undergraduates. I dare say in time his endeavours will succeed, but you are sensible that much time is required to bring about a total reformation.

I ought to beg pardon for troubling you with such impertinent matter, but I rely on your goodness, and am, dear Sir,

Your most sincere friend and humble servant,

BEAUCHAMP

From HENRIETTA SEYMOUR CONWAY, Friday 11 April 1760

Printed for the first time from a photostat of BM Add. MSS 23218, ff. 13–14.

Chichester, 11th April 1760.

Good Mr Walpole,

I HOPE these few lines will find you well, and as happy as I sincerely wish you to be. I have enjoyed that great blessing, health, thank God, better this winter than I have done for many years, which

3. 'Idle people . . . whose whole business is to fly from the painful task of thinking' (*The Student, or the Oxford and Cambridge Monthly Miscellany*, Oxford, 1750, i. 21).

4. 'A drink or dish made of milk . . . or cream, curdled by the admixture of wine, cider, or other acid, and often sweetened and flavoured' (OED *sub* 'sillabub').

5. MS, 'Xᵗ.'

6. David Gregory (1696–1767), D.D. 1732; first regius professor of modern history and languages at Oxford 1724–36; canon of Christ Church 1736–56 and dean, 1756–67.

I attribute in a great measure to the tour I took last summer and the kind reception I met with from some of my friends, and from none more so than yourself. I often traverse over in my thoughts that agreeable day I spent with you at Strawberry Hill.[1]

Now, good Sir, I am going to petition you for my Easter offering, instead of a New Year's gift, as that used to be the time I troubled you to put your name to some covers,[2] which I shall soon send to your house in Arlington Street. I beg you to take your time in doing them, as I am in no hurry for them, having a few of yours by me. I doubt you'll think me very troublesome and impertinent, as I have another favour to beg of you, I am informed Lord Clarendon's *Life*[3] is published which he gave to the University of Oxford; if so, I shall be infinitely obliged to you to get them for me. I hear they are in three volumes large octavo. I would not have them bound in leather, but, what I think they call it, half bindings. I beg they may be a large print, as my eyesight begins to fail, *infirmities* of *age* will appear,[4] so it is folly to endeavour to conceal it.

When you return the covers to Mr Compton[5] I desire you will be so good to send the books at the same time, and hope I shall have the favour of a note in the parcel, to inform me of your welfare, likewise to let me know what I am indebted to you for the books; then I shall order Mr Compton to call at your house in town to pay whoever you shall appoint to receive the money,

And beg you will believe me to be, what I really am,

Your very sincere friend and humble servant,

H. SEYMOUR CONWAY

To HENRIETTA SEYMOUR CONWAY, ca Monday 28 April 1760

Missing; received 30 April (*post* 6 May 1760).

1. Presumably in late Aug. or early Sept. 1759 (see *ante* 24 Aug. 1759).
2. I.e., to frank some covers for her as a member of Parliament.
3. *The Life of Edward, Earl of Clarendon,* written by himself, Oxford, 1759,

folio. The copy HW sent to Henrietta Seymour Conway, with his inscription, is now WSL (Hazen, *Cat. of HW's Lib.,* No. 4000). See *post* 6 May 1760.
4. She was about 49 at this time.
5. Not identified.

To Conway, Monday ?5 May 1760

Printed from *Works* v. 71 (misdated Feb. 1761). The date given in the original printing of this letter is clearly wrong since the Qualification Bill, which it mentions, was introduced into the House of Commons 13 Feb. 1760 and finally passed 2 May 1760 (*Journals of the House of Commons* xxviii. 761, 903). On Friday 15 Feb. the bill was ordered to be printed but the second reading was postponed to 22 Feb. On the Fridays of 22 and 29 Feb. the second reading was further postponed (ibid. xxviii. 768, 783, 794). On Friday 25 April the bill was reported from the committee of the whole but consideration of it was again postponed (ibid. xxviii. 889); both Conway and HW are listed as voting in the minority on 24 April (BM Add. MSS 32905, f. 70). The only Friday when Conway is known to have spoken against the bill is 2 May, when he served as a teller for the 'noes' in the division on the third reading (BM Add. MSS 32905, f. 246; *Journals of the House of Commons* xxviii. 903). Also, the final decision to send six battalions to Germany, to which HW apparently alludes in this letter, was taken 1 May (Newcastle to Hardwicke 1 May 1760, BM Add. MSS 32905, f. 196; below, n. 5).

The next most likely date for this letter would be Monday 18 Feb. 1760, but at that time Charles Townshend, who brought the news of Conway's speech to HW, lay 'dangerously ill at his house in Grosvenor Square' according to the *London Chronicle* 19–21 Feb. 1760 (vii. 177).

Monday, five o'clock, Feb. 1761 [?5 May 1760].

I AM a little peevish with you—I told you on Thursday night that I had a mind to go to Strawberry on Friday without staying for the Qualification Bill.¹ You said it did not signify— No! What if *you* intended to speak on it?² Am I indifferent to hearing you? More— Am I indifferent about acting with you?³ Would not I follow you in

1. A bill 'to enforce and render more effectual the laws relating to the qualification of members to sit in the House of Commons,' read the first time 13 Feb. and carried 2 May by 95-46; it received the royal assent 22 May (see headnote; *Journals of the House of Commons* xxviii. 741–926 *passim*). HW gives an account of the progress of the bill and describes the leading proponents and opposers, but does not mention Conway in connection with it, in *Mem. Geo. II* iii. 278–80.

2. James West's minutes for Newcastle of the meeting of the House of Commons 2 May 1760 lists Conway among the speakers against the bill and reports, 'Mr Pitt, talked very much of the happiness of be-

ing reunited . . . that the principle of the bill was right, that he would ever defend it, knew nothing of bargains and demands, which it was harsh and uncandid to him for anyone to name . . . and at last extorted from General Conway, that he thought the persons who agreed to the bargain, more to blame than those who proposed it' (BM Add. MSS 32905, f. 246).

3. James West's minutes of the meeting of the House of Commons 24 April 1760 report 'a division on the clause that contained the oath which we carried by 84 against 51. In the minority were . . . Walpole . . . Conway' (BM Add. MSS 32905, f. 70).

anything in the world?—This is saying no profligate thing. Is there anything I might not follow you in? You even did not tell me yesterday that you had spoken. Yet I will tell you all I have heard; though if there was a point in the world in which I could not wish you to succeed where you wish yourself, perhaps it would be in having you employed. I cannot be cool about your danger; yet I cannot know anything that concerns you, and keep it from you. Charles Townshend called here just after I came to town today. Among other discourse he told me of your speaking on Friday, and that your speech was reckoned hostile to the Duke of Newcastle.⁴ Then talking of regiments going abroad,⁵ he said, . . .⁶

With regard to your reserve to me, I can easily believe that your natural modesty made you unwilling to talk of yourself to me. I don't suspect you of any reserve to me: I only mention it now for an occasion of telling you that I don't like to have anybody think that I would not do whatever you do. I am of no consequence: but at least it would give me some, to act invariably with you; and that I shall most certainly be ever ready to do. Adieu!

Yours ever,

HOR. WALPOLE

4. According to HW, Newcastle was opposed to the bill, but forced to swallow it by Pitt (*Mem. Geo. II* loc. cit.). Newcastle wrote the E. of Kinnoull 15 Feb., 'We have an unfortunate affair at home. The Tories have inserted in their Qualification Bill a clause to continue the qualification the whole Parliament, and drawn very absurdly. Mr Pitt (contrary to all assurances) supports them in it. The Whigs are outrageous. The Duke of Devonshire will oppose it; and I shall oppose everything that varies from the last bill except the taking the oath in the House of Commons' (BM Add. MSS 32902, f. 194). In a letter to Hardwicke 23 Feb. Newcastle wrote, 'We might let it pass in the House of Commons, and fling it out in our House. I wish your Lordship could see Mr Pitt.—I own I am very uneasy upon this point. I should be sorry whether that the bill should pass as it is, or that we should do anything to create a coolness with Mr Pitt' (ibid. f. 338). On 4 March Newcastle wrote Hardwicke, 'I then went to Mr Pitt where I had but an uncomfortable audience—all upon the Qualification Bill. He was civil, but plainly extremely hurt . . . We differed in our opinions . . .' (BM Add. MSS 32903, ff. 82–3, 98).

5. Newcastle informed Granby 2 May of the 'resolution, which we have taken to send you immediately six of our best battalions, viz. Hodgson, Barrington, Bocland, Griffin now Carr's, Cornwallis's, and Lord Charles Hay now Griffin' (BM Add. MSS 32905, f. 230; see also ibid. ff. 181, 196, 242, 244). This is announced in the *London Chronicle* 6–8 May, vii. 446.

6. A passage has been omitted here in *Works*, so indicated by asterisks.

From BEAUCHAMP, Monday ?5 May 1760

Printed for the first time from a photostat of BM Add. MSS 23218, f. 18. Dated tentatively by the letter of 9 May 1760, which it obviously precedes; by Hertford to HW 5 June 1760, referring to HW's verses; and by HW's mention of them in 'Short Notes' (below, n. 1).

Ch[rist] Ch[urch] Monday evening.

Dear Sir,

IF I had not received too many proofs of your goodness and friendship for me to entertain the least doubt of either, I should not have ventured to trouble you again on the subject of poetry. The copy[1] is very much approved of,[2] but there is one objection raised to it, as not being in some parts of the narration sufficiently confined and directed to our marine, which they imagine sometimes is lost amidst the many interesting events by land. No one objection is raised against the absolute goodness of the piece, but as to the relative goodness of it to the thesis, some alterations and additions it is thought might make considerable improvement. I beg leave to state their opinion: 'The request of Arthur has something particular in it, he asks not of Merlin the fate of Britain as of a common kingdom, but as of one eminently distinguished by Heaven, secluded from all natural connections with the continents by its situation, and on that situation he grounds his hopes that it may one day arise the sovereign of the world and centre of universal commerce without which no sovereignty can be lasting. The conclusion from this [is] that a few verses in Arthur's speech touching the nature of the island Britain, might be an improvement. Merlin struck with the particular turn of this inquiry, fired as it were with an instantaneous afflatus of the prophetic spirit, rushes *in medias res;* that Britain will be mistress of the world and that every river will swell with the tributary offerings of subject nations; but then correcting himself laments that this great event will not be accomplished till late, that an undue attention to maritime affairs and the ambition of a dangerous rival will retard the completion of it. He shows how the

1. HW's verses 'on the destruction of the French navy,' written in April 1760 'as an exercise for Lord Beauchamp at Christ Church Oxford' ('Short Notes,' GRAY i. 35). The verses have not been found, but probably commemorated Admiral Hawke's defeat of the French invasion fleet under Marshal de Conflans at the Battle of Quiberon Bay, 20–21 Nov. 1759.

2. Presumably by Beauchamp's tutors.

English are foiled when they attend to continental wars; in this light the allusions to history will be rather more pertinent and interesting. Merlin sees a whole race of monarchs whose heroic actions deserve commendation, but none appear truly sensible of the kingdom's natural strength before Elizabeth. She puts the marine on a proper footing and lays the foundation of our future successes. The latter part, particularly the allegory of Justice, is unexceptionable.'

How many excuses ought I to make for troubling a man of such true taste with such trifling criticisms, but as my composition stands or falls by their opinion, there is a necessity of conforming thereto. I throw myself upon your generosity for pardon in thus troubling you to correct or insert what you think necessary in conformity to their objections. The composition is so really good, that I should be sorry if it was not made perfect. I am, dear Sir,

Your most sincere friend,

BEAUCHAMP

'Tis unnecessary after what has [been] said to observe that the latter part was comparatively thought rather short: whether a few verses describing the advantages we receive in commerce from our successes, might not be very proper, is submitted to Mr Walpole. If you have not got a copy of the poem I will send it to you immediately. I hope you will consign this letter to the fire, that it may not expose the liberties I take upon the assurance of your friendship.

From HENRIETTA SEYMOUR CONWAY, Tuesday 6 May 1760

Printed for the first time from a photostat of BM Add. MSS 23218, f. 15.

Chichester, 6th May 1760.

Good Mr Walpole,

I HAD the favour of yours[1] on Wednesday last[2] and on Saturday I had received your most noble and valuable present;[3] I may justly term it so, as you have made it so to me in all respects. I know no

1. *Ante* ca 28 April 1760.
2. 30 April.
3. Clarendon's *Life;* see *ante* 11 April 1760.

one so polite and generous as yourself, for which reason you should be the last I find should be employed in such a commission. I would have wrote to Lady Hyde[4] for it, but was fearful she would make me a present of it, which would look so like begging, made me choose to trouble you, but perhaps I might have been safer from that *quarter,* there being few people has so generous a spirit as yourself. It is a most charming print and very handsomely bound indeed.

I received the franks, which I am also obliged to you for. I doubt you will think me a troublesome acquaintance. How kind it is in you to send a thought after my health, which, thank God, continues pure well. I am sure no one can be gladder to hear of yours than, dear Sir,

Your most obliged humble servant,

H. SEYMOUR CONWAY

PS. You do poor old Pelham[5] a great deal of honour in remembering her; she takes the liberty of sending her duty.

To BEAUCHAMP, ca Wednesday 7 May 1760

Missing; answered *post* 9 May 1760.

From BEAUCHAMP, Friday 9 May 1760

Printed for the first time from a photostat of BM Add. MSS 23218, f. 19.

Ch[rist] Ch[urch] May the 9th.

Dear Sir,

I WAS very far from desiring so considerable an alteration as you seem to understand from my last letter. I own any request of that sort was very unreasonable after the trouble you have been so good to take, but I beg to explain my meaning lest I should seem guilty of bad taste and being excessively unreasonable. The objec-

---

4. Charlotte Capel (1721–90), dau. of William, 3d E. of Essex, by Jane Hyde, dau. of the 4th E. of Clarendon; m. (1752) Thomas Villiers, cr. (1756) Bn Hyde of Hindon and (1776) E. of Clarendon.
5. Presumably Miss Conway's maid.

tions I there stated were very far from being my own opinion; they savoured strong of the logical turn of this place which admits of no deviation even in poetry from the thesis. To obviate this I proposed inserting a few lines here and there where the descriptions of our actions on the Continent were long, to represent the state of the navy at the time being. This I imagined might make it rather more agreeable to the inspectors, but the reasons you offer against undertaking it are so good that I have laid aside all thoughts of such a revision. I can assure you the time which you gave up in so friendly a manner to my service, has not been thrown away. It fully answers my utmost wishes as a good poem and as a fresh mark of your zeal and friendship for, dear Sir,

Your most sincere friend,

Beauchamp

From Hertford, Thursday 5 June 1760

Printed for the first time from a photostat of BM Add. MSS 23218, f. 22.

London, June 5th 1760.

Dear Horry,

I HAVE just received Con's verses from Oxford as he has altered them; I have not time to read them, but just enough to enclose them to you and beg your opinion of them as they now stand. He declares he has no confidence in his own judgment; it is in yours he hopes for satisfaction. He expresses a thousand obligations for the assistance he has received from you. The objection which strikes him at present is the small extent of the latter part about our naval victories; if it appears an objection to you and his opinion is at all founded, you will add to the many [?favours] already received if you are so good to remove it by adding to that part of the poem. My son is grateful and attentive enough to own his obligations to you in a manner that I have not time to express for him. The verses are in another cover sent by this post; be so good to direct them and what you have to say to me or my son upon them to Ragley near Alcester in Warwickshire.

Excuse the hurry I am in, and believe me, dear Horry, at all times and in all places,

Most truly and affectionately yours,

Hertford

To Hertford, June 1760

Missing; answered *post* 21 June 1760.

From Hertford, Saturday 21 June 1760

Printed for the first time from a photostat of BM Add. MSS 23218, f. 23.

Ragley, June 21st 1760.

Dear Horry,

I THINK your remarks upon my son's verses just, and I hope he is persuaded to keep more to your plan. He has been advised by those who have more learning than judgment, that they were not to his purpose; that opinion, or rather that apprehension, made him take great pains to alter them with that view. It is natural now to suppose him a little unwilling to part with his own composition, but I flatter myself when the poem is finished and shown that they will not be altered in a manner to deface the original. He thinks himself under the highest obligations to you, and I hope for his sake and character no suspicion will arise that he has been well assisted.

My son desired me when I wrote to you to say from him that if you and my brother are at any time unemployed he shall be very happy to see you at Oxford. From the 7th to the 10th of next month are, as I understand, busy days there;[1] any time before the 7th or after the 11th to the 20th he shall be more at liberty, and pleased to receive you.

What account do I see in the papers of a defeat near Quebec?[2] I hope that place is not in danger of being retaken.

1. Because of the feast at Christ Church on 8 July, in honour of its founder, Cardinal Wolsey (*post* 9 July 1760).

2. News of the English defeat at the Battle of Sillery, 28 April, reached London on 17 June (Mann v. 416 and nn. 1–

In the course of next month, and I believe about the middle of it, I am to wait a week at Kensington,[3] when I shall hope to see you. Lady Hertford desires her best compliments, and I am, dear Horry, with true regard,

Very faithfully and sincerely yours,

HERTFORD

To CONWAY, Saturday 21 June 1760

Printed from the MS now WSL; first printed Wright iv. 65–7. For the history of the MS see *ante* 29 June 1744 OS. This letter may have been written on the 20th rather than the 21st; see nn. 5, 6.
Endorsed: Mr Walpole 21 June 1760.

Strawberry Hill, June 21st 1760.

THERE is nothing in the world so tiresome as a person that always says they will come to one and never does;[1] that is a mixture of promises and excuses, that loves one better than anybody, and yet will not stir a step to see one; that likes nothing but their own ways and own books, and that thinks the Thames is not as charming in one place as another, and that fancies Strawberry Hill is the only thing upon earth worth living for—all this *you* would say, if even *I* could make you peevish; but since you cannot be provoked, you see I am for you, and give myself my due. It puts me in mind of General Sutton,[2] who was one day sitting by my father at his dressing—Sir Robert said to Jones[3] who was shaving him, 'John, you cut me'—presently afterwards, 'John, you cut me'—and again, with the same patience or Conwayence, 'John, you cut me'— Sutton started up and cried, 'By God if he can bear it, I can't; if you cut him once more, damn my blood if I don't knock you down—' my dear Harry, I will knock myself down—but I fear I shall cut

5). The French besieged Quebec, but retired 17 May after an English squadron arrived on the 15th (*post* 28 June 1760).

3. Hertford was in waiting from 13 to 19 July (*post* Lady Hertford to HW 28 June; Hertford to HW 19 July).

1. HW finally visited Park Place on his return from Oxford, where he and Conway were on 15 July (*post* 28 June 1760; MONTAGU i. 288).

2. Richard Sutton (1674–1737), Lt-Gen., 1735; M.P. Newark 1708–10, 1712–37.

3. Not further identified.

you again. I wish you *sorrow* of the battle of Quebec⁴—I thought as much of losing the duchies of Aquitaine and Normandy as Canada. However, as my public feeling never carries me to any great lengths of reflection, I bound all my Quebecquian meditations to a little diversion on Geo[rge] Townshend's absurdities. The *Daily Advertiser* said yesterday that a certain great officer who had a principal share in the reduction of Quebec had given it as his opinion that it would hold out a tolerable siege.⁵ This great General has acquainted the public today in an advertisement,⁶ with what do you think, not that he has such an opinion, for he has no opinion at all and does not think that it can nor cannot hold out a siege—but in the first place, that he was *luckily* shown this paragraph, which however he does not like; in the next, that he is and is not that great general, and yet that there is nobody else that is, and thirdly lest his silence, till he can proceed in *another* manner with the printer (and indeed it is difficult to conceive what manner of *proceeding* silence is) should induce anybody to believe the said paragraph, he finds himself under a necessity of giving the public his honour that there is no more truth in this paragraph, than in some others which have tended to set the opinions of some general officers together by the ears—a thing, however inconceivable, which he has shown may be done, by the conclusion he himself has made in the King's English. For his *another manner* with the printer, I am impatient to see how the charge will lie against Matthew Jenour,⁷ the publisher of the

4. The battle of Sillery (see previous letter).

5. The paragraph appeared in the *Daily Adv.* 19 June: 'It is said that a certain great officer, who had a principal hand in the reduction of Quebec, has given his opinion, that it is able to hold out a considerable siege.'

6. Townshend's advertisement, dated 'Audley-Square, June 19,' is quoted in the *London Chronicle* 19–21 June, vii. 593–4 *sub* 20 June, as having appeared 'this morning': 'Having luckily been shown the following paragraph in the *Daily Advertiser* of yesterday, viz. [variation of quotation of n. 5 above]. Although I am very far from claiming some part of the said description, yet being the only person now in England who acted as a general officer in the late expedition against Que-

bec, I find myself under a necessity, lest my silence, until I can proceed in another manner with the printer, should induce any person to credit the said paragraph, to assure the public, upon my honour, and as a man of truth, that there is no more foundation in this paragraph, than in many other unfair and false suggestions which have appeared in some of the public papers, and been whispered about the town, tending to set the opinions of the general officers lately employed in Canada, in opposite and unfavourable lights.'

7. Either Matthew Jenour, printer of Gilt-Spur Street, London, 1707–25, who inherited the *Daily Advertiser* from his father-in-law in 1755, or his son Matthew (1707–86) who continued publishing the *Daily Advertiser* and who was Master of

Advertiser, who without having the fear of God before his eyes has forcibly, violently and maliciously, with an offensive weapon called a hearsay and against the peace of our sovereign Lord the King, wickedly and traitorously assaulted the head of George Townshend, General, and accused it of having an opinion, and him the said George Townshend, has slanderously and of malice prepense believed to be a great general—in short, to make Townshend easy, I wish, as he has no more contributed to the loss of Quebec, than he did to the conquest of it, that he was to be sent to sign this capitulation too![8]

There is a delightful little French book come out, called, *Tant mieux pour elle*—it is called Crébillon's,[9] and I should think was so—I only borrowed it, and cannot get one; *tant pis pour vous*—by the way I am not sure you did not mention it to me; somebody did.

Have you heard that Miss Pitt[10] has dismissed Lord Buckingham? *Tant mieux pour lui.* She damns her eyes that she will marry some captain—*tant mieux pour elle.* I think the forlorn Earl should match with Miss Ariadne Drury—[11] and by the time my Lord Halifax has had as many more children and sentiments by and for Miss Falkner,[12]

the Stationers' Company in 1769 (John Nichols, *Literary Anecdotes,* 1812–15, i. 290–1, iii. 726–7; GM 1853, n.s. xxxix [cxciii] . 325, xl [cxciv]. 434; H. R. Plomer et al., *Dictionary of the Printers and Booksellers . . . in England, Scotland and Ireland from 1668 to 1725,* Oxford, 1922, pp. 171–2; idem, *Dictionary of the Printers . . . from 1726 to 1775,* Oxford, 1932, p. 140).

8. Townshend had succeeded to the command of Quebec, and had signed the articles of capitulation of the town 18 Sept. 1759, after Wolfe was killed and the second-in-command, Brig.-Gen. Monckton, was wounded in the battle on 13 Sept.; see MANN v. 337–8 and nn. 1, 2.

9. It was not by Crébillon and is usually attributed to Claude-Henri Fuzée de Voisenon (1708–75) or to Charles-Alexandre de Calonne (*Biographie universelle,* 1811–62, xlix. 400, 411; BM Cat.). The book is not mentioned in Hazen, *Cat. of HW's Lib.*

10. Presumably Harriot Pitt (1745–63), dau. of George Morton Pitt, m. (1762) Brownlow Bertie, 5th D. of Ancaster. HW

mentions her engagement to Buckinghamshire in his letter to Montagu 23 Dec. 1759 (MONTAGU i. 263 and n. 9).

11. Mary Anne Drury (1740–69), whom Lord Buckinghamshire did marry 14 July 1761. She had been betrothed to Lord Halifax in April, but the engagement had been broken off at the beginning of June (ibid. i. 278 and n. 1, 300 and n. 1; CHUTE 302).

12. Anna Maria Falkner, niece of George Faulkner, the Dublin printer, who had been married (1748) and deserted by William Donaldson, had long been Halifax's mistress. According to the *Town and Country Magazine,* May 1769, i. 227, which would seem to be confirmed by this letter and by anecdotes recorded by William Cole in 1763, her tearful imposition with her child by Halifax, Anna Maria Montagu (d. *post* 1771) caused the broken engagement (CHUTE loc. cit.; MONTAGU i. 278 and n. 2, 300 and n. 1; ii. 204 and n. 14, 246, 335). He also had an illegitimate son, George, who d. 1767, but about whom nothing else seems to be known (ibid. ii. 246, n. 6).

as he can contrive to have, probably Miss Pitt may be ready to be taken into keeping. Good night.

Yours ever,

H. W.

The Prince of Wales has been in the greatest anxiety for Lord Bute,[13] to whom, he professed to Duncombe[14] and Middleton,[15] he has the greatest obligations; and when they pronounced their patient out of danger, his Royal Highness gave to each of them a gold medal of himself,[16] as a mark of his sense of their care and attention.

From CONWAY, ca Wednesday 25 June 1760

Missing; implied in HW's letter of the 28th, when he accepts the invitation to meet Conway at Chalfont.

To HERTFORD, ca Wednesday 25 June 1760

Missing; written in reply to Hertford's letter of 21 June; alluded to *post* 28 June.

---

13. Who had been ill of the epidemic fever and sore throat which was rife in London during May and June. He was reported 'quite recovered' in the *Daily Adv.* 20 June. His own account of his 'most nauseous and tormenting disease' and of the Prince's attentions is in Bute to Campbell 5 July, cited in *Letters from George III to Lord Bute 1756–1766*, ed. Sedgwick, 1939, p. 46, n. 3. See also MANN v. 416 and n. 8.

14. William Duncan (ca 1715–74), cr. (1764) Bt; physician to George III both as Prince and King.

15. David Middleton (ca 1705–85), sergeant-surgeon to the King: surgeon-general to the army (GM 1786, lvi pt i. 82).

16. Bute mentions these in the letter to Campbell cited above, n. 13.

To Conway, Saturday 28 June 1760

Printed from *Works* v. 66–7.

Strawberry Hill, June 28, 1760.

THE devil is in people for fidgeting about! They can neither be quiet in their own houses, nor let others be at peace in theirs! Have not they enough of one another in winter, but they must cuddle in summer too? For your part, you are a very priest: the moment one repents, you are for turning it to account. I wish you was in camp—never will I pity you again. How did you complain when you was in Scotland, Ireland, Flanders, and I don't know where, that you could never enjoy Park Place? Now you have a whole summer to yourself, and you are as *junkettaceous* as my Lady Northumberland.[1] Pray, what horse-race do you go to next? For my part, I can't afford to lead such a life: I have Conway papers to sort;[2] I have lives of the painters to write;[3] I have my prints to paste, my house to build,[4] and everything in the world to tell posterity.[5]—How am I to find time for all this? I am past forty, and may not have above as many more years to live; and here I am to go here and to go there.—Well, I will meet you at Chaffont[6] on Thursday; but I positively will stay but one night. I have settled with your brother[7] that we will be at Oxford on the 13th of July, as Lord Beauchamp is only loose from the 12th to the 20th.[8] I will be at Park Place on the 12th,[9] and we will go together the next day. If

1. Lady Northumberland was an indefatigable traveller; her diary for 1760 records her junkets in England and Scotland that spring and summer (*The Diaries of a Duchess*, ed. James Greig, 1926, pp. viii, 15–26).

2. The Conway family correspondence which HW had found at Ragley in Aug. 1758 (*ante* 2 Sept. 1758).

3. HW had begun writing the *Anecdotes of Painting* on 1 Jan.; he completed the first volume on 14 Aug., and the second was written between 5 Sept. and 23 Oct. ('Short Notes,' GRAY i. 34–5).

4. HW had just begun the additions to SH that were to include the Round Tower, Great Cloister, the Gallery and other rooms; the Round Tower and Great Cloister were probably completed in

1761, the rest, not until 1763 (MANN v. 410 and n. 25).

5. Writing his *Memoirs*.

6. Chalfont, Lady Mary Churchill's house. HW mentions having just returned from two days there with Conway, Lady Ailesbury, Lady Lyttelton and Mrs Shirley in his letter to Montagu 4 July (MONTAGU i. 284–5).

7. Presumably in a missing letter, ca 25 June. The date of the visit was changed to the 15th while they were at Chalfont (ibid. i. 285), as HW suggests below it might be.

8. As Hertford had told HW *ante* 21 June.

9. HW apparently did not visit Park Place until on his return from Oxford (*ante* HW to Conway 21 June 1760, n. 1).

this is too early for you, we may put it off to the 15th: determine by Thursday, and one of us will write to Lord Hertford.[10]

Well! Quebec is come to life again.[11] Last night I went to see the Holdernesses,[12] who by the way are in raptures with Park[13]—in Sion Lane: as Cibber says of the Revolution, I met the Raising of the Siege;[14] that is, I met my Lady in a triumphal car, drawn by a Manks horse thirteen little fingers high, with Lady Emily,[15]—

> —et sibi Countess
> Ne placeat, ma'amselle curru portatur eodem—[16]

Mr M_____[17] was walking in ovation by himself after the car; and they were going to see the bonfire at the alehouse at the corner. The whole procession returned with me; and from the Countess's dressing-room we saw a battery fired before the house, the mob crying, 'God bless the good news!'—These are all the particulars I know of the siege: my Lord would have showed me the journal,[18] but we amused ourselves much better in going to eat peaches from the new Dutch stoves.

The rain is come indeed, and my grass is as green as grass; but all my hay has been cut and soaking this week, and I am too much in the fashion not to have given up gardening for farming; as next I suppose we shall farming, and turn graziers and hogdrivers.

I never heard of such a Semele[19] as my Lady Stormont[20] brought

10. HW wrote directly to Beauchamp instead (post ca 4 July 1760).

11. News that the siege of Quebec had been lifted on 17 May, after the arrival of an English squadron, reached London 27 June (London Gazette Extraordinary 27 June; MANN v. 419, n. 1).

12. At Syon Hill.

13. Presumably, 'Place' is omitted.

14. 'Met the Revolution at Nottingham. Took arms on that side' (heading to Chapter III of An Apology for the Life of Mr Colley Cibber, 1740, p. 34). HW's annotated copy is Hazen, Cat. of HW's Lib., No. 450. HW also alludes to the line in letters to Mann 7 Aug. 1745 OS (MANN iii. 92) and to Lady Ossory 20 June 1783 (OSSORY ii. 402).

15. Lady Amelia Darcy (1754–84), Bns Conyers, s.j., 1778; m. 1 (1773) Francis Godolphin Osborne, M. of Carmarthen (div. 1779); m. 2 (1779) John Byron.

16. 'And may it please the Countess, Mademoiselle is carried in the same chariot.' It was the custom for a conquering hero returning to Rome to have his children with him in the chariot in the triumphal procession.

17. Wright and subsequent editors expand to 'Milbank'; one of the brothers of Sir Ralph Milbanke, M.P., who was connected with the Holdernesses (Namier and Brooke iii. 137–8; MANN iv. 172, n. 2).

18. Perhaps the letter from Gen. Murray to Pitt, printed in the Gazette Extraordinary 27 June. Holderness, as a secretary of state, would have had copies of the dispatches received.

19. Daughter of Cadmus, King of Thebes; she was destroyed by lightning when Zeus granted her request that he appear before her in his true shape (SELWYN 159, n. 3).

20. See ante 11 Oct. 1759, n. 19.

to bed in flames. I hope Miss Bacchus Murray[21] will not carry the resemblance through, and love drinking like a Pole. My Lady Lyttelton is at Mr Garrick's,[22] and they were to have breakfasted here this morning; but somehow or other they have changed their mind. Good night!

Yours ever,

Hor. Walpole

From Lady Hertford, Saturday 28 June 1760

Printed for the first time from a photostat of BM Add. MSS 23218, f. 24. Dated by the reference to HW's intended visit to Lord Beauchamp.

Ragley, Saturday the 28th.

Sir,

AS you are so good as to intend Lord Beauchamp a visit on the 13th at Oxford, we hope you will acquaint him the time of day you propose being there, that he may be ready to receive you. I wish Ragley could tempt you to come on farther, but this summer I fear we must despair of having that pleasure.[1] My Lord begins waiting on the 13th, and hopes to see you at Kensington in the course of that week. I am, Sir,

Your faithful and obedient humble servant,

I. Hertford

To Beauchamp, ca Friday 4 July 1760

Missing; answered *post* 9 July 1760. HW mentions in his letter to Montagu 4 July 1760 (MONTAGU i. 285) that he is going to write Beauchamp that he will be in Oxford on the 15th.

21. Hon. (later Lady) Elizabeth Mary Murray (18 May 1760–1825), m. (1785) George Finch Hatton (Collins, *Peerage*, 1812, v. 150; see also Mary Granville, Mrs Delany, *Autobiography and Correspondence*, ed. Lady Llanover, 1861–2, vi. 304–5; *Scots Peerage* viii. 209).

22. The villa Garrick had bought in 1754 at Hampton (MONTAGU i. 198; BERRY i. 33, n. 27).

————

1. HW visited Ragley about 20 Aug. (*post* 19 July 1760, n. 2).

From BEAUCHAMP, Wednesday 9 July 1760

Printed for the first time from a photostat of BM Add. MSS 23218, f. 25.

Ch[rist] Ch[urch] July the 9th.

Dear Sir,

THE hurry and business of yesterday when the members of our College, as usual, feasted in honour of their founder,[1] prevented me from returning you my immediate thanks for the favour you intend me. I shall be ready to receive you at three o'clock, and hope that you and Mr Conway will condescend to eat some college commons with me at Christ[2] Church. Your apprehensions of visiting Oxford at a time when it is crowded with company, are entirely groundless: for the Long Vacation commences this week and I fancy before the 15th Oxford will be entirely deserted. I do not propose leaving it till the 28th. I am, dear Sir,

Your sincere friend,

BEAUCHAMP

From HERTFORD, Saturday 19 July 1760

Printed for the first time from a photostat of BM Add. MSS 23218, f. 26.

Kensington, July 19th 1760.

Dear Horry,

I HAVE lived in hopes of seeing you here; as my week[1] ends today, I now despair, and you must give me leave to acquaint you that the Duke and Duchess of Grafton have fixed to be at Ragley on the 15th August, when Lady Hertford and I both beg you will meet them there.[2] I will not talk of ceilings and works,[3] wherein

1. Thomas Wolsey (ca 1475–1530), cardinal, received letters patent for the foundation of Cardinal College (now Christ Church) in July 1525.
2. MS, 'X^t.'

_____

1. Of waiting (*ante* Hertford to HW 21 June 1760).
2. The visit of the Graftons was sub-

sequently postponed to 20 Aug., when HW did meet them at Ragley (*post* 24 July, 10, 14 Aug.; MONTAGU i. 292–4).
3. Some of the decoration at Ragley may have been done by Francis Vassali, stuccoist (Christopher Hussey, *English Country Houses: Early Georgian 1715–1760*, 1955, p. 18).

I should be glad to have your opinion, but will acknowledge the passion of that and the time they stay at Ragley to be loo, in which you will be most useful and obliging to make one. We are very impatient here for news, but none of any consequence is come in my week. I intend going tomorrow to my brother's in my way to Ragley; and am, dear Horry,

Very affectionately and sincerely yours,

HERTFORD

To HERTFORD, ca Tuesday 22 July 1760

Missing; from Hertford's letter of the 24th, it appears that HW wrote accepting the invitation to Ragley for 15 Aug., although implying that so early a date was somewhat inconvenient.

From HERTFORD, Thursday 24 July 1760

Printed for the first time from a photostat of BM Add. MSS 23218, f. 27.
Memorandum (by HW, f. 29 verso):
'There was another person, too illustrious an lover and even practitioner of the art, to be omitted, though I find no mention of him in Vertue's MSS.'[1]

Ragley, July 24th 1760.

Dear Horry,

THIS morning Lady Hertford had a letter from the Duchess of Grafton desiring as the Chatsworth party was put off for some days on account of Darby races,[2] that we would excuse their being at Ragley till the 19th.[3] Lady Hertford answers it by this post and

1. This sentence, slightly amended, opens the account of Edward Courtenay (1526–56), 'the last Earl of Devonshire,' in the first volume of HW's *Anecdotes of Painting* (1762, p. 128), which he finished writing 14 Aug. (*ante* HW to Conway 28 June 1760, n. 3).
2. Run 5 Aug. 1760 (*Baily's Racing Register*, 1845, i. 195).
3. Hertford enclosed part of the Duch-

ess's letter: 'Wakefield Lodge, July 21st. The Duke of Grafton having yesterday received a letter from the Duke of Devonshire to desire us to put off our coming to Chatsworth a few days on account of Derby Races, this obliges us to change our whole scheme; and so to defer the pleasure of waiting on you and Lord Hertford till the 19th of August if that time is agreeable' (BM Add. MSS 23218, f. 28).

fixes the party for this place to the 20th, as I am obliged to attend Warwick races on the 19th. We hope this alteration may make it more convenient to you, as by leaving Lord Strafford's[4] a day or two sooner than you proposed, you may take Ragley on your return upon the 20th and it will be adding very little to the length of your journey upon a good post road.

I am still concerned that your inclination to oblige us should make it necessary for you to write and change your plan so often. You see it is on our part unavoidable, and we beg you will make one of the loo table at Ragley on the 20th. The party removes from Trentham here and I expect Lord Gower will adjourn with their Graces to Ragley.

I see in the papers some of the Guards are going to fill up the gap occasioned by the last mistake;[5] perhaps in time my brother may be wanted.[6]

I remain with Lady Hertford's compliments, dear Horry,

Ever truly yours,

HERTFORD

I expect my brother here to meet their Graces.[7] Enclosed you have a part of the Duchess's letter to my Lady.[8]

4. HW was planning to leave London to visit Wentworth Castle on 9 Aug., but his first serious attack of the gout caused a change in his plans and he did not go until after his visit to Ragley (MANN v. 429; CHUTE 303; post 23 Aug. 1760).

5. The defeat of the advance corps of the Allied army under the Hereditary Prince by the French at Corbach on 10 July, the news of which reached London on 21 July. They had underestimated the size of the opposing forces (London Chronicle 19–22, 22–24 July, viii. 77, 78, 80, 81; Daily Adv. 22 July; MANN v. 427 and n. 5). On the 21st orders were issued for three battalions of the Guards to ready themselves to march; on the 23d it was announced that four battalions would leave for Germany on the 28th and a review

was held in St James's Park at which they received their foreign supplies (Daily Adv. 23, 24 July; London Chronicle 19–22, 22–24 July, viii. 78, 81).

6. Conway was sent to the British army in Germany as second in command under the M. of Granby in late March 1761 (post 10 April 1761; HW to Montagu 25–30 March 1761, MONTAGU i. 350; GM 1761, xxxi. 139).

7. Conway wrote the D. of Devonshire 14 Aug., 'Both Lady A. and I are extremely unhappy the north does not lie within our reach for this year. We have promised my brother a short and it must be a very short visit at Ragley . . .' (Chatsworth MSS, 416/64).

8. See above, n. 3.

From Conway, ca Monday 4 August 1760

Missing; implied in the last two paragraphs *post* 7 Aug. 1760, where HW seems to be commenting on passages in it.

To Conway, Thursday 7 August 1760

Printed from *Works* v. 68–9.

Strawberry Hill, August 7, 1760.

I CAN give you but an unpleasant account of myself, I mean unpleasant for me; everybody else I suppose it will make laugh. Come, laugh at once! I am laid up with the gout,[1] am an absolute cripple, am carried up to bed by two men, and could walk to China as soon as cross the room. In short, here is my history: I have been out of order this fortnight, without knowing what was the matter with me; pains in my head, sicknesses at my stomach, dispiritedness, and a return of the nightly fever I had in the winter.[2] I concluded a northern journey[3] would take all this off—but behold! on Monday morning I was seized as I thought with the cramp in my left foot; however, I walked about all day: towards evening it discovered itself by its true name, and that night I suffered a great deal. However, on Tuesday I was again able to go about the house; but since Tuesday I have not been able to stir, and am wrapped in flannels and swathed like Sir Paul Pliant on his wedding-night.[4] I expect to hear that there is a bet at Arthur's which runs fastest, Jack Harris or I.[5] Nobody would believe me six years ago when I said I had the gout.[6] They would do leanness and temperance honours to which they have not the least claim.

I don't yet give up my expedition: as my foot is much swelled, I

1. HW wrote about this attack to Strafford 7 Aug. (CHUTE 303) and to Montagu 12 Aug. (MONTAGU i. 291–2).

2. In his letter to Montagu 28 Jan. HW mentions having had 'a nervous fever these six or seven weeks every night' (ibid. i. 271).

3. His projected visit to Wentworth Castle (*ante* 24 July 1760, n. 4).

4. In Congreve's *Double-Dealer*.

5. John Harris of Hayne in Devonshire, married to Mr Conway's eldest sister (HW). He was a chronic sufferer from gout (*post* 25 May 1766, 31 Dec. 1774).

6. HW mentioned this attack to Bentley 16 Nov. 1755 and 6 Jan. 1756 (CHUTE 259–60, 264).

trust this alderman distemper is going: I shall set out the instant I am able; but I much question whether it will be soon enough for me to get to Ragley by the time the clock strikes loo. I find I grow too old to make the circuit with the charming Duchess.[7]

I did not tell you about German skirmishes, for I knew nothing of them:[8] when two vast armies only scratch one another's faces, it gives me no attention. My gazette never contains above one or two casualties of foreign politics:—overlaid, one king;[9] dead of convulsions, an electorate;[10] burnt to death, Dresden.[11]

I wish you joy of all your purchases; why, you sound as rich as if you had had the gout these ten years. I beg their pardon; but just at present, I am very glad not to be near the vivacity of either Missy or Peter.[12] I agree with you much about the *Minor:*[13] there are certainly parts and wit in it. Adieu!

Yours ever,

Hor. Walpole

7. Anne Liddel Duchess of Grafton (HW). The 'circuit' was Chatsworth, Trentham and Ragley; HW had been invited to join them at the first as well as at Ragley (MANN v. 427; CHUTE 303–4).

8. The most important, after the defeat at Corbach (or Korbach) on 10 July (*ante* 24 July 1760 and n. 5), had been a minor victory by the Hereditary Prince at Emsdorf near Marburg on 16 July (MANN v. 427 and n. 6).

9. Frederick the Great, whose army had suffered a major defeat at Landeshut 23 June and who was in grave danger from Russian troops as well (ibid. v. 419 and nn. 2–3).

10. Hanover; it was expected that a de-

feat of the Allies by the French at this time would lead to the loss of Hanover and Hesse (ibid. v. 427).

11. Which Frederick the Great had burnt while besieging it in mid-July; he had, however, raised the siege on 23 July (news of which reached London 1 Aug.) and abandoned it during the night of 29–30 July (ibid. v. 428 and n. 11).

12. A favourite greyhound (HW).

13. A comedy by Samuel Foote (1720–77), satirizing Whitefield and the Methodists, which had opened at the Little Theatre in the Haymarket 28 June; see MONTAGU i. 326–7 and nn. 10–11 and *London Stage* Pt IV, ii. 801. HW's copy is Hazen, *Cat. of HW's Lib.,* No. 1810:1:1.

RAGLEY HALL,

SEAT OF THE MARQUIS OF HERTFORD.

Drawn & Engraved by T. Radclyffe

Published by W. Emans Birmingham.

From HERTFORD, Sunday 10 August 1760

Printed for the first time from a photostat of BM Add. MSS 23218, f. 30. Sent to HW at Wentworth Castle (*post* 14 Aug. 1760).

On the back page of this letter (f. 31 verso) HW has written in pencil what appears to be a draft for part of an otherwise missing letter; see HW to Unknown ca 15 Aug. 1760.

Ragley, August 10th 1760.

Dear Horry,

GIVE me leave to acquaint you that the Duke and Duchess of Grafton have now desired to be at Ragley on the 19th, having some business that will carry them back to Northamptonshire sooner than I think they at first proposed; my brother and Lady Ailesbury have likewise fixed to be here on the 19th, and if it is not inconvenient I wish you would meet them here on that day. The Hereditary Prince has been again successful[1] I find; Prince Ferdinand is fortunate in having the French for his enemy when their affairs are so ill directed.[2]

I remain with the compliments of this family, dear Horry,

Most truly yours,

HERTFORD

1. At the battle of Warburg, 31 July, news of which reached London on 8 Aug. (*London Gazette Extraordinary* 9 Aug.; *Daily Adv.* 9 Aug.).

2. The *London Chronicle* 5–7 Aug. published a French account of the battle of Emsdorf (16 July) which emphasized the general confusion and lack of organization among the French troops before and during the battle, and their non-existent reconnaissance (viii. 136).

To Hertford, Tuesday 12 August 1760

Printed for the first time from the MS now wsl. The MS was sold Sotheby's 13 [14] March 1865 ('another property' with Joseph Cottle Sale), lot 140 to Moffatt; Sotheby's 27 Oct. 1959 (George Moffatt Sale), lot 499, to Maggs, and Maggs to wsl 10 Nov. 1959.

Strawberry Hill, Aug. 12, 1760.

My dear Lord,

YOU will be surprised at a letter from hence while you are thinking me at Wentworth Castle. Alas! I am no more that volatile creature I was! I cannot now tire Lord Beauchamp, and run over Oxford from morning till night![1] I have taken my degrees under your brother Jack Harris, Professor of Gout—in short, since yesterday sennight I have been laid up with that respectable malady in both feet—My legs, by the help of flannels are grown of a very portly size, and though I cannot guess where I got any flesh to swell, have swelled, till I have been carried to bed by two servants. The pain is now almost gone, and today I walk alone with a stick, but when I shall be able to get out I know not:[2] I trust, time enough to be with you by the twentieth. You will laugh, and so do I, when I don't cry; but my chief satisfaction has been in abusing Temperance and Leanness, who have made such a fool of me, and made me think myself invulnerable and immortal. I find vices are at least honester; *their* consequences one expects—but it is woeful to be as much deceived in one's own virtues as in those of other people. I should as soon have expected to get a bad distemper, by making a vow of chastity, as the gout by the hardiness and regularity of my way of life. My dear Lord, I beg your pardon for abusing your friends the Virtues, but consider I had but one such friend in the world and see how she has served me. 'Tis shocking when one has chosen a mistress for her

1. HW told Montagu, after his return from Oxford, that he 'ferreted from morning to night' and 'fatigued' Lord Beauchamp (Montagu i. 288). The same letter mentions some of his discoveries, which are listed in greater detail in *Country Seats* 24–5.

2. Conway wrote from Park Place to the D. of Devonshire 14 Aug., 'I wish for his sake H. Walpole may be able to wait upon you but alas the poor gentleman has been laid up with the gout, an honour his friends little expected for him, and to which, though I love him, I must say he has as little pretension as any man in England. If he is able he thinks of coming here today by way of trying his wings for a longer flight but doubts much if he shall be able to reach the north, which I believe is a great mortification to him' (Chatsworth MSS, 416/64).

ugliness and meagreness, to be betrayed with as much impudence as if she was as agreeable as the poor Countess[3] in your neighbourhood.

I received a *Gazette Extraordinary* yesterday,[4] and the bells have been ringing, and the guns going off for a piece of victory; but I think it is not quite allowed. They say our army is retired, and Cassel taken by the French;[5] but I know nothing certain; I am an old gouty man, that live in my armchair and can't tell how the world passes—I have done with it—Well! What would I take to be first minister, if I had the gout as much as Mr Pitt—I have thought often that his fits were political, now I am persuaded of it. Last Friday I should have flung my standish[6] at a General Wolfe's head, if he had come to plague me with a plan for taking Quebec. Adieu! all you young creatures.

Yours ever,

H. WALPOLE

From HERTFORD, Thursday 14 August 1760

Printed for the first time from a photostat of BM Add. MSS 23218, f. 32.

Ragley, August 14th 1760.

Dear Horry,

AS I dined today at Lord Archer's[1] I have but a minute to pity your gout and to say that if you are able, as we all most heartily wish, we hope you will be here on the 19th instead of the 20th as first pro-

3. The Countess of Coventry, one of the beautiful Gunning sisters, died 30 Sept. at Croome Court, Worcs, after a long illness. Dr Wall's letter to Selwyn, 8 Aug., describes her condition (J. H. Jesse, *George Selwyn and His Contemporaries*, 1882, i. 173–5).

4. Apparently the *Gazette Extraordinary* 9 August, on the battle of Warburg, 31 July (*ante* 10 Aug. 1760, n. 1).

5. 'Notwithstanding the great advantages just gained over the French, it is reported that they are in possession of the city of Cassel. The French, upon meeting with a resistance from the troops in that

city, immediately fired into it with red-hot balls, which set fire to several houses; upon which Prince Ferdinand sent them orders to surrender the city, rather than have it destroyed by such inhuman proceedings' (*London Chronicle* 9–12 Aug., viii. 150, *sub* 12 Aug.).

6. Inkstand.

———

1. Umberslade, near Henley-in-Arden, Warwickshire. Hertford probably alludes to a tedious dinner which he and HW had once endured there, perhaps in 1751 (*post* 7 April 1765; HW to Montagu 22 July 1751, MONTAGU i. 121).

posed; the Duke and Duchess of Grafton, my brother, Lady Ailesbury etc. being expected at Ragley on the 19th by their Graces' appointment.

I wrote to you some days ago[2] to give you notice of it, and directed my letter to Wentworth Castle.

We have no stranger at present with us but Mr Varey.[3] The best wishes and compliments of this family always attend you and we hope to see you on the 19th.

Yours most truly and affectionately,

HERTFORD

To LADY AILESBURY, Saturday 23 August 1760

Printed from the MS now WSL; first printed, with omissions, *Works* v. 549–50, and in full Toynbee iv. 417–19 and *Supp.* ii. 117. The MS was sold Sotheby's 5 Dec. 1921 (Waller Sale), lot 6, to Maggs; sold by Maggs, June 1932, to WSL.

Whichnovre,[1] Aug. 23d 1760.

WELL, Madam, if I had known whither I was coming, I would not have come alone! Mr Conway and your Ladyship should have come too. Do you know, this is the individual Manor House, where married persons may have a flitch of bacon upon the easiest terms in the world?[2] I should have expected that the owners would be ruined in satisfying the conditions of the obligation, and that the Park would be stocked with hogs instead of deer—on the contrary, it is thirty years since the flitch was claimed,[3] and Mr Offley was never

2. *Ante* 10 Aug. 1760.
3. Possibly Rev. William Varey (ca 1712–94), son of James Varey, of St James's, Westminster; perhaps student at Eton 1725–8; matriculated at Christ Church, Oxford, 1729; vicar of Stillington, Yorks (Foster, *Alumni Oxon.*; R. A. Austen-Leigh, *Eton College Register 1698–1752*, Eton, 1927, p. 350; GM 1794, lxiv pt i. 386).

———

1. The name is correctly Wichnor (MONTAGU i. 294, n. 5).

2. From the time of Edward III, at least, one of the terms on which the manor of Wichnor was held was that the lord of the manor should give a flitch of bacon to any man who would swear that for a year and a day he had never regretted marrying and that he would, if free, take the same spouse again; see the references cited ibid. i. 294, n. 6.

3. HW repeats this in *Country Seats* 27, but no record apparently survives of any successful claim (MONTAGU loc. cit.).

so near losing one as when you and Mr Conway were at Ragley. He so little expects the demand, that the flitch is only hung in effigy over the hall chimney, carved in wood.[4] Are not you ashamed, Madam, never to have put in your claim? It is above a year and a day that you have been married, and I never once heard either of you mention a journey to Whichnovre. *If you quarrelled at loo every night,*[5] you could not quit your pretensions with more indifference. I had a great mind to take my oath, as one of your witnesses, that you neither of you would, if you were at liberty, prefer anybody *else, ne fairer ne fouler,* and I could easily get twenty persons to swear the same—I could almost engage as much for my Lord and Lady Hertford—but on reflection, the utmost I would venture in conscience to depose for him, is, that though I do not believe he has wished for fewer wives, I am a little afraid he may have wished for more wives. For you two, I should not have the least doubt of your being qualified to take the oath, except from your having neglected to take it. Therefore, unless you will let the world be convinced, that all your apparent harmony is counterfeit, you must set out immediately for Mr Offley's, or at least send me a letter of attorney to claim the flitch in your names, and I will send it up by the coach to be left at the Blue Boar, or wherever you will have it delivered. But you had better come in person; you will see one of the prettiest spots in the world; it is a little paradise, and the more like the antique one, as, by all I have said, the married couple seems to be driven out of it. The house is very indifferent;[6] behind is a pretty park; the situation, a brow of a hill, commanding sweet meadows, through which the Trent serpentizes in numberless windings and branches. The spires of the Cathedral of Litchfield are in front at a distance, with variety of other steeples, seats and farms, and the horizon bounded by rich hills covered with blue woods. If you love a prospect, or bacon, you will certainly come hither.

4. This is also mentioned in *Country Seats* loc. cit.

5. Probably an allusion to the D. and Ds of Grafton. HW told Montagu, 1 Sept., that the Duke had been unsuccessful at loo at Ragley and 'had some high words with Pam'; disputes over the Duchess's passion for deep gaming were a contributing cause to their growing estrangement and eventual separation and divorce (MONTAGU i. 293–4 and n. 3, 363–4, n. 9).

6. It had been built by Offley's father. HW commented in *Country Seats* 27: 'The house is very small, with a bit of garden with clipt hedges, and a pretty park. The situation charming, on the brow of a steep hill, the Trent serpentines extremely through a rich meadow at the foot. Litchfield, several other churches and seats, with hills and pendent woods, enrich the view.'

Wentworth Castle, Sunday night.

I had writ thus far yesterday, but had no opportunity of sending my letter. I arrived here last night, and found only the Duke of Devonshire who went to Hardwicke[7] this morning; they were down at the menagerie, and there was a clean little pullet, with which I thought his Grace looked as if he should be glad to eat a slice of Whichnovre bacon. We follow him to Chatsworth[8] tomorrow, and make our entry to the Public Dinner,[9] to the disagreeableness of which I fear even Lady Mary's[10] company will not reconcile me.

My Gothic building,[11] which my Lord Strafford has executed in the menagerie, has a charming effect. There are two bridges built besides;[12] but the new front is very little advanced.[13] Adieu! Madam,

Your most affectionate evidence,

HOR. WALPOLE

To CONWAY, ?Monday ?8 ?September ?1760

Printed from *Works* v. 70. This letter is placed in *Works* immediately after HW's letter of 19 Sept. 1760, but seems to belong at the beginning of Conway's period of waiting as a groom of the Bedchamber. In refusing the D. of Devonshire's invitation to Chatsworth, Conway wrote 14 Aug., 'Both Lady A. and I are extremely unhappy the north does not lie within our reach for this year. We have promised my brother a short and it must be a very short visit at Ragley after which the necessary duty of my military employment carries me into Kent and Essex which will take me up till the return of my waiting on the 7th of next month' (Chatsworth MSS, 416/64). Under Chatham, 3 Sept., the *Daily Adv.* 5 Sept. reported, 'This morning the two regiments encamped here were reviewed by General Conway, who afterwards set out for Barham Downs.' Since Conway

7. Hardwick Hall, which HW visited, and did not admire, on his return to London. See MONTAGU i. 296–8; *Country Seats* 29–30.

8. This was HW's first visit to Chatsworth, where he stayed four days. See MONTAGU i. 295–6; *Country Seats* 28–9.

9. In ibid. 29 HW mentions that 'the Duke of Devonshire keeps two public days in a week,' when he apparently entertained the families of the neighbourhood.

10. Lady Mary Coke.

11. In his notes on this visit to Wentworth Castle, ibid. 28, HW mentions 'a Gothic building in the menagerie, proposed by me and drawn by Mr Bentley, on the idea of Chichester Cross; built by this Lord.' See also HW to Bentley Aug. 1756 (CHUTE 266–7) and HW to Montagu 1 Sept. 1760 (MONTAGU i. 295 and n. 15).

12. These are also mentioned in *Country Seats* 28.

13. HW mentions this as 'begun,' ibid.

expected to be in waiting in London by Sunday 7 Sept., HW might have asked him to stop at SH on his way to London on Friday 5 Sept.

You are good for nothing; you have no engagement, you have no principles; and all this I am not afraid to tell you, as you have left your sword behind you. If you take it ill, I have given my nephew,[1] who brings your sword, a letter of attorney to fight you for me; I shall certainly not see you: my Lady Waldegrave[2] goes to town on Friday, but I remain here.[3] You lose Lady Anne Conolly[4] and her forty daughters,[5] who all dine here today upon a few loaves and three small fishes. I should have been glad if you would have breakfasted here on Friday on your way;[6] but as I lie in bed rather longer than the lark, I fear our hours would not suit one another. Adieu!

Yours ever,

HOR. WALPOLE

From CONWAY, ca Wednesday 17 September 1760

Missing; answered *post* 19 Sept. 1760.

1. Probably Edward Walpole (1737–71), natural son of HW's brother, Sir Edward Walpole (DU DEFFAND i. 253, n. 6, iii. 57, n. 1); Cornet, 1755, and Lt, 1759, in the 6th (Inniskilling) Dragoons; Capt., 1759, and Maj., 1763 in the 16th (Burgoyne's) Light Dragoons; Lt-Col., 1768, in the 19th (Drogheda's) Light Dragoons in Ireland (*St James's Chronicle* 11–13 April 1771; *Army Lists*, 1756–69 *passim*).
2. Maria Walpole (1736–1807), natural dau. of Sir Edward Walpole; m. 1 (1759) James Waldegrave, 2d E. Waldegrave; m. 2 (1766) William Henry, D. of Gloucester.
3. At Strawberry Hill (HW).
4. Sister of William, [2d] Earl of Strafford (HW); see BERRY i. 56, n. 8; MORE 196, n. 3. At this time she lived in London or at Stretton Hall in Staffordshire; later

she lived at Copt Hall about half a mile from SH.
5. She had six daughters: Catharine (d. 1771), m. (1754) Ralph Gore, E. of Ross; Anne (d. 1805), m. (1761) George Byng, M.P.; Harriet, m. (1764) Rt Hon. John Staples, M.P.; Frances (ca 1742–1817), m. (1765) Sir William Howe, 5th Vct Howe; Caroline (ca 1755–1817), m. (1770) John Hobart, 2d E. of Buckinghamshire; Jane, m. George Robert Fitzgerald (Sir Bernard Burke, *A Genealogical History of the Dormant . . . Peerages of the British Empire*, 1866, p. 577; Brian Fitzgerald, *Lady Louisa Conolly*, 1950, p. 23; GM 1805, lxxv pt ii. 1085; see also Collins, *Peerage*, 1812, iv. 371, vi. 91, viii. 152; Mervyn Archdall and John Lodge, *Peerage of Ireland*, 1789, iii. 287).
6. See headnote above.

To Conway, Friday 19 September 1760

Printed from *Works* v. 69–70.

Strawberry Hill, September 19, 1760.

THANK you for your notice, though I should certainly have contrived to see you without it. Your brother promised he would come and dine here one day with you and Lord Beauchamp. I go to Navestock[1] on Monday, for two or three days; but that will not exhaust your waiting.[2] I shall be in town on Sunday; but as that is a Court day, I will not, so don't propose it—dine with you at Kensington; but I will be with my Lady Hertford about six, where your brother and you will find me if you please. I cannot come to Kensington in the evening, for I have but one pair of horses in the world, and they will have to carry me to town in the morning.

I wonder the King expects a battle; when Prince Ferdinand can do as well without fighting, why should he fight? Can't he make the Hereditary Prince gallop into a mob of Frenchmen, and get a scratch on the nose;[3] and Johnson[4] straddle cross a river and come back with six heads of hussars in his fob, and then can't he thank all the world, and assure them he shall never forget the victory they have not gained? These thanks are sent over:[5] the *Gazette* swears that this no-success was chiefly owing to General Mostyn;[6] and the *Chronicle* protests, that it was achieved by my Lord Granby's losing his hat,[7] which he never wears; and then his Lordship sends over for

1. Lord Waldegrave's seat in Essex.

2. Mr Conway was a groom of the Bedchamber to the King, and then in waiting at Kensington (HW). His waiting began 7 Sept.; see headnote, *ante* ?8 ?Sept. ?1760.

3. The Hereditary Prince had been slightly wounded at Corbach on 10 July.

4. James Johnston (ca 1721–97), at this time Lt-Col. commanding the 1st Dragoons; Lt-Gen., 1777; Gen., 1793; Lt-Gov. of Minorca 1763–74; Gov. of Quebec, 1774 (MONTAGU i. 28, n. 19). The praise of him in Prince Ferdinand's order of thanks after the battle of Warburg (below, n. 5) had provided HW, Conway, and Lady Ailesbury with a subject about which to tease his fiancée, the Hon. (later Lady) Henrietta Cecilia West (CHUTE 305).

5. Prince Ferdinand's orders of thanks, dated 1 Aug., to the officers engaged in

the battle of Warburg 31 July, were printed in the *London Chronicle* 28–30 Aug., viii. 216 and in the *Daily Adv.* 1 Sept.

6. John Mostyn (1709–79), Col. 5th Dragoons 1758–60, 7th Dragoons 1760–3, 1st Dragoon Guards 1763–79; Maj.-Gen., 1757; Lt-Gen., 1759; Gen., 1772; M.P.; commander of the British cavalry in Germany 1759–62 and acting commander of all British forces during the winter of 1759–60. The *London Gazette* No. 10024, 5–9 Aug., printed Granby's letter to Holdernesse of 1 Aug. crediting Mostyn with the cavalry's success at Warburg.

7. The *London Chronicle* 19–21 Aug. (viii. 184) reported 'that in the affair of the 31st, the Marquis of Granby, having dropt his hat, broke the French lines three times bareheaded'; and in the issue for 13–16 Sept. (viii. 266) printed an ode

three hundred thousand pints of porter to drink his own health;[8] and then Mr Pitt determines to carry on the war for another year; and then the Duke of Newcastle hopes that we shall be beat, that he may lay the blame on Mr Pitt, and that then he shall be minister for 30 years longer; and then we shall be the greatest nation in the universe. Amen!—My dear Harry, you see how easy it is to be a hero. If you had but taken Impudence and Oatlands[9] in your way to Rochfort, it would not have signified whether you had taken Rochfort or not. Adieu! I don't know who Lady A.'s Mr Alexander[10] is.—If she curls like a vine with any Mr Alexander but you, I hope my Lady Coventry will recover[11] and be your Roxana.

Yours ever,

Hor. Walpole

From HERTFORD, Thursday 25 September 1760

Printed for the first time from a photostat of BM Add. MSS 23218, f. 33.

London, September 25th 1760.

Dear Horry,

I HAVE spoke to Lady Yarmouth as you desired me and she has most readily undertaken to obtain the King's consent for Lady Hervey's going through St James's Park.[1] No more time will be taken about it than what is necessary in form, as his Majesty signs his name to these things it seems; her Ladyship will speak tomorrow, makes no doubt about its being granted, and desired me to say

'On the Marquis of Granby's losing his Hat, and charging the French Lines bareheaded.'

8. The previous year the *London Chronicle* (17–20 Nov. 1759, vi. 486) reported, 'It is said the Hon. the Marquis of Granby has ordered some thousand barrels of porter to be sent to the army in Germany at his own expense, for the use of the private men.' A similar report after the battle of Warburg has not been found; see also W. E. Manners, *Some Account of the . . . Marquis of Granby*, 1899, p. 143.

9. Oatlands Park, Weybridge, Surrey. It belonged to the D. of Newcastle (though

it was occupied at this time by his nephew, Lord Lincoln).

10. Perhaps the same 'Mr Alexander' who is listed on the cover, *post* 20 July 1761 *bis*.

11. She died 30 Sept. of a combination of tuberculosis and white lead poisoning.

———

1. The park was open to all for walking, but special permission from the King was necessary for driving there (Hon. Mrs Evelyn Cecil, *London Parks and Gardens*, 1907, pp. 71–2). HW's suit for Lady Hervey was granted promptly; see HW to Montagu 14 Oct. 1760, Montagu i. 305.

to you she was glad to do anything wherein you interested yourself.

If I had had time today and had thought of it at the moment I saw you, which I am not sure I did, I should have been glad to have mentioned to you, as a person whom upon all occasions I esteem my friend, what has passed lately upon bringing my brother into Parliament.[2]

When I see you next I will talk to you about it; in the meantime and in great hurry, believe me, dear Horry,

Always most sincerely yours,

HERTFORD

To HERTFORD, Friday 10 October 1760

Missing; answered in the postscript, *post* 11 Oct. 1760.

From HERTFORD, Saturday 11 October 1760

Printed for the first time from a photostat of BM Add. MSS 23218, f. 34.

London, October 11th 1760.

Dear Horry,

HARRY does not command the expedition[1] if it goes, which I think at present a little doubtful and may depend on events in Germany; Kingsley[2] is recovered for it and his Majesty will not

2. Presumably a negotiation with the D. of Grafton, since Conway was returned for the borough of Thetford, where Grafton had great influence, at the general election of 1761. Conway had sat for St Mawes in the Falmouth interest in the Parliament of 1754.

1. A secret expedition (originally designed in the spring of 1760 for an attack on Mauritius in the Indian Ocean) which Pitt had revived 30 Sept. in response to pleas from Prince Ferdinand for a diversion to prevent the French from reinforcing their army in Germany. Its ob-

ject was now an immediate descent on Belle-Île. The project was strongly opposed by Newcastle, Hardwicke, and the military and naval commanders; it was further delayed by the King's death on 25 Oct., and was finally postponed in December until the following year (J. S. Corbett, *England in the Seven Years' War*, 1907, ii. 81–2, 95–104; Richard Waddington, *La Guerre de sept ans*, [1899–1914], iv. 396–7; MANN v. 437–8 and nn. 3–4). Conway had requested the command but was refused (MONTAGU i. 307; MANN v. 444).

2. William Kingsley (ca 1698–1769), Col.

send a lieutenant-general. I have taken the opportunity to express my grievances about Harry, though I feel much secret comfort when I consider the sort of service at this time of year and his peculiar circumstances.

A letter yesterday from Mr Yorke[3] informs the Ministers that the Hereditary Prince had taken possession of Clèves[4] with five hundred French prisoners, that he had invested Wesel on the 3d[5] and had prevented two regiments intended to reinforce the garrison from getting into the place;[6] on the 27th of last month Marshal Broglio is said to have made no motion, nor to have taken any visible step in consequence of this detachment under the H. Prince.

I remain, dear Horry,

Always most truly yours,

Hertford

After I had sealed my letter I received yours, and though I am in waiting I will call upon you and carry you to Leicester House as you propose.[7] The hour will be something before two and I will come to you in my chariot from Kensington; after Court you may return with me to dine at Kensington or dine with my Lady and Mr Bowman[8] in Grosvenor Street[9] as she wishes you to do.

of the 20th Foot 1756; Maj.-Gen. 1758; Lt-Gen. Dec. 1760. He had previously been appointed to command the land forces of the expedition when it was directed against Mauritius, and again kissed hands as commander of the revived expedition, 12 Oct. (GM 1760, xxx. 485).

3. His letter dated The Hague, 6 Oct., is paraphrased in the London Gazette No. 10042, 7–11 Oct.

4. 3 Oct. (ibid.)

5. This news had already reached England on the 6th or 7th, in a letter from The Hague of 4 Oct. (London Chronicle 4–7 Oct., viii. 344; London Gazette No. 10041, 4–7 Oct.).

6. 'It is said, that the two Swiss regiments of Lochman and Planta, which were on their march to reinforce the garrison of that place [Wesel], had been prevented in that design' (London Gazette No. 10042, 7–11 Oct.).

7. HW had asked Hertford to take him to thank the D. of York for his unexpected visit to SH on 10 Oct.; see HW to Montagu 14 Oct. 1760 (Montagu i. 304–7) for an account of the visit and the problems created for HW by the necessity of going to Leicester House. He did not, however, go on Sunday the 12th as he planned to do in the present letter; see post 22 Oct. 1760, n. 1.

8. Walter Bowman, who had been travelling tutor to Hertford during his Grand Tour and was later travelling tutor to Lord Beauchamp (ante 2 July 1737 OS, 24 March 1739 NS).

9. Hertford's town house (ante 14 July 1759, n. 3). Lady Hertford's twelfth child (sixth daughter) had just been born on 4 Oct. (Lloyd's Evening Post 3–6 Oct., vii. 332).

To LADY AILESBURY, ca Friday 17 October ?1760

Missing. Mentioned in HW to Selwyn 19 Oct. ?1760 (SELWYN 160): 'I have writ to my Lady Ailesbury about the commode, and have not heard from her.'

From LADY AILESBURY, ca Sunday 19 October ?1760

Missing. Mentioned in HW to Selwyn 21 Oct. ?1760 (SELWYN 161): 'My Lady Ailesbury is much obliged to you, and very glad to have the commode, without seeing it, provided I approve it.'

From LADY HERTFORD, Wednesday 22 October 1760

Printed for the first time from a photostat of BM Add. MSS 23218, f. 40. Dated by the references to HW's projected visit to Leicester House, and to Clanricarde's letter.

London, Wednesday the 22d.

Sir,

AS Lady Mary Coke tells me you intend to do right[1] and go to Leicester House next Sunday, I am sure you will be glad to know that though my Lord is out of town now, that he will be back time enough to attend you there; and I hope you will dine with us afterwards that I may hear from yourself how you have behaved. Lady Northumberland told me last night she had received a very agreeable present[2] from you and admired it vastly. I want to beg one copy, but as I own it is not for myself, you may refuse me if you have the least inclination; the person I wish to give it to is Doctor Hunter,[3] who is already an humble admirer of yours, and

1. HW had postponed his projected visit to Leicester House on 12 Oct. for reasons explained in his letter to Montagu 14 Oct. 1760 (MONTAGU i. 305–7), and had submitted his problem to 'a jury of court matrons' probably including Lady Mary Coke. He intended to go on Sunday the 26th, but the death of George II on the

25th enabled him to kiss hands on the 28th (ibid. i. 310, 313).
2. HW's *Fugitive Pieces in Verse and Prose*, printed at SH in 1758. Lady Northumberland's copy has not been located.
3. William Hunter (1718–83), M.D. 1750; anatomist and collector (see MASON ii. 86, n. 6). He attended Lady Hertford at the births of her four youngest children

must become still more so when he has had the pleasure of reading the *Fugitive Pieces*. I conclude you have heard of Lord Clanricarde's[4] extraordinary letter to the Duke of Bedford that was in last Saturday's *Chronicle*,[5] and I hope will see it. Excuse my giving you this trouble, and believe me

Very faithfully yours,

I. Hertford

From Hertford, Saturday 1 November 1760

Printed for the first time from a photostat of BM Add. MSS 23218, f. 35.

London, November 1st 1760.

Dear Horry,

BY a deed made just after the battle of Culloden and not revoked, the late King[1] has I hear left to the Duke[2] most part of his jewels and a hundred and fourscore thousand pounds; great part of which is out upon mortgage, may with difficulty be recovered, and part of it probably lost. By will he has left to the Duke, Princess Amelia and the Princess of Hesse fifty thousand. The Duke is said to have given up his share; the two sisters will jointly enjoy the interest whilst they live and the survivor is to have the whole. To Lady Yarmouth he has left a bureau with eight or nine thousand pounds in it.

(Montagu i. 238; *post* 27 Aug., 3 and 18 Dec. 1764, ?7 April 1768). HW's *Fugitive Pieces* does not appear in the catalogue of Hunter's library, although he possessed other works by HW (Mungo Ferguson, *The Printed Books in the Library of the Hunterian Museum in the University of Glasgow*, Glasgow, 1930, pp. 62, 159, 174, 175, 373, 381, 385).

4. John Smith Bourke (after 1752 De Burgh) (1720–82), 11th E. of Clanricarde.

5. Selections from Clanricarde's letter to Bedford, which had been published as a pamphlet in Dublin, were printed in the *London Chronicle* 16–18 Oct., viii. 384, with the explanation that the omitted sections were 'not fit to appear in a public paper.' The letter, dated from the

Camp at Winchester, 1 Aug. 1760, concerned the repeated challenges given Bedford by Clanricarde, which the former had ignored, and blamed all the problems of Ireland on Bedford's administration as lord lieutenant. Bedford had Clanricarde prosecuted for it; see *Mem. Geo. III* i. 24; *Bedford Corr.* ii. 427.

———

1. George II died on 25 Oct. Contemporary accounts of the details of his will, which was opened 31 Oct., vary, but those given here are generally in accord with other reliable reports; see Montagu i. 317, n. 2. HW repeats many of the details in his letter to Mann 1 Nov. (Mann v. 450).

2. Of Cumberland.

I suppose he must have spent a great deal in this war, for this will not be dying rich.

Yours most truly,

HERTFORD

To HERTFORD, December 1760

Missing; answered *post* 13 Dec. 1760.

From HERTFORD, Saturday 13 December 1760

Printed for the first time from a photostat of BM Add. MSS 23218, f. 36.

Ragley, December 13th 1760.

Dear Horry,

WHAT can I say to you from hence but that we feel vastly obliged for the news you send us from London. We are here only with our children about us; I shoot chief part of the day, and my Lady is not so well amused.

I cannot be very sorry for the Duke of Richmond;[1] I have no opinion of his Grace's judgment, and his temper will bear humbling.

My new painted ceiling is finished not ill nor very elegantly; I hope you will be satisfied with it, and with an improvement I have lately made in the front of the house which opens the meadows and a part of the river at present to our view.

My eldest sons are to be here next week. I am to leave it to be in

---

1. Who had resigned as a lord of the Bedchamber on 8 Dec. after a quarrel with King George III, in protest against the promotion of Lord Fitzmaurice to be aide-de-camp to the King over the head of Lord George Lennox, the Duke's brother (*Letters from George III to Lord Bute 1756–1766*, ed. Sedgwick, 1939, pp. 50–1). Richmond's own sister, Lady Caroline Fox, echoed Hertford's sentiments about the event: 'He had indeed made a fine *tripotage* altogether. . . . I'm glad I was angry at him before, else I should have been exceedingly hurt at this; as it is I am very sorry, for it's a thousand pities with so many good and pleasing qualities as he has, to give himself such a *travers dans le monde* and throw away the prospect (at least of a most agreeable situation in life) before him. . . . The King's behaviour has been, by what I find, very sensible, very polite and very firm' (*Leinster Corr.* i. 304). See also *Mem. Geo. III* i. 19–21.

town on Saturday[2] where I shall hope to meet you at the opera;[3] and am with Lady Hertford's best compliments, dear Horry,

Always very affectionately yours,

HERTFORD

From LADY HERTFORD, Monday ?15 December 1760

Printed for the first time from a photostat of BM Add. MSS 23218, f. 39. Placed in Dec. 1760 because of its reference to the 'disagreeably select' royal loo parties (below, n. 1) and tentatively dated the 15th since it was certainly written shortly before Hertford went to London on the 20th (*ante* 13 Dec. 1760).

Ragley, Monday night.

Sir,

MY Lord desires me to say he is very sensible of your goodness in writing to him so constantly, and I flatter myself with the hopes of meeting with the same indulgence from you when he is gone from Ragley. The post comes here every day, therefore you need not confine yourself to writing on general post-days when it is not convenient to you. Are you admitted yet into the royal loo party,[1] or is it as disagreeably select as ever? My Lord had a summons from Lady Isa[bella] Finch[2] to be at her house tomorrow night. If this happens often of an opera night, I fancy the Duchesses will grow to dislike it. Pray don't forget to visit the Duchess of Cleveland's picture.[3] My Lord is so sleepy with having been out all day a-shooting, that he can hardly keep himself awake enough to give his affectionate compliments to you. I am

Faithfully yours,

I. HERTFORD

2. 20 Dec.

3. HW shared box No. 3 on the ground tier with Hertford and others (CHUTE 350, n. 8); see *post* 20 July 1761, n. 17.

———

1. The 'wonderfully select and dignified' loo parties for Princess Amelia, the Duke of Cumberland, etc., given frequently at this time. HW attended his first at Norfolk House on 7 Jan. 1761

(MONTAGU i. 331), and thereafter became a regular member.

2. (d. 1771), the first lady of the Bedchamber to Princess Amelia (Collins, *Peerage*, 1812, iii. 401). Her house was in Berkeley Square (ibid.).

3. Probably a portrait of Lady Henrietta Finch (ca 1705–42), m. (1732) William Fitzroy, 3d D. of Cleveland; Lady Isabella Finch's sister.

From CONWAY, ca Wednesday 1 April 1761

Missing; written after his arrival in Holland and answered *post* 10 April 1761.

To CONWAY, Friday 10 April 1761

Printed from *Works* v. 72–3.

Arlington Street, April 10, 1761.

IF Prince Ferdinand had studied how to please me, I don't know any method he could have lighted upon so likely to gain my heart, as being beaten out of the field before you joined him.[1] I delight in a hero that is driven so far that nobody can follow him. He is as well at Paderborn,[2] as where I have long wished the King of Prussia, the other world. You may frown if you please at my imprudence, you who are gone with all the disposition in the world to be well with your commander; the peace is in a manner made,[3] and the anger of generals will not be worth sixpence these ten years. We peaceable folks are now to govern the world, and you warriors must in your turn tremble at our subjects the mob, as we have done before your hussars and court martials.

I am glad you had so pleasant a passage.[4] My Lord Lyttelton

1. Conway was on his way to the army in Germany (below, n. 4). Prince Ferdinand and the Allied army had been forced to retire after the Hereditary Prince was attacked and defeated near Grünberg 21 March (MANN v. 498, n. 10; MONTAGU i. 353 and n. 3).

2. He had established himself there about 1 April (MANN v. 498, n. 11; MONTAGU i. 353). Conway wrote the D. of Devonshire from Paderborn 5 May, 'I met with as favourable a reception from the Prince and as much politeness as it was possible in any reason for me to expect; which has continued the same ever since; he shows great attention, and has a manner that makes him easy and agreeable enough without entirely forgetting the

dignity of his station and character . . . I dine with him two or three times a week' (Chatsworth MSS, 416/67).

3. Negotiations for peace between England and France were about to begin on the basis of a *mémoire* and letter from Choiseul of 26 March (MANN v. 498, n. 9).

4. From Harwich to Helvoetsluys (HW). Conway and 'several officers set out in post chaises for Germany' 26 March (GM 1761, xxxi. 139; *Daily Adv.* 30 March) and Conway wrote the D. of Devonshire from 'Newmarket Friday,' 27 March, 'I could not stop at Newmarket without paying my compliments to you . . . I proposed going on board today but found our ship would not be ready till Sunday morning so had just time to run down and back

would say,[5] that Lady Mary Coke, like Venus, smiled over the waves, *et mare præstabat eunti.*[6] In truth, when she could tame me, she must have had little trouble with the ocean. Tell me how many burgomasters she has subdued, or how many would have fallen in love with her if they had not fallen asleep? Come, has she saved two-pence by her charms?[7] Have they abated a farthing of their impositions for her being handsomer than anything in the seven provinces? Does she know how political her journey is thought? Nay, my Lady A., you are not out of the scrape; you are both reckoned *des Maréchales de Guébriant,*[8] going to fetch, and *consequently* govern the young Queen.[9] There are more jealousies about your voyage, than the Duke of Newcastle would feel if Dr Shaw[10] had prescribed a little ipecacuanha[11] to my Lord Bute.[12]

again' (Chatsworth MSS, 416/65). From The Hague he wrote 10 April 'that by Lord Granby's arrival here, we are now determined upon our journey forward and shall set out in a day or two: I mean Lord Frederick [Cavendish] and I, leaving the ladies behind us' (ibid. 416/66). He left The Hague for Paderborn 14 April (GM 1761, xxxi. 186; *London Chronicle* 21–3 April, ix. 385).

5. HW often ridicules Lyttelton's pompous style (e.g., *post* 31 July 1762).

6. 'And calmed the sea for the traveller'; HW is presumably paraphrasing Ovid's line, 'Venus orta mari mare præstat amanti' ('Venus who rose from the sea calms the sea for the lover') (*Heroides* xv. 213). Lady Mary and Lady Ailesbury had accompanied Conway; he wrote the D. of Devonshire 10 April, 'Lady Mary has shone in health, spirits and good humour beyond anything. I can't say enough to commend her as a *compagne de voyage.* Lady Ailesbury too holds up her head pretty well' (Chatsworth MSS, 416/66). Gen. Mostyn wrote Newcastle from Hanover 22 April, 'We hear of General Conway, Lady Ailesbury, Lady Mary Cook, and *plusieurs autres* great personages on this side of the water and on the road to the army, but none of them are yet come up to it' (BM Add. MSS 32922, ff. 126–7).

7. Lady Mary was given to petty economies.

8. The Maréchale de Guébriant was sent to the King of Poland with the char-

acter of ambassadress by Louis XIII [XIV] to accompany the Princess Marie de Gonzague, who had been married by proxy to the King of Poland at Paris (HW). Renée du Bec-Crespin (d. 1659), m. (1632) Jean-Baptiste Budes, Comte de Guébriant, Maréchal de France. HW also alludes to her mission in his letter to Lady Hervey 3 Feb. 1766 (MORE 102 and n. 4).

9. Who had not yet been selected, although it was generally believed at this time that a Princess of Brunswick would be chosen (Henry Fox to Lady Caroline Fox 7 April, in *Life and Letters of Lady Sarah Lennox,* ed. Lady Ilchester and Lord Stavordale, 1902, i. 100), and Lady Mary had planned to go to Brunswick (below, n. 18). The most serious candidate by April 1761 was the Princess of Darmstadt, unfavourable reports having been received of the Princess of Schwedt. The eventually successful candidate, the Princess of Strelitz (*post* 11 July 1761, n. 5), was already being considered (*Letters from George III to Lord Bute 1756–1766,* ed. Sedgwick, 1939, pp. 22–3, 51–3).

10. Peter Shaw, M.D.; physician in ordinary to George II and George III (*ante* 29 Aug. 1748 OS, n. 10).

11. The root of a South American plant, much used as an emetic (OED).

12. Bute had become secretary of state, at Newcastle's suggestion, in March; the appointment was generally known by the 12th, but he was not formally sworn in until the 25th (Sir Lewis Namier, *England*

I am sorry I must adjourn my mirth, to give Lady A. a pang; poor Sir Harry Ballenden[13] is dead; he made a great dinner at Almac's for the House of Drummond, drank very hard, caught a violent fever, and died in a very few days.[14] Perhaps you will have heard this before; I shall wish so; I do not like, even innocently, to be the cause of sorrow.

I do not at all lament Lord Granby's leaving the army,[15] and your immediate succession. There are persons in the world who would gladly ease you of this burthen.[16] As you are only to take the vice-royalty of a coop, and that for a few weeks,[17] I shall but smile if you are terribly distressed. Don't let Lady A. proceed to Brunswic:[18] you might have had a wife[19] who would not have thought it so terrible to

in the Age of the American Revolution, 2d edn, New York, 1961, pp. 163–7; MANN v. 487, nn. 1–4).

13. Uncle to the Countess of Ailesbury (HW). Hon. Henry Bellenden (d. 7 April 1761), Kt, 1749; Gentleman Usher of the Black Rod, 1747; Keeper of Hurst Castle, 1745 (Scots Peerage ii. 73–4, which quotes this letter; GM 1745, xv. 389). His sister was Lady Ailesbury's mother.

14. HW gives a few details to Montagu 16 April (MONTAGU i. 359).

15. Granby arrived in London 14 April, left 25 May, and sailed from Harwich to return to Germany 1 June (GM 1761, xxxi. 186, 281; London Chronicle 11–14 April, 4–6 June, ix. 360, 542; Hist. MSS Comm., 12th Report, App. pt v, Rutland MSS, ii. 250).

16. According to HW, Conway's appointment had been opposed by the Bedford group 'in favour of General Waldegrave' (Mem. Geo. III i. 37). Conway wrote the D. of Devonshire Friday [27 March], 'I saw Lady Y[armouth] and am much obliged to your Grace for speaking to her as I found she had actually writ and was in the best humour and the civilest imaginable' (Chatsworth MSS, 416/65); and again 10 April, 'Mostyn goes over too; he is not with Lord Granby but probably on the road.—I suppose he will make some push if any accident prevents Lord G.'s return in which case I must recommend myself to your Grace's friendship to have a little care of me' (ibid. 416/66).

17. On 27 June from Soest Conway

wrote Devonshire, 'When I had the command you mention, which before the army came up here grew to be the advanced guard towards Monsieur de Soubise, Lord Granby and W[aldegrave] were not come up; it continued a good while after they did.—I suspect a little that was not quite liked, however this is mere conjecture. I have seen no sign of the least ill humour at all or from any quarter: but without that and apart from it il y a quelquefois une petite jalousie de métier. —H.S. [P. Ferdinand] told me the day the army came up [24 June], "Qu'il était très content de tous les arrangements que j'avais pris mais qu'il avait les mains un peu liées et qu'il ne pouvait pas faire tout de qui était de son inclination." He did not explain this farther.—I that day fell into the line with my command and the following night Lord Gr[anby] was detached with another: and had G. Waldegrave under him. They lie at a league and half on our left.' Conway concludes, 'I liked my command, and gave it up with some regret' (ibid. 416/68).

18. Where Lady Mary had planned to go; Conway wrote the D. of Devonshire 10 April, 'I won't say by whose fickleness it is that she [Lady Mary] has for the present, I believe, abandoned her Brunswick scheme, though Lord Granby's account of the security of the road has a little revived her former inclination' (ibid., 416/66). Lady Ailesbury remained at The Hague.

19. Lady Harrington, with whom Con-

fall into the hands (*arms*) of hussars; but as I don't take *that* to be your Countess's turn, leave her with the Dutch, who are not so boisterous as Cossacs or chancellors of the Exchequer.[20]

My love, my duty, my jealousy, to Lady Mary, if she is not sailed before you receive this—if she is, I shall deliver them myself. Good night; I write immediately on the receipt of your letter, but you see I have nothing yet new to tell you.

Yours ever,

Hor. Walpole

To Lady Ailesbury, ca Monday 25 May 1761

Missing; mentioned *post* 13 June 1761 as having been sent by Gen. Walde-grave, who left London for Germany 26 May (GM 1761, xxxi. 281).

way had been in love when she was Lady Caroline Fitzroy (*ante* 18 July NS, 20 July OS 1744).

20. Lady Harrington had been having an affair with Lord Barrington, who had become chancellor of the Exchequer during the ministerial changes in mid-March (Montagu i. 265 and n. 20, 344 and n. 20; Mann v. 490 and n. 23).

From HERTFORD, Friday ?12 June 1761

Printed for the first time from a photostat of BM Add. MSS 23218, f. 41. Placed in June 1761 because of the reference to the Hertfords' impending trip to Ireland, which began about Friday 26 June (*post* 1 July 1761); tentatively dated the 12th, since this seems to be the only Friday morning in the month on which HW could have left London, as Hertford mentions he has done. HW was at Arlington Street on Tuesday the 9th (HW to Lord Dacre 9 June 1761) and presumably still there on Thursday the 11th when he saw the Duchess of Grafton at Lady Kildare's, but was back at SH on Saturday the 13th (*post* 13 June 1761). The other Fridays are ruled out because HW intended to go to London from SH on Friday the 5th (HW to Lady Mary Coke 3 June 1761, MORE 23); a letter to Montagu from SH on Thursday the 18th makes no mention of an intention to go to London that night, as HW would have had to have done to meet the conditions of the present letter.

Grosvenor Street, Friday, three o'clock.

Dear Horry,

AS we go so soon into Ireland,[1] Lady Hertford thinks it right and would be glad to go to Court on Sunday; Lady Mary Coke and her have conversed upon it; and if equally convenient to you, will propose to dine at Strawberry on Tuesday instead of Sunday. If it is inconvenient you will freely tell me so, and we will dine with you on Sunday; if it is not, Lady Hertford will be less hurried and we shall prefer Tuesday.

I called at your house this morning and you was just gone.

Yours always most faithfully,

HERTFORD

Lady Mary, you understand, approves of Tuesday if you like it.

---

1. To Lisburn, co. Antrim, where Hertford owned estates estimated to be worth £9000 a year in 1767 ([Thomas Prior], *A List of the Absentees of Ireland*, Dublin, 1767, p. 5).

To Lady Ailesbury, Saturday 13 June 1761

Printed from the MS now WSL; first printed, with omissions, *Works* v. 551–3, and in full Toynbee v. 65–8 and *Supp.* ii. 119. For the history of the MS see *ante* 23 Aug. 1760.

Strawberry Hill, June 13th 1761.

I NEVER eat such good snuff, nor smelt such delightful bonbons, as your Ladyship has sent me. Every time you rob the Duke's[1] dessert, does it cost you a pretty snuff-box?[2] Do the pastors at The Hague[3] enjoin such expensive retributions? If a man steals a kiss there, I suppose he does penance in a sheet of Brussels lace. The comical part is, that you own the theft, and send it me, but say nothing of the vehicle of your repentance. In short, Madam, the box is the prettiest thing I ever saw, and I give you a thousand thanks for it. Don't trouble yourself about Delft[4]—nay, I am now afraid you should get any, lest you should pack it up in an old china jar, and really find a meaning for that strange auctioneer's word, a *rowwaggon*.[5]

When you comfort yourself about the operas, you don't know what you have lost—nay, nor I neither, for I was here, concluding that a serenata for a Birthday would be as dull and as vulgar as those festivities generally are—but I hear of nothing but the enchantment of it.[6] There was a second orchestra in the footman's gallery, disguised by clouds, and filled with the music of the King's Chapel. The choristers behaved like angels, and the harmony between the two bands was in the most exact time. Elisi[7] piqued himself, and beat both heaven and earth. The joys of the year do not end there. The under-actors open at Drury Lane tonight with a new comedy by Murphy[8] called, *All in the Wrong*.[9] At Ranelagh all is

1. The Duke of Richmond.
2. Possibly the 'fine old blue and white box and cover, a present from Lady Ailesbury' which HW placed in the China Closet ('Des. of SH,' *Works* ii. 413).
3. Lady Ailesbury remained at The Hague while Mr Conway was with the army during the campaign of 1761 (Mary Berry).
4. She sent him some 'old china' the following month (*post* 20 July 1761).
5. Unexplained.
6. This ode, written by William White-head, the poet laureate, and set to music by Dr Boyce, master of the King's band of musicians, was performed 4 June and printed *London Chronicle* 2–4 June, ix. 534; GM 1761, xxxi. 278.
7. Filippo Elisi, first male singer at the opera for the 1760–1 season (MANN iv. 86, n. 6; v. 459 and n. 8).
8. Arthur Murphy (1727–1805), author and dramatist.
9. It opened 15 June (*London Stage* Pt IV, ii. 871). HW's copy, now WSL, is Hazen, *Cat. of HW's Lib.*, No. 1810:2:7.

fireworks and sky-rockets. The Birthday exceeded the splendour of Haroun Alraschid, and the Arabian Nights, when people had nothing to do but to scour a lanthorn, and send a genie for a hamper of diamonds and rubies.[10] Do you remember one of those stories, where a Prince has eight statues of diamonds, which he overlooks, because he fancies he wants a ninth—and to his great surprise the ninth proves to be pure flesh and blood, which he never thought of?[11] Somehow or other Lady Sarah Lenox[12] is the ninth statue; and you will allow has better white and red, than if she was made of pearls and rubies. Lord Besborough has made some verses on her not knowing the meaning of the expression, *save one's bacon*.[13] I have not got them, nor are they very excellent. Oh! I forgot, I was telling you of the Birthday: my Lord Pomfret[14] had drunk the King's health so often at dinner, that at the ball, he took Mrs Lane[15] for a beautiful woman, and, as she says, *made an improper use of his hands*. The proper use of hers, she thought, was to give him a box on the ear, though within the verge of the Court[16]—he returned it by a push, and she tumbled off the end of the bench, which his Majesty has accepted as sufficient punishment, and she is not to lose her right hand.

10. 'There never was a more brilliant Court on any occasion. Such an amazing number of jewels as the ladies wore for nosegays in their bosoms, etc. was scarce ever before collected at one time. Most of their clothes were gold and silver brocades' (*London Chronicle* 4–6 June, ix. 537).

11. The story of King Zeyn Alasnzm. HW's copy of *The Arabian Night's Entertainment Consisting of One Thousand and One Stories*, 1736, is Hazen, *Cat. of HW's Lib.*, No. 1552.

12. (1745–1826), dau. of Charles, 2d D. of Richmond. The King was in love with her, but on the advice of Bute began 'looking in the New Berlin Almanack for Princesses' (*Letters from George III to Lord Bute 1756–1766*, ed. Sedgwick, 1939, pp. 37–40). He continued, however, to pay her marked attention, most recently at the Birthday ball, when he had conversed with her nearly to the exclusion of the other guests, so much so that the announcement on 8 July of his impending marriage caused consternation among her relatives; see particularly Lord Holland's 'Memoir' in *The Life and Letters of Lady Sarah Lennox*, ed. Lady Ilchester and Lord Stavordale, 1902, i. 26–31, 47–51; *Mem. Geo. III* i. 49–52; Lord Ilchester, *Henry Fox*, 1920, ii. 130–7; MANN v. 517, n. 14. It is possible that Henry Fox, Lady Sarah's brother-in-law, as a means of ingratiating himself with the King had encouraged Lady Sarah to play up to George with a view of becoming his mistress; see John Brooke, *King George III*, New York, 1972, pp. 95–7.

13. 'To escape injury to one's body, to keep oneself from harm' (OED 5a).

14. George Fermor (1722–85), 2d E. of Pomfret.

15. Perhaps Hon. Harriet Benson (1705–71), m. (1731) George Fox (after 1751, Fox Lane), cr. (1762) Bn Bingley.

16. Chamberlayne says 'Of Offences committed within the Verge of the King's Court': 'If any man presume to strike another within the palace where the King's royal person resideth, and by such a stroke only draw blood, his right hand shall be struck off, and he committed to perpetual imprisonment, and fined' (*Magnæ Britanniæ Notitia*, 1755, Pt I, Bk II, p. 109).

I enclose the list[17] your Ladyship desired; you will see that the plurality of *Worlds* are Moore's,[18] and of some I do not know the authors.[18a] There is a late edition[19] with these names to them.

My Duchess[20] was to set out this morning.[21] I saw her for the last time the day before yesterday at Lady Kildare's; never was a journey less a party of pleasure.[22] She was so melancholy that all Miss Pelham's oddness and my spirits could scarce make her smile—I don't think *the Uncle*[23] is what she is most sorry to leave. Towards the end of the night, and that was three in the morning, I did divert her a little. I slipped Pam into her lap, and then taxed her with having it there. She was quite confounded, but taking it up, saw he had a telescope in his hand, which I had drawn, and that the card which was split, and just waxed together, contained these lines:

> Ye simple astronomers, lay by your glasses;
> The transit of Venus[24] has proved you all asses:
> Your telescopes signify nothing to scan it;
> 'Tis not meant in the clouds, 'tis not meant of a planet:
> The Seer, who foretold it, mistook it, or deceives us,
> For Venus's transit is when Grafton leaves us.[25]

I don't send your Ladyship these verses as good, but to show you that all gallantry does not centre at The Hague.

I wish I could tell you that Stanley[26] and Bussy,[27] by crossing over

---

17. Missing.

18. Edward Moore (1712–57), dramatist; editor of the *World*, of which he wrote sixty-one of the 209 numbers. HW is echoing the title of Fontenelle's *Entretiens sur la pluralité des mondes*.

18a. In his copy of the collected edition of the *World*, 1755–7, in 6 vols 12mo (now in the Morgan Library) HW has identified the authors and made other notes; see Hazen, *Cat. of HW's Lib.*, No. 2501.

19. A third collected edition of the *World* was published in 1761.

20. Of Grafton.

21. She did so (*Daily Adv.* 15 June).

22. The Graftons were ostensibly going abroad for her health, but the real reason lay in their growing incompatibility; see MANN v. 506; MONTAGU i. 363.

23. Unexplained. Mary Berry omits this sentence.

24. Which had taken place 6 June.

25. HW transcribed one version of this epigram in his MS 'Book of Materials,' 1759, p. 106 (printed OSSORY i. 1). Another version appears in a collection of 'Fugitive Pieces, or, a Collection of Oddities' (Osborn Collection, Yale University Library MS C. 378), apparently collected by John Baynes, dated 1786:
'Philosophers, throw aside your tubes, and your glasses,
The transit of Venus will prove we're all asses.
The sage who foretold it, mistook or deceives us,
The transit of Venus is when Grafton leaves *us*.'

26. Hans Stanley, the British plenipotentiary in the peace negotiations with France; see Namier and Brooke iii. 468–9.

27. François de Bussy (1699 – ?1780), French plenipotentiary in the peace negotiations (*Dictionnaire de biographie française*, 1933– , vii. 722–3).

and figuring in,[28] had forwarded the Peace. It is no more made than Belleisle is taken.[29] However I flatter myself that you will not stay abroad till you return for the Coronation, which is ordered for the beginning of October.[30] I don't care to tell you how lovely the season is, how my acacias are powdered with flowers, and my hay just in its picturesque moment—do they ever make any other hay in Holland than bullrushes in ditches? My new buildings rise so swiftly, that I shall not have a shilling left,[31] so far from giving commissions on Amsterdam. When I have made my house so big that I don't know what to do with it, and am entirely undone, I propose, like King Pyrrhus,[32] who took such a roundabout way to a bowl of punch, to sit down and enjoy myself; but with this difference, that it is better to ruin one's self than all the world. I am sure you would think as I do, though Pyrrhus were King of Prussia. I long to have you bring back the only Hero that ever I could endure. Adieu! Madam; I sent you just such another piece of tittle-tattle[33] as this by General Waldegrave;[34] you are very partial to me, or very fond of knowing everything that passes in your own country, if you can be amused so. If you can, 'tis surely my duty to divert you, though at

28. A country-dance term. Bussy arrived in London 31 May and Stanley in Paris 4 June (MANN v. 504, nn. 2, 5; *London Chronicle* 30 May – 2 June, 9–11 June, ix. 526, 560). The *London Chronicle* notes (2–4 June, ix. 535), 'On Tuesday last [2 June] Monsieur Bussy waited on the Right Hon. William Pitt, the Earl of Bute, and his Grace the Duke of Newcastle, and afterwards went to Court.'

29. The citadel of Belle-Île capitulated 7 June. 'The news of the surrender of Belleisle was published on Saturday night [13 June] by the firing of the Tower guns about half an hour after eleven. The Mansion House was immediately illuminated, and bonfires lighted before the Admirality and War Offices. The *Extraordinary Gazette* was published on Sunday about noon [14 June]' (*London Chronicle* 13–16 June, ix. 570).

30. The *London Chronicle* 9–11 June (ix. 554) states that 'orders were given out for the Board of Works to get everything in readiness against the 6th of October next for the Coronation.' The exact date for the Coronation was not set until the Privy Council of 8 July, when it was an-

nounced for 22 Sept.; the date was publicly proclaimed 13 July (*London Gazette* No. 10120, 7–11 July; *Daily Adv.* 13 July).

31. HW had made a similar remark to Mann 9 July (MANN v. 514). The new rooms which HW paid for 6 May 1762 cost him £1,241.8*s.* (*Strawberry Hill Accounts,* ed. Toynbee, Oxford, 1927, p. 9).

32. The allusion is to a conversation between Pyrrhus, King of Epiru₃, and his friend Cineas in Plutarch's 'Life of Pyrrhus,' in which the latter asked the King what he intended to do after he had conquered the world. Pyrrhus replied that he should spend his time in feasting and pleasure, whereupon Cineas asked why not do so at once. HW paraphrases the anecdote at greater length in his letter to Lady Mary Coke ca Nov. 1771 (MORE 160–1), following Dryden's translation, with Dacier's notes, 1727, iv. 29–30. HW's copy, now WSL, is Hazen, *Cat. of HW's Lib.,* No. 1718; see also CHUTE 299 and n. 22.

33. *Ante* ca 25 May 1761, missing.

34. John Waldegrave (1718–84), 3d E. Waldegrave, 1763. He had left for Germany 26 May (GM 1761, xxxi. 281); see *ante* 10 April 1761, n. 16.

the expense of my character, for I own I am ashamed when I look back and see four sides of paper scribbled over with nothings.

Your Ladyship's most faithful servant,

Hor. Walpole

From Hertford, Wednesday 1 July 1761

Printed for the first time from a photostat of BM Add. MSS 23218, f. 42.

Carlisle, July 1st 1761.

Dear Horry,

YOU have goodness enough to interest yourself for the whole caravan and will not be sorry to hear it is got well here. The first three days of our journey were excessively hot; we had no thunder or heavy rain on our journey. The coach who did not travel with us got some of it at Grantham. We stayed two whole days at Chatsworth, and dined another at Wentworth Castle, which is a charming place full of beauties and full of taste. Tomorrow we go into Scotland and hope to be in Ireland on Sunday. Pray tell me when you can learn anything about the Coronation; it is a point in which I am interested, if it should be fixed for this year.[1]

Lady Hertford etc. desire their best compliments, and I am, dear Horry,

Yours most truly and affectionately,

Hertford

From Conway, ca Wednesday 1 July 1761

Missing; answered *post* 14 July 1761. Conway's next letter (8 July, also missing) took two weeks to reach HW and this one presumably took about as long.

---

1. The date of the Coronation had not yet been set (*ante* 13 June 1761, n. 30).

From CONWAY, Wednesday 8 July 1761

Missing; mentioned *post* 23 July 1761 as having been received on the 22d.

To LADY AILESBURY, ca Thursday 9 July 1761

Missing; mentioned *post* 14 July 1761 as having been written on the announcement of the King's marriage 8 July.

To HERTFORD, ca Thursday 9 July 1761

Missing; answered *post* 17 July 1761. Since it discussed the King's marriage, it was presumably written shortly after the announcement of it 8 July.

From LADY AILESBURY, ca Friday 10 July 1761

Missing; answered *post* 20 July 1761.

From HERTFORD, Saturday 11 July 1761

Printed for the first time from a photostat of BM Add. MSS 23218, f. 43.

Lisburn, July 11th 1761.

Dear Horry,

AFTER travelling two or three days through bad roads in Scotland, and waiting as many for a wind at the worst inn you can imagine, we are got safe and well into Ireland.[1] The passage was a little rough and of course frightened my Lady, but it was not tedious and the rest of the family was satisfied with it. I think we have

---

1. 'Belfast, July 7. Friday his Majesty's ship *Mercury*, of 24 guns, Capt. Falkingham, arrived in this harbour, and hath since sailed to the coast of Scotland, to bring over, as we hear, the Right Hon. the Earl of Hertford, who comes from London, by way of Scotland' (*London Chronicle* 16–18 July, x. 61).

enough of that part of Scotland and shall return the common road to England. From hence it is impossible you can expect me to entertain you. I can say nothing but what regards ourselves, that we are well and sociably received.

From my brother I hear nothing.[2] Fitzroy[3] is so good to write and mention him, from whence I may conclude him well, but he is not in a situation to leave my mind at ease.[4]

Are we to have peace, a Queen or a Coronation this year?[5] When you can learn, I need not say I am impatient to be informed, and I know your readiness to please your friends.

Adieu, dear Horry, with the best compliments of the family, believe me,

> Truly and affectionately yours,
>
> Hertford

To Conway, Tuesday 14 July 1761

Printed from *Works* v. 73–5.

Arlington Street, July 14, 1761.

MY dearest Harry, how could you write me such a cold letter as I have just received from you, and beginning *Dear Sir!* Can you be angry with me, for can I be in fault to you? Blameable in ten thousand other respects, may not I almost say I am perfect with regard to you? Since I was fifteen have not I loved you unalterably? Since I was capable of knowing your merit, has not my admiration been veneration? For what could so much affection and esteem change? Has not your honour, your interest, your safety been ever my

2. Conway wrote the D. of Devonshire from the camp at Soest 27 June, and at Lunderen 1 July (Chatsworth MSS, 416/68, 69).

3. Col. Charles Fitzroy, an aide-de-camp to Prince Ferdinand, was Lady Hertford's nephew.

4. News of a battle in Germany was expected momentarily, since a report stating that the armies were within a day's march of each other was published in the *London Gazette* No. 10118, 30 June – 4 July; see

HW to Montagu 10 July (Montagu i. 377). None took place, however, until the battle of Vellinghausen (or Kirch Denckern) on 15–16 July (*post* 20, 23 July 1761).

5. News of the King's announcement that he would marry Princess Charlotte of Mecklenburg-Strelitz, and that the Coronation would take place 22 Sept., made at a special meeting of the Privy Council 8 July (Mann v. 513 and nn. 1–3), had not yet reached Ireland.

first objects? Oh, Harry! if you knew what I have felt and am feeling about you, would you charge me with neglect? If I have seen a person since you went, to whom my first question has not been, 'What do you hear of the peace?' you would have reason to blame me. You say I write very seldom: I will tell you what, I should almost be sorry to have you see the anxiety I have expressed about you in letters to everybody else.[1] No; I must except Lady A., and there is not another on earth who loves you so well and is so attentive to whatever relates to you.

With regard to writing this is exactly the case: I had nothing to tell you; nothing has happened; and where you are, I was cautious of writing. Having neither hopes nor fears, I always write the thoughts of the moment, and even laugh to divert the person I am writing to, without any ill will on the subjects I mention. But in your situation that frankness might be prejudicial to you: and to write grave unmeaning letters, I trusted you was too secure of me either to like them or desire them. I knew no news, nor could I: I have lived quite alone at Strawberry; am connected with no court, ministers, or party; consequently heard nothing, and events there have been none. I have not even for this month heard my Lady Townshend's extempore gazette. All the morning I play with my workmen or animals, go regularly every evening to the meadows with Mrs Clive, or sit with my Lady Suffolk,[2] and at night scribble my painters[3]—What a journal to send you! I write more trifling letters than any man living; am ashamed of them, and yet they are expected of me. You, my Lady A., your brother, Sir Horace Mann, George Montagu, Lord Strafford—all expect I should write—Of what? I live less and less in the world, care for it less and less, and yet am thus obliged to inquire what it is doing. Do make these allowances for me, and remember half your letters go to my Lady A. I writ to her of the King's marriage,[4] concluding she would send it to you: tiresome as it would be, I will copy my own letters, if you expect it; for I will do anything rather than disoblige you. I will send you a diary of the Duke of York's balls and Ranelaghs, inform you

1. See, for example, HW to Strafford 5 July (CHUTE 308), HW to Montagu 10 July (MONTAGU i. 377).

2. Henrietta Hobart, Countess of Suffolk, then living at Marble Hill (HW).

3. HW was working on the third volume of the *Anecdotes of Painting;* he completed it 22 Aug. ('Short Notes,' GRAY i. 36–7).

4. Announced 8 July in a *London Gazette Extraordinary.*

of how many children my Lady B_____5 is with child, and how many races my nephew goes to. No; I will not, you do not want *such* proofs of my friendship.

The papers tell us you are retiring,[6] and I was glad. You seem to expect an action[7]—Can this give me spirits? Can I write to you joyfully, and fear? Or is it fit Prince Ferdinand should know you have a friend that is as great a coward about you as your wife? The only reason for my silence, that can*not* be true, is, that I forget you. When I am prudent or cautious, it is no symptom of my being indifferent. Indifference does not happen in friendships, as it does in passions; and if I was young enough or feeble enough to cease to love you, I would not for my own sake let it be known. Your virtues are my greatest pride; I have done myself so much honour by them, that I will not let it be known you have been peevish with me unreasonably. Pray God we may have peace, that I may scold you for it!

The King's marriage was kept the profoundest secret till last Wednesday, when the Privy Council was extraordinarily summoned,[8] and it was notified to them. Since that, the new Queen's[9] mother[10] is

5. Presumably, as Wright and subsequent editors have assumed, Lady Berkeley, who gave birth to triplets in 1748 (Collins, *Peerage*, 1779, iv. 30). Her current pregnancy, which was concluded before the end of the year (*post* HW to Lady Ailesbury 10 Oct. and n. 26), resulted in a daughter, Louisa, who was not recognized by her second husband, Robert Nugent. A John Waple wrote to Mrs Charles Ingram 8 Dec., 'Mr Nugent disowns Lady Berkeley's child and wanted to send it to the Foundling Hospital and insisted that she should relinquish the jointure he settled on her' (Hist. MSS Comm., *Various Collections*, 1901–14, viii. 179). See also GEC ix. 794, n. a, 795, n. a.

6. Reports to this effect, covering the night of 1–2 July, were printed in the *London Chronicle* 11–14 July, x. 46, *sub* 14 July; see also *London Gazette* No. 10121, 11–14 July.

7. From Soest 27 June Conway wrote the D. of Devonshire that Soubise was 'about 18 or 20 miles from this place.—There was an expectation yesterday that he would march *on* today. . . . If he does *now* I think it will probably bring on an affair immediately. I rather am apprehensive he'll stay till Monsieur de Broglie who is in motion comes nearer to second him' (Chatsworth MSS, 416/68). From Lunderen 1 July Conway described the the French retreating from their camp and taking a new defensive position, and commented, 'From this I conclude they don't intend to molest us, for the present, and as their post is very strong I presume we have no design to attack them' (ibid. 416/69).

8. A 'general' Council was summoned 1–2 July for meeting on the 8th, as was generally known by the 4th, but the business to be discussed was not mentioned, and it was generally thought to relate to peace with France (MANN v. 513 and nn. 1–2; GM 1761, xxxi. 330).

9. Charlotte Sophia (1744–1818), of Mecklenburg-Strelitz, m. (8 Sept. 1761) George III.

10. Elizabeth Albertine (1713 – 29 June 1761), of Saxe-Hildburghausen, m. (1738) Karl Ludwig of Mecklenburg-Strelitz (Isenburg, *Stammtafeln* i. taf. 124). News of her death reached London 12 July (*Letters from George III to Lord Bute 1756–1766*, ed. Sedgwick, 1939, pp. 57, 59–60).

dead, and will delay it a few days;[11] but Lord Harcourt[12] is to sail on the 27th,[13] and the Coronation will certainly be on the 22d of September.[14] All that I know fixed, is, Lord Harcourt Master of the Horse,[15] the Duke of Manchester[16] Chamberlain, and Mr Stone[17] Treasurer. Lists there are in abundance; I don't know the authentic: those most talked of, are, Lady Bute,[18] groom of the Stole, the Duchesses of Hamilton and Ancaster,[19] Lady Northumberland, Bolinbroke, Weymouth,[20] Scarborough,[21] Abergavenny,[22] Effingham,[23] for Ladies; you may choose any six of them you please; the four first are most probable.[24] Misses,[25] Henry Beauclerc,[26] M. Howe,[27] Meadows,[28] Wrottes-

11. The King had originally hoped that the Princess would be ready to set out 1 Aug.; after the news of her mother's death, he hoped she could arrive by 1 Sept., and a few days later, that she would set out 6 Aug. She finally left Strelitz 17 Aug. but did not reach London until 8 Sept. (ibid. 58, 60; GM 1761, xxxi. 380; *post* 9 Sept. 1761).

12. Simon Harcourt (1714–77), 2d Vct Harcourt, cr. (1749) E. Harcourt; governor to the King when he was Prince of Wales; ambassador to Strelitz to escort the Princess to England.

13. It was originally intended that he leave 20 July, but he did not sail from Harwich until 7 Aug. (Sedgwick, op. cit. 58; *London Chronicle* 9–11 July, x. 38; MANN v. 525, n. 3). The *London Chronicle* 16–18 July, x. 57, reported the hope that the fitting out of the yacht which was to carry the Princess would be finished by 26 July.

14. The date was set at the same Council at which the King's marriage was announced, 8 July (*London Gazette* No. 10120, 7–11 July).

15. He was appointed when the King named him ambassador to Strelitz 9 July (*London Chronicle* 9–11 July, x. 38).

16. Robert Montagu (ca 1710–62), 3d D. of Manchester. He did not kiss hands for his appointment until 31 July (ibid. 30 July – 1 Aug., x. 110).

17. Andrew Stone.

18. Mary Wortley Montagu (1718–94), m. (1736) John Stuart, 3d E. of Bute; cr. (1761) Bns Mount Stuart, s.j. She was not given an appointment in the Queen's household. By 'groom of the Stole' HW presumably means mistress of the Robes.

19. Mary Panton (d. 1793), m. (1750) Peregrine Bertie, 3d D. of Ancaster; mistress of the Robes and first lady of the Bedchamber to the Queen 1761–93.

20. Lady Elizabeth Cavendish Bentinck (1735–1825), m. (1759) Thomas Thynne, 3d Vct Weymouth, cr. (1789) M. of Bath; she was lady of the Bedchamber 1761–93 and mistress of the Robes 1793–1818.

21. Barbara Savile (d. 1797), m. (1752) Richard Lumley Saunderson, 4th E. of Scarbrough, 1752.

22. Henrietta Pelham (1730–68), m. 1 (1748) Hon. Richard Temple; m. 2 (1753) George Nevill, 17th Bn Abergavenny, cr. (1784) E. of Abergavenny.

23. See *ante* 11 Oct. 1759, n. 23; she was lady of the Bedchamber 1761–91.

24. The Duchesses of Hamilton and Ancaster, and Ladies Northumberland, Bolingbroke, Weymouth, Effingham, and Egremont kissed hands as ladies of the Bedchamber 2 Aug. (*London Chronicle* 4–6 Aug., x. 122; Egremont to Grenville [6 Aug.], *Grenville Papers* i. 383, MS now WSL). The appointments were not formally announced until 5 Sept. (*London Gazette* No. 10136, 1–5 Sept.). The complete list is in *Court and City Register,* 1762, pp. 99–100

25. I.e., maids of honour.

26. Diana Beauclerk (1741–1809), dau. of Lord Henry Beauclerk, 'senior maid of honour' at the time of her death (MONTAGU i. 377, n. 14).

27. Hon. Mary Howe (ca 1733–1819), m. Gen. Sir William Augustus Pitt (ibid. i. 264, n. 13).

28. Frances Meadows (d. 1769), m. (1768) Capt. Alexander Campbell, equerry to the D. of Cumberland (ibid. i. 377, n. 9).

ley,[29] Bishop,[30] etc. etc. etc.[31] Choose your maids too. Bedchamber women, Mrs Bloodworth,[32] Robert Brudenel,[33] Charlotte Dives,[34] Lady Erskine:[35] in short, I repeat a mere newspaper.

We expect the final answer of France this week.[36] Bussy[37] was in great pain on the fireworks for Quebec,[38] lest he should be obliged to illuminate his house:[39] you see I ransack my memory for something to tell you.

Adieu! I have more reason to be angry than you had; but I am not so hasty: you are of a *violent, impetuous, jealous* temper—I, *cool, sedate, reasonable*. I believe I must subscribe my name, or you will not know me by this description.

Yours unalterably,

HOR. WALPOLE

29. Mary Wrottesley (d. 1769) (ibid. i. 377, n. 8).

30. Frances Bisshopp (d. 1804), m. (1764) Sir George Warren, K.B. (ibid. i. 377, n. 13); maid of honour 1761–3.

31. Of those mentioned, all but Miss Howe reportedly kissed hands as maids of honour 2 Aug. (*London Chronicle* 4–6 Aug., x. 122). In addition Miss Evelyn and Miss Keck were reported as appointed at that time, but the final list drops Miss Evelyn and adds Miss Tryon (*London Gazette* No. 10136, 1–5 Sept.).

32. Margaret Bloodworth or Bludworth (d. 1786), Bedchamber woman until her death (MONTAGU i. 377, n. 7).

33. Anne Bisshopp (ca 1728–1803), m. (1759) Hon. Robert Brudenell (ibid. i. 140, n. 18).

34. Charlotte Dyve (*ante* 3 Dec. 1751 NS, n. 25), m. (1762) Samuel Masham, 2d Bn Masham.

35. Presumably Janet Wedderburn (d. 1767), m. (1761) Sir Henry Erskine, 5th Bt, a close friend of Bute's. Of the ladies mentioned, only Mrs Brudenell was reported to have kissed hands 2 Aug. (*London Chronicle* 4–6 Aug., x. 122); the others said to be appointed then were Mrs Dashwood and Mrs Herbert. The final list, however, also included Mrs

Bloodworth, Mrs Tracy, and Mrs Boughton (*London Gazette* loc. cit.).

36. This 'final answer' arrived on the 20th; it was not an 'answer,' but a *mémoire*, dated 13 July, outlining French terms, and was in its turn answered by a British ultimatum dispatched on the 25th (MANN v. 515, n. 2). For the subsequent stages in the negotiation, see *post* 5 Aug. 1761.

37. The Abbé de Bussy sent here with overtures of peace. Mr Stanley was at the same time sent to Paris (HW).

38. Probably a slip for Belle-Île, news of the capture of which had arrived 13 June (*ante* 13 June 1761, n. 29); nothing connected with Quebec had occurred to justify fireworks since Bussy's arrival in England.

39. In Suffolk Street (MANN v. 514, n. 5). Jenkinson wrote to Grenville 16 June, 'Bussy waited on Mr Pitt on Sunday morning, and held the same language as before; and, even added, that as Belleisle was now taken, he was to demand as a preliminary article, before they proceeded to treat on anything else, that that island should be surrendered. He would not illuminate, as Choiseul said, he had ordered him, and held a language very unfriendly and sour' (*Grenville Papers* i. 366–7, MS now WSL).

From CONWAY, Friday 17 July 1761

Missing; answered *post* 5 Aug. 1761.

From HERTFORD, Friday 17 July 1761

Printed for the first time from a photostat of BM Add. MSS 23218, f. 44.

Lisburn, July 17th 1761.

Dear Horry,

WE did not intend the King should marry so soon and I am half angry with Lady Sarah Lenox for it;[1] after so long a journey it is not pleasant to think of returning immediately,[2] but I suppose you are not serious about my being at the wedding. If you are and think it necessary, tell me; I have wrote by this post to Lord Bute upon it,[3] saying I should be glad to be excused if my personal attendance can be properly dispensed with.[4] If you think I should not be absent on the occasion you will give me your opinion freely; I wish to show every mark of personal regard and respect to his Majesty, though his Ministers have laid me under no obligation to go out of my way.[5] Lady Hertford is concerned about the Coronation and wishes to avoid it; I have told her she cannot. If you think differently she will be very glad to hear your opinion.[6]

1. It was widely believed that the King's marriage had been expedited by his mother and Bute because of his continuing attention to Lady Sarah, especially at the Birthday ball (*ante* 13 June 1761, n. 12 and references cited), but the King had already selected Princess Charlotte by 20 May, and an intimation of the intended proposal had been sent to Strelitz at the beginning of June (*Letters from George III to Lord Bute 1756–1766*, ed. Sedgwick, 1939, pp. 55–6).

2. Hertford had not yet heard of the delay in the wedding because of the death of the Princess's mother (*ante* 14 July 1761, n. 11); in any case, he did not return in time for the wedding (*post* 10 Sept. 1761).

3. Hertford's letter is missing; Bute did not reply (*post* 15 Aug. 1761).

4. Hertford, as a lord of the Bedchamber, might have been expected to participate.

5. In addition to Hertford's long-standing grievance against the government for refusing to turn the borough of Orford over to him (*ante* 1 Sept. 1755, n. 6), he had been piqued by the appointment of Halifax instead of himself as lord lieutenant of Ireland in March 1761; see Lord Holland's 'Memoir,' in *The Life and Letters of Lady Sarah Lennox*, ed. Lady Ilchester and Lord Stavordale, 1902, i. 35.

6. Because of her ill health she watched it with HW from his deputy's house at the gate of Westminster Hall (*post* 25 Sept. 1761).

We live here very sociably and are treated with great respect, and could be well satisfied to continue in this situation till my sons return to Oxford.[7] Let me hear from you, and believe me with the best compliments of the family, dear Horry,

Always very sincerely and affectionately yours,

Hertford

From Lady Ailesbury, ca Sunday 19 July 1761

Missing; mentioned *post* 20 July 1761, *sub* 22 July, and in HW to Strafford 22 July 1761 (Chute 310).

To Lady Ailesbury, Monday 20 July 1761

Printed from the MS now wsl; first printed, with omissions, *Works* v. 553–5, and in full Toynbee v. 80–3 and *Supp.* ii. 120. For the history of the MS see *ante* 23 Aug. 1760.

Strawberry Hill, July 20th 1761.

I BLUSH, dear Madam, on observing that half my letters to your Ladyship are prefaced with thanks for presents—don't mistake; I am not ashamed of thanking you, but of having so many occasions for it. Monsieur Hop[1] has sent me the piece of china;[2] I admire it as much as possible, and intend to like him as much as ever I can; but hitherto I have not seen him, not having been in town since he arrived. You tell me that if I listen to Madame Welderen,[3] I shall say you have been very wicked—without her chronicle I say so: be-

7. For Michaelmas term, which began 10 Oct. (*Court and City Register* 1761, p. 89). Lord Beauchamp was at Christ Church, 1760–2; Henry Seymour-Conway matriculated at Hertford College 19 Sept. 1761, receiving his B.A. 1764 and his M.A. (Merton) 1767 (Foster, *Alumni Oxon.*).

1. Hendrik Hop (1686–1761), Lt-Gen.; Dutch envoy extraordinary to England 1723-61 (Mann iii. 212, n. 6).

2. Two gifts of china from Lady Ailesbury are listed in 'Des. of SH,' *Works* ii. 413, 415.

3. Anne Whitwell (1721–96), m. (1759) Jan Walrad, Count van Welderen, Dutch envoy to England 1762–80 (Montagu ii. 139, n. 9; Ossory ii. 250, n. 9; Mann vii. 269–70, n. 3). She had presumably come to England with her husband, who arrived 14 July (gm 1761, xxxi. 330).

cause *The Book* did but hint at a father giving his son a stone when he asked for a fish,[4] you give me a fish when I asked for a stone: I begged a bit of Delft[5]—you send me old china.

Could I have believed that The Hague would so easily compensate for England? Nay, for Park Place! adieu! all our agreeable suppers! Instead of Lady Cecilia's[6] French songs, we shall have Madame Welderen quavering a confusion of d's and t's, b's and p's—*Bourquoi sais du blaire?*[7]—worse than that, I expect to meet all my Vanneck relations[8] at your house, and Sir Samson Gideon[9] instead of Charles Townshend. You will laugh like Mrs Tipkin[10] when a Dutch Jew tells you that he bought at two and a half per cent and sold at four. Come back, if you have any taste left. You had better be here talking robes, ermine and tissue, jewels and tresses, as all the world does, than own you are so corrupted. Did you receive my notification of the new Queen?[11] Her mother is dead, and she will not be here before the end of August.

My mind is much more at peace about Mr Conway than it was: nobody thinks there will be a battle,[12] as the French did not attack them, when both armies shifted camps;[13] and since that, Soubize has

---

4. Matthew 7. 9–10.

5. Lady Ailesbury eventually gave him some: 'Two butter-pots and plates of blue and white Delft ware; presents from Lady Ailesbury' ('Des. of SH,' *Works* ii. 411).

6. Lady [Henrietta] Cecilia West [*ante* ca 9 May 1755, n. 2], daughter of John, Earl of Delawar, afterwards [1762] married to General [James] Johnston (Mary Berry).

7. The first words of a favourite French air (Mary Berry). Although Mme Welderen was an Englishwoman, she had been in Holland before her marriage as maid of honour to Anne, Princess of Orange (Collins, *Peerage*, 1812, vi. 754).

8. HW's first cousins, Thomas and Richard Walpole, had married daughters of Joshua Vanneck in the 1750s.

9. Sir Sampson Gideon (1745–1824), son of the financier Sampson Gideon; cr. (1759) Bt, (1789) Bn Eardley of Spalding; M.P. Cambridgeshire 1770–80, Midhurst 1780–4, Coventry 1784–96, Wallingford 1796–1802.

10. A character in the *Constant Hus-*

band, or the Accomplished Fools, by Sir Richard Steele.

11. In his missing letter ca 9 July.

12. There already had been one, at Vellinghausen or Kirch Denckern 15–16 July; see postscript and *post* 23 July 1761.

13. The *London Chronicle* 14–16 July (x. 49) reported, *sub* 'Camp at Hemmerden, July 6': 'On the 1st inst. at 11 at night, our army decamped from Lunderen, and turned the enemy's left flank with a design to attack them in the rear; but it being excessively rainy, and the country full of morasses, it was found impossible to bring up the cannon, and we were forced to lay that attempt aside; upon which we continued our march along the enemy's rear, and without any interruption or loss, took post on their other flank. . . . On the 3d our whole army advanced again upon the enemy, who retired immediately behind Werle . . . and occupied the very same camp where we had been a few days before; and our army then encamped at this place, in the face of the enemy.'

entrenched himself up to the whiskers[14]—whiskers I think he has, I have been so afraid of him. Yet our hopes of meeting are still very distant; the Peace does not advance,[15] and if Europe has a *stiver*[16] left in its pockets, the war will continue; though happily all parties have been so scratched, that they only sit and look anger at one another, like a dog and cat that don't care to begin again.

We are in danger of losing our sociable box at the opera;[17] the new Queen is very musical,[18] and if Mr Deputy Hodges[19] and the City don't exert their veto, will probably go to the Haymarket— though she will be extremely surprised to find that Giardini[20] does not play on the Jew's-harp, the favourite instrument at the court of Mecklemburg. George Pitt,[21] in imitation of the Adonises in Tanzai's retinue,[22] has asked to be her Majesty's grand harper. *Dieu sait quelle râclerie il y aura!*[23] All the guitars are untuned; Birmingham and Sheffield have raised the price of iron, and if Miss Conway[24] has a mind to be in fashion at her return, she must take some David or

14. The same *London Chronicle* reported *sub* 'Hague, July 10,' 'The Allied army was got on the 8th to Hulbeck, Prince Ferdinand having made a further attempt to bring the enemy to action on the 7th, but the Prince of Soubize again declined it, marching towards Soest; at which place Marshal Broglio, after having taken possession of Warbourg and Paderborn, was said to be arrived on the 5th.'

15. HW presumably did not yet know of the arrival of the French *mémoire* that day (*ante* 14 July 1761, n. 36).

16. The Dutch coin equivalent to an English penny (OED *sub* 'stiver').

17. The Queen's fondness for opera did cause some difficulties about the box, but they were eventually adjusted (*post* 27 Sept., 28 Nov. 1761). For HW's box at the opera, see *ante* 13 Dec. 1760, n. 3.

18. HW describes music as 'her passion' in *Mem. Geo. III* i. 56. Elizabeth, Ds of Northumberland, describes the Queen's weekly concerts: 'The Queen and Lady Augusta play on the harpsichord and sing, the Duke of York plays on the violoncello, and P. William on the German flute; the King never plays in concert, but when they are alone he sometimes accompanies her on the German

flute' (*The Diaries of a Duchess*, ed. James Greig, 1926, p. 41).

19. Sir James Hodges, town clerk and deputy chamberlain of London (*ante* 19 Sept. 1758, n. 9).

20. Felice de Giardini (1716–96), violinist; manager of the Italian Opera in London; in England 1750–84, 1790 (MONTAGU ii. 73, n. 22; *London Stage* Pt IV, ii. 1007).

21. (1721–1803), of Strathfield-Say, Hants; M.P. Shaftesbury 1742–7, Dorset 1747–74; groom of the Bedchamber 1760–70; cr. (1776) Bn Rivers. The reference is obscure, but HW to Lady Ossory 15 Aug. 1765 jokes about his 'attitudes' (OSSORY i. 13).

22. In *Tanzaï et Néadarné, histoire japonaise* by Crébillon *fils*. HW's copy of the 1740 edn is Hazen, *Cat. of HW's Lib.*, No. 979.

23. HW is echoing a passage in the *Mémoires* of Gramont: 'Ce Francisque venait de faire une sarabande qui charmait ou désolait tout le monde; . . . toute la guitarerie de la Cour se mit à l'apprendre, et Dieu sait la raclerie universelle que c'était' (Chap. VIII).

24. The Honourable Anne Damer (Mary Berry).

other to teach her the new twing twang, twing twing twang. As I am still desirous of being in fashion with your Ladyship, and am over and above, very grateful, I keep no company but my Lady Denbigh and Lady Blandford, and learn every evening for two hours to mash my English. Already I am tolerably fluent in saying *she* for *he*.[25]

Good night, Madam. I have no news to send you. One cannot announce a royal wedding and a coronation every post.

Your most faithful and obliged servant,

Hor. Walpole

PS. Pray, Madam, do the gnats bite your legs? Mine are swelled as big as *one,* which is saying a great deal for me.

Another postscript. Lady Lyttelton and Mrs Shirley[26] dined here yesterday.

22d.

I had writ this, and was not time enough for the mail, when I receive your charming note,[27] and this magnificent victory![28] Oh! my dear Madam, how I thank you, how I congratulate you, how I feel for you, how I have felt for you and for myself!—but I bought it by two terrible hours today—I heard of the battle two hours before I could learn a word of Mr Conway[29]—I sent all round the world, and went half round it myself. I have cried and laughed, trembled and danced, as you bid me, my Lady Suffolk is witness—in short, I have behaved

---

25. A mistake which these ladies, who were both Dutch women, constantly made (Mary Berry).

26. Mary Sturt (d. 1800), m. (1749) Hon. George Shirley.

27. Missing; HW told Lord Strafford 22 July that it said that she had been awakened with the news that Conway was safe before she had even heard of the battle (Chute 310).

28. Of Kirchdenckircke (Mary Berry). News of the battle of Kirch Denckern (better known as Vellinghausen) 15–16 July reached London at noon on the 22d (Mann v. 515, n. 3).

29. Conway wrote the D. of Devonshire 27 July, 'I commanded a very considerable district corps and in a very important post which his H[ighness] confided entirely to me the day of the action: though it was not attacked' (Chatsworth MSS, 416/70; see Mann v. 516, n. 5). Although he was not mentioned in the first accounts in the *London Gazette Extraordinary* 22 July, the more complete accounts, which arrived on the 23d and were published in another *Gazette Extraordinary* on the 24th, reported that he had 'replaced the Prince of Anhalt between Illingen and Hohenover,' that is, in the centre of the Allied line, which had escaped the brunt of the French attack (W. E. Manners, *Some Account of the . . . Marquis of Granby,* 1899, pp. 216n., 220).

like a fool, and so Lady Vere[30] told me. If you had sent me as much old china as King Augustus[31] gave two regiments for,[32] I should not be half so much obliged to you as for your note—how could you think of me, when you had so much reason to think of nothing but yourself?—and then they say virtue is not rewarded in this world— I will preach at Paul's Cross,[33] and quote you and Mr Conway; no two persons were ever so good and so happy—in short, I am serious in the height of all my joy—God is very good to you, my dear Madam; I thank him for you; I thank him for myself; it is very unallayed pleasure we taste at this moment! Good night: my heart is so expanded, I could write to the last scrap of my paper, but I won't.

Yours most entirely,

H. Walpole

30. Mary Chambers (d. 1783), m. (1736) Lord Vere Beauclerk, cr. (1750) Bn Vere of Hanworth.

31. Frederick Augustus (1670–1733), Elector of Saxony as Frederick Augustus I 1694–1733; K. of Poland as Augustus II 1697–1704, 1709–33.

32. Mrs Toynbee quotes (v. 83, n. 11) the unpublished journal of Capt. (later Gen. Sir John) Floyd in explanation of this allusion: 'Dresden—Monday, 22nd September, 1777. *China-ware*. "Saw the collection of Dresden and Indian china . . . it contained . . . the progress of the Dresden or Meissen manufactory and 22 jars of Indian china which the late King of Prussia gave the King of Poland for eight hundred dragoons mounted and equipped." '

33. Where public preachers spoke in medieval and Tudor England.

From HERTFORD, Monday 20 July 1761

Printed for the first time from a photostat of BM Add. MSS 23218, ff. 45–6.
Memoranda (by HW, for an unidentified letter):

Hear a lean bard whose wit could never give
Himself a dinner, makes an actor live.[1]

Mr Alexander[2]
Mr Black[3]
0-15-6
Ld Hert[ford] 4 Ten

Lisburn, July 20th 1761.

Dear Horry,

THAT you may not be surprised if you should hear it by any
other way I must acquaint you that after I wrote to you last
week, Lady Hertford wrote to Lady Bute to say that she should think
herself much honoured if she was thought a proper person to be put
about the intended Queen. I suppose the application may very probably come too late;[4] if it should we shall not be grieved. Lady Hertford I thought seemed most inclined to it, though her passion for
Court is not strong, which made me not try to dissuade her from it.
Il y a du pour et du contre; from a greater indifference about Court
I am not so anxious to determine for the best, and whether she succeeds or not it is no reflection to offer herself in the way she has
done it. You know what passed between us before on this subject, and

1. This may be a line from Bentley's *The Wishes,* which HW had seen at its first performance 27 July, about the time he would have received this letter. The play was never printed, but there is a MS in the Huntington Library; see MONTAGU i. 381, n. 1. It is summarized in the *London Chronicle* 28–30 July, x. 100–1.

2. Perhaps HW noted the deaths of William Alexander 25 July and the Rev. John Black 22 July, reported in GM 1761, xxxi. 382, and the *London Chronicle* 30 July – 1 Aug., x. 105, 110. William Alexander (ca 1690–1761) was director of the Royal Bank of Scotland 1730–60, lord provost of Edinburgh 1752–4, M.P. Edin-burgh 1754–61.

3. John Black (d. 1761), chaplain of Hampton Court Palace and of Conway's 1st (or Royal) Regiment of Dragoons (*Army Lists* 1761, p. 25); according to the *London Chronicle* 30 July – 1 Aug., x. 105, 'Lately died in Germany, the Rev. Mr Black, chaplain to one of the regi-ments there, and of his Majesty's Chapel Royal at Hampton Court. He was em-inently skilled in the game of chess, and used frequently to play by desire with the Marquis de Mirepoix, the late French ambassador here, who, it is said, asked the chaplainship for him.'

4. It did; see *post* 15 Aug. 1761. Lady Hertford did not become a lady of the Bedchamber until Jan. 1768 (Coke, *Jour-nals,* ii. 174). Her correspondence with Lady Bute at this time has not survived.

what has passed since upon another;[5] I hope the difference of time will not make you disapprove what you then seemed rather disposed to acquiesce in. I wish for the sanction of my best friends in every matter where my opinion has weight, and I shall be more indifferent to the consequences. My brother's situation makes me solicitous to hear of him. Yours ever, dear Horry,

Very truly and affectionately,

HERTFORD

To CONWAY, Thursday 23 July 1761

Printed from *Works* v. 76–7.

Strawberry Hill, July 23, 1761.

WELL, *mon biau*[1] *cousin!* you may be as cross as you please now: when you beat two marshals of France and cut their armies to pieces,[2] I don't mind your pouting; but in good truth, it was a little vexatious to have you quarrelling with me, when I was in greater pain about you than I can express. I will say no more; make a peace, under the walls of Paris if you please, and I will forgive you all— but no more battles: consider, as Dr Hay said, it is cowardly to beat the French now.[3]

Don't look upon yourselves as the only conquerors in the world. Pondicherri is ours,[4] as well as the field of Kirk Denckirk. The park guns never have time to cool; we ruin ourselves in gunpowder and skyrockets.[5] If you have a mind to do the gallantest thing in the

<hr>

5. Hertford to HW *ante* 17 July mentions an exchange of letters about whether Lady Hertford should attend the Coronation, and whether Lord Hertford would be expected to attend the King's wedding. See also *post* 1 Aug.

1. A late Old French variant of *beau* (OED).

2. The victory obtained by Prince Ferdinand of Brunswic over the Maréchal de Broglio and the Prince de Soubize at Kirk Denckirk (HW). The first reports had represented the victory as a total defeat for the French, but the magnitude

was diminished in the fuller reports received on the 23d (below, n. 8; MANN v. 515 and n. 3, 518–19; MONTAGU i. 378; CHUTE 309–10).

3. HW also refers to Hay's sneer at the French in a letter to Mann 13 Dec. 1759 (MANN v. 355; see also *ante* 15 Nov. 1755, n. 19).

4. It had surrendered 15 Jan.; the news reached London 20 July and was published as a *Gazette Extraordinary* that day (MANN v. 515 and n. 1, 516 and n. 10).

5. 'About twelve [on 20 July] the guns were fired in St James's Park and at the Tower, the flags were displayed on the

world after the greatest, you must escort the Princess of Mecklenburg[6] through France. You see what a bully I am; the moment the
French run away, I am sending you on expeditions. I forgot to tell
you that the King has got the Isle of Dominique[7] and the chicken-
pox,[8] two trifles that don't count in the midst of all these festivities.
No more does your letter of the 8th, which I received yesterday: it
is the one that is to come after the 16th, that I shall receive graciously.

Friday 24th.

Not satisfied with the rays of glory that reached Twickenham, I
came to town to bask in your success; but am most disagreeably disappointed to find you must beat the French once more,[9] who seem to
love to treat the English mob with subjects for bonfires. I had got
over such an alarm, that I foolishly ran into the other extreme, and
concluded there was not a French battalion left entire upon the face
of Germany. Do write to me; don't be out of humour, but tell me
every motion you make:[10] I assure you I have deserved you should.
Would you were out of the question, if it were only that I might feel
a little humanity! There is not a blacksmith or linkboy in London

steeples, the bells rung, and the day was
concluded with bonfires, etc.' (*London
Chronicle* 18–21 July, x. 68). Similar celebrations took place on the 22d (GM 1761,
xxxi. 331).

6. Her present Majesty (HW).

7. It had fallen 7 June: the news was
published in the *London Gazette* No.
10123, 18–21 July.

8. George III was diagnosed as having
caught chicken-pox 22 July (*Letters from
George III to Lord Bute 1756–1766*, ed.
Sedgwick, 1939, p. 60).

9. HW makes similar comments to
Mann on the same day, based on the continued numerical superiority of the
French despite the defeat (MANN v. 518–
19). But Conway wrote the D. of Devonshire 27 July, 'If they mean to do anything, I imagine it must be to march to
Hanover with Broglie's now the principal
army, while Soubise guards their com-
munications with the Rhine and Main, or,
I should rather think, give us jealousy
and check us on the right flank and rear
if we advance. Anything else I can only
construe to be pacific orders from Court,

or retreat for absolute want. Some de-
serters say their army is ill paid and fed,
they desert much and are very sickly. . . .
All the accounts of the people here where
they have been agree that their loss on
the 16th was very considerable; some of
their officers have said more than at
Minden. . . . The French will be ashamed
to be beat into it [peace]; but I have no
notion how they can hold out' (Chatsworth MSS, 416/70).

10. From the camp at Borgelen Conway
wrote the D. of Devonshire 27 July, 'I
have always been at the head of one of
the principal columns in every march. . . .
Two days ago he [P. Ferdinand] took me
without any regular tour and gave me six
battalions and about 7 squadrons to cover
a general forage towards the enemy . . .
which I marched within about a league
of their army then lying at Soest. . . . We
marched from our camp at Hans Hoeno-
ver to this place about two leagues today';
and on the 28th, 'We have marched another march to Erwitte: half way to Paderborn where M. Broglie was yesterday'
(ibid.).

that exults more than I do, upon any good news, since you went abroad. What have I to do to hate people I never saw, and to rejoice in their calamities! Heaven send us peace, and you home! Adieu!

Yours ever,

HOR. WALPOLE

To HERTFORD, ca Thursday 23 July 1761

Missing; answered *post* 1 Aug. 1761.

From HERTFORD, Saturday 1 August 1761

Printed for the first time from a photostat of BM Add. MSS 23218, ff. 47–8. There is a floor plan in pencil by HW on the back of the letter (f. 48 verso), so:

apparently of the Oratory at SH, which HW mentions to Montagu 22 July 1761: 'The oratory of our Lady of Strawberries shall be dedicated next year on the anniversary of Mr Conway's safety' (MONTAGU i. 379). Under the plan is a barely legible word or words, possibly 'North oratory,' and the numeral '½'.

Lisburn, August 1st 1761.

Dear Horry,

A THOUSAND thanks for your exactness in giving me an account of the battle.[1] I had heard, by an extraordinary accident of a vessel's coming from Liverpool the day before the post, that there had been an action to our advantage, and was forced to wait with anxiety till the next morning to be assured my brother was safe; his not being named in the *Gazette*[2] which was sent to me was in the meantime some consolation. I am vastly satisfied with the general event and his security, and yet now it is over I could have wished him the honour Lord Granby[3] will receive from it. Fitzroy has prom-

---

1. Of Kirch Denckern (see *ante* HW to Lady Ailesbury 20 July 1761, n. 28).
2. The *Gazette Extraordinary* 22 July (ibid., n. 29).

3. Who had borne the main force of the French attack on both days of the battle. HW wrote Lord Strafford 22 July, 'Lord Granby, to the mob's heart's con-

ised me the particulars when he is less hurried, and I hope to receive them soon.⁴ The time has not yet allowed me to receive an answer from London about my return; I hope, as you are already informed, to avoid the wedding. At the Coronation you may expect me. My Lady's attending it is not sure; though she is pretty well she is easily disturbed with anything that hurries or affects her. I hope health, under such circumstances and her present distant situation, if her dislike to it continues, will be a reasonable excuse. I would not be suspected of failing wantonly in any point of duty or respect to the King, to whose person I am most sincerely and faithfully attached; on the other hand I am not called upon to drive my friends under much inconvenience, having little more than my own personal regard for the King to say for it. Amongst the crowd these compliments have little weight, and I will own to you that as far as my own immediate interest is concerned in such things, the edge of my ambition is much taken off by what has passed lately;⁵ I am still a courtier for the interest of a large family to a King I admire, but my inclinations are at present contracted.

We have not yet received our clothes and goods from London, which we sent before us by way of Liverpool, and we have the misfortune to hear of the loss of one of our men-servants who attended them being lost there in a small boat, which gives me much pain. Adieu, dear Horry, accept the best compliments of the family and believe me always,

Most truly and affectionately yours,

HERTFORD

tent, has the chief honour of the day—rather, of the two days' (CHUTE 310).

4. He had arrived in London 23 July with the detailed account of the battle (*London Gazette Extraordinary* 24 July).

5. Probably a reference to the appointment of Halifax instead of Hertford as lord lieutenant of Ireland, and to the government's continued refusal of Hertford's request for control over the borough of Orford (*ante* 17 July 1761, n. 5; 1 Sept. 1755, n. 6).

To Conway, Wednesday 5 August 1761

Printed from *Works* v. 77–9. The year is determined by the contents.

Strawberry Hill.

THIS is the 5th of August, and I just receive your letter of the 17th of last month by Fitzroy.[1] I heard he had lost his pocket-book with all his dispatches, but had found it again. He was a long time finding the letter for me.[2]

You do nothing but reproach me; I declare I will bear it no longer, though you should beat forty more marshals of France. I have already writ you two letters[3] that would fully justify me if you receive them; if you do not, it is not I that am in fault for not writing, but the post offices for reading my letters, content if they would forward them when they have done with them. They seem to think, like you, that I know more news than anybody. What is to be known in the dead of summer, when all the world is dispersed? Would you know who won the sweepstakes at Huntington?[4] What parties are at Woburn? What officers upon guard in Betty's fruit-shop? Whether the peeresses are to wear long or short tresses at the Coronation? How many jewels Lady ——[5] borrows of actresses? All this is your light summer wear for conversation; and if my memory were as much stuffed with it as my ears, I might have sent you volumes last week. My nieces, Lady Waldegrave, and Mrs Keppel, were here five days, and discussed the claim or disappointment of every miss in the kingdom for Maid of Honour. Unfortunately this new generation is not at all my affair. I cannot attend to what concerns them— Not that their trifles are less important than those of one's own time, but my mould has taken all its impressions, and can receive no more. I must grow old upon the stock I have. I, that was so impatient at all their chat, the moment they were gone, flew to my Lady Suffolk, and heard

1. George [*sic,* Charles] Fitzroy, afterwards created Lord Southampton (HW). The *London Chronicle* 23–5 July announced, 'We hear that Colonel Fitzroy left the army on the 18th' (x. 82).

2. He had arrived in London 23 July (*ante* 1 Aug. 1761, n. 4).

3. *Ante* 14 and 23 July.

4. The *London Chronicle* 1–4 Aug., x. 114, reported that 'At Huntingdon the

500 guineas subscription, on Tuesday last [28 July], was won by Lord Waldegrave's colt, got by Dormouse'; see also ibid. 30 July – 1 Aug., x. 110.

5. Assumed by Wright and subsequent editors to be Lady Harrington. HW mentioned to Montagu 24 Sept. that at the Coronation she was 'covered with all the diamonds she could borrow, hire, or tease' (MONTAGU i. 387).

her talk with great satisfaction of the late Queen's Coronation petti-coat.[6] The preceding age always appears respectable to us (I mean as one advances in years), one's own age interesting, the coming age neither one nor t'other.

You may judge by this account that I have writ *all* my letters, or ought to have written them; and yet, for occasion to blame me, you draw a very pretty picture of my situation: all which tends to prove that I ought to write to you every day, whether I have anything to say or not. I am writing, I am building—both *works that will outlast the memory of battles and heroes!* Truly, I believe, the one will as much as t'other. My buildings are paper, like my writings, and both will be blown away in ten years after I am dead;[7] if they had not the substantial use of amusing me while I live, they would be worth little indeed. I will give you one instance that will sum up the vanity of great men, learned men, and buildings altogether. I heard lately, that Dr Pearce,[8] a very learned personage, had consented to let the tomb of Aylmer de Valence, Earl of Pembroke,[9] a very great personage, be removed for Wolfe's monument;[10] that at first he had objected, but was wrought upon by being told that *hight* Aylmer was a Knight Templar, a very wicked set of people as his Lordship had heard, though he knew nothing of them, as they are not mentioned by Lon-ginus.[11] I own I thought this a made story, and wrote to his Lord-ship,[12] expressing my concern that one of the finest and most an-cient monuments in the Abbey should be removed, and begging, if it was removed, that he would bestow it on me, who would erect and preserve it here. After a fortnight's deliberation, the Bishop sent me

6. Presumably it was at this time that HW learned the anecdote he relates in his *Reminiscences:* 'Queen Caroline's petti-coat had jewels borrowed to the value of £100,000. . . . As the Queen's petticoat was so immensely stiff and heavy, that she could not have knelt to receive the sacra-ment, it was contrived to draw up with pullies like a little curtain, and had leads to weigh it down again' (HW, *Reminis-cences Written . . . in 1788,* ed. Toynbee, Oxford, 1924, p. 112).

7. This metaphor is echoed and im-proved upon by HW in his letter to Lady Ossory 11 Aug. 1778 (Ossory ii. 43).

8. Zachary Pearce (1690–1774), Bp of Bangor, 1748; Bp of Rochester, 1756; Dean of Westminster, 1756.

9. Aymer de Valence (ca 1270–1324), re-garded as E. of Pembroke, 1307; one of the major figures of the reign of Edward II. His tomb, on the north side of the choir of Westminster Abbey, was not re-moved.

10. Unveiled 4 Oct. 1773 (GM 1773, xliii. 524); illustrated J. F. Kerslake, 'The Likeness of Wolfe,' in *Wolfe: Portraiture and Genealogy,* Quebec House, 1959, plate 20.

11. Pearce's edition of Longinus, *De sublimitate,* first published in 1724, had reached a fourth edition by 1751. HW's copy of the 1732 edn, with two notes and occasional marginal markings, is now WSL (Hazen, *Cat. of HW's Lib.,* No. 2089).

12. HW's letter, ca 26 June, is missing.

an answer,[13] civil indeed, and commending my zeal for antiquity! but avowing the story under his own hand. He said, that at first they had taken Pembroke's tomb for a Knight Templar's. Observe, that not only the man who shows the tombs names it everyday, but that there is a draught of it at large in Dart's *Westminster;*[14] that upon discovering whose it was, he had been very unwilling to consent to the removal, and at last had obliged Wilton[15] to engage to set it up within ten feet of where it stands at present. His Lordship concluded with congratulating me on publishing learned authors at my press. I don't wonder that a man who thinks Lucan a *learned* author,[16] should mistake a tomb in his own cathedral. If I had a mind to be angry, I could complain with reason; as, having paid forty pounds for ground for my mother's tomb,[17] that the Chapter of Westminster sell their church over and over again; the ancient monuments tumble upon one's head through their neglect, as one of them did, and killed a man at Lady Elizabeth Percy's funeral;[18] and they erect new waxen dolls of Queen Elizabeth,[19] etc. to draw visits and money from the mob. I hope all this history is applicable to some part or other of my letter; but letters you will have, and so I send you one, very like your own stories that you tell your daughter: There was a king, and he had three daughters, and they all went to see the tombs; and the youngest, who was in love with Aylmer de Valence, etc.

13. Pearce to HW 10 July 1761, printed in Toynbee, *Supp.* ii. 120–2.

14. *Westmonasterium: or the History and Antiquities of the Abbey Church of St Peter's, Westminster,* 1742, by John Dart (d. 1730). HW's copy is Hazen, op. cit., No. 566.

15. Joseph Wilton (1722–1803), sculptor; see HW's *Anecdotes of Painting,* Vol. V, ed. Hilles and Daghlian, New Haven, 1937, pp. 156–7.

16. HW had published the SH edition of Lucan's *Pharsalia,* with notes by Grotius and Richard Bentley, on 8 Jan. (Hazen, *SH Bibl.* 46–50).

17. HW apparently means the monument to his mother which he had placed in the south aisle of Henry VII's chapel in 1754; in 1747 he had paid £21 (not £40) for permission to erect it ('Short Notes,' GRAY i. 25–6 and nn. 169, 170).

18. Lady Elizabeth Anne Frances Percy (1744 – 27 May 1761), only daughter of the E. and Cts of Northumberland (Collins, *Peerage,* 1812, ii. 364). 'On Friday night [5 June] two accidents happened in St Nicholas Chapel in Westminster Abbey while the corpse of Lady Elizabeth Piercy was interring: a man who had climbed up to see it, fell on the rails of an old monument, and the iron spikes ran through both of his thighs: also a stone fell from a stone screen on which some people had got, and fractured the skull of one of the persons who attended the procession' (*London Chronicle* 6–9 June, ix. 546).

19. The original funeral effigy of Queen Elizabeth had been remade in 1760 when the Gentlemen of the Choir celebrated the bicentenary of Elizabeth's foundation of the Collegiate Church of Westminster. It has been suggested that it may be closer to the original than long supposed; see R. C. Strong, *Portraits of Queen Elizabeth,* Oxford, 1963, p. 151; references in MANN ii. 193, n. 12.

Thank you for your account of the battle;[20] thank Prince Ferdinand for giving you a very honourable post,[21] which, in spite of his teeth and yours, proved a very safe one; and above all, thank Prince Soubize, whom I love better than all the German princes in the universe. Peace, I think, we must have at last, if you beat the French, or at least hinder them from beating you, and afterwards starve them.[22] Bussy's last *last* courier is expected;[23] but as he may have a last last *last* courier, I trust no more to this than to all the others.[24] He was complaining t'other day to Mr Pitt of our haughtiness, and said it would drive the French to some desperate effort; thirty thousand men, continued he, would embarrass you a little, I believe! 'Yes, truly,' replied Pitt, 'for I am so embarrassed with those we have already, I don't know what to do with them.'[25]

Adieu! Don't fancy that the more you scold, the more I will write: It has answered three times, but the next cross word you give me shall put an end to our correspondence. Sir Horace Mann's father[26] used to say, 'Talk, Horace, you have been abroad:'—you cry, 'Write, Horace, you are at home.' No, Sir, you can beat an hundred and twenty thousand French, but you cannot get the better of me. I will not write such foolish letters as this every day, when I have nothing to say.

Yours as you behave,

Hor. Walpole

20. Of Kirk Denckirk (HW).

21. Conway had replaced the P. of Anhalt as commander of the centre of the Allied line (*ante* HW to Lady Ailesbury 20 July 1761, n. 29).

22. Conway expressed this opinion to the D. of Devonshire 27 July; see *ante* 23 July 1761, n. 9. The *London Chronicle* 28–30 July (x. 101) reported *sub* Hague, 22 July, that 'the two French armies were obliged to separate immediately after their common defeat, for want of provisions. . . . "By Prince Ferdinand's position at Ham, the French who are cut off from their magazines at Cologn, Dusseldorp, and Wesel, are obliged to draw their provisions from this place [Frankfurt-am-Main], where there is but a small quantity, and consequently they must immediately give battle to the Allies." '

23. The French reply to the English ultimatum of 24 July was received in

London 6 Aug. (Mann v. 515, n. 2, 526, n. 5).

24. Negotiations dragged on until late September, when they ended in the recall of Bussy and Stanley (*post* 25 Sept. 1761).

25. The *London Chronicle* 11–13 Aug. (x. 148) reported, 'M. de B. since his last proposals were flatly rejected, seems not a little disconcerted and chagrined. . . . He lately talked of the great change the King his Master could give to the face of affairs, by throwing 10,000 men into this kingdom. The Great Minister to whom this was spoke, answered very gravely, "I should be sorry to hear of their being landed in England. Having already more French prisoners than we can well dispose of, I know not what we should do with ten thousand more." '

26. Robert Mann (d. 1752), of Linton, Kent (see Mann i. 27, n. 9).

From Hertford, Saturday 15 August 1761

Printed for the first time from a photostat of BM Add. MSS 23218, ff. 49–50.
Memoranda (by HW, probably for a missing letter):

> Lord Hunt[ingdon][1]
> Lord Cow[per][2]
> Princess Em[ily][3]

Lisburn, August 15th 1761.

Dear Horry,

LADY Hertford has received from Lady Bute a refusal,[4] but in the most polite and obliging terms, putting it entirely upon the lateness of the application, when all the ladies though not named in form have been privately acquainted with their intended appointment,[5] and the compliment to Lady Hertford's character upon refusing it is in Lord Bute's as well as her own name. From my Lord I have received no answer, so I suppose I am to take it for granted I stand excused for the wedding. To the Coronation I intend, though not with the most perfect satisfaction, to go; Lady Hertford has at present too just an excuse for absenting herself, being by no means in an easy state of health, and if you hear it called disappointment or coldness in me from any supposed reason, I beg you will contradict it. Whatever I may feel, my respect for the King is the same, and if it was not severity to recommend it too strongly to my Lady in her present state of health, when she apprehends so much from hurry and fatigue, I would, to avoid every appearance of that sort, and to satisfy my own mind, prevail upon her; at the same time that I am well assured there is not one of the royal family who knew her as well as I do that would not excuse her.

I am unhappy, I will confess, not to show every mark of respect in my power to the King, and yet under such circumstances I do not see how I can expect it from Lady Hertford. Perhaps it may be too early to talk of it, yet such is the present state of her health and disposition; and I can assure you I am concerned about it.

1. This may relate to the 'campaign opened in the Bedchamber' discussed *post* 9 Sept. 1761.
2. William Cowper (after 1762 Clavering Cowper) (1709–64), 2d E. Cowper.
3. Princess Amelia.
4. Of her application to be a lady of the Bedchamber (*ante* 20 July *bis*, n. 4, and 1 Aug.).
5. According to the *London Chronicle* 4–6 Aug. (x. 122), they had kissed hands for their appointments 2 Aug.; the list was published in the *London Gazette* No. 10136, 1–5 Sept. See *ante* 14 July 1761, n. 24.

I propose setting out from hence about the beginning of next month[6] to finish what business I have in Dublin and to secure my appearance at the Coronation. In the meantime I shall be very happy to hear from you and desire always to be thought

> Your very faithful friend,
>
> HERTFORD

From HERTFORD, Monday 31 August 1761

Printed for the first time from a photostat of BM Add. MSS 23218, f. 51.

> Lisburn, August 31st 1761.

Dear Horry,

I INTEND setting out for Dublin Wednesday next; the family and caravan will move on Friday. We hope to be in London about the 17th. My Lady will not venture I believe to undertake the Coronation; my son's attendance and my own[1] with her present state of health will I hope excuse the family. I mean always the most dutiful respect to the King, but cannot press Lady Hertford with so sufficient a reason against it to risk the fatigue of that day, without her mind changes upon finding the journey very easy to her.

> Yours ever most truly,
>
> HERTFORD

6. See *post* 31 Aug., 3 Sept. 1761.

———

1. Lord Beauchamp was one of the King's train-bearers at the Coronation; Hertford was one of the peers who held the canopy over the King at the anointing (*post* 27 Sept. 1761; GM 1761, xxxi. 420).

From HERTFORD, Thursday 3 September 1761

Printed for the first time from a photostat of BM Add. MSS 23218, f. 52.
Address: To the Honourable Hor. Walpole in Arlington Street, London.
Postmark: 9 SE. DUBLIN.

Dublin, September 3d 1761.

Dear Horry,

I AM just come to Dublin before the packet can sail; my Lady comes on Saturday. When I have done my business here we propose sailing for England; a letter to Ragley may probably catch me on my road to London, where I intend being by the Coronation.

I remain ever yours,

HERTFORD

To CONWAY, Wednesday 9 September 1761

Printed from *Works* v. 80–1.

Arlington Street, Sept. 9, 1761.

THE date of my promise is now arrived, and I fulfil it—fulfil it with great satisfaction, for the Queen is come;[1] I have seen her, have been presented to her[2]—and may go back to Strawberry. For this fortnight I have lived upon the road between Twickenham and London:[3] I came, grew impatient, returned; came again, still to no purpose. The yachts made the coast of Suffolk last Saturday,[4] on

1. She arrived at St James's at 3:15 P.M. on 8 Sept. (below; CHUTE 313; *Daily Adv.* 9 Sept.).
2. At the Drawing-Room 9 Sept. (below; MANN v. 531). The *London Chronicle* 8–10 Sept. (x. 246) reported *sub* 10 Sept., 'Yesterday there was the most brilliant Court at St James's ever known. The Spanish, Dutch, Tripolitan, and Morocco ambassadors, appeared richly dressed, as did all the other foreign ministers, among whom was Mons. Bussy. . . . The Court days are to continue today and tomorrow on the same occasion.'

3. HW planned to go to London 23 Aug. on a report that the Queen was expected on the 24th (MONTAGU i. 384). The *London Chronicle* 15–18 Aug. (x. 167) stated, 'We hear that her Majesty is to be at Stade the 20th instant, and, if the winds are fair, is expected at Greenwich on Monday next.' See also ibid. 20–2 Aug., x. 177.
4. The royal yachts had been seen off Lowestoft at 5 P.M. on 5 Sept.; the news reached London on Sunday morning (*Letters from George III to Lord Bute 1756–1766*, ed. Sedgwick, 1939, pp. 61–2).

Sunday entered the road of Harwich,[5] and on Monday morning the King's chief eunuch, as the Tripoline ambassador[6] calls Lord A.[7] landed the Princess. She lay that night at Lord Abercorn's[8] at Witham,[9] the palace of silence;[10] and yesterday at a quarter after three arrived at St James's. In half an hour one heard of nothing but proclamations of her beauty: everybody was content, everybody pleased. At seven one went to Court. The night was sultry. About ten the procession[11] began to move towards the chapel, and at eleven they all came up into the drawing-room.[12] She looks very sensible, cheerful, and is remarkably genteel.[13] Her tiara of diamonds was very pretty, her stomacher sumptuous;[14] her violet-velvet mantle and ermine so heavy, that the spectators knew as much of her upper half as the King himself.[15] You will have no doubts of her sense by what I shall tell you. On the road they wanted her to curl her toupet: she said she thought it looked as well as that of any of the ladies sent to fetch her; if the King bid her, she would wear a periwig, otherwise she would remain as she was.[16] When she caught the first glimpse of the palace, she grew frightened and turned pale; the Duchess of Hamilton[17] smiled—the Princess said, 'My dear Duchess, you may

'Yesterday morning [6 Sept.] about eight o'clock, arrived an express from Loestoffe, which was dispatched at five o'clock on Saturday afternoon, with an account of Lord Anson with the fleet, being then about five leagues from that port, with the wind about west, stretching to the southward. Upon receiving this agreeable news, the guns in the park and at the Tower were fired at noon, a new standard was hoisted at the Tower, the bells were rung, and at night the houses were finely illuminated' (*London Chronicle* 5–8 Sept., x. 234).

5. This news arrived in London on Monday morning (CHUTE 311).

6. Hüsejn (or Hasan or Hussem) Bej, Tripolitan ambassador to England 1759–61 (MANN v. 528, n. 3).

7. Anson, who had commanded the fleet bringing the Queen. HW repeats this 'witticism' to Strafford 8 Sept. (CHUTE 312) and to Mann 10 Sept. (MANN v. 528; see also *ante* 28 May 1758, 16 June 1758, n. 6).

8. James Hamilton (1712–89), 8th E. of Abercorn.

9. Near Chelmsford, Essex.

10. Lord Abercorn was notoriously taciturn (MONTAGU i. 208 and n. 1, ii. 210; MANN v. 528).

11. Described in the *London Chronicle* 8–10 Sept., x. 246; GM 1761, xxxi. 416–17.

12. Where they remained for about ten minutes, but no one was presented (MANN v. 529 and n. 13; *Mem. Geo. III* i. 56; GM 1761, xxxi. 417).

13. HW made similar comments to Mann on the 10th (MANN v. 529) and in *Mem. Geo. III* i. 56.

14. HW told Mann that it was worth 'threescore thousand pounds' (MANN v. 529). Mrs Isabella Ramsden wrote Mrs Charles Ingram 8 Aug., 'The jewels will be immense, the stomacher is worth £70,000' (Hist. MSS Comm., *Various Collections*, 1901–14, viii. 179).

15. HW told Mann that it 'dragged itself and almost the rest of her clothes half way down her waist' (MANN v. 529).

16. HW repeated this to Mann 10 Sept. (MANN v. 528–9).

17. Who had been sent to Strelitz to accompany the Queen to England (*Mem. Geo. III* i. 55).

laugh, you have been married twice, but it is no joke to me.'[18] Her
lips trembled as the coach stopped, but she jumped out with spirit,
and has done nothing but with good humour and cheerfulness. She
talks a great deal—is easy, civil, and not disconcerted. At first, when
the bride-maids and the court were introduced to her, she said, '*Mon
Dieu, il y en a tant, il y en a tant!*' She was pleased when she was to
kiss the peeresses; but Lady Augusta[19] was forced to take her hand
and give it to those that were to kiss it, which was prettily humble
and good-natured. While they waited for supper, she sat down, sung,
and played. Her French is tolerable, she exchanged much both of
that and German, with the King, the Duke, and the Duke of York.
They did not get to bed till two. Today was a Drawing-Room:[20]
everybody was presented to her; but she spoke to nobody, as she could
not know a soul. The crowd was much less than at a Birthday, the
magnificence very little more. The King looked very handsome, and
talked to her continually with great good humour. It does not promise as if they two would be the two most unhappy persons in England,
from this event. The bride-maids, especially Lady Caroline Russel, Lady Sarah Lenox, and Lady Elizabeth Keppel, were beautiful
figures. With neither features nor air, Lady Sarah was by far the
chief angel. The Duchess of Hamilton was almost in possession of
her former beauty today; and your other Duchess, your daughter,[21]
was much better dressed than ever I saw her. Except a pretty Lady
Sutherland,[22] and a most perfect beauty, an Irish Miss Smith,[23] I don't
think the Queen saw much else to discourage her; my niece,[24] Lady
Kildare, Mrs Fitzroy,[25] were none of them there. There is a ball tonight, and two more Drawing-Rooms; but I have done with them.
The Duchess of Queensberry and Lady Westmorland[26] were in the
procession, and did credit to the ancient nobility.

18. HW repeated this anecdote to
Mann 10 Sept. (MANN v. 528) and in *Mem.
Geo. III* i. 56.

19. Princess Augusta, the King's sister.

20. 'On the 9th instant, the day after
the ceremony, there was the most numerous levee of the peers and peeresses, and
gentlemen of the first distinction, with
the foreign ministers, all in their grand
dresses, that had ever been seen, to pay
their compliments to their Majesties on
their nuptials' (GM loc. cit.).

21. The Duchess of Richmond (HW).

22. Mary Maxwell (ca 1740–66), m.

(1761) William Sutherland, 18th E. of
Sutherland. HW mentions her to Montagu as a 'very pretty figure' (MONTAGU
i. 387 and n. 11).

23. Afterwards married to Mr Matthew,
now Lord Landaff (HW); Ellis *or* Elisha
Smyth (ca 1743–81), m. (1764) Francis
Mathew, cr. (1783) Bn, (1793) Vct, and
(1797) E. of Landaff.

24. The Countess of Waldegrave (HW).

25. Anne Warren (d. 1807), m. (1758)
Charles Fitzroy, cr. (1780) Bn Southampton.

26. Mary Cavendish (1698–1778), m. (ca

You don't presume to suppose, I hope, that we are thinking of you, and wars, and misfortunes and distresses, in these festival times. Mr Pitt himself would be mobbed if he talked of anything but clothes, and diamonds, and bride-maids. Oh! yes, we have wars, civil wars; there is a campaign opened in the Bedchamber.[27] Everybody is excluded but the ministers; even the lords of the Bedchamber, cabinet-counsellors, and foreign ministers: but it has given such offence that I don't know whether Lord Huntingdon must not be the scape-goat.[28] Adieu! I am going to transcribe most of this letter to your Countess.

Yours ever,

Hor. Walpole

To Lady Ailesbury, ca Wednesday 9 September 1761

Missing; mentioned in the previous letter as about to be written.

From Hertford, Thursday 10 September 1761

Printed for the first time from a photostat of BM Add. MSS 23218, f. 54.

Chester, September 10th 1761.

Dear Horry,

WE have had a very quick passage from Dublin[1] which will require at least a night's rest to recover. I observe by the papers which I found on my arrival here that Lord Anson was making dis-

1720) John Fane, cr. (1733) Bn Catherlough, 7th E. of Westmorland, 1736. HW also admired her appearance at the Coronation (*post* 27 Sept. 1761; Montagu i. 387).

27. In a letter of 5 Sept. Lady Kildare mentions 'a sad fuss among the lords of the Bedchamber and the Groom of the Stole [Lord Huntingdon] about putting on the King's shirt. This subject has almost put that of the Wedding and Coronation out of fashion' (*Leinster Corr.* i. 112). The normal procedure was that the King was dressed in levee clothes by the lord of the Bedchamber in waiting, supervised by the Groom of the Stole (John Brooke, *King George III*, New York, 1972, p. 294).

28. He remained Groom of the Stole until 1770.

———

1. 'Parkgate, Sept. 11 [*sic*]. This day arrived here the King's yacht from Dublin, with the Marquis of Kildare, Lord and Lady Hertford, Lord Beacham, and Lord Drogheda' (*London Chronicle* 15–17 Sept., x. 269).

positions for landing the Queen on the 7th,[2] by which I suppose I am to conclude the wedding over.[3] If I find by tomorrow's post that I can get to town in time for it, I intend going directly to London; if it is over I shall make Ragley in my way for the sake of my family, but shall even then be very soon in town, I believe, to pay my duty to the King.

This is my present scheme, which I hope you will approve; my head and stomach have not yet recovered the want of sleep and sickness to enable me to add more than that I am with the best compliments of the family, dear Horry,

Always most truly yours,

HERTFORD

From LADY AILESBURY, ca Monday 21 September 1761

Missing; answered *post* 27 Sept. 1761.

To CONWAY, Friday 25 September 1761

Printed from *Works* v. 82–4.

Arlington Street, Sept. 25, 1761.

THIS is the most unhappy day I have known of years: Bussy goes away![1] Mankind is again given up to the sword! Peace and you are far from England!

Strawberry Hill.

I was interrupted this morning, just as I had begun my letter, by Lord Waldegrave; and then the Duke of Devonshire sent for me to

2. The newspapers of the 7th contained many reports of the arrival of the Queen, including one of a messenger who arrived in London at five that morning with the report that Anson was making dispositions to land her at eight (*Lloyd's Evening Post* 4–7 Sept., ix. 238).

3. It took place on the evening of 8 Sept. (*ante* 9 Sept. 1761).

1. He had been recalled 17 Sept. (*London Chronicle* 26–9 Sept., x. 311–12). Peace negotiations had collapsed in a series of Council meetings and conferences between the 15th and 21st with the rejection of a French *mémoire* of 1 Sept. and accumulating evidence of a Franco-Spanish alliance (below, nn. 7, 9, 11; MANN v. 536–7 and nn. 16–17; *Hardwicke Corr.* iii. 274–7, 322–7).

Burlington House to meet the Duchess of Bedford, and see the old pictures from Hardwicke.[2] If my letter reaches you three days later, at least you are saved from a lamentation. Bussy has put off his journey to Monday[3] (to be sure, you know this is Friday): he says this is a strange country, he can get no wagoner to carry his goods on a Sunday. I am glad a Spanish war waits for a conveyance, and that a wagoner's *veto* is as good as a tribune's of Rome, and can stop Mr Pitt on his career to Mexico. He was going post to conquer it—and Beckford, I suppose, would have had a contract for remitting all the gold, of which Mr Pitt never thinks, unless to serve a City-friend. It is serious that we have discussions with Spain, who says France is humbled enough, but must not be ruined.[4] Spanish gold is actually coining in frontier towns of France;[5] and the privilege which Biscay and two other provinces have of fishing on the coast of Newfoundland,[6] has been demanded for all Spain.[7] It was refused peremptorily; and Mr Secretary Cortez[8] insisted yesterday sennight on recalling Lord Bristol.[9] The rest of the Council, who are content with the

2. Hardwick Hall, Derbyshire, a seat of the Dukes of Devonshire. HW described the pictures there in Aug. 1760 (*Country Seats* 29–31).

3. When he sailed from Dover (GM 1761, xxxi. 475).

4. 'Spain for some time had interposed officiously in behalf of France, which, said the Spaniards, was sufficiently humbled, and must not be ruined' (*Mem. Geo. III* i. 60).

5. The *London Chronicle* (3–6 Oct., x. 336) announced news from Madrid 'that the Spanish flota was safely arrived from Mexico,' and from The Hague 'that the rich flota which Spain hath long expected from Vera Cruz is arrived at Cadiz. We are told that it hath on board immense sums, the greatest part of which will be employed in executing a project which will not a little surprise, as it may possibly give a new face to the affairs of Europe.' Pitt said in the meeting of the Cabinet Council 2 Oct., 'Spain is now carrying on the worst species of war she can for France, covers her trade, lends her money and abets her in negotiation' (*Hardwicke Corr.* iii. 280; see also *Chatham Corr.* ii. 140, 142–3, n. 1).

6. Not recognized by the English, who claimed that 'Spain having never made

any settlement there [on Newfoundland], and the pretended right of the Biscayners and Guipuscoans not being at any time admitted, the King can never consent to the least concession on this article' (paper sent by E. of Bristol to Pitt 31 Aug., in Cobbett, *Parl. Hist.* xv. 1143; see also Bristol's letter to Pitt 31 Aug., ibid. 1137). The *London Chronicle* 17–19 Sept., x. 279, discusses the historical claim of the Biscayners and Guipuzcoans to fisheries on the coast of Newfoundland.

7. The French memorial delivered by Bussy to Pitt 23 July, as part of the peace terms between England and France, demanded for Spain the restitution of prizes, the privilege of fishing on the banks of Newfoundland, and the demolition of the British settlement in the Bay of Honduras (MANN v. 536, n. 15; *Mem. Geo. III* i. 62; Cobbett, op. cit. xv. 1045).

8. Mr Pitt, then secretary of state (HW).

9. The English ambassador at the Court of Madrid (HW). George William Hervey (1721–75), 2d Bn Hervey of Ickworth, 1743; 2d E. of Bristol, 1751; British ambassador to Spain 1758–61. When Pitt's demand for an immediate declaration of war against Spain on 18th Sept. was overruled by the Cabinet Council, he and Lord Temple drew up a paper recom-

world they have to govern, without conquering others, prevailed to defer this impetuosity.[10] However, if France or Spain are the least untractable, a war is inevitable: nay, if they don't submit by the first day of the session, I have no doubt but Mr Pitt will declare it himself on the Address.[11] I have no opinion of Spain intending it: they give France money to protract a war, from which they reap such advantages in their peaceful capacity; and I should think would not give their money if they were on the point of having occasion for it themselves. In spite of you, and all the old barons our ancestors, I pray that we may have done with glory, and would willingly burn every Roman and Greek historian who have done nothing but transmit precedents for cutting throats.

The Coronation is over:[12] 'tis even a more gorgeous sight than I imagined. I saw the procession[13] and the Hall;[14] but the return was in the dark.[15] In the morning they had forgot the Sword of State, the chairs for King and Queen,[16] and their canopies.[17] They used the lord mayor's for the first,[18] and made the last in the Hall: so they did not set forth till noon; and then, by a childish compliment to the King, reserved the illumination of the Hall till his entry,[19] by which

mending 'that orders be forthwith sent to the Earl of Bristol . . . to return immediately to England, without taking leave' (*Hardwicke Corr.* iii. 275, 323; MANN v. 537, n. 17). Bristol was finally recalled in mid-November (MANN v. 548 and n. 20).

10. Pitt was supported only by Lord Temple; see *post* HW to Lady Ailesbury 10 Oct. 1761, n. 11.

11. Pitt resigned over the issue 5 Oct. (*post* 10 Oct. 1761). Hardwicke wrote to Newcastle 27 Sept., 'As to the opinion [of the Council] against an immediate declaration of war against Spain, I cannot yet repent of that opinion. There were not sufficient proofs to justify the doing of it. It would have been precipitate, rash and dangerous' (*Hardwicke Corr.* iii. 328).

12. It took place 22 Sept.

13. From Westminster Hall to the Abbey. There are descriptions in GM 1761, xxxi. 418–20; *London Chronicle* 26–9 Sept., x. 305–7; and a detailed account of all the ceremonies connected with the Coronation in the *Annual Register* 1761, pp. [215]–[42].

14. Westminster Hall. HW watched the procession from the home of his deputy,

Grosvenor Bedford, which, as he says below, was at the gate of Westminster Hall.

15. The return procession apparently did not leave the Abbey until about 7:30 P.M.; the King and Queen entered the Abbey at 1:30 and the ceremony lasted six hours (GM 1761, xxxi. 420, 428). 'The return from the Abbey was so late, that the spectators could not distinguish the several degrees of the nobility; the whole not having entered Westminster Hall before 7 o'clock' (*London Chronicle* 22–4 Sept., x. 290).

16. Presumably those for use in Westminster Hall. Thomas Gray, who watched the formation of the procession from within the Hall, mentions the King and Queen taking their place in 'their chairs of state' there before the procession set out (Gray, *Correspondence*, ed. Toynbee and Whibley, Oxford, 1935, ii. 754–5).

17. Presumably those under which they walked in the procession (ibid. ii. 755).

18. 'The Sword of State had been entirely forgot; so Lord Huntingdon was forced to carry the Lord Mayor's great two-handed sword instead of it' (ibid.).

19. 'The instant the Queen's canopy en-

means they arrived like a funeral, nothing being discernible but the plumes of the Knights of the Bath, which seemed the hearse.[20] Lady Kildare, the Duchess of Richmond, and Lady Pembroke, were the capital beauties.[21] Lady Harrington, the finest figure at a distance;[22] old Westmorland, the most majestic.[23] Lady Hertford could not walk, and indeed I think is in a way to give us great anxiety.[24] She is going to Ragley to ride. Lord Beauchamp was one of the King's train-bearers. Of all the incidents of the day, the most diverting was, what happened to the Queen. She had a retiring-chamber, with *all* con-veniencies, prepared behind the altar. She went thither—in the *most convenient,* what found she but—the Duke of Newcastle![25] Lady Hardwicke died three days before the ceremony,[26] which kept away the whole House of Yorke. Some of the peeresses were dressed over-night, slept in armchairs, and were waked if they tumbled their heads. Your sister Harris's maid, Lady Peterborough,[27] was a comely figure. My Lady Cowper refused, but was forced to walk with Lady Maccles-field.[28] Lady Falmouth was not there; on which George Selwyn said, that those peeresses who were most used to *walk,* did not.[29] I carried

tered [the Hall], fire was given to all the lustres at once by trains of prepared flax, that reached from one to the other. To me it seemed an interval of not half a minute, before the whole was in a blaze of splendour' (ibid. ii. 756). GM mentions that on the Queen's entry '3000 wax lights were all lighted in less than five minutes' (1761, xxxi. 428).

20. The Knights of the Bath walked early in the procession, before all the peers (ibid. xxxi. 418).

21. HW also praises them to Lady Ailesbury (*post* 27 Sept.) and to Montagu (MONTAGU i. 387); Gray includes them, to-gether with Ladies Spencer, Harrington, and Strafford, as 'the noblest and most graceful figures among the Ladies' (Gray, op. cit. ii. 754).

22. As HW also told Lady Ailesbury and Montagu, loc. cit.

23. She had impressed HW at the Royal Wedding (*ante* 9 Sept.) as well; he also praised her appearance at the Coronation to Lady Ailesbury, Montagu and Mann (MANN v. 535).

24. See *ante* 15 Aug. 1761.

25. 'When the Queen retired while she was in the Abbey, to a sort of closet fur-nished with necessary conveniences, one of the ladies opening the door to see all was right, found the Duke of Newcastle perked up and in the very act upon the anointed velvet close-stool. Do not think I joke, it is literally true' (Gray to Brown 24 Sept., Gray, op. cit. ii. 757). HW also repeats the anecdote to Mann 28 Sept. (MANN loc. cit.).

26. On 19 Sept.; see *Hardwicke Corr.* ii. 581.

27. Robiniana Browne (d. 1794), m. (1755) Charles Mordaunt, 4th E. of Peter-borough. In calling her Mrs Harris's 'maid,' HW perhaps means 'bridesmaid.'

28. Dorothy Nesbitt (d. 1779), m. (1757, as his second wife) George Parker, 2d E. of Macclesfield. HW repeats this anecdote to Lady Ailesbury *post* 27 Sept. According to HW, Lady Macclesfield had been her husband's 'mistress, or at least other peo-ple's' and 'a common woman' (MANN vi. 211 and n. 13; MORE 10, n. 7). Lady Cowper was born a Carteret and ap-parently combined excessive family pride with prudery; see MONTAGU i. 301 and n. 6.

29. Lady Falmouth, whose origins are obscure, was notorious enough to be

my Lady Townshend, Lady Hertford, Lady Anne Connolly, my Lady Hervey, and Mrs Clive, to my deputy's[30] house at the gate of Westminster Hall.[31] My Lady Townshend said she should be very glad to see a coronation, as she never had seen one. 'Why,' said I, 'Madam, you walked at the last?'[32] 'Yes, child,' said she, 'but I saw nothing of it: I only looked to see who looked at me.' The Duchess of Queensberry walked: her affectation that day was to do nothing preposterous. The Queen has been at the opera,[33] and says she will go once a week. This is a fresh disaster to our box, where we have lived so harmoniously for three years. We can get no alternative but that over Miss Chudleigh's; and Lord Strafford and Lady Mary Coke will not subscribe, unless we can. The Duke of Devonshire and I are negotiating with all our art to keep our party together. The crowds at the opera and play when the King and Queen go, are a little greater than what I remember.[34] The late Royalties went to the Haymarket, when it was the fashion to frequent the other opera in Lincoln's Inn Fields.[35] Lord Chesterfield one night came into the latter, and was asked, If he had been at the other house? 'Yes,' said he, 'but there was nobody but the King and Queen; and as I thought they might be talking business, I came away.'

Thank you for your journals: the best route you can send me would be of your journey homewards. Adieu!

Yours most sincerely,

Hor. Walpole

featured in a 'tête-à-tête' portrait in the *Town and Country Magazine* a few years later (GEC).

30. Grosvenor Bedford (d. 1771), HW's deputy as usher of the Exchequer (GM 1771, xli. 523).

31. According to Bedford's note to HW's letter to him, 23 Sept., the party also included John Chute, Mr Raftor, a 'Master' Townshend, and 'Miss Hotham and her maid.'

32. The coronation of George II in 1727. Although her husband did not succeed his father until 1738, he had been summoned to the House of Lords in his father's barony in 1723, which would have entitled his wife to walk with the peeresses in the Coronation procession.

33. On 19 Sept., to see *Le speranze della*

terra and *Le promesse del ciels*, 'an entirely new serenata writ in order to celebrate, as far as lies in Sga Mattei's power, the late Royal Nuptials, and approaching Coronation' (*London Stage* Pt IV, ii. 889; GM 1761, xxxi. 428).

34. 'It is almost inconceivable the crowds of people that waited in the streets, quite from St James's to the playhouse, to see their Majesties [ca 14 Sept.]. . . . The house was full almost as soon as the doors were open, so that out of the vast multitude present, not a fiftieth part got in, to the infinite disappointment and fatigue of many thousands' (ibid. xxxi. 417–18).

35. In 1734, George II and Queen Caroline were strong supporters of Handel, at that time manager of the opera in

PS. If you ever hear from, or write to, such a person as Lady A., pray tell her she is worse to me in point of correspondence than ever you said I was to you,[36] and that she sends me everything but letters.

To LADY AILESBURY, Sunday 27 September 1761

Printed from the MS now WSL; first printed, with omissions, Works v. 555–8, and in full Toynbee v. 117–21 and Supp. ii. 122–3. For the history of the MS see ante 23 Aug. 1760; it was marked by HW for inclusion in Works.

Strawberry Hill, Sept. 27, 1761.

YOU are a mean mercenary woman: if you did not want histories of weddings and coronations, and had not jobs to be executed about muslins and a bit of china and counterband goods,[1] one should never hear of you. When you don't want a body, you can frisk about with greffiers and burgomasters, and be as merry in a dyke as my Lady Frog herself. The moment your curiosity is agog, or your cambric seized, you recollect a good cousin in England, and as folks said two hundred years ago, begin to write *upon the knees of your heart.*[2] Well! I am a sweet-tempered creature, I forgive you; I have already writ to a little friend in the Custom House,[3] and will try what can be done; though by Mr Amyand's[4] report to the Duchess of Richmond, I fear your case is desperate. For the genealogies, I have turned over all my books to no purpose; I can meet with no Lady Howard that married a Carey, nor a Lady Seymour that married a Caufield.

the Haymarket, while the Prince of Wales and a large group of nobility were supporting another company in opposition at Lincoln's Inn Fields; see John, Lord Hervey, *Memoirs,* ed. Sedgwick, New York, 1963, pp. 42–3.

36. Conway in letters of 27 July, 21 Aug., and 5 Oct. to the D. of Devonshire complained of the slowness of the mails and the 'idleness' of his friends (Chatsworth MSS, 416/70, 71, 72).

1. As HW to Lady Ailesbury *post* 10 Oct. in conjunction with this letter makes clear, some cloth or clothing that Lady Ailesbury had sent to England, probably for her daughter the Ds of Richmond, had been seized as contraband.

2. Not found.

3. HW describes him *post* 10 Oct. as 'one of the most sensible and experienced men in the Custom House.' The letter is missing, but it may have been addressed to Benjamin Scott (?d. before Nov. 1761), Deputy Collector of the Customs Inward for the Port of London, in which HW held a sinecure (*Court and City Register* 1761, p. 123).

4. Claudius Amyand (1718–74), M.P. Tregony 1747–54, Sandwich 1754–6; undersecretary of state 1750–6; commissioner of the customs 1756–65; receiver of land taxes for London and Middlesex 1765–74 (MONTAGU i. 138, n. 7, corrected by Namier and Brooke ii. 20).

Lettice Caufield,[5] who married Francis Staunton, was daughter of Dr *James* (not George) Caufield,[6] younger brother of the first Lord Charlemont.[7] This is all I can ascertain. For the other pedigree; I can inform your friend that there was a Sir Nicholas Throckmorton,[8] who married an Anne Carew,[9] daughter of Sir Nicholas *Carew*[10] Knight of the Garter, not Carey—but this Sir Nicholas Carew married Joan Courtney[11]—not a Howard; and besides the Careys and Throckmortons you wot of, were just the reverse; your Carey was the cock and Throckmorton the hen—mine are vice versa; otherwise, let me tell your friend, Carews and Courtneys are worth Howards any day of the week, and of ancienter blood[12]—so, if descent is all he wants, I advise him to take up with the pedigree as I have refitted it. However, I will cast a figure once more, and try if I can conjure up the Dames Howard and Seymour that he wants.

5. Lettice Caulfeild (d. after 1627), m. 1 Francis Staunton (d. after 1627); m. 2 William Peisley (John Lodge and Mervyn Archdall, *Peerage of Ireland,* 1789, iii. 134n., 135).

6. HW, who seems to be following the 1754 edn of John Lodge's *Peerage of Ireland,* which he owned (Hazen, *Cat. of HW's Lib.,* No. 660), is apparently mistaken. Although Lodge says that the 1st Bn Charlemont's successor as 2d Bn was the son of his brother James (who also had five daughters), GEC iii. 135 says that the 2d Bn was the son of George Caulfeild, Recorder of Oxford and 'elder' brother of the 1st Bn.

7. Toby Caulfeild (1565–1627), Kt, 1603; cr. (1620) Bn Charlemont.

8. (1515–71), diplomatist.

9. (d. after 1585), m. 1 (1549 *or* 1550) Sir Nicholas Throckmorton; m. 2 (1572) Adrian Stokes (ca 1536–85), who left her well off (A. L. Rowse, *Ralegh and the Throckmortons,* 1962, pp. 13–14, 57, 107; *Notes and Queries,* 1855, 1st ser. xii. 452; GEC iv. 421–2).

10. (d. 1539), of Beddington, Surrey; K.G., 1536; courtier of Henry VIII, who was executed for his share in the 'treason' of the M. of Exeter. The confusion is compounded by 'Carew' being pronounced 'Carey.'

11. Sir Nicholas Carew of Beddington, mentioned earlier in the sentence, m. (1514) Elizabeth, dau. of Thomas Bryan,

vice-chamberlain to Catherine of Aragon (DNB *sub* Sir Nicholas Carew). The 'Sir Nicholas Carew' who m. 'Joan Courtney' lived a full century earlier. He was Sir Nicholas Carew (d. 1443), lord of Carew Castle, Pembrokeshire, who m. Joan Courtenay (b. ca 1411), only daughter of Sir Hugh Courtenay (d. 1425), of Haccombe, Devon, great-grandson of the 2d E. of Devon and grandson of William, Abp of Canterbury. She m. 2 Sir Robert Vere, 2d son of Richard de Vere (?1385–1417), 11th E. of Oxford (J. L. Vivian, *The Visitations of the County of Devon,* Exeter, [1895], pp. 134, 245; Burke, *Landed Gentry,* 1925, p. 289; GEC *sub* Devon and Oxford). The connection between the Carews of Beddington, settled there since the time of Edward III, and the Carews of Carew Castle and various places in Devon is very obscure. The confusion of the two Nicholas Carews seems to have continued in HW's mind, since he later (1771) joked about his descent from the Courtenays (MORE 155). He was descended from Sir Nicholas Carew of Beddington, whose dau. Mary m. Thomas, Lord Darcy, from whom was descended Catherine Darcy, Lady Philipps, grandmother of HW's mother (OSSORY ii. 111 and n. 28), but apparently not from the earlier Sir Nicholas Carew.

12. Both claimed, apparently justly, a Norman origin; the Howards had risen to eminence in the 15th century.

My heraldry was much more offended at the Coronation with the ladies that did walk, than with those that walked out of their place; yet I was not so *perilously* angry as my Lady Cowper, who refused to set a foot with my Lady Macclesfield,[13] and when she was at last obliged to associate with her, set out on a round trot, as if she designed to prove the antiquity of her family,[14] by marching as lustily as a maid of honour of Queen Gwiniver. It was in truth a brave sight. The sea of heads in Palace Yard, the Guards, horse and foot, the scaffolds, balconies and procession, exceeded imagination. The Hall when once illuminated, was noble, but they suffered the whole parade to return into it in the dark, that his Majesty might be surprised with the quickness with which the sconces catched fire.[15] The Champion[16] acted well, the other paladins had neither the grace nor alertness of Rinaldo.[17] Lord Effingham[18] and the Duke of Bedford[19] were but untoward knights errant, and Lord Talbot[20] had not much more dignity than the figure of General Monke[21] in the Abbey.[22] The habit of the peers is unbecoming to the last degree; but the peeresses made amends for all defects. Your daughter Richmond, Lady Kildare, and Lady Pembroke were as handsome as the Graces. Lady Rochford, Lady Holderness, and Lady Lyttelton looked exceedingly well in that their day, and for those of the day before, the Duchess of Queensberry, Lady Westmorland, and Lady Albemarle were surprising. Lady Harrington was noble at a distance, and so covered with diamonds, that you would have thought she had bid *somebody* or

13. See *ante* 25 Sept. 1761 and n. 28.

14. The Carterets traced their ancestry to 1000.

15. See ibid., n. 19.

16. John Dymoke (d. 1784), Champion of England, lord of the manor of Scrivelsby, Lincs. As Champion he rode into Westminster Hall armed cap-à-pie and challenged anyone who disputed the King's rights (Montagu i. 161, n. 2, 388 and n. 25; GM 1761, xxxi. 421).

17. A chivalric figure in *Orlando Furioso* and *Jerusalem Delivered*.

18. Deputy Earl Marshal for the Duke of Norfolk, who being a Roman Catholic, could not officiate as Earl Marshal. He, Bedford, and Talbot 'in their robes, all three on horseback prancing and curvetting, like the hobby-horses in the *Rehearsal*, ushered in the courses [at the Banquet] to the foot of the haut-pas'

(Thomas Gray, *Correspondence*, ed. Toynbee and Whibley, Oxford, 1935, ii. 753, n. 3, 756).

19. Lord High Constable of England; HW told Montagu he was the least ridiculous of the three (Montagu i. 388).

20. Lord High Steward. Perhaps significantly HW does not relate here the story he tells to Montagu of Lord Talbot's horse entering backwards (ibid. i. 388–9), and which does not seem to be mentioned again until Wilkes retold it in the *North Briton* No. 12, although there are other references to his difficulty in getting the horse to back down the Hall.

21. George Monck *or* Monk (1608–70), cr. (1660) D. of Albemarle.

22. Erected in 1730, designed by William Kent and executed by Peter Scheemakers. The Duke stands to the right in armour (Nikolaus Pevsner, *London: I . . . Lon-*

other, like Falstaff, *rob me the Exchequer.*[23] Lady Northampton[24] was very magnificent too and looked prettier than I have seen her of late. Lady Spencer[25] and Lady Bolinbroke were not the worst figures there. The Duchess of Ancaster marched alone[26] after the Queen with much majesty; and there were two new Scotch peeresses that pleased everybody, Lady Sutherland and Lady Dunmore.[27] *Per contra,* were Lady Portsmouth,[28] who had put a wig on, and old Exeter,[29] who had scratched hers off; Lady Stamford,[30] the Dowager Effingham,[31] and a Lady Say and Sele[32] with her tresses coal black and her hair coal white. Well! it was all delightful, but not half so charming as its being over—the gabble one heard about it for six weeks before, and the fatigue of the day, could not well be compensated by a mere puppet-show, for puppet-show it was, though it cost a million.[33]

The Queen is so gay that we shall not want sights; she has been at the opera,[34] *The Beggar's Opera*[35] and *The Rehearsal,*[36] and two

don and Westminster, 1957, p. 382). It adjoins the monument HW had erected to his mother in the south aisle of Henry VII's Chapel. See also A. P. Stanley, *Historical Memorials of Westminster Abbey,* New York, [1882], i. 295–6, ii. 117.

23. This is another allusion to her affair with Lord Barrington, the chancellor of the Exchequer (see *ante* 10 April 1761 and n. 20).

24. Lady Anne Somerset (1741–63), m. (1759) Charles Compton, 7th E. of Northampton. At the time of her marriage, HW described her as 'rather handsome' (MANN v. 294).

25. Margaret Georgiana Poyntz (1737–1814), m. (1755) John Spencer, cr. (1761) Vct and (1765) E. Spencer. HW also praises her appearance to Montagu (MONTAGU i. 387).

26. As Mistress of the Robes.

27. Lady Charlotte Stewart (d. 1818), m. (1759) John Murray, 4th E. of Dunmore.

28. Hon. Elizabeth Griffin (1691–1762), m. 1 Henry Grey; m. 2 (1741) John Wallop, cr. (1743) E. of Portsmouth. HW tells an anecdote of her and Lady Harrington at the Coronation to Montagu 24 Sept. (MONTAGU, loc. cit.).

29. Hannah Sophia Chambers (ca 1702–65), m. (1724) Brownlow Cecil, 8th E. of Exeter. See also ibid. i. 388.

30. Lady Mary Booth (ca 1703–72), m.

(1736) Harry Grey, 4th E. of Stamford.

31. Annie Bristow (d. 1774), m. (1728) Francis Howard, 7th Bn Howard, cr. (1731) E. of Effingham.

32. Christobella Tyrrell (1695–1789), m. 1 John Knapp; m. 2 John Pigott; m. 3 (1753) Richard Fiennes, 6th Vct Saye and Sele. HW also mentions her, Lady Exeter, and Lady Effingham to Montagu as unattractive figures (MONTAGU, loc. cit.).

33. HW also discusses the high cost in his letter to Mann 28 Sept. (MANN v. 536).

34. On 19 Sept. (*ante* 25 Sept. 1761, n. 33).

35. At Covent Garden on the 24th (*London Stage* Pt IV, ii. 890–1). 'On this occasion, two magnificent boxes were prepared; one for their Majesties of a cherry-coloured velvet, the festoon enriched with a silver embroidery, lace, and fringe; in the centre was represented two hymeneal torches enclosing a heart, the device, MUTUUS ARDOR; the columns were wreathed with lace, and the canopy adorned with tassels and a crown of excellent workmanship; the whole lined with white satin. . . . The whole is said to have cost £700' (GM 1761, xxxi. 429; *London Chronicle* 24–6 Sept., x. 297).

36. At Drury Lane on the 14th (*London Stage* Pt IV, ii. 887–8); a description of the occasion is in GM 1761, xxxi. 417.

nights ago carried the King to Ranelagh[37]—I suppose next week they will go to Mrs Holman's[38]—anywhere, so they would not come to the opera and dislodge us. It will be as much as the Duke of Devonshire's good breeding and my passion for Lady Mary Coke can do, to keep the remains of our poor society together; Lord Strafford vows and Lady Mary swears they will not subscribe, unless we can have as good a box as the King's on the nights he goes; they are not content to coo up two pair of stairs over Miss Chudleigh. In short, I am so miserable with losing my Duchess,[39] and you and Mr Conway, that I believe if you should be another six weeks without writing to me, I should come to The Hague and scold you in person, for alas! my dear Lady, I have no hopes of seeing you here. Stanley is recalled,[40] is expected every hour,[41] Bussy goes tomorrow,[42] and Mr Pitt is so impatient to conquer Mexico, that I don't believe he will stay till my Lord Bristol can be ordered to leave Madrid.[43] I tremble lest Mr Conway should not get leave to come[44]—nay, are we sure he would like to ask it? He was so impatient to get to the army, that I should not be surprised if he stayed there till every sutler and woman that follows the camp was come away. You ask me if we are not in admiration of Prince Ferdinand—in truth we have thought very little of him—he may outwit Broglio ten times, and not be half so much talked of, as Lord Talbot's backing his horse down Westminister Hall.[45] The generality are not struck with anything under a complete victory—if you have a mind to be well with the mob of England, you must be knocked on the head like Wolfe, or bring home as many diamonds as Clive.[46] We live in a country where so many follies or novelties start forth every day, that we have not time to try a general's capacity by the rules of Polybius.[47]

37. This report was false; see *post* 10 Oct. 1761.

38. Not conclusively identified. The all-inclusive but fashionable assemblies at her house in Park Place provided HW with a subject for jest for several years; see especially Montagu i. 126–7 and n. 11 and Mann iv. 142.

39. The Duchess of Grafton, who was abroad (Mary Berry). See Mann v. 537.

40. On 15 Sept. (ibid. v. 536 and n. 16).

41. He left Paris 23 Sept. and arrived in London on the 29th (ibid. v. 504, n. 5).

42. He sailed from Dover on the 28th (*ante* 25 Sept. 1761, n. 3).

43. As Pitt had demanded 18 Sept., but was overruled (ibid., n. 9).

44. He did not, but remained abroad with the army all winter (Conway to D. of Devonshire 21 Aug., 5 Oct., 17 Dec. 1761, 2 Nov. 1762, Chatsworth MSS, 416/71, 72, 73, 80; Mann v. 549).

45. For more flattering accounts of Talbot's performance see Montagu i. 388–9, nn. 27–8.

46. Robert Clive (1725–74), cr. (1762) Bn Clive. He had returned to England from India in July 1760 (Mann v. 429 and n. 23).

47. Polybius believed that the statesman

I have hardly left room for my obligations, to your Ladyship for my commissions at Amsterdam, to Mrs Sally[48] for her teapots, which are likely to stay so long at The Hague that I fear they will have begot a whole set of china; and to Miss Conway and Lady George[49] for thinking of me—pray assure them of my rethinking—I don't know how to say anything to the last word of your letter—my perroquet[50] is dead! Adieu! dear Madam; don't you think we had better write oftener and shorter?

Yours most faithfully,

H. W.

To Conway, ca Tuesday 6 October 1761

Missing: 'I wrote you an account last week of his [Pitt's] resignation' (HW to Conway *post* 12 Oct. 1761).

should learn from history to avoid predictable disasters and to cope with the unpredictable strokes of Fortune. 'That men, in the infirmity of human nature, should fall into misfortunes which defy calculation, is the fault not of the sufferers but of Fortune, and of those who do the wrong; but that they should from mere levity, and with their eyes open, thrust themselves upon the most serious disasters is without dispute the fault of the victims themselves. Therefore it is that pity and sympathy and assistance await those whose failure is due to Fortune: reproach and rebuke from all men of sense those who have only their own folly to thank for it' (Polybius, *The Histories,* ed. E. S. Shuckburgh and F. W.

Walbank, Bloomington, Ind., 1962, Bk II, 7). He says that a man's virtue should be judged 'in the hour of brilliant success or conspicuous reverse. For the true test of a perfect man is the power of bearing with spirit and dignity violent changes of fortune' (ibid. Bk VI, 1).

48. Lady Ailesbury's woman (Mary Berry).

49. Lady George Lennox. Her husband, brother of Lady Ailesbury's son-in-law the D. of Richmond, was with the army in Germany as Lt-Col. of the 33d Foot (Namier and Brooke iii. 35).

50. The parakeet is also mentioned to Montagu 14 Oct. 1760 and 31 March 1761 (MONTAGU i. 306, 350) and to Strafford 5 July 1761 (CHUTE 308).

To Lady Ailesbury, Saturday 10 October 1761

Printed from the MS now wsl; first printed, with omissions, *Works* v. 558–60, and in full Toynbee v. 130–3 and *Supp.* ii. 123. For the history of the MS see *ante* 23 Aug. 1760.

Strawberry Hill, Oct. 10, 1761.

I DON'T know, what business I had, Madam, to be an economist: it was out of character. I wished for a thousand more drawings in that sale at Amsterdam,[1] but concluded they would be very dear, and not having seen them, I thought it too rash to trouble your Ladyship with a large commission.[2] As they proved so cheap, I wish I had troubled your Ladyship with a huge commission. You are so good to me, that if I had not been saving of my money, I fear I should not have been frugal of your pains. I thank you extremely for those you have bought, and shall wait for them with great patience. I suppose I writ one of the figures carelessly; it was 1229, not 1729—but it does not signify.

I wish I could give you as good an account of your commission;[3] but it is absolutely impracticable. I employed one of the most sensible and experienced men in the Custom House,[4] and all the result was, he could only recommend[5] me to Mr Amyand as the newest and consequently the most polite of the Commissioners—but the Duchess of Richmond had tried him before—to no purpose. There is no way of recovering any of your goods, but purchasing them again at the sale.

What am I doing, to be talking to you of drawings and chintzes, when the world is all turned topsy-turvy? Peace, as the poets would say, is not only returned to heaven, but has carried her sister Virtue along with her—oh! no, Peace will keep no such company—Virtue is an arrant strumpet, and loves diamonds as well as my Lady Harrington and is as fond of a coronet as my Lord Melcomb.[6] Worse! worse! She will set men to cutting throats, and pick their pockets at

1. Probably the sale of 4537 drawings and 70 prints, the property of Jacques-Gabriel Huquier (1695–1772), Parisian painter, engraver, print-merchant and collector, held at Amsterdam on 14 Sept. and the following days (Frits Lugt, *Répertoire des catalogues de ventes publiques*, La Haye, 1938–64, No. 1172).

2. HW's commission was apparently sent in a missing letter, perhaps that of ca 9 Sept.

3. About her clothes (*ante* 27 Sept. 1761).

4. Perhaps Benjamin Scott (ibid., n. 3).

5. MS, 'recommended.'

6. George Bubb Dodington, after a life-long ambition for a peerage, had finally been created Bn Melcombe 6 April 1761.

the same time. I am in such a passion, I cannot tell you what I am angry about—why, about Virtue and Mr Pitt;[7] two arrant cheats, gypsies; I believe he was a comrade of Elizabeth Canning,[8] when he lived on Enfield Wash.[9] In short, the Council were for making peace,

> But he as loving his own pride and purposes,
> Evades them with a bombast circumstance,
> Horribly stuffed with epithets of war,
> And in conclusion—nonsuits my mediators.[10]

He insisted on a war with Spain,[11] was resisted, and last Monday resigned. The City breathed vengeance on his opposers,[12] the Council quaked, and the Lord knows what would have happened; but yesterday, which was only Friday, as this giant was stalking to seize the Tower of London, he stumbled over a silver penny, picked it up, carried it home to Lady Esther,[13] and they are now as quiet, good sort of people, as my Lord and Lady Bath who lived in the vinegar bottle.[14] In fact, Madam, this immaculate man has accepted the barony of Chatham for his wife with a pension of three thousand pounds a year for three lives,[15] and though he has not quitted the House of

7. Whose resignation 5 Oct. caused a general outcry (below, n. 12).

8. (1734–73), impostor, who was convicted of perjury in 1754 and transported for false accusations that she had been kidnapped. See Chute 175.

9. Miss Canning had asserted she had been held prisoner at Enfield Wash. Pitt had occasionally lived at South Lodge in Enfield Chace between 1748 and 1756 (Earl of Rosebery, *Chatham: His Early Life and Connections*, 1910, pp. 308–10).

10. *Othello* I. i. 12–16.

11. Initially on 18 Sept., and again in the Cabinet Council 2 Oct. On both occasions every other member of the Council except Lord Temple had opposed him and favoured a delay in opening hostilities (*Hardwicke Corr.* iii. 274–80; Mann v. 537, nn. 17, 2). Newcastle wrote Bedford 2 Oct., 'Every Lord adhered to his former opinion, and spoke strongly. Lord President, the Duke of Devonshire, Lord Hardwicke, Lord Anson, Lord Ligonier, Lord Mansfield, Lord Bute, and myself, against it. My Lord Temple, and Mr Pitt, adhered to the paper, they had given to the King' (BM Add. MSS 32929, f. 29).

12. Bute wrote Newcastle 6 Oct., 'The storm runs high in the City, and I hear some of them are rash enough to say, they will have their Minister again' (ibid., f. 74; see also Mann v. 540). GM prints letters and extracts from pamphlets about Pitt's resignation (GM 1761, xxxi. 460–8, 513–20).

13. Lady Hester Grenville (1720–1803), m. (1754) William Pitt, cr. (1766) E. of Chatham; cr. (1761) Bns Chatham, s.j. The allusion is to his pension and her barony (below, n. 15; *post* 12 Oct. 1761, n. 3). Richard Rigby wrote Bedford 12 Oct., 'The City and the people are outrageous about Lady *Cheat'em*, as they call her, and her husband's pension' (*Bedford Corr.* iii. 51).

14. According to Mrs Toynbee (v. 132, n. 3), this is an allusion to the west-country tale of Mr and Mrs Vinegar 'who lived in a vinegar-bottle.' Lord Bath was embittered by his loss of popularity when he accepted a peerage in 1742 on the fall of Sir Robert Walpole.

15. His own, his wife's, and their eldest son's. Both the peerage and the pension were announced in the *London Gazette* No. 10146, 6–10 Oct., *sub* 9 Oct. According to HW, this was 'the first instance, I

Commons, I think my Lord Abercorn would now be as formidable there.[16] The pension he has left us, is, a war for three thousand lives! perhaps, for twenty times three thousand lives! but—

> Does this become a soldier? *this* become
> Whom armies follow'd, and a people lov'd?[17]

What! to sneak out of the scrape, prevent peace, and avoid the war! blast one's character, and all for the comfort of a paltry annuity, a long-necked peeress, and a couple of Grenvilles! The City looks mighty foolish, I believe, and possibly even Beckford[18] may blush. Lord Temple resigned[19] yesterday; I suppose his virtue pants for a dukedom. Lord Egremont[20] has the Seals, Lord Hardwicke, I fancy, the Privy Seal,[21] and George Grenville, no longer Speaker, is to be the Cabinet Minister in the House of Commons.[22]—Oh! Madam, I am glad you are inconstant to Mr Conway, though it is only with a barbette;[23] if you piqued yourself on your virtue, I should expect you would sell it to the master of a trackscoot.[24]

I told you a lie about the King's going to Ranelagh—no matter;

believe, of a pension ever specified in that paper' (*Mem. Geo. III* i. 64–5). See also *Hardwicke Corr.* iii. 330.

16. Abercorn was not 'formidable' at all because of his taciturnity.

17. These lines have not been traced.

18. William Beckford, Pitt's chief supporter in the City. There was a momentary reaction against Pitt in London, and the Common Council, which had been summoned to meet 13 Oct. to thank him for his services, temporarily dropped the intention (*Mem. Geo. III* i. 66; *London Chronicle* 8–10, 10–13 Oct., x. 350, 360). He had however recovered most of his popularity there by the end of October (*post* 26 Oct. 1761).

19. As Lord Privy Seal.

20. Sir Charles Wyndham (1710–63), 4th Bt; 2d E. of Egremont, 1750. As Bute's choice to succeed Pitt, he received the Seals and kissed hands 9 Oct. and was sworn in on the 12th (*Daily Adv.* 10, 14 Oct.; MANN v. 540 and nn. 8–9).

21. Newcastle proposed Hardwicke to Bute for the office 9 Oct.; Bute replied that Hardwicke 'was not the least thought of—sure he was rewarded enough by the great things which were done for his

family and with the promise of the President's [of the Council] place.' Nevertheless, it was widely reported at the time that Hardwicke would get it, and on 16 Nov. Bute did in fact offer the post to him. He declined and the D. of Bedford, Bute's own candidate, was appointed 25 Nov. (*Hardwicke Corr.* iii. 292 and n. 3, 328–9; MANN v. 541 and n. 8).

22. Grenville, at this time treasurer of the Navy and a member of the Nominal Cabinet, had been under consideration for nomination as Speaker of the House of Commons since the beginning of the year in succession to Arthur Onslow who retired in March 1761. On Pitt's resignation, however, Bute offered him the secretaryship of state with leadership of the Commons; Grenville declined to succeed his brother-in-law and begged to be allowed to go to the Chair as planned, but was finally prevailed upon to accept the leadership of the Commons with a seat in the Effective Cabinet while remaining treasurer of the Navy (Namier and Brooke ii. 538–9 and references cited).

23. 'A little dog with long curly hair, a poodle' (OED).

24. See *ante* 21 Jan. 1759, n. 9.

there is no such thing as truth. The Duchess of Marlborough[25] is dead, and Lady Berkeley has given up her jointure without dying—to avoid the ecclesiastic court.[26] Garrick exhibits the Coronation,[27] and opening the end of the stage, discovers a real bonfire and real mob; the houses in Drury Lane let their windows at threepence a head.[28] Rich is going to produce a finer Coronation,[29] nay, than the real one, for there is to be a dinner for the Knights of the Bath and the Barons of the Cinque Ports, which Lord Talbot refused them.[30]

I put your Caufields and Stauntons into the hands of one of the first heralds upon earth,[31] and who has the entire pedigree of the Careys, but he cannot find a drop of Howard or Seymour blood in the least artery about them. Good night, Madam.

Yours most faithfully,

H. Walpole

25. Hon. Elizabeth Trevor (d. 7 Oct. 1761), m. (1732) Charles Spencer, 2d D. of Marlborough.

26. Her husband, following the birth of a daughter he did not recognize as his, threatened her with divorce unless she surrendered her jointure (ante 14 July 1761, n. 5).

27. Garrick's Coronation, inserted in a performance of Shakespeare's Henry VIII, was first performed at Drury Lane 30 Sept. and repeatedly thereafter until, apparently, 4 Dec. (London Stage Pt IV, ii. 892–3, 906). A long unfavourable description mentioning the opening of the end of the stage and the real bonfire is in Thomas Davies, Memoirs of the Life of David Garrick, 1808, i. 364–7.

28. The exorbitant rentals charged for viewing the Coronation itself are given in Mann v. 536 and nn. 12–13.

29. Rich's Coronation at Covent Garden was performed for the first time on 13 Nov. (London Stage Pt IV, ii. 903).

30. He had been forced to admit two of the Knights of the Bath to their old place at the banquet and give a dinner to the rest in the Court of Requests. The claim of the Barons, who carried the canopies over the King and Queen in the procession, seems to have been rejected. See HW's anecdotes in his letter to Montagu 24 Sept. (Montagu i. 389), repeated in Mem. Geo. III i. 58–9, and, with slight variations, in Gray to Brown 24 Sept. (Gray, Correspondence, ed. Toynbee and Whibley, Oxford, 1935, ii. 757); Gray may have heard this from HW.

31. Perhaps John Chute, who had a passion for genealogy.

From HERTFORD, Saturday 10 October 1761

Printed for the first time from a photostat of BM Add. MSS 23218, f. 55.

Ragley, October 10th 1761.

Dear Horry,

I AM not yet satisfied about the resignation.[1] I cannot imagine my judgment so far mistaken as that Mr Pitt can accept either place, pension, peerage or any other honour under his present circumstances,[2] and yet his going to Court so very often[3] when he quits the helm at such a time does in my humble opinion not become him. Does Lord Temple resign?[4] If he does not I think Mr Pitt will be blamed, and if Lord Egremont is preferred[5] to the Duke of Bedford I shall not wonder at his Grace's dissatisfaction.[6] If I was a Frenchman I should rejoice in such conduct. We arrived at the great house[7] yesterday evening; Lady Hertford made a visit to Lady Ann Coventry[8] and I shot on our way home. On the road we were informed of the death of the Duchess of Marlbro'.

Lady Hertford desires her best compliments. Yours, dear Horry,

Always most sincerely,

HERTFORD

1. Of Pitt on 5 Oct.

2. Pitt's pension and the peerage for his wife were announced in the *Gazette* on the 10th (*ante* HW to Lady Ailesbury 10 Oct. 1761, n. 15), but the news had not yet reached Ragley; rumours of these awards had been circulating.

3. The newspapers reported that he had spent 'some hours' with the King on 7 Oct.; Lord Hardwicke saw him at the levee on that day and at the Queen's Drawing-Room on the 8th (*London Chronicle* 6–8 Oct., x. 343; *Daily Adv.* 8 Oct.; *Hardwicke Corr.* iii. 330).

4. He had resigned on the 9th; see previous letter.

5. Egremont's appointment as Pitt's successor as secretary of state was generally known in London on the 8th (MANN v. 540), but the news had apparently not reached Ragley.

6. Bedford's correspondence with New-

castle at this time indicates no particular dissatisfaction with the appointment of Egremont, of which he had been informed on 6 Oct. Newcastle, however, told another correspondent that he would have preferred Bedford as secretary of state; and Bute, who was responsible for Egremont's appointment, hinted at putting the privy seal in commission for a later offer to Bedford as a means of managing him (*Bedford Corr.* iii. 49; Bedford to Newcastle 7, 11 Oct., BM Add. MSS 32929, ff. 101, 192–3; Newcastle to John White 10 Oct., ibid. ff. 172–3; Newcastle to Devonshire 9 Oct., ibid. f. 139; Devonshire to Newcastle 10 Oct., ibid. f. 155).

7. His own, Ragley.

8. Probably Anne Somerset (1673–1763), Dowager Cts of Coventry, widow of Thomas, the 2d E.; she lived at Snitterfield, Warwickshire, near Ragley, and was Lady Hertford's maternal great-aunt.

To CONWAY, Monday 12 October 1761

Printed from *Works* v. 84–5.

Arlington Street, October 12, 1761.

IT is very lucky that you did not succeed in the expedition to Rochfort. Perhaps you might have been made a peer; and as *Chatham*[1] is a naval title, it might have fallen to your share. But it was reserved to crown greater glory: and lest it should not be substantial pay enough, three thousand pounds a year for three lives go along with it. Not to Mr Pitt—you can't suppose it. Why truly, not the title, but the annuity does, and Lady Hesther is the Baroness; that, if he should please, he may earn an earldom himself.[2] Don't believe me, if you have not a mind. I know I did not believe those who told it me. But ask the *Gazette* that swears it[3]—ask the King, who has kissed Lady Hesther[4]—ask the City of London, who are ready to tear Mr Pitt to pieces—ask forty people I can name who are overjoyed at it[5]—and then ask me again, who am mortified, and who have been the dupe of his disinterestedness. Oh, my dear Harry! I beg you on my knees, keep your virtue: do let me think there is still one man upon earth who despises money. I wrote you an account last week of his resignation. Could you have believed that in four days he would have tumbled from the conquest of Spain to receiving a quarter's pension from Mr West?[6] Today he has advertised his seven coach-horses to be sold[7]—three thousand a

1. The title Pitt had taken for his wife.
2. Pitt became Earl of Chatham in 1766.
3. *The London Gazette* No. 10146, 6–10 Oct., states *sub* St James's 9 Oct., 'In consideration of the great and important services of . . . Mr Pitt, his Majesty has been graciously pleased to direct, that a warrant be prepared for granting to the Lady Hester Pitt, his wife, a barony of Great Britain, by the name, style, and title, of Baroness of Chatham, to herself, and of Baron of Chatham to her heirs male; and also to confer upon the said William Pitt, Esq. an annuity of three thousand pounds sterling, during his own life, and that of Lady Hester Pitt, and their son John Pitt, Esq.'

4. Richard Rigby wrote Bedford 12 Oct., 'Lady Esther kissed hands yesterday, and Mr Pitt was at the Drawing-Room, but I am told few people took notice of him; he is, however, perfectly satisfied' (*Bedford Corr.* iii. 52).
5. In his *Memoirs* HW mentions Newcastle, Hardwicke, Bedford, Devonshire, Mansfield, and Fox as being 'not less pleased' than Bute, France, and Spain with Pitt's resignation (*Mem. Geo. III* i. 62).
6. Secretary to the Treasury (HW). James West (1703–72), M.P. St Albans 1741–68, Boroughbridge 1768–72; joint secretary to the Treasury 1746–56, 1757–62.
7. 'To be sold, seven coach horses be-

year for three lives, and fifty thousand pounds of his own, will not keep a coach and six. I protest I believe he is mad, and Lord Temple thinks so too; for he resigned the same morning that Pitt accepted the pension.[8] George Grenville is minister in the House of Commons. I don't know who will be Speaker. They talk of Prowse,[9] Hussey,[10] Bacon,[11] and even of old Sir John Rushout.[12] Delaval[13] has said an admirable thing: he blames Pitt—not as you and I do; but calls him fool; and says, if he had gone into the City, told them he had a poor wife and children unprovided for, and had opened a subscription, he would have got five hundred thousand pounds, instead of three thousand pounds a year. In the meantime the good man has saddled us with a war which we can neither carry on nor carry off. 'Tis pitiful! 'tis wondrous pitiful! Is the communication stopped, that we never hear from you? I own 'tis an Irish question. I am out of humour: my visions are dispelled, and you are still abroad. As I cannot put Mr Pitt to death, at least I have buried him: here is his epitaph:

> Admire his eloquence— It mounted higher
> Than Attic purity, or Roman fire:

longing to the Right Honourable William Pitt. Inquire at Ormond Mews, the back of St James's Square' (*London Chronicle* 10–13 Oct., x. 354; *Daily Adv.* 14 Oct.). Richard Rigby wrote Bedford 12 Oct., 'Your Grace will perceive in today's *Public Advertiser* that his coach-horses are to be sold; his house in St James's Square is also to be let: he will have no house in town, and live altogether at Hayes' (*Bedford Corr.* iii. 54).

8. Temple wrote to the Earl of Denbigh 13 Oct.: 'A reward from his sovereign for past services is christened a composition, and so on; but how he could refuse or why he ought, so honourable a confirmation from the King of what the public have so long with one voice declared, I confess passes my comprehension. I came to town on the Thursday night and resigned on Friday; surely this is a pretty good comment upon composition. Jemmy resigned yesterday' (Hist. MSS Comm., *Denbigh MSS*, 1911, p. 290).

9. Thomas Prowse (1707–67), of Compton Bishop, Somerset; M.P. Somerset 1740–67. He was the most popular candidate and was offered the nomination, but refused it because of his health (Namier

and Brooke iii. 336; see also Grenville to Prowse, 14 Oct., Prowse to Grenville 16 Oct., MSS now wsl).

10. Probably Richard Hussey (?1715–70), M.P. Mitchell 1755–61, St Mawes 1761–8, East Looe 1768–70, a prominent lawyer who was at this time attorney-general to the Queen (Namier and Brooke ii. 662–3). He does not seem to have been seriously considered for the Speakership, but was considered for solicitor-general in Dec. (ibid.). The only other possible 'Hussey' in the House at this time was Sir Edward Hussey (since 1749, Hussey Montagu) (see *ante* 24 May 1753, n. 2) who seems unlikely.

11. Edward Bacon (?1712–86), of Earlham, near Norwich; M.P. King's Lynn 1742–7, Callington 1748–54, Newport 1754–6, Norwich 1756–84; at this time a lord of Trade and chairman of the committee on elections and privileges. He was seriously considered by Newcastle for the Speakership, but was 'not liked' (Namier and Brooke ii. 36–7).

12. Who was 76; he does not appear to have been seriously considered.

13. Presumably Sir Francis Blake Delaval.

Adore his services—our lions view
Ranging, where Roman eagles never flew:
Copy his soul supreme o'er Lucre's sphere;
—But oh! beware three thousand pounds a year!

October 13.

Jemmy Grenville[14] resigned yesterday. Lord Temple is all hostility;[15] and goes to the Drawing-Room[16] to tell everybody how angry he is with the Court—but what is Sir Joseph Wittol, when Nol Bluff is pacific?[17] They talk of erecting a tavern in the City, called The Salutation: the sign to represent Lord Bath and Mr Pitt embracing. These are shameful times. Adieu!

Yours ever,

HOR. WALPOLE

From CONWAY, ca Monday 12 October 1761

Missing; answered *post* 26 Oct. 1761. From what HW says of it there it was written before Conway had learned of Pitt's resignation or had received accounts of the Coronation. Conway wrote the D. of Devonshire 5 Oct., 'I hear nothing of our Parliament or our politics, so that I feel quite absorbed in our military element; and as detached as possible from everything civil and domestic, partly from the idleness of my friends who I really think worse writers than we' (Chatsworth MSS, 416/72). In this letter he does mention the King's wedding.

14. Hon. James Grenville (1715–83), M.P. Old Sarum 1742–7; Bridport 1747–54; Buckingham borough 1754–68; Horsham 1768–70; a lord of the Treasury 1756–61; cofferer of the Household 1761. According to Henry Fox, his resignation was forced by his brother, Lord Temple ('Memoir' in *Life and Letters of Lady Sarah Lennox,* ed. Lady Ilchester and Lord Stavordale, 1902, i. 53). See J. Grenville to Bute 12 Oct., *Grenville Papers* i. 394, MS now WSL; *London Chronicle* 15–17 Oct., x. 369; *Daily Adv.* 16 Oct.

15. 'Lord Temple, who had as little decency as his brother George had judgment, was exasperated beyond measure; broke out in bitter invectives against him' (*Mem. Geo. III* i. 65). Temple refused admittance to George Grenville when he called, and at Whitehall 'turned his back upon him' (*Grenville Papers* i. 414, 415).

Temple wrote Wilkes 16 Oct., 'What fools must they be who cannot read and understand his [Pitt's] resignation, attended with the very broad comment of Jemmy's and mine' (ibid. i. 405).

16. Richard Rigby wrote to Bedford 12 Oct., after speaking of Pitt's being at the Drawing-Room: 'I saw Lord Egremont at Court, and wished him joy—I saw it, indeed, in his countenance. The reverse was as visible in Lord Temple's, who . . . does not take all this business in the same manner Mr Pitt does, and gave Mr Elliott notice that he meant to appeal to the public for his justification' (*Bedford Corr.* iii. 52–3).

17. Characters in Congreve's *The Old Batchelour;* Captain Bluffe is a blustering bully, always urging the pusillanimous Sir Joseph Wittoll to defend his honour.

To Hertford, October 1761

Missing; answered *post* 24 Oct. 1761.

From Hertford, Saturday 24 October 1761

Printed for the first time from a photostat of BM Add. MSS 23218, f. 56.

Ragley, October 24th 1761.

Dear Horry,

I SHALL this night if I have no return, have missed two fits of the ague, but I have confined myself to the house and taken the bark regularly. My next crisis will be upon trying the weather; if I can bear the air without a return I flatter myself to be soon able to get to London, and I shall now be glad to be well there, for I fear the aguish disposition of this air. It is a very unpleasant disorder. It reduces extremely, and as the cure is chiefly performed by melting away, it does not agree with us thin men. By what I hear from London our affairs are going fast into confusion.[1] My last letters from Ireland make no mention of the Money Bill,[2] but Mr Vesey[3] who is now here thinks your intelligence[4] is probably well founded.

1. Because of the revival of Pitt's influence in the City; see the following letter.

2. The long-standing controversy in Ireland between the Irish House of Commons and the Administration over the initiation of the appropriation clauses in Irish money bills had been renewed in the autumn of 1761 and now threatened to break out again, since one of the first bills designed to be laid before the Irish Parliament in the forthcoming session was to carry into law a vote of credit from the previous session. The supporters of the government in Ireland had threatened opposition, and Halifax, the Lord Lieutenant, had written to England 11 Oct., suggesting that the bill be dropped and asking for instructions; on the 20th Egremont replied, stating the unanimous decision of the Council that the bill must be laid be-fore Parliament in the form in which it had been sent to Ireland (*Calendar of Home Office Papers*, 1760–1765, ed. Joseph Redington, 1878, pp. 69–70, 71; J. A. Froude, *The English in Ireland in the Eighteenth Century*, 1872–4, ii. 4-7; *Bedford Corr.* iii. 63–4). For the subsequent course of the dispute, see *post* 14 Dec. 1761.

3. Probably Agmondesham Vesey (d. 1785), Irish politician; friend of Dr Johnson and Burke.

4. The source of HW's information is unknown; he had recently received two letters from Montagu in Dublin of 8 and 12 Oct., but neither of them mentioned the projected Money Bill (Montagu i. 393–4, 395–6), and the proceedings in the Cabinet on Halifax's correspondence do not seem to have been generally known.

Lady Hertford desires her best compliments and thanks for your letter. I remain always, dear Horry,

Most faithfully yours,

HERTFORD

To CONWAY, Monday 26 October 1761

Printed from *Works* v. 86–7.

Strawberry Hill, October 26, 1761.

HOW strange it seems! You are talking to me of the King's wedding, while we are thinking of a civil war. Why, the King's
wedding was a century ago, almost two months; even the Coronation
that happened half an age ago, is quite forgot. The post to Germany
cannot keep pace with our revolutions. Who knows but you may still
be thinking that Mr Pitt is the most disinterested man in the world?
Truly, as far as the votes of a Common Council can make him so,
he is.[1] Like Cromwell, he has always promoted the self-denying
ordinance, and had contrived to be excused from it himself.[2] The
City could no longer choose who should be their man of virtue;
there was not one left: by all rules they ought next to have pitched
upon one who was the oldest offender: instead of that, they have
re-elected the most recent; and, as if virtue was a borough, Mr Pitt
is re-chosen for it, on vacating his seat. Well, but all this is very
serious: I shall offer you a prophetic picture, and shall be very glad
if I am not a true soothsayer. The City have voted an address of
thanks to Mr Pitt, and given instructions to their members;[3] the chief
articles of which are, to promote an inquiry into the disposal of the

1. The Common Council had thanked
Pitt for his services in a letter of 22 Oct.,
printed in the *London Chronicle* 24–7
Oct., x. 402. The vote for the motion had
been carried 109 to 15 (HW to Montagu
24 Oct., MONTAGU i. 397; *Mem. Geo. III* i.
66).

2. The Long Parliament passed the
Self-Denying Ordinance 3 April 1645 (21
Car. I), discharging all members of either
house from every office or command, civil
or military, granted since 20 Nov. 1640 as

a step in creating the New Model Army
(Cobbett, *Parl. Hist.* iii. 354–5 and 326–
38). Cromwell had been a strong supporter of it to purge the army high command, but had himself been excused from
it and remained commander of the cavalry.

3. At the same time as their letter of
thanks to Pitt. The instructions are
printed *London Chronicle* 22–4 Oct., x.
398.

money that has been granted, and to consent to no peace, unless we are to retain all, or very near all, our conquests. Thus the City of London usurp the right of making peace and war. But is the government to be dictated to by one town? By no means. But suppose they are not—what is the consequence? How will the money be raised? If it cannot be raised without them, Mr Pitt must again be minister: that you think would easily be accommodated. Stay, stay; he and Lord Temple have declared against the whole Cabinet Council.[4] Why, that they have done before now, and yet have acted with them again. It is very true; but a little word has escaped Mr Pitt, which never entered into his former declarations; nay, nor into Cromwell's, nor Hugh Capet's, nor Julius Caesar's, nor any reformer's of ancient time. He has happened to say, he will *guide*.[5] Now, though the Cabinet Council are mighty willing to be guided, when they cannot help it, yet they wish to have appearances saved: they cannot be fond of being told they are to be guided; still less, that other people should be told so.[6] Here, then, is Mr Pitt and the Common Council on one hand, the great lords on the other. I protest, I do not see but it will come to this. Will it allay the confusion, if Mr Fox is retained on the side of the Court?[7] Here are no Whigs and Tories, harmless people, that are content with worrying one another for 150 years together. The new parties are, *I will*, and *You shall not*; and their principles do not admit delay. However, this age is of suppler mould than some of its predecessors; and this may come round again, by a *coup de baguette,* when one least expects it. If it should

4. In the demand for the recall of Lord Bristol and an immediate declaration of war against Spain (*ante* HW to Lady Ailesbury 10 Oct. 1761 and n. 11).

5. Pitt, in his letter to Beckford, 15 Oct., which produced the letter of thanks from the Common Council, had written: 'I resigned the Seals on Monday, the 5th of this month, in order not to remain responsible for measures which I was no longer allowed to guide' (*Chatham Corr.* ii. 158–9). According to Newcastle's account of the Cabinet meeting on 2 Oct., Pitt had made similar remarks there: 'In his station and situation he was responsible and would not continue without having the direction: that this being his case, nobody could be surprised that he

could go on no longer, and he would repeat it again, that he would be responsible for nothing but what he directed' (quoted in *Hardwicke Corr.* iii. 280).

6. Pitt's letter was printed in the newspapers, e.g. *Daily Adv.* 19 Oct. and *London Chronicle* 15–17 Oct., x. 376. HW echoes the sentiments of a satirical answer to Pitt in the *London Chronicle* 20–22 Oct. (x. 388): 'If you are to *guide* always, you *alone* constitute the *whole* Cabinet Council.' See the correspondence between Newcastle and Hardwicke on Pitt's letter (*Hardwicke Corr.* iii. 333–4), expressing special indignation at Pitt's revealing the opinions of ministers in Council.

7. Fox was not enlisted by the Court for another year; see *post* 13 Oct. 1762.

not, the honestest part one can take is to look on, and try if one can do any good if matters go too far.

I am charmed with the Castle of Hercules;[8] it is the boldest pile I have seen since I travelled in Fairyland. You ought to have delivered a princess imprisoned by enchanters in his club: she, in gratitude, should have fallen in love with you: your constancy should have been immaculate. The devil knows how it would have ended—I don't—and so I break off my romance.

You need not beat the French any more this year: it cannot be ascribed to Mr Pitt; and the mob won't thank you. If we are to have a warm campaign in Parliament, I hope you will be sent for. Adieu! We take the field tomorrow sennight.[9]

Yours ever,

HOR. WALPOLE

PS. You will be sorry to hear that Worksop is burned.[10] My Lady Waldegrave has got a daughter,[11] and your brother an ague.[12]

From CONWAY, ca Thursday 26 November 1761

Missing; mentioned *post* 10 Dec. 1761.

---

8. Alluding to a description of a building in Hesse Cassel, given by Mr Conway in one of his letters (HW).

9. Parliament opened 3 Nov. (*Journals of the House of Commons* xxxix. 6).

10. 'On Wednesday evening an express arrived at the Duke of Norfolk's, with an account, that about nine o'clock on Tuesday morning last [20 Oct.] a fire broke out at Worksop Manor, his Grace's seat in Nottinghamshire, which in a short time entirely reduced the whole building to ashes' (*Daily Adv.* 23 Oct.). The estimated loss was 'upwards of £100,000' (ibid. 24 Oct.; see *ante* 17 Sept. 1758, n. 13). Conway had visited there in 1758 (*ante* 27 Aug. 1758).

11. Lady Charlotte Maria Waldegrave (11 Oct. 1761–1808), m. (1784) George Henry Fitzroy, styled E. of Euston; 4th D. of Grafton, 1811.

12. See the previous letter.

To Lady Ailesbury, Saturday 28 November 1761

Printed from the MS now WSL; first printed, with omissions, *Works* v. 560–1, and in full Toynbee v. 145–7 and *Supp.* ii. 123–4. For the history of the MS see *ante* 23 Aug. 1760; it was marked by HW for inclusion in *Works*.

Arlington Street, Nov. 28th 1761.

Dear Madam,

YOU are so bad and so good, that I don't know how to treat you. You give me every mark of kindness but letting me hear from you; you send me charming drawings the moment I trouble you with a commission,[1] and you give Lady Cecilia[2] commissions for trifles of my writing, in the most obliging manner—I have taken the latter off her hands; the *Fugitive Pieces* and the *Catalogue of Royal and Noble Authors* shall be conveyed to you directly. Lady Cecilia and I agree how we lament the charming suppers there, every time we pass the corner of Warwick Street! We have a little comfort for your sake and our own, in believing that the campaign is at an end, at least for this year—but they tell us, it is to recommence here or in Ireland—you have nothing to do with that. Our politics, I think, will soon be as warm as our war—Charles Townshend is to be lieutenant-general to Mr Pitt.[3] The Duke of Bedford is privy seal;[4] Lord Thomond,[5] cofferer; Lord George Cavendish, comptroller.[6]

Diversions, you know, Madam, are never at high-water mark before Christmas: yet operas flourish pretty well: those on Tuesdays

1. See *ante* 27 Sept. 1761.

2. Lady Cecilia Johnston (HW).

3. Townshend, who had been secretary at war since March, had been offended by Grenville's appointment to leadership of the Commons, and, according to Henry Fox, by the King's refusal to appoint his wife to the Queen's Bedchamber. He had criticized the King's Speech at a meeting before Parliament opened, but when pressure was immediately applied by the King and some of the other ministers, he moderated his opposition for the time being (Sir Lewis Namier and John Brooke, *Charles Townshend*, 1964, pp. 67–9).

4. Announced in the *London Chronicle* 21–4 Nov., x. 502; see also *ante* HW to

Lady Ailesbury 10 Oct. 1761, n. 21, Hertford to HW 10 Oct. 1761, n. 6, *Bedford Corr.* iii. 58, 59. Bedford held this post until 22 April 1763.

5. Percy Wyndham (after 1741 Wyndham O'Brien) (?1723–74), cr. (1756) E. of Thomond. He had been treasurer of the Household, and was made cofferer in place of James Grenville at George Grenville's request (Namier and Brooke iii. 667-8; *London Chronicle* 26–8 Nov., x. 518). False reports that Lord Melcombe and the E. of Powis had been appointed appeared ibid. 3–5, 21–4 Nov., x. 434, 502.

6. Announced ibid. 21–4, 26–8 Nov., x. 502, 518.

are removed to Mondays,[7] because the Queen likes the burlettas, and the King cannot go on Tuesdays, his post days. On those nights we have the middle front box, railed in, where Lady Mary[8] and I sit in trist state like a lord mayor and lady mayoress. The night before last there was a private ball at Court,[9] which began at half an hour after six, lasted till one, and finished without a supper. The King danced the whole time with the Queen, Lady Augusta[10] with her four younger brothers. The other performers were, the two Duchesses of Ancaster and Hamilton, who danced little, Lady Effingham and Lady Egremont,[11] who danced much, the six maids of honour,[12] Lady Susan Stewart,[13] as attending Lady Augusta, and Lady Caroline Russel and Lady Jane Stewart,[14] the only women not of the family. Lady Northumberland is at Bath, Lady Weymouth lies in;[15] Lady Bolinbroke was there in waiting, but in black gloves and breeding,[16] so did not dance. The men, besides the royals,[17] were Lord March and Eglinton, of the Bedchamber; Lord Cantelupe,[18] vice-chamberlain; Lord Huntingdon;[19] and four strangers, Lord Mande-

7. In connection with the performance on 21 Nov., it had been announced that 'the comic operas will be performed for the future on Mondays instead of Tuesdays, and the serious operas are to continue on Saturdays as usual.' The first Monday performance was 23 Nov. (*London Stage* Pt IV, ii. 904).

8. Lady Mary Coke (HW).

9. HW also describes the ball to Montagu 28 Nov. (Montagu i. 405–6), and made lists of the guests on the backs of two letters from Montagu (ibid. i. 402, 403).

10. (1737–1813), sister of George III, m. (1764) Karl Wilhelm Ferdinand, Hereditary Prince of Brunswick-Wolfenbüttel.

11. Alicia Maria Carpenter (d. 1794), m. 1 (1751) Charles Wyndham, 2d E. of Egremont; m. 2 (1767) Hans Moritz, Gräf von Brühl; lady of the Bedchamber 1761–94 (see *ante* 14 July 1761, n. 24).

12. Frances Bisshopp, Mary Wrottesley, Diana Beauclerk, Frances Meadows, Charlotte Keck, Mary Tryon (ibid. nn. 26, 28–31).

13. Lady Susanna Stewart (ca 1731–1805), m. (1768) Granville Leveson Gower, 2d E. Gower, cr. (1786) M. of Stafford; lady of the Bedchamber to the Princess Augusta.

14. Lady Jane Stuart (1742–1828), m. (1768) George Macartney, Kt, 1764, K.B. 1772, cr. (1776) Bn, (1792) Vct, and (1794) E. Macartney. The King's request that they should be at the ball is in a letter to Bute printed *Letters from George III to Lord Bute 1756–1766*, ed. Sedgwick, 1939, p. 71.

15. Her second daughter, Charlotte, was born 7 Nov. 1761 (d. 19 May 1764) (Collins, *Peerage*, 1812, ii. 510). The Countess Cowper wrote 20 Aug., 'Lady Weymouth will be too near her time to walk at the Coronation, which I conclude is a mortification to her' (Mary Granville, Mrs Delany, *Autobiography and Correspondence*, ed. Lady Llanover, 1861–2, iv. 6). She was a lady of the Bedchamber 1761–93.

16. She was in mourning for her mother, the Ds of Marlborough, who had died 7 October (*ante* 10 Oct. 1761); in Feb. or early March she gave birth to a daughter, Charlotte, who died young (GM 1762, xxxii. 144; Collins, op. cit. vi. 61).

17. The King and his brothers.

18. John West (*ante* ca 9 May 1755, n. 2), styled Vct Cantelupe; 2d E. de la Warr, 1766.

19. Groom of the Stole.

ville,[20] who pulled off his weepers[21] (which the Duke of Marlbro[22] and Lord Charles Spenser[23] excused themselves from doing),[24] Lord Northampton,[25] Lord Suffolk[26] and Lord Grey.[27] No sitters-by, but the Princess, the Duchess of Bedford and Lady Bute.

If it had not been for this ball, I don't know how I should have furnished a decent letter. Pamphlets on Mr Pitt are the whole conversation, and none of them worth sending cross the water;[28] at least I, who am said to write some of them,[29] think so, by which you may perceive I am not much flattered with the imputation. There must be new personages at least, before I write on any side—Mr Pitt and the Duke of Newcastle! I should as soon think of informing the world that Miss Chudleigh is no vestal. You will like better to see some words which Mr Gray has writ, at Miss Speed's[30] request, to an old air of Geminiani;[31] the thought is from the French.

1.

Thyrsis, when we parted, swore
     E'er the spring he would return.
Ah! what means yon violet-flower,
     And the buds that deck the thorn?
'Twas the lark that upward sprung,
'Twas the nightingale that sung.

20. George Montagu (1737–88), styled Vct Mandeville; 4th D. of Manchester, 1762.

21. Strips of white linen or muslin formerly worn by men on their sleeve-cuffs as a sign of mourning (OED).

22. George Spencer (1739–1817), 3d D. of Marlborough.

23. Lord Charles Spencer (1740–1820), M.P. Oxfordshire 1761–1801.

24. They were in mourning for their mother. 'I find from what Lady Boling-broke said the other day none of that family chose dancing in their black gloves for their mother' (George III to Lord Bute, loc. cit.). Lord Mandeville's relationship to the late Ds of Marlborough was rather distant, she being by marriage his second cousin once removed.

25. Charles Compton (1737–63), 7th E. of Northampton.

26. Henry Howard (1739–79), 12th E. of Suffolk.

27. George Harry Grey (1737–1819), styled Lord Grey; 5th E. of Stamford, 1768; cr. (1796) E. of Warrington. All these men are mentioned in George III's letter to Bute about the ball (Sedgwick, loc. cit.).

28. HW preserved only two of them (Montagu i. 397 and n. 8).

29. HW also mentioned these reports in a letter to Montagu 30 Dec. (ibid. i. 416). No confirmation has been found.

30. Henrietta Jane Speed (1728–83), m. (12 Nov. 1761) Francesco Maria Giuseppe Giustino, Barone di la Perrière, Conte di Viry, 1766; a friend of Gray (Thomas Gray, Correspondence, ed. Toynbee and Whibley, Oxford, 1935, ii. 770–1 and nn. 12–16; Montagu i. 330, n. 12, 406 and n. 10).

31. Francesco Geminiani (ca 1680–1762), Italian violinist, teacher and composer, who had settled in London in 1714.

2.

Idle notes! untimely green!
     Why this unavailing haste?
Western gales and skies serene
     Speak not always winter past
Cease my doubts, my fears to move;
Spare the honour of my love.

Your Ladyship may go to any shop of old china or Dresden; Sir Compton Domville[32] is given over.[33] Adieu! Madam,

Your most faithful servant,

Hor. Walpole

To Hertford, ca Tuesday 8 December 1761

Missing; answered *post* 10 Dec. 1761.

From Hertford, Thursday 10 December 1761

Printed for the first time from a photostat of BM Add. MSS 23218, f. 57.

Ragley, December 10th 1761.

Dear Horry,

HAVING little to tell you, as you will easily conceive from your knowledge of this place, I shall flatter myself and take it for granted you will be glad to hear I do not propose to go yet into Ireland;[1] I intend seeing whether we are to have a Spanish War[2] or a perpetual militia[3] to defend us before I settle there.

32. Sir Compton Domvile (ca 1686–1768), 2d Bt, of Templeogue, co. Dublin.

33. As HW had been informed in a letter from Montagu written at Dublin 19 Nov. (Montagu i. 403). The news would be of the greatest interest to Conway and Lady Ailesbury, since Conway had the reversion of Domvile's place of Clerk of the Crown and Hanaper in the Court of Chancery of Ireland. Domvile re-covered, however, so Conway did not come into the place until 1768.

1. A report had been current in Dublin in October that Hertford had taken a house there for the winter (Montagu to HW 8 Oct. 1761, Montagu i. 393).

2. England finally declared war on Spain on 4 Jan. 1762.

3. As the Militia Act of 1757 expired

I had a letter from my brother today, possibly of the same date as yours.[4] It contains little but instructions about the place in Ireland,[5] in case the life upon it, which is now in danger, should drop.

I was told by a friend in London, which I forgot to mention to you before I left it, that my brother was commended for all instances of his conduct and behaviour in the army, except in giving such long directions in orders to the sergeants and noncommissioned officers that they could not understand them; and G. Townshend was suspected to be the author of the intelligence. When I write to him I propose acquainting him with the charge but not with the author's name.

My Lady is very well in this airy situation. I am sorry that Lady Mary Coke is out of order.[6] She was very obliging to make you write; it is absolute charity to do it to a friend in the country, and I do not intend staying so long here as to be very troublesome.

Is Lord Orford come to town? I do not think you intended to solicit for him.[7] Yours always, dear Horry,

Most faithfully,

HERTFORD

To HERTFORD, ca Saturday 12 December 1761

Missing; answered *post* 14 Dec. 1761.

in 1762, some form of extension had become necessary, but the measure was so generally unpopular that the government planned to ask only a short extension. Pitt and his friends, however, in an attempt to embarrass the administration, bound themselves at a meeting in the St Alban's Tavern on 25 Nov. 1761 to support an act making the militia perpetual. A bill to this effect was introduced in the Commons by Lord Strange on 14 Dec., but eventually was amended to a seven years' extension and passed in this revised form on 26 March 1762 (*Mem. Geo. III* i. 78–9, 112; MANN v. 552 and nn. 3–7).

4. Both of these letters are missing.

5. See *ante* 28 Nov. 1761, n. 33.

6. A few days later she was suffering from St Anthony's fire (erysipelas) in her cheek, an event HW commemorated in some verses, 20 Dec. (MONTAGU i. 413; 'Short Notes,' GRAY i. 37).

7. Presumably for some sinecure, since Orford was encumbered with debts. In the following year, he was made Ranger of St James's and Hyde Parks (HW to Orford 22 Nov. 1762, FAMILY 36–7).

From HERTFORD, Monday 14 December 1761

Printed for the first time from a photostat of BM Add. MSS 23218, ff. 58–9.

Ragley, December 14th 1761.

Dear Horry,

I THANK you a thousand times in my Lady's and my own name for the accounts you have sent us from London. I see you are all going into confusion,[1] and I hear from Ireland there is now a fair prospect of their doing the same, which may complete our case, especially if we go to war with Spain.

Lord Halifax on his going first over[2] left the three Justices[3] to retrieve their reputation with English Government[4] by the good behaviour of their friends in Parliament. The Secretary, Mr Hamilton, laid himself out entirely for such intimacy with the heads of Opposition as might save him trouble in the House from the irregulars, whilst the main body did their business. One of these,[5] a very popular and ready orator, he gained by the place of prime sergeant with £500 a year additional salary. He soon became a favourite, and from favourite a minister.[6] The old servants of Gov-

1. Probably as a result of the acrimonious debates on the German war and Spain in the House of Commons on 9, 10, and 11 Dec.; see *Mem. Geo. III* i. 79–96.

2. He had arrived in Dublin as lord lieutenant on 6 Oct. (GM 1761, xxxi. 476).

3. George Stone, Archbishop of Armagh; Henry Boyle, E. of Shannon; and John Ponsonby, Speaker of the Irish House of Commons, had been Lord Justices (Regents) of Ireland between the departure of Bedford in May 1760 and the arrival of Halifax.

4. Which they lost by their refusal to send over the heads of a money bill in the autumn and early winter of 1760–1, for which they had twice been reprimanded by the English Privy Council, and by their unceasing opposition to the government of the D. of Bedford; see *Mem. Geo. III* i. 23–5; *Bedford Corr.* ii. 427–9, iii. 1–6. On Halifax's arrival, however, they had given him 'the strongest assurances of their intentions to support his Majesty's Government, unqualified by any

terms or conditions whatever' (*Calendar of Home Office Papers*, 1760–1765, ed. Joseph Redington, 1878, p. 69).

5. John Hely Hutchinson (1724–94), lawyer and politician. He had begun his Parliamentary career in 1759 as a vigorous 'patriot' in opposition to Bedford, but made his peace with Halifax on a visit to England in Sept. 1761 and soon became an intimate of Hamilton. His patent as prime sergeant was not issued until 11 Dec., but reports were that he was to have the office were current in Dublin by 20 Oct. (*Lloyd's Evening Post* 26–8 Oct., ix. 409; Hist. MSS Comm., 12th Report, App. pt ix, *Donoughmore MSS*, 1891, pp. 231–2; Rowley Lascelles, *Liber munerum publicorum Hiberniae*, [1852], i pt ii ['Lodge's Patentee Officers']. 72). The order for the increase in his salary had been issued on 25 Nov. (Redington, op. cit. 137).

6. He and Hamilton had taken the lead in pushing the Money Bill through the Irish House of Commons in November (ibid. 78).

ernment grew jealous and a question which you knew was lost[7] put his Excellency in a passion, and explained to the Justices by what tenure they held their favour;[8] however they still continued their labours and carried for him the Money Bill,[9] which had been originally the work of their own hands.[10] This procured them no thanks, no change in their tenure.

Intimation was sent of four regiments to be raised;[11] to each of the Justices four companies were to be given. The rest with the changes arising from these commissions he[12] reserved to himself; thus

7. A resolution referring to the fact that the pensions on the Irish Establishment for two years (military excluded) exceeded the whole charge of the Civil List by £35,129 3s. 3½d. It had been passed in the Committee of Accounts, appointed 30 Oct., before 3 Nov. and, despite Halifax's immediate remonstrance, was reported from the Committee to the House on 11 Nov. and approved *nem. con. (Journals of the House of Commons . . . Ireland*, Dublin, 1753–71, xii. 196–9, 448–9; Redington, op. cit. 74).

8. On learning of the resolution, Halifax had summoned the Lords Justices and requested a 'full explanation.' He told them that 'he was greatly concerned that the first resolution the Irish Parliament had come to was such an one as must reflect on the manner in which his Majesty had exercised one of the undoubted branches of his prerogative; that this attack would confirm the unfavourable impressions so long and so justly entertained in England; and that either the influence of the late Lords Justices was not so great as they represented, or they had failed to use it.' The Justices had assured him that the resolution had been as much of a surprise to them as to him, and that there would be no repetition. On 20 Nov., having received approval for his lecture from England, Halifax again summoned the Justices and told them 'that no partial or occasional support will be accepted as a performance of their engagements, nor entitle them or their friends to His Majesty's favour.' They again promised to do their best to defeat any further attack, and Halifax concluded by reminding them that a contrary conduct would affect nobody so much as themselves (ibid. 74–5, 76, 79–80, 81).

9. The first reading was carried on 14 Nov. by a vote of 170–42 (according to Halifax, 172–44), and the third reading on the 19th by 147–37 (*Journals of the House of Commons . . . Ireland*, xii. 503, 520; Redington, op. cit. 78, 79). Halifax commented that the Lords Justices had been 'most assiduous' on both occasions (ibid.).

10. When the Money Bill was first discussed in October, Egremont had reminded Halifax that the King was particularly surprised at the threat of opposition, as he had already 'in order to remove all difficulties, graciously condescended to accept the Bill in the form proposed by the late Lords Justices, who are, therefore, in honour bound to support it' (ibid. 71).

11. Hertford appears to have been misinformed about the regiments. On 26 Nov. Halifax had forwarded proposals to London made by Lt-Cols Pomeroy, Horne, Elphinstone, Cunninghame, and Gisborne to raise four battalions of 700 men each at no expense to the government except for arms and supplies, by selling their present commissions in return for command of the new regiments. The only condition that Halifax proposed was that the new commissions not be granted until the officers had raised at least part of their men. The proposal was laid before the King by 5 Dec. and further proposals were forwarded by Halifax 11 and 18 Dec., but the final plan was not approved until the 26th, when Lt-Col. Mackay was added to the list, though the report was current in Dublin by 1 Dec. that the new regiments were to be raised 'immediately' (ibid. 81–2, 84, 86, 88, 91–2; *London Chronicle* 5–8 Dec., x. 550).

12. Halifax.

the power of rewarding their troops is limited extremely. A Septennial Bill has been since brought into the House,[13] a thing destruc-
tive to that country, and no way honourable to the Crown, but yet
popular. His Excellency it seems concluded the Justices would throw
it out for their own sakes as this Parliament is of their modelling, so
he allowed his new Minister[14] and Mr Perry[15] to take the popular side
whilst Mr Hamilton declared to everybody his indifference about
it.[16] The Lords Justices, seeing through this artifice, resolved not
to support[17] it against the inclinations of Government, and directed
all their friends to divide with those employed by Government, by
which means the Bill had an easy passage.[18] There is however one
clause still depending,[19] and his Lordship has taken the alarm; new
measures are now to be taken[20] to do with a bad grace what might

13. On 28 Oct., by Dr Charles Lucas,
when the heads of the bill were read
and committed (*Journals of the House
of Commons . . . Ireland,* xii. 169). Under the existing law the Irish Parliament
was elected only at the beginning of each
reign.

14. John Hely Hutchinson. His support
was only lukewarm, however, for he was
teller for the ayes on a motion of 3 Dec.
to attach a qualification clause to the
bill that would destroy its appeal, and
teller for the nays in a division on 9 Dec.
that prevented the bill from being laid
before the Lord Lieutenant by the
Speaker accompanied by the whole House
(ibid. xii. 548, 565–6; J. A. Froude, *The
English in Ireland in the Eighteenth
Century,* 1872–4, ii. 8–9).

15. Edmond Sexton Pery (1719–1806),
cr. (1785) Vct Pery; Speaker of the Irish
House of Commons 1771–85. At this time
he usually opposed the vice-regal government, and it is doubtful whether any
lord lieutenant had much influence on
his conduct.

16. Halifax and Hamilton did not commit themselves on the Septennial Bill because they had no instructions from England and did not know the government's
attitude; see Froude, op. cit. ii. 8, and
Redington, op. cit. 84.

17. *Sic* in MS, but Hertford must mean
'oppose.'

18. Hertford means the passage of the
heads of the bill through committee,
where they were discussed on 7 Nov.,
3 Dec., and 8 Dec. They were not re-

ported back to the House until 9 Dec.
and then there was no division on the
heads themselves, though there was on
the method of presenting them to the
Lord Lieutenant (*Journals of the House
of Commons . . . Ireland,* xii. 288, 548,
564, 565–6). The next sentence in the
letter shows that Hertford had not yet
learned of the final passage.

19. A qualification clause, making possession of an estate of £600 a year necessary for holding a county seat, and one
of £300 a year for a borough, had been
referred to the committee on the heads
of the bill after a 69–62 division on 3
Dec. (ibid. xii. 548). The government and
the Lords Justices supported the clause
in hopes that the heavy condition of
eligibility would cause rejection of the
bill (Redington, op. cit. 85–6, 87, 89–90;
Froude, op. cit. ii. 8).

20. Probably an attempt to stop the bill
in the Irish Privy Council before it was
referred to England, but the initiative in
these was taken by the Lords Justices rather than by Halifax. The bill was eventually invalidated in England because of
a blunder in the drafting that made it
unworkable, and nothing further was
heard of it in the present session of the
Irish Parliament, except for a resolution
27 April 1762 denying reports that the
bill would have been rejected even had
it been returned from England with no
material changes (Froude, op. cit. ii. 9–
10; *Journals of the House of Commons
. . . Ireland,* xii. 913).

have been done at first with credit and dignity, and in this instance the Justices must be entirely acquitted, since there never was a time in which business might have been more easily or more reputably done. By this misconduct there is now some danger of their going all to pieces again. Thus for want of better I have treated you with Irish news; if it does not entertain you, it will at least prove my desire of doing it, and I hope you will ever believe me, dear Horry,

Most truly yours,

HERTFORD

Lady Hertford's best compliments attend you.

To Henrietta Seymour Conway, Thursday 21 January 1762

Missing; answered *post* 8 June 1762.

From Lady Ailesbury, ca March 1762

Missing; acknowledged *post* 15 March 1762 (postscript 16 March).

From Beauchamp, Wednesday 10 March 1762

Printed for the first time from a photostat of BM Add. MSS 23218, ff. 37–8. Dated by HW's reply, 13 March.

Christ Church, Wednesday.

Dear Sir,

I DELAYED thanking you for a very kind present[1] till I had made myself acquainted with its real value—Be not afraid—I am not writing a letter of compliment—that is a style I hope we never shall

---

1. The first two volumes of HW's *Anecdotes of Painting*, published 15 Feb. (*Journals of the Printing Office at Straw-* *berry Hill*, ed. Toynbee, 1923, p. 10; Hazen, *SH Bibl.* 55).

converse in—yet I cannot preclude myself from telling you agreeable truths. I confess I was at first prejudiced against the subject of your work—it appeared dry, and I doubted even of your ability to render the laborious compilations of an antiquary[2] both amusing and instructive to a common reader. I wished your leisure had been employed in explaining some problem in English story, in exploding old errors, and setting mistaken characters in a new point of view. But how agreeably was I surprised to find a methodical history of a fine art under the modest title of *Anecdotes.* The subject is indeed worthy of the pen that has undertaken it—a pen which finishes while it seems only to sketch. The world in general is indebted to you for a curious work—the antiquaries in particular for giving grace to their labours and dignity to their anecdotes— the painters for kindly rescuing their names from oblivion. May I not offer one and perhaps not a very far-fetched reason for the scarcity of English painters? They never yet had a Félibien,[3] a De Pile,[4] to immortalize them—their own perishable works were the only support of their reputation, and when they suffered the injuries of time, their names perished with them. Was not this discouragement sufficient to check the faint efforts of an infant art? In Italy deification and plenty, in England poverty and a transient fame has been the painter's lot. But the fine arts may now expect better days, when the Throne is become the altar of the Graces and Mr Walpole deigns to pay his adorations there.[5] I am, dear Sir, with great truth

Your affectionate humble servant

BEAUCHAMP

2. George Vertue (1684–1756), whose MS collection of painters in England formed the basis of *Anecdotes of Painting.*

3. André Félibien (1619–95), Sieur des Avaux et de Javercy, architect and author of many books, including *Entretiens sur les vies et sur les ouvrages des plus excellents peintres anciens et modernes,* 1666. HW's copy of the 1725 edition is Hazen, *Cat. of HW's Lib.,* No. 1294.

4. Roger de Piles (1635–1709), painter, engraver, and writer on art, whose *Abrégé de la vie des peintres . . . et un traité du peinture parfait,* 1699 (2d edn 1715), was translated into English in 1706 under the title of *The Art of Painting, and the Lives of the Painters . . . to Which Is* *Added an Essay towards an English School;* 2d edn 1744; 3d edn [?1750]–54 (E. Bénézit, *Dictionnaire . . . des peintres, sculpteurs, dessinateurs, et graveurs,* 1948– 55, vi. 684; Bibl. Nat. Cat.; BM Cat.; Yale Cat.). HW's copies of the second French edition and the third English edition are Hazen, *Cat. of HW's Lib.,* Nos 308, 350.

5. Beauchamp is echoing a sentence in the 'Preface' to the *Anecdotes of Painting:* 'The Throne itself is now the altar of the Graces, and whoever sacrifices to them becomingly, is sure that his offering will be smiled upon by a Prince, who is at once the example and patron of accomplishments' (i. p. xiii).

To Beauchamp, Saturday 13 March 1762

Printed for the first time from the MS, now wsl. The history of the MS is untraced until its sale at Sotheby's 28 April 1937 (property of Capt. W. J. W. C. Barrow), lot 635, to Maggs for wsl.

Arlington Street, March 13, 1762.

My dear Lord,

IF the letter I have received from you had been writ to anybody but myself, I should say it was the genteelest and most charming composition of the kind I ever saw; but unluckily being sensible how little foundation there is for such compliments, your judgment loses with me as much as your art gains, and I am forced to ascribe to your good nature what your heart is too upright to let me attribute to too much civility. The book is very trifling, and so is anything I have ever writ. I only meant to try if I could not redeem antiquarian works from the deserved imputation of being the worst books that are written. If I have succeeded, I am content; if I have amused you, I am pleased.[1] I pretend to no more, nor do I think myself qualified to treat any subject of much importance. I am not serious enough, nor am I tempted to the trial. The world is not easily cured of prejudices, nor does it love truth, which I can honestly say has always been in my view. Even on idle subjects, I thought one might instill some truths. I am too grateful for the blessing of liberty not to wish to transmit it to others, and one can act on few better principles. Grave folly, error and interest will misrepresent one's motives, but worthy men in all times will do justice to the intention, and if they do not, the satisfaction of one's own mind is ample reward.

I beg your pardon for being so serious; you have made me so, and it is a pleasure to me to find that I need not much beg your pardon for it. It is rather your age than your understanding to which I should apologize. I am no solemn counsellor, and all the advice I will ever give you is to continue what you are. Continue to improve your mind, but keep your heart exactly as it is; I mean, don't let

1. A sentiment that HW repeated to Cole three years later apropos the *Castle of Otranto:* 'You will laugh at my earnestness, but if I have amused you by re- tracing with any fidelity the manners of ancient days, I am content, and give you leave to think me as idle as you please' (COLE i. 88).

artificial improvements impose on the integrity of your nature. One may add to the treasures of one's head, but for our virtue and honesty we have nothing to do but to watch that they are not perverted. You see, my Lord, how little I value all that is to be *acquired,* and therefore may believe me when I assure you I am far from vain of anything of that kind. Fame and parts are agreeable amusements, but indeed they are no more. I am not young enough to make a rash judgment, nor old and morose enough to speak from mortification and humour: my philosophy, you know, is not very severe, and therefore I don't believe there is a more persuasive witness, than one who generally laughs, and yet assures you there is little satisfaction but in the goodness of one's heart. You have the best in the world by nature and inheritance; if you had not, you would be exceedingly tired of this letter, the sole drift of which is to tell you, that I prefer your friendship even to your commendations. Adieu! my dear Lord.

Yours most faithfully,

Hor. Walpole

To Lady Ailesbury, Monday 15 March 1762

Printed from the MS now wsl; first printed, with omissions, *Works* v. 562–3. For the history of the MS see *ante* 23 Aug. 1760.

The letter is misdated 'Strawberry Hill, March 5th' by HW. In a letter to Montagu, 'Arlington Street, March 9th' (Montagu ii. 20–1), HW wrote, 'I have not been at Strawberry above a month,' so that the present letter could not have been written on the 5th; also, the earliest assurances of an eventual victory at Martinique, alluded to in the letter, apparently did not reach London until 9 March (see n. 5 below). Since the postscript is dated 'Tuesday, 6th,' but 6 March 1762 fell on a Saturday, HW apparently miswrote '5th' and '6th' for '15th' and '16th', dates which fell on Monday and Tuesday, respectively.

Strawberry Hill, March [1]5th, 1762.

Madam,

ONE of your slaves, a fine young officer,[1] brought me two days ago a very pretty medal[2] from your Ladyship. Amidst all your triumphs you do not I see forget your English friends, and it makes

1. Not identified.
2. Possibly one of the 36 'German

medals, various, in white metal,' sold SH x. 84 for £1.8s.

me extremely happy. He pleased me still more, by assuring me that you return to England when the campaign opens.[3] I can pay this news by none so good as by telling you that we talk of nothing but peace.[4] We are equally ready to give law to the world or peace, Martinico[5] has not made us intractable. We and the new Czar[6] are the best sort of people upon earth; I am sure, Madam, you must adore him; he is willing to resign all his conquests,[7] that you and Mr Conway may be settled again at Park Place. My Lord Chesterfield, with the despondence of an old man and the wit of a young one, thinks the French and Spaniards must make some attempt

3. Hostilities commenced 'on the night between the 10th and 11th of March,' when 'a body of 3000 French sallied forth from Gottingen, and fell upon the line of the Allies at break of day' (*Operations of the Allied Army under . . . Prince Ferdinand* [1757–62], 1764, p. 243). The British troops, however, remained in winter quarters until May, Conway receiving on the 8th 'les marches-routes et ordres' from Prince Ferdinand 'pour les nouveaux cantonnements' (Conway to Maj.-Gen. de Reden, 8 May, MS copy now WSL); the troops were ordered to march 'from the 11th to the 15th' (Conway to 'Mr Thomas, surveyor of the hospital,' 8 May, MS copy now WSL). On the 16th Conway wrote to Prince Ferdinand from his new quarters at Hertford that 'my Lady Ailesbury . . . partit hier pour la Hollande, sur son voyage pour l'Angleterre' (MS copy now WSL); she arrived back in England ca 30 June (More 25; Mann vi. 47), presumably after some protracted stops along the way. See Sir Reginald Savory, *His Britannic Majesty's Army in Germany during the Seven Years' War*, Oxford, 1966, pp. 362–6.

4. On 5 Feb. in the House of Lords the Duke of Bedford had moved 'that it is the opinion of this House, that the war . . . in Germany is necessarily attended with a great and enormous expense . . . and that the bringing the British troops home from Germany would . . . carry on with vigour the war against the united forces of France and Spain . . . to procure a safe and honourable peace' (*Journals of the House of Lords* xxx. 155).

5. In a letter dated 'Martinico, Jan. 20,' and received 'Whitehall, March 9,' Maj.-Gen. Monckton wrote that 'the troops

continue healthy . . . and are in the highest spirits, and I don't in the least doubt but that I shall be able to execute this principal object of his Majesty's commands [i.e., the capture of Fort Royal]' (printed *London Gazette* No. 10189, 6–9 March; reprinted *London Chronicle* 9–11 March, xi. 233). Printed in the same newspapers is a letter from Rear-Adm. Rodney to Clevland, dated 'Martinico, the 19th of Jan.,' also attesting to the 'perfect health . . . spirit and harmony' of the army and navy (see also Lady Hervey to the Rev. Edmund Morris, 9 March, in her *Letters*, 1821, pp. 285–6). Ft Royal surrendered 4, and most of the island capitulated 7 Feb. (Monckton's dispatch of 9 Feb., printed *London Gazette Extraordinary* 23 March).

6. Peter III (1728–62), who had succeeded his aunt, Elizabeth, as Czar of Russia, 5 Jan. NS.

7. In a declaration of 23 Feb. NS, sent 'to the Imperial, French, and Swedish ministers, residing at Petersbourgh,' Peter stated that in order to secure peace, he was 'ready to make a sacrifice of the conquests made by the arms of Russia in this war' (text in GM 1762, xxxii. 103). On 16 March NS an armistice was signed between Russia and Prussia (*Recueil des traités . . . par la Russie avec les puissances étrangères*, ed. F. Martens, St Petersburg, 1874–1909, v. 356–67), and on 5 May NS, a definitive peace treaty was concluded, in which Peter promised 'de restituer à sa Majesté le roi de Prusse tous les états, pays, villes, places et forteresses appartenantes à sa Majesté le roi de Prusse qui ont été occupées par les armées russiennes pendant le cours de cette guerre' (Article VI, ibid. 371–2).

upon these islands, and is frightened lest we should not be so well prepared to repel invasions as to make them; he says, 'What will it avail us if we gain the whole world and lose our own soul?'

I am here alone, Madam, and know nothing to tell you; I came from town on Saturday for the worst cold I ever had in my life, and what I care less to own even to myself, a cough. I hope Lord Chesterfield will not speak more truth in what I have quoted, than in his assertion, that one need not cough if one did not please. It has pulled me extremely, and you may believe I do not look very plump, when I am more emaciated than usual. However, I have taken James's powder[8] for four nights, and have found great benefit from it, and if Miss Conway[9] does not come back with *soixante et douze quartiers,*[10] and the hauteur of a landgravine, I think I shall still be able to run down the precipices at Park Place with her—this is to be understood, supposing that we have any summer. Yesterday was the first moment that did not feel like Thule: not a glimpse of spring or green, except a miserable almond-tree, half opening one bud, like my Lord Powerscourt's[11] eye.

It will be warmer, I hope, by the King's Birthday,[12] or the old ladies will catch their deaths. There is a court-dress to be instituted (to thin the Drawing-Rooms) stiff-bodied gowns, and bare shoulders. What dreadful discoveries will be made both on fat and lean! I recommend to you the idea of Mrs Cavendish,[13] when half-stark; and I might fill the rest of my paper with such images, but your imagination will supply them; and you shall excuse me though I

8. HW's favourite remedy, the fever powder and cure-all of Dr Robert James (1705–76) (COLE i. 337, n. 1). HW was soon to suffer his third major attack of the gout; see *post* 20 May 1762; MONTAGU ii. 29, 31.

9. Who was with her parents at Osnabrück, winter quarters of the English infantry (*Operations of the Allied Army,* p. 241).

10. *Quartier* here signifies 'chaque degré de descendance dans une famille noble, tant du côté paternel que du côté maternel' (Littré, *Dictionnaire,* 1962, vi. 672). HW is perhaps alluding to a passage in Chapter XV of *Candide* (published 1759; HW's copy Hazen, *Cat. of HW's Lib.,* No. 1307): 'Vous, insolent! répondit le baron, vous auriez l'impudence d'épouser

ma sœur, qui a soixante-douze quartiers.'

11. Edward Wingfield (1729–64), 2d Vct Powerscourt; M.P. Stockbridge 1756–61.

12. 4 June.

13. Elizabeth Cavendish (d. 1779), m. (1732) Richard Chandler, later Cavendish (SELWYN 270, n. 13). HW, in a letter to Lady Hervey, 3 Oct. 1765, refers to the 'more' than 'common size' of Mrs Cavendish (MORE 53), and in his copy (now in the New York Public Library) of a satiric print published 2 July 1772 by J. Brotherton, entitled 'Masquerade Scene, Kensington Gardens,' identifies her as the enormously fat woman (who is a sailor in disguise) pursuing a young woman (ibid., n. 18). HW jokes about her size also *post* 17 June 1771.

leave this a short letter, but I wrote merely to thank your Ladyship
for the medal, and as you perceive have very little to say, besides that
known and lasting truth, how much I am Mr Conway's and your
Ladyship's faithful humble servant,

Hor. Walpole

Tuesday [1]6th.

I am this moment come to town and find a letter[14] from your
Ladyship with a most delightful regiment of all nations;[15] but it is
so late, I shall not save the post[16] if I tell you how much I like them
and Madame Pagantzkar of Osnaburg.[17] My compliments to Miss
Conway's drawing.

From Hertford, Thursday 20 May 1762

Printed for the first time from a photostat of BM Add. MSS 23218, f. 64.

London, May 20th 1762.

My dear Horry,

BOTH Lady Hertford and myself rejoice to hear you are
so well, and we shall be glad to see you on Saturday; I should
have sent sooner to inquire after you if my servant had been well.
The Duke of Newcastle's resignation I now believe is determined,[1]
but does not take place till Wednesday next; in the meantime I hear
his friends think so little that he retires from choice, that they are already in the coffee-houses deciding how men will vote and the general
members stand next winter. There are officers going and to go every

14. Missing.
15. Four sketches on cards, by Anne
Seymour Conway, of a 'Dutch officer,' an
'English officer in his morning dress,' a
'German officer,' and a 'French officer and
English alehouse-man' (pasted, with HW's
MS notes, in his extra-illustrated copy,
now wsl, of A Description of . . . Strawberry Hill, 1774).
16. 'The mails go out . . . to . . . Germany . . . Tuesday and Friday' (Court
and City Register, 1762, p. 129).
17. A sketch of 'Madame Paganzikar
of Osnabrück by Miss A. Conway now

Mrs Damer' (HW's MS note in A Description of . . . Strawberry Hill, 1774).

———

1. Newcastle had first informed the
King on 7 May of his intention to resign
at the end of the session (Letters from
George III to Lord Bute 1756–1766, ed.
Sedgwick, 1939, p. 101; Hardwicke Corr.
iii. 356–7). He did so on Wednesday, 26
May. For a full account of the affair, see
L. B. Namier, England in the Age of the
American Revolution, 1961, pp. 318–26.

packet to Germany, and I am sure your letters will be always entertaining.[2]

I know no other news and am, dear Horry,

Always most truly yours,

Hertford

From Beauchamp, Thursday 27 May 1762

Printed for the first time from a photostat of BM Add. MSS 23218, f. 20. The year has been determined by the reference to the reports of new creations of peers.

Memoranda (by HW):   Cook
Posting house
Father
W[illegible]
Trick
Bench
Door
Cherry seat
H[illegible]
Cistern

Christ Church, May the 27th.

Dear Sir,

I HAVE just received the enclosed transcripts[1] from the Ashmolean librarian:[2] how well he has executed your commission, I know not, having not had a moment's time to compare them with the originals, but I should suppose they have been transcribed accurately

2. Probably HW had asked about sending letters to Conway and his family at Osnabrück.

1. Missing. As far as their contents can be inferred from those specifically mentioned in this letter, many of them apparently related to material that HW had begun to assemble for his proposed 'Collections for a History of the Manners, Customs, Habits, Fashions, Ceremonies, etc. etc. etc. of England, begun February 21, 1762,' following a suggestion made by Lord Bute in a letter of ca 13 Feb. See *Works* v. 400–2; HW to Bute 15 Feb. 1762; Gray ii. 122.

2. William Huddesford (1732–72), antiquary; keeper of the Ashmolean Museum 1755–72. The list of transcripts that HW had requested, as the numbers mentioned below show, was compiled from his *Catalogus librorum manuscriptorum . . . Antonii à Wood, Oxford, 1761.*

enough. The account of the Duke of Buckingham's[3] entertainment in France seems curious—such anecdotes as throw light on the manners and economy of our ancestors can never be contemptible. What think you of Anthony Wood's[4] rigmarole about Lord Leycester and his Lady?[5] Is the story founded on fact? I am too little versed in the history of that age to determine.

The numbers[6] 8485.23,[7] 8489,[8] 8494.15,[9] 8495,[10] 8518,[11] are writ in so execrable an hand, that the librarian begs some time may be allowed him in deciphering them. 8543 is printed;[12] he will therefore

3. George Villiers, 2d D. of Buckingham; ambassador to France 1670, 1671, 1672. The account was item 8494.27 in the *Catalogus*, p. 40: 'A Relation of the Duke of Buckingham's Entertainment in France A.D. 1671.' It is now MS Wood F 32, f. 114 in the Bodleian Library.

4. Anthony à Wood (1632–95), antiquary and historian.

5. This probably refers to a transcript of an account of the death of Amy Robsart (ca 1532–60), m. (1549) Robert Dudley, cr. (1564) E. of Leicester; now printed in *The Life and Times of Anthony Wood*, ed. Andrew Clark, Oxford, 1891–1900, i. 260–3. The account is mentioned in the *Catalogus*, p. 53, in the description of item 8518, as 'Cumner, Berks. Account of the Manor House there belonging to Robert Dudley, E. of Leicester, etc.'; it is now MS Wood D 4, f. 97 (Falconer Madan *et al.*, *A Summary Catalogue of Western Manuscripts in the Bodleian Library*, ii pt ii [1937]. 1179), not f. 351 pt 2 as cited in Clark, op. cit. i. 260n.

6. All but one of the numbers in the following list refer to entire volumes of manuscripts in the *Catalogus;* but in view of Beauchamp's query about transcribing two other 'very bulky' items which had been requested, it seems unlikely that HW had asked for transcripts of whole volumes. In the absence of his original request to Beauchamp, however, the specific items desired from the various volumes cannot be distinguished.

7. 'A collection of several papers by Dr Kettle sometime President of Trinity Coll[ege]', a volume of 100 pages (now MS Wood F 23), containing many papers relating to the proposed Spanish marriage of Charles I, described in the *Catalogus*, pp. 21–2, and in Madan, op. cit. ii pt ii.

1168. HW may have been interested in some copies of Charles's verses to the Infanta which are included in the volume.

8. A volume of 260 leaves (now MS Wood F 27), containing papers mostly relating to Oxford and its libraries. The contents are described in the *Catalogus*, pp. 23–7, and in Madan, op. cit. ii pt ii. 1171–2.

9. 'Expenses for a fish meal for the King, Queen, and their Majesties' Household (tem. Phil. and Mariæ)' (now MS Wood F 32, f. 77); it is printed in [John Gutch], *Collectanea curiosa*, Oxford, 1781, ii. 1–3.

10. A volume of 284 leaves (now MS F 33), containing mainly arms and genealogies. It is described in the *Catalogus*, pp. 40–3, and in Madan, op. cit. ii pt ii. 1174–5.

11. A volume of some 300 leaves (now MS Wood D 4 and D 11), containing notes on the foundations, lists of masters, 'and other material toward the history of several free schools in England'; accounts of arms and epitaphs; and some miscellaneous material. It is described in the *Catalogus*, pp. 50–3, and in Madan, op. cit. ii pt ii. 1178–80.

12. '8543 [now MS Wood D 33]. The Life, Deeds, and Death of Sir John Perrott Lord Deputy of Ireland in the Time of Queen Elizabeth.' It was edited and published as *The History of that Most Eminent Statesman, Sir John Perrott, Knight of the Bath, and Lord Lieutenant of Ireland*, 1728 [1727]; the editing is usually ascribed to Richard Rawlinson (1690–1755), but this attribution is dismissed as 'absurd' in Madan, op. cit. ii pt ii. 1186. HW's copy is Hazen, *Cat. of HW's Lib.*, No. 1688.

not undertake it till he receives your commands. The numbers 8563 and 8568 are very bulky[13]—would you have them transcribed? Perhaps it may be useless to say that the expense of the enclosed transcripts is but ⟨7⟩ shillings. So much for A. Wood.

The papers inform us that the peerage is again to be augmented.[14] Is it possible? Will Lord B[ute] fill the House of Lords with old-fashioned country bobs? Even the Tories of this place are disgusted at this measure which by removing so many men of property from the House of Commons may insensibly (they think) destroy the balance of our constitution; but I have no business to make remarks. I am, dear Sir,

Your faithful humble servant,

Beauchamp

From Henrietta Seymour Conway, Tuesday 8 June 1762

Printed for the first time from a photostat of BM Add. MSS 23218, ff. 65–6.

Chichester, 8th June 1762.

Good Mr Walpole,

YOUR most obliging letter dated the 21st of January[1] did not come to hand till the 28th of May, which you will be astonished at till I explain it. The reason was your packet laid at Mr Compton's, waiting till I ordered some things to come from him, else what an ungrateful creature I must have been, not to have acknowledged so friendly and kind a letter. I am sensible you are a great deal too *partial* to me, the consequence of which will be that I shall grow vain, though in the decline of life, as I am confident that you are all

---

13. 8563 (now MS Wood D 18) is a collection of miscellaneous papers in 220 leaves, described in the *Catalogus*, pp. 71–3, and in Madan, op. cit. ii pt ii. 1183–5. 8568 (now MS Wood D 19 [4]) as 'some materials toward a history of the lives and compositions of all English musicians; drawn up according to alphabetical order in 210 pages by A. W.' (*Catalogus*, p. 77).

14. 'We hear that the following persons will soon be created peers, viz. Sir John Phillips, Sir John Hind Cotton, Sir Charles Kemis Tynte, and Sir Francis Dashwood, Barts. Mr Norborne Berkeley, Mr James West, and Mr Ryder, son of the late Sir Dudley Ryder' (*London Chronicle* 22–5 May, xi. 493). The rumour was false but gained currency because of extensive creations at the end of April; see MANN vi. 31–2.

1. Missing.

sincerity and never say a thing you do not really think. Well, all I can say in return is that it is impossible for any mortal to have a higher esteem and regard than I have for you, as I am sensible you are endowed with all the merit and good qualities that can be united in one person.

Though the news is so old, I must give you joy of our taking Martinico; as you very justly observe we have been a very successful people in this instant and many others. God send us grace to be thankful for all these blessings. Do you think the Spaniards, with all their boasting, can do us much harm? I fear them not, for they are an ungrateful set of people and their proceedings can never prosper. There was a report here a little while ago that our army in Germany was to be recalled,[2] but I fear without foundation as I had a letter about a fortnight ago from our dear relation the General[3] who mentioned nothing of it, and told me Lady Ailesbury was coming over. So I will not trespass any longer upon your time, which I know is always precious with you, only return you my best thanks for your kind intention in serving my friend, had it been in your power, and likewise for the franks, and believe me to be, good Sir, at all times

Your sincere affectionate friend and humble servant,

H. Seymour Conway

PS. Pelham desires her most respectful thanks for the honour you do her in remembering her.

2. See *ante* 15 March 1762, n. 4.   3. Conway; his letter is missing.

From HERTFORD, Wednesday 30 June 1762

Printed for the first time from a photostat of BM Add. MSS 23218, f. 67.

Address: To the Honourable Horatio Walpole at Strawberry Hill, near Twickenham, Middlesex.

Postmark: 30 IV.

June 30th 1762.

Dear Horry,

I CAN only tell you that an officer[1] is arrived from Germany with an account of a glorious victory[2] (for that is the expression) by Prince Ferdinand over the French army. All our generals[3] are safe. Harry Townshend[4] and another officer[5] of the Guards are killed; Monsieur Stainville,[6] a French general, is thought to be killed, and two of their first corps, the Grenadiers de France and Royaux, are taken.[7]

This is all I am able to learn; thank God my brother is safe.

Yours ever,

HERTFORD

1. Lt-Col. Robert Boyd (1710–94), K.B. 1785; first aide-de-camp to Prince Ferdinand; Col. (39th Foot), 1766; Gen., 1793; governor of Gibraltar, 1790. He brought the dispatches of the victory (*London Gazette Extraordinary* 30 June).

2. The battle of Wilhelmsthal, 24 June; see MANN vi. 46–7; Sir Reginald Savory, *His Britannic Majesty's Army in Germany during the Seven Years' War,* 1966, pp. 366–75, 509, 510, 514.

3. Including Conway.

4. Lt-Col. Henry Townshend (d. 24 June 1762), aide-de-camp to P. Ferdinand (*ante* 4 June 1758, n. 21). Lord Pembroke wrote to Chase Price from Gudensberg 29 Oct.: 'His company was in the Foot Guards, who . . . went off rather early in the day. . . . Harry would not submit to follow them, but went to the Grenadiers of the line, who behaved like angels. Like them he was shot through the body'

(Price MSS in the possession of the Marquess of Salisbury, cited Namier and Brooke iii. 552–3).

5. William Middleton (1738–95), of Belsay Castle, Northumberland; 5th Bt 1768; M.P. Northumberland 1774–95; Lt, 1759, Capt., 1762, in the 'Blues'. He was erroneously reported to have been killed (Conway to Grafton 25 June, Grafton, *Autobiography,* ed. Anson, 1898, p. 39; MANN, loc. cit.).

6. Jacques-Philippe de Choiseul (d. 1789), called Comte de Stainville; brother of the Duc de Choiseul; Lt-Gen. and commander of the Grenadiers de France (La Chenaye-Desbois v. 663; DU DEFFAND i. 217). He escaped unhurt.

7. They had formed the French rearguard and had been taken only after 'a most desperate hand to hand fight'; see W. E. Manners, *Some Account of the . . . Marquis of Granby,* 1899, pp. 242–3.

To HERTFORD, Wednesday 30 June 1762

Missing. 'I have told my Lord Hertford that I expect to hear your Ladyship has made a triumphant entry into our headquarters, and that with becoming dignity you have obtained from our general the liberty of the two hundred French officers, a proper way of resenting your confinement' (HW to Lady Mary Coke, 30 June 1762, MORE 25). HW had learned of the battle on the evening of the 30th, before receiving Hertford's letter (ibid. 27).

From HERTFORD, Thursday 29 July 1762

Printed for the first time from a photostat of BM Add. MSS 23218, f. 69. The pencil sketches on the cover are by HW.

London, July 29th 1762.

Dear Horry,

AS you may have got no letter by the last mail I enclose you one[1] I received from my brother last night, which you will be so good to return me.

There have been two councils to consider of the last proposals from France;[2] in the first there was said to be difference of opinion. The decision does not transpire.

I intend going to Ragley with my family on Monday, where I shall be very[3] happy to hear from you, being, dear Horry,

Always affectionately yours,

HERTFORD

The letters today from Holland mention the Czar's[4] being deposed,[5] which would not surprise you. They likewise mention the

1. Missing.
2. New proposals for peace had been received from France on 24 July. The Cabinet met upon them on the 26th and 28th, but at the first meeting nearly all the members, except Lord Bute, considered them unacceptable. On the 28th, however, the terms were accepted and it was agreed to send a plenipotentiary (Bedford) to Paris to conclude peace, pro-

vided that if peace were not concluded between England and Spain, France would not help Spain and would make peace with Portugal (*Letters from George III to Lord Bute 1756–1766*, ed. Sedgwick, 1939, pp. 124–8; see also MANN vi. 55, nn. 24, 25).

3. Written over 'always' in the MS.
4. Peter III.
5. 9 July, by his wife, Catherine the

French army as being upon the point of withdrawing towards Franc-fort.[6]

To Lady Ailesbury, Saturday 31 July 1762

Printed from the MS now WSL; first printed *Works* v. 563–4. For the history of the MS see *ante* 23 Aug. 1760; it was marked by HW for inclusion in *Works*.

Strawberry Hill, July 31st 1762.

Madam,

MAGNANIMOUS as the fair soul of your Ladyship is, and plaited with superabundance of Spartan fortitude, I felicitate my own good fortune who can circle this epistle with branches of the gentle olive, as well as crown it with victorious laurel—this pompous paragraph, Madam, which in compliment to my Lady Lyttelton I have penned in the style of her Lord, means no more, than that I wish you joy of the castle of Waldeck,[1] and more joy on the Peace, which I find everybody thinks is concluded. In truth I have still my doubts; and yesterday came news, which, if my Lord Bute does not make haste, may throw a little rub in the way. In

Great. 'An express is arrived from Sir Joseph Yorke, with an account that letters, received at The Hague from Berlin, had brought advice that the Emperor of Russia had been dethroned by the Empress; and that the army under the command of General Romanzow (which was destined against Denmark) had taken the oath of allegiance to her Imperial Majesty. What is become of the Emperor, or who were the principal persons concerned in bringing about this revolution, or when it happened, is not mentioned. Nor are there (as far as I can learn) any particulars relating to it yet known here' (Hugh Valence Jones to Newcastle 29 July, '3 o'clock', BM Add. MSS 32941, f. 92). See also 'Intelligence from The Hague,' 27 July, ibid. f. 64, and *London Chronicle* 29–31 July, xii. 105. The news was confirmed 3 Aug. (ibid. 31 July – 3 Aug., xii. 120). For a fuller account of the dethronement, see MANN vi. 56–9.

6. 'The same express [received from Sir Joseph Yorke on 29 July] adds, that the French marshals had sent away part of their heavy baggage, and artillery towards Francfort. By which it was supposed that the army would soon take that route' (Hugh Valence Jones to Newcastle, 29 July, loc. cit.).

———

1. Which surrendered to Conway 'the 11th instant, after a brisk bombardment for two days' (*London Chronicle* 27–9 July, xii. 99). Conway wrote to Devonshire, 21 July, that 'I was sent with three battalions of Brunswick grenadiers to take Waldeck, and performed it; it cost me two days but the French don't shine at these defences . . . they let me frighten them out by marching up with scaling ladders, when my ammunition was out' (Chatsworth MSS, 416/78). See MANN vi. 55–6, and n. 31; Sir Reginald Savory, *His Britannic Majesty's Army in Germany during the Seven Years War*, Oxford, 1966, pp. 380–1 and n.

short, the Czar is dethroned; some give the honour to his wife,[2] others, who add the little circumstance of his being murdered too, ascribe the revolution to the Archbishop of Novogorod,[3] who like other priests, thinks assassination[4] a less affront to heaven than three Lutheran churches.[5] I hope the latter is the truth, because in the honeymoonhood of Lady Cecilia's[6] tenderness, I don't know but she might miscarry at the thought of a wife preferring a crown, and scandal[7] says a regiment of grenadiers,[8] to her husband.

2. Catherine II (1729–96) the Great, m. (1745) the future Peter III of Russia; Empress of Russia 1762–96. See *ante* 29 July 1762, n. 5.

3. Daniil Andreievich Sechenov (1709–67), known in religion as Dmitriï; Abp of Novgorod 1757; Metropolitan of Novgorod and Velikie Luki, 8 Oct. 1762. He officiated at Catherine II's coronation (MANN vi. 64, n. 8).

4. According to Mercy-Argenteau (the Austrian ambassador at St Petersburg), the Archbishop, when told by the Czar that saints' pictures and images, except those of Christ and the Virgin, should be banned by the Greek Church, had warned that, if these reforms were enforced, Peter ran the danger that one night he might be murdered by the populace (to Kaunitz, 28 May OS, *Sbornik imperatorskago russkago istoricheskago obshchestva*, 1876, xviii. 372; *Daily Adv.* 12 July, *sub* 'Petersbourg . . . 8th . . . June'). Perhaps this warning, interpreted as a veiled threat, is the ultimate source of the rumour that the Archbishop had had the Czar assassinated (at the time of the present letter, the fate of the Czar was still unknown in England).

5. 'Petersbourg, June 18. The Archbishop of Novgorod . . . strongly opposed the construction of a Lutheran church, which the Emperor had resolved to build in his palace, for the convenience of his subjects of Holstein' (*London Chronicle* 20–22 July, xii. 77); the Archbishop 'was banished, but recalled eight days after' (ibid.). In her manifesto of 28 June OS, Catherine proclaimed that the first motive for the revolution was that 'the foundations of our orthodox Greek religion have been shaken, and its traditions exposed to total ruin; so that there was absolutely ground to fear that the Faith . . . would

be entirely changed, and a foreign religion introduced' (printed *London Chronicle* 31 July – 3 Aug., xii. 120, *sub* 3 Aug.). For further accounts of Peter's establishment of a Lutheran chapel at Oranienbaum, and of the Archbishop's opposition to it, see the dispatches from Mercy-Argenteau to Kaunitz, 18 June OS, and from Béranger to Choiseul, 2 July OS, *Sbornik*, 1876, xviii. 391, 1912, cxl. 1.

6. Lady Henrietta Cecilia West, who had married Col. (later Gen.) James ('Irish') Johnston the 4th of May (GM 1817, lxxxvii pt i. 281).

7. Catherine was already notorious for her amours; see P. W. Sergeant, *The Courtships of Catherine the Great*, 1905, and A. Polovtsoff, *Les Favoris de Catherine la Grande*, 1939.

8. The Preobazhenskiï Guards, later the Imperial Body Guard. HW wrote to Mann (31 July, in the postscript dated 4 Aug.) that he had heard 'from very good authority' that Catherine 'threw herself upon the gallantry of the Preobazinsky (or Praetorian) guards, who in Russia are the most polite and compassionate cavaliers in the world' (MANN vi. 57–8). HW had written earlier (to Mann 6 Aug. 1744 OS, ibid. ii. 495) that the Empress Elizabeth likewise had 'grappled with all her own grenadiers,' whom she had led personally the night of the *coup d'état* of 6 Dec. 1741 OS (ibid., n. 8). In the present *coup*, according to Robert Keith, the British ambassador at St Petersburg, Catherine actually went first to 'the Ismaelowsky Guards, which she found under arms ready to receive her,' then 'to the Simonowsky Regiment,' and finally 'to that of Preobasinsky, and was by the whole conducted to the palace' (Keith's dispatch of 1 July OS to Grenville, *Sbornik*, 1873, xii. 4).

I have a little meaning in naming Lady Lyttelton and Lady Cecilia, who I think are at Park Place. Was not there a promise that you all three would meet Mr Churchill and Lady Mary here in the beginning of August?[9] Yes indeed was there, and I put in my claim—not confining your heroic and musical Ladyships to a day or a week; my time is at your command; and I wish the rain was at mine, for if you or it do not come soon,[10] I shall not have a leaf left. Strawberry is browner than Lady Bel Finch.[11]

I was grieved, Madam, to miss seeing you in town on Monday, particularly as I wished to settle this party. If you will let me know when it will be your pleasure, I will write to my sister.

I am your Ladyship's most faithful servant,

HOR. WALPOLE

From CONWAY, ca August 1762

Missing; answered *post* 9 Sept. 1762.

To HERTFORD, ca Wednesday 4 August 1762

Missing; answered *post* 7 Aug. 1762. It contained an account of the Czar's deposition, confirmation of which reached England on 3 Aug. (*London Chronicle* 31 July – 3 Aug., xii. 120).

9. Lady Ailesbury and 'a party' had visited SH by 9 Sept., after putting 'it off for a month' (*post* 9 Sept. 1762).

10. 'We have not had a tea-cup full of rain till today for these six weeks' (HW to Strafford 5 Aug. 1762, CHUTE 315); 'Our drought continues, though we have had one handsome storm' (HW to Montagu 10 Aug. 1762, MONTAGU ii. 38).

11. HW wrote to Montagu, 18 May 1749 OS, that 'the turf is as brown as Lady Bell Finch' (ibid. i. 82). The Finch family were notorious for their swarthiness; 'the sable Finches' is a frequent expression with HW.

From HERTFORD, Saturday 7 August 1762

Printed for the first time from a photostat of BM Add. MSS 23218, ff. 70–1.

Ragley, August 7th 1762.

Dear Horry,

IS it her Grace's passions, the intrigue of his old friends, or the Duke's wishes for the first time of following them that carries my Lord of Bedford to Paris?[1] Do not imagine when I say this that I am angry enough to feel much disappointed;[2] I have known it too long to be surprised, and think too humbly of myself to contend with a Duke of Bedford of his character[3] at such a time as this. Still I think some explanation due to me, though I do not expect it; grandeur and state have so few charms for me that I should have made a sacrifice of my own inclinations to my children's advantage. I have hardly another wish to gratify, and in that respect I feel some concern in not going to Paris if the Peace succeeds.

I intend without much philosophy to go to town when the Queen lies in,[4] and I have besides private business and my old trust to finish; my Lady will not attend me. Why should I stay in town on the Czar's deposition when you tell me more than I might have heard in London?[5]

I have now my twelve children with me and receive no small satisfaction from what I can discover of them.

Do not think me growing old and peevish from talking so much of my family; you are my friend and can forgive my weaknesses. The best compliments of all here attend you, and you will believe me always, dear Horry,

Very affectionately yours,

HERTFORD

1. The Cabinet had decided, 28 July, to send Bedford to Paris as plenipotentiary to conclude the peace (*ante* 29 July 1762, n. 2).

2. Hertford had been nominated ambassador to France in Feb. 1755 (CHUTE 207; MANN iv. 468; *Mem. Geo. II* ii. 2). As he did not go to Paris at that time because of the deteriorating relations between the two Courts, he had some claim to be appointed when diplomatic relations were resumed.

3. Probably a reference to Bedford's known enthusiasm for peace.

4. Her first child, later George IV, was born 12 Aug. (*post* 14 Aug. 1762, n. 22).

5. Confirmation of the deposition had reached England on 3 Aug. HW had also heard details of the 'Muscovite history . . . from very good authority' by 4 Aug. (*London Chronicle* 31 July – 3 Aug., xii. 120; MANN vi. 57).

To Lady Hertford, ca Thursday 12 August 1762

Missing; answered *post* 14 Aug. 1762.

From Lady Hertford, Saturday 14 August 1762

Printed for the first time from a photostat of BM Add. MSS 23218, f. 72. Dated by the memoranda. A sketch of what appears to be a window or picture frame with the numbers '2–6' and '2' is on the cover.

Memoranda (by HW):

[Deaths in Aug.–Sept. 1762]	[Letters written][13]	
Mr Nunez[1]	Mr Sharp[14]	
Lady Portsmouth[2]	Lady Lyttel[ton]	18
Mr Knight[3] son of	Lord Hertford	
Lord Lux[borough]	Mr Bateman[15]	19
Mrs Redish,[4] coz. to	Mr Warton[16]	21
Lady Town[shend]	Mr Boone[17]	23
Gen. Caesar[5]	Mr Mont[agu][18]	
Lady Mary Wortley[6]	Mr Conw[ay]	26
Dow. Lady Fane[7]	Mr Bate[man]	
Lord Westmorland[8]	Sir H[orace] Man[n]	29
Miss Poyntz[9]	Lady Ailesb[ury]	
Adm. Smith[10]	Serg. Whitaker[19]	30
———	Mr Selwyn	
Mr Penton[11]	Lord Hert[ford]	4
Capt. Ogle[12]	Mr Conw[ay]	9 X

[Unexplained]
¼ guinea
French books
auct. of books
Lady Bute Pr[ince]ss[20]
Hogarth[21]

1. Isaac Fernandez Nunez, a Jewish neighbour of HW's at Twickenham, who shot himself through the head in August; see Cole ii. 368 and Hilda F. Finberg, 'Jewish Residents in Eighteenth-Century Twickenham', Jewish Historical Society of England, *Transactions*, xvi [1952]. 133–5.
2. Died 13 Aug.
3. The Hon. Henry Knight (1728 – 15

Aug. 1762); M.P. Great Grimsby 1761–2; only son of Robert Knight (1702–72), cr. (1745) Bn Luxborough of Shannon and (1763) E. of Catherlough.
4. Not identified.
5. Julius Caesar (d. 7 Aug.), Major-Gen. 1759; commander of the brigade of English Guards. He was killed by a fall from his horse (Edmund Lodge, *Life of*

Ragley, Saturday the 14th.

Sir,

I AM sorry to make so unworthy a return as to send you a few dull lines in answer to a very entertaining letter I had the pleasure of receiving from you this morning; but so it must be without I am quite silent and leave you to think that I am undeserving of your goodness to me. I admire the rocker you have found out for our royal child,[22] for it seems to be the only situation he is now fit for. There are many reasons that would make me glad not to go to Paris, and yet there is one that outweighs almost every other, which would

Sir Julius Caesar, 1827, p. 63; *London Chronicle* 17–19 Aug., xii. 170).

6. Lady Mary Wortley Montagu, d. 21 Aug.

7. Mary Stanhope (ca 1686 – 21 Aug. 1762), m. (1707) Charles Fane, cr. (1718) Vct Fane.

8. Died 26 Aug.

9. 'Lately died in the south of France, whither she went for the recovery of her health, Miss [Louisa] Poyntz, sister to the Lady Viscountess Spencer' (*London Chronicle* 28–31 Aug., xii. 211).

10. Thomas Smith (d. 28 Aug.), admiral 1757.

11. Henry Penton (?1705 – 1 Sept. 1762), letter-carrier to the King; M.P. Tregony 1734–47, Winchester 1747–61.

12. A lunatic, burned to death in Newgate 7 Sept., who had been before 1756 'captain of dragoons on the Irish Establishment' (GM 1756, xxvi. 202), and was possibly the Capt. Robert Ogle who in 1740 was captain in Lord Tyrawley's Fifth Horse (Society for Army Historical Research, *Army List of 1740,* 1931, p. 63): 'Yesterday morning, about two o'clock, a fire broke out at the back of a staircase in the Press Yard, Newgate, which in a few hours consumed all the apartments in that place, greatly damaged the chapel, and the back part of a house belonging to a stocking trimmer in Phoenix Court, Newgate Street. There were two unfortunate prisoners in the rooms which were burnt down who perished in the flames; Capt. Ogle was one (in whose apartment it is said it first began); he was tried some

time ago [1756] for the murder of the master of the Vine Tavern, near Dover Street, Piccadilly, and being found a lunatic, was ordered to remain in prison' (*Daily Adv.* 8 Sept.). See also GM loc. cit. for his trial.

13. Of the letters mentioned in this list, those to Warton 21 Aug., to Mann 29 Aug., to Selwyn 30 Aug. (actually dated 31 Aug.), and to Conway 9 Sept. survive. The rest have not been located. The list is not all-inclusive, as HW's letter to Cole, 19 Aug., which survives, is not mentioned.

14. John Sharp (ca 1729–72), Fellow of Corpus Christi College, Cambridge, 1753–72 (GRAY ii. 104, n. 2). He had written to HW 13 Aug.

15. Richard Bateman (ca 1705–73), collector and antiquary (COLE i. 90, n. 11).

16. Thomas Warton (1728–90), historian of English poetry.

17. Charles Boone (?1729–1819), M.P., a friend of Lord Orford's (MANN viii. 47, n. 15).

18. George Montagu (ca 1713–80).

19. William Whitaker (d. 1777), prime sergeant and treasurer of Serjeant's Inn (GM 1777, xlvii. 508).

20. Probably Augusta, Princess Dowager of Wales, allegedly Lord Bute's mistress.

21. William Hogarth (1697–1764), painter.

22. The Prince of Wales, later George IV, born 12 Aug. (see MANN vi. 64, 72). Possibly Hertford, in his capacity as lord of the Bedchamber, had asked HW to find an appropriate gift for himself and Lady Hertford to present to the Queen.

have made me wish at this time to have gone.²³ I hope you will be charitable and visit my Lord while he is in London; I was very sorry to let him go alone, and yet as I had all the twelve²⁴ here, I could not with any sort of convenience leave them. You are very good to think of Spa for me;²⁵ next summer I will go there, or anywhere else that you advise. Accept the best wishes of all your friends here, and believe me

> Faithfully yours,
>
> I. HERTFORD

From HERTFORD, Wednesday 18 August 1762

Printed for the first time from a photostat of BM Add. MSS 23218, ff. 74–5.

London, August 18th 1762.

Dear Horry,

I BELIEVE the peace between France and England is settled,¹ and the news of today will probably include Spain.² A ship is arrived at Dover from Carolina, who sends an express³ to the Admiralty informing their Lordships that before she sailed from thence the *Bonetta* sloop was arrived there with news that we had then taken a troop of Spanish horse intended to reinforce the garrison of the Havanna. We had taken a 64-gun ship and three frigates, on

23. Probably Hertford's disappointment at not being made ambassador; see *ante* 7 Aug. 1762, *post* 21 Aug. 1764.

24. The Hertfords' children.

25. Lady Hertford was apparently ailing. HW had written to Lady Mary Coke, 30 June 1762: 'If you had not had my heart before, you would have won it by your kind attention to Lady Hertford; but I fear all is in vain. She will not hear of Spa, and is gone today to Ragley, and I doubt will go to Ireland. Nothing touches her about herself; she is as indifferent to that, as active and anxious about her family' (MORE 27).

1. A messenger had arrived from France, 16 Aug., with the French acceptance of the last British offer, even if Spain did not consent; but the French insisted on postponing the exchange of ministers until they received a reply from Madrid (Barrington to Newcastle 16 Aug.; Jones to Newcastle 16 Aug.; Barrington to Newcastle 17 Aug.; 'Heads of what passed with C[ount] V[iry]' 18 Aug., BM Add. MSS 32941, ff. 249, 253–4, 266, 270–4).

2. Bedford told Newcastle on 18 Aug. that the reply from Spain was not expected until 2 Sept. (Newcastle to Hardwicke 19 Aug., ibid., f. 302).

3. Which had arrived in London that day (ibid., ff. 282–93). An extract from the letter, containing all the information mentioned by Hertford, is printed in the *London Chronicle* 17–19 Aug., xii. 174.

board of one of which was a million sterling, and we had taken four of the forts, and must be in possession of the place by the 7th of last month.[4] The Spaniards had sunk two of their large ships and a frigate in the harbour's mouth and had four or five more large men-of-war in the harbour.

The Duke of Bedford is preparing to set out;[5] I hear it has been proposed that he should go to The Hague to negotiate,[6] but I suppose that will not be admitted. When he goes to Paris, if I am out of town, I will beg you to offer him what I bought of Lord Arbermarle's,[7] which I will leave with my porter directed for you whenever you shall send for it. It may be an advantage to his Grace as well as to me, but if he has any economy about it I am very indifferent. The account is a very particular one and I have never touched anything except the vis-à-vis,[8] which was resold, and must of course not be charged; the goods are in the hands and under the care of the Lambert[9] family at Paris.

News is hourly expected of a battle in Germany,[10] which is supposed to have been fought on the 9th or 10th instant; still I have some hopes that the French generals may have orders to avoid it.

I must not forget to tell you that the Duchess of Bedford's negotiations have succeeded; the Duke of Marlborough marries Lady Caroline[11] next week.

4. This was confidently predicted in the express (ibid.), but Havana did not fall until 13 Aug.; the news finally reached London 29 Sept. (*post* 28 Sept. 1762, postscript 30 Sept.).

5. This was the conclusion generally drawn from his conduct at Court 15 Aug. (Devonshire to Newcastle 16 Aug.; Jones to Newcastle 16 Aug., BM Add. MSS 32941, ff. 251, 254), but he did not leave London until 5 Sept. (*London Chronicle* 4–7 Sept., xii. 234).

6. This proposal is not mentioned in the correspondence relating to the negotiation in the Newcastle Papers or in any published correspondence.

7. William Anne van Keppel (1702–54), 2d E. of Albemarle, ambassador to France 1749–54. Hertford had apparently purchased his Paris equipage in 1755 when he had been nominated ambassador to France (*ante* 7 Aug. 1762, n. 2).

8. 'A light carriage for two persons

sitting face to face' (OED); see MANN viii. 260, n. 4.

9. Sir John Lambert (1690–1772), 2d Bt; English banker in Paris.

10. No battle, only a few skirmishes, took place. The report was founded on intelligence from The Hague of 13 Aug. (received 17 Aug.), that Prince Ferdinand, on the 8th, had been about to attack the French army and that Lord Granby had actually begun to do so (Barrington to Newcastle 17 Aug., BM Add. MSS 32941, f. 266; *London Gazette* No. 10235, 14–17 Aug.). Further developments are discussed ibid., No. 10237, 21–24 Aug. See Sir Reginald Savory, *His Britannic Majesty's Army in Germany during the Seven Years' War*, Oxford, 1966, pp. 391–401.

11. Lady Caroline Russell, daughter of the 4th D. of Bedford. m. (23 Aug.) George Spencer, 3d D. of Marlborough. According to HW, Marlborough was in love with her but had been unwilling

The christening[12] is fixed for the 8th and the installation[13] for the 22d; if you love sights you may be entertained, and if you was of the Bedchamber you might be often respectfully employed in attendance at St James's.

I propose going again into the country some time tomorrow, and am, dear Horry, always

Most sincerely yours,

Hertford

To Hertford, Thursday 19 August 1762

Missing; mentioned in the memoranda *ante* 14 Aug. 1762.

To Conway, Thursday 26 August 1762

Missing; mentioned in the memoranda *ante* 14 Aug. 1762.

To Lady Ailesbury, Monday 30 August 1762

Missing; mentioned in the memoranda *ante* 14 Aug. 1762.

To Hertford, Saturday 4 September 1762

Missing; mentioned in the memoranda *ante* 14 Aug. 1762.

to marry her because he disliked her mother (Mann vi. 73, n. 31).

12. Of the Prince of Wales; see *post* 9 Sept. 1762.

13. Of Prince William Henry, later Duke of Gloucester, and Lord Bute as Knights of the Garter; see *post* 28 Sept. 1762.

To Conway, Thursday 9 September 1762

Printed from *Works* v. 87–90.

Strawberry Hill, Sept. 9, 1762.

Nondum laurus erat, longoque decentia crine
Tempora cingebat de qualibet arbore Phœbus.[1]

THIS is a hint to you, that as Phœbus, who was certainly your superior, could take up with a chestnut garland, or any crown he found, you must have the humility to be content without laurels, when none are to be had: you have hunted far and near for them, and taken true pains to the last in that old nursery-garden Germany, and by the way have made me shudder with your last journal:[2] but you must be easy with *qualibet*[3] other *arbore;* you must come home to your own plantations. The Duke of Bedford is gone in a fury to make peace,[4] for he cannot be even pacific with temper; and by this time I suppose the Duke de Nivernois[5] is unpacking his portion of olive *dans la rue de Suffolk Street.*[6] I say, I suppose—for I do not, like my friends at Arthur's, whip into my post-chaise to see every novelty. My two sovereigns, the Duchess of Grafton and Lady Mary Coke, are arrived,[7] and yet I have seen neither Polly nor Lucy.[8] The

1. 'Not yet was the laurel, and his temples, comely with long locks, Phœbus was apt to wreathe with a garland from any tree' (Ovid, *Metamorphoses,* i. 450–1).
2. Missing.
3. 'Any.'
4. As minister plenipotentiary and ambassador extraordinary to Paris, where he arrived 12 Sept.; see MANN vi. 69, n. 2. 'On Tuesday [7 Sept.] sailed from Dover . . . the Duke of Bedford, for Calais' (*London Chronicle* 7–9 Sept., xii. 246).
5. Louis-Jules-Barbon Mancini-Mazarini (1716–98), Duc de Nivernais; French ambassador to Rome 1749–52, to England 1762–3, minister without portfolio 1787–9; friend and correspondent of HW (MANN iv. 286, n. 11).
6. Nivernais reached London 12 Sept. (*London Chronicle* 11–14 Sept., xii. 262; see also MANN vi. 70, n. 3). HW, in a MS note to his copy of Pennant's *Of London,* 1790 (Hazen, *Cat. of HW's Lib.,* No. 3928), says that Suffolk Street 'used to be known for the residence of foreigners,

who were but ill lodged here: of late years hotels have been introduced where they are better accommodated and in better streets' (quoted in H. B. Wheatley and Peter Cunningham, *London Past and Present,* 1891, iii. 331). Actually, Nivernais settled in Albemarle Street (*Court and City Register,* 1763, p. 113; Edward Gibbon's *Journal,* ed. D. M. Low, 1929, p. 200).
7. 'On Wednesday night [1 Sept.] the Duke and Duchess of Grafton arrived at their house in New Bond Street from Harwich' (*Daily Adv.* 3 Sept.); 'On Sunday night [5 Sept.] Lady Mary Coke . . . arrived at her house in Berkeley Square from France' (ibid. 7 Sept.). The Duke and Duchess had been abroad since June, 1761 (see *ante* 13 June 1761; *Daily Adv.* 15 June 1761), Lady Mary since June of the present year (see *London Chronicle* 15–17 June, xi. 569).
8. Polly Peachum and Lucy Lockit, the two inamoratas of Macheath in Gay's *The Beggar's Opera.*

former, I hear, is entirely French;[9] the latter as absolutely English.

Well! but if you insist on not doffing your cuirass, you may find an opportunity of wearing it. The storm thickens. The City of London are ready to hoist their standard;[10] treason is the *bon ton* at that end of the town; seditious papers pasted up at every corner:[11] nay, my neighbourhood is not unfashionable; we have had them at Brentford and Kingston.[12] The Peace is the cry; but to make weight, they throw in all the abusive ingredients they can collect.[13] They talk of your friend the Duke of Devonshire's resigning;[14] and, for the Duke of Newcastle, it puts him so much in mind of the end of Queen Anne's time,[15] that I believe he hopes to be minister again[16] for another forty years.

In the meantime there are but dark news from the Havannah:[17]

9. George Selwyn wrote likewise to Henry Fox, 15 Sept., that 'I have not seen the Duchess of Grafton, but hear she is very much frenchified' (*Letters to Henry Fox*, ed. Lord Ilchester, Roxburghe Club, 1915, p. 160); HW later wrote to Mann 26 Sept. 1762 (MANN vi. 80) that 'I have seen my Duchess. . . . She is not dressed French, but Italian, that is, over-French.'

10. In opposition to the terms of the peace (see *ante* 29 July 1762), by which England was felt to be making too great concessions to France (for a detailed discussion of the negotiations towards peace and English dissent over them, see L. B. Namier, *England in the Age of the American Revolution*, 1961, pp. 283–418). Newcastle wrote to Devonshire, 4 Sept., that 'the City is in the highest rage, particularly with . . . the Duke of Bedford, who goes to negotiate such a peace, and Mr Fox, who is supposed to be the adviser and supporter of my Lord Bute; and against my Lord Bute himself. Nothing can be stronger than the run is, and indeed violences are to be apprehended from both quarters' (BM Add. MSS 32942, ff. 174–5).

11. 'The Exchange was prostituted to the posting up of papers that were a disgrace to the police of any civilized nation' (Symmer to Mitchell 10 Sept., quoted in O. A. Sherrard, *Lord Chatham and America*, 1958, p. 64).

12. 'The clamour stirred up against peace has been very great, both in the country as well as in London' (Rigby to Bedford, 16 Sept., *Bedford Corr.* iii. 123).

13. Examples of extreme personal abuse are to be found, for example, in the *North Briton* No. XIV, 4 Sept. First Bute is abused: 'A minister of mean and narrow genius, who finds himself embarrassed in the management of an important war, is from necessity drove to ask peace for the preservation of his own power, and the concealment of his incapacity from his master.' Then, further on in the same article, Bedford is satirized and branded as a French sympathizer who will laugh with the French over 'our loss of Newfoundland.'

14. Devonshire resigned his office of lord chamberlain 28 Oct.; see *post* 30 Oct. 1762.

15. The *North Briton*, loc. cit., draws this same parallel: 'This was exactly the state of England at the latter end of Queen Anne's reign, after the change of the glorious ministry, which had preserved Europe from the universal monarchy of the House of Bourbon. Our arms had then too . . . been crowned with astonishing success,' etc., etc.

16. Newcastle had resigned 26 May (*ante* 20 May 1762).

17. Between 9 and 11 Sept. letters from Lord Albemarle (commander of the army at Havana) to Lord Egremont, 13 and 17 July, were received, via Sir James Douglas, together with a 'Journal of the Siege of Havannah, 1762,' from 6 June to 16 July, the last published in the *London Gazette* No. 10242, 7–11 Sept.; in the letter of 13 July, Albemarle says that 'the increasing sickness of the troop, the intense heat of the weather, and the ap-

the *Gazette*,[18] who would not fib for the world, says, we have lost but four officers: the world, who is not quite so scrupulous, says, our loss is heavy.[19]—But what shocking notice to those who have *Harry Conways* there! The *Gazette* breaks off with saying, that they were to storm the next day![20] Upon the whole, it is regarded as a preparative to worse news.[21]

Our next monarch was christened last night, George Augustus Frederic;[22] the Princess,[23] the Duke of Cumberland, and Duke of Mecklenburgh,[24] sponsors;[25] the ceremony performed by the Bishop of London.[26] The Queen's bed, magnificent, and they say in taste, was placed in the great drawing-room:[27] though she is not to see company in form,[28] yet it looks as if they had intended people should have been there,[29] as all who presented themselves were admitted, which were very few, for it had not been notified; I suppose to pre-

proaching rainy season, are circumstances which prevent my being too sanguine about our future success against the town' (printed in 'Papeles sobre la toma de La Habana por los Ingleses en 1762,' *Publicaciones del Archivo Nacional de Cuba*, 1948, xviii. 80).

18. *London Gazette Extraordinary* 9 Sept., *sub* 'return of the killed, wounded, and missing . . . on . . . Cuba to the 13th of July.'

19. See *post* 28 Sept. 1762.

20. 'Captain Urry . . . who left the Havannah the 18th of July . . . reports, that . . . it was intended to storm the place [Moro Castle] that night, or the night following' (*London Gazette Extraordinary* 9 Sept., *sub* 'Admiralty Office, September 8').

21. News of the surrender of Havana 13 Aug. arrived 29 Sept.; see *post* 28 Sept. 1762, postscript 30 Sept.

22. See *London Chronicle* 7–9 Sept., xii. 246.

23. Augusta, Princess Dowager of Wales.

24. Adolph Friedrich IV (1738–94), Duke of Mecklenburg-Strelitz 1752, the Queen's brother.

25. Ibid.

26. Richard Osbaldeston (1690–1764), Bp of Carlisle, 1747; of London, 1762. The ceremony was actually performed by the Archbishop of Canterbury (ibid.; see also *post* 28 Sept. 1762).

27. 'A grand state bed is put up in the Great Council Chamber at St James's,

for her Majesty to sit on to receive the quality' (*London Chronicle*, loc. cit.); 'The Queen appeared as in bed; and in the finest bed I ever saw, placed where the canopy usually stands' (Barrington to Newcastle 8 Sept., BM Add. MSS 32942, f. 202).

28. Though the Duke of Devonshire, lord chamberlain, wanted the Queen 'to see company on her bed some evenings,' George III and Bute 'agreed it was unnecessary' (George III to Bute, 5 Sept., *Letters from George III to Lord Bute 1756–1766*, ed. Sedgwick, 1939, p. 132), and Devonshire wrote to Newcastle, 7 Sept., that 'the Queen does not see company but will appear in the Drawing-Room on Sunday' (BM Add. MSS 32942, f. 194).

29. Barrington wrote to Newcastle, loc. cit., that 'peers, peeresses, and privy councillors were invited' to the christening. As for those not invited, George III wrote to Bute, 5 Sept., that the Duke of Devonshire 'is desirous to know in what manner he shall stop people from coming to the christening, for that the world is now so ill-bred that nothing less than locking the doors will stop them' (Sedgwick, loc. cit.). Whatever precautions Devonshire may have taken were of no avail; for example, George Selwyn wrote to Henry Fox, 15 Sept., that 'the means of my being at the christening . . . was my insatiable curiosity . . . the means of my admittance an *air de protection* that very often imposes upon those who ought to

vent too great a crowd—all I have heard named, besides those in waiting, were the Duchess of Queensberry, Lady Dalkeith, Mrs Grenville,[30] and about four more ladies.

My Lady A. is abominable: she settled a party to come hither, and put it off for a month;[31] and now she has been here and seen my Cabinet,[32] she ought to tell you what good reason I had not to stir. If she has not told you that it is the finest, the prettiest, the newest and the oldest thing in the world, I will not go to Park Place on the 20th, as I have promised.[33] Oh! but tremble you may for me, though you will not for yourself—all my glories were on the point of vanishing last night in a flame! The chimney of the new Gallery,[34] which chimney is full of deal-boards, and which Gallery is full of shavings, was on fire at eight o'clock. Harry[35] had quarrelled with the other servants, and would not sit in the kitchen; and to keep up his anger had lighted a vast fire in the servants' hall, which is under the gallery. The chimney took fire; and if Margaret[36] had not smelt it with the first nose that ever a servant had, a quarter of an hour had set us in a blaze. I hope you are frightened out of your senses for me: if you are not, I will never live in a panic for three or four years for you again.

I have had Lord March and the Rena[37] here for one night, which does not raise my reputation in the neighbourhood, and may usher me again for a Scotchman into *The North Briton*.[38] I have had too a

demand my credentials. . . . I walked up, and then on to the *sanctum sanctorum* without the least opposition; I know no more of my manner of admittance than that' (Ilchester, op. cit. 159).

30. Elizabeth Wyndham (d. 1769), m. (1749) the Hon. George Grenville (OSSORY i. 38, n. 9).

31. HW had reminded Lady Ailesbury, *ante* 31 July 1762, of 'a promise' that she, Lady Lyttelton, Lady Cecilia Johnston, Charles Churchill, and Lady Mary Churchill would all meet at SH 'in the beginning of August.'

32. The Cabinet (later called Chapel and Tribune) at SH was described by HW to Mann, 1 July 1762 (MANN vi. 49) as 'on the point of being completed,' and 'really striking beyond description.' Due to workmen's strikes, however, it was not completed until April 1763 (see MONTAGU ii. 64).

33. See *post* 28 Sept. 1762.

34. The Gallery, likewise delayed by strikes, was not completed until August 1763 (see *post* 9 Aug. 1763; COLE i. 44).

35. Henry Jones, HW's servant 1752 (MONTAGU i. 132) to 1762. The same day as the present letter (9 Sept.), HW wrote to Grosvenor Bedford that 'my servant, Henry Jones, is grown old and wants to retire,' setting forth the qualifications and duties of a successor, who 'is to be steward and butler.' As of 28 Sept., however, Jones was still in HW's employ (*post* 28 Sept. 1762, *sub* 30 Sept.).

36. Margaret Young (fl. 1760–86), HW's housekeeper.

37. Mistress to Lord March. HW, in a footnote to his letter to Mann of 14 April 1769 (MANN vii. 106, n. 7), identifies her as wife of a Florentine wine-merchant and former mistress of Lord Pembroke.

38. Lord March was a Scottish peer. HW's praise of the Scots in the advertisement to the Scottish and Irish sections

letter[39] from a German[40] that I never saw, who tells me, that, hearing by chance how well I am with my Lord Bute, he desires me to get him a place. *The North Briton* first recommended me for an employment,[41] and has now given me interest at the backstairs. It is a notion, that whatever is said of one, has generally some kind of foundation: surely I am a contradiction to this maxim! yet, was I of consequence enough to be remembered, perhaps posterity would believe that I was a flatterer! Good night!

Yours ever,

HOR. WALPOLE

From HERTFORD, Friday 10 September 1762

Printed for the first time from a photostat of BM Add. MSS 23218, f. 76.

London, September 10th 1762.

Dear Horry,

COME away, as I hear with pleasure from G. Selwyn[1] that you are able, and play at loo with your favourite Duchess.[2] She has a party tomorrow night and goes to Lord Ravensworth's[3] on Monday.

The Duke of Bedford is gone to Paris with his usual acclamations, hissed through the towns he passed.[4] He is now in more safety in France, where I hear he proposes staying about a year. The Duchess, whom I saw last night, follows him when the Peace is sure.[5] The French are retired to Hanau and Berghen,[6] and I hope by such a march finish the German campaign.

of *The Royal and Noble Authors* had drawn upon him ironical praise from the anti-Scottish *North Briton* (No. 2, 12 June): 'How faithful is this masterly pen of Mr Walpole! How unlike the odious sharp and strong incision pen of Mr Swift,' etc.

39. Missing.

40. Not identified.

41. 'I beg to recommend Mr Walpole . . . for so very particular a compliment . . . and I entreat his Lordship [Bute] to put him on the list immediately after my countrymen' (ibid.).

———

1. Selwyn had presumably visited SH with Lord March and the Rena a few days previously (SELWYN 166; *ante* 9 Sept. 1762).

2. Grafton, who had returned to London from the Continent 1 Sept. (ibid., n. 7).

3. Ravensworth Castle, Durham, seat of her father, Bn Ravensworth.

4. HW mentions in *Mem. Geo. III*, i. 151, that Bedford was hissed as he passed through the principal streets of London on his way to France.

5. She finally left London 30 Sept.; see *post* 28 Sept. 1762.

6. 'We have advice of the 29th from Frankfort that the French marshals had

My Lady is in the country, but proposes on account of her family friends to see the installation. Adieu, dear Horry, and believe me always

Most truly yours,

HERTFORD

From HERTFORD, Tuesday 21 September 1762

Printed for the first time from a photostat of BM Add. MSS 23218, f. 77.

London, September 21st 1762.

Dear Horry,

IN the present demand for tickets[1] I am happy to have been able to send one to your friend.

There is no news but what you may read in the papers.

The Duchess of Bedford is I hear going to Paris,[2] but yet the armies are too near[3] for the slowness of the present negotiation. Her Grace I hear has not been invited to Blenheim.[4]

My best compliments at Park Place;[5] when I see my Lady I will acquaint you when I can come to Straberry, but I think it must be after my Suffolk expedition.[6]

Yours in great haste, dear Horry

HERTFORD

already their headquarters at Hanau, with the corps of Generals Stainville and Guerchy at Bergen; the whole country is employed in transporting forage and provisions to them, of which they were in great want' ('Intelligence from The Hague,' 3 Sept., BM Add. MSS 32942, f. 137). See also *London Gazette* No. 10242, 7–11 Sept. The Allies had actually been defeated by the French in a minor battle on 30 Aug., but the news had not yet arrived.

1. To the installation of the Knights of the Garter at Windsor, 22 Sept.; see *post* 28 Sept. 1762. The 'friend' has not been identified.

2. 'Monday next [27 Sept.] . . . the Duchess of Bedford will embark for Paris' (*London Chronicle* 21–3 Sept., xii. 289). She did not leave until the 30th (*post* 28 Sept. 1762).

3. The two armies were still facing each other just east of Frankfurt-am-Main (*London Chronicle* 16–18, 18–21 Sept., xii. 280, 281).

4. To visit her newly-married daughter, the Duchess of Marlborough. See Gladys Scott Thomson, *The Russells in Bloomsbury*, 1940, pp. 368–9.

5. Where HW was visiting Lady Ailesbury; he returned to SH on the 22nd or 23rd (MONTAGU ii. 44). See *post* 28 Sept. 1762.

6. To visit his seat at Sudbourne (CHUTE 247; *post* 28 Sept. 1762).

To Conway, Tuesday 28 September 1762

Printed from *Works* v. 90–2.

Strawberry Hill, Sept. 28, 1762.

TO my sorrow and your wicked joy,[1] it is a doubt whether Monsieur de Nivernois will shut the temple of Janus. We do not believe him quite so much in earnest, as the dove[2] we have sent, who has summoned his turtle to Paris. She sets out the day after tomorrow,[3] escorted, to add gravity to the embassy, by George Selwyn.[4] The stocks don't mind this journey of a rush, but draw in their horns every day.[5] We can learn nothing of the Havannah,[6] though the axis on which the whole treaty turns.[7] We believe, for we have never seen them,[8] that the last letters thence[9] brought accounts of great loss,[10] especially by the sickness.[11] Colonel Burgoyne[12] has given a little fillip[13] to the Spaniards, and shown them, that though they can take Portugal from the Portuguese, it will not be entirely

1. An allusion to Conway's eagerness for battle; see *post* 4 Oct. 1762.

2. The Duke of Bedford, then ambassador at Paris (HW).

3. The Duchess dined at Rochester the 30th, passed through Canterbury 1 Oct., and arrived at Paris 4 Oct. (*Leinster Corr.* i. 344; MANN vi. 78, n. 4).

4. See Lady Holland to Lady Kildare, 1 Oct., *Leinster Corr.*, loc. cit.

5. For example, South Sea stock fell from 94½ (22 Sept.) to 91 (27 Sept.) to 90 (28 Sept.) (GM 1762, xxxii. 450).

6. See below, postscript, 30 Sept.

7. See MANN vi. 77, n. 1.

8. Albemarle's letter of 13 July to Egremont for example, by which 'the expedition seems very near failing,' was ordered by George III 'to be communicated to no one' but Lord Bute, 'and then to be laid by, for it would be highly improper that either this people, or the enemy should know that every day may bring us Lord Albemarle's retreat' (George III to Bute, n.d., *Letters from George III to Lord Bute 1756–1766*, ed. Sedgwick, 1939, p. 135).

9. From Albemarle to Egremont, 13 and

17 July; see *ante* 9 Sept. 1762, n. 17; MANN vi. 77–8.

10. Through 13 Aug., the day Havana surrendered, the 'killed, wounded, missing, and dead' totalled 1822 (*London Gazette Extraordinary* 30 Sept.).

11. Albemarle's letter to Egremont of 13 July mentions 'the increasing sickness of the troops.' By Oct. 4700 were dead from disease, well over a third of the whole force (J. S. Corbett, *England in the Seven Years' War*, 1907, ii. 282).

12. Colonel, afterwards General Burgoyne, with the Comte de Lippe, commanded the British troops sent to the relief of Portugal (HW). John Burgoyne (1723–92), dramatist and army officer; Lt-Gen. 1777; commander-in-chief in Ireland, 1782–4; M.P. At the time of the taking of Valencia he was Lt-Col., commandant of the 16th Light Dragoons, but was promoted to Col. for this exploit in October (*Army Lists*, 1763, p. 40; Bute to Burgoyne, 2 Nov., in E. B. de Fonblanque, *Political and Military Episodes in the Latter Half of the Eighteenth Century*, 1876, p. 49).

13. The capture of Valencia de Alcántara on 27 Aug.; see MANN vi. 78, n. 3.

so easy to wrest it from the English. Lord Pulteney,[14] and my nephew,[15] Lady Waldegrave's brother, distinguished themselves.[16] I hope your Hereditary Prince is recovering of the wounds[17] in his loins; for they say he is to marry Princess Augusta.[18]

Lady A. has told you, to be sure, that I have been at Park Place.[19] Everything there is in beauty; and, I should think, pleasanter than a campaign in Germany. Your Countess is handsomer than fame; your daughter improving every day; your plantations more thriving than the poor woods about Marburg and Cassel.[20] Chinese pheasants swarm there.—For Lady Cecilia,[21] I assure you, she sits close upon her egg, and it will not be her fault if she does not hatch a hero.[22] We missed all the glories of the installation,[23] and all the false, and all the frowning faces there. Not a knight was absent, but the lame and the deaf.

Your brother, Lady Hertford, and Lord Beauchamp, are gone from Windsor into Suffolk.[24] Henry,[25] who has the genuine in-

14. Only son of William Pulteney, Earl of Bath. He died before his father (HW). He was Lt-Col. in the 85th Foot (*Army Lists*, 1763, p. 150).

15. Edward, only son of Sir Edward Walpole. He died in 1771 (HW). He was Capt. in Burgoyne's regiment, and later Lt-Col. (*Army Lists*, 1763, p. 40).

16. In a letter of 30 Aug. to Egremont (printed *London Gazette* No. 10246, 21–5 Sept.), the Graf von Schaumburg-Lippe, commander-in-chief of the English forces in Portugal, mentions 'the valorous behaviour of the British grenadiers, under Lord Pulteney's command'; and, prior to the action of Valencia, in a letter of 26 June to Charles Townshend, secretary at war (quoted in F. J. Hudleston, *Gentleman Johnny Burgoyne*, 1927, p. 19, from W.O. 1/165), Burgoyne already speaks favourably of Walpole's 'behaviour since his arrival in Portugal, where he has been trusted with a separate command,' and recommends him for promotion to Major (granted 19 March 1763, *Army Lists*, 1765, p. 40).

17. Suffered in a minor battle on 30 Aug. 'The ball entered on the right side, a little above the hip bone, which it grazed; and came out in the back part of his body, about four inches below' (*Lon-*

don Chronicle, 14–16 Sept., xii. 265). The *Chronicle* for 25–8 Sept., xii. 305, reported that the Prince 'continued in a fair way of recovery.'

18. Sister of George III, m. (16 Jan. 1764) Karl Wilhelm Ferdinand, Hereditary Prince of Brunswick-Wolfenbüttel.

19. 20 to 22 or 23 Sept. (*ante* 9, 21 Sept. 1762).

20. Enemy strongholds besieged by the Allied army.

21. Lady Henrietta Cecilia Johnston, who had married Col. James Johnston 4 May (*ante* 31 July 1762 and n. 6).

22. She had three children: Caroline Georgina (ca 1764–1823), m. (1780) Francis Evelyn Anderson; Hester Maria, who died in her infancy; and Henry George (1766–1809), army officer (CHUTE 474, n. 10).

23. An installation [22 Sept. at Windsor] of Knights of the Garter (HW): Prince William Henry (later D. of Gloucester) and Lord Bute (*London Chronicle* 23–5 Sept., xii. 298). A detailed account of the ceremony is given ibid. 28–30 Sept., xii. 313–15.

24. To visit their seat at Sudbourne (*ante* 21 Sept. 1762).

25. [The Hon. (after 1793, Lord)] Henry Seymour Conway [(1746–1830), later known as Lord Henry Seymour], second son of

difference of a *Harry Conway,* would not stir from Oxford[26] for those pageants. Lord Beauchamp showed me a couple of his letters, which have more natural humour and cleverness than is conceivable. They have the ease and drollery of a man of parts who has lived long in the world—and he is scarce seventeen![27]

I am going to Lord Waldegrave's[28] for a few days, and, when your Countess returns from Goodwood,[29] am to meet her at Cecilia's. Lord Strafford,[30] who has been terribly alarmed about my Lady,[31] mentions, with great pleasure, the letters he receives from you. His neighbour and cousin,[32] Lord Rockingham, I hear, is one of the warmest declaimers at Arthur's against the present system.[33] Abuse continues in much plenty, but I have seen none that I thought had wit enough to bear the sea.[34] Good night. There are satiric prints enough to tapestry Westminster Hall.

Yours ever,

Hor. Walpole

Stay a moment: I recollect telling you a lie in my last,[35] which, though of no consequence, I must correct. The Right Reverend Midwife, Thomas Secker,[36] Archbishop, did christen the babe,[37] and not the Bishop of London,[38] as I had been told by matron

Francis, Earl and afterward Marquis of Hertford (HW); M.P. Coventry 1766–74, Midhurst 1774–80, Downton 1780–4.

26. Where he had matriculated 19 Sept. 1761. He received a B.A. 1764, and an M.A. 1767 (Foster, *Alumni Oxon.*).

27. He would be sixteen 15 Dec.

28. James, second Earl of Waldegrave, Knight of the Garter, had married Maria, second daughter of Sir Edward Walpole (HW).

29. In Sussex, seat of the Richmonds.

30. William Wentworth, Earl of Strafford, married Lady Anne Campbell, third daughter of John Duke of Argyll (HW).

31. Lady Strafford suffered from epilepsy, dying in 1785 after falling into the fire during a fit (Ossory ii. 460; Lady Louisa Stuart, *Selections from Her Manuscripts,* ed. Home, Edinburgh, 1899, pp. 43, 46).

32. Rockingham's great-grandmother was a niece of Strafford's great-grandfather, making them third cousins, once removed.

33. Rockingham resigned his office of lord of the Bedchamber 3 Nov., following Devonshire's resignation of his office of lord chamberlain 28 Oct.; see *post* 30 Oct. 1762; Mann vi. 97, n. 18.

34. That is, that was worth sending across the water (see *ante* 28 Nov. 1761).

35. *Ante* 9 Sept. 1762.

36. (1693–1768), Bishop of Oxford 1737; Archbishop of Canterbury 1758. The canard of Secker's having been bred a man-midwife, which HW repeats *post* 16 Dec. 1763, in *Mem. Geo. II* i. 65 and elsewhere, apparently arose from the fact that Secker, descended from dissenting minor gentry, had once studied medicine at Leyden, where he took an M.D. in 1721 (DNB).

37. The Prince of Wales, christened 8 Sept. (*ante* 9 Sept. 1762).

38. Richard Osbaldeston (ibid., n. 26).

authority. Apropos to babes: Have you read Rousseau[39] on education?[40] I almost got through a volume at Park Place, though impatiently; it has more tautology than any of his works, and less eloquence. Sure he has writ more sense and more nonsense than ever any man did of both! All I have yet learned from this work is, that one should have a tutor for one's son to teach him to have no ideas, in order that he may begin to learn his alphabet as he loses his maidenhead.

Thursday noon, 30th.

Io Havannah! Io Albemarle![41] I had sealed my letter, and given it to Harry[42] for the post; when my Lady Suffolk sent me a short note from Charles Townshend, to say the Havannah surrendered on the 12th of August,[43] and that we have taken twelve ships of the line in the harbour.[44] The news came late last night. I do not know a particular more. God grant no more blood be shed! I have hopes again of the peace. My dearest Harry, now we have preserved you to the last moment, do take care of yourself. When one has a whole war to wade through, it is not worthwhile to be careful in any one battle; but it is silly to fling one's self away in the last. Your character is established; Prince Ferdinand's letters are full of encomiums on you;[45] but what will weigh more with you, save yourself for another war, which I doubt you will live to see, and in which you may be superior commander, and have space to display your talents. A second in service is never remembered, whether the honour of the victory be owing to him, or he killed. Turenne[46] would have

39. Jean-Jacques Rousseau (1712–78).

40. *Émile, ou de l'éducation;* an advertisement in the *London Chronicle* 2–4 Sept., xii. 232, reads: 'Just imported . . . *Émile, ou de l'éducation.* Par J. J. Rousseau. 4 Vol. Paris 1762.' HW's copy, published Frankfurt, 1762, is Hazen, *Cat. of HW's Lib.,* No. 818.

41. Commander of the army at Havana.

42. Henry Jones, HW's servant (*ante* 9 Sept. 1762).

43. 13 Aug.; see MANN vi. 82.

44. According to a list in the *London Gazette Extraordinary* 30 Sept., nine ships 'surrendered with the city,' while three

were 'sunk in the entrance of the harbour.'

45. Conway wrote to Devonshire, 9 Sept.: 'What has made me particularly happy in the course of this campaign is that I have through the whole of it been honoured with a great increase of favour and confidence by [Prince Ferdinand] . . . who has employed me a good deal and with such marks of trust and satisfaction as were extremely flattering' (Chatsworth MSS, 416/79).

46. Henri de la Tour d'Auvergne (1611–75), Vicomte de Turenne; general; Maréchal de France.

a very short paragraph, if the Prince of Condé[47] had been general, when he fell.[48] Adieu.

To CONWAY, Monday 4 October 1762

Printed from *Works* v. 92–3.

Arlington Street, October 4, 1762.

I AM concerned to hear you have been so much out of order,[1] but should rejoice your sole command disappointed you,[2] if this late cannonading business[3] did not destroy all my little prospects. Can one believe the French negotiators are sincere, when their marshals are so false?[4] What vexes me more is to hear you seriously tell your brother that you are always unlucky, and lose all opportunities of fighting. How can you be such a child? You cannot, like a German, love fighting for its own sake. No: you think of the mob of London, who, if you had taken Peru, would forget you the first Lord Mayor's Day, or for the first hyena that comes to town. How can one build on virtue and on fame too? When do they ever go together? In my passion, I could almost wish you were as worthless and as

47. Louis II de Bourbon (1621–86), Prince de Condé, called 'le Grand Condé'; general.

48. While preparing to make an attack upon Montecuculli at Sasbach. Turenne served under Condé at the victories of Freiburg (1644) and Nördlingen (1645), but later fought against him, defeating him at the Faubourg Saint-Antoine (1652) and at the battle of the Dunes (1658) (M. Weygand, *Turenne*, 1929, pp. 51, 67, 89, 238–9).

———

1. Conway wrote to Devonshire 9 Sept., that 'I have had a little illness which has discomposed and interrupted me in a thousand things' (Chatsworth MSS, 416/ 79).

2. In the same letter Conway wrote that he had at the end of August been charged by Prince Ferdinand with the siege of Marburg. 'I had opened ground, begun to fire on the place and should I believe have probably had it in a few days,' when developments elsewhere led the Prince

to call him back. 'You may imagine I was mortified not a little, but there was no remedy.' See Sir Reginald Savory, *His Britannic Majesty's Army in Germany during the Seven Years' War*, Oxford, 1966, pp. 403, 408 and n. 1.

3. Between Granby's forces and those of Gen. Zastrow, 21 Sept., near Amöneburg, reported in the *London Gazette* No. 10249, 2–5 Oct., from The Hague: 'The whole affair lasted fourteen hours, without one moment's intermission.' Granby's account of the 'furious cannonading between the two armies on the 21st past across the Ohm' is mentioned by Yorke in his 'Advices' from The Hague, 1 Oct. (BM Add. MSS 32943, f. 1). See also HW to Mann 3 Oct. 1762, MANN vi. 86.

4. 'The Prince of Soubise's letter to my Lord Granby, that the peace would be concluded by the 25th, and then attacking him the 21st was very extraordinary' (Newcastle to Yorke 5 Oct., BM Add. MSS 32943, f. 56).

great as the King of Prussia! If conscience is a punishment, is not it a reward too? Go to that silent tribunal, and be satisfied with its sentence.

I have nothing new to tell you. The Havannah is more likely to break off the peace than to advance it. We are not in a humour to give up the world; *anzi,* are much more disposed to conquer the rest of it. We shall have some cannonading here, I believe, if we sign the peace. Mr Pitt, from the bosom of his retreat, has made Beckford[5] mayor. The Duke of Newcastle, if not taken in again, will probably end his life as he began it—at the head of a mob.[6] Personalities and abuse, public and private, increase to the most outrageous degree, and yet the town is at the emptiest. You may guess what will be the case in a month. I do not see at all into the storm: I do not mean that there will not be a great majority to vote anything;[7] but there are times when even majorities cannot do all they are ready to do. Lord Bute has certainly great luck, which is something in politics, whatever it is in logic: but whether peace or war, I would not give him much for the place he will have this day twelve-month. Adieu! The watchman goes past one in the morning; and as I have nothing better than reflections and conjectures to send you, I may as well go to bed.

5. William Beckford, elected lord mayor of London 29 Sept. (*London Chronicle* 28–30 Sept., xii. 317–18). HW writes in *Mem. Geo. III* i. 153, that his being elected was 'a mark of their [the nation's] good-will to his friend, Mr Pitt.'

6. HW wrote in *Mem. Geo. II* i. 163 that Newcastle 'early distinguished himself for the House of Hanover, and in the last years of Queen Anne retained a great mob of people to halloo in that cause.'

7. The administration was anxious to secure a majority in the House of Commons to approve the Peace; see *post* 13 Oct. 1762, nn. 1, 4. HW is alluding to the corruption of the House and charges, with great exaggeration, in *Mem. Geo. III* i. 157 that later on 'in a single fortnight a vast majority was purchased.'

From HERTFORD, Wednesday 13 October 1762

Printed for the first time from a photostat of BM Add. MSS 23218, f. 78.

London, October 13th 1762.

Dear Horry,

MR Fox[1] undertakes the management of the House of Commons and keeps the place he now has,[2] his health, as he is pleased to say, not permitting him to accept the Seals;[3] Mr Grenville[4] retires quietly to the Admiralty and is succeeded by Lord Halifax,[5] who possibly may keep the government of Ireland till a new arrangement takes place; at least no successor is yet named for him.

The armies in Germany remain as they did;[6] my brother I hear is well. We go into the country on Saturday and are sorry our time and business will not allow us to see you and Strawberry before we go.

When Mr Fox is out and the Duke of Newcastle is in you shall let me know it. The Parliament is really to meet on the 11th.[7] I remain, dear Horry,

Always most truly yours,

HERTFORD

The Duke of Bedford is I hear doing as well in France as he did in Ireland, with the advantage of being more popular there.

1. Henry Fox. The King, at Bute's suggestion, had offered him the leadership of the House of Commons on 7 Oct.; he kissed hands for his new post on the 13th (Lord Ilchester, *Henry Fox*, 1920, ii. 189–90, 199). The object of the change was to force the projected peace through a recalcitrant House of Commons.

2. Paymaster-General of the Forces, which he had held since 1757 and kept until 1765.

3. The King had pressed him to take the Seals as secretary of state, but Fox told him that 'my declining health would not admit of my taking the Seals and acting a busy part in the House of Commons too' (ibid. ii. 190).

4. George Grenville. He had been leader of the House of Commons since Oct. 1761, and had succeeded Bute as secretary of state for the north in May 1762, but his resistance to certain sections of the projected treaty determined the King and Bute to remove him to a less sensitive office. He accepted the change with little enthusiasm; see *Letters from George III to Lord Bute 1756–1766*, ed. Sedgwick, 1939, p. 145; *Grenville Papers* i. 451–2, 482–5.

5. Who, though still lord lieutenant of Ireland (which he remained until April 1763), had been first lord of the Admiralty since June. He served as secretary of state until 1765.

6. 'The situation of the armies in Hesse continues upon the same footing along the Ohme and Lahne, the French having been constantly disappointed in their attempts to open a communication with Cassel' (*London Gazette*, No. 10251, 9–12 Oct.).

7. Parliament had been prorogued 9

From CONWAY, ca Sunday 17 October 1762

Missing; answered *post* 29 Oct. 1762. Dated midway between HW's letters to Conway of 4 Oct. and 29 Oct. by HW's mentioning in the later letter Conway's taking kindly his philosophy in the earlier.

To HERTFORD, ca Thursday 28 October 1762

Missing; answered *post* 30 Oct. 1762.

To CONWAY, Friday 29 October 1762

Printed from *Works* v. 93–6.

Strawberry Hill, Oct. 29, 1762.

YOU take my philosophy[1] very kindly, as it was meant; but I suppose you smile a little in your sleeve to hear me turn moralist. Yet why should not I? Must every absurd young man prove a foolish old one? Not that I intend, when the latter term is quite arrived, to profess preaching; nor should, I believe, have talked so gravely to you, if your situation had not made me grave. Till the campaign is ended, I shall be in no humour to smile. For the war, when it will be over, I have no idea.[2] The peace is a jack-o'lantern that dances before one's eyes, is never approached, and at best seems ready to lead some folks into a woeful quagmire.

As your brother was in town, and I had my intelligence from him,[3] I concluded you would have the same, and therefore did not tell you of this last revolution, which has brought Mr Fox[4] again upon the scene.[5] I have been in town but once since; yet learned

Sept. to 9 Nov., but on 17 Sept. the Cabinet ordered it prorogued again until the 11th; however, before this order could be carried into effect, the Cabinet issued (3 Nov.) a new order proroguing Parliament till the 25th (*Journals of the House of Commons* xxix. 352; *London Chronicle* 4–6 Nov., xii. 448).

1. In his letter to Conway *ante* 4 Oct. 1762; Conway's reply is missing.
2. The preliminary treaty of peace between England, France, and Spain was signed at Fontainebleau 3 Nov. (MANN vi. 95 and n. 1).
3. In his letter to HW *ante* 13 Oct. 1762.
4. Henry Fox.
5. See ibid.

enough to confirm the opinion I had conceived, that the building totters, and that this last buttress will but push on its fall. Besides the clamorous opposition already encamped, the world talks of another, composed of names not so often found in a mutiny. What think you of the great Duke,[6] and the little Duke,[7] and the old Duke,[8] and the Derbyshire Duke,[9] banded together against the favourite?[10] If so, it proves the Court, as the late Lord G——[11] wrote to the mayor of Litchfield,[12] will have a majority in everything but numbers. However, my letter is a week old before I write it: things may have changed since last Tuesday. Then the prospect was *des plus* gloomy. Portugal at the eve of being conquered[13]—Spain preferring a diadem to the mural[14] crown of the Havannah—a squadron taking horse for Naples, to see whether King Carlos[15] has any more private bowels than public, whether he is a better father than brother.[16] If what I heard yesterday be true, that the

6. Of Cumberland (HW).

7. Of Bedford (HW).

8. Of Newcastle (HW).

9. Of Devonshire (HW).

10. John Stuart Earl of Bute (HW). Writing to Bute ca 5 Oct. of Devonshire's refusal to attend Council (see *post* 30 Oct. 1762, n. 7), George III expressed his opinion that 'this meant open opposition to the Crown,' and that this step had the approval of Cumberland and Newcastle (*Letters from George III to Lord Bute 1756–1766*, ed. Sedgwick, 1939, p. 143; see also Newcastle to Charles Yorke 25 Oct., printed *Hardwicke Corr.* iii. 426). The rumour of Bedford's being in collusion with the three other Dukes presumably arose from reports of differences between him and the administration over the handling of the peace negotiations: 'The D. of Bedford seems ready to yield everything, and indeed give reason to the voice now of faction' (George III to Bute 16 Oct., Sedgwick, op. cit. 147); 'A letter is arrived from the D. of Bedford which gives me great concern . . . the directions, or sentiments of a Court are never disputed by a minister, I wish the Duke had some friend that would try to prevent his continuing so ill-humoured or the negotiations probably will suffer by it' (idem to idem 23 Oct., ibid. 150–1). Bedford's political agent, Rigby, was dis-

patched to Paris 26 Oct. (*post* 30 Oct. 1762; MANN vi. 92, n. 9).

11. Presumably John Leveson Gower (1694–1754), 2d Bn Gower, cr. (1746) E. Gower.

12. In Staffordshire. Lord Gower was lord lieutenant of Staffordshire 1742–54.

13. 'It is this day rumoured that the King, with his prime minister, hath fled from Lisbon' ('Extract of a letter from The Hague, Oct. 21,' *London Chronicle* 23–6 Oct., xii. 408). 'We learn from Lisbon, that that unhappy city is under the utmost confusion; and that every person is secreting their most valuable effects' (*Daily Adv.* 26 Oct.).

14. I.e., 'embattled' (OED *sub* 'mural' a[1] 1b).

15. Charles III (1716–88), King of Spain 1759–88.

16. His son was King of Naples, his sister Queen of Portugal. HW wrote to Mann 9 Nov. 1762 (MANN vi. 95) that prior to the signing of the preliminary treaty 3 Nov. (n. 2 above), 'a bombarding fleet was destined' to Naples, which manœuvre, he believed, had induced Spain to relinquish her hopes of annexing Portugal. In wondering whether Charles 'has any more private bowels than public,' HW may be thinking of Charles's reaction, as reported to him by Mann 31 July 1762 (MANN vi. 51), to the news of the

Parliament is to be put off till the 24th,[17] it does not look as if they were ready in the green-room, and despised catcalls.

You bid me send you the flower of brimstone, the best things published in this season of outrage. I should not have waited for orders, if I had met with the least tolerable morsel. But this opposition ran stark mad at once, cursed, swore, called names, and has not been one minute cool enough to have a grain of wit. Their prints are gross, their papers scurrilous; indeed the authors abuse one another more than anybody else. I have not seen a single ballad or epigram. They are as seriously dull as if the controversy was religious. I do not take in a paper of either side, and being very indifferent, the only way of being impartial, they shall not make me pay till they make me laugh. I am here quite alone, and shall stay a fortnight longer, unless the Parliament prorogued lengthens my holidays. I do not pretend to be so indifferent, to have so little curiosity, as not to go and see the Duke of Newcastle frightened *for* his country—the only thing that never yet gave him a panic. Then I am still such a schoolboy, that though I could guess half their orations, and know *all* their meaning, I must go and hear Cæsar and Pompey scold in the Temple of Concord. As this age is to make such a figure hereafter, how the Gronoviuses[18] and Warburtons[19] would despise a senator that deserted the forum when the masters

loss of the Spanish register ship, the *Hermione*: 'The case is that he was so struck with the news that he hardly spoke for two days.'

17. On 3 Nov. the Cabinet ordered Parliament to be prorogued to the 25th, after its having initially been prorogued to the 9th (*ante* 13 Oct. 1762, n. 7).

18. A family of Dutch classical scholars; the most famous were the philologists Joannes Fridericus (1611–71) and his son Jacobus (1645–1716). HW owned Joannes's edition of Caius Plinius Secundus, *Naturalis historiæ tomus primus*, Leyden, 1699 (Hazen, *Cat. of HW's Lib.*, No. 2207:34), and Jacobus's editions of Titus Livius, *Historiarum quod extat*, Amsterdam, 1679 (ibid., No. 2207:22), and Herodotus, *Historiarum libri IX*, Leyden, 1715 (ibid., No. 3815). See A. J. van der Aa, *Biographisch woordenboek der Nederlanden*, Haarlem, 1852–78, v. 134–7.

19. William Warburton (1698–1779), Bishop of Gloucester 1759, writer on the-ological history, notorious for his attacks upon his scholarly contemporaries. HW wrote in his 'Short Notes' for 1762 that 'I had been told [by John Hawkins, for one, in a letter of 1 March 1762] that Bishop Warburton resented something in the chapter of architecture in . . . my *Anecdotes of Painting*, and that he intended to abuse me in the new edition of Mr Pope's works which he proposed to have printed at Birmingham' (GRAY i. 38). The Bishop's resentment was unjustified (ibid. i. 39–40, n. 265), and HW subsequently calls him in various places 'all-arrogant and absurd' (ibid. i. 39), a 'turncoat hypocritic infidel' (MONTAGU ii. 150), etc. It is possible that HW is also referring here to John Warburton (1682–1759), herald and antiquary, author of *London and Middlesex Illustrated by . . . Names, Residence, Genealogy, and Coat Armour of the Nobility, Principal Merchants*, etc., 1749; HW's copy is Hazen, *Cat. of HW's Lib.*, No. 2979.

of the world harangued! For, as this age is to be historic, so of course it will be a standard of virtue too; and we, like our wicked predecessors the Romans, shall be quoted, till our very ghosts blush, as models of patriotism and magnanimity. What lectures will be read to poor children on this era! Europe taught to tremble, the great King humbled, the treasures of Peru diverted into the Thames, Asia subdued by the gigantic Clive! for in that age men were near seven feet high; France suing for peace at the gates of Buckingham House, the steady wisdom of the Duke of Bedford drawing a circle round the Gallic monarch, and forbidding him to pass it till he had signed the cession of America;[20] Pitt more eloquent than Demosthenes, and trampling on proffered pensions like—I don't know who;[21] Lord Temple sacrificing a brother[22] to the love of his country; Wilkes[23] as spotless as Sallust,[24] and the Flamen[25] Churchill[26] knocking down the foes of Britain with statues of the gods![27]—Oh! I am out of breath with eloquence and prophecy, and truth and lies: my narrow chest was not formed to hold inspiration; I must return to piddling with my painters: those lofty subjects are too much for me. Good night!

Yours ever,

HOR. WALPOLE

20. By Articles II and VI of the preliminary treaty (n. 2 above), France ceded to England Canada and all the territory she had previously claimed east of the Mississippi, except New Orleans.

21. A thrust at Pitt for accepting, after his resignation as secretary of state in Oct. 1761, a pension of £3000 a year for three lives, as well as the title of Baroness Chatham for his wife (see Chatham Corr. ii. 151–3; ante 10 Oct. 1761).

22. George Grenville, from whom Lord Temple had become estranged after resigning office with Pitt in Oct. 1761; Grenville remained treasurer of the navy, and accepted the lead in the House of Commons. On 17 Oct. 1761, Bute had told Hardwicke 'that Geo. G. had teased him out of his life for these two days past. That his brother, my Lord Temple, was most hostile and outrageous against him; that he had deserted the family; that he would never let him come within his doors, nor see his face more' (Hardwicke

to Newcastle 17 Oct. 1761, BM Add. MSS 32929, f. 334). They were reconciled in 1765 (post 20 May 1765).

23. John Wilkes (1727–97), author of the scurrilous, anti-administration North Briton (see ante 9 Sept. 1762).

24. Caius Sallustius Crispus (86–34 B.C.), Roman historian.

25. Quintus Claudius Flamen (fl. 209–206 B.C.), Roman general, whose interception of letters to Hannibal saved Rome, 207 B.C. (NBG).

26. Charles Churchill [1731–64] the poet (HW), collaborator with Wilkes on the North Briton.

27. The editor of The Political Controversy or Weekly Magazine, 1762–3, writes in No. II, 26 July 1762 (i. 44, n.) that as Churchill 'is of a robust and athletic make and constitution, some of his enemies . . . have favoured him with the appelation of a bully; and sometimes declared their opinion of his readiness to pull the cassock off in case of an affront

PS. I forgot to tell you that Gideon,[28] who is dead worth more than the whole land of Canaan, has left the reversion of all his milk and honey, after his son[29] and daughter[30] and their children, to the Duke of Devonshire, without insisting on his taking the name, or even being circumcised.[31]

Lord Albemarle is expected home in December.[32] My nephew Keppel[33] is Bishop of Exeter,[34] not of the Havannah, as you may imagine,[35] for his mitre was promised the day before the news came.[36]

---

and drop all the consequence of the clergyman, to assume the spirit of the *bruiser';* while HW, in *Mem. Geo. III* i. 143, characterizes Churchill as 'this bacchanalian priest . . . protecting his gown by the weight of his fist.'

28. Sampson Gideon (1699 – 17 Oct. 1762), Jewish financier. He had left the reversion of his estates, valued at £580,000, to the Duke of Devonshire (who was one of his executors, with a legacy of £1000), if his own children died without issue (John Nichols, *Illustrations of the Literary History of the Eighteenth Century*, 1817–58, vi. 283).

29. Sir Sampson Gideon (afterwards Eardley), 1st Bt (*ante* 20 July 1761), m. (1766) Maria Marowe Wilmot (1743–94), by whom he had two sons and three daughters.

30. Gideon had two daughters: the elder 'died unmarried in 1784' (John Nichols, *Literary Anecdotes of the Eighteenth Century*, 1812–15, ix. 643; GM 1784, liv pt ii. 638), while the younger, Elizabeth (ca 1739–83), m. (1757) William Hall Gage, 2d Vct Gage, by whom she had no issue.

31. Gideon had married Jane Ermell, daughter of an English Protestant, and though he himself was never converted to Christianity, he raised his children as Christians; see HW to Richard Bentley 9 July 1754, CHUTE 178–9.

32. He returned home in Feb. 1763 (*London Chronicle* 19–22 Feb. 1763, xiii. 184).

33. Frederick Keppel, youngest brother

of George Earl of Albemarle, who commanded at taking the Havannah, had married Laura, eldest daughter of Sir Edward Walpole (HW).

34. 'The Hon. and Rev. Dr Keppel, brother to the Earl of Albemarle has kissed the King's hand, on his being appointed Bishop of Exeter' (*London Chronicle* 14–16 Oct. 1762, xii. 369).

35. Keppel had three brothers commanding at the taking of Havana: Lord Albemarle, commander of the army and 'chief favourite' of the influential Duke of Cumberland, who was 'transported' at the news of Albemarle's success (*Mem. Geo. II* i. 82; MANN vi. 94 and n. 15); Capt. (afterwards Admiral) Augustus Keppel, commodore and second-in-command of the navy; and Maj.-Gen. William Keppel (ibid. vi. 82 and n. 4).

36. The news had come 29 Sept. (*ante* 28 Sept. 1762, postscript 30 Sept.). HW here wishes to refute the notion that the preferment had been bestowed upon Keppel because of the success of his brothers at Havana; Keppel (through his father-in-law, Sir Edward Walpole) had applied unsuccessfully for a bishopric in 1761 (*Chatham Corr.* ii. 135). In Jan. 1762 George III had pronounced Keppel 'very fit for the Deanery of Exeter' (Sedgwick, op. cit. 79), and upon the death of Keppel's predecessor as Bishop, George Lavington, on 13 Sept. (*London Chronicle* 14–16 Sept., xii. 270), Keppel was presumably a leading candidate to replace him.

From HERTFORD, Saturday 30 October 1762

Printed for the first time from a photostat of BM Add. MSS 23218, f. 79.

Ragley, October 30th 1762.

Dear Horry,

I THANK you for your letter;[1] your intelligence is always news in Warwickshire, whatever you may think of it in Middlesex, and we rejoice when we can discover your hand in the postbag.

My brother in his last letter[2] desires I will provide for his return to England when the campaign is over,[3] to which he thinks he has an equitable claim, as he was the only English Lt-General who stayed in Germany last winter. Having occasion since I received his letter to write to Charles Townshend,[4] I hope you will approve my having mentioned it to him as a thing we should expect if the continuance of the war made it necessary for Government to come to any resolution about the winter quarters of that part of our army. Shall we have peace or not?[5] I hear Mr Rigby[6] is gone to Paris.

The Duke of Devonshire's resignation[7] is earlier than I expected it.

1. Missing.
2. Missing.
3. Conway wrote to Devonshire, 2 Nov.: 'You ask me whether I don't think of going to England this winter and if I should not take my precautions early. I wrote to my brother on that head some time ago' (Chatsworth MSS, 416/80). Following Hertford's advice, Conway had also written a letter to Lord Bute inquiring in general terms about his future in the peace-time establishment (ibid.); Bute's non-committal reply, the 'driest' Conway had ever seen, as he characterized it in a letter to Hertford of 29 Oct. (MS now WSL), made him suspect that he was not in fashion and therefore he begged Hertford in a letter of 2 Nov. (MS now WSL) to see the matter of his return to England 'secured for me if possible *immediately;* Lord Granby will or has transmitted me among those who apply and he acknowledges *my right,* as being the only lieutenant-general who stayed here last

winter. However, as he advises me to apply to my friends in England, I am doubtful whether he will lay any stress upon my claim and my brethren may perhaps be pressing and have friends of consequence.' The permission was apparently granted, and Conway started for home, but was recalled by Granby's illness and was left in Germany to bring home the troops, an honour which he felt to be a slightly veiled persecution, particularly since he was subjected to a series of rebukes from the government at home for his conduct (MANN vi. 103 and n. 17; Conway to Hertford 2, 23 Feb. 1763, MSS now WSL).

4. At this time secretary at war. Hertford's letter has not been found.

5. See *ante* 29 Oct. 1762, n. 2.

6. Richard Rigby, Bedford's political agent. He had left for Paris 26 Oct. (ibid., n. 10).

7. He had resigned as lord chamberlain on 28 Oct. before the King had a chance

Lady Hertford has not been well for some days, but is now some-thing better.

Next week we expect Lord and Lady Powis[8] at Ragley: the fol-lowing week we intend being in town, though we suppose we shall hear the Parliament is further adjourned.[9] Gideon's will[10] is un-accountable in every part of it. I remain, dear Horry,

Always most truly and affectionately yours,

HERTFORD

From CONWAY, Saturday 19 February 1763

Missing; answered *post* 28 Feb. 1763.

To CONWAY, Monday 28 February 1763

Printed from *Works* v. 96–7.

Strawberry Hill, February 28, 1763.

YOUR letter of the 19th[1] seems to postpone your arrival rather than advance it;[2] yet Lady A. tells me that to her you talk of being here in ten days.[3] I wish devoutly to see you, though I am not departing myself; but I am impatient to have your disagreeable function[4] at an end, and to know that you enjoy yourself after such fatigues, dangers, and ill-requited services.[5] For any public satisfac-

to dismiss him, and was dismissed from the Privy Council 3 Nov., thus concluding a crisis that had begun when he refused to attend a Cabinet meeting to consider the peace terms at the beginning of the month (*Letters from George III to Lord Bute 1756–1766*, ed. Sedgwick, 1939, pp. 143, 152–3, 155). For full particulars about Devonshire's resignation, see L. B. Namier, *England in the Age of the American Revolution*, 1961, pp. 369–74.

8. Henry Arthur Herbert (ca 1703–72), cr. (1743) Bn Herbert of Chirbury, and (1748) E. of Powis; m. (1751) Barbara Herbert (1735–86).

9. See *ante* 29 Oct. 1762, n. 17.
10. See ibid., n. 28.

———

1. Missing.
2. In his letter to Hertford of 23 Feb. (MS now WSL), Conway writes that 'I don't exactly know the time I shall leave.'
3. Conway's letter to Lady Ailesbury is missing. He reached England 1 April (*Daily Adv.* 2 April; MONTAGU ii. 55).
4. The re-embarkation of the British troops from Flanders after the peace (HW), which Conway supervised.
5. See *ante* 30 Oct. 1762, n. 3.

tion you will receive in being at home, you must not expect much. Your mind was not formed to float on the surface of a mercenary world. My prayer (and my belief) is, that you may always prefer what you always have preferred, your integrity to success. You will then laugh, as I do, at the attacks and malice of faction or ministers. I taste of both;[6] but, as my health is recovered,[7] and my mind does not reproach me, they will perhaps only give me an opportunity, which I should never have sought, of proving that I have some virtue—and it will not be proved in the way they probably expect. I have better evidence than by hanging out the tattered ensigns of patriotism. But this and a thousand other things I shall reserve for our meeting. Your brother has pressed me much to go with him, if he goes, to Paris.[8] I take it very kindly, but have excused myself, though I have promised either to accompany him for a short time at first, or to go to him if he should have any particular occasion for me:[9] but my resolution against ever appearing in any public light is unalterable. When I wish to live less and less in the world here, I cannot think of mounting a new stage at Paris. At this moment I am alone here, while everybody is balloting in the House of Commons. Sir John Philips proposed a commission of accounts, which has been converted into a select committee of 21, eligible by ballot.[10]

6. In his letter to Montagu of 20 Dec. 1762, HW complains that 'my poor neutrality . . . subjects me . . . to affronts,' giving an example of one such affront, committed by Princess Amelia at one of her loo parties (MONTAGU ii. 49–50).

7. In December HW had complained of the 'flying gout' in his stomach and breast, but by the end of January he was quite recovered, thanks, he thought, to extremely cold weather (MANN vi. 110, 116).

8. As ambassador (HW). Hertford was named ambassador to France in April as part of the changeover in the ministry following the resignation of Bute. He arrived there in Oct. (ibid. vi. 130; post 9 April, 15 Oct. 1763).

9. HW did not go to France until Sept. 1765, just after Hertford had left.

10. On 11 Feb. Philipps, apparently acting on his own initiative, moved 'that this House . . . resolve itself into a committee of the whole House to consider of the most proper and effectual method of

examining' the expenditure of public funds during the war (Journals of the House of Commons, xxix. 452; Bedford Corr. iii. 208–9); and on 22 Feb., in the committee of the whole, he proposed a commission of accounts, his aim, as a supporter of Bute, apparently being to discomfit Newcastle (though he denies this in a letter to Barrington, 10 Feb., BM Add. MSS 32946, f. 369). However, his proposal met with little enthusiasm from either side; see Letters from George III to Lord Bute 1756–1766, ed. Sedgwick, 1939, p. 190 and Mem. Geo. III i. 191. He subsequently substituted Dashwood's proposal to appoint a select committee to examine all accounts (Bedford Corr. iii. 209; Journals of the House of Commons, xxix. 491). On 23 Feb. it was resolved 'that the number of the said committee be one-and-twenty,' and that it 'be chosen by way of balloting' (ibid. xxix. 491, 513, 527). The half-measure of a select committee was proposed by the administration as a means of 'throwing off the

As the ministry is not predominant in the *affections* of mankind, some of them may find a jury elected that will not be quite so complaisant as the House is in general when their votes are given *openly*.[11] As many may be glad of this opportunity, I shun it; for I should scorn to do anything in secret, though I have some enemies that are not quite so generous.

You say you have seen the *North Briton* in which I make a capital figure.[12] Wilkes, the author, I hear, says, that if he had thought I should have taken it so well, he would have been damned before he would have written it—but I am not sore where I am not sore.

The theatre at Covent Garden has suffered more by riots than even Drury Lane.[13] A footman of Lord Dacre has been hanged for murdering the butler.[14] George Selwyn had great hand in bringing him to confess it. That Selwyn should be a capital performer in a scene of that kind is not extraordinary:[15] I tell it you for the strange coolness which the young fellow, who was but nineteen, expressed: as he was

unpopularity of rejecting' Philipps' proposal for a commission (George III to Bute, ca 22 Feb., Sedgwick, loc. cit.), and, as was intended, the inquiry died in this committee.

11. But, as it turned out, the members of the committee (listed in *Journals of the House of Commons* xxix. 527) were almost all supporters of the ministry.

12. The *North Briton* No. 36, 5 Feb., contains a lengthy attack on HW's panegyric on Fox, written originally in 1748 as a letter to Lady Caroline Fox, and published with minor changes as a *World Extraordinary* on 4 Jan. 1757 (SELWYN 131, n. 2). The attack implies, among other things, that HW is a flatterer and a bad judge of character, while reserving its sharpest barbs for Fox. Apparently HW drew this attack intentionally upon himself and Fox: 'When Lord Holland was engaged in his bitter persecution of the Whigs under Lord Bute, I sent an anonymous letter to Wilkes, pointing out a very advantageous character of Lord Holland that I had formerly written in the paper called *The World*, and inciting the *North Briton* to take notice both of the author and the subject of the character. Wilkes caught at the notice, said but little of me, and fell severely on Lord Holland, as I had foreseen he would' (*Mem. Geo. III* ii.

20n). HW had been one of the objects of the persecution of the Whigs by Fox; when in Nov. HW had failed to vote for the ministry after Fox's offer of the Rangership of St James's and Hyde Parks to his nephew, Lord Orford, Fox had retaliated by holding up the payments of HW's place as usher of the Exchequer. See R.W. Ketton-Cremer, *Horace Walpole*, 1940, pp. 238–40; SELWYN 341.

13. 'The damage done to Covent Garden . . . was the greatest ever known' (*Daily Adv.* 26 Feb.). The riots (25 and 26 Jan. at Drury Lane, and 24 Feb. at Covent Garden) were caused by the managers' refusing to admit spectators at half price after the third act. See MANN vi. 120–1, and nn. 7–12.

14. On 24 Feb., at the Old Bailey, Daniel Blake 'was capitally convicted . . . for the wilful murder [1 Feb.] of John Murcott, late butler to Lord Dacre' (*Daily Adv.* 2, 3, 25 Feb.). He was executed 26 Feb. (ibid. 28 Feb.). For a full account of the murder, see GM 1763, xxxiii. 94.

15. HW wrote in 1752 that Selwyn 'loves nothing upon earth so well as a criminal except the execution of him' (MONTAGU i. 133), and in 1750 that his 'passion is to see coffins and corpses and executions' (MANN iv. 181).

writing his confession, 'I murd—' he stopped, and asked, 'How do you spell *murdered?*'

Mr Fox is much better than at the beginning of the winter;[16] and both his health and power seem to promise a longer duration than people expected. Indeed I think the latter is so established, that Lord Bute would find it more difficult to remove him, than he did his predecessors, and may even feel the effects of the weight he has made over to him;[17] for it is already obvious that Lord Bute's levee is not the present path to fortune.[18] Permanence is not the complexion of these times—a distressful circumstance to the votaries of a court, but amusing to us spectators. Adieu!

Yours ever,

Hor. Walpole

From Hertford, Saturday 9 April 1763

Printed for the first time from a photostat of BM Add. MSS 23218, ff. 84–5.

London, April 9th 1763.

Dear Horry,

IT is not a panic or a sudden thought upon which Lord Bute retires, but a measure determined some time ago,[1] though my Lord has certainly failed in judgment in making his resolution

16. In Oct. Fox had declined taking the seals as secretary of state because of his health (see *ante* 13 Oct. 1762 and n. 3); in Jan. his wife wrote that 'he is far from well and very nervous' (*Leinster Corr.* i. 358; Selwyn 170).

17. However, in April Fox resigned as leader of the House to take a peerage, which in effect marked the end of his political career; see *post* 9 April 1763.

18. Bute resigned 8 April; see ibid.

———

1. Bute resigned as first lord of the Treasury on 8 April. He had informed the King as early as November 1762 of his desire to resign, had repeatedly declared to his friends his intention of doing so as soon as the peace was concluded,

and had begun arrangements with Fox for executing his decision as early as 2 March. But he did not inform the secretaries of state of his intention until 1 April, nor the world at large until the 6th (*Letters to Henry Fox*, ed. Lord Ilchester, Roxburghe Club, 1915, p. 172; *Letters from George III to Lord Bute 1756–1766*, ed. Sedgwick, 1939, pp. 166, 171, 196–207; *Hardwicke Corr.*, iii. 457; Montagu ii. 59 and n. 2; Mann vi. 128–9; *Mem. Geo. III* i. 201–2). HW, who confuses some details in these transactions, clung to the explanation of panic even after receiving this letter, especially in Montagu ii. 64–5 and Mann vi. 133, but less strongly in *Mem. Geo. III* i. 201–2.

known in a way and at a moment to make it liable to much suspicion.

Lord Bute retires, as he says himself[2] to his friends, not to come in again, and that he has too much spirit to act behind the curtain; that from his attachment to the King he wished to serve him, but that finding his health unequal to the fatigue and his character growing every day by faction's artful means more unpopular, he could not persuade himself to stand between the King and his people and lessen that popularity which his Majesty deserved from them; that therefore when the Ministry was formed, he should retire, leaving the King his best wishes. It is likewise as certain, however incredulous you may be to such an improbable contract, that Mr Fox agreed with Lord Bute, when he undertook the management of the House of Commons for this winter, that he should retire at the end of the sessions,[3] serving as many friends as he could before he left it, and it was stipulated to be kept secret till the Parliament was prorogued and the business done. Lord Hardwicke was at Court yesterday and well received;[4] it is said proposals have been made to him,[5] and that perhaps he may not dine with Opposition next Tuesday.[6] The bearskin,[7] when it is within the reach of politicians, always

---

2. Hertford's account of Bute's explanation for his resignation is very similar to that given by Bute himself to Bedford in a letter of 2 April and to Charles Yorke, the attorney-general, in a long interview on 9 April (*Bedford Corr.* iii. 223–6; *Hardwicke Corr.* iii. 385–8). He had also told the secretaries of state (so they reported) that 'he would take no other place nor remain at all about the Court to have the imputation of being a minister behind the curtain' (ibid. iii. 457). His failure to leave the political scene soon gave him precisely this imputation.

3. It had been agreed, when Fox accepted the leadership of the House of Commons in October 1762, that he should retire with a peerage at the end of the session (Lord Ilchester, *Henry Fox*, 1920, ii. 223, 230, 232; *Hardwicke Corr.* iii. 388; *Bedford Corr.* iii. 224; *Leinster Corr.* i. 363).

4. 'I am just come from the King's levee, where I had determined to go before anything was said of this change, otherwise I should have chose another

day. His Majesty said a very few words civilly as usual, and looked in much better humour than I expected' (Hardwicke to Newcastle 8 April, BM Add. MSS 32948, f. 54, printed in *Hardwicke Corr.* iii. 457).

5. There is no evidence that any proposals were made to Hardwicke at this time. His son Charles, in his account of an interview with Bute on 9 April, explicitly states that no mention was made of his father or the other Opposition leaders (ibid. iii. 388). See also HW to Montagu 14 April, MONTAGU ii. 64.

6. The younger members of the Opposition, with Newcastle's eventual blessing, organized a political dinner club in the winter of 1762–3; see L. B. Namier, *England in the Age of the American Revolution*, 1961, pp. 416–18.

7. Apparently a mat placed under the feet of state officers. In Mann's letter to HW of 10 Jan. 1742 NS, he mentions Braitwitz's honouring him by putting him 'into his state chair in the Great Duke's box' at the opera and giving him 'the

divides them. The Opposition are like the rest of the world, and I suppose may soon be as inconsistent as the Ministers. I wish the King well and easier than I think he will be for some time.

Adieu, dear Horry; you have always my best wishes and I am sorry you have any occasion to form the melancholy party now at Strawberry.[8] Dissolve it as soon as you can and come amongst us for your own and your friends' sakes.

Yours ever,

HERTFORD

To CONWAY, Sunday 1 May 1763

Printed from *Works* v. 97–9.

Strawberry Hill, May 1, 1763.

I FEEL happy at hearing your happiness; but, my dear Harry, your vision is much indebted to your long absence, which

Makes bleak rocks and barren mountains smile.[1]

I mean no offence to Park Place, but the bitterness of the weather makes me wonder how you can find the country tolerable now. This is a May day for the latitude of Siberia! The milkmaids should be wrapped *in the motherly comforts of a swanskin petticoat*.[2] In short, such hard words have passed between me and the north wind today, that, according to the language of the times, I was very near abusing it for coming from Scotland, and to imputing it to Lord Bute. I don't know whether I should not have written a *North Briton* against it, if the printers were not all sent to Newgate, and

state bearskin under my feet' (MANN i. 259).

8. HW had taken his niece, Lady Waldegrave, and her sisters to SH immediately after her husband's death from smallpox 8 April (MANN vi. 126–7; MONTAGU ii. 63).

———

1. A paraphrase of one of HW's favourite lines, from Addison's *A Letter from Italy, to the Right Honourable Charles Halifax*, l. 140: 'And makes her barren rocks and her bleak mountains smile.' HW paraphrases it also to Mann,

20 June 1743 OS (MANN ii. 255) and to Mason, 17 Sept. 1773 (MASON i. 108).

2. HW may be recalling the following passage from Richardson's *Pamela*: 'I bought two flannel undercoats; not so good as my swanskin and fine linen ones, but what will keep me warm, if any neighbour should get me to go out to help 'em to milk, now and then, as sometimes I used to do formerly' (Vol. I, Letter XX). For the May Day celebration by milkmaids see W. S. Lewis, *Three Tours through London in the Years 1748, 1776, 1797*, New Haven, 1941, p. 78.

Mr Wilkes to the Tower—ay, to the Tower, *tout de bon*.[3] The new ministry[4] are trying to make up for their ridiculous insignificance by a *coup d'éclat*. As I came hither yesterday, I do not know whether the particulars I have heard are genuine—but in the Tower he certainly is, taken up by Lord Halifax's warrant for treason;[5] *vide* the *North Briton* of Saturday was sennight. It is said he refused to obey the warrant,[6] of which he asked and got a copy from the two messengers,[7] telling them he did not mean to make his escape, but sending to demand his habeas corpus,[8] which was refused.[9] He then went to Lord Halifax, and thence to the Tower; declaring they should get nothing out of him but what they knew.[10] All his papers have been seized.[11] Lord Chief Justice Pratt,[12] I am told, finds great fault with the wording of the warrant.[13]

3. 'On Friday [29 April], the publisher and printer of the *North Briton*, being taken into custody, were examined at Lord Halifax's office; and on Saturday [30 April] John Wilkes . . . being charged with being concerned in publishing a seditious libel, highly reflecting on the honour and dignity of the Crown, in . . . the North Briton [No. 45, Saturday, 23 April] . . . was brought from his house by two of the King's messengers to Lord Halifax's office, and from thence sent prisoner to the Tower' (*London Chronicle* 30 April – 3 May, xiii. 424). For the nature of the libel, see MANN vi. 136 and n. 20.

4. See MANN vi. 130.

5. There were two principal warrants issued, the first by Halifax authorizing the messengers to seize 'the authors, printers, and publishers' of the libel, and the second by Halifax and Egremont authorizing the close confinement of Wilkes in the Tower (printed *London Chronicle* 5–7 May, xiii. 436–7); also there was a third, issued by Halifax and Egremont, authorizing two additional messengers to transfer Wilkes to the Tower (printed Wilkes, *Correspondence*, ed. Almon, 1805, i. 105).

6. 'It is said, that Mr. Wilkes disputed at first the authority of the messengers to put him under arrest' (*London Chronicle* 30 April – 3 May, xiii. 424).

7. See 'The Case of John Wilkes, Esq. on a Habeas Corpus,' in T. B. Howell, *Complete Collection of State Trials*, 1816–

26, xix. 981–2. The two messengers HW refers to were presumably James Watson and Robert Blackmore, who held Wilkes in custody at his house in Great George Street, prior to taking him to Lord Halifax's house (H. Bleackley, *Life of John Wilkes*, 1917, p. 99). The warrant of arrest itself was directed to Watson, Blackmore, Nathan Carrington, and John Money; of the latter two, Carrington excused himself on account of illness (R. W. Postgate, *That Devil Wilkes*, New York, 1929, p. 53), while Money apparently had become separated from Watson and Blackmore by the time Wilkes was brought under arrest to his house (see Hist. MSS Comm., 10th Report, App. pt i, *Underwood MSS*, 1885, p. 357).

8. In the Court of Common Pleas.

9. It was not refused; however, see below, n. 22.

10. Wilkes wrote to Grafton, 12 Dec. 1767, that upon being examined by Halifax and Egremont at Halifax's house, he had declared that 'at the end of my examination, all the quires of paper on their Lordships' table should be as milk-white as at the beginning' (Wilkes, op. cit. iii. 204).

11. See Bleackley, op. cit. 103–4.

12. Sir Charles Pratt (1714–94), Kt, 1761; cr. (1765) Bn and (1768) E. Camden; lord chief justice of the Common Pleas 1761–6; lord chancellor 1766–70; M.P. Downton 1757–61.

13. Upon examining the copy of the

I don't know how to execute your commission for books of architecture, nor care to put you to expense, which I know will not answer. I have been consulting my neighbour young Mr Thomas Pitt,[14] my present architect: we have all books of that sort here, but cannot think of one which will help you to a cottage or a greenhouse. For the former you should send me your idea, your dimensions;[15] for the latter, don't you rebuild your old one, though in another place? A pretty green-house I never saw; nor without immoderate expense can it well be an agreeable object. Mr Pitt thinks a mere portico without a pediment, and windows removeable in summer, would be the best plan you could have. If so, don't you remember something of that kind, which you liked, at Sir Charles Cotterel's[16] at Rousham? But a fine green-house must be on a more exalted plan. In short, you must be more particular, before I can be at all so.

I called at Hammersmith yesterday about Lady A.'s tubs; one of them is nearly finished, but they will not both be completed these ten days. Shall they be sent to you by water? Good-night to her Ladyship and you, and the Infanta,[17] whose progress in waxen statuary[18] I hope advances so fast, that by next winter she may rival

warrant of arrest obtained from the messengers, Pratt said that he thought 'the warrant . . . a very extraordinary one; I know no law that can authorize it, nor any practice that it can be founded on' ('The Chief Justice's Words on the Warrant,' on the verso of 'a true copy' by J. Watson of the warrant of arrest, BM Add. MSS 32948, f. 170).

14. Afterwards created Lord Camelford (HW). Thomas Pitt (1737–93), cr. (1784) Bn Camelford; M.P. Old Sarum 1761–3, 1774–83; Okehampton 1768–74; nephew of the elder William Pitt. He took a house at Twickenham near HW in 1762. HW wrote Mann 13 April that Pitt 'draws Gothic with taste, is already engaged on the ornaments of my cabinet and gallery' (MANN vi. 25; *ante* 9 Sept. 1762, nn. 32, 34; *post* 9 Aug. 1763; *Strawberry Hill Accounts*, ed. Toynbee, Oxford, 1927, pp. 108–9). HW credits him in 'Des. of SH' with designing the chimney-piece of the Gallery (together with John Chute) and the grated door of the Tribune (*Works* ii. 461, 471). Chute's drawings at Far-

mington show no signs of this collaboration.

15. Later in the year HW wrote that 'the works at Park Place go on bravely; the cottage will be very pretty' (to Montagu 3 Oct. 1763, MONTAGU ii. 104). For a photograph of the cottage as it appeared ca 1900, see Percy Noble, *Park Place*, 1905, p. 40.

16. Sir Charles Cottrell Dormer (d. 1779), Kt; master of the ceremonies. HW and Conway had visited Rousham together in 1760 (MONTAGU i. 290).

17. Anne Seymour Conway.

18. HW records in his 'Book of Visitors,' 1784–96, that 'Mrs Damer gave the first symptom of her talent for statuary, when she was but ten years old. She was reading Spenser, and with bits of wax candle and silk and feathers and tinsel picked out of silks, she made a knight and his esquire, not so long as a finger, in the perfect costumes of the description. A few years after she made a portrait of a shock dog in bas-relief in wax small, and then heads in wax in the manner of Gosset' (BERRY ii. 273).

Rackstrow's[19] old man.[20] Do you know that, though apprised of what I was going to see, it deceived me, and made such impression on my mind, that, thinking on it as I came home in my chariot, and seeing a woman steadfastly at work in a window in Pall Mall, it made me start to see her move. Adieu!

Yours ever,

HOR. WALPOLE

Arlington Street, Monday night.

The mighty commitment set out with a blunder; the warrant directed the printer, and all concerned (unnamed) to be taken up.[21] Consequently Wilkes had his habeas corpus of course, and was committed again; moved for another in the Common Pleas, and is to appear there tomorrow morning.[22] Lord Temple being, by another strain of power, refused admittance to him, said, 'I thought this was the Tower, but find it is the Bastille.'[23] They found among Wilkes's papers an unpublished *North Briton*, designed for last Saturday.[24] It contained advice to the King not to go to St Paul's on

19. Benjamin Rackstrow (d. 1772), sculptor (Rupert Gunnis, *Dictionary of British Sculptors 1660–1851*, Cambridge, Mass., 1954, p. 314).

20. 'A whole figure of an elderly man sitting, cast in plaister of Paris and coloured,' displayed in the 1763 exhibition of the Free Society (HW's MS note in one of his copies of the catalogue, Hazen, *Cat. of HW's Lib.*, No. 3885:3, now WSL). It was 'so very near to life that everybody mistook it for real,' and 'was removed, on having frightened an apothecary' (ibid.). Before it was removed, it was No. 172 in the catalogue, 'a figure of a gentleman, sitting, as large as life.'

21. See above, n. 5. The only person named in the warrant of arrest was Kearsley, the publisher.

22. Though a writ of habeas corpus was granted by Pratt the afternoon of the day of Wilkes's arrest (*London Chronicle* 30 April–3 May, xiii. 424), by the time it was delivered, Wilkes was no longer in the custody of Watson and Blackmore, to whom it was directed, but in the custody of the secretaries of state, so that a new writ had to be obtained. In the meantime the secretaries prepared a new warrant

(mentioned above, n. 5) authorizing the constable of the Tower of London to keep Wilkes under close confinement. By this evasive action Wilkes was kept incommunicado in the Tower until Tuesday, 3 May, when his case was brought up before the Court of Common Pleas (*London Chronicle*, loc. cit.; Bleackley, op. cit. 102, 104–5). For the decision of the Court, see *post* 6 May 1763.

23. Temple was one of the friends to whom Wilkes had sent word the day of his arrest to obtain a writ of habeas corpus. For his zealous efforts in Wilkes's behalf, he was later (7 May) dismissed from the lord lieutenancy of Buckinghamshire, after having first been forced to strip Wilkes of his commission in the militia (5 May) (MANN vi. 138 and nn. 9, 10).

24. The King wrote to Bute, Saturday, 30 April, that 'Balf [the current printer of the *North Briton*] on being taken up . . . declared that the N. Brit. Number 45 was wrote in Mr Wilkes hand as also the one to have been published this morning which he delivered in that rascal's hand' (*Letters from George III to Lord Bute 1756–1766*, ed. Sedgwick, 1939,

the thanksgiving, but to have a snug one in his own chapel; and to let Lord George Sackville carry the sword.[25] There was a dialogue in it too between Fox[26] and Calcraft:[27] the former says to the latter, 'I did not think you would have served me so, Jemmy Twitcher.'[28]

To CONWAY, Friday 6 May 1763

Printed from *Works* v. 99–101.

Arlington Street, May 6, very late, 1763.

THE complexion of the times is a little altered since the beginning of this last winter. Prerogative, that gave itself such airs in November, and would speak to nothing but a Tory, has had a rap this morning that will do it some good, unless it is weak enough to do itself more harm. The judges[1] of the Common Pleas have unani-

p. 232). The *North Briton* which Balf delivered may have been the proof sheets, wrongly numbered and dated, of the issue for 30 April, bearing MS corrections by Wilkes (BM Cat.). This issue was never published; however, it was later clandestinely reprinted in part (and falsely attributed to the SH Press) as a 'Fragment of a North Briton in the Possession of the . . . Earls of Egremont and Halifax. Number XLVI . . . Saturday, April the 30th, 1763' (title reproduced from photostat in Yale Library of the copy now at the University of Chicago; see Hazen, *SH Bibl.* 270–2).

25. 'The humiliating circumstance of giving up so many and important conquests . . . [should not] be attended with parade or ostentation. . . . I hope, therefore, that on the day of thanksgiving for the Peace, his Majesty will only go to chapel, and that all bloody iron swords being now sheathed and laid aside, the peaceful wooden sword of state will be carried by that excellent peace-officer, Lord George Sackville' ('Fragment'). The reference to Sackville alludes to his failure to bring up the British cavalry at the Battle of Minden in 1759 (on the grounds that his superior's orders were contra-

dictory and imprecise), for which he was subsequently dismissed from the service (see *ante* 14 Aug. 1759), and to the King's lenient attitude towards him (see Sedgwick, op. cit. 43; Lord Fitzmaurice, *Life of . . . Shelburne*, 1912, i. 168; Hist. MSS Comm., *Stopford-Sackville MSS*, 1904–10, i. 58).

26. HW had not yet got accustomed to Fox's new title, Lord Holland, which he obtained on 17 April.

27. John Calcraft (1726–72), politician; M.P. Calne 1766–8; Rochester 1768–72.

28. This dialogue is not in the 'Fragment.' The allusion is to Calcraft's turning upon Fox, his long-time patron, to support Shelburne's contention that on becoming a peer, Fox was pledged to relinquish the pay office (Namier and Brooke ii. 172; see also *post* 6 May 1763, n. 4). 'Jemmy Twitcher' is a character in *The Beggar's Opera* who betrays his comrade Macheath.

———

1. Sir Charles Pratt, lord chief justice (*ante* 1 May 1763); Sir Edward Clive (1704–71); Hon. Henry Bathurst, later 2d E. Bathurst and lord chancellor (*post* 7 Nov. 1774); and Sir Henry Gould (1710–94) (*Court and City Register*, 1764, p. 116).

mously dismissed Wilkes from his imprisonment, as a breach of privilege;[2] his offence not being a breach of the peace, only tending to it.[3] The people are in transports; and it will require all the vanity and confidence of those able ministers Lord S. and Mr C.[4] to keep up the spirits of the Court.

I must change this tone, to tell you of the most dismal calamity that ever happened. Lady Molesworth's house, in Upper Brook Street, was burned to the ground between four and five this morning.[5] She herself, two of her daughters, her brother, and six servants, perished. Two other of the young ladies jumped out of the two pair of stairs and garret windows: one broke her thigh, the other (the eldest of all) broke hers too, and has had it cut off. The fifth daughter is much burnt. The French governess leaped from the garret, and was dashed to pieces. Dr Molesworth and his wife, who were there on a visit, escaped; the wife by jumping from the two pair of stairs, and saving herself by a rail; he by hanging by his hands, till a second ladder was brought, after a first had proved too short. Nobody knows how or where the fire began; the catastrophe is shocking beyond what one ever heard; and poor Lady Molesworth, whose character and conduct were the most amiable in the world, is universally lamented. Your good hearts will feel this in the most lively manner.

I go early to Strawberry tomorrow, giving up the new opera,[6]

2. See *London Chronicle* 5–7 May, xiii. 436.

3. 'We are all of opinion that a libel is not a breach of the peace. It tends to the breach of the peace, and that is the utmost' (judgment of the Court as delivered by Lord Chief Justice Pratt, in 'The Case of John Wilkes, Esq. on a Habeas Corpus,' T. B. Howell, *Complete Collection of State Trials*, 1816–26, xix. 990).

4. Probably Lord Shelburne (*post* 2 Dec. 1763) and John Calcraft, whom HW regarded as opportunists interested only in their own advancement. 'Lord Shelburne, who had negotiated between . . . [Fox] and Lord Bute, when Fox undertook the conduct of the House of Commons, had told the Earl that Fox would quit the pay office for a peerage; but Fox had only stipulated to give his support for that reward. . . . The probability was, that Shelburne intended to slip into the pay

office himself' (*Mem. Geo. III* i. 203). 'In the discussion, and during the defending and proving what . . . [Fox] had or had not said relative to the cession of the paymaster's office, Calcraft, his own creature, his cousin raised from extreme indigence and obscurity to enormous wealth . . . took part with Lord Shelburne, and witnessed to the latter's tale' (ibid. i. 207–8).

5. HW repeats his account of the calamity in greater detail to Mann 10 May 1763, MANN vi. 138–41.

6. The new opera, *Zanaida*, libretto by G. G. Bottarelli and music by J. C. Bach, opened at the King's Opera House in the Haymarket 7 May, and was performed to full houses five more times until the season closed 11 June (*Daily Adv. passim*; Sir George Grove, *Dictionary of Music and Musicians*, 5th edn, ed. Blom, 1954–61, i. 330; *London Stage* Pt IV, ii. 995–1000; Allardyce Nicoll, *History of English*

Madame de Boufflers,[7] and Mr Wilkes, and all the present topics. Wilkes, whose case has taken its place by the side of the seven bishops,[8] calls himself the eighth—not quite improperly, when one remembers that Sir Jonathan Trelawney,[9] who swore like a trooper, was one of those confessors.

There is a good letter in the *Gazetteer* on the other side, pretending to be written by Lord Temple, and advising Wilkes to cut his throat, like Lord E[ssex],[10] as it would be of infinite service to their cause.[11] There are published, too, three volumes of Lady Mary Wortley's[12] letters,[13] which I believe are genuine, and are not unentertaining—But have you read Tom Hervey's letter to the late King?[14] That beats everything for madness, horrid indecency, and folly, and yet has some charming and striking passages.

I have advised Mrs H[arris][15] to inform against Jack, as writing

Drama 1660–1900, 4th edn, Cambridge, 1952–65, iii. 363).

7. Marie-Charlotte-Hippolyte de Campet de Saujon (1725–1800), m. (1746) Édouard, Comte (Marquis, 1751) de Boufflers-Rouverel; called Comtesse de Boufflers (MANN vi. 135, n. 10). She had arrived in England 23 April (ibid.), and visited SH 17 May (MONTAGU ii. 70).

8. The seven bishops who protested against James II's second declaration of indulgence, and were imprisoned in the Tower in 1688. Their acquittal, like Wilkes's, met with great popular acclaim. Chief Justice Pratt referred to the case of the seven bishops in delivering the verdict of the Court on Wilkes (Howell, loc. cit.). For a full account of the trial of the seven bishops, see *The Proceedings and Trial in the Case of . . . William Lord Archbishop of Canterbury [et al.] . . . in the Court of King's Bench . . . 1688*, 1689.

9. Sir Jonathan Trelawny (1650–1721), 3d Bt, Bp of Bristol, 1685; Exeter, 1689; Winchester, 1707.

10. Arthur Capell (1631–83), 2d Bn Capell, 1649; cr. (1661) E. of Essex; conspirator. Imprisoned for complicity in the Rye House plot, he was found dead in the Tower with his throat slashed. Though the Whigs accused the Court of murder, it is more probable that he took his own life (DNB).

11. 'I put it to [our friends] . . . how this lucky event [Wilkes's imprisonment in the Tower] might be still farther improved to the advantage of the general cause? And after the most mature deliberation, we are all, *nem. con.*, of opinion, that nothing could throw so great an odium upon the Ministry . . . as, on Thursday evening next, for you to cut your own throat, which we have no manner of doubt you will be overjoyed to do, remembering the wonderful effect the like behaviour in Lord Essex formerly produced. . . . I shall come to see you on Friday morning, when I hope to find it done, as if nothing had happened, and I have already wrote down in my pocket-book, what reflections, insinuations, and suspicions, I shall throw out upon finding you murdered. . . . [signed] yours till death, T.' (*Gazetteer and London Daily Advertiser* 6 May).

12. Lady Mary Wortley Montagu.

13. See MANN vi. 141 and n. 31; HW's copy, now WSL, is Hazen, *Cat. of HW's Lib.*, No. 814.

14. *A Letter from the Hon. Thomas Hervey to the Late King*, published April, 1763 (HW's MS note in his copy, ibid. No. 1609:6:3, now WSL).

15. Anne Seymour Conway, sister of Henry Seymour Conway, m. (1755) John Harris.

in the *North Briton;* he will then be shut up in the Tower, and may be shown for old Nero.[16] Adieu!

Yours ever,

Hor. Walpole

To Conway, Saturday 21 May 1763

Printed from *Works* v. 101–3.

Arlington Street, May 21, 1763.

YOU have now seen the celebrated Madame de Boufflers. I dare say you could in that short time perceive that she is agreeable, but I dare say too that you will agree with me that vivacity is by no means the *partage* of the French—bating the *étourderie* of the *mousquetaires* and of a high-dried petit-maître or two, they appear to me more lifeless than Germans. I cannot comprehend how they came by the character of a lively people. Charles Townshend has more *sal volatile* in him than the whole nation. Their king is taciturnity itself; Mirepoix[1] was a walking mummy; Nivernois has about as much life as a sick favourite child; and Monsieur Dusson[2] is a good-humoured country gentleman, who has been drunk the day before, and is upon his good behaviour.[3] If I have the gout next year and am thoroughly humbled by it again, I will go to Paris, that I may be upon a level with them: at present, I am *trop fou* to keep them company. Mind, I do not insist that, to have spirits, a nation should be as frantic as poor ——,[4] as absurd as the Duchess of Queensberry, or as dashing as the Virgin Chudleigh. Oh, that you

---

16. An old lion there, so called (HW). 'The largest and oldest lion in the Tower' (*An Historical Description of the Tower of London and Its Curiosities,* 1760, p. 15). The public were admitted to see the animals in the Tower menagerie at sixpence per person (ibid. 13).

———

1. Who was French ambassador to England, 1749–55.
2. Pierre-Chrysostome d'Usson de Bonac (1724–82), Comte d'Usson; French ambassador to Sweden 1774–82. He was visiting

England with his wife (Mann vi. 135; *post* 18 Oct. 1763).

3. Lady Holland wrote, 22 April, that 'le Comte d'Usson, who has been here all winter, is much liked' (*Leinster Corr.* i. 367).

4. Probably Frances Pelham, whose 'oddness' HW mentions, *ante* 13 June 1761. HW had attended an entertainment given by her at Esher Place 18 May (Montagu ii. 72). She was notorious for her passion for gambling and her ungovernable temper (ibid. i. 53, n. 7).

had been at her ball t'other night! History could never describe it and keep its countenance. The Queen's real birthday, you know, is not kept:[5] this maid of honour[6] kept it—nay, while the Court is in mourning,[7] expected people to be out of mourning; the Queen's family really was so, Lady Northumberland[8] having desired leave for them. A scaffold was erected in Hyde Park for fireworks. To show the illuminations without to more advantage, the company were received in an apartment totally dark, where they remained for two hours— If they gave rise to any more birthdays, who could help it? The fireworks were fine, and succeeded well. On each side of the court were two large scaffolds for the Virgin's tradespeople. When the fireworks ceased, a large scene was lighted in the court, representing their Majesties; on each side of which were six obelisks, painted with emblems, and illuminated; mottos beneath in Latin and English: 1. For the Prince of Wales, a ship, *Multorum spes.*[9] 2. For the Princess Dowager, a bird of paradise, and *two* little ones, *Meos ad sidera tollo.*[10] People smiled. 3. Duke of York, a temple, *Virtuti et honori.*[11] 4. Princess Augusta, a bird of paradise, *Non habet parem*[12]—unluckily this was translated, *I have no peer.* People laughed out, considering where this was exhibited.[13] 5. The three younger Princes,[14] an orange-tree, *Promittit et dat.*[15] 6. The two younger Princesses,[16] the flower crown-imperial. I forget the Latin: the translation was silly enough, *Bashful in youth, graceful in age.* The lady of the house made many apologies for the poorness of the performance, which she said was only oil-paper, painted by one of her servants; but it really was fine and pretty. The Duke of Kingston

---

5. The Queen's birthday, 19 May, being too close to the King's (4 June), was for the benefit of trade and public convenience, kept 18 Jan. instead (John Watkins, *Memoirs of . . . Sophia-Charlotte, Queen of Great Britain,* 1819, i. 152: Isenburg, *Stammtafeln* i. taf. 124, ii. taf. 65; GM 1763, xxxiii. 44).

6. To the Princess Dowager of Wales.

7. From 1 to 22 May for Friedrich, Margrave of Brandenburg-Bayreuth, who had died 26 Feb. (*London Gazette* Nos 10308, 10311, 26–30 April, 7–10 May; Isenburg, *Stammtafeln* i. taf. 65; *Genealog. hist. Nachrichten* 1763–4, 3d ser. ii. 805).

8. One of the ladies of the Bedchamber.

9. 'The hope of the multitude.'

10. 'I raise my own to the stars.'

11. Probably meant in the specific sense

of military courage, valour, bravery, etc., York being a naval officer.

12. 'She has no equal.'

13. The festivities were held at Elizabeth Chudleigh's house in Knightsbridge, where the most frequent guest was presumably the Duke of Kingston, whose mistress she had been for some years (Elizabeth Mavor, *The Virgin Mistress,* 1964, p. 79).

14. William Henry (1743–1805), cr. (1764) D. of Gloucester; Henry Frederick (1745–90), cr. (1766) D. of Cumberland; and Frederick William (1750–65).

15. 'It promises and it gives.'

16. Louisa Ann (1749–68); and Caroline Matilda (1751–75), m. (1766) Christian VII, K. of Denmark 1766–1808.

was in a frock, *comme chez lui*. Behind the house was a cenotaph for the Princess Elizabeth,[17] a kind of illuminated cradle; the motto, *All the honours the dead can receive.* This burying-ground was a strange codicil to a festival; and, what was more strange, about one in the morning, this sarcophagus burst out into crackers and guns. The Margrave of Anspach[18] began the ball with the Virgin. The supper was most sumptuous.

You ask, when I propose to be at Park Place. I ask, Shall not you come to the Duke of Richmond's masquerade, which is the 2d of June?[19] I cannot well be with you till towards the end of that month.

The enclosed[20] is a letter which I wish you to read attentively, to give me your opinion upon it, and return it. It is from a sensible friend of mine in Scotland,[21] who has lately corresponded with me on the enclosed subjects, which I little understand; but I promised[22] to communicate his ideas to George Grenville,[23] if he would state them—are they practicable?[24] I wish much that something could be done for those brave soldiers and sailors, who will all come to the gallows, unless some timely provision can be made for them.[25]— The former part of his letter relates to a grievance he complains of, that men who have *not* served,[26] are admitted into garrisons, and then into our hospitals, which were designed for meritorious sufferers. Adieu!

Yours ever,

Hor. Walpole

17. Who had died in 1759, age 18 (*ante* 13 Sept. 1759; GM 1740, x. 622).

18. Karl Alexander (1736–1806), Margrave of Brandenburg-Ansbach 1757–91; of Brandenburg-Bayreuth, 1769–91; Count of the Empire, 1801 (Isenburg, *Stammtafeln*, i. taf. 66).

19. The masquerade was put off till 6 June, due to the Duke of Richmond's sore throat and fever (MONTAGU ii. 80). It is described in HW's letter to Mann of 5–7 June 1763, MANN vi. 148–9, where Conway is not mentioned, though he apparently intended to be there (see *post* 28 May 1763).

20. Dalrymple's letter to HW is missing.

21. Sir David Dalrymple (1726–92), Bt, of Hailes; judge with title of Lord Hailes, 1776–92; antiquary.

22. In his reply, 2 May 1763, to Dalrymple's letter (DALRYMPLE 88–90).

23. HW was on good terms with Grenville at the moment, but turned against him after the negotiation with Conway, discussed *post* 9 Dec. 1763 and 22 Jan. 1764.

24. Grenville did not consider them so. His objections are stated in HW's letter to Dalrymple, 1 July 1763 (DALRYMPLE 90–1). Dalrymple was apparently unable to answer them.

25. Dalrymple had wanted some provision to be made for ex-soldiers and sailors who were forced by the unavailability of honest employment to become highwaymen.

26. 'Fictitious invalids' HW calls them (ibid. 88); Dalrymple wanted a peremptory order for dismissing them.

To Conway, Saturday 28 May 1763

Printed from *Works* v. 103. Dated by the reference to the Duke of Richmond's masquerade, which was originally scheduled to take place 2 June (below, n. 1).

Arlington Street, Saturday evening.

NO, indeed I cannot consent to your being a dirty Philander.[1]
Pink and white, white and pink! and both as greasy as if you
had gnawed a leg of a fowl on the stairs of the Haymarket with a
bunter[2] from the Cardigan's Head![3] For heaven's sake don't produce
a tight rose-coloured thigh, unless you intend to prevent my Lord
Bute's return from Harrowgate.[4] Write, the moment you receive
this, to your tailor to get you a sober purple domino as I have done,
and it will make you a couple of summer waistcoats.

In the next place, have your ideas a little more correct about us
of times past. We did not furnish our cottages with chairs of ten
guineas apiece. Ebony for a farm-house![5] So, two hundred years
hence some man of taste will build a hamlet in the style of George
the Third, and beg his cousin Tom Hearne[6] to get him some chairs

1. At the masquerade given by the
Duke of Richmond on the 6th of June,
1763, at his house in Privy Garden
(Mary Berry). See *ante* 21 May 1763 and
n. 19.

2. 'A cant word for a woman who picks
up rags about the street; and used, by
way of contempt, for any low vulgar
woman' (Samuel Johnson, *Dictionary*,
1755).

3. A notorious bagnio at Charing Cross.
Its sign, depicting the head and torso of
a figure identified as the 'Earl of Cardi-
gan,' is shown in Hogarth's picture of
'Night,' from 'The Four Times of the
Day' (engravings published 1738; see H. B.
Wheatley, *Hogarth's London*, 1909, pp.
138–40).

4. That is, unless Conway wants to replace Lord Bute in the affections of the
Princess Dowager. According to HW, Bute
was inordinately fond of his figure and
had made his 'conquest' of the Princess in
part by displaying to her the 'beauty' of
his legs (*Mem. Geo. II* i. 47, ii. 205; in the

fair copy of the MS 'beauty' has been substituted for 'veins in the calf'). Lord and
Lady Bute had set out for Harrogate the
2d of May, where they proposed to reside
'about a month' (*London Chronicle* 30
April – 3 May, xiii. 424).

5. Mr Conway was at this time fitting
up the little building beautifully situated
on the brow of the hill at Park Place,
and called the Cottage [see *ante* 1 May
1763 and n. 15], though indeed containing a very good room towards the prospect in the Gothic style, for which he
had consulted Mr Walpole on the propriety of ebony chairs (Mary Berry). Conway may have had in mind HW's purchasing for him some ebony chairs at an
auction HW was to attend later; see
Montagu ii. 76–7.

6. Thomas Hearne (1678–1735), antiquary. HW compares himself to Hearne
also in his letters to Lady Ossory 25 June
1776 and 10 Nov. 1782 (Ossory i. 297, ii.
368).

for it of mahogany gilt, and covered with blue damask. Adieu! I have not a minute's time more.

Yours, etc.,

Hor. Walpole

From Conway, August 1763

Missing; answered *post* 9 Aug. 1763.

To Conway, Tuesday 9 August 1763

Printed from *Works* v. 104–5.

Strawberry Hill, August 9, 1763.

MY Gallery claims your promise; the painters and gilders finish tomorrow, and next day it washes its hands. You talked of the 15th; shall I expect you then,[1] and the Countess,[2] and the Contessina,[3] and the Baroness?[4]

Lord Digby is to be married immediately to the pretty Miss Fielding;[5] and Mr Boothby,[6] they say, to Lady Mary Douglas.[7] What more news I know I cannot send you; for I have had it from Lady Denbigh and Lady Blandford,[8] who have so confounded names, genders, and circumstances, that I am not sure whether Prince Ferdinand is not going to be married to the Hereditary Prince. Adieu!

Yours ever,

Hor. Walpole

1. See the postscript below.
2. Of Ailesbury (HW).
3. Miss Anne Seymour Conway (HW).
4. Elizabeth Rich, second wife of George Lord Lyttelton (HW).
5. Elizabeth (ca 1742–65), daughter of Hon. Charles Feilding; m. (4 Sept. 1763) Henry Digby (1731–93), 7th Bn Digby, cr. (1790) E. Digby (GM 1763, xxxiii. 465).
6. HW's third cousin, Charles Boothby Skrymsher (Clopton after 1792) (ca 1740–

1800) (Berry ii. 201, n. 16; Mann v. 431, n. 14).
7. (1737–1816), daughter of James, 13th E. of Morton, m. (1774) Charles Gordon, 4th E. of Aboyne (*Scots Peerage* vi. 382, ix. 141).
8. They were both Dutch women, and spoke very bad English (HW). HW had joked about their bad English *ante* 20 July 1761.

PS. If you want to know more of me, you may read a whole column of abuse upon me in the *Public Ledger* of Thursday last; where they inform me that the Scotch cannot be so sensible as the English, because they have not such good writers.[9] Alack! I am afraid *the most sensible* men in any country do *not* write.

I had writ this last night. This morning I receive your paper of evasions,[10] *perfide que vous êtes!* You may let it alone, you will never see anything like my Gallery—and then to ask me to leave it the instant it is finished! I never heard such a request in my days!—Why, all the earth is begging to come to see it: as Edging[11] says, I have had offers enough from blue and green ribbands to make me a falbala apron.[12] Then I have just refused to let Mrs Keppel and her Bishop[13] be in the house with me, because I expected all you— It is mighty well, mighty fine![14]—No, Sir, no, I shall not come; nor am I in a humour to do anything else you desire: indeed, without your provoking me, I should not have come into the proposal of paying Giardini.[15] We have been duped and cheated every winter for these twenty years by the undertakers of operas, and I never will pay a farthing more till the last moment, nor can be terrified at their puffs; I am astonished you are. So far from frightening me, the kindest thing they could do, would be not to let one have a box to hear their old threadbare voices and frippery thefts; and as for Giardini him-

9. This has not been found. In the advertisement to the Scottish and Irish sections of his *Catalogue of the Royal and Noble Authors*, 1758, HW had called the Scots 'the nation to which, if any one country is endowed with a superior partition of sense, I should be inclined to give the preference in that particular' (ii. 182). HW's praise of the Scots in this advertisement had the previous year drawn an attack from the *North Briton* (see *ante* 9 Sept. 1762).

10. Missing. Conway wrote to Devonshire, 29 Aug., that 'I am so tied to my bridge that I never stir a moment from it. . . . I have even quarrelled with H. Walpole for not going to him for a single day' (Chatsworth MSS, 416/83). This was a stone bridge which Conway was in the process of constructing at Park Place; see MONTAGU ii. 104–5 and nn. 7, 8.

11. Mrs Edging, woman to Lady Easy in Cibber's *The Careless Husband*.

12. 'I have had as many blue and green ribbons after me, for aught I know, as would have made me a falbala apron' (Act I).

13. Of Exeter.

14. However, the Conways apparently visited SH in early Sept. (see MONTAGU ii. 99, 100).

15. He had been manager of the Italian opera in London 1756–9, and resumed the direction for the upcoming season (Sir George Grove, *Dictionary of Music*, 5th edn, ed. Blom, 1954–61, iii. 627–8). In his letter to Devonshire of 29 Aug. (n. 10 above), Conway wrote that 'Mr Walpole was shabby and thought it ridiculous in us to talk of paying the money and to be bullied as he called it by Giardini's advertisement. We have certainly done very nobly to pay the whole subscription . . . we secure our box and the support of an opera . . . I think a most public-spirited and laudable action.'

HON. GEORGE SEYMOUR-CONWAY,
LATER LORD GEORGE SEYMOUR, BY SIR JOSHUA REYNOLDS

o cross the room to hear him play to eternity. I
ould frighten nobody but Lady Bingley[16] by a

RTFORD, Saturday 20 August 1763

ime from a photostat of BM Add. MSS 23218, f. 86.
[H]onourable Horatio Walpole, at Strawberry Hill, near
x.

London, August 20th 1763.

[fri]ghtened at my proposal; you are still at liberty.
[...]ng[1] is at my house tomorrow evening and you
[...] if you attend it; none of the sponsors stand in
[...] to be represented, and the Bishop of Exeter
performs the ceremony. Mr Pitt was at Court yesterday and I think
better received than usual.[2]

I have heard no public news since I returned to town.

Yours ever,

HERTFORD

16. Harriet Benson (ca 1705–71), m. (1731) George Fox (afterwards Fox Lane), cr. (1762) Bn Bingley.

17. Lady Bingley was apparently an ardent admirer of Giardini. In a letter to Mrs Delany of 30 April ?1770, Mrs Boscawen writes that 'Lady Bingley summonses the world to Giardini's concert tonight' (Mary Granville, Mrs Delany, *Autobiography and Correspondence*, ed. Lady Llanover, 1861–2, iv. 260).

1. Of his seventh son and thirteenth child, the Hon. (after 1793 Lord) George Seymour-Conway (21 July 1763–1848), army officer 1779–ca 1797; M.P. Orford 1784–90, Totnes 1796–1801; chairman of the Board of Excise 1822–33 (BERRY ii. 40, n. 11). 'Yesterday evening [21 Aug.] the son of the Earl of Hertford was baptized at his Lordship's house in Grosvenor Square. The King, by his proxy the Earl of Denbigh, stood godfather' (*London Chronicle* 20–23 Aug., xiv. 177).

2. 'Yesterday [19 Aug.] the Right Hon. William Pitt, Esq. and several of the nobility, who came to town on purpose from their respective country seats, waited on his Majesty with their congratulations on the safe delivery of the Queen, and the birth of a Prince' (ibid. 18–20 Aug., xiv. 174; *Lloyd's Evening Post* 19–22 Aug., xiii. 177).

With the Compliments of the Editor

W. S. Lewis

From HERTFORD, Saturday 27 August 1763

Printed for the first time from a photostat of BM Add. MSS 23218, f. 88.
Address: To the Honourable Horatio Walpole, at Strawberry Hill, near Twickenham, Middlesex.

London, August 27th 1763.

Dear Horry,

IF you are not tired of political news you may be glad to hear that Mr Pitt has been today near three hours with the King at Buckingham House.[1]

The success is not yet known; the Duke of Grafton who dined with me is gone to Mr Pitt, but I have yet heard nothing.

Yours ever,

HERTFORD

From HERTFORD, Tuesday 30 August 1763

Printed for the first time from a photostat of BM Add. MSS 23218, f. 90.
Address: To the Honourable Horatio Walpole, at Strawberry Hill, near Twickenham, Middlesex.

London, August 30th 1763.

Dear Horry,

I HEAR from common report, but I have no other authority for it, that the treaty is at present broke off,[1] and Mr Pitt returned to Hayes.[2] The conditions required from the King are said to have been general restitution and no kind of communication with Lord Bute:[3] difficult terms to accept at the first notice, but from what has

1. Contemporary accounts of what passed at this interview and in the succeeding stages of this negotiation with Pitt are in many cases contradictory, those originating with Pitt giving one version and those with the King, another. For a detailed study of the affair see D. A. Winstanley, *Personal and Party Government 1760–1766*, Cambridge, 1910, pp. 167–83.

1. The King terminated the negotiations at the end of a two-hour interview with Pitt on 29 Aug.

2. After the interview on the 29th; however, he returned to London on the 30th (Pitt to Newcastle [30 Aug. 1763], BM Add. MSS 32950, f. 298).

3. There is no evidence that Pitt demanded the total exclusion of Bute, although he apparently did refuse to act in

passed I shall now conclude Mr Pitt to be the minister of this country whether he kisses hands this week or the next.[4] If he is sent for again before I seal my letter you shall have it in the postscript.

Yours ever,

HERTFORD

From HERTFORD, Saturday 15 October 1763

Printed for the first time from a photostat of BM Add. MSS 23218, ff. 92–3.

Montreuil,[1] October 15th 1763.

Dear Horry,

WE left Dover at nine o'clock on Friday morning and landed about eight that evening at Boulogne.[2] The easterly wind would not suffer us to approach Calais, by which means we lost a very fine entertainment and ball that the Prince de Croÿ[3] had prepared for us; I was likewise to have been received with a speech from some lawyer of the town, which I am very glad to have been excused answering without any preparation. I received at Boulogne a very polite letter from the Comte de Guerchi[4] acquainting me that he had declined sailing with a very fair wind in order to have seen me at Calais.[5]

office with those responsible for the Peace. He also urged the general restitution of the 'great Whig families and persons which had been driven from his Majesty's Council and service' (*Hardwicke Corr.* iii. 526, 530).

4. Pitt did not return to office until July 1766, though he was always the centre and the great imponderable of the several negotiations discussed in the following letters.

———

1. Montreuil-sur-Mer, 23½ miles south of Boulogne on the road to Paris.

2. Hertford, who had been named ambassador to France in April (*ante* 28 Feb. 1763, n. 8), had left London for Paris with his entourage on 13 Oct. (MANN vi. 175; *Mem. Geo. III* i. 240).

3. Emmanuel de Croÿ (1718–84), Prince and (1768) Duc de Croÿ, Prince de Solre and de Mœrs; commander of the troops in Artois Picardie, Calaisis, and Boulonnais. He had just given 'un souper de quarante couverts, suivi d'un bal' to his late wife's brother-in-law, the Comte de Guerchy, French ambassador to England, at Calais, and presumably planned a similar entertainment for Hertford (Emmanuel, Duc de Croÿ, *Journals inédit*, ed. Grouchy and Cottin, 1906–7, ii. 123n.).

4. Claude-Louis-François de Regnier (1715–67), Comte de Guerchy; French ambassador to England 1763–7. The letter is missing.

5. Guerchy reached Dover on Sunday morning, 16 Oct., and London on the 18th (*Daily Adv.* 18, 19 Oct.).

Hitherto we have come on extremely well, and to[6] this place English language with English guineas is well understood. My Lady and I are the only two of our company that escaped seasickness. Mr Hume[7] is well prepared for a change of diet.

The country through which we have passed is much better cultivated and improved than I expected to see it, and has by no means that I can discover a worse appearance for the war; if we had not made peace till France was reduced to the state I have heard supposed of this and some parts of her country, we should have had nothing in England but public debts.

Mr Hume who sees me write says he is determined to make you the best answer he can to your inquiry about the cause of the Jesuits' disgrace.[8]

We hope to be at Paris on Monday night and shall think ourselves very happy when we hear from you.

Accept the best compliments of all the family and believe me, dear Horry,

Always sincerely and affectionately yours,

HERTFORD

---

6. I.e., 'as far as.'

7. David Hume (1711–76). Hertford, though personally unacquainted with him, had invited Hume to accompany him to Paris, with the prospect of becoming secretary to the Embassy, an arrangement that caused considerable comment because of the contrast between Hertford's piety and Hume's infidelity. See Hume, *Letters*, ed. Greig, Oxford, 1932, i. 392–3; *Letters to Henry Fox*, ed. Lord Ilchester, Roxburghe Club, 1915, p. 186; *Mem. Geo. III* i. 209.

8. Hume's promise of collecting materials on the destruction of the Jesuits in France, also mentioned in the following letter, was apparently never fulfilled. The campaign against the order, which had begun with the trial of Father La Vallette, 1756–61, reached a climax in the *arrêt* of the parliament of Paris, 6 Aug. 1761, which suppressed the Society and confiscated its property. For details, see the account in H. Carré, *Le Règne de Louis XV* (*Histoire de France*, ed. E. Lavisse, Vol. VIII, Pt II), 1909, pp. 319–26, and the bibliography there given. The final steps in the destruction of the order are mentioned *post* 8 March 1764.

To Hertford, Tuesday 18 October 1763

Printed from *Works* ix. 1–4. The address is printed from a photostat of the MS kindly supplied by the late Sir John Murray; since it is detached, it could belong to this or any of HW's subsequent letters to Hertford at Paris.

Address: À son Excellence Monsieur le Comte de Hertford ambassadeur de sa Majesté Britannique à Paris.

Arlington Street, Oct. 18, 1763.

My dear Lord,

I AM very impatient for a letter from Paris, to hear of your outset, and what my Lady Hertford thinks of the new world she is got into, and whether it is better or worse than she expected. Pray tell me all: I mean of that sort, for I have no curiosity about the Family Compact,[1] nor the harbour of Dunkirk.[2] It is your private history— your audiences, reception, comforts or distresses, your way of life, your company—that interests me; in short, I care about my cousins and friends, not, like Jack Harris, about my Lord Ambassador.[2a] Consider you are in my power. You, by this time, are longing to hear from England, and depend upon me for the news of London. I shall not send you a tittle, if you are not very good, and do not (one of you, at least) write to me punctually.

This letter, I confess, will not give you much encouragement, for I can absolutely tell you nothing. I dined at Mr Grenville's[3] today, where, if there had been anything to hear, I should have heard it; but all consisted in what you will see in the papers—some diminutive battles in America,[4] and the death of the King of Poland,[5]

1. The third treaty of that name had been signed between France and Spain 15 Aug. 1761. Hertford's instructions had ordered close cooperation between him and Lord Rochford, ambasssador to Spain, in observing relations between the two Courts (S.P. 78/258, ff. 83–4, printed in *British Diplomatic Instructions 1689–1789*, Vol. VII: France, Pt IV, 1745–89, ed. L. G. Wickham Legg, 1934, pp. 86–7).

2. The demolition of which had been ordered by Article XIII of the Treaty of Paris. Hertford's instructions ordered him to press the execution of this article (S.P. 78/258, ff. 86–7, printed Legg, op. cit. 88).

2a. Harris, Hertford's brother-in-law, was evidently partial to persons of rank.

3. George Grenville.

4. Battles with the Indians near Fort Detroit, 31 July, and at Edghill near Bushy Run, 5–6 Aug. Details had reached London on 14 Oct. in a dispatch from General Sir Jeffrey Amherst, dated New York, 3 Sept. (*London Gazette* No. 10356, 11–15 Oct.; *Daily Adv.* 17 Oct.).

5. Frederick Augustus (1696 – 5 Oct. 1763), Elector of Saxony as Friedrich August II and K. of Poland as August III 1733–63 (Isenburg, *Stammtafeln*, i. taf. 55, ii. taf. 86). News of his death was reported

which you probably knew before we did. The town is a desert; it is like a vast plain, which, though abandoned at present, is in three weeks to have a great battle fought upon it.[6] One of the colonels, I hear, is to be in town tomorrow, the Duke of Devonshire.[7] I came myself but this morning, but as I shall not return to Strawberry till the day after tomorrow, I shall not seal my letter till then. In the meantime, it is but fair to give you some more particular particulars of what I expect to know. For instance, of Monsieur de Nivernois's cordiality;[8] of Madame Dusson's[9] affection for England; of my Lord Holland's joy at seeing you in France,[10] especially without your secretary;[11] of all my Lady Hertford's cousins,[12] at St Germains; and I should not dislike a little anecdote or two of the late embassy,[13] of which I do not doubt you will hear plenty. I must trouble you

in the newspapers, 18 Oct., from letters from Hamburg and Holland, and confirmed in the *Gazette* on the same day (*Daily Adv.* 18 Oct.; *London Gazette* No. 10357, 15–18 Oct.).

6. Parliament was to meet on 15 Nov.

7. He did not arrive until Thursday, 20 Oct., which was his original intention, though his brother had assured Newcastle that he could arrive on Wednesday, and apparently wrote urging him to do so (two letters from Lord Frederick Cavendish to Newcastle 17 Oct., and Newcastle to Devonshire 19 Oct., BM Add. MSS 32952, ff. 32, 34, 40; *London Chronicle* 20–22 Oct., xiv. 385).

8. HW is apparently being ironical here, as he is in the rest of his queries. In *Mem. Geo. III* he comments on the ill-disguised 'disgust' Nivernais showed to England (i. 152), while Hertford subsequently insists that the many attentions of Nivernais and his wife to him and Lady Hertford 'sufficiently contradict every bad impression that may have been conceived in England on their indifference of behaviour to the nation' (*post* 19 Nov. 1763). Gray quotes Nivernais as saying of England, on his return to France: 'Quel roi, quel peuple, quelle société' (Gray, *Correspondence*, ed. Toynbee and Whibley, Oxford, 1935, ii. 828).

9. Margaretha Cornelia van de Poll (1726–93), m. 1 (1743) Cornelius Munter; m. 2 Pierre-Chrysostome d'Usson de Bonac, Comte d'Usson (*ante* 21 May 1763). Dur-

ing her visit to England the past spring with her husband, HW entertained her at SH and complimented her in verses from the SH Press (Montagu ii. 71; Hazen, *SH Bibl.* 179–81; HW's MS note to the verses in his set of 'Detached Pieces,' now wsl). Hertford mentions *post* 11 Nov. 1763 that she was 'generally thought to love abuse,' a trait to which HW probably refers in his query.

10. Holland had been on the Continent with his family since the middle of May (*Leinster Corr.* i. 371–2).

11. Through Holland's influence, his wife's brother-in-law, Thomas Charles Bunbury (1740–1821), 6th Bt 1764, M.P. Suffolk 1761–84, 1790–1812, had been named secretary to the embassy in April 1763 without Hertford's knowledge or approval. Hertford, though ostensibly acquiescing in the appointment, treated his secretary with 'such obstinate coldness' (going so far, according to Hume, as to refuse to see or to transact business with him), that Bunbury was constrained to remain in England, though he retained the salary of his office. HW considered the whole affair but another instance of Holland's treating Hertford as a 'personal enemy' (*Mem. Geo. III* i. 209; Hume, *Letters*, ed. Greig, Oxford, 1932, i. 422).

12. The Fitzjames family; the Duc de Fitzjames was a grandson of James II, Lady Hertford, a great-granddaughter of Charles II.

13. Bedford's.

with many compliments to Madame de Boufflers,[14] and with still more to the Duchesse de Mirepoix,[15] who is always so good as to remember me. Her brother, Prince de Beauvau, I doubt has forgotten me.[16] In the disagreeableness of taking leave, I omitted mentioning these messages. Good-night for tonight— Oh! I forgot— pray send me some *café au lait:* the Duc de Picquigny[17] (who by the way is somebody's son, as I thought)[18] takes it for snuff; and says it is the new fashion at Paris; I suppose they drink rappee[19] after dinner.

Wednesday night.—

I might as well have finished last night, for I know nothing more than I did then, but that Lady Mary Coke arrived this evening.[20] She has behaved very honourably, and not stolen the Hereditary Prince.[21]

Mr Bowman[22] called on me yesterday before I came, and left word that he would come again today, but did not. I wished to hear of you from him, and a little of my old acquaintance at Rheims.[23] Did you find Lord Beauchamp much grown? Are all your sons to be like those of the Amalekites?[24] who were I forget how many cubits high.

14. Who had visited England the past spring (*ante* 6, 21 May 1763), and had dined the same day as Mme d'Usson at SH, where HW had saluted her also with verses from the SH Press (above, n. 9).

15. Anne-Marguerite-Gabrielle de Beauvau (1707–91), m. 1 (1721) Jacques-Henri de Lorraine, Prince de Lixin; m. 2 (1739) Gaston-Charles-Pierre-François de Levis de Lomagne, Duc de Mirepoix, Maréchal de France. HW had known her when her husband was ambassador to England 1749–55.

16. HW had known him in Italy (MANN i. 11; Beauvau to HW 19 Oct. 1740).

17. Marie-Joseph-Louis d'Albert d'Ailly (1741–93), Duc de Pecquigny; later Duc de Chaulnes.

18. HW is perhaps alluding to an item that had recently appeared in the newspapers: 'The Duke of Pecquigny, son of the Duke of Chaulnes, and son-in-law of the Duke of Chevreuse, Governor of Paris, is arrived in England, where he proposes to make a stay sufficient to learn the language, customs, etc.' (*London Chronicle* 11–13 Oct., xiv. 358; *Daily Adv.* 13 Oct.).

19. A coarse kind of snuff (OED).

20. She had been at Spa in Aug., and at Hanover in Sept. (*Leinster Corr.* i. 385, 387; Coke, *Journals* i. 5–6).

21. Lady Mary, to her disappointment, had missed seeing the Hereditary Prince at Spa, and though she was invited to Brunswick in Sept., was unable to go (*Leinster Corr.* i. 382, 385; Coke, loc. cit.). HW is alluding to Lady Mary's notorious infatuation with Edward, Duke of York, to whom she later pretended she had been secretly married.

22. Lord Beauchamp's travelling tutor (*ante* 11 Oct. 1760).

23. HW had spent three months at Rheims in the summer of 1739 (see *ante* i. 42). Presumably Bowman had been there with Beauchamp during the summer.

24. HW has apparently confused the Amalekites with the Anakim, perhaps

Pray remind Mr Hume of collecting the whole history of the expulsion of the Jesuits.[25] It is a subject worthy of his inquiry and pen. Adieu! my dear Lord.

Yours ever,

H. WALPOLE

From HERTFORD, Friday 28 October 1763

Printed for the first time from a photostat of BM Add. MSS 23218, ff. 94–6.
Memoranda (by HW):   Deon

Ireland[1]

[badly smudged, illegible names]

Gov. Wharton[2]

Fontainbleau,[3] October 28th 1763.

Dear Horry,

AS you desire, I will mention neither Family Compact nor Dunkirk, but proceed directly to our own history.

Lady Hertford's will be very short; I think she seems to like France better than she expected.[4] I will not say more, but she has yet seen no more of it than what she can judge from her journey or from the visits she has received at Paris. Her dress is not yet prepared for Court; it is expected to be ready in a very few days and in the meantime she is advised not to appear in public but to confine herself to her Paris visits which cannot be very numerous. All the great world is here.[5] Madame de Mirepoix and the Duchess of Niver-

from Numbers 13. 29–33 where the two tribes, both enemies of the ancient Jews, are discussed together. None of the other references to the Amalekites mentions their size, but the great height of the 'sons of Anak' is alluded to in the passage in Numbers and also in Deuteronomy 2. 10–11, 21 and 9.2. HW does compare Hertford's sons with the sons of Anak in his letter to Conway *post* 3 June 1781.

25. The Jesuits had not yet been expelled, merely suppressed (*ante* 15 Oct. 1763, n. 8).

———

1. Both the Chevalier d'Éon and Ireland

are mentioned in HW to Hertford, *post* 25 Nov. 1763.

2. Not identified.

3. Hertford had arrived in Paris on 20 Oct., and on the 22d had gone to Fontainebleau to join the Court (Hertford to Halifax, 26 Oct., S.P. 78/258, f. 195; *Daily Adv.* 29 Oct.).

4. It was Lady Hertford's first visit; Hertford had been there in 1739 during his grand tour (Thomas Gray, *Correspondence*, ed. Toynbee and Whibley, Oxford, 1935, i. 101–13, *passim*; GRAY i. 166 and n. 34).

5. At Fontainebleau.

nois[6] are her directors; the Duchess de Fitzjames,[7] her relation,[8] who it seems might otherways have expected it from the forms of this country, is at Toulouse with her husband.[9] The first of the ladies I have named is all civility and attention, but she is here and therefore cannot be so immediately useful to her. When she returns to Paris she has promised me to be very useful and to direct all our supper-parties that the companies may be well mixed.

Lady Hertford's ceremonial[10] is now lying by me and I must pity her, it is a dreadful one; but still everything will go better than I believe she imagined. The French language is easier to her than she expected, and the people not so formidable, and I think her plain unaffected manner will please more here than if she presumed farther upon the customs of her own country.

The Duchess of Richmond[11] and Lady Caroline Fox[12] have been vastly civil to her and without constraint.[13]

My own history and that of my son's[14] are very different. We have lived entirely *dans le grand monde,* and I am confined by letters from England to this place.[15] At Paris I went twice to the Italian comedy,

6. Hélène-Angélique-Françoise Phélypeaux de Pontchartrain (1715–82), m. (1730) Louis-Jules-Barbon Mancini-Mazarini, Duc de Nivernais.

7. Victoire-Louise-Sophie de Goyon de Matignon (1722–77), m. (1741) Charles, Duc de Fitzjames, Maréchal de France.

8. By marriage; see *ante* 18 Oct. 1763, n. 12.

9. Charles (1712–87), Duc de Fitzjames; Maréchal de France; governor of the Limousin and commandant of Languedoc. He had been sent on a special mission to Toulouse to force the parliament of that place to register the financial edicts of April 1763; for subsequent developments see *post* 28 Dec. 1763, 23 Jan. 1764.

10. For her presentation at Court. Details, though for an earlier period in the century, are given in Jean Dumont, Baron de Carlscroon, *Cérémonial diplomatique des cours de l'Europe,* ed. Rousset, Amsterdam, 1739, i. 49–50, 57–8 (*Corps universelle diplomatique, Supplement,* Vol. IV).

11. She and her husband had been in France since late June, though they had already left Paris for England by the date of this letter; they reached London

31 Oct. (*St James's Chronicle* 25–8 June; *Leinster Corr.* i. 391; *Daily Adv.* 2 Nov.).

12. Bns Holland, Lady Hertford's cousin. Hertford disregards both her husband's recent title and the fact that she had been created *suo jure* Bns Holland in 1762.

13. Written presumably to assure HW that the Duchess and Lady Holland apparently bore no ill-will towards Lady Hertford, in spite of Hertford's treatment of Bunbury, brother-in-law of Lady Holland and the Duke of Richmond; see *ante* 18 Oct. 1763, n. 11.

14. Lord Beauchamp (see below).

15. A dispatch from Halifax of 21 Oct. directed Hertford to 'press, in the most earnest manner, with the French ministers, the full performance of his Most Christian Majesty's engagements with respect to the demolition' of the harbour of Dunkirk, 'and that it be now set about in earnest, and without further delay' (S.P. 78/258, f. 169). Also, another dispatch of the same date directed Hertford to continue pressing the 'two affairs still depending at the Court of France, of the Brunswick hostages, and Hessian artillery' (ibid. f. 171).

which is a very pretty entertainment, and I supped at the d'Ussons' with French ladies, whom I found extremely easy. We played at cards and talked of trifles, where any man may acquit himself tolerably well that is not bashful. As soon as I came here I waited on the Duke de Praslin,[16] where I was invited to sup and pass the evening; the next morning had been before appointed for my audience.[17] The King of France was most particularly gracious to me. I made my speech to him without hesitation, and after I had finished he kept me half an hour in the Closet talking to me upon different subjects, and was pleased to tell me that the King my master could not in his Court have chosen a person to represent him more agreeable to him than myself; at the next levee I was so much distinguished by him, that it struck the English who were present. Lord Holland indeed did not tell me so, but he was present; and with the French, if I am to judge by their first behaviour, it will be an advantage to me whilst I am in this country. His Majesty is observed to talk to me with ease, which is the greatest compliment he can pay; in return I have been twice a-hunting, once in my coach and once on horseback, and I believe by his behaviour to me the compliment was well judged. The Queen[18] is a very good woman, who says but little. The Mesdames[19] are well behaved; I made my speeches to them without any difficulty. The Dauphin and Dauphiness[20] I have not yet seen; the King of Poland's death has kept them at Versailles.[21]

I have likewise had half an hour at least alone with Madame de Pompadour and have found her most polite and obliging, with a great deal more sense and conversation than I expected; Monsieur de Choiseuil[22] is a man of lively parts; the Duke de Praslin is a man of sense. They are very different and easily discover the difference of

---

16. César-Gabriel de Choiseul (1712–85), Duc de Praslin; secretary of state for foreign affairs.

17. 'Fontainbleau, October 26. On the 23rd instant the Earl of Hertford, his Britannic Majesty's ambassador at this Court, had a private audience of the King to present his letters of credence' (*Daily Adv.* 5 Nov.). Hertford's account here of his various audiences parallels closely that which he gives in his dispatch to Halifax of 26 Oct. (S.P. 78/258, ff. 195–6).

18. Marie-Catherine-Sophie-Félicité Le-

szczyńska (1703–68), m. (1725) Louis XV, K. of France.

19. Marie-Adélaïde (1732–1800); Victoire-Louise-Marie-Thérèse (1733–99); Sophie-Philippine-Élisabeth-Justine (1734–82); and Louise-Marie (1737–87), daughters of Louis XV.

20. Louis (1729–65), m. (1747) Marie-Josèphe (1731–67) of Saxe.

21. The Dauphiness was a daughter of the late King of Poland.

22. Étienne-François de Choiseul-Stainville (1719–85), Duc de Choiseul; principal minister.

A PARTY AT SIR HORACE MANN'S IN FLORENCE,
BY THOMAS PATCH

their nature in treating the same subject in business with more or less frankness or reserve.²³

The women here are some of them very handsome, but they are in general more pleasing than beautiful. My son is vastly admired for his good sense, his figure and behaviour,²⁴ and he talks French amazingly for the time he has been in France.

Mr Hume says he is driven out of company *à coup de compliments* upon his knowledge and writings.²⁵

I must now finish and go on with our history on another occasion, having letters to dispatch to the Secretary of State.²⁶

I remain, dear Horry,

Always affectionately yours,

Hertford

Believe me when I tell you that I am in a constant hurry with business and visits and entertainments. Be so good to give my brother some account of me; I have not time to write.

To Hertford, ca Friday 11 November 1763

Missing; 'a long comfortable letter' answered *post* 19 Nov. 1763. HW usually wrote to Hertford on Friday.

23. In one of his dispatches to Halifax of 28 Oct. (n. 26 below), Hertford mentions 'the open and sanguine humour of M. de Choiseul,' and 'the cautious and reserved temper of M. de Pralin [*sic*]' (S.P. 78/258, f. 219).

24. See illustration. The English in Paris were less enthusiastic about Lord Beauchamp. Lady Holland wrote in December that 'he has a pretty figure and address, is sensible, but too self-sufficient for his age, and too wise. I will always take boys' word for character at Eton, tho' much commended by the masters he was not liked by the boys' (*Leinster Corr.* i. 398). Neither was he liked at Oxford; see *ante* 3 March 1760, n. 7.

25. Hume, writing on the same day to

Adam Smith, comments: 'During the two last days in particular, that I have been at Fontainebleau, I have suffered (the expression is not improper) as much flattery as almost any man has ever done in the same time: but there are few days in my life, when I have been in good health, that I would not rather pass over again' (Hume, *Letters*, ed. Greig, Oxford, 1932, i. 409).

26. Two letters, dated 28 Oct. In the first Hertford discusses his conferences with Choiseul and Praslin concerning chiefly the demolition of the harbour at Dunkirk; and in the second he offers a suggestion for facilitating the exchange of dispatches between himself and Halifax (S.P. 78/258, ff. 219-23).

From HERTFORD, Friday 11 November 1763

Printed for the first time from a photostat of BM Add. MSS 23218, ff. 97–100.

Paris, November 11th 1763.

Dear Horry,

I CAME from Fontainbleau last night after having been there near three weeks; the King leaves it on the 14th and the foreign ministers are not thought deficient in duty to their own Courts nor to want respect to this if they leave it three or four days sooner. I was therefore very glad to take the first opportunity I could with propriety, though I have passed my time extremely well at Fontainbleau.

My family is, properly, not settled here; I was obliged to follow the Court before I could give orders for many things I shall want here. The Paris way of living is extremely magnificent; a great deal is expected from ambassadors in return for the civilities shown to them; the English minister is perhaps more particularly the object of their attention, and I cannot think of bringing any disgrace upon myself or my country by an ill-placed economy in so public a situation.[1] Lady Hertford is to go to Versailles on Tuesday sennight when the Court will be settled there; the forms of her presentation will be long and very fatiguing; I am not surprised she fears them. The Emperor's minister's wife,[2] who you would think with me never feared anything, pretends to have been so much alarmed as not to be able to speak to the King; I cannot give her entire credit, she speaks French as fluently as you do English, and wears too much red to be ashamed. When Lady Hertford tries it I think she will find it less terrible than she expects. The King himself is one of the best-natured men in the world, and has already talked to me with great ease upon Lady Hertford's timidity, which I have admitted, and thrown as much as I could on the want of language. The Queen seems a good old woman that will fatigue no person with too many questions; her Court is pretty numerous, and the worst part of the whole from the gravity which attends it;[3] the King and Dauphin

1. Hertford's parsimony was notorious; see GEC vi. 511, n. 'g.'
2. Maria Franziska von Salm-Salm (1731–1806), m. (1761) Georg Adam,

Fürst von Starhemberg, Imperial ambassador to France 1754–66.
3. The Queen's court took its tone from its mistress's pedantry and piety;

love talking when they can receive answers easily, but the want of language is so usual in this country where they see so many strangers that it is not thought or treated as a singular thing. The Mesdames seem the stiffest part of the whole, but as they are not the most considerable, it is of less consequence.

The Princes of the Blood[4] I know only by sight and from their general characters; having not yet seen the Dauphiness I have not made them the first and almost only visit which form allows me as an ambassador.[5] The Prince of Conti, as having the most sense, is the prince most generally respected. He seems to be upon bad terms with the Court.[6] He came but once to Fontainbleau whilst I was there; that was to a great ball, and I believe he left it without going to the King's levee. The affectation of his dress is very singular in this country: his hair is almost without a curl, his stockings rolled as they were worn twenty years ago, his coat an old one, and his bag[7] and solitaire[8] you would not think good enough for your footman; under all these disadvantages he is an handsome well-looking prince. Madame de Boufflers is I hear still in his good graces; an Englishman who happened to be at Isle-Adam could I hear swear for the truth of it if it was necessary, his Altesse not being particularly prudent in the choice of the place and couch he took to give her a proof of his affection.

The Duchess of Nivernois has been all goodness and attention to Lady Hertford; nothing can exceed hers and her daughter's[9] civility; they have bought and ordered all her clothes and make a point of having her appear here as she should. The Duke has been very polite and properly attentive to me; but I will not disguise from you that I can see French *fierté* through his behaviour. Madame d'Usson is very polite and obliging, but I do not find that she is upon any footing here as a person of consequence, and she is generally thought to love abuse. Madame de Boufflers has been with Lady Hertford and

see the brief but sweeping characterization in H. Carré, *Le règne de Louis XV* (*Histoire de France*, ed. E. Lavisse, Vol. VIII, Pt II), 1909, p. 135.

4. At this time they were the Ducs d'Orléans and de Chartres, the Princes de Condé and de Conti, the Comtes de Clermont and de la Marche, and the legitimated descendants of Louis XIV, the Comte d'Eu and the Duc de Penthièvre.

5. See *post* 30 Nov. 1763, and nn. 3, 4.

6. Because of his support of the parliaments against the Court.

7. 'A small silken pouch to contain the back-hair of a wig' (OED).

8. 'A loose neck-tie of black silk or broad ribbon worn by men in the 18th century' (ibid.).

9. Hélène-Julie-Rosalie Mancini-Mazarini (1740–80), m. (1753) Louis-Marie Fouquet de Belle-Isle, Comte de Gisors; see *post* 19 Nov. 1763.

speaks with great propriety in all companies of the English. Do not tell Lady Mary Coke what I have said about her; I do not love scandal though I commit myself to you.

I saw Lord Holland at Fontainbleau. He was very polite and attentive to me; I showed him the respect due to him from the English ambassador as far as that situation would allow it, which indeed was very limited. I had the honour of speaking to him twice or thrice at Court, and I had no family settled there;[10] I fancy we understood one another very well, and what we owed publicly to each other. If you hear me abused at any time in London I desire to know it; hitherto I have done the business of my Court with particular attention and have hardly had an opportunity to err in point of form; during my absence from Paris, Lady Hertford has had almost all her travelling countrymen to dinner or supper, and I have been introducing them to balls and operas, and doing their little jobs at Court. Lady Holland and the Duke and Duchess of Richmond have been very polite and attentive to Lady Hertford; young Fox[11] is a very good creature without guile or design.

His Grace asked Lady Hertford a most improper question from him, I think:[12] whether Mr Hume was my friend or my secretary. Lady Hertford knew how to answer, by painting the *friend* in strong colours. Lady Holland has affected, I hear, to talk of Bunbury's not coming here as if it arose from the occasion ministers might have for his service in Parliament.[13] Adieu, dear Horry, my courier is going and I must conclude my history by assuring you that I am always

Most sincerely and affectionately yours,

HERTFORD

10. Which presumably freed Hertford from private attentions to Holland.

11. Stephen Fox (1745–74), 2d Bn Holland, 1774. He was in Paris with his family.

12. Because Bunbury, Hertford's official secretary, was the Duke's brother-in-law.

13. Lady Holland's conversation was well founded. Two letters from Sandwich to Holland (26 Sept., 14 Oct.) mention the Ministry's desire to keep Bunbury in England for the opening of the session, and on 16 Oct. Lady Sarah Bunbury informed a friend that they would remain in London until Christmas 'for Lord Halifax wrote Mr B. word that he must attend part of the session' (*Letters to Henry Fox*, ed. Lord Ilchester, Roxburghe Club, 1915, pp. 184, 190; *Life and Letters of Lady Sarah Lennox*, ed. Lady Ilchester and Lord Stavordale, 1902, i. 133).

To Hertford, Thursday 17 November 1763

Printed from *Works* ix. 5–16.

Arlington Street, Nov. 17, 1763.

IF the winter keeps up to the vivacity of its *début,* you will have no reason to complain of the sterility of my letters. I do not say this from the spirit of the House of Commons on the first day, which was the most fatiguing and dull debate I ever heard, dull as I have heard many; and yet for the first quarter of an hour it looked as if we were met to choose a King of Poland, and that all our names ended in *isky.*[1] Wilkes,[2] the night before, had presented himself at the Cockpit:[3] as he was listening to the speech, George Selwyn said to him, in the words of the *Dunciad,* 'May heaven preserve the ears you lend!'[4] We lost four hours debating whether or not it was necessary to open the session with reading a bill,[5] the opposite sides, at the same time, pushing to get the start, between the King's Message, which Mr Grenville stood at the bar to present, and which was to

1. That is, the confusion in the House resembled that which usually prevailed in the tumultuous assembly that was supposed to elect unanimously a king of Poland. Frequent paragraphs in the newspapers in the month preceding this letter, reporting manœuvres for the election to the recently vacated crown of Poland, had reminded the English of the disorder, usually breaking out in civil war, that always accompanied this event. See *Daily Adv.* 19, 20, 29 Oct.; 4, 11 Nov.

2. At the moment the centre of a political storm occasioned by his arrest for a seditious libel in the *North Briton* No. 45, and by his previously successful defiance of the King and ministry over the issue (see *ante* 1, 6 May 1763).

3. An assembly room, formerly part of the old Whitehall Palace. It was frequently used in the 18th century for political meetings, particularly one on the eve of a Parliamentary session when the King's speech was read. Though it was usually attended primarily by administration supporters, it was open to all. Grenville described the meeting of 14 Nov., attended by 254 or 255 members, as 'in

all respects a very good one, except that Mr Wilkes thought fit to make his appearance there, and was, as I am informed, universally avoided' (Geo. III's *Corr.,* ed. Fortescue, i. 63).

4. 'So may the Fates preserve the ears you lend' (*Dunciad,* iii. 214). A reference to William Prynne (1600–69), Puritan pamphleteer, who twice had his ears cropped for libelling Charles I and Henrietta Maria.

5. The debate turned on whether a complaint of breach of privilege had priority over the usual form of opening the session by reading a bill. The Opposition wanted the complaint to come first so that Wilkes could speak prior to the reading of the King's Message on the *North Briton.* HW gives a brief account of the debate in *Mem. Geo. III* i. 249–50; a full list of the speakers (and brief accounts of the positions of some) is in Fortescue, op. cit. i. 54–6. See also *Journals of the House of Commons* xxix. 667 for the exact wording of the successive questions and amendments moved during the course of the debate.

acquaint us with the arrest of Wilkes and all that affair,[6] and the complaint which Wilkes himself stood up to make.[7] At six we divided on the question of reading a bill.[8] Young Thomas Townshend[9] divided the House injudiciously, as the question was so idle; yet the whole argument of the day had been so complicated with this question, that in effect it became the material question for trying forces. This will be an interesting part to you, when you hear that your brother[10] and I were in the minority. You know *him*, and therefore know he did what he thought right; and for *me*, my dear Lord, you

6. The King's Message is printed ibid. xxix. 667–8. It brought before the House the question (over the extent of Parliamentary privilege) raised by Wilkes's arrest in April 1763 for a 'most seditious and dangerous libel' and his subsequent release from the Court of Common Pleas and his successful defiance of orders to attend proceedings in the Court of King's Bench on the grounds of his privilege as a member of the House of Commons.

7. Wilkes made his complaint immediately after the motion of thanks for the King's Message had been made and seconded (*Mem. Geo. III* i. 250; Fortescue, op. cit. i. 56), not after the *North Briton* had been condemned, as is implied in the *Journals of the House of Commons* xxix. 668. His complaint was first printed by himself in *A Complete Collection of the Genuine Papers, Letters, etc. in the Case of John Wilkes*, Paris, 1767, pp. 51–4, and subsequently reprinted in eighteenth-century collections of debates, in Cobbett, *Parl. Hist.* xv. 1360–1, and in Wilkes, *Correspondence*, ed. Almon, 1805, ii. 4–7.

8. The division was on whether an amended amendment should be added to the question for reading a bill to open the session, so that the question would read 'that a bill prepared by the clerk for the opening the session . . . be read the first time before the House will receive the message relating to the privileges of this House, which Mr Chancellor of the Exchequer has signified that he has in command from his Majesty to deliver to the House, and before the complaint of a breach of the privilege of this House, which John Wilkes, Esquire, has in his place offered to make, be heard.' The original amendment had been moved by

Pitt to give Wilkes priority to make his complaint immediately after the reading of the bill (the Opposition having apparently conceded that the reading of the bill come first), while the amendment to the amendment was moved by Lord North to give priority to the King's Message. The amendment in this revised form passed the House without a division, suggesting government approval. However, upon the question being put to add the revised amendment to the question for reading a bill, the House did divide, and the question was defeated, 300-111, with the Court majority voting *against* the revised amendment, and with the Opposition minority voting for it, suggesting that the latter now *approved* of the King's Message's priority over Wilkes's complaint (*Journals of the House of Commons* xxix. 667; Fortescue, op. cit. i. 54–6). In the absence of a full report on the debate, the manœuvres that led to this double reversal of position (and particularly those leading to the reversal of the Opposition) remain obscure.

9. (1733–1800), cr. (1783) Bn and (1789) Vct Sydney; M.P. Whitechurch 1754–83. He had been clerk of the Board of Green Cloth 1760-2, but had been summarily dismissed in the general purge of those who had voted against the Peace in Dec. 1762 (*Mem. Geo. III* i. 185), and remained in Opposition, except for the years 1765–8, until 1782. He was usually called 'young' or 'Tommy' to distinguish him from his father, Thomas Townshend (1701–80), M.P. Winchelsea 1722–7, Cambridge Univ. 1727–74.

10. Conway had also spoken during the debate on reading a bill (Fortescue, op. cit. i. 55).

must know that I would die in the House for its privileges, and the liberty of the press. But come, don't be alarmed: this will have no consequences.[11] I don't think your brother is going into Opposition; and for me, if I may name myself to your affection after *him,* nothing but a question of such magnitude can carry me to the House at all. I am sick of parties and factions, and leave them to buy and sell one another. Bless me! I had forgot the numbers: they were 300, we 111.

We then went upon the King's Message; heard the *North Briton* read; and Lord North,[12] who took the prosecution upon him and did it very well, moved to vote it a scandalous libel, etc., *tending to foment treasonable insurrections.*[13] Mr Pitt gave up the paper, but fought against the last words of the censure.[14] I say *Mr Pitt,* for indeed, like Almanzor,[15] he fought almost singly, and spoke forty times:[16] the first time in the day with much wit,[17] afterwards with little energy.[18] He had a tough enemy too; I don't mean in parts or

11. On the contrary, the King, when notified by Grenville that Conway (a lord of the Bedchamber) had twice voted with the Minority, wrote: 'Gen. Conway's conduct is amazing. I am hurt for Lord Hertford; I shall propose to Mr Grenville the dismissing instantly, for in this question I am personally concerned.' Grenville, however, had a further discussion of the subject with the King on 16 Nov. and 'advised his Majesty to defer it till the whole affair was concluded relating to Mr Wilkes, and Mr Conway's conduct thoroughly known upon it. The King said Mr Grenville was right in his opinion, and he would follow it' (ibid. i. 54; *Grenville Papers* ii. 162, 223–4). The subsequent steps leading to Conway's dismissal appear in the following letters.

12. Frederick North (1732–92), styled Lord North 1752–90, 2d E. of Guilford, 1790; first lord of the Treasury 1770–82; at this time a junior lord of the Treasury.

13. Lord North's motion, carried after the division on the amendment, read: 'that the paper, entitled, "The *North Briton,* No. 45" is a false, scandalous, and seditious libel, containing expressions of the most unexampled insolence and contumely towards his Majesty, the grossest aspersions upon both Houses of Parliament, and the most audacious defiance of the authority of the whole legislature; and

most manifestly tending to alienate the affections of the people from his Majesty, to withdraw them from their obedience to the laws of the realm, and to excite them to traitorous insurrections against his Majesty's government' (*Journals of the House of Commons* xxix. 668).

14. Pitt objected to Wilkes's motion to omit the word 'false' from the motion, but moved to omit the words 'and to excite them to traitorous insurrection against his Majesty's government' (Fortescue, op. cit. i. 56; *Journals of the House of Commons* xxix. 668). HW gives a report of his speech in *Mem. Geo. III* i. 250–1.

15. The hero of Dryden's *Conquest of Granada.*

16. According to Grenville's list of speakers, Pitt spoke twenty-one times during the debate; Grenville also told the King that 'both of the divisions were chiefly supported by Mr Pitt and the latter almost by him alone' (Fortescue, op. cit. i. 53–7).

17. Apparently the speech in defence of the priority of a complaint of breach of privilege over the reading of a bill, which HW reports in *Mem. Geo. III* i. 250.

18. Pitt was, as usual, suffering from the gout, though at the moment he was 'tolerably well' except for lameness in one hand (Pitt to Newcastle [16 Nov.], [17

argument, but one that makes an excellent bulldog, the Solicitor-General Norton.[19] Legge was, as usual, concise;[20] and Charles Townshend, what is not usual, silent. We sat till within few minutes of two,[21] after dividing again;[22] we, our exact former number, 111; they, 273; and then we adjourned to go on the point of privilege the next day:[23] but now

> Listen, lordings, and hold you still;
> Of doughty deeds tell you I will.[24]

Martin,[25] in the debate, mentioned the *North Briton,* in which he himself had been so heavily abused;[26] and he said, 'Whoever stabs a

Nov.], BM Add. MSS 32952, ff. 376, 378). In addition to the speeches of Pitt reported by HW, Grenville mentions ones in which there passed between himself and Pitt 'personal altercation' in which the latter was 'extremely warm'; and that Pitt also made 'a very abusive attack upon the late Attorney-General [Charles Yorke] and the Solicitor [Norton]' (*Grenville Papers* ii. 223).

19. Sir Fletcher Norton (1716–89), Kt 1762; cr. (1782) Bn Grantley; M.P. Appleby 1756–61, Wigan 1761–8, Guildford 1768–82; solicitor-general 1762–3; attorney-general 1763–5; speaker of the House of Commons 1770–80. He had replied to the speech in which Pitt moved the amendment to the resolution condemning the *North Briton* (Fortescue, op. cit. i. 56). He had also spoken once in the debate on reading a bill and twice, once directly in answer to Pitt, on the adjournment (ibid. i. 56–7).

20. He had spoken once, in the debate on reading a bill (ibid. i. 55).

21. The newspapers agree with HW, but both Grenville and the *Journals* of the House mention the adjournment as being agreed upon 'near one o'clock' (*Daily Adv.* 17 Nov.; Fortescue, op. cit. i. 54; *Journals of the House of Commons* xxix. 668).

22. A motion being made, asserting in part that the *North Briton* No. 45 tended 'to alienate the affections of the people from his Majesty . . . and to excite them to traitorous insurrections against his Majesty's government,' an amendment was proposed to leave out the words, 'and to excite them,' etc.; the House divided on

the question 'that those words stand part of the question' (ibid.).

23. Actually, to continue consideration of the King's Message with the understanding that as soon as proceedings on that were over, the House would then consider Wilkes's complaint (Fortescue, op. cit. i. 54, 57–8).

24. HW may be quoting from a version of 'The Rising in the North,' a ballad about the insurrection led by the Earls of Northumberland and Westmorland in 1569 to free Mary, Queen of Scots, and restore the Catholic religion. One extant version (in *Bishop Percy's Folio Manuscript,* ed. J. W. Hales and F. J. Furnivall, 1867–8, ii. 210) begins:
'Listen, liuely lordings all,
    & all *that* beene this place within!
if youle giue eare vnto my songe,
    I will tell you how this geere did begin.'

25. Samuel Martin, secretary to the Treasury 1758–63 (*ante* 15 Nov. 1755). In April 1763 he had been given the reversion of HW's ushership of the Exchequer (Montagu ii. 65; *Mem. Geo. III* i. 210).

26. The passages attacking Martin were in the *North Briton* Nos 37 (12 Feb. 1763) and 40 (5 March 1763); 'The secretary of a certain board, a very apt tool of ministerial persecution, with a spirit worthy of a Portuguese inquisitor, is hourly looking for carrion in every office to feed the maw of the insatiable vulture.' 'With respect to the letter mentioned in the Memorial [of John Ghest, quoted in the *North Briton* No. 40], I should guess that it was at the time suppressed from the

reputation in the dark, without setting his name, is a cowardly, malignant, and scandalous scoundrel.'[27] This, looking at Wilkes, he repeated twice, with such rage and violence, that he owned his passion obliged him to sit down. Wilkes bore this with the same indifference as he did all that passed in the day. The House too, who from Martin's choosing to take a public opportunity of resentment, when he had so long declined any private notice, and after Wilkes's courage was become so problematic,[28] seemed to think there was no danger of such champions going further;[29] but the next day, when we came into the House, the first thing we heard was that Martin had shot Wilkes:[30] so he had; but Wilkes has six lives still good.[31] It seems Wilkes had writ, to avow the paper, to Martin, on which the latter challenged him.[32] They went into Hyde Park about noon,

Treasury; or, perhaps, in violation of every rule of honour, and of every right of office, with papers of the utmost moment, conveyed away to a patron very similar and worthy of him, by the most treacherous, base, selfish, mean, abject, low-lived and dirty fellow that ever wriggled himself into a secretaryship' (*The North Briton*, 1769, pp. 122–3, 132).

27. Martin had spoken three times in the debate (Fortescue, op. cit. i. 55–6). In the letter he wrote to Wilkes the following day challenging him, he quoted himself as saying 'that the writer of the *North Briton*, who had stabbed me in the dark, was a cowardly as well as a malignant and infamous scoundrel' (Wilkes, op. cit. ii. 13).

28. Because of his questionable conduct in avoiding a duel with Captain John Forbes at Paris the previous August, behaviour that HW consistently implies to have bordered on cowardice (MANN vi. 162; *Mem. Geo. III* i. 223–4). In adopting this attitude, HW was merely following general opinion, for Wilkes's friends had been unable to allay suspicions that his initial excuse for declining the duel—a previous engagement with Lord Egremont —was specious, that his subsequent conduct of negotiations with Forbes was calculated to make the projected duel known to the Parisian police so that they would (as they did) intervene and forbid it, and that his later over-publicized attempts (following Egremont's death) to meet Forbes at Menin and elsewhere were

calculated in the knowledge that Forbes was unable to make the rendezvous. See, for example, the controversy on the subject in the *London Chronicle*, Sept.–Oct., xiv. 216, 271–2, 310–11, 322, 335, 352, 368. But the passages relating to the affair in Wilkes's correspondence with Charles Churchill (*The Correspondence of John Wilkes and Charles Churchill*, ed. E. S. Weatherly, New York, 1954, pp. 63–4, 66–9, 71–2) tend to vindicate Wilkes's intentions and to justify the accounts given by his friends at the time, and later in Wilkes, op. cit. i. 213–23.

29. The House usually intervened to forbid duels when personalities exchanged in the House threatened to result in one (*Mem. Geo. III* i. 252).

30. 'The next day [16 Nov.], when I went down to the House, I found all the members standing on the floor in great hubbub, questioning, hearing, and eagerly discussing I knew not what. I soon learned that Wilkes about two hours before had been dangerously wounded by Martin in a duel' (*Mem. Geo. III* i. 251–2). The details of the account HW gives in this letter and in the *Memoirs* (i. 252) closely correspond with those given in the full accounts of the duel in the newspapers (*London Chronicle* 15–17 Nov., xiv. 480; *Lloyd's Evening Post* 16–18 Nov., xiii. 485; *St James's Chronicle* 15–17 Nov.).

31. This was Wilkes's third duel; see the last sentence in this paragraph.

32. The letters exchanged, together with an account of the duel, were published by

Humphrey Coates,[33] the wine-merchant, waiting in a post-chaise to convey Wilkes away if triumphant. They fired at the distance of fourteen yards: both missed. Then Martin fired and lodged a ball in the side of Wilkes,[34] who was going to return it, but dropped his pistol. He desired Martin to take care of securing himself, and assured him he would never say a word against him, and he allows that Martin behaved well.[35] The wound yesterday was thought little more than a flesh wound, and he was in his old spirits.[36] Today the account is worse, and he has been delirious:[37] so you will think when you hear what is to come.[38] I think, from the agitation his mind must be in, from his spirits, and from drinking, as I suppose he will, that he probably will end here.[39] He puts me in mind of two lines of *Hudibras,* which, by the arrangement of the words combined with Wilkes's story, are stronger than Butler[40] intended them—

But he that fights and runs away,
May live to fight another day.[41]

Wilkes himself in *A Complete Collection* (above, n. 7), pp. 54–9; reprinted, with additions to the account, in Wilkes, op. cit. ii. 12–17.

33. Humphrey Cotes (d. 1775), politician; friend of Wilkes and Lord Temple; wine-merchant in Mincing Lane until he went bankrupt in 1767; unsuccessful candidate for Westminster, 1774 (SELWYN 225, n. 6).

34. The force of the ball was stopped by Wilkes's coat and waistcoat buttons. It 'entered his belly about half an inch below the navel, and sunk obliquely, on the right side, towards the groin, but did not penetrate the abdomen' (Wilkes, op. cit. ii. 17). An admirer preserved the buttons in a silver box with a patriotic inscription; see Percy Fitzgerald, *The Life and Times of John Wilkes,* 1888, i. 222, n.

35. All the contemporary accounts, and Wilkes's own (though written later), pay tribute to Martin's offers of service after the duel (references cited above, n. 30). The *St James's Chronicle* 15–17 Nov. also has Wilkes expressly declaring that 'his antagonist had behaved like a gentleman.' The discovery a few days later that Martin had been long practising at a target subsequently dampened the admiration.

36. 'I apprehend Mr Wilkes's wound is *not* dangerous. . . . He is in very good spirits and does not seem to think himself in any danger' (Dr Hawkins to Newcastle 16 Nov. 'past nine at night,' BM Add. MSS 32952, f. 383). 'Mr Wilkes seemed quite easy on Wednesday, after the ball was extracted and the wound dressed, rested well that night, and was yesterday [17 Nov.] thought to be in a fair way of recovery' (*Daily Adv.* 18 Nov.).

37. 'We hear from good authority, that a gentleman of distinction, who fought a duel yesterday . . . lies dangerously ill at his house in Great George Street, being delirious, and in great agony, occasioned from the wound received' ('Postscript' to the *St James's Chronicle* 15–17 Nov.). Wilkes thought himself in such danger that he returned Martin's challenge to protect Martin in case of his death (Wilkes, op. cit. ii. 16).

38. The account of the *Essay on Woman,* which HW gives below.

39. Wilkes soon recovered.

40. Samuel Butler (1612–80).

41. These lines, though commonly attributed to Butler, are not in *Hudibras:* the same sentiment, however, is expressed in Part III, canto iii, ll. 243–4:

His adventures with Lord Talbot,[42] Forbes,[43] and Martin, make these lines history.

Now for part the second. On the first day, in your House, where the Address was moved by Lord Hillsborough and Lord Suffolk, after some wrangling between Lord Temple, Lord Halifax, the Duke of Bedford, and Lord Gower,[44] Lord Sandwich[45] laid before the House the most blasphemous and indecent poem that ever was composed, called 'An Essay on Woman, with notes by Dr Warburton.'[46] I will tell you none of the particulars: they were so exceedingly bad, that Lord Lyttleton begged the reading might be stopped. The House was amazed; nobody ventured even to ask a question: so it was easily voted everything you please, and a breach of privilege into the bargain.[47] Lord Sandwich then informed your Lordships that Mr Wilkes

'For those that fly may fight again
Which he can never do that's slain.'
The source of the lines HW quotes is uncertain, though the sentiment itself, expressed in various ways, can be traced back to antiquity; a contemporary citation of the lines is included in anonymous verses in J. Newbery, *The Art of Poetry on a New Plan*, 1762, ii. 147.

42. Wilkes had fought a duel with him on 5 Oct. 1762.

43. John Forbes (d. 1809) of Skellater, a Scotsman first in the French and then in the Portuguese service. He 'married a princess of the blood-royal of Portugal, and rose to be a field marshal in the Portuguese service. He was a distinguished soldier, and acted with great success against the Spaniards. He accompanied the royal family to the Brazils, where he died in 1809' (*The New Statistical Account of Scotland*, 1845, xii. 541–2; William Anderson, *The Scottish Nation*, Edinburgh, 1872–4, ii. 234). He was said to be 'a young man of three and twenty' at the time of the challenge to Wilkes (*London Chronicle* 27–9 Sept., xiv. 311), but another account said Forbes was 'only nine years of age at the time of the rebellion,' which would make his age 27 (ibid. 15–17 Sept., xiv. 272).

44. The 'diverting' passages in the Lords' debate which HW quotes below apparently occurred during this skirmish; see the brief account of the debate in *Mem. Geo. III* i. 245.

45. At this time secretary of state for the north.

46. The obscene parody of Pope's *Essay on Man*, with notes ascribed to William Warburton, Bp of Gloucester, Pope's editor, was revealed to the world in this debate. Controversy has raged ever since over the true text and authorship; for a discussion and attempt to solve the problems by the use of additional manuscript material, see Raymond Postgate, *That Devil Wilkes*, New York, 1929, pp. 70–8.

47. 'It is resolved, by the lords spiritual and temporal in Parliament assembled, that a printed paper, entitled *An Essay on Woman*, with the notes; and another printed paper, entitled *The Veni Creator Paraphrased*, highly reflecting upon a member of this House, is a manifest breach of the privilege thereof; and is a most scandalous, obscene, and impious libel; a gross profanation of many parts of the Holy Scripture; and a most wicked and blasphemous attempt to ridicule and vilify the person of our Blessed Saviour' (*Journals of the House of Lords* xxx. 415). Accounts of the debate, adding details to the account HW gives here and in *Mem. Geo. III* i. 247–8, are in a misdated letter from Halifax to George III in Fortescue, op. cit. i. 50–1, and in a letter from Warburton to Ralph Allen in *A Selection from Unpublished Papers of . . . Warburton*, ed. F. Kilvert, 1841, pp. 227–9.

was the author.[48] Fourteen copies alone[49] were printed, one of which the ministry had bribed the printer[50] to give up. Lord Temple then objected to the manner of obtaining it,[51] and Bishop Warburton, as much shocked at infidelity[52] as Lord Sandwich had been at obscenity,[53] said, 'The blackest fiends in hell would not keep company with Wilkes when he should arrive there.'[54] Lord Sandwich moved to vote Wilkes the author; but this Lord Mansfield stopped, advertising the House that it was necessary first to hear what Wilkes could say in his defence.[55] Today, therefore, was appointed for that purpose;

48. It is now generally accepted that most of the *Essay* was written by Thomas Potter, an attribution that HW had already heard by the date of this letter, while Wilkes probably contributed the notes, some additions and alterations, and the poems at the end; see Postgate, op. cit. 72–4 and Mann vi. 184. However, for an attempt to prove that Wilkes was indeed the original author, see E. R. Watson, 'John Wilkes and the "Essay on Woman,"' *Notes and Queries*, 1914, 11th ser. ix. 121–3, 143–5, 162–4, 183–5, 203–5, 222–3, 241–2.

49. See Mann vi. 185, n. 22.

50. Michael Curry (ca 1732–88) (GM 1788, lviii pt ii. 752). Postgate states, op. cit. 68, presumably from material in the Crown Solicitor's papers at the Guildhall, that Curry received £233 6s. 6d. in bribes.

51. 'Temple rose up, and said he had as great an abhorrence of the parodies as any lord in the House (when it is generally reported and believed, that he had them in his possession, showed them to others, and was much delighted with them); but that the legality of the method by which they were obtained ought to be inquired into; that the liberty of the subject was concerned in it; and a great deal of nonsense to that purpose. He spoke wretchedly ill, as usual, and was as wretchedly seconded by Lord Sandys, who is gone over to the Opposition. They were answered by the Duke of Bedford, Lord Halifax, Lord Sandwich, and by the Chancellor with his usual heat. Still Temple hung upon it, and I believe rose up half a dozen different times, till Lord Mansfield, finding there would be no end, rose up, and, as he always does, ended the dispute at once. . . . He said

nothing was more absurd than the objection. The coming by evidence illegally does not make that evidence illegal in the trial of a criminal. . . . In short, he exposed and ridiculed the objection so effectually, that the House called out to *go on*' (Kilvert, op. cit. 228–9). See also *Mem. Geo. III* i. 247–8.

52. Warburton's many ventures into controversial theology had produced charges of infidelity from his opponents; HW shared this opinion (*Mem. Geo. II* iii. 239). HW also records that when he informed Pitt of what was going on in the Lords, Pitt replied 'Why do not they search the Bishop of Gloucester's study for heresy?' (*Mem. Geo. III* i. 248).

53. Sandwich's earlier approval of the *Essay* was generally rumoured by this time, together with other examples of his profanity, one of which HW mentions in his letter to Mann of 17 Nov. 1763 (Mann vi. 185).

54. Warburton's speech is printed in Kilvert, op. cit. 281–3. The words as HW quotes them here and in *Mem. Geo. III* i. 247 do not appear in the speech, but they are an obvious reworking of Warburton's conclusion that in Wilkes's parodies 'there is so foul a mixture of bestiality interlarding his fearful blasphemies, that the hardiest inhabitant of hell would blush as well as tremble to hear repeated.' Warburton had been privy to the proceedings against the *Essay* since 5 Nov. (*Grenville Papers* ii. 154; Kilvert, op. cit. 225).

55. 'The House proceeded to the severest vote against the criminal. But here again Lord Mansfield interposed, and said he had his doubts whether it was regular to come to that vote till Wilkes had been

but it has been put off[56] by Martin's *lodging a caveat*. This bomb was certainly well conducted, and the secret, though known to many,[57] well kept. The management is worthy of Lord Sandwich, and like him. It may sound odd for me, with my principles, to admire Lord Sandwich; but besides that he has in several instances been very obliging to me,[58] there is a good humour and an industry about him that are very uncommon.[59] I do not admire politicians; but when they are excellent in their way, one cannot help allowing them their due. Nobody but he could have struck a stroke like this.

Yesterday we sat till eight on the Address,[60] which yet passed without a negative: we had two very long speeches from Mr Pitt and Mr Grenville; many fine parts in each.[61] Mr Pitt has given the latter some strong words, yet not so many as were expected.[62] Tomorrow we go on the great question of privilege;[63] but I must send this away, as we have no chance of leaving the House before midnight, if before next morning.

This long letter contains the history of but two days; yet if two

---

heard. On which Lord Sandwich said, if he had such doubts, he would defer the vote to this day [17 Nov.]' (ibid. 229).

56. Until 22 Nov. and then again postponed because of Wilkes's inability to appear (*Journals of the House of Lords* xxx. 421, 422).

57. Warburton states that 'only two or three of the Cabinet Council' besides himself knew of the government's intention to bring forward the *Essay;* and the only persons mentioned as privy to the secret in the one published letter relating to the preparation of the attack are Sandwich, Halifax, Lord Chancellor Henley and Bishop Warburton (Kilvert, op. cit. 227; *Grenville Papers* ii. 153–5). But it is evident that several of the subordinate agents engaged in obtaining the copy of the verses and the legal officers of the Crown, particularly P. C. Webb, must have known what was going on; see Postgate, op. cit. 66–7.

58. For example, he presented HW with a portrait of Ninon de Lenclos, given by that lady herself to Sandwich's grandmother (see Sandwich to HW 22 July 1757 and *ante* 4 June 1758).

59. 'His industry to carry any point he had in view was so remarkable, that for a

long time the world mistook it for abilities' (*Mem. Geo. II* i. 187). HW mentions his 'partiality' for Sandwich in even stronger terms in a letter to Montagu of 20 Nov. 1763 (MONTAGU ii. 111).

60. Of thanks for the King's speech at the opening of the session, not for the message on privilege, consideration of which was deferred on Grenville's motion to 18 Nov., when the Ministry learned of Wilkes's duel (*Grenville Papers* ii. 224; *Journals of the House of Commons* xxix. 669; West to Newcastle [16 Nov.], BM Add. MSS 32952, f. 372).

61. HW describes them in *Mem. Geo. III* i. 253–4; there are a few more details in *Grenville Papers* ii. 224–5.

62. Grenville found the personalities in this speech much less objectionable than those on the previous day, and described it as 'totally different from the tone of the preceding debate' (ibid. ii. 223, 224). Pitt's speech actually discomfited his friends and pleased his enemies; see the letter of Lord Barrington to Andrew Mitchell quoted *Chatham Corr.* ii. 262, n. and *Grenville Papers* ii. 164–5.

63. Because of the Speaker's illness, the debate was postponed to Wednesday, 23 Nov.

days furnish a history, it is not my fault. The Ministry, I think, may do whatever they please. Three hundred, that will give up their own privileges, may be depended upon for giving up anything else. I have not time or room to ask a question, or say a word more.

Yours, ever,

H. W.

Nov. 18, Friday.

I have luckily got a holiday, and can continue my dispatch, as you know dinner-time is my chief hour of business. The Speaker,[64] unlike Mr Onslow,[65] who was immortal in the chair,[66] is taken very ill, and our House is adjourned to Monday.[67] Wilkes is thought in great danger:[68] instead of keeping him quiet, his friends have shown their zeal by visiting him,[69] and himself has been all spirits and riot, and sat up in his bed the next morning to correct the press for tomorrow's *North Briton*.[70] His bons mots are all over the town, but too gross, I think, to repeat; the chief are at the expense of poor Lord George.[71] Notwithstanding Lord Sandwich's masked battery, the tide runs violently for Wilkes, and I do not find people in gen-

64. Sir John Cust (1718–70), 3d Bt; M.P. Grantham 1743–70; speaker of the House of Commons 1761–70.

65. Arthur Onslow, speaker of the House of Commons 1727–61.

66. The *St James's Chronicle*, 22–4 Nov., mentions that Onslow in 35 years as Speaker missed only one day in the House, and that on account of the death of his brother.

67. Cust was unable to attend the House until Wednesday, 23 Nov., so that the adjournment was extended to then.

68. So the newspapers reported, mentioning a fever on the 18th; but on that very day Wilkes informed his daughter that his physician and surgeon had declared him out of danger (*Daily Adv.* 19 Nov.; *St James's Chronicle* 17–19 Nov., postscript; Wilkes, op. cit. ii. 27).

69. 'His Grace the Duke of Bolton, the Right Hon. Earl Temple, and Mr Pitt, etc. waited on Mr Wilkes the moment he was carried home after receiving his wound' (*St James's Chronicle* 15–17 Nov.; *Annual Register*, 1763, p. 111). The in-

clusion of Pitt in the list, in view of his explicit denunciation of Wilkes on 24 Nov., is probably a piece of propaganda on the part of Wilkes's friends rather than a statement of fact.

70. A false rumour; the last *North Briton* to be published, No. 46, had appeared on Saturday, 12 Nov. (Wilkes, op. cit. i. 224–38), and there is no evidence that others were planned for the subsequent Saturdays.

71. Sackville. They probably concerned the allegedly homosexual relations between Lord George, George Stone, Primate of Ireland, and Col. Robert Cuninghame (later 1st Bn Rossmore), which had been the subject of much scandal in 1752 (MANN iv. 315–16; passage in foul copy of *Mem. Geo. II* for 1752, omitted in fair copy and in Holland's edition at i. 281). There is an allusion to Lord George and the Primate at the bottom of the title-page of what seems most likely to be the true copy of the *Essay on Woman* in the Dyce Collection (Fitzgerald, op. cit. i. 196, n.).

eral so inclined to excuse his Lordship as I was. One hears nothing but stories of the latter's impiety, and of the concert he was in with Wilkes on that subject.[72] Should this hero die, the Bishop of Gloucester[73] may doom him whither he pleases, but Wilkes will pass for a saint and a martyr.

Besides what I have mentioned, there were two or three passages in the House of Lords that were diverting.[74] Lord Temple dwelled much on the Spanish Ministry being devoted to France.[75] Lord Halifax replied, 'Can we help that? We can no more oblige the King of Spain to change his ministers, than his Lordship can force his Majesty to change the present administration.' Lord Gower, too, attacking Lord Temple on want of respect to the King, the Earl replied, he never had wanted respect for the King: he and his family had been attached to the House of Hanover *full as long* as his Lordship's family had.[76]

You may imagine that little is talked of but Wilkes, and what relates to him. Indeed, I believe there is no other news, but that Sir George Warren marries Miss Bishop,[77] the maid of honour. The Duchess of Grafton is at Euston, and *hopes*[77a] to stay there till after Christmas. Operas do not begin till tomorrow sennight;[78] but the Mingotti is to sing, and that contents me.[79] I forgot to tell you, and you may wonder at hearing nothing of the Reverend Mr Charles

72. HW reports some of these stories in his letters to Mann 17 Nov. 1763 (Mann vi. 185) and to Montagu 20 Nov. 1763 (Montagu ii. 111), and in *Mem. Geo. III* i. 248. He declined to report them to Hertford (*post* 9 Dec. 1763).

73. Warburton.

74. During the 'wrangling' after the King's speech had been read (above, n. 44).

75. Gen. Richard Wall, the pro-British Spanish minister for foreign affairs, had resigned in Sept. in favour of the Marquis Grimaldi, Spanish ambassador to France, negotiator of the Family Compact, and an ardent supporter of Franco-Spanish unity.

76. Lord Gower's father, the 1st E. Gower, had intrigued much with the Jacobites in his youth, and had once been considered the head of that party in England. He had gone over to the government in the early 1740s, remained firm during the ''45,' and was rewarded with his earldom. Lord Temple's an-

cestors had been staunch supporters of the Hanoverians from the beginning.

77. Frances Bisshopp, maid of honour 1761–3 (*ante* 14 July 1761, n. 30), m. (3 Feb. 1764) Sir George Warren (1735–1801) of Stockport and Poynton, Cheshire; K.B. 1761; M.P. Lancaster borough 1758–80, 1786–96, Beaumaris 1780–4 (GM 1801, lxxi pt ii. 861). They were separated in 1772 after airing their differences in the ecclesiastical courts, but were later reconciled; see GM loc. cit.; 1804, lxxiv pt i. 190; *Annual Register*, 1804, xlvi. 468; and the London newspapers, particularly the *St James's Chronicle* for 1771–2, which gives an almost day by day account of their feud.

77a. An allusion to the growing incompatibility of the Duke and Duchess.

78. 26 Nov.

79. She had been performing in London since the season of 1754–5 (*London Stage* Pt IV, i. pp. lxviii, 437 *et passim*).

Pylades,[80] while Mr John Orestes[81] is making such a figure: but Dr Pylades, the poet, has forsaken his consort[82] and the Muses, and is gone off with a stonecutter's daughter.[83] If he should come and offer himself to you for chaplain to the Embassy![84]

The Countess of Harrington[85] was extremely alarmed last Sunday, on seeing the Duc de Prequigny[86] enter her assembly: she forbade Lady Caroline[87] speaking to such a debauched young man, and communicated her fright to everybody. The Duchess of Bedford observed to me that as Lady Berkeley and some other matrons of the same stamp were there, she thought there was no danger of any violence being committed.[88] For my part, the sisters are so different, that I conclude my Lady Hertford has not found any young man in France wild enough for *her*.[89] Your counterpart, Monsieur de Guerchy, takes extremely. I have not yet seen his wife.

I this minute receive your charming long letter of the 11th,[90] and

80. Charles Churchill, the poet and intimate friend of Wilkes (*ante* 29 Oct. 1762, n. 26). Pylades was the proverbial friend of Orestes.

81. Wilkes.

82. Martha Scott or Scot, an otherwise almost completely obscure woman with whom Churchill had contracted a Fleet Street marriage about 1749. They had been separated since 1760 or 1761, according to HW because they had 'tired of each other,' and she had become first the housekeeper and then the mistress of Gen. Tatton, while Churchill had entered upon 'all his debaucheries' (DU DEFFAND v. 374; Wallace Cable Brown, *Charles Churchill*, Lawrence, Kansas, 1953, pp. 17, 28–29, 219–20, n. 27).

83. Elizabeth Carr (b. ca 1748). She has been identified as Elizabeth Cheere, a daughter of Sir Henry Cheere (1703–81), Kt 1761, cr. (1766) Bt, an eminent sculptor, on the basis of an explicit statement to that effect by Mrs Montagu; but this identification has been questioned by Churchill's most recent biographer on the certainty that the lady's name is consistently spelled 'Carr' and that a daughter can in no way be connected with the well-documented life of Sir Henry Cheere (Joseph M. Beatty, Jr, 'Mrs Montagu, Churchill and Miss Cheere?,' *Modern Language Notes*, 1926, xli. 384–6; Brown,

op. cit. 178–9). Brown suggests no alternative identification, but it seems possible that she may have been an otherwise unmentioned daughter of Joseph Carr (fl. 1754–68), a sculptor and stone-mason with a yard at Mill Bank, Westminster (Rupert Gunnis, *Dictionary of British Sculptors, 1660–1851*, [1953], pp. 83–4). All that is certainly known of Elizabeth Carr is incorporated in the account of her affair with Churchill in Brown, op. cit. 172–81.

84. HW is probably hinting at a rumour, current in London by early December, that Churchill had gone to France (*St James's Chronicle* 6–8 Dec.). The same report was current in Paris late in Dec. (*post* 28 Dec. 1763). Churchill's exact whereabouts is unknown after early Nov., but according to Brown, op. cit. 182–3, 'in all probability' he did not go to France.

85. Lady Hertford's sister.

86. *Sic* in *Works;* correctly 'Pecquigny.'

87. Lady Caroline Stanhope, the Countess's eldest daughter.

88. Lady Berkeley was notorious for her gallantries.

89. HW is being ironic; Lady Harrington was as notorious for her vulgarity and exhibitionism as her sister was famous for her virtue and decorum.

90. The letter was presumably brought

give you a thousand thanks for it. I wish next Tuesday[91] was past, for Lady Hertford's sake. You may depend on my letting you know if I hear the least rumour in your disfavour. I should do so without your orders, for I could not bear to have you traduced and not advertise you to defend yourself. I have hitherto not heard a syllable; but the newspapers talk of your magnificence,[92] and I approve extremely your intending to support their evidence; for though I do not think it necessary to scatter pearls and diamonds about the streets like their Vice-Majesties of Ireland,[93] one owes it to one's self and to the King's choice to prove it was well made.

The colour given at Paris to Bunbury's stay in England has been given out here too. You need not, I think, trouble yourself about that; a majority of 300 will soon show, that if he was detained, the reason at least no longer subsists.

Hamilton[94] is certainly returning from Ireland.[95] Lord Shannon's son is going to marry the Speaker's daughter,[96] and the Primate[97] has begged to have the honour of joining their hands.[98]

by the messenger who arrived from France on 18 Nov. carrying dispatches from Hertford (St James's Chronicle 17–19 Nov.). This and the following paragraph answer various points in Hertford's letter.

91. The day of Lady Hertford's presentation, according to Hertford's letter of the 11th; the date was changed to Sunday, 20 Nov. (post 19 Nov. 1763).

92. 'Paris, Nov. 4. My Lord Hertford, the British ambassador, makes a great figure here, and his retinue is as numerous as brilliant. Mr Hume, the author of the History of England and of several other celebrated works, is his secretary' (Daily Adv. 16 Nov.: St James's Chronicle 15–17 Nov.).

93. The Earl and Countess of Northumberland. Northumberland had succeeded Halifax as lord lieutenant of Ireland in April 1763, and had arrived in Dublin 22 Sept. (Calendar of Home Office Papers 1760–1765, ed. J. Redington, 1878, p. 307; Elizabeth, Duchess of Northumberland, The Diaries of a Duchess, ed. Greig, 1926, p. 57). HW mentions that his 'profusion and ostentation had been so great, that it seemed to lay a dangerous precedent for succeeding governors, who must risk unpopularity if more parsimonious; or the ruin of their fortune,

should they imitate his example' (Mem. Geo. III i. 332).

94. William Gerard ('Single Speech') Hamilton, chief secretary to the lord lieutenant of Ireland 1761–4.

95. Though on increasingly bad terms with Northumberland and the rest of the Irish government, he remained at his post until May 1764, when he was finally dismissed in favour of the Earl of Drogheda; see post 2 Dec. 1763, n. 35. HW's Irish intelligence at this time seems to be based on hearsay rather than solid information, since many of his reports contain serious errors of fact; see, in addition to the notes on the Irish passages in his correspondence with Hertford below, his letter to Montagu 12 Nov. 1763, n. 4 (Montagu ii. 108), and the correspondence between Northumberland and Halifax in Redington, op. cit. 314 ff.

96. Catherine Ponsonby (1746–1827), daughter of John Ponsonby, speaker of the Irish House of Commons; m. (15 Dec. 1763) Richard Boyle, styled Vct Boyle 1756–64, 2d E. of Shannon 1764; son of Henry Boyle, 1st E. of Shannon.

97. George Stone.

98. HW had been informed of the projected alliance by Montagu on 15 Nov. 1763 (Montagu ii. 110), with the sig-

This letter is woefully blotted and ill-written, yet I must say it is print compared to your Lordship's. At first I thought you had forgot that you was not writing to the Secretary of State, and had put it into cipher. Adieu! I am neither dead of my fever[99] nor apoplexy, nay, nor of the House of Commons. I rather think the violent heat of the latter did me good. Lady Aylesbury was at Court yesterday, and benignly received; a circumstance you will not dislike.[100]

Yours, most cordially,

Hor. Walpole

PS. If I have not told you all you want to know, interrogate me, and I will answer the next post.

From Hertford, Saturday 19 November 1763

Printed for the first time from a photostat of BM Add. MSS 23218, ff. 101–2.

Paris, November 19th 1763.

My dear Horry,

I MUST thank you for a long comfortable letter[1] I have received from you before I attend Lady Hertford to Versailles. We sup this evening with the Duchess of Praslin,[2] and tomorrow her Excellency is to be presented to the royal family of France,[3] attended by the English gentlemen here, who still make a very considerable number.

nificant addition that the Primate 'hates the alliance,' a 'fact' that HW did not send on to Hertford. The explanation of these somewhat obscure allusions is probably that marriage would unite two of the three lords justices in a family alliance, thus weakening the influence of Stone, the third and most powerful lord justice, in Irish affairs, but that Stone would publicly bless the alliance to demonstrate the unity of the lords justices in resisting any program of directing Irish politics from the Castle through any means but themselves.

99. HW mentions the return of his 'nightly fever' to Montagu 12 Nov. 1763 (ibid. ii. 109).

100. Because it supposedly showed that no resentment was felt at the votes of her husband, Gen. Conway, against the government.

———

1. Missing; written ca 11 Nov.

2. Anne-Marie de Champagne-la-Suze (1713–84); m. (1732) César-Gabriel de Choiseul, Duc de Praslin, secretary of state for foreign affairs.

3. The date of presentation had apparently been changed, as Hertford had previously informed HW that it would take place on Tuesday, 22 Nov. (ante 11 Nov. 1763).

LADY ISABELLA FITZROY, COUNTESS OF HERTFORD,
BY ALEXANDRE ROSLIN

Lord Holderness is to be at the head of this procession.[4] He returned here three or four days ago from his tour through the southern provinces.[5] Both him and Lady Holdernesse[6] dined with us yesterday; they dined with us again today, and his Lordship attends us this evening to the manufacture at Sève and from thence to Versailles.

Lady Hertford is magnificently prepared for the ceremony; her own dress is ordered by the Duchess of Nivernois, and is beautiful; her pages, *officiers* or men out [of] livery, with the servants in livery, are all dressed for the occasion, and it is nobly done. Do not think my head is turned and that I am grown so young as to forget I have thirteen children; I mean to act with all proper economy, but since I have undertaken this commission I will not in any instance suffer disgrace from it though it is an expensive one.

The Maréchale[7] goes this evening likewise to Versailles. She has attended Lady Hertford upon her visits and is, with the Duchess of Nivernois and Madame de Gisors,[8] quite interested that everything should go right. I must not upon this occasion omit doing justice to the Nivernois family; their attention to Lady Hertford and the trouble they have undertaken by choice on her account, will sufficiently contradict every bad impression that may have been conceived in England on their indifference of behaviour to the nation.[9] Lady Hertford begins to summon all her powers in the French language and will do very well. She speaks it with modesty and not with impropriety, and the French are satisfied to understand her. If she presumed to dictate in better language she might be worse heard,[10] and yet she has spirit enough for her situation. My son and

4. The custom of gentlemen accompanying an ambassador's wife at her presentation is not mentioned in the protocol for the ceremony in Jean Dumont, Baron de Carlscroon, *Cérémonial diplomatique des cours de l'Europe*, ed. Rousset, Amsterdam, 1739, i. 49–50, 57–8 (*Corps universelle diplomatique, Supplement*, Vol. IV), though it gives directions that her other servants (discussed in the next paragraph) proceed with her in the procession from the entrance chamber to the antechamber of the Queen's reception chamber (i. 49).

5. He and Lady Holdernesse had been on the Continent since late July (*St James's Chronicle* 21–3 July).

6. She subsequently caused something of a furore by being presented to the French Court, thus defying the usual custom of English ladies; see *post* 7 Dec., 16 Dec. 1763 *bis*.

7. Mme de Mirepoix (*ante* 28 Oct. 1763).

8. The widowed daughter of Mme de Nivernais (*ante* 11 Nov. 1763, n. 9).

9. For the source of this impression, see *ante* 18 Oct. 1763, n. 8.

10. Probably a reference to the Duchess of Bedford, who had been unpopular in France (*Leinster Corr.* i. 397).

I go on very well I hope, our language will pass, and we visit all the town, which you must conceive if you can to be a great pleasure, for it is the most constant occupation of the French. They do not begin to play till they get into their select parties for supper about nine o'clock. They then play for a quarter of an hour before they sup and finish the party when they rise from table. The rest of the time is all passed in conversation upon the most common subjects; a knowledge of the royal family and some study of their plays and spectacles are necessary for a man who would shine in company.

What is become of Déon?[11] I suppose he fears the Bastile more than the *petites maisons*[12] and therefore remains in England. He is generally treated here as a madman,[13] which is the most charitable way of treating him in his present circumstances.[14] What the Minis-

11. Charles-Geneviève-Louis-Auguste-André-Timothée de Beaumont (1728–1810), Chevalier d'Éon; French diplomatist who subsequently caused a sensation by posing as a woman. He had been secretary to Nivernais during the latter's embassy to England and then, pending the arrival of Guerchy, temporary minister plenipotentiary to England. The sudden elevation had gone to his head with results mentioned below and discussed in succeeding letters.

12. Madhouses.

13. Even by Louis XV himself, who had to some extent secretly encouraged d'Éon's behaviour; he wrote to one of his secret agents as early as 11 Oct. that d'Éon's appointment as minister had apparently turned his head (*Correspondance secrète inédite de Louis XV*, ed. E. Boutaric, 1866–8, i. 299).

14. D'Éon had received his letters of recall on Guerchy's arrival, but had refused to present them, to obey orders to turn over his papers to the new ambassador, or to return to France. Guerchy protested, and on 4 Nov. Praslin, in the King's name, sent to the English ministry a demand for d'Éon's extradition, a demand impossible to fulfil under English law, but which removed d'Éon's official character. He still remained in London, however, in open defiance of the orders of the French ministry, and evaded all attempts to seize his papers, with results described in subsequent letters in the present correspondence. The history of the affair, which has never been wholly explained, is complicated by the fact that d'Éon, in addition to his official capacity, served as an agent of Louis XV's secret diplomacy, and had had the tacit approval of the King in the first stages of his refusal to turn over his papers. But a famous letter from the King to d'Éon, 4 Oct. 1763, ordering him to disregard the recall, to disguise himself as a woman, and to remain in England incognito, is in all probability a forgery, since the subsequent correspondence of the King with his other secret agents makes it clear that he had acquiesced in the first recall and the order for extradition, and that he expected d'Éon to return to France—though perhaps significantly, he never ordered him expressly to do so. The King's correspondence is printed ibid. i. 298ff.; d'Éon's own version is given at length in the first volume of his *Mémoires*, 1836; and full discussions of the affair, from conflicting points of view, are in J. B. Telfer, *The Strange Career of the Chevalier d'Éon de Beaumont*, 1885, pp. 90ff., where the discussion is extremely pro-d'Éon; and in E. A. Vizetelly, *The True Story of the Chevalier d'Éon*, 1895, pp. 149ff., where the discussion is more critical in its treatment of some vital evidence.

ters may intend I do not know, but he is a Frenchman and must obey their orders if he means ever to serve the King of France.

I desire you will pay my compliments to Lady Mary Coke and acquaint her that upon hearing from an acquaintance of hers in Paris that there was some difficulty in sending a gown to England for her, that I took charge of it, and the Prince de Masseran[15] will I hope deliver it to her next week.[16] Write to me for the future by directing your own letters to Paris; the couriers are uncertain.

Yours etc.,

HERTFORD

To HERTFORD, Friday 25 November 1763

Printed from *Works* ix. 17–22.

Arlington Street, Nov. 25th 1763.

YOU tell me, my dear Lord, in a letter I have this moment received from you, that you have had a comfortable one from me; I fear it was not the last: you will not have been fond of your brother's voting against the Court. Since that he has been told by different channels that they think of taking away regiments from opposers.[1] He heard it, as he would the wind whistle; while in the

15. Vittorio Filippo Ferrero di Biella (1713–77), Principe di Masserano; Spanish ambassador to England 1763–72, ca 1775–7 (DU DEFFAND iv. 203, n. 10).

16. Masserano landed at Dover on 24 Nov., reached London on the 26th, and presented his credentials as ambassador on the 30th (*Daily Adv.* 28 Nov., 1, 5 Dec.). The gown proved to be the wrong dress (*post* 2 Dec. 1763).

1. On the same day that HW wrote this letter, the King told Grenville that Bedford and 'many others' had 'pressed much' the dismissing of some of those who had voted in the minority, and that he himself did not 'differ much with them in this.' He then singled out Conway for immediate dismissal from his military and civil posts (along with Fitzherbert from his civil one), presumably because Conway had voted again against the government (for the earlier instances, see *ante* 17 Nov. 1763 and n. 11), in the divisions on 23 Nov. for postponing the debate on privilege, and again on the 24th on the question whether privilege of Parliament extended to libels. Grenville, however, again counselled moderation, as he had done 16 Nov. in discussing Conway's earlier votes with the King—at least to the extent of delaying any dismissal until Christmas, and then extending it to Barré and 'some others' (*Grenville Papers* ii. 166, 229).

shape of a threat he treats it with contempt: if put into execution, his scorn would subside into indifference. You know he has but one object—doing what is right; the rest may betide as it will. One or two of the ministers, who are honest men, would, *I have reason to believe,* be heartily concerned to have such measures adopted; but they are not directors.[2] The little favour *they* possess, and the desperateness of their situation, oblige them to swallow many things they disapprove, and which ruin their character with the nation; while others, who have no character to lose, and whose situation is no less desperate, care not what inconveniences they bring on their master, nor what confusion on their country, in which they can never prosper, except when it is convulsed. The nation, indeed, seems thoroughly sensible of this truth. They are unpopular beyond conception: even of those that vote with them there are numbers that express their aversion without reserve. Indeed, on Wednesday,[3] this went farther: we were to debate the great point of privilege: Wilbraham[4] objected that Wilkes was involved in it, and ought to be present.[5] On this, though, as you see, a question of slight moment, fifty-seven[6] left them at once: they were but 243 to 166. As we had sat, however, till eight at night,[7] the debate was postponed to next day. Mr Pitt, who had a fever and the gout, came on crutches, and wrapped in flannels:[8] so he did yesterday, but was obliged to retire

2. From *post* 9 Dec. 1763 and 16 Dec. 1763 *bis* it seems that HW means Grenville and Halifax (though he subsequently changed his opinion of Grenville; see *Mem. Geo. III* i. 272). Grenville had so far certainly shown himself averse to precipitate dismissals; as for Halifax, however, in Grenville's account of the division of opinion in the Cabinet on the subject when it was again discussed, 30 Nov., he mentions that Halifax was 'eager for the measure' (*Grenville Papers* ii. 230–1).

3. 23 Nov.

4. Randle Wilbraham (1694–1770), barrister; M.P. Newcastle-under-Lyme 1740–7, Appleby 1747–54, Newton 1754–68; 'the Gamaliel of the Jacobites' (*Mem. Geo. III* i. 258).

5. HW gives an account of the debate, ibid. i. 257–9; there are further details in Geo. III's *Corr.,* ed. Fortescue, i. 61–2, where Grenville attributes the defection

from the government to Wilbraham's intervention; a list of the speakers is in L. B. Namier, *Additions and Corrections to Sir John Fortescue's Edition of the Correspondence of King George III* (*Vol. I*), Manchester, 1937, pp. 82–4.

6. Of their majority of 300 in the first division on 15 Nov.; of these 55 apparently joined the minority, since it was increased by that number.

7. According to Grenville, the division did not take place until nine (*Grenville Papers* ii. 228).

8. On the 24th Pitt wrote to Newcastle by an amanuensis that he had returned from the debate 'extremely fatigued'; that he had 'passed the night in a great deal of pain; continues still in pain, and is much lamer than he was yesterday'; and that his hand was still so weak that he could not hold his pen (Pitt to Newcastle 24 Nov., BM Add. MSS 32953, f. 45).

at ten at night,[9] after making a speech of an hour and fifty minutes;[10] the worst, I think, I ever heard him make in my life.[11] For our parts, we sat till within ten minutes of two in the morning.[12] Yet we had but few speeches,[13] all were so long. Hussey,[14] solicitor to the Princess of Wales, was against the Court, and spoke with great spirit, and true Whig spirit.[15]

Charles Yorke shone exceedingly.[16] He had spoke and voted with us the night before;[17] but now maintained his opinion against Pratt's.[18] It was a most able and learned performance, and the latter part, which was oratoric, uncommonly beautiful and eloquent. You find I don't let partiality to the Whig cause blind my judgment. That speech was certainly the masterpiece of the day. Norton would not have made a figure, even if Charles Yorke had not appeared; but giving way to his natural brutality, he got into an ugly

9. Pitt again informed Newcastle the morning after this debate that he had 'passed a night of much pain and continues still in pain' (Pitt to Newcastle, Friday [25 Nov.], ibid. f. 59).

10. An abstract of Pitt's speech, in which he opposed the proposed limitation of privilege but roundly abused Wilkes and dissociated himself from him, is in [John Debrett], The History, Debates, and Proceedings of Both Houses of Parliament . . . 1743 to . . . 1774, 1792, iv. 149–50. Some details, omitted in the abstract, of Pitt's abuse of the legal profession in this speech, which added to the difficulties of the Opposition in their attempts to reconcile Pitt and Charles Yorke, are in A Selection from Unpublished Papers of William Warburton, ed. F. Kilvert, 1841, p. 232; and Hardwicke Corr. iii. 556–7.

11. Grenville supports HW's criticism; Pitt's speech, he informed the King, 'made no impression on the House' (Grenville Papers ii. 229).

12. Confirmed by Grenville and the newspapers (Daily Adv. 26 Nov.; Fortescue, op. cit. i. 63).

13. Eighteen speakers participated in the debate (Namier, op. cit. 85). HW gives an account of the debate in Mem. Geo. III i. 259–61.

14. Richard Hussey (ca 1715–70), lawyer and politician; M.P. St Michael 1755–61, St Mawes 1761–8, East Looe 1768–70; attorney-general to the Queen 1761–70. HW

is in error both here and in Mem. Geo. III i. 259 in naming his Court office.

15. 'An excellent speech in behalf of privilege and liberty' (ibid.); 'the finest speech that ever was heard, for us' (G. Onslow to Newcastle, 9 o'clock [24 Nov.], in Hardwicke Corr. iii. 556). His opposition on this occasion seems to have caused no comment among members of the government.

16. Supporters of both government and Opposition echo HW's praise of the speech; see Fortescue, op. cit. i. 62; Hardwicke Corr. iii. 557; Kilvert, op. cit. 232. Onslow, however, informed Newcastle that it was 'not half so well received' in the House as Hussey's speech had been (Hardwicke Corr. iii. 556).

17. On the question of postponing the debate on privilege; see ibid. iii. 556. He privately informed Grenville that he had done so out of respect to Wilbraham, whom he had persuaded to support the government on the main question of privilege (Fortescue, op. cit. i. 62).

18. Sir Charles Pratt, Chief Justice of the Common Pleas. In discharging Wilkes on 6 May 1763 he had ruled that privilege of Parliament extended to libels, on the grounds that privilege extended to all cases not treason, felony, or breach of the peace, and that a libel was not a breach of the peace but only tended thereunto. See ante 6 May 1763 and n. 3.

scrape. Having so little delicacy or decency as to mention a cause in which he had prosecuted Sir John Rushout (who sat just under him) for perjury, the tough old knight (who had been honourably acquitted of the charge) gave the House an account of the affair; and then added, 'I was assured the prosecution was set on foot by that *honest gentleman;* I hope I don't call him out of his name—and that it was in revenge for my having opposed him in an election.'[19] Norton denied the charge, upon his honour, which did not seem to persuade everybody.[20]

Immediately after this we had another episode. Rigby, totally unprovoked either by anything said or by the complexion of the day, which was grave and argumentative, fell upon Lord Temple, and described his behaviour on the commitment of Wilkes.[21] James Grenville, who sat behind him, rose in all the acrimony of resentment:[22] drew a very favourable picture of his brother, and then one of Rigby, conjuring up the bitterest words, epithets, and circumstances that he could amass together: told him how interested he was, and how ignorant: painted his journey to Ireland to get a law place,[23] for which he was so unqualified; and concluded with affirming he had fled from thence to avoid the vengeance of the people.[24] The passive Speaker suffered both painters to finish their works, and would have let them carry their colours and brushes into Hyde

19. Perhaps the Evesham election of 1761, in which Rushout and his son were returned after a hard contest. James West wrote, 12 Oct. 1762, that 'Sir J. Rushout has been . . . harassed with prosecutions against himself and friends' on account of this election (Namier and Brooke iii. 384). HW gives a similar account of his altercation with Norton in *Mem. Geo. III* i. 260.

20. 'The shout of the House did justice on Norton' (ibid.).

21. 'Rigby, looking at Lord Temple, who was sitting at the end of the House to hear the debate, as he constantly practised, drew a picture of that incendiary peer, described him in his blue riband encouraging mobs from windows of coffeehouses; and more particularly as the instigator of Wilkes' (ibid.).

22. HW gives more details of Grenville's behaviour on this occasion, ibid.

23. Rigby had been made Master of the Rolls in Ireland in Nov. 1759, and reappointed under a new patent in Feb. 1761, at which time provision had been made for him to take the oaths of office *in absentia* (R. Lascelles, *Liber munerum publicorum Hiberniae (1152–1827); or, The Establishment of Ireland*, Dublin, 1824–30 [1852], i pt ii. 20; pt iii. 61; *Calendar of Home Office Papers 1760–1765*, ed. J. Redington, 1878, p. 133). Presumably it had become necessary for him to take the oaths in person, for he made a trip to Dublin in June 1763 (*London Chronicle* 18–21 June 1763, xiii. 589; R. J. S. Hoffman, *Edmund Burke, New York Agent*, Philadelphia, 1956, p. 308).

24. Charles O'Hara, who saw much of Rigby in Dublin, reported that he 'was more caressed than ever man was in a country where people thought he would not be well received' (ibid.).

Park the next morning, if other people had not represented the
necessity of demanding their paroles that it should go no farther.
They were both unwilling to rise: Rigby did at last, and put an end
to it with humour and good humour.[25] The numbers were 258 to
133.[26] The best speech of all those that were *not* spoken was Charles
Townshend's. He has for some time been informing the world that
for the last three months he had constantly employed six clerks to
search and transcribe records, journals, precedents, etc.[27] The pro-
duction of all this mountain of matter was a mouse, and that mouse
still-born; he has voted with us, but never uttered a word.

We shall now repose for some time; at least I am sure I shall. It
has been hard service; and nothing but a Whig point of this magnitude could easily have carried me to the House at all, of which I
have so long been sick. Wilkes will live, but is not likely to be in a
situation to come forth for some time. The Blasphemous Book has
fallen ten times heavier on Sandwich's own head than on Wilkes's:
it has brought forth such a catalogue of anecdotes as is incredible![28]
Lord Hardwicke fluctuates between life and death.[29] Lord Effingham is dead suddenly,[30] and Lord Cantelupe has got his troop.[31]

These are all our news; I am glad yours go on so smoothly. I take
care to do you justice at Monsieur de Guerchy's for all the justice
you do to France, and particularly to the House of Nivernois. D'Éon
is here still: I know nothing more of him but that the honour of
having a hand in the Peace[32] overset his poor brain. This was evident

25. He replied that his office was a
sinecure and that 'a man as ignorant as
he was might execute the office' (*Mem.
Geo. III* i. 261).

26. On the question 'that privilege of
Parliament does not extend to the case of
writing and publishing seditious libels,
nor ought to be allowed to obstruct the
ordinary course of the laws, in the speedy
and effectual prosecution of so heinous
and dangerous an offence' (*Journals of
the House of Commons*, xxix. 675).

27. 'As to the question of privilege, it is
an intricate matter. The authorities are
contradictory, and the distinctions to be
reasonably made on the precedents are
plausible and endless' (letter from Townshend to Dr Brocklesby, written two
months before Parliament met, quoted by

Croker in a note on this passage, *Works*
ix. 20, n. 11).

28. See *ante* 17 Nov. 1763.

29. He had been ill since early October,
apparently suffering from cancer (*Hardwicke Corr.* iii. 482–3). He subsequently
rallied, but soon relapsed, and died 6
March 1764. Details of his illness and day-
to-day reports of his condition abound
in the Newcastle Papers for the whole period of his illness.

30. He died 19 Nov.

31. He succeeded Effingham as Col. of
the 1st troop of horse guards.

32. He had been brought to England
by Nivernais as his secretary, made courier of the peace, and then left as *chargé
d'affaires* with the character of minister
when Nivernais returned to France.

on the fatal night at Lord Halifax's:[33] when they told him his behaviour was a breach of the peace, he was quite distracted, thinking
it was the *peace* between his country and this.[34]

Our operas begin tomorrow. The Duchess of Grafton is come for
a fortnight only. My compliments to the Ambassadress, and all your
Court.

Yours, my dear Lord,

Most faithfully,

Hor. Walpole

From Hertford, Wednesday 30 November 1763

Printed for the first time from a photostat of BM Add. MSS 23218, ff. 103–4.

Paris, November 30th 1763.

My dear Horry,

YOU are the best correspondent in the world and I have a thousand thanks to return you for the constant intelligence you send
me from England. What relates to your own and my brother's conduct on the opening of the Parliament does not make me happy; I
fear the King will too naturally upon this occasion think himself involved in the question.[1] It is the sort of opposition not meant, and
I am the more concerned it can have that appearance. Mr Wilkes's
is a species of writing I never can approve, and though I am a Whig

---

33. 26 Oct., when it had been necessary
for Halifax to summon the Guards to
force d'Éon to sign a promise not to fight
one de Vergy (whom d'Éon believed had
been brought to England to assassinate
him) after d'Éon had publicly announced
his intention of doing so. D'Éon's own
version of the events of the evening in his
Mémoires, 1836, i. 324–9 (followed by all
of his biographers) is rather less sensational than that given by HW in *Mem.
Geo. III* i. 242, and corresponds more
closely with the details of the movements
of the troops summoned and the departure of the principals given in two letters

from H. V. Jones to Newcastle, 27 and
28 Oct., BM Add. MSS 32952, ff. 110–11,
117. The latter also suggest that HW had
had to rely on some of the many conflicting rumours afloat about what had happened in the House, since Jones states
that all the witnesses had been bound to
secrecy and that it was impossible to discover what had actually happened.

34. HW repeats this anecdote as a note
to *Mem. Geo. III* i. 242.

1. As the King had done; see *ante* 17
Nov. 1763, n. 11.

and have all the regard I owe in justice both to yours and my brother's principles and judgment, I cannot discover a member of Parliament should be more at liberty to write a seditious libel than another man. I have seen the government since I have lived in the world unhinged by these treatises, and though I am a friend to liberty, I am against the abuse of it in profligate hands.

Having said that, I will not tire you by saying any more upon a subject which you must be sick of long ago; I think in a little time I shall hate the name of parties as much as you do.

Pray tell me the anecdotes which you have heard of Lord Sandwich; I fancy a war between him and Wilkes must be entertaining. Tell me likewise what is Lord Hardwicke's illness. In return I will talk to you of ourselves and our interest. You are so good to prefer our cause to that of the parliaments of France, though they are growing Whigs apace and are obtaining powers which may make great alterations in this constitution.[2]

Our visits are now far advanced and it is a business here; I have been today with the Duke of Orléans in form, and could wish from what I can judge of him in our first interview to be able to see more of him than the present forms are likely to allow. You know the difficulties which subsist between the Princes of the Blood and foreign ministers.[3] They are of the Prince of Conti's creating;[4] the Duke of Orléans would wish to remove them, but I believe it will be difficult now they have once been made. Lady Hertford receives French visits with almost as much ease as she did English ones, and receives them without any assistance from us; ministers, bishops, all ranks and sexes visit her with seeming satisfaction. In the course of this week I hope to have entertained all my countrymen and some

2. Hertford discusses the affairs of the French parliaments in detail, *post* 23 Jan. 1764. At the moment, the parliament of Rouen was leading the campaign, its members all having resigned 19 Nov.—a move met by the King's refusal to accept the resignation on the 28th, accompanied by a promise to make some alterations in the financial edicts that had occasioned the resistance.

3. Due to the pretensions of the princes in matters of form; see D. B. Horn, *The British Diplomatic Service 1689–1789*, Oxford, 1961, p. 209. According to Hertford,

ante 11 Nov. 1763, etiquette seldom allowed an ambassador more than one visit to them.

4. However, the Princes of the Blood had been adamant about punctilios of form at least since the previous century, and the Prince of Conti's own father had once refused to make a formal visit to the new English ambassador because the latter had declined to receive him at the foot of the outer staircase and had remained at the top of the stairs (Horn, loc. cit.).

few French. We have likewise some engagements abroad. I have likewise proposed parties to the ministers' wives, who are the first persons I should ask, and as they are generally engaged at Versailles, I am at liberty to begin with my dinners and suppers, which I intend doing next week, by Monsieur de Nivernois and those who have been most attentive to us. My livery is prodigiously approved, I speak to you from a confidence in your good wishes, and I flatter myself in general that our début is approved. You may answer for me that I mean to support it whilst I am in Paris.

One of my boys[5] at Tours is ill—the pretty one—and distresses us much. It is a disorder in his bowels attended with some fever; I hope in God he will soon be better. Adieu, my dear Horry; between business and dissipation I am constantly employed.

Yours ever affectionately,

HERTFORD

To HERTFORD, Friday 2 December 1763

Printed from *Works* ix. 23–7.

Arlington Street, Dec. 2d 1763.

I HAVE been expecting a letter all day, as Friday is the day I have generally received a letter from you, but it is not yet arrived, and I begin mine without it. Monsieur de Guerchy has given us a prosperous account of my Lady Hertford's audience: still I am impatient to hear it from yourselves. I want to know, too, what you say to your brother's being in the minority. I have already told you that unless they use him ill, I do not think him likely to take any warm part. With regard to dismission of officers, I hear no more of it;[1] such a violent step would but spread the flames, which are

5. Probably the Hon. Hugh Seymour-Conway (1759–1801), known from 1794 as Lord Hugh Seymour; naval officer; a lord of the Admiralty 1795–8 (BERRY i. 261–2, nn. 2–4). He was considered the best-looking of Hertford's sons (see *post*

3 June 1781) and was the right age at this time for the designation 'pretty' (also, Hertford calls him, *post* 21 Dec. 1763, 'my little boy').

———

1. The plans for dismissing officers were

already fierce enough. I will give you an instance: last Saturday, Lord Cornwallis[2] and Lord Allen[3] came drunk to the opera: the former went up to Rigby in the pit, and told him in direct words that Lord Sandwich was a pickpocket. Then Lord Allen, with looks and gestures no less expressive, advanced close to him, and repeating this again in the passage, would have provoked a quarrel, if George West had not carried him away by force. Lord Cornwallis, the next morning in Hyde Park, made an apology to Rigby for his behaviour, but the rest of the world is not so complaisant. His[4] pride, insolence, and overbearingness, have made him so many enemies, that they are glad to tear him to pieces for his attack on Lord Temple, so unprovoked, and so poorly performed. It was well that with his spirit and warmth he had the sense not to resent the behaviour of those two drunken young fellows.

On Tuesday,[5] your Lordship's House sat till ten at night, on the resolutions we had communicated to you;[6] and you agreed to them by 114 to 35;[7] a puny minority indeed, considering of what great names it was composed![8] Even the Duke of Cumberland voted in it; but

proceeding rapidly in secret. It was definitely decided, 30 Nov., at Grenville's urging, to dismiss Barré and Calcraft from their employments, though the King temporarily postponed doing so until a decision was reached about Conway. On 2 Dec., the day that HW writes, the King took a further step and ordered Grenville to have an interview with Conway to discover 'whether he did actually mean to join the Opposition, or that the votes he had given upon the late questions were merely from opinion, and that in other measures he would fairly and roundly support the King's government.' Grenville's first step was to send Thomas Pitt to HW to arrange a meeting with Conway, an interview that must have taken place on 3 Dec., since HW is obviously writing this letter late on 2 Dec., and HW's interview with Grenville, arranged in his interview with Pitt, took place the next day (Grenville Papers ii. 230–2; Mem. Geo. III i. 271–2).

2. Charles Cornwallis (1738–1805), 2d E. Cornwallis, cr. (1792) M. Cornwallis; army officer; later commander in America dur-

ing the Revolution; governor-general of Bengal 1786–93, 1797, 1805; and lord lieutenant of Ireland 1798–1801.

3. Joshua Allen (1728–1816), 5th Vct Allen; army officer; M.P. Eye 1762–70.

4. Rigby's.

5. 29 Nov.

6. On 24 Nov. the resolutions voted 15 Nov. condemning the North Briton and ordering it to be burned by the hangman, and the resolution voted 24 Nov. withdrawing privilege of Parliament in cases of writing and publishing seditious libels, were ordered communicated to the Lords; this was done at a conference on the 25th (Journals of the House of Commons xxix. 675, 677). The first resolution, condemning the North Briton, was agreed to by the Lords nem. con. on the same day (Journals of the House of Lords xxx. 425).

7. The division took place on the third resolution, withdrawing privilege.

8. Lists of the minority are in BM Add. MSS 32953, ff. 109, 111; only 17 of these 35 lords signed the protest against the vote (Journals of the House of Lords xxx. 429).

Mr Yorke's speech in our House,[9] and Lord Mansfield's in yours, for two hours, carried away many of the Opposition, particularly Lord Lyttelton,[10] and the greater part of the Duke of Newcastle's bishops.[11] The Duke of Grafton is much commended. The Duke of Portland[12] commenced, but was too much frightened. There was no warmth nor event; but Lord Shelburn,[13] who they say spoke well, and against the Court,[14] and as his friends had voted in our House,[15] has produced one, the great Mr Calcraft[16] being turned out yesterday, from some muster-mastership; I don't know what.

Lord Sandwich is canvassing to succeed Lord Hardwicke, as High Steward of Cambridge;[17] another egg of animosity. We shall, however, I believe, be tolerably quiet till after Christmas, as Mr Wilkes will not be able to act before the holidays. I rejoice at it: I am heartily sick of all this folly, and shall be glad to get to Strawberry again, and hear nothing of it. The ministry have bought off Lord Clive with a bribe that would frighten the King of France himself:

9. 24 Nov. (*ante* 25 Nov. 1763).

10. Lyttelton's speech on the occasion is printed in [John Debrett], *The History, Debates and Proceedings of Both Houses of Parliament . . . from . . . 1743 . . . to 1774*, 1792, iv. 231–6, 'from his Lordship's copy' and reprinted in Cobbett, *Parl. Hist.* xv. 1365–71. Throughout he deferred to the opinions expressed in Mansfield's previous speech.

11. So called because most of them owed their mitres to Newcastle. Only three of them, Lichfield, St Asaph, and Chichester (by proxy) voted with the minority, and of these only Lichfield signed the protest (BM Add. MSS 32953, ff. 109, 111; *Journals of the House of Lords* xxx. 429). The Bishop of Norwich, one of Newcastle's intimates, explained to the Duke in some detail that his leaving the House without voting 'was wholly owing to the most full conviction of conscience' (Bp of Norwich to Newcastle [30 Nov.], 22 Dec., BM Add. MSS 32953, f. 129; 32954, ff. 152–3).

12. William Henry Cavendish Bentinck (1738–1809), 3d D. of Portland; later first lord of the Treasury 1783, 1807–9. He signed the protest (*Journals of the House of Lords* xxx. 429).

13. William Petty (1737–1805), 2d E. of Shelburne; cr. (1784) M. of Lansdowne. He had been president of the Board of

Trade April–August 1763 in the Grenville administration.

14. He spoke and voted against the restriction of privilege, but 'making a compliment to Lord Bute . . . and flattering the Crown' (*Grenville Papers* ii. 230). He did not sign the Lords' protest.

15. Shelburne's brother Thomas Fitzmaurice, Col. Barré, and Calcraft had all voted against the restriction of privilege on 24 Nov. (ibid. ii. 229).

16. John Calcraft (*ante* 1 May 1763, nn. 27, 28). He was removed as deputy commissary-general of musters, a very lucrative post which he had held since 1755 or 1756, on 1 Dec. (*Grenville Papers* ii. 231; *Court and City Register*, 1756 et seq.). His successor, Welbore Ellis Agar, was actually appointed 30 Nov., the very day that the King consented to Calcraft's removal (*Calendar of Home Office Papers, 1760–1765*, ed. J. Redington, 1878, p. 346).

17. The Cabinet approved Sandwich's candidacy on 22 Nov. Lord Temple heard of it 'from good authority' the same day and immediately informed Newcastle (*Grenville Papers* ii. 227–8; BM Add. MSS 32953, f. 3). The Duke thereupon began an extensive correspondence (which occupies the better part of four volumes in his papers) in behalf of the candidacy of Hardwicke's son, Lord Royston (BM Add. MSS 32953–32957). Some events in the

they have given him back his £25,000 a year.[18] Walsh[19] has behaved nobly: he said he could not in conscience vote with the administration, and would not vote against Lord Clive, who chose him: he has, therefore, offered to resign his seat.[20] Lady Augusta's[21] fortune was to be voted today, and Lord Strange[22] talked of opposing it;[23] but I had not the curiosity to go down. This is all our politics, and indeed all our news; we have none of any other kind. So far you will not regret England. For my part, I wish myself with you. Being perfectly indifferent who is minister and who is not, and weary of laughing at both, I shall take hold of the first spring to make you my visit.[24]

contest are mentioned in subsequent letters from HW to Hertford.

18. HW exaggerates the extent of the government's offers and services to Clive, probably following a contemporary rumour like that in the *Gazetteer* a few days later 'that Lord Clive has agreed with the East India Company for his claim on one of the nabobs of India for the sum of three hundred thousand pounds' (quoted *London Chronicle* 6–8 Dec., xiv. 550, but expressly denied in the following issue, 8–10 Dec., xiv. 554). At the date of this letter these offers and services do not seem to have extended beyond an offer to mediate between Clive and the Company in the affair of Clive's *jagir* of £27,000 a year, payment of which had been stopped immediately after his defeat in an attempt to gain control of the Company in April 1763. In return for this mediation, Clive, who had previously supported the Opposition, had pledged his Parliamentary following to the administration—a bargain that remained good even when the government's intervention failed to obtain the return of the *jagir*, as discussed *post* 29 Dec. 1763. The part played by the *jagir* in contemporary politics is fully described in Lucy S. Sutherland, *The East India Company in Eighteenth Century Politics*, Oxford, 1952, pp. 82–132, especially pp. 113–15, where HW's statement in this letter is called a 'combination of inside information and picturesque exaggeration' (p. 113). Further details of Clive's activity in English Parliamentary politics are in L. B. Namier, *The Structure of Politics at the Accession of George III*, 1929, ii. 352–63.

19. John Walsh (1726–95), secretary to Clive and man of science; M.P. Worcester city 1761–80.

20. The offer was not accepted; according to HW (*Mem. Geo. III*, i. 262) Walsh thereupon 'abstained from attendance on the House,' but Dame Lucy Sutherland observes that he overcame his scruples and 'was soon in full support of Grenville's administration' (op. cit. 113, n. 4).

21. Eldest sister of George III. Frederick, P. of Wales, had reverted to the old English style of 'Lady' for his daughters instead of the style 'Princess', which had been introduced by the Hanoverian dynasty (*Letters from George III to Lord Bute 1756–66*, ed. Sedgwick, 1939, p. 30n). Lady Augusta's 'fortune' was her dowry for her approaching marriage; she was given £80,000 (*Annual Register*, 1763, p. 115). HW also mentions annuities of £5000 a year on Ireland and £3000 a year on Hanover (*Mem. Geo. III* i. 276).

22. James Smith Stanley, erroneously styled Lord Strange.

23. He does not appear to have opposed the grant during the debate. His probable ground for considering opposition was that Augusta, merely the eldest daughter of a Prince of Wales, was being given the same dowry as had previously been given only to the eldest daughter of a King, while the other princesses had received only £40,000 (ibid.). In view of Strange's eccentricities, it is also possible that he considered opposing the grant merely because Augusta was attached to the Opposition while he had recently become a member of the government.

24. HW did not go to Paris until Sept. 1765, after Hertford had returned.

Our operas do not succeed.[25] Giardini,[26] now become *Minister*, and having no exchequer to buy an audience, is grown unpopular. The Mingotti, whom he has forced upon the town, is as much disliked as if he had insisted on her being first lord of the Treasury. The first man,[27] though with sweet notes, has so weak a voice that he might as well hold his tongue like Charles Townshend. The figurantes are very pretty, but can dance no more than Tommy Pelham.[28] The first man dancer[29] is handsome, well made, and strong enough to make his fortune *anywhere;*[30] but you know, fortunes made in private are seldom agreeable to the public. In short, it will not do; there was not a soul in the pit the second night.

Lady Mary Coke has received her gown by the Prince de Masseran, and is exceedingly obliged to you, though much disappointed; this being a slight gown made up, and not the one she expected, which is a fine one bought for her by Lady Holland, and which you must send somehow or other: if you cannot, you must dispatch an ambassador on purpose. I dined with the Prince de Masseran, at Guerchy's, the day after his arrival,[31] and if faces speak truth, he will not be our ruin. Oh! but there is a ten times more delightful man— the Austrian minister:[32] he is so stiff and upright, that you would think all his mistress's diadems were upon his head, and that he was afraid of their dropping off.

I know so little of Irish politics, that I am afraid of misinforming you, but I hear that Hamilton,[33] who has come off with honour in a

25. Dr Burney described the season on the whole as being 'inauspicious' (Charles Burney, *A General History of Music*, ed. F. Mercer, 1935, ii. 867).

26. Currently manager of the Italian opera in London; see *ante* 9 Aug. 1763, n. 15.

27. Presumably Antonio Manziotti, who sang the role of Demetrius to the Mingotti's Cleonice in *Cleonice*, 'a new serious opera' which opened at the Haymarket 26 Nov. (*London Stage* Pt IV, ii. 1023).

28. Thomas Pelham (1728–1805), cousin of the D. of Newcastle; 2d Bn Pelham, 1768; cr. (1801) E. of Chichester.

29. Presumably Pietro Sodi, the director of dances for the new opera (ibid.); see Mann ii. 104, n. 19.

30. An allusion to Bute who, according

to HW, was extremely vain of his own figure; see *ante* 28 May 1763, where HW makes the same kind of allusion to Bute.

31. Probably at the 'grand entertainment' given by Guerchy 'to all the foreign ministers and a great number of the nobility at his house in Piccadilly' on 28 Nov., actually two days after Masserano's arrival (*London Chronicle* 26–9 Nov., 29 Nov.–1 Dec., xiv. 514, 526).

32. Christian August (1717–1801), Graf von Seilern; Austrian ambassador to England 1763–9; chief justice (Justiz-Präsident) in Vienna 1779–91 (Montagu ii. 138, n. 8). He had arrived in England on 23 Oct. (*London Chronicle* 25–7 Oct., xiv. 401).

33. William Gerard Hamilton, the chief secretary.

squabble with Lord Newton, about the latter's wife,[34] speaks and votes with the Opposition against the Castle.[35] I don't know the meaning of it, nor, except it had been to tell you, should I have remembered it.

Well! your letter will not come, and I must send away mine. Remember, the holidays are coming, and that I shall be a good deal out of town. I have been charming hitherto, but I cannot make brick without straw. Encore, you are almost the only person I ever write a line to.[36] I grow so old and so indolent that I hate the sight of a pen and ink.

Yours ever,

H. Walpole

From Beauchamp, Monday 5 December 1763

Missing; not sent. See *post* 13 Feb. 1764.

34. Lady Jane Rochfort (1737–1828), m. 1 (1754) Brinsley Butler, styled Lord Newtown Butler or Lord Newtown 1756–68; 2d E. of Lanesborough 1768; m. 2 (ca 1785) John King (Mann ix. 601, n. 12). Croker, who was apparently acquainted with the affair, states that 'in the affair here alluded to, Lord Newtown exhibited at first an extreme jealousy, and subsequently what was thought an extreme facility in admitting Mr Hamilton's exculpatory assurances' (*Works* ix. 27, n. 23).

35. A false report. Hamilton was on bad terms with the government and had taken little part in the business of the session, but there is no evidence in Northumberland's dispatches or elsewhere that he had gone into open opposition. Hamilton's own explanation of his unpopularity with the government

and his lack of activity in its behalf was that he had earned, for reasons he professed not to understand, the ill-will of Lady Northumberland, and that the lord-lieutenant and his advisers had determined to reverse the methods of Halifax, the previous lord-lieutenant, and entrust the management of affairs to Primate Stone (with whom Hamilton was on bad terms), while excluding Hamilton and his lieutenant, John Hely Hutchinson, from all confidence. See Hamilton's letters to James Oswald in explanation and defence of his conduct in *Memorials of the Public Life and Character of . . . James Oswald*, Edinburgh, 1825, pp. 450–75.

36. Only six of HW's letters are known during the previous two months, one to Cole, two to Mann, and three to Montagu.

From HERTFORD, Wednesday 7 December 1763

Printed for the first time from a photostat of BM Add. MSS 23218, ff. 105–6.

Paris, December 7th 1763.

Dear Horry,

I HAVE just a minute before supper to thank you for the last long letter[1] I have received today. It is a great satisfaction to hear what is passing amongst our friends and in a country where all our chief interests are seated, and yet you are the only friend at present that seem[s] to recollect we are in France; for the last three or four posts my friends are immersed in politics, very idle or very forgetful, for I have not heard a word from any of them.

Pray tell Lady Mary Coke there is another public minister[2] already engaged to carry over the gown she now speaks of, and that I shall be always happy to execute any commands of hers.

Lady Holderness has been presented at Versailles and was well received.[3] I do not know how you will approve it in England. There are certain forms observed here at Court to which not only the English ladies of quality but the Germans will not submit;[4] *elle a franchi le pas*,[5] but you will not know it from me when you talk of it.

I have had today at dinner the house of Nivernois, the Bishop of Soissons,[6] Lady Hertford's relation, who is in disgrace,[7] and a considerable number of the foreign ministers at this Court. Madame de

1. That of 2 Dec.
2. Domenico Caracciolo (1715–89), Marchese Caracciolo; Neapolitan ambassador to England 1764–71; ambassador to France 1771–81; Viceroy of Sicily, and Secretary of State (MONTAGU ii. 216, n. 8). He had agreed to carry the dress, but the arrangements were subsequently altered (*post* 16 Dec. 1763).
3. 'They write from Versailles, that on the 30th past the Countess of Holdernesse was presented to the French King, Queen, and the rest of the royal family, by Madame la Maréchale de Mirepoix' (*London Chronicle* 10–13 Dec., xiv. 566).
4. Lady Holland also alludes to the restrictive forms of the French Court and the English ladies' ban on being presented there: 'I regret that *malgré* the etiquette of us English peeresses, I was

not presented when I came here, as I should have seen more of the Court, and they want us English ladies to be presented vastly, I find. After all why should I not be contented to be on the same footing at Court as the Duke of Fitzjames, or any other duke's sister or great lady that is not duchess, particularly as they won't give our duchesses the *tabouret*' (*Leinster Corr.* i. 393).
5. I.e., she has set a precedent.
6. Francis Fitzjames (1709–64), brother of the Duc de Fitzjames; Bp of Soissons, 1739; first almoner to the King, 1742–8.
7. Having forced the King to discard his mistress Mme de Châteauroux in 1744, the Bishop subsequently had been exiled to his diocese, and was never again restored to favour; see MANN ii. 504, n. 1; 523, n. 23; 544, n. 27.

Praslin is already engaged to supper,[8] and I will do in that very essential point all sorts of right things. I miss no English gentleman of any rank or name, and I invite them all to dine with me; my servants' table, etc., are as they should be for the representation I have undertaken. This you may venture to say: the living is certainly very expensive, but when I can afford it no longer, considering the state of my family, I will sooner return to England than[9] be deficient in what my post requires.

Lady Hertford improves vastly in her French and seems to be much approved here.

I shall be very happy to see you next spring. I think you are warmer than ever with your politics in England; I wish the King well and am not very solicitous about particular persons, though I am glad to hear who is commended and who is abused. Adieu, dear Horry, I have not a minute more to say anything.

Yours ever affectionately,

HERTFORD

To HERTFORD, Friday 9 December 1763

Printed from *Works* ix. 28–33.

Friday, Dec. 9, 1763.

YOUR brother has sent you such a full account[1] of his transaction with Mr Grenville,[2] that it is not necessary for me to add a syllable, except, what your brother will not have said himself,

8. The Hertfords had supped with her, 19 Nov. (*ante* 19 Nov. 1763).

9. The rest of this sentence has been substituted for 'disgrace myself.'

1. Conway to Hertford, dated 5 Dec., but written in part on 4 Dec., in part on the 6th, and finished on the 8th (MS now WSL).

2. Conway had had a long interview with George Grenville in the late evening of 4 Dec. after two days of preliminary conferences between HW and Thomas Pitt and HW and Grenville and the exchange of several notes. Conway assured Grenville of his general good wishes to administration, though he refused to commit himself to support, while Grenville on his side professed himself satisfied with Conway's attitude and later persuaded the King to abandon plans for dismissing him. The possibility of dismissal was not mentioned in the conversation between Conway and Grenville, but was strongly hinted at, even threatened, in the preliminary interviews with HW. Grenville's version of the negotiation is in *Grenville Papers* ii. 231–6; the

that he has acted as usual with the strictest honour and firmness, and has turned this negotiation entirely to his own credit. He has learned the ill wishes of his enemies, and what is more, knows who they are:[3] he has laughed at them, and found at last that their malice was much bigger than their power. Mr Grenville, as you would wish, has proved how much he disliked the violence of his associates, as I trust he will, whenever he has an opportunity, and has at last contented himself with so little or nothing, that I am sure you will feel yourself obliged to him.[4] For the measure itself, of turning out the officers in general who oppose, it has been much pressed, and what is still sillier, openly threatened by one set; but they dare not do it, and having notified it without effect, are ridiculed by the whole town, as well as by the persons threatened, particularly by Lord Albemarle, who has treated their menaces with the utmost contempt and spirit.[5] This mighty storm, like another I shall tell you of, has vented itself on Lord Shelburn and Colonel Barré,[6]

letters exchanged between Grenville and Conway are printed ibid. ii. 176–80; HW's version is in *Mem. Geo. III* i. 271–4; and Conway's in the letter described in the preceding note. The details given of the various conversations agree at nearly every point, but nevertheless a dispute subsequently arose over exactly what had been said; see HW to T. Pitt 5 June 1764, T. Pitt to HW 25 May, 10 June 1764; *Grenville Papers* ii. 320–7, 353–60; and *Mem. Geo. III* ii. 8–9.

3. Conway was less certain who his enemies were than HW thought. In his account of the negotiation with Grenville, he wrote, rather vaguely, to his brother, 'You'll easily guess, I believe, from what quarter this violence against me proceeds; I think I do, and I foresee almost that I shall not long be able to stem it. I wonder Mr G. who I believe is not the author has the weakness to give way to such a manifest injustice' (letter of 4–8 Dec., now WSL). Hertford in his missing reply (21 Dec.) to this letter (and presumably also influenced by HW's comment above) inquired who the suspects were. Conway replied, 'I really can't fix on any one with any degree of certitude; the shyness and distance of Lord Holland's behaviour, which seemed unnatural from the family connection between us [Lady

Ailesbury's daughter had married the D. of Richmond, Lady Holland's brother], and from the civility and personal attention I have always endeavoured to show him, have [made] me often suspect him. . . . If not him I should think some of the Bedford party . . . —I can only speak of mere suspicion' (letter of 1 Jan. 1764, now WSL).

4. HW's sentiments here towards Grenville are considerably at variance with those expressed in the *Memoirs* where he writes that from the hour of his interview with Thomas Pitt on 3 Dec. all his 'prejudices in Grenville's favour were dispelled' (*Mem. Geo. III* i. 272), an attitude that does not appear in HW's letters until *post* 22 Jan. 1764.

5. Albemarle's name does not appear in any of the discussions of possible dismissals mentioned in the *Grenville Papers* nor does Albemarle himself mention the possibility of it in his letters to Newcastle in the Newcastle Papers.

6. Isaac Barré (1726–1802), army officer and politician; M.P. He had been made adjutant-general and governor of Stirling Castle, posts worth £4000 a year, on 14 May 1763, shortly after Shelburne had joined the government (*Calendar of Home Office Papers 1760–1765*, ed. J. Redington, 1878, p. 378). Letters exchanged between

who were yesterday[7] turned out; the first from aide-de-camp to the King,[8] the latter from adjutant-general and governor of Stirling.[9] Campbell,[10] to whom it was promised before, has got the last; Ned Harvey,[11] the former. My present expectation is an oration from Barré, in honour of Mr Pitt;[12] for those are scenes that make the world so entertaining. After that, I shall demand a satire on Mr Pitt, from Wilkes;[13] and I do not believe I shall be balked, for Wilkes has already expressed his resentment on being given up by Pitt,[14] who, says Wilkes, ought to be expelled for an impostor.[15] I do not know whether the Duke of Newcastle does not expect a *palinodia*

him and Shelburne on their dismissals are printed in Lord Fitzmaurice, *Life of . . . Shelburne*, 2d edn rev., 1912, i. 212–14.

7. Probably on Wednesday, 7 Dec., the day first set for their dismissal (*Grenville Papers* ii. 236).

8. 'Lord Shelburne was turned out for the praises given to my Lord Bute [in his speech of 29 Nov.], and his personal compliments to his Majesty, which, they thought, might be interpreted, that his Lordship pleased the King by the encomiums given to my Lord Bute; and therefore his Lordship was made the sacrifice. There are those who think that that sacrifice has hurt Mr Pitt most extremely' (Newcastle to Devonshire 19 Dec., BM Add. MSS 32954, ff. 64–5). The King's ready consent (5 Dec.) to Grenville's suggestion that Shelburne be dismissed, and his comment that 'he has acted like a worthless man, and has broke his word with me' suggest that the measure was in no way forced upon him (*Grenville Papers*, loc. cit.).

9. Also from his lieutenant-colonelcy in the army.

10. James Campbell (formerly Livingston) (d. 1788), 3d Bt 1771; M.P. Stirlingshire 1747–68; governor of Stirling Castle, 1763. He informed Barré at this time that he would not ask for the post, but Barré told Shelburne that it had been 'settled at Lutton' (that is, by Bute) to give it to him (Lord Fitzmaurice, op. cit. i. 212). A prior decision in the disposal of the post is suggested by the fact that Campbell's appointment is dated 7 Dec. (Redington, op. cit. 377).

11. Edward Harvey (1718–78), 3d son of William Harvey of Chigwell, Essex; army

officer; adjutant-general 1765–78; lieutenant-general 1772; governor of Portsmouth 1773–8; M.P. Gatton 1761–8, Harwich 1768–78. According to Barré, Harvey learned of his good fortune directly from the mouth of his predecessor, who hoped he would refuse it—a questionable story, since Harvey's appointment is dated 7 Dec. (Lord Fitzmaurice, op. cit. i. 212–13; Redington, op. cit. 346).

12. Barré had opened his Parliamentary career in Dec. 1761 with violent abuse of Pitt; see *Mem. Geo. III* i. 86–7, 94–6, and *Chatham Corr.* ii. 170–1n.

13. HW's demand was eventually satisfied by the publication as a pamphlet of Wilkes's *Letter to . . . the Duke of Grafton* (dated 12 Dec. 1766), much of which was devoted to abuse of Pitt.

14. In his speech on 24 Nov., Pitt 'condemned the whole series of *North Britons*: he called them illiberal, unmanly, and detestable. . . . The author did not deserve to be ranked among the human species— he was the blasphemer of his God, and the libeller of his King. He had no connection with him: he had no connection with any such writer. He neither associated nor communicated with any such' (Cobbett, *Parl. Hist.* xv. 1364).

15. Particularly because of Pitt's denial of any connection with Wilkes, when he had apparently encouraged the *North Briton* through Temple, had frequently seen and conversed with Wilkes himself, and had even (according to Wilkes, writing in 1767) sent messages of amused approval of Wilkes's parodies; see Raymond Postgate, *That Devil Wilkes*, New York, 1929, pp. 50–1, 72, 85.

from me.[16] T'other morning at the Duke's[17] levee he embraced me, and hoped I would come and eat a bit of Sussex mutton with him. I had such difficulty to avoid laughing in his face that I got from him as fast as I could. Do you think me very likely to forget that I have been laughing at him these twenty years?

Well! but we have had a prodigious riot:[18] are not you impatient to know the particulars? It was so prodigious a tumult, that I verily thought half the administration would have run away to Harrowgate.[19] The *North Briton* was ordered to be burned by the hangman at Cheapside, on Saturday last.[20] The mob rose;[21] the greatest mob, says Mr Sheriff Blunt,[22] that he has known in forty years. They were armed with that most bloody instrument, the mud out of the kennels: they hissed in the most murderous manner; broke Mr Sheriff Harley's[23] coach glass in the most frangent manner; scratched his forehead, so that he is forced to wear a little patch in the most becoming manner; and obliged the hangman[24] to burn the paper with a link, though faggots were prepared to execute it in a more solemn manner. Numbers of gentlemen, from windows and balconies, encouraged the mob, who, in about an hour and half, were so undutiful to the ministry, as to retire without doing any mischief, or giving

16. He subsequently received one, for HW recants some of his previous criticism of Newcastle, *post* 3 Aug. 1764, *sub* 4 Aug., when he describes a visit to the Duke at Claremont.

17. Of Cumberland. His most recent levee had been 6 Dec. (*Grenville Papers* ii. 236).

18. *Works* ix. 30 reads 'rest,' but the misprint is obvious.

19. Where Bute had retired after his resignation the past April.

20. 3 Dec.

21. HW's account of the riot follows that in the *London Chronicle* 3–6 Dec., xiv. 537. Other accounts, such as those in the *Daily Adv.* 5 Dec. and in the *St James's Chronicle* 1–3 Dec., that of J. Twells to Newcastle, Sunday [4 Dec.] (BM Add. MSS 32953, f. 194), and the sheriffs' testimony before the House of Lords 6 Dec. (*Journals of the House of Lords* xxx. 437) suggest rather more violence, especially to the hangman; they also all (including the *London Chronicle*) describe

the mob as throwing billets and sticks as well as mud and filth.

22. Richard Blunt (ca 1706 – 30 Dec. 1763), distiller; alderman of Vintry Ward 1761–3; sheriff of London, 1763. 'He was no less active in the administration of justice, than he has been acknowledged to be in carrying the laws into execution. He was a man of strong understanding, strict integrity, and firm resolution, and was excelled by none in the character of a good husband, a tender parent, a sincere friend; and it may be truly said, that by his death, the public, as well as his family and friends, have sustained a real loss' (*Daily Adv.* 31 Dec. 1763, 2 Jan. 1764; A. B. Beaven, *Aldermen of . . . London*, 1908–13, ii. 132).

23. Hon. Thomas Harley (1730–1804), 4th son of the 3d E. of Oxford; sheriff of London 1763–4; lord mayor 1767–8; M.P. London 1761–74, Hereford 1776–1802.

24. Thomas Turlis (d. 1771), hangman 1752–71 (H. Bleackley, *The Hangmen of England*, 1929, pp. 93–110).

Mr Carteret Webbe[25] the opportunity of a single information, except against an ignorant lad,[26] who had been in town but ten days.

This terrible uproar has employed us four days. The sheriffs were called before your House on Monday,[27] and made their narrative.[28] My brother Cholmondeley,[29] in the most pathetic manner, and suitably to the occasion, recommended it to your Lordships, to search for precedents of what he believed never happened since the world began. Lord Egmont, who knows of a plot, which he keeps to himself, though it has been carrying on these twenty years, thought more vigorous measures ought to be taken on such a crisis, and moved to summon the mistress of the Union Coffee-house.[30] The Duke of Bedford thought all this but piddling, and at once attacked Lord Mayor,[31] Common Council, and charter of the City,[32] whom, if he had been supported, I believe he would have ordered to be all burned by the hangman next Saturday. Unfortunately for such national justice, Lord Mansfield, who delights in every opportunity

25. Philip Carteret Webb (?1700–70), antiquary, lawyer, and politician; M.P. Haslemere 1754–68; joint solicitor to the Treasury 1756–65 and one of the leaders in the prosecution of Wilkes.

26. John Franklin. 'The young man who was committed on Saturday to Newgate . . . is son of a person of reputation in the country. He came to town for the first time a fortnight ago, and made application to a merchant in Cannon Street for employment, who had procured him a berth as steward, or clerk, to the captain of a West-Indiaman, and he was to embark as this day' (London Chronicle 3–6 Dec., xiv. 531, 542). Franklin was eventually tried and convicted at the Old Bailey, 22 Feb. 1764, for assaulting and wounding the Hon. Thomas Harley in the execution of his office of sheriff of the City. 'When the trial was over, Mr Harley observed, that, for his own part, he had forgiven the affront to his person; that justice requiring a prosecution, it had been, by the conviction of the offender, in part satisfied, and therefore he requested the court to mitigate his punishment: accordingly, the court were pleased to order, that he should be imprisoned only three months, pay a fine of 6s. 8d. and give surety for his good be-

haviour for one year' (GM 1764, xxxiv. 96; London Chronicle 21–3 Feb. 1764, xv. 182).

27. The sheriffs were ordered to attend on Monday, 5 Dec., but actually did so on Tuesday, 6 Dec. (Journals of the House of Lords xxx. 436, 437).

28. Printed ibid. xxx. 437–8, together with the questions asked them and their replies. HW had attended the debate (Cole i. 52).

29. George Cholmondeley (1703–70), 3d E. of Cholmondeley. He had married HW's elder sister Mary.

30. The city marshal, Osmond Cooke, had informed the House of Lords that the 'well-dressed' persons encouraging the mob had done so from the windows and balcony of the Union Coffee-house, a bit of information confirmed by Alexander Fall, another witness (Journals of the House of Lords xxx. 437, 438).

31. William Bridgen (ca 1709–79), wine merchant; alderman of Farringdon Within, 1754; sheriff 1756–7; lord mayor 1763–4 (GM 1779, xlix. 519; A. B. Beaven, Aldermen of . . . London, 1908–13, i. 152; ii. 131, 199).

32. HW quotes from Bedford's speech and describes the debate that followed in Mem. Geo. III i. 263–4.

of exposing and mortifying the Duke of Bedford, and Sandwich, interposed for the magistracy of London, and after much squabbling, saved them from immediate execution. The Duke of Grafton, with infinite shrewdness and coolness, drew from the witnesses that the whole mob was of one mind;[33] and the day ended in a vote of general censure on the rioters.[34] This was communicated to us at a conference,[35] and yesterday we acted the same farce;[36] when Rigby trying to revive the imputation on the Lord Mayor, etc. (who, by the by, *did* sit most tranquilly at Guildhall during the whole tumult) the ministry disavowed and abandoned him to a man, vindicating the magistracy, and plainly discovering their own fear and awe of the City,[37] who feel the insult, and will from hence feel their own strength. In short, to finish this foolish story, I never saw a transaction in which appeared so little parts, abilities, or conduct; nor do I think there can be anything weaker than the administration except it is the Opposition: but an Opposition, bed-rid and tongue-tied, is a most ridiculous body. Mr Pitt is laid up with the gout; Lord Hardwicke, though much relieved by a quack medicine,[38] is still very ill; and Mr Charles Townshend is as silent as my Lord Abercorn[39]—that they two should ever be alike!

This is not all our political news; Wilkes is an inexhaustible fund: on Monday[40] was heard in the Common Pleas, his suit against

33. 'I must tell you of a good question asked by the D. of Grafton today in examining the witnesses at the Bar. They talked of the vast and numerous mob that were present (the Marshal of the City was I think the man). "You have been used to see mobs, Sir," said the Duke, "there are commonly dissensions among them some on one side, some on the other, pray did you perceive any such difference on the present occasion, or were they in appearance unanimous?" He said he perceived no dissension' (Conway to Hertford [4–8 Dec.], MS now WSL). HW repeats the anecdote, *Mem. Geo. III* i. 263; the question is phrased somewhat differently in the formal report of the examination (*Journals of the House of Lords* xxx. 437).

34. 'Resolved, *nemine contradicente* . . . that all persons concerned in the riot at the burning of "The North Briton, No. 45" on Saturday last, their aiders and

abettors, are perturbators of the public peace, dangerous to the liberties of this country, and obstructers of national justice' (ibid. xxx. 438).

35. 7 Dec. (ibid. xxx. 439–40; *Journals of the House of Commons* xxix. 696).

36. The formal proceedings of the House are ibid. xxix. 698–9.

37. 'Mr Grenville was not for urging the blame upon the Mayor, and the King was strongly against the doing anything that might exasperate the City' (*Grenville Papers* ii. 235).

38. Which he had taken on 30 Nov. (C. Yorke to Newcastle [30 Nov.], BM Add. MSS 32953, ff. 117–18). His improvement can be followed ibid. ff. 148, 175, 204, 227, 232.

39. Some examples of Abercorn's laconic utterances are in GM 1789, lix pt ii. 961, and *post* 22 Jan. 1764.

40. Tuesday, 6 Dec.

Mr Wood,[41] when, after a trial of fourteen hours, the jury gave him damages of £1,000; but this was not the heaviest part of the blow. The Solicitor-General[42] tried to prove Wilkes author of the *North Briton,* and failed in the proof. You may judge how much that miscarriage adds to the defeat. Wilkes is not yet out of danger: they think there is still a piece of coat or lining to come out of the wound.[43] The campaign is over for the present, and the troops going into country quarters. In the mean time the House of Harrington has supplied us with new matter of talk. My Lord[44] was robbed about three o'clock in the night between Saturday and Sunday last, of money, bills, watches, and snuff-boxes, to the amount of three thousand pounds.[45] Nothing is yet discovered, but that the guard in the Stable Yard saw a man in a greatcoat and white stockings, come from thereabouts, at the time I have named. The servants have all been examined over and over to no purpose. Fielding[46] is all day in the house, and a guard of his at night. The bureau in my Lord's dressing-room (the little red room where the pictures are) was forced open. I fear you can guess *who* was at first suspected.[47]

41. Robert Wood (ca 1717–71), traveller, antiquary, and politician. As under-secretary of state, he had seized Wilkes's papers under the general warrant, 30 April 1763; Wilkes thereupon brought an action for trespass against him. The trial is reported at length in T. B. Howell, *Complete Collection of State Trials,* 1816–26, xix. 1154–68.

42. Sir Fletcher Norton.

43. 'Saturday night [10 Dec.] another operation was performed on Mr Wilkes, by cutting and laying the wound entirely open, when several more pieces of the coat and waistcoat were extracted; since which, although everything is in a fair way of doing well, he has been in the most extreme pain, and rested very little' (*London Chronicle* 13–15 Dec., xiv. 569).

44. Lady Hertford's brother-in-law.

45. 'The Earl of Harrington's house, in the Stable Yard, St James's, was robbed of a large red leather pocket book, with a silver clasp; a smaller ditto, with a gold clasp and gold pee, containing two drafts upon Mess. Blackwell and Co. for £20 each, a note of Mess. Drummond for £50, a draft of Mr Compton's of Derby on Bracey and Co. for £200, two round tin cases, of the size of a guinea, and about six inches long, filled with guineas; a rich gold snuff-box, enamelled red; another enamelled blue; a square gold snuff-box, of curious workmanship; a repeating watch in a transparent case, and a diamond hasp, gold chain and seal; an antique seal set in gold; a silver ink-standish; the whole valued at upwards of £3000. This robbery is the more remarkable as no place was broke open where the robbers could enter, and as the money was brought in but the day before by his Lordship's order, to pay tradesmen' (GM 1763, xxxiii. 614). The case was not solved until the following autumn; see the account of the robbery in the *Annual Register,* 1764, pp. 149–54, and *post* 3 Dec. 1764, 10 Jan. 1765.

46. Sir John Fielding.

47. Possibly Lady Harrington herself. However, John Wesket (d. 1765), Harrington's porter, 'was chiefly suspected . . . as the only person in the house, except the steward and a maid or two, that knew the drawers where the bills and money were' (*Annual Register,* 1764, p. 151). He was afterwards convicted of the robbery and executed (ibid. 154; *post* 3 Dec. 1764, 10 Jan. 1765).

I have received yours, my dear Lord, of Nov. 30th, and am pleased that my Lady Hertford is so well reconciled to her ministry. You forgot to give me an account of her audience, but I have heard of the Queen's good-natured attention to her.[48]

The anecdotes about Lord Sandwich are numerous; but I do not repeat them to you, because I know nothing how true they are, and because he has, in several instances, been very obliging to me; and I have no reason to abuse him. Lord Hardwicke's illness, I think, is a rupture and consequences.[49]

I hope to hear that your little boy is recovered. Adieu! I have filled my gazette, and exhausted my memory. I am glad such gazettes please you: I can have no other excuse for sending such tittle-tattle.

Yours, ever,

H. W.

From HERTFORD, Friday 16 December 1763

Printed for the first time from a photostat of BM Add. MSS 23218, ff. 107–8.

Paris, December 16th 1763.

My dear Horry,

YOU have raised my curiosity and my brother has not satisfied it: I have not had a word from him these three weeks.[1] In the meantime I am happy to hear of any negotiations or anything which does him credit. I am likewise pleased to know Mr Grenville is not amongst the number of his enemies; I have a good opinion of him and should be sorry to find it ill-placed.

You will not expect me to be very sorry for Lord Shelburne or Colonel Barré; however I may disapprove these measures of revenge for votes given in Parliament, I cannot think a storm better directed than upon a very intriguing young man[2] who wanted by artful management to change an administration who have now disposed of him, in order at five-and-twenty to be a very insufficient

48. By darkening the apartment until part of the ceremony was over (*post* 16 Dec. 1763).

49. More probably internal cancer (*ante* 25 Nov. 1763, n. 29).

1. Hertford finally received Conway's letter of 4–8 Dec. on 21 Dec. (*post* 21 Dec. 1763, postscript).

2. Shelburne.

minister himself.[3] If it does not extend farther I will excuse it; I could almost change my way of thinking to see such a gentleman drove from the King's person. Without any partiality for a particular set of men, I would wish such gentlemen to be always disappointed.

I admire your idea about the Duke of Newcastle, and I can easily suppose how willing his Grace may be to flatter himself that any vote given in Opposition is a proof of good wishes for his future power.

I had agreed as I told you[4] with Monsieur Caraccioli, a foreign minister, to take over Lady Mary Coke's gown, but my Lady now tells me that Lady Lambert[5] has found some other method of conveyance for it; I shall therefore desire you to acquaint Lady Mary with the alteration determined by Lady Lambert and that I shall deserve no blame if any accident happens.

I wish in return for all the news you send me so constantly from England, that I could entertain you from Paris; you surprise me by saying I did not acquaint you with Lady Hertford's presentation. I am very sure I meant to do it; however I find you have been well informed by having heard that the Queen's apartment was darkened till a part of the ceremony was over in order to make it more easy to her. It had I believe a contrary effect upon Lady Hertford by being more melancholy when her spirits were agitated; but still the Queen's goodness and attention were not less remarkable. She has been since at Court with great ease to herself, and the Queen, Dauphiness and Mesdames behaved to her in a most obliging manner. When I talk of the King's behaviour I must speak of myself. You may have heard that he is bashful or at least very cold and reserved to strangers; with me he is observed to be particularly easy, and I will give you proof of it by telling you that at Court last Tuesday he took hold of my ribbon[6] (which I wear here under my coat) with the greatest ease and good nature, saying it could scarce be seen with the blue coat which I then wore with it.

The *contrôleur*[7] has resigned because he was not popular with

3. Hertford refers to Shelburne's prominent part in the negotiations with Pitt in Aug. 1763; see Lord Fitzmaurice, *Life of . . . Shelburne*, 2d edn, rev., 1912, i. 198–210.

4. *Ante* 7 Dec. 1763.

5. Anne Holmes (d. 1794), m. (ca 1728) Sir John Lambert, 2d Bt, English banker in Paris.

6. Of the Garter.

7. Henri-Léonard-Jean-Baptiste Bertin (1720–92), administrator; contrôleur général des finances 1759–8 Dec. 1763 (*Dictionnaire de biographie française*, 1933– , vi. 244–5; *Répertoire . . . de la Gazette de France*, ed. de Granges de Surgères, 1902–6, i. 353).

the parliament,[8] and a Monsieur de la Vardie[9] succeeds because he is a favourite of that assembly,[10] a man unknown till this event. Now that his history is public, he is found to be of very mean extraction[11] with indefatigable application. He has been warm in opposition to the Jesuits[12] and the measures of the Court, a singular reason you will perhaps think for the choice of a minister in this country, but so it is; and if I am to form my opinion from common conversation the spirit in favour of parliaments is increasing strongly here. If you knew the ladies of this place I might perhaps divert you better. They are more attended than any ministers.

I remain, dear Horry,

Always affectionately yours,

HERTFORD

To HERTFORD, Friday 16 December 1763

Printed from *Works* ix. 34–7.

Arlington Street, Dec. 16, 1763.

ON the very day I wrote to you last,[1] my dear Lord, an extraordinary event happened, which I did not then know. A motion was made in the Common Council,[2] to thank the sheriffs for their behaviour at the riot, and to prosecute the man who was apprehended for it. This was opposed, and the previous question being put, the numbers were equal; but the casting vote of the Lord Mayor[3] was given against putting the first question[4]—a pretty strong proceeding; for though, in consequence and in resentment of the

8. Which he had alienated by attempts to continue the old taxes and to raise new ones; see the brief survey of his difficulties in H. Carré, *Le Règne de Louis XV* (*Histoire de France*, ed. E. Lavisse, Vol. VIII, Pt II), 1909, pp. 365–7.

9. Clément-Charles-François Del'Averdi (or de Laverdy or de l'Averdy or de la Verdy) (1720 or 1723–93), Chevalier, contrôleur général des finances 16 Dec. 1763–1768 (MANN vii. 164, n. 7; de Granges de Surgères, op. cit. iii. 284).

10. He was a councillor of the parliament of Paris.

11. La Chenaye-Desbois vi. 801–4 gives

his descent as being from a noble Milanese family settled in France since the middle of the 16th century; his immediate ancestors had been advocates in the parliament.

12. He had moved the *arrêts* against the Jesuits, promulgated 6 Aug. 1761 (Carré, op. cit. 322).

———

1. 9 Dec.

2. An account of the proceedings is in the *London Chronicle* 8–10 Dec., xiv. 558.

3. Bridgen.

4. According to Grenville, Bridgen justified his vote by stating that he should

Duke of Bedford's speech, it seemed to justify his Grace, who had accused the Mayor and magistracy of not trying to suppress the tumult; if they will not prosecute the rioters it is not very unfair to surmise that they did not dislike the riot. Indeed, the City is so inflamed, and the ministry so obnoxious, that I am very apprehensive of some violent commotion. The Court have lost the Essex election,[5] merely from Lord Sandwich interfering in it,[6] and from the Duke of Bedford's speech; a great number of votes going from the City on that account to vote for Luther.[7] Sir John Griffin,[8] who was disobliged by Sandwich's espousing Conyers,[9] went to Chelmsford, at the head of 500 voters.

One of the latest acts of the ministry will not please my Lady Hertford: they have turned out her brother, Colonel Fitzroy:[10] Fitzherbert,[11] too, is removed,[12] and, they say, Sir Joseph Yorke

look upon thanking the sheriffs 'as prejudging Mr Wilkes's cause' (*Grenville Papers* ii. 237).

5. 12–14 Dec., when John Luther defeated John Conyers. An item in the newspapers estimated that the expense on both sides 'has not been less than £40,000' (*London Chronicle* 15–17 Dec., xiv. 577).

6. Several reports and anecdotes of ministerial interference appear in the newspapers (*The Ledger,* quoted *London Chronicle,* loc. cit.; *Lloyd's Evening Post* 14–16 Dec., xiii. 580; *St James's Chronicle* 13–15 Dec.), while the *Public Advertiser* printed an explicit denial of any such intervention, stating that 'the most exact neutrality has been observed, notwithstanding the repeated solicitation of both the candidates' (quoted in *London Chronicle* 15–17 Dec., xiv. 583). In fact, while both Grenville and Sandwich had been applied to for government support, Grenville had remained neutral, whereas Sandwich openly 'acted for Conyers' (Sandwich to Rigby, 28 Oct., Sandwich MSS, quoted in Namier and Brooke i. 275, where it is admitted that the unpopularity of Sandwich may well have been one of the deciding factors in the election).

7. John Luther (?1739–86), of Myles's, Essex; M.P. Essex 1763–84. Accounts of the sudden appearance of large numbers of voters in his favour are in *Lloyd's Evening Post* 12–14 Dec., xiii. 575, and *St James's Chronicle* loc. cit.

8. Sir John Griffin Griffin (until 1749

John Griffin Whitwell) (1719–97), K.B. 1761; 4th Bn Howard de Walden, 1784; cr. (1788) Bn Braybrooke; army officer; M.P. Andover 1749–84; a great landowner in Essex where he had inherited the estates of Saffron Walden and Audley End from his aunt.

9. John Conyers (1717–75), of Copt Hall, Essex; M.P. Reading 1747–54, Essex 1772–5 (MONTAGU i. 92–3, nn. 14–17).

10. Charles Fitzroy (after 1749 Fitzroy Scudamore) (?1713–82), natural son of 2d D. of Grafton, and half-brother of Lady Hertford; army officer until 1748; M.P. Thetford 1733–54; 1774–82; Hereford city 1754–68; Heytesbury 1768–74; Groom Porter to the King 1743–63; Master of the King's Tennis Courts 1733–63. He 'resigned' his two Court offices 14 Dec., and was promptly replaced by Francis Buller (*London Chronicle* 15–17 Dec., 17–20 Dec., xiv. 584, 592).

11. William Fitzherbert (1712–72), of Tissington Hall, Derbyshire; friend of the Cavendishes and of Dr Johnson; M.P. Bramber 1761–2, Derby borough 1762–72; commissioner of trade and plantations 1765–72 (Burke, *Peerage*, 1928, p. 942; Boswell's *Life of Johnson*, ed. Hill and Powell, 1934–50, *passim*, esp. iii. 497).

12. From the post of gentleman usher, which he had held since 1759 (*London Chronicle* 13–15 Dec., xiv. 576). 'Lord Gower told him, *that the King* had ordered him to dismiss him, but gave no reason for it. His Lordship had told the

recalled.[13] I must do Lord Halifax and Mr Grenville the justice to say that these violences are not imputed to them. It is certain that the former was the warmest opposer of the measure for breaking the officers; and Mr Grenville's friends take every opportunity of throwing the blame on the Duke of Bedford and Lord Sandwich.[14] The Duchess of Bedford, who is too fond a wife not to partake in all her husband's fortunes, has contributed her portion of indiscretion. At a great dinner, lately, at Lord Halifax's, all the servants present, mention being made of the Archbishop of Canterbury, Monsieur de Guerchy asked the Duchess, 'Est-il de famille?' She replied, 'Oh! mon Dieu, non, il a été sage-femme.' The mistake of *sage-femme* for *accoucheur,* and the strangeness of the proposition, confounded Guerchy so much, that it was necessary to explain it: but think of a minister's wife telling a foreigner, and a Catholic, that the Primate of her own church had been bred a man-midwife![15]

The day after my last, another verdict was given in the Common Pleas, of £400 to the printers;[16] and another episode happened, relating to Wilkes: one Dunn,[17] a mad Scotchman, was seized in Wilkes's house,[18] whither he had gone intending to assassinate him. This was complained of in the House of Commons,[19] but the man's frenzy was verified;[20] it was even proved that he had notified his

King that—Fitzherbert was an old acquaintance of Wilkes's' (Newcastle to Devonshire 19 Dec., BM Add. MSS 32954, f. 65).

13. The report of his recall from his embassy at The Hague was false, though it had been widely circulated (*Mercure historique,* 1763, clv. 558). It had been urged by Halifax and Sandwich shortly before Parliament opened in Nov., but opposed by Grenville, who persuaded the King that leniency to Sir Joseph would be a means of conciliating the rest of the Yorke family (*Grenville Papers* ii. 219–22).

14. However, in Grenville's account of the division of opinion in the Cabinet on the subject of dismissals, 30 Nov., he mentions that both secretaries (Sandwich *and* Halifax) were 'eager for the measure' while Bedford agreed with Grenville in opposing the dismissal of Conway (ibid. ii. 230–1).

15. See *ante* 28 Sept. 1762, n. 36.

16. 10 Dec. in the case of Dryden Leach

and several of his men vs. the King's messengers. A summary of the trial, attributed to Wilkes's friends, is in the *London Chronicle* 10–13 Dec., xiv. 562. Further details are in the account of the second action on the same subject, 17 May 1765, in T. B. Howell, *Complete Collection of State Trials,* 1816–26, xix. 1001–1028; see also MANN vi. 188, n. 20.

17. Alexander Dunn, late a lieutenant in the marines (below, n. 20).

18. 8 Dec. Several letters and documents relating to the affair were published in the *London Chronicle* 10–13 Dec., xiv. 561–2, *sub* 12 Dec.; and reprinted, with comments, by Wilkes in *A Complete Collection of the Genuine Papers, Letters, etc. in the Case of John Wilkes,* Paris, 1767, pp. 74–94; see also Wilkes, *Correspondence,* ed. Almon, 1805, i. 165–75.

19. 9 Dec. (*Journals of the House of Commons* xxix. 701).

20. 10 Dec. (ibid. xxix. 702). 'The following account of Mr Dunn may be re-

design in a coffee-house, some days before.[21] The mob, however, who are determined that Lord Sandwich shall answer for everybody's faults, as well as his own, believe that he employed Dunn. I wish the recess, which begins next Monday, may cool matters a little, for indeed it grows very serious.

Nothing is discovered of Lord Harrington's robbery, nor do I know any other news, but that George West is to marry Lady Mary Grey.[22] The Hereditary Prince's wound is broken out again,[23] and will defer his arrival. We have had a new comedy,[24] written by Mrs Sheridan,[25] and admirably acted; but there was no wit in it, and it was so vulgar that it ran but three nights.[26]

lied on as genuine . . . that Alexander Dunn was a lieutenant of marines on board the *Bienfaisant*, Captain Balfour, where he gave such evident proofs of his insanity, that the Captain was obliged to confine him. Dunn was set on shore at Gibraltar, and put under the care of the physician of the hospital there, who considered him . . . in a very high state of lunacy, and indeed, among other marks of it, he made some attempts upon his own life, insomuch that they were forced to confine him more closely. Dunn was discharged from the hospital, as being incurable, and came home in the *Blenheim*. It is but a very short time ago (a few days, it is believed) that Dunn's father was so sensible of the insane state of his son, that he wrote to an eminent surgeon in town, desiring him to . . . put him into some proper place of restraint, fit for persons in his unhappy condition. And with respect to Dunn's declarations, it is observable that at the time, almost in the same breath that he used menaces against Mr Wilkes's life (in the presence of numbers of people) he likewise declared that it was necessary for him to save his (Mr Wilkes's) life' (*London Chronicle* 10–13 Dec., xiv. 562). Dunn was much in the news two months later, as well, for a briefly successful escape from King's Bench prison, another abortive attempt to do so, and finally for setting the gaol on fire (GM 1764, xxiv. 94; *London Chronicle* 16–18, 18–21 Feb. 1764, xv. 166, 174).

21. Wilkes was notified by a letter from M. Darly on 7 Dec. that Dunn had de-

clared at a coffee-house the previous evening that he and thirteen more Scots were associating for his destruction. The fact of this notification is mentioned, in a slightly garbled form, *sub* 10 Dec. in the *London Chronicle* 8–10 Dec., xiv. 558; Darly's letter is printed in full *sub* 12 Dec., ibid. 10–13 Dec., xiv. 561.

22. (1739–83), daughter of 4th E. of Stamford; m. (24 Feb. 1764) Hon. George West.

23. This report is without foundation, though it was in general circulation; see Newcastle to Devonshire 19 Dec., BM Add. MSS 32954, f. 65. It apparently originated with the Dutch minister's wife, who told Mrs Grenville on 15 Dec. that the Hereditary Prince 'had overheated himself at Potsdam by dancing, and afterwards taking too hasty a journey to Brunswick, which made it feared his wound would break out again, which must retard the marriage' (*Grenville Papers* ii. 245). The Prince finally arrived in London, 13 Jan. 1764, and the marriage took place on the 16th.

24. *The Dupe* (Allardyce Nicoll, *A History of English Drama 1660–1900*, 4th edn, 1952–65, iii. 305; *London Stage* Pt IV, ii. 1025). HW's copy, now WSL, is Hazen, *Cat. of HW's Lib.*, No. 1810:5:6. HW wrote 'Mrs Sheridan' on the title page and noted that the play was 'acted for the first time Dec. 10th 1763.'

25. Frances Chamberlaine (1724–66), m. (1747) Thomas Sheridan; novelist and dramatist.

26. Mrs Sheridan asserted that it was withdrawn because of a cabal, but the

Poor Lady Hervey desires you will tell Mr Hume how incapable she is of answering his letter.[27] She has been terribly afflicted for these six weeks with a complication of gout, rheumatism, and a nervous complaint. She cannot lie down in her bed, nor rest two minutes in her chair. I never saw such continued suffering.

You say in your last, of the 7th, that you have omitted to invite no Englishman of rank or name. This gives me an opportunity, my dear Lord, of mentioning one Englishman,[28] not of great rank, but who is very unhappy that you have taken no notice of him.[29] You know how utterly averse I am to meddle, or give impertinent advice, but the letter[30] I saw was expressed with so much respect and esteem for you, that you would love the person. It is Mr Selwyn, the banker. He says, he expected no favour, but the great regard he has for the amiableness of your character, makes him miserable at being totally undistinguished by you. He has so good a character himself, and is so much beloved by many persons here, that you know, that I think you will not dislike my putting you in mind of him. The letter was not to me, nor to any friend of mine, therefore, I am sure, unaffected. I saw the whole letter, and he did not even hint at its being communicated to me.

I have not mentioned Lady Holdernesse's presentation, though I by no means approve it, nor a Dutchwoman's[31] lowering the peerage of England. Nothing of that sort could make me more angry, except a commoner's wife taking such a step; for you know I have all the pride of

contemporary criticism supports HW's explanation. 'The truth is, that the comedy of The Dupe is a very poor performance, lame and defective, not to add gross and indelicate, in fable, characters and sentiments, and remarkably coarse and inelegant in dialogue. . . . If, however, a bad play can be supported by good acting, we may promise this comedy at least a nine days life, and that is a bold word' (St James's Chronicle 10–13 Dec.). See also the attack on the play in Lloyd's Evening Post, 12–14 Dec., xiii. 571, and other contemporary comments quoted in London Stage, loc. cit.

27. Hume's letter is missing. Lady Hervey had given him letters of introduction before he left England; she

finally replied to his letter 1 and 9 Jan. 1764 (Letters of Eminent Persons Addressed to David Hume, ed. J. H. Burton, Edinburgh, 1849, pp. 24–7; J. Y. T. Greig and H. Beynon, Calendar of Hume MSS in the Possession of the Royal Society of Edinburgh, Edinburgh, 1932, p. 77).

28. Charles Selwin, English banker in Paris.

29. Hertford had already entertained Selwin at dinner 'some time ago' (post 21 Dec. 1763).

30. Missing; it was forwarded to HW by Anne Pitt; see HW to Anne Pitt 10 Dec. 1763 (More 31–2).

31. Lady Holdernesse was daughter of Francis Doublet, of Groeneveldt.

—A citizen of Rome, while Rome survives:[32]

In that respect my name is thoroughly

HORATIUS

From HERTFORD, Wednesday 21 December 1763

Printed for the first time from a photostat of BM Add. MSS 23218, ff. 109–11.

Paris, December 21st 1763.

Dear Horry,

I CANNOT send off my courier without informing you that your friends in France are well, though the number of dinners and suppers to which we are invited is enough to destroy us.

I hope the entertainments for an ambassador upon his first arrival are as long again as they will continue to be when the society becomes more easy. The time we spend at table is too considerable. Faro and birabi[1] are now fashionable games here, and they are very useful because they employ a great many persons. I do not know whether you are acquainted with the last of them, nor can I find out from whence it was imported—I imagine by the name from Italy— and it is unequal enough to satisfy any gamester in that country. Lady Hertford plays at both, but not so deep as Madame de Mirepoix, who still loves play as much as ever,[2] though she is not given up to it as we remember her in England.[3]

The women here are not in general I think so handsome as in England, though there are some pretty ones amongst the women of fashion; but even the homely ladies, after they have passed the first bloom of youth, are so much better dressed and ornamented that it requires a close inspection not to think them pretty. They are very easy and agreeable in their manner, at least in my opinion, but I do

32. 'A senator of Rome, while Rome
    survived
  Would not have match'd his daugh-
    ter with a King . . .'
        (Addison, *Cato*, V. iv)

1. Properly *biribi*; it was still being played in 1777 (DU DEFFAND iv. 388).

2. For her continued passion for gambling and its disastrous effects on her finances, see ibid., *passim*.

3. HW had told Mann in 1750 that Mme de Mirepoix 'likes nothing but gaming' (MANN iv. 106).

not think Lady Hertford means to adopt the plan. She sometimes calls it freedom, and my son and I take the ladies' behaviour under our protection.

For the French young men I have little to say. They are fashionably polite, and have all the Paris phrases on such occasions ready for every hearer, but they are scandalously uninformed. My son passes here I believe for a young man of extraordinary knowledge for his time of life and rank, and I do not know that I may not be esteemed the fitter man to serve my country for playing well at whist.

We have strange reports here calculated of course for the meridian of Paris, that the savages in Canada have destroyed 20,000 British in America and are in possession of all the western ports and strong passes in his Majesty's colonies.[4] That thirteen men are associated for the destruction of Mr Wilkes,[5] and that the town of Edinborough have expressed their joy upon the news of his safety from a wound in a duel, by bonfires and other public demonstrations.[6]

The King of France goes today to Choisi[7] to play at trille for two or three days; do not you think it of consequence? If you do not, you might pass for a stupid fellow here, for I may possibly hear of it twenty times within these three days.

My little boy who was ill is recovering,[8] thank God; I hear of no remaining complaint but weakness.

I have not yet received any letter from my brother either on the subject you mention or indeed on any other for a considerable time.

If you can discover it, do endeavour to know what the ministers

4. In his dispatch to Halifax of 18 Dec., Hertford wrote that 'the news of Paris have assembled in Canada forty thousand savages, with whom they have fought the English, and killed them twenty thousand men. They have, in consequence of this great success, put these savages into possession of all the western sea ports, and most of the lakes, and strong passes of his Majesty's different colonies in America' (S.P. 78/259, ff. 156–7). A 'translation of a letter handed about at Paris,' dated from Canada, 3 Oct., giving this intelligence is printed in the *London Chronicle* 20–22 Dec., xiv. 599–600. See also the quotation from the Utrecht *Gazette* in the *Daily*

Adv. 20 Dec. The story is obviously an exaggeration of the very real Indian attacks on the American frontier during the summer and autumn of 1763; see *ante* 18 Oct. 1763, n. 4.

5. A version of Dunn's remarks in the coffee-house (*ante* 16 Dec. 1763 *bis*, n. 21).

6. Probably a version of reports from Edinburgh printed in the London papers, describing such celebrations on learning that Wilkes had been wounded but recovered; see *St James's Chronicle* 3–6 Dec.

7. Choisy, a favourite residence of Louis XV, on the Seine southeast of Paris (DU DEFFAND i. 122, n. 9).

8. See *ante* 30 Nov. 1763, and n. 5.

think of my letters and my negotiations from this place and at Versailles. Adieu, dear Horry,

Yours always most affectionately,

HERTFORD

Mr Selwyn has dined with me some time ago. I like the man and have done everything I could to be civil; the first moments of hurry should excuse a man.

My brother's letter is just arrived.

I[9] do not know that my brother's crimes are not already fallen or falling on me. I have received a kind of refusal for the expenses of my journey to Paris;[10] a demand that may be refused, I admit *à la lettre*, but was granted for near double the sum to the Duke of Bedford,[11] and the extravagance of this place will well justify the payment. Mr Grenville I do not suspect of being personally disinclined to me though this is in some measure, almost entirely I suppose, an affair of his department.[12]

9. The rest of this letter is written on a separate sheet, probably for greater privacy.

10. Hertford, in a private letter to Halifax of 18 Dec., acknowledged receipt of Halifax's private letter of 13 Dec. (S.P. 78/259, f. 126), 'to inform me, that his Majesty upon seeing an order of the late King's, did not think proper to pay my demand for my journey from London to Paris' (ibid. f. 164).

11. 'Lord Albemarle and the Duke of Bedford were my immediate predecessors; the first had five hundred pounds allowed him in the late King's time for this journey, and the Duke of Bedford had nine hundred pounds given him on this account, by his present Majesty's commands, clear of all deductions' (ibid.).

12. In turning down Hertford's demand a second time, Halifax offered the following explanation of the refusal: 'Though some few deviations have been made, in extraordinary cases, from the rule established by the late King (of which however the Earl of Albemarle's journey *out* was not one, having preceded that rule) it is his Majesty's pleasure that it should be observed more strictly for the future; and in consequence thereof, no such allowance will be made either to your Excellency, or to the Earl of Rochford, or to Lord Stormont' (3 Jan. 1764, S.P. 78/260, f. 4).

From HERTFORD, Wednesday 28 December 1763

Printed for the first time from a photostat of BM Add. MSS 23218, ff. 112–13.

Paris, December 28th 1763.

My dear Horry,

THE last English post brought us no news nor any letter from you. All our correspondents agree in saying that the society of London is interrupted by the violence of the present parties. What do you intend to do or where are you to stop? Is there to be a duel every day the House meets, or will the City take arms against the present ministry? Some letters talk of coalitions,[1] but mine mention none, and I do not give any credit to the present report. Apropos to duels, Mr Martin is at Paris.[2] He has dined with me and given me a very modest account of the whole transaction between himself and Wilkes; I could not find out why he should leave England upon it, since Wilkes was not likely to die, and he agreed with me, though he said he was always liable to be put into Newgate by a justice of peace's warrant. He said he had taken his friends' opinion, and amongst them Lord Granby's, and they had determined it so, after which he thought it became him to acquiesce under it. He has been at Lisle and in other places and is but just come to Paris; next week he returns to England.[3]

Churchill is said to be here[4] after having sworn that he was the author of the infamous paper ascribed to Wilkes,[5] but as I have not seen him nor do not imagine such a trick would save the latter, I do not believe it.

1. None were in prospect. Charles Yorke, in a conversation with Grenville, 17 Dec., had urged the 'taking in aids from the Opposition,' but Grenville had rejected anything but receiving detached individuals (*Grenville Papers* ii. 239). Attempts were also being made in the ranks of Opposition to heal the breach between Pitt and the Yorke family, but at the time the reports Hertford mentions must have been sent to Paris, nothing significant had been accomplished (*Hardwicke Corr.* iii. 557–60).

2, He had been on the Continent since early Dec., having arrived at Brussels on 6 Dec. (*Daily Adv.* 20 Dec., *sub* Brussels 12 Dec.).

3. Martin arrived at Dover, 8 Jan. (*St James's Chronicle* 10–12 Jan. 1764; MANN vi. 198).

4. Probably a false report, based on a rumour current in London early in Dec. that Churchill had gone to France; see *ante* 17 Nov. 1763, n. 84.

5. Churchill never swore to the authorship of any of Wilkes's works; the story is probably based on a rumour mentioned in a London paper that 'a celebrated poetical genius will be tried as one of the publishers of the *Essay on*

Lady Hertford visits alone amongst the French without any apparent unwillingness,[6] and does very well in conversation. You will of course suppose her language much improved.

We do not any of us go much to spectacles. You would not suspect her Ladyship if I did not say so, but perhaps it may be more necessary to tell you that I can pass my evenings very well by going fashionably from one house to another and conversing till nine o'clock. The mornings here are too short. I have some thoughts of lengthening mine by leaving off my own dinner in great measure, and I shall at the same time be better enabled to perform a very necessary duty with the French at supper.

The parliaments here are not quite so lively as they are in England, but they are improving so fast as to be already very troublesome to the ministers of this country. Indeed if there was more firmness in the gentlemen who direct these councils, perhaps the steps taken by parliament might not be so bold as they are. But still they are encouraged by the general disposition and conversation of the country, and in every place they talk and reason with more freedom than they used to do in France. The Duke of Fitzjames, Governor at Toulouse, is *décrété de prise du corps* by the parliament of that place.[7] The peers are offended at this step taken against one of their own body, and are to assemble tomorrow upon the occasion;[8] in the meantime it is doubted whether the parliament of Paris, who is the most flexible, will not on this occasion take the side of parliament.[9]

In the midst of all this, everybody lives here as if there was the

Woman' (*St James's Chronicle* 1–3 Dec.).

6. Lady Holland formed a rather different impression of Lady Hertford's attitude; she wrote to Lady Kildare, 21 Dec.: 'The Hertfords go on pretty well; Lady Hertford hates it, and suffers from her own shyness still more to see what her pretty daughter suffers' (*Leinster Corr.* i. 398).

7. 17 Dec. The *arrêt* ordering his arrest is printed (though misdated) in *Mercure historique*, 1764, clvi. 40–4; an English translation is in GM 1764, xxxiv. 41. For a full account of the conflict leading to this action and its consequences, see J. B. Dubédat, *Histoire du Parlement de Toulouse*, 1885, ii. 457–513; and *post* 23 Jan. 1764.

8. The peers had already met at the Duc d'Orléans's, 22 or 23 Dec., and had decided to carry their complaint to a *grand'chambre* (a session of the parliament of Paris augmented by the formal presence of the peers of France) on 29 Dec. This was done, but because of a procedural irregularity, action on the complaint had to be delayed until the 30th when the *arrêt* was invalidated; see *post* 23 Jan. 1764, n. 38.

9. The parliament of Paris supported the complaint of the peers and consented to the annulment of the decree on the grounds that it alone, and not the parliament of Toulouse, was empowered to proceed against peers of France (Dubédat, op. cit. ii. 503–4; É. Glasson, *Le Parlement de Paris*, 1901, ii. 288–9, where the date of the decision is misprinted 3 Dec.).

most perfect harmony. Parties are not yet sufficiently established for the interruption of all society.

Adieu, dear Horry,

Yours ever,

H.

To HERTFORD, Thursday 29 December 1763

Printed from *Works* ix. 38–43.

Arlington Street, Dec. 29th 1763.

YOU are sensible, my dear Lord, that any amusement from my letters must depend upon times and seasons. We are a very absurd nation (though the French are so good at present as to think us a very wise one, only because they, themselves, are now a very weak one); but then that absurdity depends upon the almanac. Posterity, who will know nothing of our intervals, will conclude that this age was a succession of events. I could tell them that we know as well when an event, as when Easter, will happen. Do but recollect these last ten years. The beginning of October, one is certain that everybody will be at Newmarket, and the Duke of Cumberland will lose, and Shafto[1] win, two or three thousand pounds. After that, while people are preparing to come to town for the winter, the ministry is suddenly changed,[2] and all the world comes to learn how it happened, a fortnight sooner than they intended;

1. Jenison Shafto (ca 1728–71), of Wratting Park, Cambs; M.P. Leominster 1761–8, Castle Rising 1768–71; a well-known sportsman and owner of horses whose luck was proverbial. HW may be thinking in particular of a famous wager won by Shafto in 1761: 'In 1761, a match was made between Jennison Shafto, and Hugo Meynel, Esquires, for two thousand guineas; Mr Shafto to get a person to ride one hundred miles a day (on any one horse each day) for twenty-nine days together: to have any number of horses not exceeding twenty-nine. The person chose by Mr Shafto was Mr John Woodcock, who started on Newmarket-heath, the fourth of May, 1761, at one o'clock in the morning, and finished (having used only fourteen horses) on the first of June, about six in the evening' (*Sporting Magazine*, 1792, i. 56); see also HW to Lord Dacre 9 June 1761 and n. 4).

2. Major changes had occurred in Nov. 1755, Nov. 1756, Oct. 1761, and Oct. 1762.

and fully persuaded that the new arrangement cannot last a month. The Parliament opens; everybody is bribed; and the new establishment is perceived to be composed of adamant. November passes, with two or three self-murders, and a new play. Christmas arrives; everybody goes out of town; and a riot happens in one of the theatres. The Parliament meets again; taxes are warmly opposed; and some citizen makes his fortune by a subscription.[3] The Opposition languishes; balls and assemblies begin; some master and miss begin to get together, are talked of, and give occasion to forty more matches being invented; an unexpected debate starts up at the end of the session, that makes more noise than anything that was designed to make a noise, and subsides again in a new peerage or two. Ranelagh opens and Vauxhall; one produces scandal, and t'other a drunken quarrel. People separate, some to Tunbridge, and some to all the horse races in England; and so the year comes again to October. I dare to prophesy, that if you keep this letter, you will find that my future correspondence will be but an illustration of this text; at least, it is an excuse for my having very little to tell you at present, and was the reason of my not writing to you last week.

Before the Parliament adjourned,[4] there was nothing but a trifling debate[5] in an empty House, occasioned by a motion from the ministry, to order another physician and surgeon[6] to attend Wilkes: it was carried by about 70 to 30,[7] and was only memorable by producing Mr Charles Townshend, who, having sat silent through the question of privilege, found himself interested in the defence of Dr Brocklesby![8] Charles ridiculed Lord North extremely, and had warm words with George Grenville.[9] I do not look upon this as

3. Probably a subscription to a private lottery.

4. 19 Dec., to 16 Jan. (*Journals of the House of Commons* xxix. 712).

5. 16 Dec. (ibid. xxix. 709). Some details of the debate are in a letter from G. Onslow to Newcastle Sunday [18 Dec.], BM Add. MSS 32954, ff. 35–6.

6. The physician ordered to attend Wilkes was Dr William Heberden (1710–81), M.D., 1739; the surgeon, Caesar Hawkins (1711–86), cr. (1778) Bt; sergeant-surgeon to the King.

7. 71 to 30 (*Journals of the House of Commons* loc. cit.).

8. Dr Richard Brocklesby (1722–97), M.D. 1745; Wilkes's physician; friend of Dr Johnson and Burke. He was much connected with the Opposition, so that the appointment of other doctors to attend Wilkes had political overtones; he was also a personal friend of Townshend, who was therefore anxious to defend him.

9. Onslow told Newcastle that Townshend 'most handsomely ridiculed Lord North, and worked George Grenville, who, he said, "he hoped whenever they differed, which he thought they were

productive of consequential speaking for the Opposition;[10] on the contrary, I should expect him sooner in place, if the ministry could be fools enough to restore weight to him, and could be ignorant that he can never hurt them so much as by being with them. Wilkes refused to see Heberden and Hawkins,[11] whom the House commissioned to visit him; and to laugh at us more, sent for two Scotchmen, Duncan[12] and Middleton.[13] Well! but since that, he is gone off himself:[14] however, as I did in D'Éon's case,[15] I can now only ask news of him from you, not tell you any; for you have got him. I do not believe you will invite him, and make so much of him, as the Duke of Bedford did.[16] Both sides pretend joy at his being gone; and for once I can believe both. You will be diverted, as I was, at the cordial esteem the ministers have for one another: Lord Waldegrave[17] told my niece,[18] this morning, that he had offered a shilling, to receive an hundred pounds when Sandwich shall lose his head!

very likely often to do this session . . . would use just such arguments as he had used that day" ' (G. Onslow to Newcastle, loc. cit.). A day later, Onslow again told the Duke that 'Townshend declares open war against G. Grenville' (ibid. f. 82). Early in Jan., however, he 'expressed great regret' for his attack, and began sending friendly messages to Grenville (*Grenville Papers* ii. 482–3).

10. These doubts were shared by the leaders of Opposition; see Newcastle to Devonshire 19 Dec., and Rockingham to Newcastle 20 Dec., BM Add. MSS 32954, ff. 64, 98–9.

11. The letters exchanged among Brocklesby, Heberden, Hawkins, and Wilkes were printed in the newspapers, 23 Dec. (*Daily Adv.* 23 Dec.; *London Chronicle* 22–4 Dec., xiv. 601, *sub* 23 Dec.). They were reprinted by Wilkes in *A Complete Collection of the Genuine Papers, Letters, etc. in the Case of John Wilkes*, Paris, 1767, pp. 59–69.

12. William Duncan, physician to George III.

13. David Middleton, sergeant-surgeon to the King. 'I hear that Mr Wilkes does not choose to allow the power the House of Commons have assumed of sending physicians and surgeons to examine his wound; but in order to satisfy the curi-

osity of our great men, he has written to Mr Middleton the surgeon, that he may take a view of him whenever he pleases to call upon him. He has chosen a Scotchman for this office, as thinking that his report will not be suspected of partiality, but must produce universal conviction' (John Roberts to Newcastle 20 Dec., BM Add. MSS 32954, f. 115).

14. Wilkes left London on 24 Dec. to visit his daughter in Paris. The first reports of his departure had him going to Aylesbury or to Humphrey Cotes's seat in Surrey, but his true destination was generally known on the 27th (*Daily Adv.* 26, 28 Dec.; *London Chronicle* 24–7 Dec., xiv. 609, 616).

15. HW mentioned that he knew virtually nothing of d'Éon, *ante* 25 Nov. 1763.

16. The Duke had visited Wilkes and invited him twice to dinner during his visit to Paris in April 1763; Hertford describes his reception of Wilkes *post* 6 Jan. 1764 and in a letter to Grenville of 4 Jan. 1764 (*Grenville Papers* ii. 249–50).

17. Waldegrave was not a minister, but was closely connected with the ministers through his wife, sister of the Duchess of Bedford.

18. Maria Walpole, widow of the 2d E. Waldegrave and sister-in-law of the 3d Earl.

what a good opinion they have of one another! apropos to losing heads, is Lally[19] beheaded?

The East India Company have come to an unanimous resolution[20] of not paying Lord Clive the three hundred thousand pounds, which the ministry had promised him in lieu of his nabobical annuity. Just after the bargain was made, his old rustic of a father[21] was at the King's levee; the King asked where his son was; he replied, 'Sire, he is coming to town, and then your Majesty will have another vote.' If you like these franknesses, I can tell you another. The Chancellor[22] is chosen a governor of St Bartholomew's Hospital:[23] a smart gentleman, who was sent with the staff,[24] carried it in the evening, when the Chancellor happened to be drunk. 'Well, Mr Bartlemy,'[25] said his Lordship, snuffling, 'what have you to say?' The man, who had prepared a formal harangue, was transported to have so fair opportunity given him of uttering it, and with much dapper gesticulation, congratulated his Lordship on his health, and the nation on enjoying such great abilities. The Chancellor stopped him short, crying, 'By God, it is a lie; I have neither health nor abilities;

19. Thomas Arthur Lally (1702–66), Count Lally; Irish officer in the French service; commander-in-chief of the French forces in India during the Seven Years' War. HW's inquiry was probably prompted by a report in the *London Chronicle* 24–7 Dec. (xiv. 614) that 'a gentleman who arrived from Paris on Sunday night [25 Dec.] says that General Lally . . . was beheaded there privately, early in the morning of Thursday the 22nd instant.' The report was premature; Lally had been on trial before the parliament of Paris since July 1763 on capital charges arising from his administration in India, but he was not sentenced and executed until May 1766 (NBG).

20. 14 Dec., when the Court of Directors unanimously rejected Clive's proposed settlement of his *jagir* claim, despite government support of his propositions. The terms suggested had been a grant of the *jagir* for ten or twelve years (i.e., total payments of approximately £300,000) in return for which Clive would abstain from interfering in the Com-

pany's affairs (Lucy S. Sutherland, *The East India Company in Eighteenth Century Politics*, Oxford, 1952, pp. 114–15). The government's share in these negotiations is discussed *ante* 2 Dec. 1763.

21. Richard Clive (ca 1693–1771), M.P. Montgomery 1759–71.

22. Sir Robert Henley (ca 1708–72), Kt, cr. (1760) Bn Henley and (1764) E. of Northington; lord keeper 1757–61; lord chancellor 1761–6; M.P. Bath 1747–57.

23. Presumably on 21 Sept., St Matthew's Day, the usual day for elections of governors of the Hospital (Norman Moore, *The History of St Bartholomew's Hospital*, 1918, ii. 188–9).

24. 'Every governor on his election is given a staff, shaped like a billiard cue and painted green—the heraldic tincture of the Tudors—and bearing the arms of the hospital, "Per pale argent and sable a chevron counterchanged" . . . , with the letters "St. B. H." below it in white' (Sir D'Arcy Power, *A Short History of St Bartholomew's Hospital 1123–1923*, 1923, p. 64).

25. I.e., Bartholomew.

my bad health has destroyed my abilities.' The late Chancellor[26] is much better.

The last time the King was at Drury Lane, the play given out for the next night was *All in the Wrong:*[27] the galleries clapped, and then cried out 'Let *us* be all in the right! Wilkes and Liberty!'[28] When the King comes to a theatre, or goes out, or goes to the House, there is not a single applause; to the Queen there is a little: in short, *Louis le bien-aimé*[29] is not French at present for King George.

The town, you may be sure, is very empty; the greatest party is at Woburn,[30] whither the Comte de Guerchy and the Duc de Pecquigny are going. I have been three days at Strawberry, and had George Selwyn, Williams,[31] and Lord Ashburnham;[32] but the weather was intolerably bad. We have scarce had a moment's drought since you went, no more than for so many months before. The towns and the roads are beyond measure dirty, and everything else under water. I was not well neither, nor am yet, with pains in my stomach:[33] how-ever, if I ever used one, I could afford to pay a physician. T'other day, coming from my Lady Townshend's, it came into my head to stop at one of the lottery offices, to inquire after a single ticket I had, expecting to find it a blank, but it was five hundred pounds—thank you! I know you wish me joy. It will buy twenty pretty things when I come to Paris.

I read, last night, your new French play, *Le Comte de Warwic,*[34] which we hear has succeeded much.[35] I must say, it does but con-

26. Lord Hardwicke.

27. By Arthur Murphy (*ante* 13 June 1761).

28. This incident, as HW describes it, cannot have happened in the presence of the King, who saw *All in the Wrong* at Drury Lane 15 Dec. (*Lloyd's Evening Post* 14–16 Dec., xiii. 583). The outcry possibly occurred on 14 Dec. when the command performance would have been announced, but it is not mentioned elsewhere.

29. The nickname given to Louis XV in his youth.

30. Bedfordshire, seat of the D. of Bedford.

31. George James ('Gilly') Williams (1719–1805), wit.

32. Ashburnham was at this time connected with the Opposition.

33. HW mentions in a letter to Montagu, 11 Jan. 1764, that on 2 Jan. 'I

was excessively out of order with a pain in my stomach which I had had for ten days' (MONTAGU ii. 115).

34. *Le Comte de Warwick, tragédie . . . répresentée pour la première fois par les Comédiens Français ordinaires du Roi, le 7 Novembre 1763*, 1764, by Jean-François de la Harpe (1739–1803), author and critic. Despite the date on the title-page, the play was published in late Nov. or early Dec. 1763 (Grimm, *Correspondance*, ed. Tourneux, 1877–82, v. 416; Gabriel Peignot, *Recherches historiques, litter-aires et bibliographiques sur la vie et les ouvrages de M. de la Harpe*, Dijon, 1820, p. 19). HW's spelling, 'Warwic,' follows that adopted by Hume in the second volume of his *History of England from the Invasion of Julius Cæsar to the Accession of Henry VII*, 1762.

35. 'Elle aura vraisemblablement quinze

firm the cheap idea I have of you French: not to mention the preposterous perversion of history in so known a story,[36] the Queen's[37]
ridiculous preference of old Warwick to a young King;[38] the omission of the only things she ever said or did in her whole life worth re-
cording, which was thinking herself too low for his wife, and too high
for his mistress;[39] the romantic honour bestowed on two such savages
as Edward and Warwick: besides these, and forty such glaring absurdities, there is but one scene that has any merit, that between
Edward and Warwick in the third act.[40] Indeed, indeed, I don't
honour the modern French: it is making your son but a slender
compliment, with his knowledge, for them to say it is extraordinary.
The best proof I think they give of their taste, is liking you all three.
I rejoice that your little boy is recovered. Your brother has been at
Park Place this week, and stays a week longer:[41] his hill is too high
to be drowned.

Thank you for your kindness to Mr Selwyn: if he had too much

représentations et c'est aujourd'hui le plus
haut degré de gloire auquel un poète
puisse prétendre' (Grimm, loc. cit., *sub* 1
Dec. 1763).

36. Except for the names of his principal characters, La Harpe's treatment of
the subject of his tragedy—Edward IV's
decision to marry Elizabeth Woodville and
the consequent fall and death of the Earl
of Warwick—bears no resemblance to
the actual historical situation; rather it
is based on a purely fictitious passage in
the Abbé Prévost's *Histoire de Marguerite d'Anjou, reine d'Angleterre*, Amsterdam [Paris], 1740, ii. 40–62, which por-
trays Warwick as so infatuated with Elizabeth that Marguerite is able to use her
as a lure in an abortive attempt to destroy him. La Harpe exaggerates this
false situation still further by making
Elizabeth and Warwick plighted lovers,
ignoring the famous story of Elizabeth's
courtship by Edward, and then com-
presses Edward's decision to marry Elizabeth and the fall of Warwick into a
single event, whereas they were separated
by several years. The actual history was,
as HW says, well known, most recently
through the account in the second volume of Hume's *History* (n. 34 above). A
similar criticism of the historical absur-

dity of the tragedy is made in Grimm,
op. cit. v. 403–7, *sub* 1 Nov. 1763, but obviously written after its first performance
on 7 Nov.

37. Elizabeth Woodville.

38. Ridiculous in the dramatic rather
than in the historical situation; Elizabeth was about 27 when the marriage
took place in 1464, Warwick, 36, and
Edward, only 22.

39. This reply to Edward's early solicitation seems to have been first attributed to Elizabeth, in somewhat different
words, in More's *History of Richard III*
whence it was incorporated into Hall's
and Holinshed's *Chronicles* and so into
3 Henry VI, III. ii. 97–8. According to
Croker's notes on the present letter
(*Works* ix. 42 and errata sheet), it has
also been attributed to Mlle de Mont-
morency, later Princess de Condé, in reply
to solicitations of Henri IV, and to Mlle
de Rohan, later Duchesse de Deux Ponts.

40. Scene iii.

41. Conway wrote to Hertford from
Park Place, 1 Jan. 1764, 'I have been here
with Lady Ailesbury ever since last
Wednesday sennight [21 Dec.] . . . I believe we shall not quite stay out the
holidays but return towards Wednesday
or Thursday' (MS now WSL).

impatience, I am sure it proceeded only from his great esteem for you.

I will endeavour to learn what you desire; and will answer, in another letter, that and some other passages in your last. Dr Hunter is very good, and calls on me sometimes. You may guess whether we talk you over or not. Adieu!

Yours ever,

H. Walpole

PS. There has not been a death, but Sir William Maynard's,[42] who is come to life again; or a marriage, but Admiral Knollys's,[43] who has married his divorced wife[44] again.

From Hertford, Friday 6 January 1764

Printed for the first time from a photostat of BM Add. MSS 23218, ff. 114–16.

Paris, January 6th 1764.

Dear Horry,

I HAVE with this letter sent you by Mr Webb,[1] an English officer, a small parcel containing two small mustard-pots of Sève china.[2] You are not to imagine 'em particularly pretty; if you do you will be deceived when you open them. They are such things as are given here on the New Year's Day, nor have they any other merit but novelty, till you give it by accepting them.

42. (1721–72), 4th Bt; M.P. Essex 1759–72. His death was reported in the newspapers, 22 Dec., but contradicted the following day (*Daily Adv.* 22, 23 Dec.; *London Chronicle* 20–2 Dec., in the postscript; 22–4 Dec., *sub* 23 Dec., xiv. 600, 601).

43. Admiral Charles Knowles.

44. His second wife, Maria Magdalena Theresa de Bouget (d. 1796), whom he had married the first time in 1750. He had divorced her for adultery with Capt. Gambier in 1757; see *Trial of Capt. G[ambier] for Crim. Con. with Admiral Knoly's Lady*, 1757. The only other record of their remarriage is a veiled report in the *St James's Chronicle* 22–4 Dec.: 'We hear that a gentleman of distinction, who some time ago was divorced from his lady for incontinency, was a few days since married again to the said lady.'

1. Not certainly identified, but perhaps Charles Webb, Capt. in the army 1755, in the 36th Foot 1756; major in the army 1762 (*Army Lists*, 1763, pp. 17, 89). The other Webbs in the *Army Lists* at this time are either ensigns, or, in the case of Daniel Webb, a Major-Gen.

2. HW placed them in the China Room: 'Two mustard pots and plates, of Sève china; given by Lord Hertford' ('Des. of SH,' *Works* ii. 406).

Apropos to *étrennes*[3] I must beg you to acquaint Lady Hervey that I have sent her by the Comtesse d'Egmont's[4] orders a parcel which she sent to me to be forwarded to England. I believe it may contain a small table or some such thing.[5] It was too large to be sent by a messenger or by a private hand. I have therefore sent it, as the safest way and least liable to accidents, by water, and it will be consigned to a merchant at Rouen[6] who will take care to forward it with another parcel[7] to the Princess Amelia by the first safe occasion. The only difficulty which can occur is at the custom-house, but that difficulty is not to be removed by my name; however I suppose Lady Hervey cannot have much trouble if she thinks proper to apply about such a trifle.

Mr Wilkes is here.[8] He came soon after his arrival to my door.[9] I was not at home or not visible,[10] and he left his name; on Sunday[11] he was at the chapel in my house, which divine service makes free, but I was then at Versailles. When we came back from thence Mr Hume told Mr Trail[12] he must have been strangely puzzled to preach against any sin without offending him, but as I do not love mischief you shall not repeat it. I inquired in the house from those who had served the Duke of Bedford and Mr Neville[13] what they had done in the same circumstances. His Grace had visited him and invited him twice to dinner;[14] Mr Neville had left his name or had it left at his door.[15] The last I thought the most becoming example for his

3. New Year's gifts.

4. Henriette-Julie de Durfort-Duras (1696–1779), m. (1717) Procope-Charles-Nicolas-Augustin-Léopold Pignatelli, Comte d'Egmont. For her friendship with Lady Hervey, see HW's correspondence with Lady Hervey in MORE.

5. It was apparently some sort of library table since HW and Hertford subsequently refer to it both as a *bibliothèque* and as a table; it was not delivered until mid-April (*post* 8, 27 March; 5, 15, 20 April 1764). Lady Hervey had asked HW to have Hertford carry to the Comtesse half a dozen bottles of honey water when he went to Paris (Lady Hervey to HW 31 Aug. 1763, MORE 30–1).

6. Not identified.

7. Containing trees (*post* 8, 27 March; 5, 15, 20 April 1764).

8. He arrived in Paris, 28 Dec. (Wilkes, *Correspondence*, ed. Almon, 1805, ii. 35).

9. 30 Dec. (ibid. ii. 21).

10. In the account of his relations with Wilkes which Hertford sent to Grenville, 4 Jan., he explained that he had had Wilkes turned away because he 'did not think it proper to admit him.' The rest of the account is the same as that in the present letter (*Grenville Papers* ii. 249–50).

11. 1 Jan.

12. Hertford's chaplain (*ante* 22 Jan. 1756).

13. Richard Neville Aldworth Neville (1717–93), politician and diplomatist; M.P. Reading 1747–54, Wallingford 1754–61, Tavistock 1761–74; secretary to the embassy at Paris under Bedford 1762–3; minister plenipotentiary to France May–Nov. 1763.

14. During Wilkes's visit to Paris in April 1763.

15. Neville also exchanged visits with

Majesty's representative, and in consequence my name has been carried to the Swiss[16] of his hôtel[17] in form, nor do I think myself at liberty (with all the inclination in the world to be personally civil) to show this gentleman in his circumstances any kind of countenance or protection from my representation, so if you hear it named you will know this to be the case, whatever may be said about it; but perhaps nothing may, and I shall like it the better.[18] Wilkes went to see Martin here and talked to him with his usual gay freedom for an hour, as if their acquaintance had never been interrupted by any quarrel.[19] He talks here of being in London I hear by the 16th;[20] his wound is still open, but I fancy not at all dangerous if his way of treating his constitution and running about does not make it so.[21]

The parliaments in this country begin to give some amusement to the world and a great deal of trouble to the ministers, but except to men very curious, which I think you are not, these transactions are hardly worth relating. At present I must endeavour to be informed for the satisfaction of my Court,[22] but I do not intend to trouble you with it till you tell me your taste is altered.[23]

Apropos to parliaments, I hear the ministry in England is well

Wilkes at Compiègne during the latter's visit to France in the summer of 1763 (*Grenville Papers* ii. 99).

16. So called because the porters of the large houses in Paris were usually Swiss.

17. Wilkes was staying at the Hôtel de Saxe, Rue du Colombier, Faubourg St-Germain (Wilkes, op. cit. ii. 35).

18. Wilkes sent his own account of his reception by Hertford to his friend Humphrey Cotes on the same day: 'I have been to make my bow to Lord Hertford; who, of course, was not at home, but, to my surprise, returned my visit. I left a card for the private secretary, David Hume; who returned my visit likewise; and today I met him at Baron Holbach's where we laughed much. . . . I went last Sunday [1 Jan.] to the ambassador's chapel, and go again next Sunday to take my leave of a dull preacher there' (ibid. ii. 35–6).

19. The notes they exchanged previous to the visit, 30 Dec., are printed ibid. ii. 19–21. Martin, on his return to England, described the interview as 'a friendly conference of about an hour'

(*Gazetteer,* quoted *London Chronicle* 19–21 Jan., xv. 65).

20. Wilkes wrote to Cotes the same day as the present letter that he intended to set out for England on the 13th, and would be glad to be back in England 'though I am to go through the fire ordeal of both Lords and Commons' (Wilkes, op. cit. ii. 36). On the 11th he wrote that he was 'now too ill to undertake the journey' (ibid. ii. 37–8), and forwarded certificates to this effect at the same time (ibid. ii. 41–4).

21. The wound became inflamed and Wilkes developed a fever (ibid. ii. 40, 41, 44).

22. Hertford had included in his dispatch to Halifax of 2 Jan. an account 'of the present interior circumstances of the Kingdom of France' (acknowledged by Halifax 10 Jan., S.P. 78/260, f. 10; Hertford's dispatch is not in S.P. 78).

23. HW in his missing reply to this letter apparently asked for details of the affairs of the parliaments, since Hertford wrote him at length on the subject, 23 Jan.

established and the Opposition quite disjointed; is it true?[24] I admire what you have told me from your niece, and I can easily believe Lord W[aldegrave] said it of Lord Sandwich in the zeal of friendship.

I am sorry the King grows impopular; I love him and do not think he deserves it.

Le Comte de Warwick is abominable; I abused it when I saw it pretty well acted.

Adieu, my dear Horry. I deserve no thanks for civility to Mr Selwyn; I really meant it all to himself and feel he deserves it. You know you may under any circumstances command me. The best compliments of the family attend you.

Yours ever,

Hertford

24. HW combats the reports of disunion in the Opposition *post* 22 Jan. 1764, but the leaders of the Opposition themselves tended to support them. Devonshire wrote to Newcastle, 2 Jan.: 'The prospect . . . I own appears to me very gloomy; on the side of the ministry I see everything that is bad; precipitate, daring and ready to pursue any measure to satisfy their revenge and carry their points, and I fear supported by a majority that will follow them too implicitly. On our side no concert but disunion, arising from jealousy and impracticability in some; and in others coolness and ill-humour from resentment and other personal considerations' (BM Add. MSS 32955, f. 11). On the 5th Newcastle wrote to Rockingham in similar terms, complaining of Pitt's impracticability (ibid. ff. 70–1).

To Hertford, ca Friday 13 January – Friday 20 January 1764

At least one, and probably two letters are missing. The first, to which Hertford replies on 23 Jan., contained an account of George Grenville and a request for an account of the proceedings of the French parliaments, and was probably written around 13 Jan. in immediate reply to Hertford's letter of the 6th. HW mentions, however, in his letter of 22–5 Jan. that in his 'last' letter, he had said he would send a private letter through a 'particular friend,' a promise not alluded to in Hertford's letter of the 23rd. HW also makes no mention in his long letter of 22–5 Jan., except retrospectively, of the expulsion of Wilkes from the House of Commons, 19 Jan., nor of any other event before 20 Jan. It seems probable that he dealt with them in a letter written either after he returned at eleven from the debate in the House on the 19th, or on the morning of 20 Jan. Hertford could hardly have received it on the 23d, while he had obviously received one letter from HW since that of 29 Dec. 1763. There is, however, no hint in any of Hertford's later letters that he received one from HW on Wilkes's expulsion.

To Hertford, Sunday 22 January 1764

Printed from *Works* ix. 44–56.

Arlington Street, Jan. 22d 1764.

MONSIEUR Monin,[1] who will deliver this to you, my dear Lord, is the particular friend I mentioned in my last,[2] and is, indeed, no particular friend of mine at all, but I had a mind to mislead my Lord Sandwich, and send you one letter which he should not open.[3] This I write in peculiar confidence to you, and insist upon your keeping it entirely to yourself from every living creature. It will be an answer to several passages in your letters, to which I did not care to reply by the post.

Your brother was not pleased with your laying the stopping your

1. Not identified. He was apparently a friend of Selwyn and Lord March (J. H. Jesse, *George Selwyn and his Contemporaries*, 1882, i. 272).
2. Missing.
3. HW feared that Sandwich, a sup-

porter of the measure to dismiss Conway for voting with the Opposition (see *ante* 16 Dec. 1763 *bis* and n. 14), was opening his letters to Hertford in hopes of finding proof of Conway's attachment to the Opposition, which Conway had denied.

bills[4] to his charge.[5] To tell you the truth, he thinks you as too much inclined to Courts and ministers, as you think him too little so.[6] So far from upbraiding him on that head, give me leave to say you have no reason to be concerned at it. You must be sensible, my dear Lord, that you are far from standing well with the Opposition, and should any change happen, your brother's being well with them, would prevent any appearance that might be disagreeable to you. In truth, I cannot think you have abundant reason to be fond of the administration. Lord Bute never gave you the least *real* mark of friendship.[7] The Bedfords certainly do not wish you well: Lord Holland has amply proved himself your enemy: for a man of your morals, it would be a disgrace to you to be connected with Lord Sandwich: and for George Grenville, he has shown himself the falsest and most contemptible of mankind.[8] He is now the intimate tool of the Bedfords,[9] and reconciled to Lord Bute,[10] whom he has

4. For the expenses of his trip to Paris.

5. Hertford had done so in the postscript *ante* 21 Dec. 1763. He had written to Conway on the same day but apparently did not mention the grievance; at least Conway does not allude to it in his reply, 1 Jan. 1764 (MSS now WSL).

6. These sentiments are implicit in Conway's letter to Hertford at this time: 'I don't much admire stubbornness, in any mode of thinking or in any walk of life, because there is in all human minds such a propensity to error, that it seldom becomes us; but yet that sort of politic *flexibility* which has its foundations in our interest I can't but think a much worse fault. If I err from ignorance of the world and a false judgment of mankind, as you seem to think, I doubt I am a little too old in error to correct now . . . if I see the generality of mankind either wandering thro' life without any principle at all, or following a bad one, I shall certainly have more satisfaction in leaving the herd than joining them' (ibid.).

7. Others did not think that Bute had neglected Hertford's interest; James West told Lord Lyttelton at the end of 1767 that the 'great object' of the Bedford group at the moment was 'to get the better of Lord Hertford's credit in the

Closet, which would not be easily done, as his Lordship had a strong root of personal favour there, which he cultivated and improved by being a most assiduous courtier to Lord Bute' (*Grenville Papers* iv. 251).

8. In *Mem. Geo. III*, HW states that all his prejudices in Grenville's favour had been dispelled at his first interview with Thomas Pitt on 3 Dec. (i. 272), but he still speaks well of Grenville *ante* 9 Dec. 1763.

9. HW overstates Grenville's servility to the Bedfords. Though Grenville and the Duke were on rather better terms than they had been during the autumn, they were still quarrelling over patronage at the time of this letter (*Grenville Papers* ii. 485–6, 489).

10. Grenville's diary suggests that his relations with Bute were improving, but that they were not yet reconciled. On 16 Jan. he had approved a message from Bedford to Bute discouraging the latter's return to town as 'very prejudicial to the King's affairs' despite Bute's declaration not to meddle in politics; and on the 28th he told Jenkinson 'that he had not been the means of Lord Bute's retreat, nor could he be so of keeping him in exile, but that his opinion was that his return might, in many ways, be prej-

served and disserved just as occasion or interest directed. In this situation of things, can you wonder that particular marks of favour are withheld from you, or that the expenses of your journey are not granted to you as they were to the Duke of Bedford?

You ask me how your letters please:[11] it is impossible for me to learn, now I am so disconnected with everything ministerial. I wish you not to make them please too much. The negotiations with France must be the great point on which the nation will fix its eyes: with France we must break sooner or later. Your letters will be strictly canvassed: I hope and firmly believe that nothing will appear in them but attention to the honour and interest of the nation; points, I doubt, little at the heart of the present administration, who have gone too far not to be in the power of France, and who must bear anything rather than quarrel. I would not take the liberty of saying so much to you, if, by being on the spot, I was not a judge how very serious affairs grow, and how necessary it is for you to be upon your guard.

Another question you ask[12] is, whether it is true that the Opposition is disunited. I will give you one very necessary direction, which is, not to credit any Court stories. Sandwich is the father of lies, and every report is tinctured by him. The administration give it out, and trust to this disunion. I will tell you very nearly what truth there is or is not in this. The party in general is as firmly and cordially united as ever party was. Consider, that without any heads or leaders at all, 102 men stuck to Wilkes,[13] the worst cause they could have had, and with all the weight of the Yorkes against them.[14] With regard to the leaders there is a difference. The old Chancellor[15] is

---

udicial at this time to the King's affairs, and that he had always understood that his Lordship meant to absent himself during the session of Parliament' (ibid. ii. 483–4, 488–9). Whatever the state of Grenville's relations with Bute may have been at this time, HW overestimates the extent of Bute's influence (see below, n. 28).

11. Hertford had made this request *ante* 21 Dec. 1763; and HW had promised to attempt to find out *ante* 29 Dec. 1763.

12. *Ante* 6 Jan. 1764.

13. In the first division during the debate on Wilkes's expulsion, 19 Jan., the minority had divided 102 to the ministe-

rial 239 in a futile attempt to adjourn the debate. Their numbers steadily diminished in the subsequent divisions because many of their supporters, including HW, left the House (*Journals of the House of Commons* xxix. 722; *Mem. Geo. III* i. 278; MANN vi. 199).

14. The Yorkes (and Charles Townshend as well) voted with the government in the second division on 19 Jan. on the question that Wilkes was guilty of contempt of the House and that the House would proceed to hear evidence (*Chatham Corr.* ii. 274), and probably voted with them in the other divisions as well.

15. Lord Hardwicke.

violent against the Court: but, I believe, displeased that his son was sacrificed to Pratt in the case of privilege.[16] Charles Yorke resigned,[17] against his own and Lord Royston's inclination,[18] is particularly angry with Newcastle for complying with Pitt in the affair of privilege,[19] and not less displeased that Pitt prefers Pratt to him for the Seals;[20] but then Norton is attorney-general,[21] and it would not be graceful to return to Court, which he has quitted, while the present ministers remain there. In short, as soon as the affair of Wilkes and privilege is at an end, it is much expected that the Yorkes will take part with the Opposition.[22] It is for that declaration that Ch[arles] Townshend says he waits.[23] He again broke out strongly on Friday last against the ministry, attacking George Grenville,[24] who seems his object. However, the childish fluctuation of his temper, and the vehemence of his brother George for the Court,[25] that is for himself, will forever make Charles little to be depended

16. The Opposition had supported Pratt's opinion that privilege of Parliament extended to libels, while Charles Yorke steadily opposed this interpretation; see *ante* 25 Nov. 1763.

17. As attorney-general, 3 Nov. 1763.

18. An interpretation borne out in Lord Royston's later account of the resignation (*Hardwicke Corr.* iii. 475–6), though Charles Yorke managed to put a rather better face on it at the time (ibid. iii. 539–52 *passim*).

19. Charles Yorke's correspondence and interviews with Newcastle during the autumn show increasing irritation on this subject; finally, he became so cold and distant in his treatment of the Duke that the latter wrote to him 14 Jan., accusing him of neglect and of suggesting to himself or allowing someone to suggest to him 'some jealousy or suspicion of me and my attention to your interest.' Yorke sent a conciliatory reply and relations apparently began to improve (ibid. iii. 539–61 *passim*; BM Add. MSS 32955, ff. 172, 174–5).

20. Pitt told Newcastle in October 'that there was never a moment since the King came to the Crown when he would not have preferred my Lord Chief Justice Pratt to Mr Yorke' for lord chancellor (*Hardwicke Corr.* iii. 537).

21. He had replaced Yorke as attorney-general on 16 Dec.

22. They did so in the debate on general warrants; see *post* 15 Feb. 1764.

23. Townshend had carried on a brief flirtation with the government around 10 Jan., sending messages through a Mr Bindley proclaiming his respect for the abilities and talents of Grenville and Halifax and his disgust at the rest of the Opposition (*Grenville Papers* ii. 482–3).

24. 'Friday, 20th. . . . Mr Charles Townshend took occasion, in this day's debate, to make a personal attack on Mr Grenville, insinuating that some transactions during the summer made it particularly necessary to be watchful upon every breach of privilege, and the liberty of the subject. Mr Grenville, in his reply, took notice of these words, and said he had but one answer to give, which was to desire the instances might be named which deserved such an insinuation. . . . Mr Townshend sat silent, and that evening repented of what he had done; went home in low spirits; said he had spoke very ill, and had given some offence in his speech to Mr Grenville, for which he was very sorry' (ibid. ii. 484–5).

25. One of the latter's letters, urging vigour against the City on the occasion of the riots on 3 Dec., is printed ibid. ii. 175–6.

on. For Mr Pitt, you know, he never will act like any other man in Opposition, and to that George Grenville trusts: however, here are such materials, that if they could once be put in operation for a fortnight together, the present administration would be blown up. To this you may throw in dissensions among themselves: Lord Halifax and Lord Talbot are greatly dissatisfied.[26] Lord Bute is reconciled to the rest;[27] sees the King continually;[28] and will soon want more power, or will have more jealousy than is consistent with their union. Many single men are ill-disposed to them, particularly Lord G. Sackville:[29] indeed nobody is with them, but as it is farther off, from, or nearer to, quarter-day:[30] the nation is unanimous against them: a disposition, which their own foolish conduct during the episode of the Prince of Brunswick, to which I am now coming, has sufficiently manifested.

[31]The fourth question put to him[32] on his arrival was, 'When do you go?' The servants of the King and Queen were forbid to put on their new clothes for the wedding,[33] or Drawing-Room, next day,[34] and ordered to keep them for the Queen's birthday.[35] Such pains

26. This is probably an exaggeration. It was being 'whispered' about, early in January, that Halifax had slighted his colleagues by avoiding the party at Woburn during the holiday (H. V. Jones to Newcastle 5 Jan., BM Add. MSS 32955, f. 69). He had also on 6 Jan. had a rather angry discussion with Grenville on the method of paying salaries in America (*Grenville Papers* ii. 481), but Grenville's diary at this time contains no other indication that Halifax was seriously discontented. No complaints by Lord Talbot are mentioned in the diary.

27. Not to Grenville or Bedford (above, n. 10).

28. 'Lord Bute is supposed to come frequently to town *incog.*; and my intelligencers say, that his power and influence continue full as great as ever!' (John Roberts to Newcastle 5 Jan., BM Add. MSS 32955, f. 86). There is no foundation to the report; rather, Bute was trying to obtain, without success, ministerial permission to come to London (*Grenville Papers* ii. 483–4).

29. Who threw in his lot with the Opposition on 3 Feb. (*post* 6 Feb. 1764). He was particularly discontented at the min-

istry's refusal to restore him to the posts he had lost after his court martial.

30. I.e., nearer to the time when their supposed secret pensions would be due.

31. This paragraph probably, and the next certainly, was written on Tuesday, 24 Jan; see below, n. 39.

32. By the King. The Prince had his first audience on 14 Jan. (*London Chronicle* 14–17 Jan., xv. 49).

33. 16 Jan.

34. The 'splendid court at St James's to compliment their Majesties on the marriage of her Royal Highness the Princess Augusta' (ibid., 17–19 Jan., xv. 58). Mrs Montagu, in a letter to her husband, describes it as 'the greatest and most brilliant crowd . . . that I ever saw' (Reginald Blunt, *Mrs Montagu*, [1923], i. 86).

35. 'I have learnt . . . that a list of *proper* persons to dine with him is also made out; and likewise another list of those houses to which he will be permitted to go. Lord Berkeley goes to meet him, as Constable of the Tower, and consequently the properest person to take care of a state prisoner' (G. Onslow to Newcastle, Sunday [7 Jan.], BM Add. MSS

were taken to keep the Prince from any intercourse with any of the Opposition, that—he has done nothing but take notice of them. He not only wrote to the Duke of Newcastle[36] and Mr Pitt,[37] but has been at Hayes to see the latter,[38] and has dined *twice*[39] with the Duke of Cumberland; the first time on Friday last,[40] when he was appointed to be at St James's at half an hour after seven, to a concert. As the time drew near, Ferronée[41] pulled out his watch; the

32955, f. 109). Nevertheless, Opposition continued to make plans to fête the Prince, and on 10 Jan. James Stuart Mackenzie, Bute's brother, wrote to Grenville of their preparations 'as I take it for granted you would not wish that the Prince should (for want of being put upon his guard) fall into the company of those who, under pretence of opposing the ministry, are thwarting every measure which his Majesty may judge proper to pursue' (*Grenville Papers* ii. 251–2). In practice, the restrictions on the Prince seem to have consisted of having his dinner guests chosen by the Lord Steward (Mann vi. 197; *Mem. Geo. III* i. 276) and a full schedule of royal festivities to fill his time, restrictions which the Prince, as HW points out, successfully evaded. The explanation given out for the restrictions at his table was that 'as our nobility are numerous and all could not be entertained at it, to avoid distinctions none are invited except the nobility of the King's household, except Lord Bath, whom the King desires to dine with his Serene Highness every day' (Blunt, op. cit. i. 86, 89).

36. His letter to Newcastle, 14 Jan., is in BM Add. MSS 32955, f. 166; Newcastle's reply is ibid. f. 168.

37. His letter to Pitt, 14 Jan., is printed in *Chatham Corr.* ii. 271–2.

38. 22 Jan. (*London Chronicle* 21–4 Jan., xv. 80; *Chatham Corr.* ii. 278; *Grenville Papers* ii. 487, 488). The 'friends of government' subsequently denied that the visit had taken place, even to the point of offering wagers against it (which supporters of Opposition returned); but the visit is established by Pitt's letter of thanks to the Prince, 23 Jan., and Féronce's reply, 31 Jan. (Alexander Fall to Jenkinson 29 Jan., in *The Jenkinson Papers, 1760–1766,* ed. N. S. Jucker, 1949,

p. 259; *Chatham Corr.* ii. 277–9, 283–4). See also Newcastle to Lady Yarmouth 14 Feb., BM Add. MSS 32955, f. 472.

39. Either 19 or 20 Jan. (see next note) and 24 Jan. (*London Chronicle* 21–4, 24–6 Jan., xv. 78, 81). HW's reference to a second dinner suggests that this paragraph was written (the next certainly was) on Tuesday evening, 24 Jan., though it seems somewhat doubtful that HW would refer to a dinner that was going on at the time of writing, or had been recently concluded, in this manner; he may be referring instead to an apparently mythical dinner that Opposition supporters added to the two known ones when they insisted that the Prince had dined 'three times' with the Duke of Cumberland (Jucker, op. cit. 258).

40. 20 Jan. The *London Chronicle* 19–21 Jan., xv. 65 (*sub* 20 Jan.), however, places the dinner on Thursday, 19 Jan., the day that the Prince accompanied the royal family to the theatre, not the day he attended the concert; GM 1764, xxxiv. 44–5, tends to support this alternate date. If the 19th is the correct date for the dinner, the anecdote HW relates cannot have happened because the Prince would have had to have been at St James's well before 7:30 P.M., to say nothing of delaying until 8:30, since the plays began at six (W. J. Lawrence, 'The Drama and the Theatre,' in *Johnson's England,* ed. A. S. Turberville, Oxford, 1933, ii. 173). Accounts of the events of Friday, 20 Jan., also conflict with the details of HW's anecdote (see *London Chronicle* 21–4 Jan., xv. 74, *Daily Adv.* 21 Jan., and *St James's Chronicle* 19–21 Jan., *sub* 21 Jan.), and the only other mention of so pointed an offence to the King is in *Mem. Geo. III* i. 277.

41. Jean-Baptiste Feronce von Rotenkreuz (1723–99); of Genevese extraction;

Duke took the hint, and said, 'I am sorry to part with you, but I fear your time is come.' He replied, 'N'importe'; sat on, drank coffee, and it was half an hour after eight before he sat out from Upper Grosvenor Street for St James's. He and Princess Augusta have felt and shown their disgusts so strongly, and his suite have complained so much of the neglect and disregard of him, and of the very quick dismission of him, that the people have caught it, and on Thursday, at the play,[42] received the King and Queen without the least symptom of applause, but repeated such outrageous acclamations to the Prince,[43] as operated very visibly on the King's countenance. Not a gun was fired for the marriage, and Princess Augusta asking Lord Gower[44] about some ceremony, to which he replied, it could not be, as no such thing had been done for the Prince of Orange;[45] she said, it was extraordinary to quote that precedent to her in one case, which had been followed in no other.[46] I could tell you ten more of these stories, but one shall suffice. The royal family went to the opera on Saturday:[47] the crowd not to be described:[48] the Duchess of Leeds,[49]

diplomat in the service of Brunswick; finance minister of Brunswick 1773–99. He had negotiated the subsidy treaty between England and Brunswick in 1759 and had returned to England in 1762 as minister plenipotentiary to negotiate the marriage between the Hereditary Prince and Princess Augusta (*Allgemeine Deutsche Biographie*, Berlin, 1967–71, vi. 717–19).

42. 'Last night [19 Jan.] their Majesties, accompanied by their Serene and Royal Highnesses, the Prince and Princess of Brunswick, and others of the royal family, were at Covent Garden Theatre to see the last new comedy, called, *No One's Enemy but His Own* [by Arthur Murphy], and the revived pantomime of *Perseus and Andromeda*. . . . There never was known so great a concourse of people to see any person go to the theatres as yesterday to see the Prince and Princess of Brunswick go to Covent Garden' (*London Chronicle* 19–21 Jan., xv. 65). Some ladies allegedly 'offered five guineas each for a seat in the boxes' to see the Prince (ibid. xv. 69). See also MANN vi. 199 and n. 13, and *London Stage* Pt IV, ii. 1034.

43. HW gives details of the repeated applause to the Prince in his letter to Mann 18 Jan. 1764, MANN vi. 199–200.

44. At this time lord chamberlain of the Household.

45. William IV (1711–51), Prince of Orange, m. (1734) Princess Anne, eldest daughter of George II.

46. The only other marriages of royal daughters since the accession of the Hanoverians had been those of the Princess Mary to the Landgrave of Hesse-Cassel in 1740, and of the Princess Louise to Frederick V, K. of Denmark, in 1743.

47. 21 Jan. to see *Leucippo*, 'a new opera set to music by [Mattia] Vento' (*London Chronicle* 19–21 Jan., xv. 70; *London Stage* Pt IV, ii. 1032, 1034–5; Sir George Grove, *Dictionary of Music*, 5th edn, ed. Blom, 1954–61, viii. 721).

48. 'Saturday night the crowd was so great at the Opera House to see the Hereditary Prince that the coaches of the quality could not come near the door, which obliged the ladies to get out and walk to the House. . . . When the company did get in, the crowded house presented such a multitude of genteel and elegantly dressed people, as was scarce ever seen before' (*London Chronicle* 21–4 Jan., xv. 74).

49. Lady Mary Godolphin (1723 – 3 Aug. 1764), m. (1740) Thomas Osborne, 4th D. of Leeds.

Lady Denbigh,[50] Lady Scarborough,[51] and others, sat on chairs between the scenes: the doors of the front boxes were thrown open, and the passages were all filled to the back of the stoves; nay, women of fashion stood on the very stairs till eight at night. In the middle of the second act, the Hereditary Prince, who sat with his wife and her brothers in their box, got up, *turned his back* to King and Queen, pretending to offer his place to Lady Tankerville[52] and then to Lady Susan.[53] You know enough of Germans and their stiffness to etiquette, to be sure that this could not be done inadvertently; especially as he repeated this, only without standing up, with one of his own gentlemen, in the third act.[54]

I saw him, without any difficulty, from the Duchess of Grafton's box. He is extremely slender, and looks many years older than he is: in short, I suppose it is *his manner* with which every mortal is captivated, for though he is well enough for a man, he is far from having anything striking in his person.[55] Today (this is Tuesday)[56] there was a Drawing-Room at Leicester House, and tonight there is a subscription ball for him at Carlisle House, Soho,[57] made *chiefly* by the Dukes of Devonshire and Grafton. I was invited to be of it, but not having been to wait on him, did not think it civil to meet him there. The Court, by accident or design, had forgot to have a bill passed for naturalizing him. The Duke of Grafton undertook it, on which they adopted it, and the Duke of Bedford moved it;[58] but the Prince sent word to the Duke of Grafton, that he should not have liked the compliment half so well, if he had not owed it to his Grace. You may judge how he will report of us at his return!

With regard to your behaviour to Wilkes, I think you observed

---

50. Probably Isabella de Jong, widow of the 5th E. of Denbigh and not her daughter-in-law, Mary Cotton (d. 1782), m. (1757) Basil Feilding, 6th E. of Denbigh, 1755.

51. Either the widow of the 3d Earl of Scarbrough, or her daughter-in-law, wife of the 4th Earl (*ante* 14 July 1761, n. 21).

52. Alicia Astley (1716–91), m. (1742) Charles Bennet, 3d E. of Tankerville; lady of the Bedchamber to Princess Augusta.

53. Lady Susanna Stewart, later Cts Gower and then Marchioness of Stafford; lady of the Bedchamber to Princess Augusta.

54. HW repeats his account of this 'insult' to the King in *Mem. Geo. III*, where he adds that the Prince carried his displeasure to the point of 'even going away during half the representation' (i. 277). Actually, the latter incident had occurred at Covent Garden, 19 Jan., when the Prince left the Theatre for a brief visit to the Royal Society (MANN vi. 199).

55. See HW's description of his appearance ibid. vi. 198.

56. 24 Jan.

57. HW describes the ball in greater detail in the third paragraph below.

58. 23 Jan. (*Journals of the House of Lords* xxx. 457).

the just medium: I have not heard it mentioned:[59] if they should choose to blame it, it will not be to me, known as your friend and no friend of theirs. They very likely may say that you did too much, though the Duke of Bedford did ten times more. Churchill has published a new satire, called *The Duellist*,[60] the finest and bitterest of his works. The poetry is glorious; some lines on Lord Holland, hemlock:[61] charming abuse on that scurrilous mortal, Bishop Warburton:[62] an ill-drawn, though deserved, character of Sandwich;[63] and one, as much deserved, and better, of Norton.[64]

Wednesday after dinner [25 Jan.].

The Lord knows when this letter will be finished; I have been writing it this week, and believe I shall continue it till old Monin sets out. Encore, the Prince of Brunswick. At the ball, at Buckingham House, on Monday;[65] it had begun two hours before he arrived. Except the King's and Queen's servants, nobody was there but the Duchesses of Marlborough[66] and Ancaster,[67] and Lord Bute's two daughters.[68] No supper. On Sunday evening the Prince had been to

59. A correspondent of Jenkinson's informed him 29 Jan., that friends of the Opposition 'say that Wilks [*sic*] visited Lord Hertford at Paris who returned his visit (this I believe is truth)' (Jucker, op. cit. 259).

60. Published 20 Jan. (*Daily Adv.* 20 Jan.). The subject of the poem is a conspiracy of Sandwich, Warburton, and Norton against Wilkes, the result of which was Wilkes's duel with Martin.

61. Most of Book I is a virulent, though somewhat disguised, attack on Holland. He is not directly mentioned until l. 128 when his 'innocent' sleep is ironically contrasted with the troubled rest of those guilty of the villainies previously described, most of which have already been attributed to him by relatively clear allusions. There then follows (ll. 143–4) an ironic allusion to the execution of Holland's steward, John Ayliffe, for forgery in 1759, an event previously hinted at in l. 66. This execution was a favourite subject of Churchill, who made the most of suspicions that Holland had allowed the law to take its course because Ayliffe knew too much; he alludes to it in the *Epistle to Ho-*

garth (l. 140) and later advertised a projected poem to be entitled 'Ayliffe's Ghost'; see Wallace Cable Brown, *Charles Churchill*, Lawrence, Kansas, 1953, pp. 103–4 and Lord Ilchester, *Henry Fox*, 1920, ii. 112.

62. Book III, ll. 125–268.

63. Book III, ll. 345–406.

64. Book III, ll. 269–344.

65. 23 Jan. 'Last night the Prince and Princess of Brunswick, with several of the royal family, supped with their Majesties at the Queen's Palace, and afterwards there was a grand concert of music and a ball' (*London Chronicle* 21–4 Jan., xv. 78, *sub* 24 Jan.).

66. Daughter of the Duke of Bedford and hence in favour.

67. Mistress of the Robes to Queen Charlotte.

68. Presumably his two eldest unmarried daughters, Lady Jane Stuart (*ante* 28 Nov. 1761), and Lady Anne Stuart (1746 – ca 1818), m. 1 (1764) Hugh Percy, styled Lord Warkworth 1750–66 and Earl Percy 1766–86, 2d D. of Northumberland 1786 (divorced 1779); m. 2 (1780) Baron Friedrich Karl Hans Bruno von Poellnitz. For the latter daughter, see Warren H.

Newcastle House,[69] to visit the Duchess. His speech to the Duke of Bedford, at first, was by no means so strong as they gave it out:[70] he only said, 'Milord, nous avons fait deux métiers bien différents; le vôtre a été le plus agréable: j'ai fait couler du sang, vous l'avez fait cesser.' His whole behaviour, so much *à la minorité,* makes this much more probable. His Princess thoroughly agrees with him. When Mr Grenville objected to the greatness of her fortune, the King said, 'Oh! it will not be opposed, for Augusta is in the Opposition.'[71]

The ball, last night, at Carlisle House, Soho, was most magnificent:[72] one hundred and fifty men subscribed, at five guineas each, and had each three tickets. All the beauties in town were there, that is, of rank, for there was no bad company. The Duke of Cumberland was there too; and the Hereditary Prince so pleased, and in such spirits, that he stayed till five in the morning. He is gone to-

Smith, *Originals Abroad,* New Haven, 1952, pp. 141-54.

69. 22 Jan. 'Sunday the Prince of Brunswick dined with the Duke of Newcastle, at Newcastle House, in Lincoln's Inn Fields' (*London Chronicle* 21–4 Jan., xv. 78). 'S[on] A[ltesse] S[erenissimé] m'a fait l'honneur de passer deux fois ici, et une fois d'une telle manière, que me fournissait une occasion de lui présenter la duchesse de Newcastle, qui languit extrêmement, et qui en est charmée, pour pouvoir assurer S.A.S. de ses très humbles respects' (Newcastle to Lady Yarmouth 14 Feb., BM Add. MSS 32955, ff. 471-2). The visit displeased the King (*Grenville Papers* ii. 488).

70. The ministerial version of the Prince's remark to Bedford has not been found; presumably HW had reported it to Hertford in one of his missing letters.

71. This incident is not mentioned by Grenville in his diaries. HW possible exaggerates the behaviour of the Princess and her husband, as Grenville reports, with no adverse reflections, a long conversation with the Princess on 22 Jan. in which she insisted that she did not meddle in politics and that her husband had entered into no party (ibid. ii. 486–7). Grenville's entry in his diary for 26 Jan. (ibid. ii. 488) shows that he was not entirely convinced, but nowhere does he

mention any of the more obvious insults to the King or favours to the Opposition that HW attributes to the Prince. It seems likely that HW, who reports all the incidents involving the Prince, except his visit to the Opera, from hearsay, has been led into exaggeration by the wishful thinking of his informants and by his own sympathies with the Opposition.

72. 'On Tuesday night [24 Jan.] there was a grand entertainment and ball given to the Prince of Brunswick at Mrs Conolly's Concert Room in Soho Square [Carlisle House, tenanted by Theresa Cornelys 1763–78]; at which were present his Royal Highness the Duke of Cumberland, and upwards of 250 of the nobility and persons of distinction. The ball was opened by the Prince of Brunswick and the Duchess of Richmond, and continued till yesterday morning six o'clock' (*London Chronicle* 24–6 Jan., xv. 85, quoting *Daily Adv.* 26 Jan.). The government apparently tried to deny the ball, since a previous paragraph in the same issue of the *London Chronicle* mentions a rumour having been circulated that the Prince had intended to go to Drury Lane *incognito* that evening, but denies it, asserting that the Prince was at Leicester House 'where an elegant entertainment and ball was provided for him' (ibid.).

day,[73] heartily sorry to leave everything but St James's and Leicester House. They lie tonight at Lord Abercorn's, at Witham, who does not *step from his pedestal*[74] to meet them. Lady Strafford said to him, 'Soh! my Lord, I hear your House is to be royally filled on Wednesday.'—'And *serenely*,' he replied, and closed his mouth again till next day.

Our politics have been as follow. Last Friday[75] the Opposition moved for Wilkes's complaint of breach of privilege to be heard as today:[76] Grenville objected to it,[77] and at last yielded, after receiving some smart raps from Charles Townshend[78] and Sir George Saville.[79] On Tuesday[80] the latter, and Sir William Meredith,[81] proposed to put it off to the 13th of February, that Wilkes's servant,[82] the most material evidence, might be here. George Grenville again opposed it, was not supported, and yielded.[83] Afterwards[84] Dowds-

73. Many details of the Prince's departure are in the *London Chronicle* 24–6 Jan., xv. 85.

74. Presumably an allusion to Abercorn's excessive pride and stiffness of manner, and to his taciturnity (see *ante* 9 Dec. 1763 and GM 1789, lix pt ii. 961).

75. 20 Jan.

76. The order stated that the complaint would be heard on Thursday, 26 Jan. (*Journals of the House of Commons* xxix. 723).

77. Grenville's account of his attitude is rather different: 'Mr Grenville desired, by all means, that . . . [the complaint] should come on immediately, and proposed the Monday following [23 Jan.]; but they [the Opposition] desired it might be postponed 'till Thursday, to which Mr Grenville consented' (*Grenville Papers* ii. 484).

78. HW mentions this speech in an earlier portion of the present letter.

79. Sir George Savile (1726–84), 8th Bt; politician.

80. The postponement of the order for hearing Wilkes's complaint was moved, debated, and ordered on Monday, 23 Jan. (*Journals of the House of Commons* xxix. 729), as HW correctly states in *Mem. Geo. III* i. 280.

81. (ca 1725–90), 3d Bt; M.P. Wigan 1754–61, Liverpool 1761–80. He was a recent convert to the Opposition, apparently as a result of a quarrel with the ministry over customs appointments in Liverpool; see his letter to Jenkinson, 5 Nov. 1763, in Jucker, op. cit. 214–16. HW, in describing these debates, calls him 'a convert from Jacobitism,' and he appears in Newcastle's division lists for the debate on general warrants in Feb. as one of the 'original forces who voted with us' (*Mem. Geo. III* i. 279; BM Add. MSS 32956, f. 116).

82. Matthew Brown, Wilkes's butler. He had given testimony regarding the seizure of Wilkes's papers in Wilkes's suit against Wood, 6 Dec. 1763, and again gave evidence before the House of Commons on the same subject, 13 Feb. (T. B. Howell, *Complete Collection of State Trials*, 1816–26, xix. 1155–7; *Mem. Geo. III* i. 286). He arrived in London from Paris 4 Feb. (*London Chronicle* 4–7 Feb., xv. 125).

83. Accounts of the debate and details of Grenville's speech are in *Mem. Geo. III* i. 280, a letter from E. Temple to Lady Chatham 25 Jan. (*Chatham Corr.* ii. 279), and a letter from James Grenville to Pitt, 24 Jan. misdated 3 Feb. in ibid. ii. 284–6. Temple's and James Grenville's letters represent George Grenville as 'deserted by the whole House,' but HW says that he yielded even though 'the minority on putting the question were not loud for it.'

84. Tuesday, 24 Jan.

well[85] moved for a committee on the Cider Bill;[86] and, at last, a committee was appointed for Tuesday next, with powers to report the grievances of the Bill, and suggest amendments and redress, but with no authority to repeal it.[87] This the administration carried but by 167 to 125.[88] Indeed, many of their people were in the House of Lords, where the Court triumphed still less. They were upon the *Essay on Woman*.[89] Sandwich proposed two questions; 1st, that Wilkes was the author of it; 2dly, to order the Black Rod[90] to attach him. It was much objected by the Dukes of Devonshire, Grafton, Newcastle,[91] and even *Richmond*,[92] that the first was not proved, and might affect him in the courts below. Lord Mansfield tried to explain this away, and Lord Marchmont and Lord Temple had warm words.[93] At last Sandwich, artfully, to get something, if not all, agreed to melt both questions into one, which was accepted; and the vote passed, that *it appearing* Wilkes was the author, he should

85. William Dowdeswell (1721–75), M.P. Tewkesbury 1747–54; Worcester county 1761–75; chancellor of the Exchequer 1765–6. As member for one of the 'cider counties,' he took a major part in the attempt to repeal the Cider Act.

86. Which had been enacted as 3 Geo. III, c. 12: 'An act for granting to His Majesty several additional duties upon wines imported into this kingdom; and certain duties upon all cider and perry; and for raising the sum of three millions five hundred thousand pounds, by way of annuities and lotteries, to be charged on the said duties.' It met with violent opposition and was eventually amended in the present session of Parliament by 4 Geo. III, c. 7.

87. Dowdeswell's original motion had given the committee of the whole House power 'to consider so much of an act, passed in the last session of Parliament, as lays a new duty of excise on cider and perry, to be paid by the maker thereof.' This general power had been restricted by an amendment striking out the 'so much' and substituting 'such alterations and amendments as may be proper to be made in such part' (*Journals of the House of Commons* xxix. 737). Another order was also voted referring petitions stating grievances against the Bill to the committee (ibid.). An account of the debate is in *Chatham Corr.* ii. 281–3.

88. The division took place on a question that the words 'so much' stand part of the question, so that the 125 'ayes' were voting for full powers for the committee (*Journals of the House of Commons* xxix. 737).

89. The formal proceedings of the Lords are in *Journals of the House of Lords* xxx. 458–9. The debate lasted four hours (*Chatham Corr.* ii. 279).

90. Sir Septimus Robinson (1710–65), Kt, 1761, gentleman usher of the Black Rod (DNB *sub* Richard Robinson [1709–94]; W. A. Shaw, *Knights of England*, 1905, ii. 290; *Court and City Register*, 1764, p. 76). Among the various duties of the Black Rod is the custody of delinquents committed by the Lords.

91. 'The Duke of Devonshire supported me with three or four sentences, uttered with great dignity, and which carried great weight. The Dukes of Grafton and Newcastle likewise spoke' (Temple to Lady Chatham 25 Jan., *Chatham Corr.* ii. 279–80).

92. At this time a fairly steady courtier, though he soon drifted into Opposition and by the time of the change of ministry in 1765 had completely broken with his old connections.

93. In *Mem. Geo. III*, HW states that the altercation followed Marchmont's remark that 'though Wilkes was gone, he had left his gang behind him' (i. 282).

be taken into custody by the Usher.[94] It appearing, was allowed to mean *as far as appears*. Then a committee was appointed to search for precedents how to proceed on his being withdrawn.[95] That dirty dog Kidgel[96] had been summoned[97] by the Duke of Grafton, but as they only went on the breach of privilege, he was not called. The new club,[98] at the house that was the late Lord Waldegrave's, in Albemarle Street, makes the ministry very uneasy; but they have worse grievances to apprehend!

Sir Robert Rich is extremely angry with my nephew, the Bishop of Exeter, who, like his own[99] and wife's family, is tolerably warm.

94. 'Resolved, by the lords spiritual and temporal in Parliament assembled, that it appearing to this House, that John Wilkes, Esquire, of Great George Street, Westminster, is the author and publisher of "The Essay on Woman" with Notes; and of another paper, entitled, "The Veni Creator Paraphrased," he be, for the said offence, taken into the custody of the Gentleman Usher of the Black Rod' (*Journals of the House of Lords* xxx. 459).

95. 'Ordered, that all the lords this day present be appointed a committee to search precedents, as to what punishments have been inflicted, or methods taken to vindicate the honour of this House, in cases of any breach of their Lordships' privilege, or contempts of this House; and to report to the House. Their Lordships, or any five of them, to meet on Tuesday the 7th day of February next, at ten o'clock in the forenoon, in the Prince's lodgings near the House of Peers, and to adjourn as they please' (ibid.).

96. John Kidgell (1722—?90), rector of Godston and Horne, 1762; chaplain to the E. of March. He had been instrumental in securing the copy of the *Essay on Woman* for the government, and had then completed the ruin of his character by publishing *A Genuine and Succinct Narrative of a Scandalous, Obscene, and Exceedingly Profane Libel, entitled "An Essay on Woman"* in Dec. 1763; see GRAY ii. 130–1, n. 2 and MANN vi. 187 and n. 7.

97. 19 Jan. (*Journals of the House of Lords* xxx. 453).

98. Wildman's. Reports of the forma-

tion of 'a numerous and formidable society of persons of distinction, property, abilities, and influence in the nation . . . which society is to be called *The Cotery of Revolutionists*, or *Anti-Ministerialists*, from the French word *coterie*, vulgarly called a *club* in English' and that Wildman 'is fitting up [the late Lord Waldegrave's house] in an elegant manner . . . for the reception . . . of the noblemen and gentlemen in the minority' appear in the newspapers in early Jan. (e.g., *London Chronicle* 3–5, 5–7 Jan., xv. 14, 21). By the middle of the month Newcastle's friends were signing the membership list, and by 9 Feb. the club had 106 members (Bessborough to Newcastle 16 Jan., BM Add. MSS 32955, f. 192; membership list, 9 Feb., ibid. ff. 409–10). HW does not appear on the list. The government's concern, or what the Opposition hoped was the government's concern, was reflected in such rumours as: 'It is pretended that it has been intimated to the naval and military officers of condition, that they must not think of being ever seen in the new tavern opened in Albemarle Street for the reception of the noblemen and gentlemen of the Opposition, and that no favour will even be granted to any person who shall enter that house' (printed in the *St James's Chronicle* 28–31 Jan., but contradicted ibid. 31 Jan.–2 Feb.).

99. The head of the Keppel family was the Earl of Albemarle, who according to HW had been threatened with dismissal (*ante* 9 Dec. 1763).

They were talking together at St James's, when A'Court[100] came in. 'There's poor A'Court,' said the Bishop. 'Poor A'Court!' replied the Marshal, 'I wish all those fellows that oppose the King were to be turned out of the army!' 'I hope,' said the Bishop, 'they will first turn all the old women out of it!'

The Duc de Pecquigny was on the point of a duel with Lord Garlies,[101] at Lord Milton's ball,[102] the former handing the latter's partner down to supper. I wish you had this Duke again, lest you should have trouble with him from hence: he seems a genius of the wrong sort. His behaviour on the visit to Woburn[103] was very wrong-headed, though their treatment of him was not more right. Lord Sandwich flung him down in one of their horse-plays, and almost put his shoulder out. He said the next day there, at dinner, that for the rest of his life he should fear nothing so much as a *lettre de cachet* from a French secretary of state, or a *coup d'épaule*[104] from an English one. After this he had a pique with the Duchess, with whom he had been playing at whisk. A shilling and sixpence were left on the table, which nobody claimed. He was asked if it was his, and said no. Then they said, 'Let us put it to the cards': there was already a guinea. The Duchess, in an air of grandeur said, as there was gold for the groom of the Chambers, the sweeper of the room might have the silver, and brushed it off the table. The Pecquigny took this to himself, though I don't believe meaned, and complained to the whole town of it, with large comments, at his return. It is

100. William A'Court (after 1768 Ashe A'Court or A'Court Ashe) (ca 1708–81); M.P. Heytesbury 1751–81; Maj.-Gen.; Lt-Col. of 2d Foot Guards. He was dismissed from the latter post at the end of Dec. not only because of his votes against the ministry in the House, but also, according to Conway, 'because he gave his interest on the Whig side in the county of Essex.' His dismissal seemed particularly vindictive to the Opposition because he was the least well-connected and politically significant of the general officers who had voted against the government and because the loss of his command left him with 'a wife and family and £200 a year' (Conway to Hertford 1 Jan., MS now WSL; *Mem. Geo. III* i. 268). He was subsequently restored by the Rock-

ingham ministry, becoming Lt-Gen. and Col. of the 11th Foot, 1765, and Gen., 1778.

101. John Stewart (1736–1806), styled Lord Garlies 1746–73; 7th E. of Galloway 1773.

102. 'Lord Milton gave on Monday night [16 Jan.] a grand ball, at his house near Chesterfield Street, to near 400 persons of distinction; and afterwards, an elegant supper of 200 covers, in honour of the royal nuptials' (*London Chronicle* 17–19 Jan., xv. 58).

103. For the house party at New Year's; see *ante* 29 Dec. 1763.

104. A pun; *donner un coup d'épaule* means figuratively 'to come to the assistance of.'

silly to tell you such silly stories, but in your situation it may grow necessary for you to know the truth, if you should hear them repeated. I am content to have you call me gossip, if I prove but of the least use to you.

Here have I tapped the ninth page! well! I am this moment going to Monsieur de Guerchy's, to know when Monin sets out, that I may finish this eternal letter. If I tire you, tell me so: I am sure I do myself. If I speak with too much freedom to you, tell me so: I have done it in consequence of your questions, and mean it most kindly. In short, I am ready to amend anything you disapprove; so don't take anything ill, my dear Lord, unless I continue after you have reprimanded me. The safe manner in which this goes, has made me, too, more explicit than you know I have been on any other occasion. Adieu!

Wednesday night, late.

Well, my letter will be finished at last. Monsieur Monin sets out on Friday; so does my Lord Holland:[105] but I affect not to know it, for he is not just the person that you or I should choose to be the bearer of this. You will be diverted with a story they told me tonight at the French ambassador's. When they went to supper, at Soho, last night,[106] the Duke of Cumberland placed himself at the head of the table. One of the waiters tapped him on the shoulder, and said, 'Sir, your Royal Highness can't sit there; that place is designed for the Hereditary Prince.' You ought to have seen how everybody's head has been turned with this Prince, to make this story credible to you. My Lady Rockingham,[107] at Leicester House, yesterday, cried great sobs for his departure.

Yours, ever,

Page the Ninth

---

105. Who was returning to Paris to join his family.

106. At the subscription ball of the P. of Brunswick (above, n. 72).

107. Mary Bright (1735–1804), m. (1752) Charles Watson Wentworth, 2d M. of Rockingham (Edmund Burke, *Correspondence*, Vol. I, ed. Copeland, Cambridge, 1958, p. 267, n. 2).

From Hertford, Monday 23 January 1764

Printed for the first time from a photostat of BM Add. MSS 23218, ff. 117–21.

Paris, January 23d 1764.

Dear Horry,

WHEN I complained of some of my correspondents[1] I did not mean to include you, nor indeed many others who have been very good to me without attaining to your degree of perfection. Fitzroy[2] has been very bad; I desire you will scold him for me. My brother has atoned for a great deal by sending me lately three of his letters at the same time.[3] Your account of G. Grenville is charming, and I am inclined to think the spirit of intrigue and party has a most animating effect upon an English constitution.

Wilkes is still here. He talked of being in England for his expulsion; since that he has been reported ill from the neglect of his wound, and I believe sent an attestation of it to England.[4] He is now again about the town and talks of returning this week or the next to London.[5] He asked Mr Selwyn[6] the other day if I had been informed that a bill was found against C. Webb for perjury,[7] and added that he had some hopes I should hear of it in the first instance by a question at Versailles.[8] He has behaved very properly by me

1. He had done so *ante* 7 Dec. 1763, though the reference may be to a passage in some missing letter.

2. Col. Charles Fitzroy (*ante* 11 July 1761), who seems to have been a regular correspondent of Hertford's.

3. The only one of these that has been found is that of 1 Jan., now wsl.

4. The attestation, 11 Jan., is printed in *Journals of the House of Commons* xxix. 721–2 and Wilkes, *Correspondence*, ed. Almon, 1805, ii. 43–4. It was read in the House, 19 Jan. (together with Wilkes's letter to the Speaker requesting postponement of his appearance), but disregarded, apparently because it was not properly witnessed (*Journals of the House of Commons* xxix. 721–2; Wilkes, op. cit. ii. 44–5). Wilkes, on learning of this, forwarded another copy of the doctors' certificate, properly notarized, and accompanied by an attestation of the signatures by Hert-

ford. The latter document, together with some astringent comments by Wilkes on its vagueness, is printed ibid. ii. 45–7.

5. Wilkes's letter to Humphrey Cotes, 20 Jan., makes it clear that he no longer seriously intended to return to England at the moment (ibid. ii. 48–55).

6. Charles Selwin, the banker.

7. 13 Jan. (*London Chronicle* 12–14 Jan., xv. 48). An indictment against Philip Carteret Webb for wilful perjury in some of the evidence he had given in Wilkes's trial against Wood in Dec. had been presented to a grand jury about 7 Jan.; they retained a true bill on the 13th. The trial did not come on until 10 and 21 May, when Webb was acquitted; see the report of the proceedings in T. B. Howell, *Complete Collection of State Trials*, 1816–26, xix. 1172–6.

8. That is, from the King or the ministers.

since he has been here in not trying to put me under any difficulties upon his account.

Our charming French opera begins tomorrow, and I have a place in one of the best boxes. Do tell Lady Mary[9] she should be very welcome to sit before me and I would allow you to be on my left hand; I go with the Marchioness's brother.[10] The Duke d'Ayen[11] who passes here for a wit and a satirist is reported to have said to the King at play upon Cardinal Bernis's[12] recall from banishment: 'Sire, je ne jouerai plus avec vous; pour la première fois vous prenez dans votre écart.'[13] The game I suppose may have been piquet, and it would be so far just in the allusion that this cardinal is the first disgraced minister whom the King has yet received. I believe however it[14] is *sans conséquence.*[15] He is returned to his diocese,[16] and the Duke de Choiseuil is said to have been instrumental in recalling him.[17]

Lady Hertford has now another family of her relations come to Paris: the Duke and Duchess of Berwick,[18] who are as Spanish

9. Lady Mary Coke.

10. Presumably Abel-François Poisson (1727–81), Marquis de Marigny, 1754; youngest brother of Mme de Pompadour; director-general of the buildings, gardens, arts, and manufactures of the King, 1746–73 (NBG; *Répertoire . . . de la Gazette de France*, ed. de Granges de Surgères, 1902–6, iii. 522).

11. Louis de Noailles (1713–93), Duc d'Ayen, 1737; Duc de Noailles, 1766; 'célèbre par ses bons mots' (HW's note to Mme du Deffand's MS *Recueil de lettres*, quoted DU DEFFAND ii. 288, n. 4).

12. Jean-Joachim de Pierre de Bernis (1715–94), cardinal 1758, minister of foreign affairs 1756–8, had resigned his offices in Oct. 1758 in favour of Choiseul when he found his advice was no longer followed, and had been exiled to his château of Vic-sur-Aisne near Soissons. The terms of his banishment were gradually eased; at the beginning of 1763 he was allowed to establish himself at the château du Plessis near Senlis, about 30 miles from Paris; and finally, 9 Jan. 1764, he was again received at Court (Frédéric Masson, *Le Cardinal de Bernis depuis son ministère*, 1884, pp. 1–33; de Granges

de Surgères, op. cit. i. 344; *Mercure historique*, 1764, clvi. 177–8).

13. 'Sire, I shall not play with you any more; for the first time you are taking from your discard.'

14. The recall of Bernis, not the Duc's bon mot.

15. Hertford may have been informed officially, as the French ambassador abroad had been, that the recall of Bernis portended no change in the administration; rumour, however, had made him about to become either first minister or Archbishop of Paris. See, in addition to the material quoted by Masson, op. cit. 32–4, the *London Chronicle* 14–17, 24–6 Jan., xv. 49, 81; and *Mercure historique*, loc. cit.

16. Bernis returned to the château du Plessis, the property of one of his relatives, immediately after his reception at Court (Masson, op. cit. 29, 34). He had no diocese at this time as he held no bishopric.

17. An explanation accepted by Masson, op. cit. 32.

18. James Francis Edward Stuart-Fitzjames (1718–85), 3d D. of Berwick; m. (1738) Maria Teresa de Silva (1716–90), daughter of the Count de Galve.

except in speaking a little French as if they had never been here.

I have been lately most magnificently and politely entertained with Lady Hertford by the Duke de Bouillon,[19] and I can assure you there is not even a picture of the Pretender[20] in the house that I could discover; but there are some of much greater value and of more ancient date which you would look at with pleasure.

How shall I satisfy your curiosity about the parliaments here? The subject is become such a very copious one I shall hardly know where to begin nor where to end. You do not want my opinion upon such measures; your own judgment will probably be more just. I will therefore confine myself by relating merely the decisions of the parliaments since I have been here and the measures of administration in consequence of them;[21] either at least[22] [or] both of them will I think persuade you that the spirit of liberty is gaining fast upon this country, and that it has not been discouraged by the disgraces of the late war or the union and strength of Council since the Peace.

The parliament of Rouen petitioned for the power of levying the taxes of the province and offered the King five millions additional revenue.[23] They repined that a scheme calculated for the interest both of King and people should be rejected,[24] and refused to register

19. Charles-Godefroi de la Tour d'Auvergne (1706–71), Duc de Bouillon; grand chamberlain of France; Gov. of Auvergne 1728–71.

20. The Old Pretender. Bouillon was closely related to him by marriage, as they had both married grand-daughters of John Sobieski, K. of Poland; the Duchess de Bouillon, however, seems to have regarded her husband's family with undisguised contempt, and as she had abandoned her husband to return to Poland, the family tie was unquestionably weak (*Dictionnaire de biographie française*, 1933–   , vi. 1323).

21. Some of the events that Hertford mentions below, particularly those relating to the beginning of the conflict with the parliament of Rouen, occurred before his arrival in Paris, though all of them were confirmed by other acts of the parliament during Nov. and Dec.; see the succeeding notes.

22. 'At least' written over 'or both' in the MS.

23. Hertford is mistaken. The remonstrance of the parliament of Rouen, 5 Aug. 1763, against the financial edicts of April 1763, suggests in general terms a return of taxation that would replace the multitudinous national levies with a blanket assessment on each province, leaving the means of raising the sum to the province itself (i.e., to the parliament or to the provincial estates where they still existed) (*Mercure historique*, 1763, clv. 289). The theory was developed in greater detail in the remonstrances of the Cour des Comtes, Aides, et Finances of Normandy, 30 July (Armand-Thomas Hue de Miromesnil, *Correspondance*, ed. Le Verdier, Rouen and Paris, 1899–1903, ii, p. lxxviii, n. 1), but there is no mention in the detailed discussions of the proceedings of the parliament of Rouen at this time of a petition reducing the theory to a specific proposal.

24. Hertford has apparently confused the rejection of the supposed petition with the summary rebuke administered

the edicts for the *centième denier*, the prolongation of the second *vingtième* and the *deux sous par livre*;[25] their governor, the Duc d'Harcourt,[26] employed force to oblige them. They resolved unanimously to resign their gowns.[27]

The parliament of Toulouse took fire on the same question of the edicts;[28] their governor, the Duke de Fitzjames, threw some of the members into prison.[29] The Chambers refused to meet.[30]

to the parliament by the King's order, 10 Aug., for their remonstrance of the 5th; see ibid. ii, p. lxx.

25. Taxes provided for in the financial edicts of April and the King's declaration of 4 April; a *précis* of their contents is in *Mercure historique* 1763, cliv. 637–40.

26. Anne-Pierre d'Harcourt (1701–83), Duc d'Harcourt 1750; Lt-Gen. of Haute-Normandie 1716–64; named Gov. of Normandy 26 May 1764 (La Chenaye-Desbois x. 321–2).

27. 19 Nov. 1763. Hertford has telescoped events. The first refusal to register the edicts occurred 18 Aug. 1763. When Harcourt ordered the registration, all the members of the parliament, except the premier président and two other officers compelled to assist by *lettres de cachet*, left the chamber. Harcourt proceeded to enroll the edicts, but as soon as he had left the hall, the members returned, declared the registration null and void, and strengthened their resistance by voting further resolutions against Harcourt's proceedings, 19 Aug. The parliament then adjourned to Nov. On 25 Aug. Harcourt, again under royal command and with the forced assistance of the premier président, struck the *arrêts* of 18 and 19 Aug. out of the registers of the parliament and reinserted the registration of the April edicts. After the parliament reassembled on 16 Nov. they annulled Harcourt's proceedings of 25 Aug. and reaffirmed their original resolutions of 18 and 19 Aug. These measures were promptly annulled by an edict of the Council of State, and on 19 Nov. Harcourt again forcibly struck them from the registers of the parliament and again inserted the registration of the edicts of April. Upon this, all the members of the parliament, except the premier président

Miromesnil, resigned their posts. See the full narrative of the events in Miromesnil, op. cit. ii, pp. lxiii–lxxviii, iii, pp. vi–xiii; and A. Floquet [Pierre Amable], *Histoire du parlement de Normandie*, Rouen, 1840–2, vi. 537–56.

28. Events followed much the same course at Toulouse as at Rouen. The parliament, when ordered to register the edicts, published a remonstrance against them instead. Fitzjames was then sent to compel the registration, as Harcourt had done at Rouen, and delivered his orders to the effect, 13 Sept. The members of the parliament thereupon left the chamber and Fitzjames proceeded to the registration. As soon as he had left the hall, the members returned, annulled the registration, and attempted to prolong their session. They were foiled in the last attempt, and forced to adjourn for the vacation. Then, 25 Sept., Fitzjames struck out the *arrêts* of 13–14 Sept. and again registered the edicts of April. On the reassembly of the parliament in Dec., it annulled, 9 Dec., Fitzjames's act of 25 Sept. and then proceeded against him personally as mentioned *ante* 28 Dec. 1763 and discussed further below. See J.-B. Dubédat, *Histoire du parlement de Toulouse*, 1885, ii. 461–501.

29. He placed most of the members under house arrest, 19 Sept. (ibid. ii. 483–4), but none of these were actually imprisoned. Fitzjames's orders for the house arrest are printed *Mercure historique*, 1763, clv. 639–41.

30. The members actually made an attempt to prolong their session in Sept., but were forced to adjourn for their usual vacation (Dubédat, op. cit. ii. 475–83). Hertford may have confused the different meanings of *proroger*, which can signify either 'to prolong' or 'to adjourn.'

The parliament of Aix adhered to that of Toulouse and applied for the liberty of the confined members.[31]

The parliament of Grenoble passed a sentence against Monsieur du Menil,[32] their commandant.

The parliament of Bourdeaux refused to register the edicts.[33]

After many fruitless attempts to accommodate matters the ministry, who dreaded a junction between those parliaments and that of Paris, thought it expedient to present a declaration[34] to that assembly inviting them to interpose with their advice in all affairs that regard the finances, and placing the sinking fund under their inspection.[35] They likewise resolved to gratify all the other parliaments as well as that of Paris in their pretensions. The Duke de Fitzjames and Monsieur du Menil were recalled.[36] The acts of power which the former had exercised in Toulouse succeeded so ill that the parliament of the province passed a sentence against him called a *décret de prise du corps*[37] by which he was to surrender himself a prisoner and stand his trial, or in case of non-compliance he was declared outlawed and of course incapable of exercising any civil function.

31. 17 Oct. 1763, when they passed declarations protesting the methods of compelling registration of the edicts, with special reference to the proceedings at Toulouse (*Mercure historique*, 1763, clv. 642–3; P.-Albert Robert, *Les Remontrances et arrêtés du parlement de Provence au dix-huitième siècle*, 1912, p. 250).

32. Charles-Louis-Joachim de Chastellier du Mesnil (ca 1700 – 1 Mar. 1764), Marquis du Mesnil; Lt-Gen.; inspector-general of the cavalry; Lt-Gen. and commandant of the Dauphiné (La Chenaye-Desbois v. 310; de Granges de Surgères, op. cit. ii. 299). He had been *décrété de prise de corps*, 14 Oct. 1763, after a course of action parallel to those at Rouen and Toulouse (J. Egret, *Le Parlement de Dauphiné*, Grenoble, 1942, i. 103–4).

33. 7 Sept.; reaffirmed 14 Nov. 1763. Events had followed the same course at Bordeaux as at Rouen and Toulouse; see C.-B.-F. Boscheron des Portes, *Histoire du parlement de Bordeaux*, 1877, ii. 294–6.

The proceedings of 14 Nov. are printed in *Mercure historique*, 1763, clv. 643–6.

34. 21 Nov. 1763, printed ibid., 1763, clv. 647–66. It was sent to the parliament of Paris, 25 Nov., which registered it, together with letters patent explaining it, 1 Dec. The latter are printed ibid., 1764, clvi. 32–5.

35. These powers were granted particularly by Articles I and IV of the declaration and enforced by the letters patent (ibid., 1763, clv. 652, 654; 1764, clv. 32–5).

36. Del'Averdi, contrôleur général des finances, wrote to Miromesnil, premier président of the parliament of Rouen, 18 Jan., that 'le Roi vient d'écrire à M. de Fils de James de se rendre auprès de sa personne, et il vient d'en faire écrire autant à M. Dumesnil' (Miromesnil, op. cit. iii. 105–6). However, Fitzjames, fearing prosecution by the parliament of Toulouse, had already left there 14 Jan. (Dubédat, op. cit. ii. 504–5). See also Egret, op. cit. i. 112–13.

37. 17 Dec. See *ante* 28 Dec. 1763, n. 7.

The Princes of the Blood and peers were offended at a provincial parliament's assuming so much authority over one of their order, and assembled on the 22d December to canvass this irregularity. The King was invited to this as well as to a second meeting which they had on the day following, but refused to be present at either.[38] The parliament however proceeded almost unanimously to annul the sentence of the parliament of Toulouse as unprecedented and irregular, and the reason assigned for this decree was that the peers met in parliament at Paris were his sole and legal judges, and that it belonged only to them to pass any sentence for his imprisonment or outlawry.[39]

But as this decree afforded the Duke of Fitzjames only a temporary relief (the articles of charge against him being still to be discussed), the King thought proper to put a stop to these proceedings of the peers and parliament of Paris by a message desiring them to send to him that night[40] the first *président*[41] and two *présidents à mortier*. To these magistrates he acknowledged the Duke de Fitzjames's conduct to be derived from orders issued from the throne.[42] This avowal

---

38. Hertford has telescoped and confused the proceedings between the meeting he dates 22 Dec. and the formal annulment of the decree against Fitzjames. Some sort of assembly, consisting only of dukes and ecclesiastical peers, met at the Duc d'Orléans's 22 or 23 Dec., at which it was decided to carry the complaint about the decree against Fitzjames to a *grand'chambre*, a formal meeting of the parliament of Paris augmented by the Princes of the Blood and the peers. This was not done until 29 Dec. (not the day following the meeting at Orléans's, as Hertford implies), and even then, because of some procedural irregularity in summoning the peers, the parliament could not act as a *grand'chambre* that day. The *grand'chambre* was then formally convoked for 30 Dec.; the King was invited, but declined to attend. Not until this third meeting, 30 Dec., did the parliament proceed to annul the decree of the parliament of Toulouse (*Mercure historique*, 1764, clvi. 44–6; *London Chronicle* 3–5 Jan. 1764, xv. 16; É. Glasson, *Le Parlement de Paris*, 1901, ii. 288–9,

where the meeting of the 30th is misprinted the 3d).

39. The *arrêt* annulling the decree of the parliament of Toulouse is printed *Mercure historique*, 1764, clvi. 45; see also Glasson, loc. cit.

40. 30 Dec.

41. René-Nicolas-Charles-Augustin de Maupeou (1714–92), premier président of the parliament of Paris 12 Nov. 1763–1768; chancellor 1768–74, in which office he was responsible for the suppression of the parliaments.

42. Slightly different versions of the King's speech to the premier président and his colleagues are given in *Remontrances du parlement de Paris au dix-huitième siècle*, ed. Flammermont and Tourneux, 1888–98, ii. 424, and *Mercure historique*, 1764, clvi. 45–6; both versions quote the King as stating directly that Fitzjames had only obeyed the orders he had received. See also Glasson, op. cit. ii. 289. A slightly garbled version of the event had already appeared in London from letters from Paris, 6 Jan. (*London Chronicle* 17–19 Jan., xv. 61).

has in great measure saved the Duke, but it has produced strong remonstrances from the peers and parliament.[43]

There is now another affair on the carpet which may tend much to inflame the minds of the public. The Archbishop of Paris,[44] a man of courageous and inflexible temper, leading a very strict regular life which recommends him to the people, has with an indiscreet zeal adopted the cause of the Jesuits and printed a *mandement*[45] or pastoral letter blaming the suppression of that religious order and exhorting the people to pray for its restoration and to use their endeavours for that purpose. This *mandement* has been *dénoncé* by the parliament[46] and they are now setting upon it; in the meantime it is said that the King will banish him to his estate[47] in order to save him from the parliament.

43. The King in his speech to the premier président, 30 Dec., gave the parliament permission to make a remonstrance on the orders given to Fitzjames. After a debate, 31 Dec., it was resolved to do so by a vote of 82 to 56 and a committee was appointed to draw it up (Flammermont and Tourneux, loc. cit.; *Mercure historique*, 1764, clvi. 46). An *arrêt* expressing the objects of the remonstrance was voted 16 Jan. (printed ibid., 1764, clvi. 140–65; and also printed separately), and the remonstrance itself (printed Flammermont and Tourneux, op. cit. ii. 424–38), was presented 19 Jan. The King replied on the 20th that he would send letters patent to the parliament the following day settling the complaints. These ordered another registration of the declaration of 21 Nov. (above, n. 34) and imposed a silence on all previous proceedings on the subject of finances. The parliament accepted and registered these, 21 Jan., and voted *arrêts* thanking the King and communicating the victory to the other parliaments; and then the points in dispute were temporarily compromised (Flammermont and Tourneux, op. cit. ii. 439–40; *Mercure historique*, 1764, clvi. 165–71). See also Glasson, op. cit. 289–93.

44. Christophe de Beaumont du Repaire (1703–81), Bp of Bayonne 1741–5, Abp of Vienne 1745–6, of Paris 1746–81.

45. *Instruction pastorale de Monsei-*gneur *l'Archévêque de Paris sur les atteintes données à l'autorité de l'église par les jugements des tribunaux séculiers dans l'affaire des Jésuites*, 1763; dated Conflans 30 Oct. 1763.

46. The *Instruction pastorale* was complained of before the parliament, 16 Jan.; on the 21st it was formally condemned and ordered to be burnt, a sentence executed 24 Jan. The King, on learning of the condemnation, promptly forbad the parliament to proceed further in their charges against the Archbishop, as he had already been punished, but when this order was reported to the parliament on 23 Jan., they immediately appointed a committee to draw up remonstrances complaining of the withdrawing of culprits from their jurisdiction and explaining further their conduct in the case. These remonstrances were not completed until 29 Feb. and were presented to the King 4 March (Flammermont and Tourneux, op. cit. ii. 440–4; *Mercure historique*, 1764, clvi. 172–7; Glasson, op. cit. ii. 293–5). The remonstrances finally presented are printed in Flammermont and Tourneux, op. cit. ii. 444–85.

47. The Archbishop had already been banished by a *lettre de cachet*, 20 Jan., to the Abbey of Sept-Fonds and later to the Abbey of La Trappe, after arrangements made with his consent, 18 Jan. In Sept. he was permitted to resume residence at Conflans, and finally, in Dec.

I am asked sometimes about our forms of proceedings, for as yet they know little of them; but the peers seem to relish the air of business, and if the army would let them proceed, the spirit of liberty would I think show itself still more apparently.

Are not you tired of the commission you have given me? I think you have enough for some time of the history of these parliamentary proceedings. If you can decipher it from my hand do show it to my brother and then burn it.

I remain, dear Horry, with the best compliments of the family,

Most sincerely and affectionately yours,

HERTFORD

From HERTFORD, Sunday 29 January 1764

Printed for the first time from a photostat of BM Add. MSS 23218, ff. 122–3.

Paris, January 29th 1764.

Dear Horry,

I HAVE wrote you a long letter which has been ready to go by a messenger these three or four days, but I wait for some business from Versailles which I have not yet received. I shall therefore keep it for the messenger which I hope to be able to send off on my return from Versailles, and shall write you a few words to tell you how very distinguishing a mark I have lately received of the King of France's favour.

Do not be frightened for me; it is unsought and undeserved on my part, which makes the favour greater. I must introduce it by explaining the occasion, and that in as few words as possible, having not a moment to spare. I have been lately in treaty with the Duke of Chaulnes, the proprietor of the house which I now inhabit,[1] for

1764, he was freed from all restrictions (ibid. ii. 441, 485; *Mercure historique,* 1764, clvi. 174–5). Rather curiously, the *London Chronicle* 3–5 Jan. had published reports from Paris of 23 Dec. that the parliament of Paris had already complained to the King of the Archbishop's pastoral letter, and that he had already

been banished to his abbey of Conflans (xv. 14).

———

1. The Hôtel de Grimbergh, Rue St-Dominique, Faubourg St-Germain, listed as the residence of both Bedford and Hertford in the *Almanach royal,* 1763, p. 131; 1764, p. 134.

a renewal of the lease, and in my behaviour upon the occasion I endeavoured to show that spirit and generosity which I think becomes my present situation. The Duke seemed to be sensible he might expect it from me or one of my brother ambassadors, and treated me accordingly; however, not to have the trouble and expense of changing, I was submitting even under unpleasant circumstances, till the manner piqued me and made me alter my intention.[2] The story was before known to some of the French noblemen who come to this house; it was now generally diffused all over the town, and the Duke de Chaulnes's conduct as generally disapproved. It could not be known here and be long a secret at Versailles. It came to the King's knowledge, upon which he ordered one of his ministers to write to me[3] and say that he heard I might be distressed for a house, that the Hôtel de Belleisle,[4] belonging to the Crown, was now at liberty, and that he would order it to be furnished for me out of his own wardrobe till I could find one that would do for my family. This is a most extraordinary compliment to me and a justification of the French way of thinking in general upon such negotiations. I hope to be able to find another house before this lease is out,[5] but I in every case am equally sensible of this mark of the King's personal favour.

I remain, dear Horry,

Always most affectionately yours,

Hertford

2. 'Lord Hertford lodges at the Hôtel de Grimshergen [sic]. The owner of the Hotel wanted to extort a thousand crowns more from his Lordship, or force him to decamp. The French King, as soon as he was informed of it, offered the Ambassador the Hôtel de Belleisle, and said, that he had ordered it to be furnished immediately, that his Lordship might not suffer a moment's inconvenience from any of his subjects' (St James's Chronicle 15–17 March).

3. The letter has not been found.

4. Rue de Lille. It had apparently come into the hands of the Crown on the death of the Duc de Belle-Isle in 1761; it was later inhabited by the Duc and Duchesse de Praslin (Charles Lefeuve, Histoire de Paris rue par rue, 5th edn, 1875, iv. 417).

5. Hertford did so, the Hôtel de Brancas, Rue de l'Université; see post 22 March 1764.

To Hertford, Monday 6 February 1764

Printed from *Works* ix. 56–63.

Arlington Street, February 6, 1764.

YOU have, I hope, long before this, my dear Lord, received the immense letter that I sent you by old Monin.[1] It explained much, and announced most part of which has already happened; for you will observe that when I tell you anything very positively it is on good intelligence. I have another much bigger secret for you,[2] but that will be delivered to you by word of mouth. I am not a little impatient for the long letter you promised me. In the meantime thank you for the account you give me of the King's extreme civility to you.[3] It is like yourself, to dwell on that, and to say little of Monsieur de Chaulnes's dirty behaviour; but Monsieur and Madame de Guerchy have told your brother and me all the particulars.

I was but too good a prophet when I warned you to expect new extravagancies from the Duc de Chaulnes's son. Some weeks ago he lost £500 to one Virette,[4] an equivocal being, that you remember here. Paolucci,[5] the Modenese minister, who is not in the odour of honesty, was of the party. The Duc de Pecquigny said to the latter, 'Monsieur, ne jouez plus avec lui, si vous n'êtes pas de moitié.' So far was very well. On Saturday, at the Maccaroni Club[6] (which is composed of all the travelled young men who wear long curls and spying-glasses), they played again: the Duc lost, but not much. In

1. HW's letter of 22–5 Jan.; Hertford did not receive it until ca 18 Feb. (*post* 18 Feb. 1764).
2. Not explained.
3. By the offer of the Hôtel de Belle-Isle (*ante* 29 Jan. 1764).
4. Not completely identified. A letter of the 3d D. of Rutland to a relative in Lausanne, 15 Feb., about the present quarrel, describes him as 'a Suisse, or Geneva, gentleman named Vivret' (quoted in W. E. Manners, *Some Account of the . . . Marquis of Granby*, 1899, p. 300). HW also relates an anecdote of 'one Virette, a Swiss' who had originally been 'a kind of toad-eater' to the mysterious Comte de St-Germain, and who was denounced as a spy to Lord Holdernesse in

1755, but saved by the intervention of his friend Hans Stanley (Mann iii. 182, n. 35).
5. Marchese Giuseppe Paolucci (1726–85), diplomatist; Modenese envoy to England 1754–7, 1763–4; special envoy to France 1760–3; Modenese minister of commerce and agriculture, 1767 (Vittorio Spreti, *Enciclopedia storico-nobiliare italiana*, Milan, 1928–36, v. 116–17; *Repertorium der diplomatischen Vertreter aller Länder*, Vol. II, ed. Friedrich Hausmann, Zurich, 1950, pp. 225, 226).
6. The earliest use of the word *macaroni* in the sense of fop recorded in the OED. The Club was located in King Street, St James's Square; for what is known of it, see Montagu ii. 139 and n. 11.

the passage at the Opera, the Duc saw Mr Stuart[7] talking to Virette, and told the former that Virette was a *coquin,* a *fripon,* etc. etc. Virette retired, saying only, 'Voilà un fou.' The Duc then desired Lord Tavistock[8] to come and see him fight Virette, but the Marquis desired to be excused. After the opera, Virette went to the Duc's lodgings, but found him gone to make his complaint to Monsieur de Guerchy, whither he followed him; and farther this deponent knoweth not.[9] I pity the Count (de Guerchy), who is one of the best-natured amiable men in the world, for having this absurd boy upon his hands!

Well! now for a little politics. The Cider Bill has not answered to the minority, though they ran the ministry hard;[10] but last Friday[11] was extraordinary. George Grenville was pushed upon some navy bills.[12] I don't understand a syllable, you know, of money and accounts; but whatever was the matter, he was driven from entrenchment to entrenchment by Baker[13] and Charles Townshend.[14] After that affair was over, and many gone away, Sir W[illiam] Meredith moved for the depositions on which the warrant against Wilkes had

7. Possibly James ('Athenian') Stuart (1713–88), well-known painter and architect, referred to elsewhere in HW's correspondence and notes as simply 'Stuart' or 'Mr Stuart' (ibid. i. 401, ii. 230; Mason ii. 184, n. 13; 268).

8. Francis Russell (1739–67), styled M. of Tavistock; eldest son of the D. of Bedford.

9. HW's account of Pecquigny is continued in the second part of this letter. Mrs Montagu, in a letter to Mrs Carter sometime after 6 Feb., describes the incident in similar terms: 'Mr Virette who you saw in Holland and the young Duke of Pecquigny quarrelled in the Opera House the other night, the Duke not caring to pay Virette the money he had lost to him at play' (Reginald Blunt, *Mrs Montagu,* [1923], i. 81–2).

10. Though the minority had failed to carry their motion giving unlimited powers to the committee of the whole House on the Cider Bill, 24 Jan. *(ante* 22 Jan. 1764), they continued their fight against the Bill in the committee, 31 Jan. Dowdeswell 'moved a question against excise, though without naming it'; his motion was thrown out 172–152, with 'seven of the minority being shut out when the

question was putting' *(Mem. Geo. III* i. 282; *Journals of the House of Commons* xxix. 772–3).

11. 3 Feb.

12. In the committee of the whole House on ways and means, to which had been returned that day 'an account of navy, victualling, and transport bills, which were made out on or before the 31st day of December 1762, and have not been converted into annuities, after the rate of £4 *per centum per annum,* pursuant to an act made in the last session of Parliament [3 Geo. III, c. 9]' (ibid. xxix. 786). The account had been presented to the House, 26 Jan. (ibid. xxix. 748) and is printed ibid. xxix. 751.

13. Sir William Baker (1705–70), Kt, 1760; London merchant; M.P. Plympton Erle 1747–68.

14. 'Yesterday there was a great debate about the £180,000 navy bills unsubscribed. Sir Wm Baker and Chas Townshend spoke extremely well; and showed (as I am informed) great ability and knowledge; and it was agreed to give them twelve months to subscribe, but no force or compulsion to be used' (Newcastle to Legge 4 Feb., BM Add. MSS 32955, f. 360).

been granted.[15] The ministers complained of the motion being made so late in the day;[16] called it a surprise; and Rigby moved to adjourn, which was carried but by 73 to 60.[17] Had a surprise been intended, you may imagine the minority would have been better provided with numbers; but it certainly had not been concerted: however, a majority, shrunk to thirteen, frightened them out of the small senses they possess. Heaven, earth, and the Treasury, were moved to recover their ground today, when the question was renewed. For about two hours the debate hobbled on very lamely,[18] when on a sudden your brother rose, and made such a speech—but I wish anybody was to give you the account except me, whom you will think partial: but you will hear enough of it, to confirm anything I can say. Imagine fire, rapidity, argument, knowledge, wit, ridicule, grace, spirit; all pouring like a torrent, but without clashing. Imagine the House in a tumult of continued applause: imagine the ministers thunder-struck; lawyers abashed and almost blushing, for it was on their quibbles and evasions he fell most heavily, at the same time answering a whole session of arguments on the side of the Court.[19] No, it was unique; you can neither conceive it, nor the exclamations it occasioned.[20] Ellis,[21] the forlorn hope, Ellis presented himself in

15. 'A motion was made . . . that an humble address be presented to his Majesty, that his Majesty will be graciously pleased to give direction that the proper officers do lay before this House, copies of the warrants of commitment and apprehension, whereby John Wilkes, Esquire, was apprehended, and afterwards committed to the Tower of London; and also of all information and examinations, whereupon such warrants were severally granted' (*Journals of the House of Commons* xxix. 786).

16. 5:30 P.M., according to ibid.

17. Ibid.

18. HW gives a much fuller account of this part of the debate in *Mem. Geo. III* i. 282–3; except for four sentences summarizing Conway's speech, he gives no details, beyond a list of the speakers, of the part of the debate described in the present letter.

19. 'General Conway added, that if the information [on which the warrants had been issued] was the defence of Wood and the others, how would it hurt them? But, said he, this matter is treated as too high for our inspection. I thought I lived

in a free country. We have already chosen to give up our own privilege, and now are afraid to inquire on what grounds it is taken from us' (ibid. i. 284).

20. 'Conway, Lord G. Sackville and C. Townshend made the three finest speeches that ever were heard; and have made a run on the ministry, which they will feel' (G. Onslow to Newcastle [6 Feb.], BM Add. MSS 32955, f. 366). 'They say, General Conway spoke for the question, with more strength and ability than ever was known, as a gentleman, as a lawyer, and a great Parliament man' (Newcastle to Legge 7 Feb., ibid. f. 381). 'Your Royal Highness knows that no man ever spoke with more weight and knowledge than General Conway did the other day, and it had a most prodigious good effect. Charles Townshend [whom Newcastle had seen 10 Feb.] was very full of General Conway's speech and of Lord George Sackville's, and his own, and seemed I thought to found some expectations upon it' (Newcastle to Cumberland 12 Feb., ibid. f. 448).

21. Welbore Ellis.

the gap, till the ministers could recover themselves, when on a sudden Lord George Sackville *led up the Blues;*[22] spoke with as much warmth as your brother had, and with great force continued the attack which he had begun.[23] Did not I tell you he would take this part?[24] I was made privy to it; but this is far from all you are to expect. Lord North in vain rumbled about his mustard-bowl,[25] and endeavoured alone to outroar a whole party: him and Forrester,[26] Charles Townshend took up, but less well than usual.[27] His jealousy of your brother's success, which was very evident, did not help him to shine. There were several other speeches, and, upon the whole, it was a capital debate; but Plutus[27a] is so much more persuasive an orator than your brother or Lord George, that we divided but 122 against 217.[28] Lord Strange, who had agreed to the question, did not dare to vote for it, and declared off;[29] and George Townshend, who actually voted for it on Friday,[30] now voted against us. Well! upon the whole, I heartily wish this administration may last: both their characters and abilities are so contemptible, that I am sure we can be in no danger from prerogative when trusted to such hands!

22. An allusion to Sackville's conduct at the battle of Minden, for which he had been disgraced and court-martialled because he failed to bring up the Blues (the Royal Horse Guards) when ordered to do so. See *ante* 14 Aug. 1759.

23. 'Lord George Sackville spoke strongly, and with great applause, for the question' Newcastle to Legge 7 Feb., BM Add. MSS 32955, f. 381). His speech is given equal prominence with those of Conway and C. Townshend in the other Opposition accounts of the debate (above, n. 20).

24. HW had described Sackville as 'particularly' ill-disposed to the ministry, *ante* 22 Jan. 1764.

25. '. . . 'Tis yours to shake the soul
With thunder rumbling from the mustard bowl'
(Pope, *Dunciad,* ii. 225–6)
Pope's note on the lines begins: 'The old way of making thunder [for stage productions] and mustard were the same; but since, it is more advantageously perform'd by troughs of wood with stops in them' (Pope's *Dunciad,* ed. J. Sutherland, 2d edn, rev., 1943, p. 127).

26. Alexander Forrester (?1711–87), lawyer, Scotsman settled in England; barrister of the Inner Temple 1731; M.P. Dunwich 1758–61, Okehampton 1761–8, New-

castle-under-Lyme 1768–74; political adherent of the D. of Bedford.

27. Newcastle told Legge that Townshend had done 'inimitably' (7 Feb., BM Add. MSS 32955, f. 381); see also Sir Lewis Namier and John Brooke, *Charles Townshend,* 1964, p. 113.

27a. I.e., money.

28. Upon the question 'that an humble address be presented to his Majesty, that his Majesty will be graciously pleased to give directions that the proper officers do lay before this house, a copy of the warrant of apprehension, whereby John Wilkes, Esquire, then a member of this house, was apprehended.' Earlier, an amendment, striking out the requests for the informations on which the warrant was granted, had been carried without a division (*Journals of the House of Commons* xxix. 792).

29. 'Lord Strange was at first for having the warrant produced; but soon retracted, and said the complaint ought to be discharged, as the suit was depending at common law' (*Mem. Geo. III* i. 283).

30. HW mentions, ibid., George Townshend's supporting his brother Charles on the first motion, 3 Feb., for producing the informations on which Wilkes had been seized.

Before I have done with Charles Townshend, I must tell you one of his admirable bons mots. Miss Draycote,[31] the great fortune,[32] is grown very fat: he says her *tonnage* is become equal to her *poundage*.[33]

There is the devil to pay in Nabob-land,[34] but I understand Indian histories no better than stocks. The Council rebelled against the Governor,[35] and sent a deputation,[36] the Lord knows why, to the Nabob,[37] who cut off the said deputies' heads,[38] and then, I think, was dis-Nabob'd himself,[39] and Clive's old friend[40] reinstated. There is another rebellion in Minorca, where Johnson[41] has renounced

31. Anna Maria Draycott (formerly Delagard) (ca 1736–87), m. (3 May 1764) George Fermor, 2d E. of Pomfret.

32. She had inherited a great fortune from Lady Jane Coke in 1761; Lord Barrington on her marriage called her 'that deep-laden rich aquapulca' (Hist. MSS Comm., *Lothian MSS*, 1905, p. 250).

33. The joke is enhanced by tonnage and poundage being very profitable customs duties levied on both imports and exports.

34. Bengal. Intelligence of serious trouble there had reached England 3 or 4 Feb.; no 'official version' was published in the newspapers until 9 Feb., but in the interval various contradictory reports appeared, some of which HW incorporates here (GM 1764, xxxiv. 94; *London Chronicle* 4–7, 7–9 Feb., xv. 121, 125, 136; G. Onslow to Newcastle 4 Feb., BM Add. MSS 32955, f. 362).

35. Henry Vansittart (1732–?70), Gov. of Bengal 1760–4; M.P. Reading 1768–?70. The quarrel was over the private trading privileges of the Company's servants in Bengal, which some members of Vansittart's Council had extended so far in internal trade that they had come into all but open conflict with the Nawab. Vansittart attempted to compromise the dispute, but his Council voted him down and took affairs into their own hands, with disastrous results. See H. H. Dodwell, 'Bengal, 1760–72,' *Cambridge History of India*, New York, Vol. V, ed. Dodwell, pp. 170–3, and [India] Imperial Record Department, *Calendar of Persian Correspondence*, Calcutta, 1911–59, Vol. I, *passim*.

36. To dictate their terms to the Nawab; see their instructions 28 March and 1 April 1763, printed in Vansittart's

Narrative of the Transactions in Bengal, 1766, iii. 128–35.

37. Mīr Qāsim 'Alī Khān (d. 1777), Nawab of Bengal 1760–3; son-in-law of Mīr Ja'far (C. E. Buckland, *Dictionary of Indian Biography*, 1906, p. 292).

38. The deputies were William Hay (d. 1763) and Peter Amyatt (d. 1763), chief of the English factory at Patna, 1759 (ibid. 13; Dodwell, op. cit. 173, 660, 669). Amyatt was put to death in a massacre near Murshidabad 3 July 1763; Hay was killed in another massacre in October (*London Chronicle* 7–9 Feb., xv. 136, postscript; Vansittart, op. cit. iii. 325–6; [India] Imperial Record Department, op. cit. i. 228, 249).

39. The Bengal Council deposed him and set up Mīr Ja'far in his place, 7 July 1763 (Vansittart, op. cit. iii. 328–9), but a full scale military campaign was necessary before Mīr Qāsim was finally driven out of Bengal in Oct. 1763 (Dodwell, op. cit. v. 173; [India] Imperial Record Department, loc. cit.). News of the final success of the Company's troops had, of course, not yet reached England; HW's optimistic version is probably based on a prediction like that incorporated in the East India Company's 'official' version of the war—that because the full force of the Company's troops were advancing against Mīr Qāsim when the last advices came away, there was 'little doubt' of the English success (*London Chronicle* 7–9 Feb., xv. 136).

40. Mīr Ja'far Alī Khān (1691–1765), Nawab of Bengal 1757–60, 1763–5 (Buckland, op. cit. 292). He had been set up in the first instance by Clive, who was granted in return his *jagir* of some £27,000 *per annum*.

41. James ('Irish') Johnston (ca 1724–

his allegiance to Viceroy Dick Littleton,[42] and set up for himself. Sir Richard has laid the affair before the King and Council;[43] Charles Townshend first, and then your brother[44] (you know why I am sorry they should appear together in that cause)[45] have tried to deprecate Sir Richard's wrath; but it was then too late. The silly fellow has brought himself to a precipice.[46]

I forgot to tell you that Lord George Sackville carried into the minority with him his own brother Lord Middlesex;[47] Lord Milton's brother;[48] young Beauclerc;[49] Sir Thomas Hales;[50] and Colonel Irwine.[51]

We have not heard a word yet of the Hereditary Prince and Princess. They were sent away in a tempest, and I believe the best one can hope is, that they are driven to Norway.[52]

97), army officer; Lt-Gov. of Minorca 1763–74; Gov. of Quebec 1774 (Record of Old Westminsters, ed. G. F. Russell Barker and A. H. Stenning, 1928, i. 521; memoir of Johnston printed at the end of Vol. VI of Wright's 2d edn (1846) of HW's letters).

42. Sir Richard Lyttelton, commander-in-chief and governor of Minorca 1762–6. His duties as governor were performed by his deputy, Johnston, since he himself was incapacitated by the gout (Mann vi. 247; Namier and Brooke iii. 75).

43. In a letter to Grenville of 15 Oct. 1764, Lyttelton mentions that 'petitions from the magistrates or universities of Mahon, etc., containing matter of high charge against Colonel Johnston, for arbitrarily and illegally, and of his own authority solely, laying impositions upon shipping, to the great prejudice of his Majesty's subjects, and the trade and navigation in Minorca, and for other matters of very serious nature complained of by them, have been transmitted through me, as their Governor, to the Earl of Halifax, to be laid before the King in Council' (Grenville Papers ii. 449).

44. Conway and Johnston were close friends, and Johnston had been Lt-Col. in Conway's regiment since 1759 (Army Lists 1761, p. 25). Conway 'was godfather to General Johnston's only son; and their friendship, which had commenced in their earliest military career, continued unabated to the last days of their existence' (memoir of Johnston, loc. cit.).

45. Not explained.

46. However, Johnston was apparently acquitted by a court martial, and the petitions to the King in Council never considered; see post 27 May 1764, n. 14.

47. See Namier and Brooke iii. 389.

48. John Damer (1720–83), M.P. Dorchester 1762–80. Lord Milton was Sackville's brother-in-law.

49. Hon. Aubrey Beauclerk (1740–1802), 5th D. of St Albans 1787; M.P. Thetford 1761–8, Aldborough 1768–74.

50. Sir Thomas Pym Hales (ca 1726–73), 4th Bt; M.P. Downton 1762–8, Dover 1770–3.

51. John Irwin (ca 1728–88), Col. 74th Ft (disbanded 1762); Maj.-Gen. 1762; Gov. of Gibraltar 1765–7; M.P. East Grinstead 1762–83. These names are listed with four others in the Newcastle Papers in a separate column headed 'besides for the question' in the 'list of those, who voted upon the motion, for the warrant of apprehension of Mr Wilkes, on Monday February 6th 1764' (BM Add. MSS 32955, ff. 405, 407).

52. After a delay of three days because of 'stormy and tempestuous' weather, the Prince and Princess sailed from Harwich 30 Jan. 'with a fair wind' (Daily Adv. 30 Jan., 7 Feb.); however, the Daily Advertiser of 3 Feb. carried the report of 'a captain of a ship arrived at Harwich . . . that on Monday evening [30 Jan.] he passed by the yachts with the Prince and Princess of Brunswick on board, off Orfordness; and that the weather was then so tempestuous, with the wind at

Good night, my dear Lord; it is time to finish, for it is half an hour after one in the morning: I am forced to purloin such hours to write to you, for I get up so late, and then have such a perpetual succession of nothings to do, such auctions,[53] politics, visits, dinners, suppers, books to publish or revise,[54] etc., that I have not a quarter of an hour without a call upon it; but I need not tell you, who know my life, that I am forced to create new time, if I will keep up my correspondence with you. You seem to like I should, and I wish to give you every satisfaction in my power.

Yours ever,

H. W.

Tuesday, February 7th, four o'clock.

I tremble whilst I continue my letter, having just heard such a dreadful story! A captain of a vessel has made oath before the Lord Mayor, this morning, that he saw one of the yachts sink on the coast of Holland;[55] and it is believed to be the one in which the Prince was. The City is in an uproar; nor need one point out all such an accident may produce, if true; which I most fervently hope it is not. My long letter will help you to comments enough, which will be made on this occasion. I wish you may know, at this moment, that our fears are ill-placed. The Princess was not in the same yacht with her husband.[56] Poor Fanshawe,[57] as clerk of the Green Cloth, with his wife[58] and sister,[59] was in one of them.

S.S.W. that he apprehended they would be obliged to put into some port on that coast.'

53. Chief among these was the first Sir Clement Cottrell Dormer sale of prints, 19–28 Jan.; see also *post* 11 March 1764, n. 2.

54. HW had published the third volume of *Anecdotes of Painting* and the *Catalogue of Engravers* on the day of this letter; he had finished the printing of the *Life of Lord Herbert of Cherbury*, 27 Jan.; and he was corresponding with Lady Temple about his projected edition of her poems (Hazen, *SH Bibl.* 55, 70, 72; HW to Lady Temple 28 Jan. 1764).

55. A variant of this report is in the *London Chronicle*: 'On Tuesday [7 Feb.] a report was most industriously propagated that a captain of a vessel had made oath before the lords of the Admiralty

that he saw the yacht sink on which the Princess of Brunswick was on board' (7–9 Feb., xv. 132). However, authentic news of their safe arrival in Holland reached London on the 9th (*post* 15 Feb. 1764, n. 61).

56. The *Daily Adv.* 7 Feb. *sub* 'Harwich, Feb. 3,' reported that the Prince and Princess 'embarked on board different yachts.'

57. Simon Fanshawe (1716–77) of Fanshawe Gate, Derbyshire; M.P. Old Sarum 1751–4, Grampound 1754–68; comptroller of the Board of Green Cloth 1761–7.

58. Althea Snelling (d. 1805), daughter of William Snelling; m. (1753) Simon Fanshawe (*Miscellanea genealogica et heraldica*, 1876, ii. 14).

59. Probably Ann Fanshawe (1717–93) (Owen Manning, *History . . . of Surrey*, 1804–14, ii. 246).

Here is more of the Duc de Pecquigny's episode. An officer was sent yesterday to put Virette under arrest.[60] His servant disputed with the officer on his orders, till his master made his escape. Virette sent a friend, whom he ordered to deliver his letter in person, and see it read, with a challenge, appointing the Duc to meet him at half an hour after seven this morning, at Buckingham Gate, where he waited till ten to no purpose, though the Duc had not been put under arrest. Virette absconds, and has sent Monsieur de Pecquigny word, that he shall abscond till he can find a proper opportunity of fighting him. Your discretion will naturally prevent your talking of this; but I thought you would like to be prepared, if this affair should anyhow happen to become your business, though your late discussion with the Duc de Chaulnes will add to your disinclination from meddling with it.

I must send this to the post before I go to the opera, and therefore shall not be able to tell you more of the Prince of Brunswick by this post.

Adieu!

From Hertford, Monday 13 February 1764

Printed for the first time from a photostat of BM Add. MSS 23218, ff. 124–5.

Paris, February 13th 1764.

My dear Horry,

BY the post, which has just brought me yours of the 6th February, I have received directions to send back to England one of the messengers which attend me here.[1] I therefore take the opportunity

---

60. HW, relating the further history of this quarrel, *post* Feb. 1764, says that Pecquigny had also been placed under arrest. A paragraph in the *London Chronicle*, 7–9 Feb., also gives a slightly different account from HW's account in the present letter: 'On Monday night [6 Feb.] a gaming quarrel happening at a tavern near St James's, between two foreigners of distinction; to prevent a duel, notice was immediately given to the secretaries of state, and they were both put under arrest' (xv. 129). Mrs Montagu, in her letter to Mrs Carter quoted above, n. 9,

also states that 'they were both put under arrest' (Blunt, op. cit. i. 82).

---

1. In his dispatch to Hertford of 7 Feb., Halifax instructs him to send home immediately Bullock, 'the messenger who is attending your Excellency,' since he is 'a material witness in some trials, which are to commence next week, concerning the publication of the *Essay on Woman*, and the *North Briton* No. 45' (S.P. 78/260, f. 72). This was James Bullock, King's messenger ca 1756–76 (*Court and City Register* 1756–76 *passim*).

(though I have not a moment to spare) to acknowledge it and to acquaint you that the letter which you sent me by Mr Monin has never been sent to me; Lady Hertford received two from him and I another, but yours was not amongst them. I have sent this afternoon in the most civil and guarded manner to get it explained, but as he is gone to Versailles I must endeavour to explain it tomorrow when I go there, and to recover your letter, which I am impatient to receive.

The King has been pleased to express his satisfaction upon the distinguished civility shown me by the King of France.[2] My son[3] is now with me and has produced out of his pocket a letter[4] wrote to you on the 5th December which he forgot to send. I have asked his leave but he will not allow me to enclose it; he has desired me to send you the enclosed paper[5] copied on purpose for your satisfaction.

Lord Holland is arrived at Paris;[6] I have seen him at Lord Holdernesse's for a few minutes. He took the opportunity of acquainting me that he was to be at Versailles tomorrow. He seems much disposed to be civil to me here. Lady Holland said last night at supper that they proposed returning to England in April.[7]

I am always vastly happy to hear of my brother's success; I know his abilities and I wish him now and then to show them in Parliament.

We go on as usual and have all the reason in the world to be satisfied with the entertainment and civility we meet with here.

The best compliments of the family attend you and I am, dear Horry,

Always most faithfully and affectionately yours,

HERTFORD

2. 'I received, on Saturday last [4 Feb.], your Excellency's letter of the 29th, and have laid it before the King, who is much pleased with the distinguished civility, which his Most Christian Majesty has been pleased to show you, in ordering the Hôtel de Belleisle for your reception' (Halifax to Hertford, 7 Feb., loc. cit.).

3. Lord Beauchamp.

4. Missing.

5. Missing.

6. He left England 1 Feb. (*London Chronicle* 2–4 Feb., xv. 118).

7. They returned at the end of April (*Life and Letters of Lady Sarah Lennox*, ed. Lady Ilchester and Lord Stavordale, 1902, i. 140).

To Hertford, Wednesday 15 February 1764

Printed from *Works* ix. 64–79.

Arlington Street, Wednesday, February 15, 1764.

My dear Lord,

YOU ought to be witness to the fatigue I am suffering, before you can estimate the merit I have in being writing to you at this moment. Cast up eleven hours in the House of Commons on Monday, and above seventeen hours yesterday—ay, seventeen at length—and then you may guess if I am tired! nay, you must add seventeen hours that I may possibly be there on Friday, and then calculate if I am weary. In short, yesterday was the longest day ever known in the House of Commons—why, on the Westminster election at the end of my father's reign,[1] I was at home by six.[2] On Alexander Murray's affair,[3] I believe, by five[4]—on the militia, twenty people, I think, sat till six,[5] but then they were only among themselves, no heat, no noise, no roaring. It was half an hour after seven this morning before I was at home.[6] Think of that, and then brag of your French parliaments!

What is ten times greater, Leonidas and the Spartan *minority* did not make such a stand at Thermopylæ, as we did. Do you know, we had like to have been the *majority?* Xerxes[7] is frightened out of his senses;[8] Sysigambis[9] has sent an express to Luton[10] to forbid

1. 22 Dec. 1741 OS; see MANN i. 250–2.

2. HW wrote at the time: 'We sat till half an hour after four in the morning; the longest day that ever was known' (ibid. i. 252).

3. 6 Feb. 1751 OS, when the Hon. Alexander Murray (1712–78), cr. (1759) E. of Westminster in the Jacobite peerage, was committed to Newgate for interfering in the Westminster election and for contempt of the House of Commons. See *Mem. Geo. II* i. 26–31; MANN iv. 223–5.

4. In *Mem. Geo. II*, HW says that the House adjourned at two (i. 31).

5. 10 May 1756, when the first militia bill had passed the House of Commons (ibid. ii. 191; *Journals of the House of Commons* xxvii. 600; Basil Williams, *Life of William Pitt*, 1913, ii. 279).

6. Even so, HW mentions below that he left before the House rose; the time given for the adjournment in the *Journals* is 7:30 A.M.; by Grenville, 8:00 A.M. (*Jour-*

nals of the House of Commons xxix. 843; *Grenville Papers* ii. 264).

7. George III.

8. When Grenville saw the King after the debate, 'he found his Majesty angry, but not alarmed, saying the Opposition might, for what he knew, carry the question upon the warrants on Friday . . . but that would make no change in him in regard to his present administration, which he meant to support to the utmost; he had no job to ask of his people, nor nothing to conceal, and therefore was not afraid, and that firmness and steadiness was what alone could get the better of the state of anarchy which seemed to threaten Government, and that it must be shown' (ibid. ii. 491).

9. The Princess Dowager of Wales. Sysigambis was mother of the Persian emperor, Darius II.

10. Bute's seat in Bedfordshire.

Phraates[11] coming to town tomorrow;[12] Norton's impudence has forsaken him;[13] Bishop Warburton is at this moment reinstating Mr Pitt's name in the dedication to his sermons, which he had expunged for Sandwich's; and Sandwich himself is—at Paris, perhaps, by this time, for the first thing I expect to hear tomorrow is, that he is gone off.

Now are you mortally angry with me for trifling with you, and not telling you at once the particulars of this *almost-revolution*. You may be angry, but I shall take my own time, and shall give myself what airs I please both to you, my Lord Ambassador, and to you, my Lord Secretary of State,[14] who will, I suppose, open this letter— if you have courage enough left. In the first place, I assume all the impertinence of a prophet, ay, of that great curiosity, a prophet, who really prophesied before the event, and whose predictions have been accomplished. Have I, or have I not, announced to you the unexpected blows that would be given to the administration?[15]— come, I will lay aside my dignity, and satisfy your impatience. There's moderation.

We sat all Monday[16] hearing evidence against Mr Wood, that dirty wretch Webb, and the messengers, for their illegal proceedings against Mr Wilkes.[17] At midnight, Mr Grenville offered us to adjourn or proceed.[18] Mr Pitt humbly begged not to eat or sleep till so great a point should be decided.[19] On a division, in which though

11. Bute. Presumably the allusion is to Phraates IV, King of Parthia ca 38–2 B.C., a tyrant who was temporarily driven from his kingdom by a revolt of his subjects, and who was finally assassinated by one of his wives and his son by her.

12. Grenville mentions, 12 Feb., that Lady Bute was stating publicly that her husband was coming to London on Thursday, 16 Feb.; but he was later informed that she had said on Tuesday, the 14th, that 'no time was fixed' for his return (ibid. ii. 490, 491). There is no evidence that Bute received an express from the Princess, but he did delay his return until 19 March (ibid. ii. 498; *post* 27 March 1764).

13. He had recovered it by the time of the debate on Friday; see the anecdote below in the third part of this letter.

14. Sandwich.

15. HW had done so *ante* 22 Jan. 1764.

16. 13 Feb.

17. Accounts of the proceedings of the House and the debate of the 13th are in *Mem. Geo. III* i. 286–7; West to Newcastle, '½ past 10' [13 Feb.], G. Onslow to Newcastle [13 Feb], '11 o'clock' [13 Feb.], BM Add. MSS 32955, ff. 458 (partly printed in *Hardwicke Corr.* iii. 562), 460, 462; *Journals of the House of Commons* xxix. 838–9.

18. Grenville's offer was made before 10:30 and the division took place before 11:00; see West to Newcastle, '½ past 10' [13 Feb.], and Onslow to Newcastle, '11 o'clock' [13 Feb.], loc. cit. HW gives 11:45 as the time of the final adjournment that day in *Mem. Geo. III* i. 287.

19. 'Mr Pitt rose, and declared that notwithstanding his ill state of health and the time of night yet in a matter of such high [*sic*] to the rights of the people of England, he would neither live [*sic*] nor

many said *ay* to adjourning, nobody would go out for fear of losing their seats, it was carried by 379 to 31, for proceeding[20]—and then—half the House went away. The ministers representing the indecency of this, and Fitzherbert saying that many were within call, Stanley[21] observed, that after voting against adjournment, a third part had adjourned themselves, when, instead of being within *call*, they ought to have been within *hearing:* this was unanswerable, and we adjourned.

Yesterday we fell to again. It was one in the morning before the evidence was closed.[22] Carrington,[23] the messenger, was alone examined for seven hours. This old man, the cleverest of all ministerial terriers, was pleased with recounting his achievements, yet perfectly guarded and betraying nothing. However, the *arcana imperii* have been woefully laid open.

I have heard Garrick, and other players, give themselves airs of fatigue after a long part—think of the Speaker, nay, think of the clerks taking most correct minutes for sixteen hours, and reading them over to every witness; and then let me hear of fatigue! Do you know, not only my Lord Temple—who you may swear never budged as spectator—but old Will Chetwynd,[24] now past eighty, and who had walked to the House, did not stir a single moment out of his place, from three in the afternoon till the division at seven in the morning. Nay, we had *patriotesses,* too, who stayed out the whole: Lady Rockingham and Lady Sondes the first day;[25] both again the second day, with Miss Mary Pelham, Mrs Fitzroy,[26] and the Duchess

sleep till he knew, whether we had a constitution or not' (West to Newcastle, '½ past 10' [13 Feb.], loc. cit.). See also *Mem. Geo. III* i. 286.

20. *Journals of the House of Commons* xxix. 839.

21. Hans Stanley, at this time a lord of the Admiralty.

22. A brief account of the proceedings on the evidence is in *Mem. Geo. III* i. 287; more details are in West to Newcastle, '½ past 8' [14 Feb.], BM Add. MSS 32955, f. 456, a letter endorsed 13 Feb., but clearly referring to the early part of the proceedings on Tuesday, the 14th, not to those of Monday. See also *Journals of the House of Commons* xxix. 842-3.

23. Nathan Carrington (d. 1777), King's Messenger from about 1732 until his

death, by which time he was senior messenger (GM 1777, xlvii. 508; V. Wheeler-Holohan, *The History of the King's Messengers,* 1935, p. 272). He had been one of the four messengers to whom the general warrant leading to Wilkes's arrest had been directed, but had excused himself on account of illness (*ante* 1 May 1763, n. 7).

24. William Richard ('Oronooko') Chetwynd (?1683–1770), 3d Vct Chetwynd, 1767; M.P. Stafford 1715–22, 1734–70, Plymouth 1722–7; Master of the Mint 1744–69.

25. Monday, 13 Feb.

26. Anne Warren (d. 1807), daughter of Adm. Sir Peter Warren; m. (1758) Charles Fitzroy, cr. (1780) Bn Southampton.

of Richmond, as patriot as any of us.[27] Lady Mary Coke, Mrs George Pitt,[28] and Lady Pembroke,[29] came after the opera, but I think did not stay above seven or eight hours at most.

At one, Sir W[illiam] Meredith moved a resolution of the illegality of the warrant,[30] and opened it well.[31] He was seconded by Lord[32] Darlington's brother,[33] a convert to us. Mr Wood, who had shone the preceding day by great modesty, decency, and ingenuity,[34] forfeited these merits a good deal by starting up (according to a ministerial plan) and very arrogantly, and repeatedly in the night, demanding justice and a previous acquittal,[35] and telling the House he scorned to accept being merely *excused;* to which Mr Pitt replied, that if he disdained to be *excused,* he would deserve to be *censured.*[36] Mr Charles Yorke (who, with his family, have come roundly to us for support against the Duke of Bedford on the Marriage Bill)[37]

27. 'Her Grace the Duchess of Richmond, the Marchioness of Rockingham, and Lady Sondes, it is said, attended at the debates of a certain great assembly, till eight o'clock on Wednesday morning' (*London Chronicle* 16–18 Feb., xv. 161).

28. Penelope Atkins (d. 1795), m. (1746) George Pitt, cr. (1776) Bn Rivers.

29. Either the Hon. Mary Fitzwilliam, widow of the 9th E. of Pembroke, or her daughter-in-law, Lady Elizabeth Spencer, wife of the 10th E.

30. 'That a general warrant for apprehending and seizing the authors, printers, and publishers of a seditious libel, together with their papers, is not warranted by law' (*Journals of the House of Commons* xxix. 843). He also moved that the seizing of members of Parliament by such warrants was a breach of privilege of Parliament, but this motion is not entered in the *Journals;* see, however, *Mem. Geo. III* i. 288 and *Grenville Papers* ii. 262.

31. HW reports his speech in *Mem. Geo. III* i. 287–8.

32. 'Old' in *Works;* but since the reference is clearly not to a brother of the previous Lord Darlington, and the present Lord Darlington was only about 38, presumably 'old' is a misreading of HW's MS 'Ld.'

33. Hon. Frederick Vane (1732–1801), M.P. Durham Co. 1761–74; brother of the 2d E. of Darlington. He appears in Jenkinson's list of dissenting friends of gov-

ernment for this period (Namier and Brooke iii. 572).

34. James West told Newcastle that Robert Wood had made his defence 'in a sensible and judicious manner' on the 13th (BM Add. MSS 32955, f. 460).

35. I.e., to have the complaint against him for a breach of privilege discharged before a vote on the legality of general warrants.

36. HW repeats this interchange in *Mem. Geo. III,* but separates Wood's statement and Pitt's reprimand by a long period of debate and a division (i. 289–90).

37. 26 George II (1753), c. 33, 'an act for the better preventing of clandestine marriages,' originally carried largely through the exertions of Lord Hardwicke. His family felt bound to defend it, and when an attempt to repeal it was made in 1764, fought every step with the general support of Opposition. As of the date of this letter they had already unsuccessfully divided the House 130–30, on a motion for setting a date for consideration of the Bill in a committee of the whole, 27 Jan.; again, 157–79, after a long debate on going into this committee, 9 Feb.; and yet again, 70–40, on the same day, on a motion setting a day for further consideration of the Bill (*Journals of the House of Commons* xxix. 762, 826; *Mem. Geo. III* i. 282, 285–6). Because of the debates on general warrants, further con-

proposed to adjourn. Grenville and the ministry would have agreed to adjourn the debate on the great question itself, but declared they would push this acquittal. This they announced haughtily enough —for as yet, they did not doubt of their strength. Lord Frederic Campbell was the most impetuous of all,[38] so little he foresaw how much *wiser* it would be to follow your brother. Pitt made a short speech, excellently argumentative, and not bombast, nor tedious, nor deviating from the question.[39] He was supported by your brother,[40] and Charles Townshend,[41] and Lord George;[42] the two last of whom are strangely firm,[43] now they are got under the cannon of your brother.[44] Charles, who must be extraordinary, is now so in romantic nicety of honour. His father,[45] who is dying, or dead, at Bath, and from whom he hopes two thousand a year,[46] has sent for him—he has refused to go—lest his *steadiness* should be questioned. At a quarter after four we divided.[47] *Our* cry was so loud,

sideration was delayed until 6 March, at which time the committee reported in favour of repeal; a bill to this purpose was introduced, 20 March, but allowed to expire in committee, and not passed during the session (*Journals of the House of Commons* xxix. 842, 849–50, 875, 887, 967).

38. Grenville says he spoke 'with great spirit, and extremely well,' HW, 'with much warmth,' for discharging the complaint of breach of privilege before debating the general question (*Grenville Papers* ii. 262; *Mem. Geo. III* i. 288).

39. 'Pitt replied, that if the second question [the declaration that general warrants were illegal] should pass, it would be impossible entirely to acquit the accused. They could not be acquitted or condemned till the general question should be affirmed or condemned. If the warrant should be declared illegal, he would extenuate their behaviour as having acted by precedent' (ibid. i. 288–9).

40. 'General Conway observed justly, that if the accused were acquitted first, the general question would not be left entire; for could the House vote that general warrants were illegal, after it should have voted that they who executed those warrants were blameless?' (ibid. i. 290).

41. 'Charles, more decently than the rest, said the questions were the same

and required the same discussion: he would not consent to divide them' (ibid. i. 289).

42. Sackville. He told Wood 'that intentionally he had done right, but was not ready to say that he had done legally right' (ibid.).

43. Townshend's conduct was still giving alarm to the Opposition, for he had absented himself from a meeting on 11 Feb. that was to draw up the motion on the general warrants. 'To the great surprise of everybody, Charles Townshend was not at the meeting. I saw him last Friday [10 Feb.]; I found he did not approve Mr Pitt's question, and seemed disposed, or seemed disposed [*sic*] to approve of anything Mr Pitt did' (Newcastle to Cumberland 12 Feb., BM Add. MSS 32955, f. 448).

44. HW exaggerates the extent of Conway's influence on Townshend and Sackville.

45. 3d Vct Townshend, d. 12 March (*post* 18 March 1764).

46. His father left him nothing (ibid.).

47. Over the question that the words 'and the further consideration of the matter of this complaint' be inserted after the word 'debate' in the question 'that the said debate be adjourned till this day, at twelve of the clock' (*Journals of the House of Commons* xxix. 843).

that both we and the ministers thought we had carried it. It is not to be painted, the dismay of the latter—in good truth not without reason, for *we* were 197, they but 207. Your experience can tell you, that a majority of *but* ten is a defeat. Amidst a great defection from them, was even a white staff, Lord Charles Spencer[48]—now you know still more of what I told you was preparing for them!

Crestfallen, the ministers then proposed simply to discharge the complaint; but the plumes which they had dropped, Pitt soon placed in his own beaver. He broke out on liberty,[49] and, indeed, on whatever he pleased, uninterrupted. Rigby sat feeling the vice-treasurership[50] slipping from under him. Nugent[51] was not less pensive—Lord Strange, though not interested, did not like it. Everybody was too much taken up with his own concerns, or too much daunted, to give the least disturbance to the Pindaric. Grenville, however, dropped a few words,[52] which did but heighten the flame. Pitt, with less modesty than ever he showed, pronounced a panegyric on his own administration, and from thence broke out on the *dismission of officers.*[53] This increased the roar from us. Grenville replied, and very finely, very pathetically, very animated. He painted Wilkes and faction, and, with very little truth, denied the charge of menaces to officers.[54] At that moment, General A'Court walked up the House—think what an impression such an incident must make, when passions, hopes, and fears, were all afloat—think, too, how

48. Comptroller of the Household 1763–5. The white staff was the symbol of his office.

49. 'Pitt, roused by this swell of his party, and feeling the weight of so large a minority, poured forth one of his finest rhapsodies on liberty, though at that late hour, and after the fatigue of so long an attendance and attention' (*Mem. Geo. III.* i. 290).

50. The joint vice-treasurership of Ireland. He had held the post since Dec. 1762 and continued in it until July 1765.

51. Robert Nugent. He had been joint vice-treasurer of Ireland since 1760.

52. He asked why the present persons were blamed, and not their predecessors, for the issue and execution of general warrants—a reflection on Pitt who had issued two during his administration (ibid. i. 290–1).

53. 'Pitt, still rising in fire and impor-

tance, took the whole debate on himself, asking what he had done, but in a war which he was called upon to invigorate? He had never turned out officers; he had sought for merit in those who *now* held precarious commissions, not by military service. They had not only saved their country, but him, who had been undone if they had not saved their country' (ibid. i. 291).

54. 'Grenville . . . replied ably and finely. He knew, he said, the nation was left on the brink of ruin. The ministers had had enough to do without hunting in alleys for libels. He then painted faction, first setting England against Scotland; then reviving party names, and drawing the line between the Parliament and people. Look! said he, look at Wilkes's letters, where he talks of rare combustibles' (ibid. i. 291; HW does not mention there his remarks about the officers).

your brother and I, had we been ungenerous, could have added to these sensations![55] There was a man not so delicate. Colonel Barré rose—and this attended with a striking circumstance; Sir Edward Deering,[56] one of *our* noisy fools, called out, 'Mr Barré.' The latter seized the thought with admirable quickness, and said to the Speaker, who, in pointing to him, had called him *Colonel,* 'I beg your pardon, Sir, you have pointed to me by a title I have no right to,' and then made a very artful and pathetic speech on his own services and dismission;[57] with nothing bad but an awkward attempt towards an excuse to Mr Pitt for his former behaviour.[58] Lord North, who will not lose his *bellow,* though he may lose his place, endeavoured to roar up the courage of his comrades, but it would not do—the House grew tired, and we again divided at seven for adjournment; some of our people were gone, and we remained but 184, they 208;[59] however, you will allow our affairs are mended, when we say, *but* 184. *We* then came away, and left the ministers to satisfy Wood, Webb, and themselves, as well as they could.[60] It was eight this morning before I was in bed; and considering that, this is no very short letter. Mr Pitt bore the fatigue with his usual spirit—and even old Onslow, the late Speaker, was sitting up, anxious for the event.

On Friday we are to have the great question, which would prevent my writing; and tomorrow I dine with Guerchy, at the Duke of Grafton's, besides twenty other engagements. Today I have shut myself up, for with writing this, and taking notes yesterday all day, and all night, I have not an eye left to see out of—nay, for once in my life, I shall go to bed at ten o'clock.

I am glad to be able to contradict two or three passages in my last letter. The Prince and Princess of Brunswick are safely landed,[61]

55. By revealing their interviews with Thomas Pitt and Grenville in early Dec.

56. Sir Edward Dering (1732–98), 6th Bt; M.P. New Romney 1761–70, 1774–87.

57. HW relates, ibid., the anecdote of Barré's reply to the Speaker and reports him as continuing that the incident 'gave him occasion to ask why he had been dismissed? what had his Majesty done on his accession? He looked out if any man had been whispered out of his service, and did him ample justice. . . . Himself, he said, was of no consequence, but let ministers take care how they deprived the

Crown of other faithful servants at the end of a glorious war. *Non de vectigalibus agitur, sed de anima nostra res agitur.* Precedents did not justify: Charles I had acted on precedents.'

58. Barré had begun his Parliamentary career with a violent attack on Pitt (*ante* 9 Dec. 1763, n. 12).

59. *Journals of the House of Commons,* loc. cit.

60. The complaints were discharged (ibid.).

61. 2 Feb. at Hellevoetsluis; the news reached London on 9 Feb. (P. Stephens to

though they were in extreme danger.[62] The Duc de Pecquigny had not only been put in arrest late on the Sunday night,[63] which I did not know, but has retrieved his honour. Monsieur de Guerchy sent him away,[64] and at Dover, Virette found him, and whispered him to steal from D'Allonville[65] and fight. The Duc first begged his pardon, owned himself in the wrong, and then fought him, and was wounded, though slightly, in four places in the arm; and both are returned to London with their honours as white as snow.[66]

Sir Jacob Downing[67] is dead, and has left every shilling to his wife;[68] *id est,* not sixpence to my Lord Holland;[69] a mishap, which being followed by a minority of 197, will not make this a pleasant week to him.

Well! now would you believe how I feel and how I wish? I wish *we* may continue the minority. The desires of some of my associates, perhaps, may not be satisfied, but mine are. Here is an Opposition

Newcastle, 9 Feb., BM Add. MSS 32955, f. 395).

62. The *Daily Adv.,* 11 Feb., reported that 'during the whole time' they were at sea (four days), there was 'violent tempestuous weather,' and that 'the yacht which the Prince of Brunswick was on board of, had her mast carried away in the passage.'

63. 5 Feb.

64. It was reported that he and Virette were going to Liège to fight (letter of D. of Rutland 15 Feb., quoted in W. E. Manners, *Some Account of the . . . Marquis of Granby,* 1899, p. 300).

65. Perhaps Antoine-Charles-Augustin, Chevalier d'Allonville (1733 or 5 – 92), army officer; maréchal de camp 1784; sub-governor to the Dauphin and royal children 1789–92 (*Dictionnaire de biographie francaise,* 1933–   , ii. 233–4; Henri Woelmont, Baron de Brumagne, *Notices généalogiques,* 1923–35, vii. 21–2); or one of his brothers.

66. 'On Monday [13 Feb.] a duel was fought at Dover, between a French nobleman and Mr V——, a Swiss: where the former was wounded. This quarrel has been in agitation for some time' (*London Chronicle* 14–16 Feb., xv. 158). 'Since what I have mentioned above relating to the Duke of Pecquigny and Monsieur Vivret [*sic*], the affair has been decided at

Dover. Monsieur Vivret disarmed the Duke at the first onset, and a second being insisted on, Monsieur Vivret skewered his hand, lower, and upper part of his arm to his body, which put an end to the dispute' (letter of D. of Rutland, 16 Feb. quoted Manners, loc. cit.). See also *St James's Chronicle* 11–14 Feb.

67. Sir Jacob Garrard Downing (ca 1717 – 6 Feb. 1764), 4th Bt; M.P. Dunwich 1741–7, 1749–61, 1763–4.

68. Margaret Price (d. 1778), m. 1 (1750) Sir Jacob Downing, 4th Bt; m. 2 (1768) George Bowyer, cr. (1794) Bt (GEC *Baronetage,* iii. 280). The estates had actually devolved on the University of Cambridge by the will of the 3d Bt, but protracted litigation, lasting until 1800, was necessary to get them from Lady Downing and her heirs (DNB *sub* Sir George Downing [?1684–1749]).

69. Downing was a friend of Holland, and had written him in 1759 that the borough of Dunwich would 'during your life be absolutely under your directions and consequently the choice of the members in your option' (Namier and Brooke ii. 335). He arranged for Holland (then Fox) to sit for the borough in 1761, and left a condition in his will that the borough should remain under Holland's control (Lord Ilchester, *Henry Fox,* 1920, i. 152–3).

formidable enough to keep abler ministers than messieurs the present gentlemen in awe. They may pick pockets, but they will pick no more locks. While we continue a minority, we shall preserve our characters, and we have some too good to part with. I hate to have a camp to plunder; at least, I am so Whig, I hate all spoils but the *opima spolia*.[70] I think it, too, much more creditable to control ministers, than to *be* ministers—and much more creditable than to become *mere* ministers ourselves.[71] I have several other excellent reasons against our success, though I could combat them with as many drawn from the insufficience of the present folk, and from the propriety of Mr Pitt being minister, but I am too tired, and very likely so are you, my dear Lord, by this time, and therefore good night,

Yours most affectionately,

Hor. Walpole

Friday, noon [17 Feb.].

I had sealed my letter, and break it open again on receiving yours of the 13th, by the messenger. Though I am very sorry you had not then got mine from Monin, which would have prepared you for much of what has happened, I do not fear its miscarriage, as I think I can account for the delay. I had, for more security, put it into the parcel with two more volumes of my *Anecdotes of Painting;*[72] which, I suppose, remained in Monin's baggage; and he might not have unpacked it when he delivered the single letters. If he has not yet sent you the parcel, you may ask for it, as the same delicacy is not necessary as for a letter.

I thank Lord Beauchamp much for the paper, but should thank him much more for a letter from himself. I am going this minute to the House, where I have already been to prayers, to take a place.[73] It was very near full then, so critical a day it is![74] I expect we shall be beaten—but we shall not be so many times more.

70. The spoils of honour.

71. I.e., the tools of Bute and the King.

72. The third volume of the *Anecdotes,* written between 29 June and 22 Aug. 1761 and printed 28 June – 8 Oct. 1762, and the *Catalogue of Engravers,* written 2 Aug. – 10 Oct. 1762 and printed 9 Oct. 1762 – 9 May 1763. They were pub-

lished 6 Feb. 1764 (Hazen, *SH Bibl.* 55). Hertford's copies have not been found.

73. Attendance at prayers reserved a seat for the day (Thomas Erskine May, *Treatise upon the Law . . . of Parliament,* 2d edn, 1851, p. 185).

74. The day for the adjourned debate on the legality of general warrants.

Lord Granby, I hear, is to move the previous question[75]—they are reduced to their heavy cannon.

Sunday evening, 19th.

Happening to hear of a gentleman who sets out for Paris in two or three days, I stopped my letter, both out of prudence (pray admire me!) and from thinking that it was as well to send you at once the complete history of our Great Week. By the time you have read the preceding pages, you may, perhaps, expect to find a change of the ministry in what I am going to say. You must have a little patience; our Parliamentary war, like the last war in Germany, produces very considerable battles, that are not decisive. Marshal Pitt has given another great blow to the subsidiary army, but they remained masters of the field, and both sides sing *Te Deum*. I am not talking figuratively, when I assure you that bells, bonfires, and an illumination from the Monument,[76] were prepared in the City, in case we had had the majority. Lord Temple was so indiscreet and indecent as to have faggots ready for two bonfires, but was persuaded to lay aside the design, even before it was abortive.

It is impossible to give you the detail of so long a debate as Friday's.[77] You will regret it the less when I tell you it was a very dull one.[78] I never knew a day of expectation answer. The impromptus and the unexpected are ever the most shining. We love to hear ourselves talk, and yet we must be formed of adamant to be able to talk day and night on the same question for a week together. If you had seen how ill we looked, you would not have wondered we did not speak well. A company of colliers emerging from damps and darkness could not have appeared more ghastly and dirty than we did on Wednesday morning; and we had not recovered much bloom on Friday. We spent two or three hours on corrections of, and additions to, the question of pronouncing the warrant illegal, till the ministry had contracted it to fit scarce anything but the individual

75. See below, n. 104.

76. 'We are informed, that, provided an important popular question had last week been determined to the public satisfaction, a patriotic citizen intended to have finely illuminated the Monument at his own expense' (*London Chronicle* 18–21 Feb., xv. 174, quoted from *Gazetteer*).

77. HW gives a very full account in *Mem. Geo. III* i. 293–302.

78. Grenville also informed the King that 'the debate in general was but an indifferent one' (*Grenville Papers* ii. 266).

case of Wilkes,[79] Pitt not opposing the amendments because Charles Yorke gave in to them; for it is wonderful what deference is paid by both sides to that House.[80] The debate then began by Norton's moving to adjourn the consideration of the question for four months, and holding out a promise of a bill, which neither they mean, nor, for my part, should I like: I would not give prerogative so much as a definition. You are a peer, and, therefore, perhaps, will hear it with patience—but think how *our* ears must have tingled, when he told us, that should we pass the resolution, and he were a judge, he would mind it no more than the resolution of a drunken porter![81]—Had old Onslow been in the chair, I believe he would have knocked him down with the mace. He did hear of it during the debate,[82] though not severely enough; but the town rings with it. Charles Yorke replied, and was much admired.[83] Me he did not please; I require a little more than palliatives and sophistries. He excused the part he has taken by pleading that he had never seen the warrant, till after Wilkes was taken up—yet he then pronounced the No. 45 a libel, and advised the commitment of Wilkes to the Tower. If you advised me to knock a man down, would you excuse yourself by saying you had never seen the stick with which I gave the blow?[84] Other speeches we had without end, but none good, except from Lord George Sackville,[85] a short one from Elliot,[86] and one from Charles Townshend, so fine that it *amazed, even from him.*[87] Your brother had spoken with excellent sense against the corrections, and began well again in the debate, but with so much rapidity that he confounded himself

79. HW discusses this part of the debate in *Mem. Geo. III* i. 293–7; the series of amendments is given in *Journals of the House of Commons* xxix. 846.

80. Of Yorke; HW frequently applies the designation to the Yorke family.

81. HW repeats this anecdote in *Mem. Geo. III* i. 298; see also MANN vi. 208, n. 14.

82. Charles Townshend rebuked him in his speech, as did Charles Yorke (*Mem. Geo. III* i. 300; MANN, loc. cit.).

83. His speech is summarized in *Mem. Geo. III* i. 298–9; see also MANN vi. 208, nn. 13, 14.

84. HW makes the same reflection on Yorke's conduct in *Mem. Geo. III* i. 299.

85. Reported ibid. i. 299–300.

86. Gilbert Elliot (1722–77), 3d Bt, 1766; M.P. Selkirkshire 1753–65; Roxburgh 1765–77; treasurer of the Chambers 1762–70. HW reports his speech ibid. i. 302.

87. Grenville thought it the best Opposition speech; HW in *Mem. Geo. III* describes it as 'a most capital speech, replete with argument, history, and law, though severe on the lawyers; a speech like most of his, easier to be described than detailed' (*Grenville Papers* ii. 266; *Mem. Geo. III* i. 300). See also the comments in Newcastle to C. Townshend 18 Feb. and T. Townshend to Newcastle 18 Feb., BM Add. MSS 32956, ff. 27, 29, and in James Harris's MS Journal, cited in Sir Lewis Namier and John Brooke, *Charles Townshend*, 1964, p. 114.

first, and then was seized with such a hoarseness that he could not proceed. Pitt and George Grenville ran a match of silence, striving which should reply to the other. At last, Pitt, who had three times in the debate retired with pain, rose about three in the morning, but so languid, so exhausted, that, in his life, he never made less figure.[88] Grenville answered him; and at five in the morning we divided.[89] The Noes were so loud, as it admits a deeper sound than Ay, that the Speaker, who has got a bit of *nose*[90] since the Opposition got numbers, gave it for us. They went forth; and when I heard our side counted to the amount of 218,[91] I did conclude we were victorious; but they returned 232. It is true we were beaten by fourteen, but we were increased by twenty-one;[92] and no ministry could stand on so slight an advantage, if we could continue above 200.

We may, and probably shall, fall off: this was our strongest question—but our troops will stand fast; their hopes and views depend upon it, and their spirits are raised. But for the other side it will not be the same. The lookers-out will be stayers away, and their very subsidies will undo them.

They bought two single votes that day with two peerages;[93] Sir R. Bampfylde[94] and Sir Charles Tynte[95]—and so are going to light up the flame of two more county elections—and that in the west, where surely nothing was wanting but a tinder-box.[96]

You would have almost laughed to see the spectres produced by both sides; one would have thought that they had sent a search-warrant for members of Parliament into every hospital. Votes were brought down in flannels and blankets, till the floor of the House looked like the pool of Bethesda. 'Tis wonderful that half of us are not dead—I should not say *us*; Herculean I[97] have not suffered the

88. Grenville thought him 'very faint and languid' (*Grenville Papers*, loc. cit.).

89. On the question 'that the . . . debate be adjourned till this day four months' (*Journals of the House of Commons*, loc. cit.).

90. Cust's nose was rather short; see the portrait in Arthur I. Dasent, *Speakers of the House of Commons*, 1911, opp. p. 274. HW jokes about Cust's nose also to Montagu, 7 Nov. 1761 (Montagu i. 401).

91. A list of the minority is in BM Add. MSS 32956, ff. 68–71.

92. Over the 197 that had voted with them in the first division on the 14th.

93. HW says at the end of the letter that this report had since been contradicted.

94. Sir Richard Warwick Bampfylde (1722–76), 4th Bt; M.P. Exeter 1743–7, Devonshire 1747–76. He never received a peerage.

95. Sir Charles Kemys Tynte (1710–85), 5th Bt; M.P. Monmouth 1745–7, Somerset 1747–74. He also never received a peerage.

96. Because of the unrest caused by the Cider Act.

97. Probably an echo of Tom Hervey's phrase that he was no 'Herculean la-

least, except that from being a Hercules of ten grains, I don't believe I now weigh above eight. I felt from nothing so much as the noise, which made me as drunk as an owl—you may imagine the clamours of two parties so nearly matched, and so impatient to come to a decision.

The Duchess of Richmond has got a fever with the attendance of Tuesday—but on Friday we were forced to be unpolite. The Amazons came down in such squadrons, that we were forced to be denied.[97a] However, eight or nine of the patriotesses dined in one of the Speaker's rooms, and stayed there till twelve—nay, worse, while their dear country was at stake, I am afraid they were playing at loo!

The Townshends, you perceive by this account, are returned; their father not dead.[98] Lord Howe and the Colonel[99] voted with us; so did Lord Newnham,[100] and is likely to be turned out of doors for it.[101] A warrant to take up Lord Charles Spenser was sent to Blenheim from Bedford House, and signed by his brother,[102] and returned for him;[103] so he went thither—not a very kind office in the Duke of Marlborough to Lord Charles's character. Lord Granby refused to make the motion, but spoke for it.[104]

Lord Hardwicke is relapsed;[105] but we do not now fear any consequences from his death. The Yorkes, who abandoned a triumphant administration, are not so tender as to return and comfort them in their depression.

bourer' (A Letter . . . to Sir Thomas Hanmer, Bart, [1741], p. 51), which HW frequently quotes; see SELWYN 101; ante 2 Sept. 1758.

97a. I.e., the galleries were closed.

98. He lived until 12 March.

99. William Howe (1729–1814), brother of Lord Howe; 5th Vct Howe, 1799; Col. 1762; later commander-in-chief in America during the American Revolution; M.P. Nottingham 1758–80.

100. George Simon Harcourt (1736–1809), styled Vct Nuneham 1749–77; 2d E. Harcourt 1777; M.P. St Albans 1761–8; HW's correspondent.

101. By his father, who was lord chamberlain to the Queen. See Lord Harcourt's letters to Charles Jenkinson (18 Feb.) and the King (18 Feb) attempting to excuse his son's vote, and the King's reply on the same day (Jenkinson Papers 1760–1766, ed. N. S. Tucker, 1949, pp. 266–7; Harcourt Papers, ed. E. W. Harcourt, Oxford, [1880–1905], iii. 99–100).

Nuneham himself seems to have considered that the vote produced nothing more serious than a 'little coolness' (ibid. viii. 74).

102. The Duke of Marlborough.

103. That is, the Duke of Bedford asked his son-in-law, the Duke of Marlborough, to summon his brother, Lord Charles, to Blenheim to prevent him from again voting against the government as he had done 14 Feb., and Marlborough did so.

104. 'It had been proposed that Lord Granby should move the adjournment; he refused, and yet spoke for it,—and was immediately rewarded with the lieutenancy of Derbyshire, which the Duke of Devonshire had resigned, and wished, from the rivalship between their families in that county, to see in any other hands' (Mem. Geo. III i. 298).

105. 'Lord Hardwicke has too much fever after this last discharge of bile; and the return of it, before he had recovered

The chief business now, I suppose, will lie in *souterrains* and intrigues. Lord Bute's panic will, probably, direct him to make application to us.[106] Sandwich will be manufacturing lies, and Rigby negotiations. Some change or other, whether partial or extensive, must arrive. The best that can happen for the ministers, is to be able to ward off the blow till the recess, and they have time to treat at leisure; but in just the present state it is impossible things should remain.[107] The Opposition is too strong, and their leaders too able to make no impression.

Adieu! pray tell Mr Hume that I am ashamed to be thus writing the history of England, when he is with you!

PS. The new baronies are contradicted, but may recover truth at the end of the session.[108]

From HERTFORD, Saturday 18 February 1764

Printed for the first time from a photostat of BM Add. MSS 23218, ff. 126–9.

Paris, February 18th 1764.

Dear Horry,

I THANK you for a most friendly long letter by Monsieur Monin;[1] by a visit to the Temple[2] I have at last recovered it with the books you have been so good to send me. I have not yet had time to look farther into them than the title-pages, nor do I know when I shall; my time here is fully employed; when I do, I dare say I shall be pleased. It does not require the partiality and affection I have for you to be fond of your writings.

I thank you particularly for the freedom with which you treat the different questions I submitted to your opinion, and indeed it re-

his strength, seems to make an impression upon his spirits' (C. Yorke to Newcastle 18 Feb., BM Add. MSS 32956, f. 31).

106. A rumour had been afloat as early as the end of January that the Dukes of Richmond and Grafton were saying that 'it was in their power to come into office in a week's time whenever they pleased, with Lord Bute in their hands' (*Grenville Papers* ii. 490). Further rumours of negotiations between Bute and Pitt were

afloat in early March (ibid. 494–5), but do not seem to have had any foundation.

107. No important changes took place in the administration until July 1765, in part at least because Opposition failed to follow up the advantage they had won at this time.

108. They did not.

———

1. *Ante* 22–5 Jan. 1764.
2. Residence of the Prince de Conti.

quires no excuse on your part. I do not feel myself so tender on any subject as not to hear the truth, and particularly with respect to politics, to which I grow every day more indifferent. The factions and corrupted system which I have seen equally prevail in every set of men, both in and out of place, has disgusted me. The constant changes would make the first places in the kingdom lose great part of their value in my ideas, and the impossibility of agreeing with a number of friends and relations crown the whole. I feel independent in my fortune though I may have many wishes for the sake of my children, but yet I know that men do not grow rich at Courts, and that if I should be disgraced by any set of men either in or out of favour perhaps I may serve them as well in greater retirement. I am therefore not anxious for any system and I am far from having obligations enough to attach me to any party. The present ministers I know but little. Mr Grenville is a late acquaintance; he was obliging to me before I left England about Mr Bunbury and Mr Hume,[3] and he has lost a part of that merit in disallowing the bill for my journey here. With Lord Halifax I have no other connection whatever than the formal correspondence of one minister to another, nor have I ever been in a situation to experience either favour or prejudice from him.[4] With Lord Sandwich I have not the most distant connection.

With the leaders of Opposition I have as little intimacy. The Duke of Newcastle I have no reason to think my friend,[5] and his enmities[6] are equally extended to all who are not attached to him.

3. Passages in the correspondence between Grenville and Hertford in late Dec. and early Jan. make it clear that Grenville had actively interceded to prevent Bunbury's being sent to Paris; the rapidity with which Hume was assured of a pension and given a promise of the secretaryship of the embassy in due course also undoubtedly owed much to Grenville (*Grenville Papers* ii. 186–7, 247–8; Hume, *Letters*, ed. Greig, Oxford, 1932, i. 392, 394, 398).

4. By Sept. 1764, Halifax had developed a distaste for Hertford: 'Lord Halifax is discontented with Lord Hertford; says he is cold and insufficient, and wants to have him recalled; the King is by no means disposed to recall him, in which Mr Grenville entirely concurs in opinion with

his Majesty . . . Mr Grenville has great difficulty in combatting Lord Halifax's eagerness on this subject, as well as many others. . . . When Mr Grenville and Lord Halifax were alone they had a little warmth upon the subject of Lord Hertford. Lord Halifax wished, if he was not recalled, that some of his friends should write to advise him to ask to come home. Mr Grenville said no friend of Lord Hertford's would do so, and besides, who had Lord Halifax to replace him? His Lordship named nobody' (*Grenville Papers* ii. 514–15).

5. Probably because of his steady opposition to Hertford's designs on the borough of Orford.

6. 'Enmities' written over 'friendships' in the MS.

He is a good-natured old man and I am indifferent to him. To Mr Pitt I owe great civility and attention, and I respect his character and abilities. The confidence of the great men[7] of the same party I believe you know I never had. I have seen every doubtful character always trusted before me. I have therefore no reason as you see to be either partial or prejudiced in the present contest.

I am in my own person as indifferently circumstanced in this respect as an Englishman can be,[8] and the interest I have taken in it was chiefly for my brother's sake. He must therefore at least acquit me of self-interested views in what I have said about his Parliamentary conduct. When I talked about the non-allowance of my expenses to Paris I did not mean seriously to ascribe it to his behaviour in public. I should be ashamed to receive any advantage of that sort which I could owe only to such a compliance, and I hope he cannot suspect me of being so mean as to propose he should alter his conduct to recommend me to this or indeed to any set of men. When I said it I meant only to reflect on those who had disallowed it if such a motive could have any influence on their conduct. The sum refused was too indifferent to give me five moments' thought; I meant only to express my resentment, and he misunderstood me. In regard to my attachment to the King I may be faulty, but I am not more so now than I have been all my life; a connection with the present ministers can hardly be supposed after what I have said. His Majesty has done no one act that I know of since he came to the throne for which he deserves the censure of his people; I cannot therefore in justice set myself in opposition to his government, and I will confess to you that it would be in my opinion an act of passion, not of patriotism, to oppose his government because he has thought proper to employ one set of men in preference to another. I dare say they will have their turn, and in the meantime I cannot to a friend who asks my opinion say that I have either obligation or disobligation enough to any man or set of men to alter my opinion for them about the Prince upon the throne. I have no occasion myself fortunately to take any part. I am heartily glad of it though I fear neither, and when I gave my opinion it was to serve my brother. He should therefore forgive the mistake as it arose from affection; I will

7. Presumably the Duke of Devonshire, Lord Rockingham, and the Duke of Cumberland.

8. Meaning probably that he could afford to ignore the scramble for offices.

not call it judgment. He knows his own affairs best. I meant to lead him into no party; I wished him only to avoid opposition to the King, from thinking as I have shown you I do, but there is nothing so dangerous as meddling with our cursed politics even to our best friends, and it is that which makes me detest them.

I am extremely obliged to you for the advice you have given me about my negotiations at this Court, and I am perfectly satisfied how just it is; in answer I can assure you I have not made the smallest compliment since I have been here to any minister.[9] I have done my duty to the best of my judgment by my country. I have always fore-seen the delicacy of my situation, and was it not for some expressions which are unavoidable in a correspondence of this sort about the ministers of this country, I did not care how soon you had them before the House of Commons.[10] What I meant was whether the style and manner of writing was approved. I did not mean I had anxiety whether they were pleasing to the palate of any particular minister, to whose taste I am pretty indifferent. I beg you will con-tinue to write with the greatest freedom; you cannot oblige me more.

I have just received a message that there is a gentleman going to set out for England[11] who will carry anything for me. I shall there-fore finish this letter sooner than I intended, that I may not lose the opportunity.[12] It is Mr Luther who has sent to me, though it is not himself who is going. What has brought him here? He is a very pretty sort of man.

The King of France asked me the other day, pretty emphatically, as I thought, whether the Hereditary Prince did not leave England in very bad weather. I have no more time and therefore must leave

9. In his letter of 4 Jan., Hertford had congratulated Grenville on the success he had had in Parliament, but had done so rather coldly (ibid. ii. 249).

10. That is, he did not care whether a motion were made and carried for his dispatches to be laid on the table of the House for investigation.

11. Possibly Richard Watson (1737–1816), later Bishop of Llandaff, who wrote in his memoirs: 'On the 12th of February, 1764, I received a letter inform-ing me that a separation had taken place between my friend Mr Luther, then one of the members for Essex [see *ante* 16 Dec. 1763 *bis*], and his wife, and that he was gone hastily abroad. . . . I saw he was deserted and unhappy, and I flew to give him, if possible, some consolation. I set off from Cambridge on the same day I had received the account' (*Anecdotes of the Life of Richard Watson, Bishop of Landaff*, 1817, p. 27). After crossing over to France twice, Watson finally brought Luther 'back to his country and his family' (ibid. 28). See *post* 18 March 1764.

12. On his first trip over, Watson 'did not stay above twelve hours in Paris, but immediately returned to England' (Wat-son, loc. cit.).

the rest that I should have said for another opportunity. I remain, dear Horry,

Always most truly and affectionately yours,

HERTFORD

To HENRIETTA SEYMOUR CONWAY, Thursday 23 February 1764

Missing; answered *post* 27 April 1764.

To HERTFORD, Friday 24 February 1764

Printed from *Works* ix. 80–3.

Arlington Street, Feb. 24th 1764.

AS I had an opportunity, on Tuesday last, of sending you a letter of eleven pages by a very safe conveyance, I shall say but few words today; indeed, I have left nothing to say, but to thank you for the answer I received from you this morning to mine, by Monsieur Monin. I am very happy that you take so kindly the freedom I used: the circumstances made me think it necessary; and I flatter myself, that you are persuaded I was not to blame in speaking so openly, when two persons[1] so dear to me were concerned. Your indulgence will not lead me to abuse it. What you say on the caution I mentioned, convinces me that I was right, by finding your judgment correspond with my own—but enough of that.

My long letter, which, perhaps, you will not receive till after this (you will receive it from a lady),[2] will give you a full detail of the last extraordinary week. Since that, there has been an accidental suspension of arms. Not only Mr Pitt is laid up with the gout, but the Speaker has it too. We have been adjourned till today, and as he is not recovered, have again adjourned till next Wednesday.[3] The

1. Hertford and Conway.
2. The Duchesse de Rohan; see *post* 25 Feb. 1764.
3. The House adjourned on Wednesday, 22 Feb., to Friday, the 24th, met and transacted business as usual that day, and then adjourned to Wednesday, the 29th (*Journals of the House of Commons* xxix. 871–80).

events of the week have been, a complaint made by Lord Lyttelton in your House,[4] of a book called *Droit le Roy*,[5] a tract written
in the highest strain of prerogative, and drawn from all the old
obsolete law books on that question. The ministers met this complaint with much affected indignation, and even on the complaint
being communicated to us,[6] took it up themselves; and both Houses
have ordered the book to be burned by the hangman.[7] To comfort themselves for this forced zeal for liberty, the *North Briton*,
and the *Essay on Woman*, have both been condemned by juries in
the King's Bench;[8] but that triumph has been more than balanced
again, by the City giving their freedom to Lord Chief Justice Pratt,[9]
ordering his picture to be placed in the King's Bench,[10] thanking
their members for their behaviour in Parliament on the warrant,[11]

4. Lyttelton had announced his intention of making the complaint, 17 Feb.
and did so 21 Feb. (*Journals of the House
of Lords* xxx. 477; *Mem. Geo. III* i. 304–
6). The Opposition intended the complaint to embarrass the government; see
the letters of Rockingham to Newcastle
16 Feb., Dartmouth to Newcastle [16
Feb.], Rockingham to Newcastle [17 Feb.],
and Newcastle to Legge 18 Feb. (BM Add.
MSS 32956, ff. 1–2, 9, 17, 37), in which
they prepare the campaign.

5. *Droit le Roi*, or a *Digest of the
Rights and Prerogatives of the Imperial
Crown of Great Britain*, published 16 Jan.
1764 (*Daily Adv.* 13, 16 Jan.). It was compiled by Timothy Brecknock (d. 1786), a
versifier and lawyer of dubious character
who was eventually executed for murder
with his patron, George Fitzgerald; see the
anecdotes about him in *European Magazine* 1786, ix. 392, and the account of his
trial, ibid. 390–1. HW has written the
compiler's name and the date of publication on the title-page of his copy (now
WSL, Hazen, *Cat. of HW's Lib.*, No.
1609:7:2), and a brief account of the
proceedings against the book on the half-
title (MONTAGU ii. 153, n. 11). For HW's
attitude toward the royal prerogative, see
A. S. Foord, 'The Only Unadulterated
Whig,' in *Horace Walpole: Writer, Politician, and Connoisseur*, ed. W. H. Smith,
New Haven, 1967, p. 35 *et seq.*

6. At a conference, 24 Feb.; the House
of Commons promptly concurred with the
Lords (*Journals of the House of Com-

mons* xxix. 874, 875; *Journals of the
House of Lords* xxx. 481, 482, 483). According to Foord, op. cit. 42, n. 71, this
was the only issue of any constitutional
significance in the eighteenth century
upon which all members present in the
Lords and Commons voted unanimously.

7. The sentence was executed before
Westminster Hall, 25 Feb., and at the
Royal Exchange, 27 Feb. (GM 1764, xxxiv.
96; HW's note in his copy of *Droit le Roi*).

8. 21 Feb.; some details of the trials,
with lists of the jurors, are in *London
Chronicle* 21–3 Feb., xv. 184. Wilkes was
found guilty of reprinting and publishing
the *North Briton* No. 45 and of printing
and publishing the *Essay on Woman*.

9. At a meeting of the Common Council, 21 Feb. 'Resolved, That . . . this
court, in manifestation of the just sense
we entertain of the inflexible firmness and
integrity of the Right Honourable Sir
Charles Pratt, Lord Chief Justice of his
Majesty's Court of Common Pleas, doth
direct that the freedom of this city be
presented to his Lordship' (ibid.).

10. 'And that he be desired to sit for
his picture to be placed in Guildhall, in
gratitude for his honest and deliberate
decision upon the validity of a warrant'
(ibid.).

11. At the meeting of the Common
Council, 21 Feb. 'Resolved, That the
thanks of this court be presented to Sir
Robert Ladbroke, Kt, Sir Richard Glynn,
Bart, William Beckford, Esq. and the
Honourable Thomas Harley, Esq. the

and giving orders for instructions to be drawn for their future conduct.[12]

Lord Granby is made lord lieutenant of Derbyshire,[13] but the vigour of this affront was woefully weakened by excuses to the Duke of Devonshire, and by its being known that the measure was determined two months ago.

All this sounds very hostile,—yet, don't be surprised if you hear of some sudden treaty. Don't you know a little busy squadron that had the chief hand in the negotiation last autumn?[14] Well, I have reason to think that Phraates[15] is negotiating with Leonidas[16] by the same intervention.[17] All the world sees that the present ministers are between two fires. Would it be extraordinary if the artillery of both should be discharged on them at once? But this is not proper for the post: I grow prudent the less prudence is necessary.

We are in pain for the Duchess of Richmond, who, instead of the jaundice, has relapsed into a fever. She was blooded twice last night, and yet had a very bad night. I called at the door at three o'clock, when they thought the fever rather diminished, but spoke of her as very ill. I have not seen your brother, or Lady Aylesbury to-day, but found they had been very much alarmed yesterday evening.

Lord Suffolk, they say, is going to be married to Miss Trevor Hampden.[18]

Your brother has told me, that among Lady Hertford's things

representatives of this city, for their zealous and spirited endeavours to assert the rights and liberties of the subject by their laudable attempt to obtain a seasonable and Parliamentary declaration, that a general warrant for apprehending and seizing the authors, printers, and publishers of a seditious libel, together with their papers, is not warranted by law' (ibid.).

12. No order to this effect is quoted in the *London Chronicle;* HW probably refers to the last sentence in the resolution of thanks: 'And to express to them our warmest exhortations, that they steadily persevere in their duty to the Crown, and use their utmost endeavours to secure the homes, papers and persons of the subject from arbitrary and illegal violations' (ibid.).

13. He was gazetted as such, 21 Feb. (*London Gazette* No. 10393, 18–21 Feb.).

14. Shelburne had been the minister appointed to arrange the meeting between the King and Pitt the previous August (*ante* 27, 30 Aug. 1763), and his supporter, Calcraft, had also been employed in this task (Namier and Brooke ii. 172); presumably HW refers to these two, plus Barré and possibly Thomas Fitzmaurice, Shelburne's brother, these latter also being generally supposed to be under Shelburne's influence (Lord Fitzmaurice, *Life of . . . Shelburne,* 1912, i. 211).

15. Bute (*ante* 15 Feb. 1764).

16. Pitt.

17. Such rumours were afloat, but they seem to have been without foundation (ibid., n. 106).

18. Hon. Maria Constantia Trevor (1744–67), daughter of 1st Vct Hampden; m. (25 May 1764) Henry Howard, 12th E. of Suffolk.

seized at Dover,[19] was a packet for me from you.[20] Mr Bowman has undertaken to make strict inquiry for it. Adieu, my dear Lord,

Yours most faithfully,

H. Walpole

PS. We had, last Monday,[21] the prettiest ball that ever was seen at Mrs Ann Pitt's,[22] in the compass of a silver penny. There were one hundred and four persons, of which number fifty-five supped. The supper room was disposed with tables and benches back to back in the manner of an ale-house. The idea sounds ill, but the fairies had so improved upon it, had so *be-garlanded,* so *sweet-meated,* and so *desserted* it, that it looked like a vision. I told her she could only have fed and stowed so much company by a miracle, and that, when we were gone, she would take up twelve basketsful of people. The Duchess of Bedford asked me before Madame de Guerchy, if I would not give them a ball at Strawberry? Not for the universe!—What! turn a ball, and dust, and dirt, and a million of candles into my charming new Gallery![23] I said, I could not flatter myself that people would give themselves the trouble of going eleven miles for a *ball*—(though I believe they would go fifty)—'Well, then,' says she, 'it shall be a *dinner*'—'With all my heart, I have no objection; but no *ball* shall set its foot within my doors.'

19. Some items of Hertford's, 'chiefly small presents of Lady Hertford's to her friends,' had been confiscated by the Custom House officers at Dover early in Feb.; see Hertford's letter of complaint to Grenville, 11 Feb. (*Grenville Papers* ii. 260–1).

20. Possibly Hertford's long letter of 23 Jan., which he was still holding on 29 Jan. to send by messenger (*ante* 29 Jan. 1764).

21. 20 Feb.

22. Anne Pitt (1712–81), sister of William Pitt; keeper of the Privy Purse to the Ps of Wales 1751–72; HW's correspondent. See HW's letter to her, 21 Feb. 1764, praising her ball and applying *Paradise Lost* I. 775–88 to her accomplishment (More 33).

23. The Gallery at SH had been completed in August 1763 (*ante* 9 Aug. 1763).

From Hertford, Saturday 25 February 1764

Printed for the first time from a photostat of BM Add. MSS 23218, ff. 130–2.

Paris, February 25th 1764.

Dear Horry,

I HAVE now another very long letter to acknowledge from you. It was sent to me yesterday in a most polite and obliging manner by the Duchess of Rohan[1] without telling me by what means it came into her hands; when I have answered it I propose going in person to thank her. You are the best creature in the world to take such pains to inform me of what you are doing; after the fatigue you had undergone I am very sensible of the obligation. Can you preserve the numbers you have collected for this particular occasion, or will many of them return to their ancient standard? I can imagine all my friends and acquaintance very busy and very anxious.

The next division in Parliament upon a new subject will probably be critical, and I fancy you are the only person in Opposition who does not wish or design to make one or more ministers out of it. I will confess to you that I feel a satisfaction in being out of this battle. Whether old age and indifference have overtaken me or whether I see clearer for being farther removed from the smoke I cannot say, but I do not feel at present as if I could ever again enjoy a political contest at Westminster. I am still like the old libertine, pleased with the history and excessively obliged to you for the accounts you send me.

I wrote you a very long letter in answer to the one I received by Monsieur Monin; I have therefore nothing more political to add about myself. I have a great partiality for his present Majesty, which I desire you as one of my best friends to think well placed.

The carnival entertainments here are more sociable than I think they can be in London in a political winter. There is no separation from Arthur's to a new coffee-house,[2] but everyone can dine, sup and dance with pleasure in any company. Do not think me changed for the worse if I should wish this life to be consistent with English

1. Probably Émilie de Crussol (1732–91), m. (1758) Louis-Marie-Bretagne-Dominique, Duc de Rohan-Chabot.
2. As there had been in London by the foundation of the club at Wildman's Tavern for the members of Opposition (*ante* 22 Jan. 1764).

freedom. The French, as I have often repeated, treat us with great respect and civility, and we live much with them. There is no want of balls, dinners, suppers and all kinds of parties, and I have the pleasure of hearing in return for these invitations that my house is just what it should be for the English ambassador. I have not yet been able to give a ball. My house is an excuse for this carnival if the custom made it necessary, which it does not.

I have seen but little of Lord Holland. He was invited to dine here and was engaged. He was likewise invited with Lady Holland and his son[3] to a very great family party of Berwicks and Fitzjameses, but he did not stay supper; it seems he never does; and I have dined once at his house but was obliged to come home about business immediately after dinner. I think he does not seem to amuse himself much here. He looks grave and sleepy and seems depressed by his constitution. Lady Holland seems happier here than in England and does very well with the French.[4] The son is a good-natured boy.

I have not seen Madame d'Usson this month or six weeks by living in different societies. Madame de Bouflers I see oftener, but Madame de Mirepoix is the French lady I have known in England whom I see most frequently; she is to be seen in every great house at Paris almost, and loves faro as well as ever.

The Duke of Bucleugh[5] dined with me here in his way to Toulouse,[6] and I admire him much.

Lady Hertford and my son desire their best compliments, and I remain always, dear Horry,

Very sincerely and affectionately yours,

HERTFORD

---

3. Stephen.

4. Lady Holland wrote to Lady Kildare from Paris, ?1764, that 'I shall not, I own, leave this place without regret. I'm not French like Lady Hervey, but I do think they are the only people who know how to put society on an easy agreeable foot. . . . Upon the whole, I think every woman past thirty that really lives a Paris life among the French, and understands the language, and who likes conversation better than cards, will prefer Paris to London' (*Leinster Corr.* i. 399–400).

5. Henry Scott (1746–1812), 3d D. of Buccleuch; 5th D. of Queensbury, 1810.

6. Where he remained for 18 months, except for excursions, pursuing his studies (DNB *sub* Adam Smith).

To HERTFORD, Friday 2 March 1764

Missing; answered *post* 8 March 1764.

From HERTFORD, Thursday 8 March 1764

Printed for the first time from a photostat of BM Add. MSS 23218, ff. 133–4.

Paris, March 8th 1764.

Dear Horry,

I THANK you for a most comfortable letter of the 2d which I received in a very short time. You deserve every sort of return from me for your very kind attention in acquainting us so exactly with what passes in London, and indeed that is my chief motive for not allowing a courier to go for England without writing a few words to you, for I have very little to say.

Madame Pompadour's illness[1] has been the chief object of Paris for these last ten days; it has been so serious as to interrupt in some degree both the business and diversions of Versailles. She is at Choisi where the King has stayed to attend her; her disorder has been a fever and oppression upon her breast. It is now said she will recover,[2] but she is still ill. The King himself has set up I hear three nights with her, the Duke of Orléans one, and the Prince of Condé another. The Prince of Conti is the only one who will not bow to this influence, and he is rather in ridicule than esteem for it, such is the way of reasoning in this country, though the parliament intend if they can to change it.

1. 'La maladie de Mme de Pompadour arrêtait tout, et faisait un bien grand événement. Cela avait commencé le 29 février à Choisy, par une grosse fluxion qui avait fait une fluxion sur la poitrine, le septième jour de la maladie. On la croyait hors d'affaire. Il s'y joignit une fièvre miliaire, et, le onzième, il se déclara une fièvre putride, et elle fut mal. L'inquiétude redoubla. Le Roi y était presque toujours. Le 10 mars, elle fut à la mort' (Emmanuel, Duc de Croÿ, *Journal inédit*, ed. Grouchy and Cottin, 1906–7, ii. 132–3).

2. She relapsed 8 April and died the 15th; see *post* 15 April 1764. Information reaching England slightly later mentioned that 'on the 8th [March] she was much better, but in the evening of the 18th [11th], the illness had returned, and she was imagined to be in very great danger, and an eruption which had appeared gave little hopes of her recovery' (*London Chronicle* 17–20 March, xv. 269). She was convalescing by the 22d, however, and continued to improve until her relapse 8 April (*post* 22 March, 15 April 1764).

In the meantime the Queen is crying for her Jesuit and confessor.[3] The parliament some days ago had banished them,[4] but I hear that today the sentence is to be softened and that they will be permitted to stay in France upon condition they leave Paris and go to their different provinces. The parliament has likewise declared that they will oblige the bishops who have no particular office at Court to reside at their several dioceses;[5] the number at present proclaimed is forty-seven.[6]

But in the midst of all these reformations the society of Paris does not suffer, and from the indifference with which everything that is not pleasure is generally received here, I think it will be some considerable time before the parliamentary spirit has any great effect upon the genius of the people or the constitution of the government.

I beg you will take some opportunity of explaining to the Princess Amelia that I am not to blame for sending the trees I received from Madame de Bouflers by long sea,[7] which is always a tedious passage. The packet was so long and so heavy that it was hardly possible to send it by any land carriage without breaking the trees. If they should fail, which from the length of time is too probable, her R. H.

3. ——— Bieganski. He is described as a Jesuit in the *Almanach royal* until the suppression of the order, and continues to be listed as the Queen's confessor even after the banishment of the Jesuits, though it was generally reported that she had sent for another Pole (*Mercure historique*, 1764, lvi. 289; *London Chronicle* 15–17 March, xv. 264).

4. The parliament of Paris, 22 Feb., had issued an *arrêt* ordering all former Jesuits in France to take an oath not to live according to the constitution of their order, to refrain from all correspondence with the superiors of the order, and to swear that they considered the doctrine of the *Recueil des assertions* to be impious (*Mercure historique*, 1764, lxi. 286–7; *London Chronicle* 1–3 March, xv. 216). They were not formally banished, however, until 9 March when the parliament ordered that all who refused to take the oath, as most of them had done, must leave the kingdom within a month (É. Glasson, *Le Parlement de Paris*, 1901,

ii. 277; *London Chronicle* 15–17 March, xv. 264).

5. 'Notice being taken in the parliament of Paris, on the third instant, by one of the members, of the great number of bishops in that capital, it was ordered that the King's attorney-general should see the ordinances and *arrêts* touching the non-residency of archbishops and bishops carried into execution, and report what he had done in this matter to the House in a fortnight' (*London Chronicle* 8–10 March, xv. 240). See also the account of the Attorney-General's report in *St James's Chronicle* 31 March–3 April.

6. This number is also given in an item from Paris ibid. 22–4 March.

7. They had been sent through a merchant at Rouen early in January, but did not arrive in England until around 20 April (*ante* 6 Jan.; *post* 27 March, 5, 15, 20 April 1764). Presumably they were shipped up the Seine to Le Havre, and thence across the Channel and up the Thames to London, bypassing Dover.

may command my services in forming proper parcels of such sorts as to be procured here which she may wish to have. The box to Lady Harvey must be justified by similar reasoning; the couriers who ride cannot carry them.

My old friend Fuentes[8] is come to Paris, and has been excessively obliging and friendly to me about the house. He has taken one here,[9] but would not fix upon it till he had offered it to me. You may imagine I did not accept it, indeed it was one my Lady had seen before and did not approve, but I am in no fear of being lodged either where I now am or in some other good habitation. I remain, dear Horry,

Ever faithfully yours,

HERTFORD

To HERTFORD, Sunday 11 March 1764

Printed from *Works* ix. 84–8.

Strawberry Hill, Sunday, March 11th 1764.

My dear Lord,

THE last was so busy a week with me, that I had not a minute's time to tell you of Lord Hardwicke's death.[1] I had so many auctions,[2] dinners, loo parties,[3] so many sick acquaintance, with the addi-

8. Juan Joaquín Atanasio Pignatelli de Aragón (1724–76), Conde de Fuentes; Spanish ambassador to England 1760–1, to France 1764–73 (DU DEFFAND ii. 367, n. 18; MANN v. 417, n. 12; *Almanach royal* 1773, p. 146; 1774, p. 148; *Genealog. hist. Nachrichten* 1774–5, 3d ser. xiii. 312). He presented his credentials to the King 25 Feb. (*London Chronicle* 1–3 March, xv. 213).

9. The Hotel de Broglie, Rue de Varenne, where he was living when the *Almanach royal* for 1765 was published (p. 134).

___

1. 6 March.

2. HW purchased a pair of gloves worn by James I and a watch given to Gen. Fairfax by Parliament after the Battle of Naseby, at the sale of Thoresby's Museum,

5–7 March (Frits Lugt, *Répertoire des catalogues de ventes publiques*, La Haye, 1938–64, Vol. I, No. 1355; 'Des. of SH,' *Works* ii. 422–3, 499). On 9 March he bought at the second Cottrell Dormer Sale Thuanus, *Historia sui temporis*, 1733, [lot 2590], 7 vols extended to 14; this corrects COLE i. 60, n. 4. Other auctions which HW may have attended included sales of prints and drawings collected by Sir Thomas Brand, 5–8 March; stained glass 7 March; pictures including works by Rembrandt and Van Dyck, 7–8 March; antique gems 8–9 March; Italian, French, and Latin books, 8–9 March; and pictures including a large view of Twickenham, 9–10 March (*Daily Adv.* 5–10 March).

3. Conway wrote to Hertford somewhat later: 'Loo is revived I think with

tion of a long day in the House of Commons[4] (which, by the way, I quitted for a sale of books),[5] and a ball,[6] that I left the common newspapers to inform you of an event, which two months ago would have been of much consequence. The Yorkes are fixed, and the contest at Cambridge[7] will but make them strike deeper root in Opposition. I have not heard how their father has portioned out his immense treasures.[8] The election at Cambridge is to be on Tuesday, 24th;[9] Charles Townshend is gone thither,[10] and I suppose, by this time, has ranted, and romanced, and turned every one of their ideas topsy-turvy.[11]

Our long day was Friday, the opening of the budget. Mr Grenville spoke for two hours and forty minutes;[12] much of it well,[13] but too long, too many repetitions, and too evident marks of being galled by reports, which he answered with more art than sincerity. There were a few more speeches, till nine o'clock,[14] but no division. Our armi-

its usual vivacity and our parties got in train again, in spite of parties and politics: the Duchess of Grafton, the Duchess of Bedford, etc., etc., the Duke and Duchess of Marlborough are also become loo players and sometimes of our parties' (Conway to Hertford 31 March, MS now WSL).

4. Friday, 9 March; see the next paragraph.

5. Probably the Cottrell Dormer Sale, mentioned above, n. 2.

6. Given by the Duchess of Queensbury; see the second paragraph below.

7. For the post of High Steward of the University, left vacant by the death of Lord Hardwicke, and contested between the new Lord Hardwicke and Lord Sandwich.

8. 'It is said, the late Earl of Hardwicke died worth upwards of six hundred thousand pounds in money and lands' (*St James's Chronicle*, 10–13 March).

9. *Sic* in *Works;* the 24th fell on a Saturday, not a Tuesday. Ellison, the vice-chancellor of the University, had scheduled the election for Thursday, the 22d; however, he later postponed it to Friday, the 30th (Ellison to Newcastle 8 March, Newcastle to Ellison 17 March, BM Add. MSS 32956, f. 277, 32957, f. 135). For the results of the election, see *post* 5 April 1764 *bis*.

10. He went to Cambridge 8 March on

behalf of Hardwicke's candidacy (H. Thomas to Newcastle 9 March, BM Add. MSS 32956, f. 318).

11. Newcastle, writing of Townshend's efforts at Cambridge, told Legge that he had proved himself 'a most admirable negotiator' (13 March, BM Add. MSS 32957, f. 5). See Sir Lewis Namier and John Brooke, *Charles Townshend*, 1964, pp. 115–16.

12. Three hours and a quarter according to Newcastle (Newcastle to C. Townshend 10 March, BM Add. MSS 32956, f. 342; Newcastle to Legge 13 March, loc. cit.). HW reports Grenville's speech in *Mem. Geo. III* i. 309–10. The budget he described included plans for raising a revenue in America, in order to make the Americans pay for the British troops stationed there.

13. 'The King told Mr Grenville that he heard from everybody that no man had ever spoke so well as he had done, the Friday, in the House of Commons' (*Grenville Papers* ii. 495). See also Namier and Brooke ii. 542.

14. 'If Mr Pitt's health, Mr Yorke's circumstances, or Charles Townshend's necessary absence in supporting our course at Cambridge . . . had not prevented their attendance, the House would have sat, at least, until midnight, perhaps far advanced in the night' (Newcastle to Legge 13 March, loc. cit).

stice, you see, continues. Lord Bute is, I believe, negotiating with both sides; I know he is with the Opposition,[15] and has a prospect of making very good terms for himself, for patriots seldom have the gift of perseverance. It is wonderful how soon their virtue thaws!

Last Thursday, the Duchess of Queensberry gave a ball,[16] opened it herself with a minuet, and danced two country dances; as she had enjoined everybody to be with her by six, to sup at twelve, and go away directly. Of the Campbell sisters, all were left out but Lady Strafford.[17] Lady Rockingham and Lady Sondes, who having had colds, deferred sending answers, received notice that their places were filled up, and that they must not come; but were pardoned on submission. A card was sent to invite Lord and Lady Cardigan, and Lord *Beaulieu,* instead of Lord Montagu.[18] This, her Grace protested, was by accident. Lady Cardigan was very angry, and yet went. Except these flights, the only extraordinary thing the Duchess did, was to do nothing extraordinary, for I do not call it very mad that some pique happening between her and the Duchess of Bedford, the latter had this distich sent to her,

> Come with a whistle, and come with a call,
> Come with a good will, or come not at all.

15. There seems to have been no real foundation to these reports, though they were wide-spread. Although pressed to do so, Grenville adamantly refused to enter into any negotiations with Bute, who had set in motion the manœuvre for bringing Pitt back into power the previous August (see *Grenville Papers,* ii. 493, 495–6), while the King told Lord Mansfield, ca 10 March, that 'he did not believe that any transaction had passed between the Opposition and Lord Bute, but that if any had . . . he knew nothing of it' (ibid. 495); his remark was made in response to a rumour that Beckford, who had attempted to see Lord Bute, had been 'sent there by Mr Pitt, charged with some negotiation from the Opposition' (ibid. 494).

16. 'Thursday [8 March] the Duke of Queensbury gave an entertainment to a great number of the nobility and gentry at his house in Burlington Street, and afterwards a ball' (*London Chronicle* 8–10 March, xv. 238).

17. The other sisters were Lady Dalkeith, wife of Charles Townshend; Lady Elizabeth Stuart Mackenzie, sister-in-law of Lord Bute; and Lady Mary Coke.

18. John Brudenell (after 1749 Montagu) (1735–70), son of Lord and Lady Cardigan; styled Lord Brudenell 1735–62; cr. (1762) Bn Montagu of Boughton; styled M. of Monthermer 1766–70. In 1762 there had been a dispute between Lady Cardigan and her sister, the Dowager Duchess of Manchester, co-heiresses of the 2d Duke of Montagu, over who should be given the Montagu title; the Duchess wanted it for her husband, Sir Edward Hussey Montagu, but upon Lady Cardigan's objecting, it was given to the latter's son, while Hussey Montagu was created Lord Beaulieu instead. Apparently Lady Cardigan thought that the Duchess of Queensbury's confusion of names was intentional, and that she meant to imply that Lord Beaulieu should have received the Montagu title. See Montagu ii. 27 and Namier and Brooke ii. 664–5.

I do not know whether what I am going to tell you did not border a little upon Moorfields.[19] The gallery where they danced was very cold. Lord Lorn, George Selwyn, and I, retired into a little room, and sat comfortably by the fire. The Duchess looked in, said nothing, and sent a smith to take the hinges of the door off. We understood the hint, and left the room, and so did the smith the door. This was pretty legible.

My niece Waldegrave talks of accompanying me to Paris, but ten or twelve weeks may make great alteration in a handsome young widow's plan: I even think I see some[20] who will—not forbid banns, but propose them. Indeed, I am almost afraid of coming to you myself. The air of Paris works such miracles, that it is not safe to trust one's self there. I hear of nothing but my Lady Hertford's rakery, and Mr Wilkes's religious deportment, and constant attendance at your chapel.[21] Lady Anne,[22] I conclude, chatters as fast as my Lady Essex[23] and her four daughters.[24]

Princess Amelia told me t'other night, and bade me tell you, that she had seen Lady Massarene[25] at Bath, who is warm in praise of you, and said that you had spent £2000 out of friendship, to support her son[26] in an election.[27] She told the Princess too, that she had found a rent-roll of your estate in a farm-house, and that it is £14,000 a year. This I was ordered, I know not why, to tell you too. The Duchess of

19. Madness, from Bedlam being in Moorfields.

20. Especially the Duke of Portland; see *post* 22 March 1764.

21. Hertford had mentioned Wilkes's attending his chapel *ante* 6 Jan. 1764, and wrote, *post* 25 March 1764, that Wilkes was attending every Sunday, but was in the habit of 'laughing frequently during the time of service.'

22. Lady Anne Seymour-Conway (1744–84), m. (1766) Charles Moore, 6th E. of Drogheda, cr. (1791) M. of Drogheda; Hertford's eldest daughter. She was apparently quite shy (see *Leinster Corr.* i. 398); HW is being ironical about her, as he is about Lady Hertford and Wilkes.

23. Lady Elizabeth Russell (d. 1784), daughter of 2d D. of Bedford; m. (1726) as his second wife William Capel, 3d E. of Essex.

24. Lady Essex had had four daughters,

but as two of them died young (Collins, *Peerage*, 1812, iii. 484), HW is presumably referring to her two surviving daughters and to the two surviving daughters of her husband's first wife (d. 1724). Her daughters were Lady Diana Capel (1728–1800) and Lady Anne Capel (1730–1804); her step-daughters, Lady Charlotte Capel (1721–90), m. (1752) Hon. Thomas Villiers, cr. (1776) E. of Clarendon; and Lady Mary Capel (1722–82), m. (1758) Adm. the Hon. John Forbes.

25. Anne Eyre (ca 1716–1805), m. (1741) Clotworthy Skeffington (d. 1757), 5th Vct Massereene, cr. (1756) E. of Massereene.

26. Clotworthy Skeffington (1743–1805), 2d E. of Massereene, 1757.

27. Probably for one of the constituencies in County Antrim, Ireland, where both Lord Massereene and Lord Hertford had large holdings.

Bedford has not been asked to the loo parties at Cavendish House[28] this winter, and only once to whisk there, and that was one Friday when she is at home herself. We have nothing at the Princess's but silver loo, and her Bath and Tunbridge acquaintance. The *trade* at our gold loo[29] is as contraband as ever. I cannot help saying, that the Duchess of Bedford would mend our silver loo, and that I wish everybody played like her at the gold.

Arlington Street, Tuesday [13 March].

You thank me, my dear Lord, for my gazettes (in your letter of the 8th) more than they deserve. There is no trouble in sending you news, as you excuse the careless manner in which I write anything I hear. Don't think yourself obliged to be punctual in answering me: it would be paying too dear for such idle and trifling dispatches. Your picture of the attention paid to Madame Pompadour's illness, and of the ridicule attached to the mission of that homage, is very striking. It would be still more so by comparison.— Think if the Duke of Cumberland was to set up with my Lord Bute!

The East India Company, yesterday, elected Lord Clive—Great Mogul; that is, they have made him governor-general of Bengal,[30] and restored his *jaghuire*.[31] I dare to say he will put it out of their power to ever take it away again. We have had a deluge of disputes

28. Princess Amelia's house, in Cavendish Square.

29. Presumably gold loo was played for higher stakes than silver loo.

30. HW's news is somewhat premature; see *post* 18 March 1764. What actually happened is made clear by a report in the *London Chronicle:* After much discussion at a meeting of the Council of Proprietors of India Stock, a motion was made '"That Lord Clive be requested by this court to take upon him the presidency of Bengal, and the command of the military forces there, upon his arrival in that province." This seeming to be the sense of a great majority, Lord Clive stood up, and in a very handsome speech signified, that though happily his present fortune rendered such an offer a matter of indifference to him in a lucrative view, and though his future schemes of life were totally different; yet if he should

be called upon by the general voice of the proprietors, and matters could be "settled so that he could proceed with any degree of prudence, supported by a friendly and united direction, he would once more stand forth in their service." After a short debate, the question was put, and carried without a division' (10–13 March, xv. 248). See also *St James's Chronicle* 10–13 March; GM 1764, xxxiv. 145.

31. This report, which HW contradicts *post* 18 March 1764, was still current on the 17th when the *London Chronicle* reported 'that his Lordship is not only to have the payments which have been stopped of his jaghire, but also to receive of the company a sum of money, in lieu of the continuation of the annual payment of it, at the rate of 14 years purchase; which amounts to £420,000' (15–17 March, xv. 264).

and pamphlets[32] on the late events in that distant province of our empire, the Indies. The novelty of the manners diverts me: our governors there, I think, have learned more of their treachery and injustice, than they have taught them of our discipline.

Monsieur Helvétius[33] arrived yesterday. I will take care to inform the Princess, that you could not do otherwise than you did about her trees. My compliments to all your Hôtel.

Yours, most sincerely,

Hor. Walpole

To Hertford, Sunday 18 March 1764

Printed from *Works* ix. 89–92.

Sunday, March 18th 1764.

YOU will feel, my dear Lord, for the loss I have had,[1] and for the much greater affliction of poor Lady Malpas.[2] My nephew went to his regiment[3] in Ireland before Christmas, and returned but last Monday.[4] He had, I suppose, heated himself in that bacchanalian country, and was taken ill the very day he set out, yet he came on, but grew much worse the night of his arrival; it turned to an inflammation in his bowels, and he died last Friday. You may imagine the distress where there was so much domestic felicity, and where the deprivation is augmented by the very slender circumstances in which

32. Five of them are discussed in an article in GM 1764, xxxiv. 51–6; see also *London Chronicle* 28 Feb.–1 March, xv. 204–5. The newspapers also contain many letters, accounts, etc. of the affair. HW bound five of them in his 'Tracts of . . . Geo. 3d,' Hazen, *Cat. of HW's Lib.*, No. 1609:7. All but one have a February date in his hand on the title-pages.

33. Claude-Adrien Helvétius (1715–71), 'philosophe.' Details of his visit are in his letters to his wife, printed in *Le Carnet historique et littéraire*, 1900, vi. 441–6, 481–6; see also Ian Cumming, *Helvétius*, 1955, Chap. VIII, and Albert Keim, *Helvétius: sa vie et son œuvre*, 1907, pp. 486–95.

———

1. The death of his nephew George Cholmondeley (1724–15 March 1764), styled Vct Malpas 1733–64; M.P. Bramber 1754–61, Corfe Castle 1761–4.

2. Hester Edwardes (ca 1728–94), m. (1747) George Cholmondeley, styled Vct Malpas.

3. Malpas had been Col. of the 65th Foot since 1760.

4. At the special request of the government, which was anxious for his vote in Parliament; see E. of Northumberland to Grenville 2 March in *Grenville Papers* ii. 274–5.

he could but leave his family,[5] as his father—[6] such an improvident father—is living! Lord Malpas himself was very amiable, and I had always loved him—but this is the cruel tax one pays for living, to see one's friends taken away before one!—It has been a week of mortality. The night I wrote to you last,[7] and had sent away my letter, came an account of my Lord Townshend's death.[8] He had been ill treated by a surgeon in the country, then was carried improperly to the Bath, and again back to Rainham, though Hawkins, and other surgeons and physicians, represented his danger to him. But the woman he kept,[9] probably to prevent his seeing his family, persisted in these extravagant journeys, and he died in exquisite torment the day after his arrival in Norfolk.[10] He mentions none of his children in his will, but the present Lord, to whom he gives £300 a year that he had bought, adjoining to his estate. But there is said, or supposed to be, £50,000 in the funds in his mistress's name, who was his housemaid. I do not aver this, for truth is not the staple commodity of that family. Charles is much disappointed and discontented—not so, my Lady, who has to £2,000 a year already, another £1000 in jointure, and £1500 her own estate in Hertfordshire.[11] We conclude, that the Duke of Argyle will abandon Mrs Villiers[12] for this richer widow; who will only be inconsolable, as she is too cunning, I believe, to let anybody console her. Lord Macclesfield[13] is dead too; a great windfall for Mr Grenville, who gets a teller's place for his son.[14]

5. His estate was turned over to the administration of a creditor; Malpas had protested having to leave Ireland 'not only on account of leaving his own private affairs in a very unsettled state, but his regiment, which is lately come from America in great confusion, as his lieutenant-colonel is now actually in arrest, in order to be tried by a court martial on many complaints that are lodged against him' (GEC; *Grenville Papers* ii. 275). All his property was advertised in the *London Chronicle* throughout May to be sold at auction beginning 13 June.

6. Lord Cholmondeley.

7. 13 March.

8. Which occurred 12 March.

9. HW to Mann, 18 March 1764, describes her as 'a housemaid, by whom he had three children' (MANN vi. 211).

10. The *St James's Chronicle* 13–15

March reported that he died 'on the road coming from Bath.'

11. Balls Park.

12. Probably Mary Fowke (d. 1767), daughter of Capt. Thomas Fowke and sister of Lt-Gen. Thomas Fowke, m. Henry Villiers, nephew of the 1st E. of Jersey (GM 1767, xxxvii. 47; Burke, *Peerage*, 1928, pp. 970, 1303; Collins, *Peerage*, 1812, iii. 791).

13. George Parker (ca 1697 – 17 March 1764), 2d E. of Macclesfield.

14. George Grenville (later Nugent-Temple-Grenville) (1753–1813), 2d E. Temple, 1779; cr. (1784) M. of Buckingham. Through his father he had obtained, 2 March 1763, the reversion of the tellership of the Exchequer, which Macclesfield had held since 1719; see GEC ii. 406; *Grenville Papers* ii. 496–7.

There is no public news: there was a longish day on Friday[15] in our House, on a demand for money for the new bridge from the City.[16] It was refused, and into the account of contempt, Dr Hay[17] threw a good deal of abuse on the Common Council[18]—a nest of hornets, that I do not see the prudence of attacking.

I leave to your brother to tell you the particulars of an impertinent paragraph in the papers on you and your embassy;[19] but I must tell you how instantly, warmly, and zealously, he resented it. He went directly to the Duke of Somerset,[20] to beg him to complain of it to the Lords. His Grace's bashfulness made him choose rather to second the complaint, but he desired Lord Marchmont to make it,[21] who liked the office, and the printers[22] are to attend your House tomorrow.[23]

I went a little too fast in my history of Lord Clive, and yet I had it

15. 16 March.

16. The Common Council had voted, 19 Jan., to petition Parliament for additional funds (£19,000) for the completion of repairs to London Bridge. The petition was presented 27 Jan. with the King's express commendation, and referred to a committee which reported favourably 6 March; but the additional grant was refused in the committee on supply, 16 March by a vote of 94–64 (*London Chronicle* 19–21 Jan., 17–20 March, xv. 65, 265; *Journals of the House of Commons* xxix. 758–9, 911–12, 959; *Mercure historique*, 1764, clvi. 414).

17. George Hay (*ante* 15 Nov. 1755).

18. HW gives an account of the debate in *Mem. Geo. III* i. 311; the Opposition apparently 'exulted at the spirit of the Common Council . . . in the measures they have lately taken to oppose administration' (James Rosseter to Charles Jenkinson, 21 March, in *The Jenkinson Papers*, ed. N. S. Jucker, 1949, p. 275). See also the *Plain Dealer*, No. 39, quoted in *St James's Chronicle* 4–7 Feb., for further abuse of the Common Council over their application.

19. 'Although Lord Hertford is nominal ambassador at Paris, yet the affairs of our Court are taken care of by David Hume, Esq. (the author); and the Rev. Mr Trail, a Scottish Presbyterian, reads (as well as he can) the liturgy of our Church, and administers to the English

subjects there in spirituals.' The paragraph appeared in the *London Evening Post* 13–15 March and the *Gazetteer* 16 March (*Journals of the House of Lords* xxx. 508; *Mem. Geo. III* i. 311). Conway's letter to Hertford on this subject is missing. Hertford suspected Wilkes of being the author (*post* 25 March 1764).

20. Edward Seymour (1718–92), 9th D. of Somerset; Hertford's cousin.

21. The complaint was made 16 March, at which time the printers of the paper were ordered to attend on the 19th (*Journals of the House of Lords*, loc. cit.).

22. John Meres, printer of the *London Evening Post* 1761–72; John Gretton, bookseller in Old Bond Street; and Charles Green Say (d. 1775), publisher of the *Gazetteer*, were ordered to attend (*Journals of the House of Lords* xxx. 508, 511; H. R. Plomer *et al.*, *A Dictionary of Printers and Booksellers . . . 1726–1775*, 1932, pp. 110, 167, 222).

23. When they were examined and ordered confined in Newgate until they paid a fine of £100 each after the paragraph had been voted 'false, malicious, and scandalous, a gross and wanton breach of the privilege of this House, and tending to the dishonour of the nation' (*Journals of the House of Lords* xxx. 511). HW gives an account of the debate on the punishment to be given in *Mem. Geo. III*, loc. cit.

from Mr Grenville himself. The *jaghire* is to be decided by law, that is, in the year 1900. Nor is it certain that his Omrahship[24] goes; that will depend on his obtaining a board of directors to his mind, at the approaching election.[25] I forgot, too, to answer your question about Luther;[26] and now I remember it, I cannot answer it. Some said his wife[27] had been gallant. Some, that he had been too gallant, and that she suffered for it. Others laid it to his expenses at his election; others again, to political squabbles on that subject between him and his wife[28]—but in short, as he sprung into the world by his election, so he withered when it was over, and has not been thought on since.

George Selwyn has had a frightful accident, that ended in a great escape. He was at dinner at Lord Coventry's and just as he was drinking a glass of wine, he was seized with a fit of coughing, the liquor went wrong, and suffocated him: he got up for some water at the side-board, but being strangled, and losing his senses, he fell against the corner of the marble table with such violence, that they thought he had killed himself by a fracture of his skull. He lay senseless for some time, and was recovered with difficulty. He was immediately blooded, and had the chief wound, which is just over the eye, sewed up—but you never saw so battered a figure. All round his eye is as black as jet, and besides the scar on his forehead, he has cut his nose at top and bottom. He is well off with his life, and we with his wit.

Yours most sincerely,

H. Walpole

PS. Lord Macclesfield has left his wife threescore thousand pounds.

---

24. An omrah was 'a lord or grandee of a Mohammedan court, esp. that of the Great Mongul' (OED).

25. Held 11 April; see *post* 12 April 1764.

26. Which Hertford had asked *ante* 18 Feb.

27. Levinia Bennet (living 1819), daughter of Bennet Alexander (later Bennet Alexander Bennet), m. (1762) John Luther (Philip Morant, *History . . . of Essex*, 1768, ii. 129, 187; T. Faulkner, *History and Antiquities of Brentford*, 1845, p. 485; John Burke, *Genealogical and Heral-*

dic History of the Commoners, 1836–8, iv. 10; Namier and Brooke ii. 130, iii. 63).

28. Luther's friend Watson, in his account of the separation (*ante* 18 Feb. 1764, n. 11), writes that though 'Luther was a thorough honest man . . . his temper was warm, and his wife (a very deserving woman) had been overpersuaded to marry him,—had she loved him as he loved her, she would have borne with his infirmity of temper' (*Anecdotes of the Life of Richard Watson, Bishop of Landaff*, 1817, p. 28).

From Beauchamp, ca Tuesday 20 March 1764

Printed for the first time from a photostat of BM Add. MSS 23219, ff. 175–6. Dated approximately by the reference to the order for the expulsion of the Jesuits for refusing to take the oath, which was decreed by the parliament of Paris 9 March (*ante* 8 March 1764, n. 4), and by this letter's probably being the one from Beauchamp HW mentions he will answer, *post* 27 March 1764.

My dear Sir,

PERMIT me to interest your humanity in favour of a poor Jesuit;[1] do not be shocked at his profession! He has none of the vices which we heretics attribute so indiscriminately to the Society. The case is this: The parliament of Paris has lately given the Jesuits the *coup de grâce* in enjoining them to take an oath inconsistent with their honour, or in case of disobedience to leave the kingdom before the 10th of next month. They are already upon the wing. My friend wishes to take refuge in England. Do you think he can find any resources in London? He has been professor of belles-lettres at the great college here, he knows the English and German, and is a very good scholar. He would submit to translate English books into French, to teach the French, to be preceptor to young people, in short he wants to have a certain subsistence which the tyranny of his countrymen has deprived him of. Pray let me know your thoughts upon the subject, and believe me ever, dear Sir,

Your affectionate friend and servant,

Beauchamp

---

1. From the description Beauchamp gives below of the person, he is probably Antoine-Remy Arnoult (b. 1734), professor of the humanities at the Collège de Louis le Grand, 1761 until the suppression of the Jesuit faculty in 1762 (G. Dupont-Ferrier, *Du Collège de Clermont au Lycée Louis-le-Grand (1563–1920)*, 1921–5, iii. 56). There is no record that he came to England.

From Hertford, Thursday 22 March 1764

Printed for the first time from a photostat of BM Add. MSS 23218, ff. 135–6.

Paris, March 22d 1764.

My dear Horry,

WE are not likely now to have a new first mistress for this kingdom. Madame de Pompadour is recovering.[1] The physicians think her danger over for the fever; the risk she has to run is from her lungs. The disorder was chiefly seated there. If she had died we should have had many competitors for her place. Some think it would have fallen upon a young woman[2] by whom the King has had a son[3] who is now two years old; others tell you that she would not have had sense enough to have employed the very many idle hours his Majesty has to trifle away, and that her youth would have been no recommendation, since there are always handsome girls kept at Versailles[4] for the King's amusement in that way when he is so disposed; but that he must have taken a woman of sense in whose apartment he might have gone sixty times a day as he now does to unburthen his mind and receive advice. Others think he might have fallen into devotion and the hands of the clergy. His Majesty has been very constant in his attendance upon the Marchioness during her illness, and yet in her greatest danger he preserved a gaiety very incompatible with affection. His attachment therefore I

1. 'By the last advices from Paris, bearing date the 23d of March, it appears, that Madame Pompadour's illness was considerably abated, the fever with which she had been afflicted being much less violent, and all the other unfavourable symptoms decreasing, so that they were at that time not without great hopes of her recovery' (*St James's Chronicle* 31 March–3 April). Another correspondent attributed the recovery to Hertford: 'A letter from Paris, to a gentleman in the neighbourhood of Reading, says, that Madame Pompadour had been extremely ill, and thought past recovery, on which account the King was inconsolable; but that Lord Hertford, the British ambassador, had sent her some of Dr James's Powder;

which she took and has since mended every day; so that at present there is no appearance of danger' (*London Chronicle* 3–5 April, xv. 327).

2. Anne Couppier (1737–1808), called Mlle de Romans, m. (1772) Gabriel de Siran, Marquis de Cavanac (MANN vi. 4, n. 23).

3. Louis-Aimé de Bourbon (1762–87); see ibid.

4. In an apartment of the château or in *petites maisons* in the Parc-aux-Cerfs; the young girls so kept were sold into bondage by their parents or guardians, and were under the direction of Madame de Pompadour (Maurice, Comte Fleury, *Louis XV intime et les petites maîtresses*, 1909, pp. 189–90 *et passim*).

take to be mere *habitude*, which would soon have found relief in some other person.

I am just come from Madame d'Usson's where I found Madame de Bouflers. We talked of you and your journey to Paris. We talked likewise of your niece, and I found they were better informed than me, for they told me the Duke of Portland was the likely man to prevent her journey here.

Has my brother told you that I have hired the best house at Paris?[5] It is charming. It is upon the river; it has a very large garden; it has the finest apartment, and is town and country, exactly what it should be for an ambassador who is to make a show and to live in it both summer and winter. Monsieur de Lauragais[6] who is the proprietor has acted as handsomely as my present landlord acted ill, and yet you may be told that he has a *mauvaise tête*. He has indeed had some family disputes[7] that do not do him credit, but he is a man of parts with some knowledge[8] and he has done well by me.

I saw last night at the French comedy *Olimpie*,[9] a tragedy of Voltaire's which of course you know. It is well acted and well received, though the piece is in itself not much admired.

I have government letters[10] to finish to send by the messenger[11]

5. 'The Earl of Hertford has taken the Hotel de Lauragnais [sic] at Paris, formerly the Hotel de Lassay, at £500 sterling a year. The Count de Lauragnais reserves the pavillion which he used to occupy' (*London Chronicle* 22–4 March, xv. 288). It was apparently known officially as the Hôtel de Brancas, Rue de l'Université (*Almanach royal*, 1765, p. 134).

6. Louis-Léon-Félicité de Brancas (1733–1824), Comte de Lauraguais, later Duc de Brancas.

7. Though married since 1755, around 1761 Lauraguais began a liaison with the actress, Sophie Arnould, by whom he had three sons, the last in 1764; his wife demanded a separation in 1765, which he refused (*Dictionnaire de biographie française*, 1933– , vii. 145). HW wrote in 1766 that Lauraguais was also 'at variance with his father' (COLE i. 110).

8. He was a scientist and miscellaneous writer who had been elected *mécanicien adjoint* of the Académie des Sciences in 1758, had composed a tragedy, *Clytem-*

nestra, in 1761, and published a *Mémoire sur l'Inoculation* in 1763 (*Dictionnaire de biographie française*, loc. cit.; NBG).

9. 'On the 17th instant was acted at Paris, a tragedy by Voltaire, entitled, *Olimpie*, which, notwithstanding the disorder and tumult that always accompany the first representation of a new play, gave great pleasure, and was allowed to be in every respect worthy of the author' (*London Chronicle* loc. cit.). However, one spectator, Sir Alexander Macdonald, described it as 'a very bad play, founded on an improbable story, full of inconsistencies, without one good character; and yet it was so well acted that it has had a remarkable success' (Reginald Blunt, *Mrs Montagu*, [1923], i. 97).

10. Hertford's letter to Halifax, 22 March, about a conference he had had that day with Praslin, is in S.P. 78/260, ff. 247–8.

11. William Pollock (ibid. f. 248), listed as a King's messenger in the *Court and City Register* through 1779.

who carries this. I shall therefore only add the best compliments of the family with the assurance of being, dear Horry,

Always most sincerely and affectionately yours,

HERTFORD

From HERTFORD, Sunday 25 March 1764

Printed for the first time from a photostat of BM Add. MSS 23218, ff. 137–8.

Paris, March 25th 1764.

Dear Horry,

MY brother has acquainted me with the insult offered to my character in his[1] two papers, and the zeal and tenderness he has shown in resenting it. The attack I suspect must have come from Wilkes, who is every Sunday at my chapel here and has betrayed the idea to me by laughing frequently during the time of service, for which he seems in this dirty paragraph to have furnished a key by expressing his dissatisfaction at Mr Trail's reading the liturgy.[2] If it did not come from him I should be at a loss to account for the author.[3] I have not particularly offended any set of men nor am I of consequence enough to be unjustly abused by party; on the other hand I have given no person cause[4] to be so far my private enemy as to give this very unjust wound to my character.

It must therefore be the act of some madman who scatters darts and firebrands without reflection, or the more premeditated act of some villain to indulge private pique and resentment. My behaviour to Mr Wilkes has been, notwithstanding this, very inoffensive, and he has declared himself at different times much satisfied with it; but

1. 'His' written over (?) 'my' in the MS.
2. Wilkes mentions in a letter to Churchill having 'learned Erse' from his attendance at Trail's services (*The Correspondence of John Wilkes and Charles Churchill*, ed. E. H. Weatherly, New York, 1954, p. 87).
3. Hertford had apparently already received an explicit denial from Wilkes of the authorship of the paragraph, since

Conway, answering a letter from Hertford of the same date as this one, writes: 'As to Mr Wilkes and his denial, I think it very indifferent whether that impertinence was his or anybody's else. It has only brought shame to them' (Conway to Hertford 31 March, MS now WSL).
4. 'Cause' written over 'reason' in the MS.

in talking of my suspicion to Mr Hume, who has now and then conversed with Wilkes here, he has increased it extremely by acquainting me that he once said to him when they were joking together that it was more prudent to be upon friendly terms, as the contrary might produce paragraphs which it would be very easy to send to England, that might be extremely unpleasant to the embassy here. This then I suspect is the first specimen of some dislike, and as there is no principle to restrain it I wish it may not be followed by others. Till I am more sure I shall however speak little of my suspicion, and in the meantime my warmest wishes will be exerted for the removal of this firebrand from Paris.

The House of Lords have done me great honour and made me the best reparation that a wounded man can receive. I am happy in discovering the share I have in the esteem of so many great persons and in the public testimony of the House of Peers. The rest of my consolation must arise from seeing that my enemy is a low one from his manner of acting, and that everyone who serves the Crown is subject to this sort of tax.

I am very sorry for Lord Malpas, for whom I now wear mourning.

We have now a great number of our countrymen here; my chapel was crowded yesterday to hear Doctor Sterne[5] preach. I remain, dear Horry, with the best compliments of the family,

Most truly and affectionately yours,

HERTFORD

---

5. Laurence Sterne (1713–68). His sermon on this occasion is printed in *The Sermons of Mr Yorick*, ed. Wilbur L. Cross, New York, 1904 (*The Works of Laurence Sterne*, Vol. V.), i. 269–84. See also idem, *The Life and Times of Laurence Sterne*, New Haven, 1925, ii. 32–4 for an account of Sterne's day at the embassy.

TO HERTFORD, Tuesday 27 March 1764

Printed from *Works* ix. 93-9.

Tuesday night, March 27th 1764.

YOUR brother has just told me, my dear Lord, at the opera, that Colonel Keith,[1] a friend of his, sets out for Paris on Thursday.[2] I take that opportunity of saying a few things to you, which would be less proper by the common post; and if I have not time to write to Lord Beauchamp too, I will defer my answer[3] to him till Friday, as the post office will be more welcome to read that.

Lord Bute is come to town,[4] has been long with the King alone, and goes publicly to Court and the House of Lords,[5] where the barony of Bottetourt[6] has engrossed them some days, and of which the town thinks much, and I not at all, so I can tell you nothing about it. The first two days, I hear, Lord Bute was little noticed, but today much court was paid to him, even by the Duke of Bedford.

1. Robert Murray Keith (1730–95), K.B. 1772; army officer and diplomatist. Conway mentioned him to his brother as 'a friend of mine whom I must particularly recommend to you and I think you'll like him, as he is lively, sensible and honest; he is one of our German companions, where he commanded one of the Highland Corps, and son to Vienna Keith whom you know' (Conway to Hertford, 31 March, MS now WSL).

2. He was apparently delayed, as Conway mentions, ibid., that he will send his letter (not finished until at least 1 April) by Keith.

3. Presumably to Beauchamp's letter of ca 20 March 1764.

4. 19 March. On the 20th Bedford told Grenville that he had heard 'from undoubted authority' that Bute 'had been with the King that morning from seven till eleven' (*Grenville Papers* ii. 498). An item on his return in the *St James's Chronicle* 20-2 March mentions a 'conference with his Majesty upwards of three hours' on the 20th.

5. 'The great Northern Star has again appeared at Court, at the private levee at the Queen's House; and, this day, at the House of Lords, to attend Mr Norborne Berkeley's peerage. I was myself a great while in the House . . . and did not know, that the Aurora Borealis had shined upon the House, till I came home; no noise in the streets, no curiosity to see it, no coming, or going from it, so as to raise my curiosity to ask, what was the matter, and what had created any extraordinary motion in the House. In short, hitherto, I don't hear, what effect this appearance has had, either at Court, or anywhere else. The influence of its light is, however, acknowledged everywhere. Upon who it will shine, is not yet known, or guessed; I believe, *none* of our friends will find themselves in a way of being scorched by it' (Newcastle to Legge 23 March, BM Add. MSS 32957, ff. 232-3).

6. Which had been in abeyance since 1407. Norborne Berkeley claimed the title as heir to a third of the barony; see the genealogical chart in GEC ii. 234. The House passed a resolution recognizing his claim 10 April and he was summoned by the title 13 April (*Journals of the House of Lords* xxx. 561, 572).

Why this difference, I don't know: that matters are somehow adjusted between the Favourite not Minister, and the Ministers not Favourites, I have no doubt. Pitt certainly has been treating with him, and so threw away the great and unexpected progress which the Opposition had made.[7] They, good people, are either not angry with him for this, or have not found it out. The Sandwiches and Rigbys, who feel another half year coming into their pockets, are not so blind. For my own part, I rejoice that the Opposition are only fools, and by thus missing their treaty, will not appear knaves. In the meantime, I have no doubt but the return of Lord Bute must produce confusion at Court. He and Grenville are both too fond of being ministers, not to be jealous of one another. If what is said to be designed proves true, that the King will go to Hanover,[8] and take the Queen with him, I shall expect that clamour (which you see depends on very few men, for it has subsided during these private negotiations) will rise higher than ever. The Queen's absence must be designed to leave the regency in the hands of another lady:[9] connect that with Lord Bute's return, and judge what will be the consequence! These are the present politics, at least mine, who trouble myself little about them, and know less. I have not been at the House this month; the great points which interested me are over,[10] and the very stand has shut the door. I might like some folks *out,* but there are so few that I desire to see *in,* that indifference is my present most predominating principle. The busier world are attentive to the election at Cambridge, which comes on next Friday,[11] and I think, now, Lord Sandwich's friends have little hopes. Had I a vote,[11a] it would not be given for the new Lord Hardwicke.

7. Conway, in his letter to his brother of 31 March, is noncommittal about this report; after mentioning Pitt's gout as the ostensible reason for the political armistice, he says 'though certain warm politicians I find imagine his inactivity is political, one must lie deep in the secret to know the truth of such mysteries.'

8. 'It is reported his Majesty will this spring visit his German dominions' (*London Chronicle* 10–13 March, xv. 241). 'We hear his Majesty will certainly visit his German dominions, soon after the rising of the Parliament, and that he will be accompanied in his journey by his brother Prince Henry' (*St James's Chronicle* 13–15 March).

9. The Princess Dowager of Wales.

10. 'For want of better sport in Parliament we have been lately piddling with little matters of trade etc.; there has not been a party question in the House the Lord knows when; the American bills are passed almost without opposition, except in the single article of the drawbacks on linen, which the government gave up to the German merchants' (Conway to Hertford 31 March).

11. 30 March.

11a. HW did not have one as he had never proceeded M.A.

But we have a more extraordinary affair to engage us, and of which *you* particularly will hear much more, indeed, I fear must be involved in. D'Éon has published (but to be sure you have already heard so) a most scandalous quarto,[12] abusing Monsieur de Guerchy outrageously, and most offensive to Messieurs de Praslin and Nivernois. In truth, I think he will have made all three irreconcilable enemies. The Duc de Praslin must be enraged as to the Duke's carelessness and partiality to D'Éon, and will certainly grow to hate Guerchy, concluding the latter can never forgive *him*. D'Éon, even by his own account, is as culpable as possible, mad with pride, insolent, abusive, ungrateful, and dishonest, in short, a complication of abominations, yet originally ill-used by his Court,[13] afterwards too well; above all, he has great malice, and great parts to put that malice in play. Though there are even many bad puns in his book, a very uncommon fault in a French book, yet there is much wit too.[14] Monsieur de Guerchy is extremely hurt, though with the least reason of the three, for his character for bravery and good nature is so established, that here, at least, he will not suffer. I could write pages to you upon this subject, for I am full of it—but I will send you the book. The Council have met today to consider what to do upon it.[15] Most people think it difficult for them to do anything. Lord Mansfield thinks they can—but I fear he has a little alacrity on the severe side in such cases. Yet I should be glad the law would allow severity in the present case. I should be glad of it, as I was in your case last week; and considering the present constitution of things, would put the severity of the law in execution. You will wonder at this sentence out of my mouth, but not when you

12. *Lettres, mémoires et négociations particulières du Chevalier d'Éon*, London, 1764, published 23 March (MANN vi. 216, n. 4). HW's copy, with several extra illustrations and his arms on the side, is now WSL (Hazen, *Cat. of HW's Lib.*, No. 2374).

13. Probably a reference to d'Éon's failure to get reimbursed for expenses contracted while carrying treaties from St Petersburg to Vienna and Versailles in 1757 and 1760; see MANN vi. 217 and nn. 8, 9, 12.

14. 'Hor. Walpole has been before me in sending you Monsieur d'Éon's book; what say you to such an attack upon your brother ambassador– This is rather worse than yours I told you of t'other day. But was ever anything so mad? H. W. admires it much as a work. I can't say I am much of his mind. There are few madmen without some wit; but there is surely a great predominancy of folly' (Conway to Hertford 31 March).

15. The meeting upon the d'Éon affair apparently did not take place until 30 March; see the letters exchanged between the Lord Chancellor and Grenville, 31 March, discussing possible courses of action which had been referred to the law officers of the Crown for consideration, in *Grenville Papers* ii. 280–3.

have heard my reason. The liberty of the press has been so much abused, that almost all men, especially such as have weight, I mean, grave hypocrites and men of arbitrary principles, are ready to demand a restraint. I would therefore show, that the law, as *it already stands,* is efficacious enough to repress enormities. I hope so, particularly in Monsieur de Guerchy's case, or I do not see how a foreign minister can come hither; if, while their persons are called *sacred,* their characters are at the mercy of every servant that can pick a lock and pay for printing a letter. It is an odd coincidence of accidents that has produced abuse on you and your tally in the same week—but yours was a flea-bite.

Thank you, my dear Lord, for your anecdotes relative to Madame Pompadour, her illness, and the pretenders to her succession. I hope she may live till I see her; she is one of the greatest curiosities of the age, and I am a pretty universal virtuoso. The match of my niece with the Duke of P[ortland] was, I own, what I hinted at, and what I then believed likely to happen. It is now quite off, and with very extraordinary circumstances; but if I tell it you at all, it must not be in a letter, especially when D'Éons steal letters and print them. It is a secret, and so little to the lover's advantage, that I who have a great regard for his family, shall not be the first to divulge it.[16]

We had, last night, a magnificent ball at Lady Cardigan's;[17] three sumptuous suppers in three rooms. The house, you know, is crammed with fine things, pictures, china, japan, vases, and every species of curiosity.[18] These are much increased even since I was in

16. HW, mentioning the attachment in *Mem. Geo. III,* shifts the blame for breaking it off to Lady Waldegrave; 'she slighted the subject, and aspired to the brother of the Crown' (iii. 268). This version is followed by Portland's biographer, but he prints in addition an undated letter from Portland's sister to the Duke that suggests HW's version here is more accurate: 'I have just been with Lady W[aldegrave]. I have endeavoured to say in the best manner I could what you desired. I have got her leave—that when you see her in public you may make her a bow, but as for speaking she desires you will not, and she says to everybody that asks her about you, that she found it was become the talk of the town that she was to be married to you, and as she

did not choose that, she had forbid you speaking to her, and desires that you will say the same, and that is all she shall say, and never shall name you. I assured her you would never say anything but name her with the greatest respect' (A. S. Turberville, *A History of Welbeck Abbey and Its Owners,* 1938–9, ii. 44).

17. 'Last night the Earl of Cardigan gave a grand entertainment and a ball at his house in Privy Gardens' (*London Chronicle* 24–7 March, xv. 293).

18. Lord Cardigan's private accounts in the 1750s contain a number of sums 'for freight and duty on foreign pictures and "pictures from Holland"' (Joan Wake, *The Brudenells of Deene,* 2d edn, rev., 1954, p. 279).

favour there,[19] particularly by Lord Montagu's importations.[20] I was curious to see how many quarrels my Lady must have gulped before she could fill her house—truly, not many (though some), for there were very few of her own acquaintance, chiefly recruits of her son and daughter.[21] There was not the *soupçon* of a Bedford, though the town has married Lord Tavistock and Lady Betty—but he is coming to you to France.[22] The Duchess of Bedford told me how hard it was, that I, who had personally offended my Lady Cardigan, should be invited, and that she, who had done nothing, and yet had tried to be reconciled, should not be asked. 'Oh, Madam,' said I, 'be easy as to that point, for though she has invited me, she will scarce speak to me'[23]—but I let all such quarrels come and go as they please: if people, so indifferent to me, quarrel with me, it is no reason why I should quarrel with them, and they have my full leave to be reconciled when they please.

I must trouble you once more to know to what merchant you consigned the Princess's trees, and Lady Hervey's *bibliothèque*—I mean for the latter. I did not see the Princess last week, as the loss of my nephew kept me from public places. Of all public places, guess the most unlikely one for the most unlikely person to have been at. I had sent to know how Lady Macclesfield did: Louis[24] brought me word that he could hardly get into St James's Square, there was so great a crowd to see my Lord lie in state. At night I met my Lady Milton[25] at the Duchess of Argyle's, and said in joke, 'Soh, to be sure, you have been to see my Lord Maclesfield lie in state!' thinking it impossible—she burst out into a fit of laughter, and owned she had. She and my Lady Temple had dined at Lady Betty's,[26] put on hats and cloaks, and literally waited on the steps of the house in the thick

19. HW had once been very intimate with Lady Cardigan, but she had 'broke' with him because of his comments on her grandfather, the 1st Duke of Marlborough, in the first edition of *The Royal and Noble Authors*, 1758; see BERRY i. 105, and MONTAGU ii. 89.

20. Paintings and antique bronzes bought in Rome in 1758, described by John Fleming, 'Lord Brudenell and his Bear-Leader,' *English Miscellany*, 1958, ix. 134–41.

21. Lady Elizabeth Montagu (1743–1827), m. (1767) Henry Scott, 3d D. of Buccleuch.

22. He left London 2 April and reached Paris 4 April (*post* 5 April 1764).

23. In *Works* the quotation is mistakenly carried to the end of the sentence.

24. (d. 1767), HW's Swiss servant (MONTAGU ii. 241).

25. Lady Caroline Sackville (1718–75), m. (1742) Joseph Damer, cr. (1753) Bn Milton and (1792) E. of Dorchester.

26. Probably Lady Elizabeth (or Betty) Berkeley (1680–1769), m. (1706) Sir John Germain; Lady Temple's aunt and close friend of the Sackvilles. She lived in St James's Square as had the E. of Macclesfield.

of the mob, while one posse was admitted and let out again for a second to enter, before they got in.

You will as little guess what a present I have had from Holland— only a treatise of mathematical metaphysics from an author I never heard of,[27] with great encomiums on my taste and knowledge. To be sure, I am warranted to insert this certificate among the *testimonia authorum,* before my next edition of the *Painters.* No,[28] I assure you, I am much more just—I have sent the gentleman word what a perfect ignoramus I am, and did not treat my vanity with a moment's respite. Your brother has laughed at me, or rather at the poor man who has so mistaken me, as much as ever I did at his *absence* and flinging down everything at breakfast. Tom, your brother's man, told him today, that *Mister Helvoetsluys* had been to wait on him—now you are guessing—did you find out this was Helvétius?

It is piteous late, and I must go to bed, only telling you a bon mot of Lady Bel Finch. Lord Bath owed her *half a crown;* he sent it next day, with a wish that he could give her *a crown.* She replied, that though he could not give her *a crown,* he could give her *a coronet,* and she was very ready to accept it.

I congratulate you on your new house, and am,

Your very sleepy humble servant,

Hor. Walpole

From Hertford, Thursday 5 April 1764

Printed for the first time from a photostat of BM Add. MSS 23218, ff. 139–40.

Paris, April 5th 1764.

Dear Horry,

LORD Tavistock arrived last night and went immediately to the Temple[1] to supper. The Prince de Conti, whom I have seen today, has just told me that he left London on Monday night, was

27. Possibly Andreas Böhm (1720–90), German mathematical philosopher, whose *Metaphysica* was published at Giessen in 1763 (NBG); see Hazen, op. cit., No. 552.
28. 'Nor' in *Works.*

1. The residence of the Prince de Conti. 'I arrived just in time to sup at the Temple on Wednesday last, where I was most extremely well received, and have great reason to be satisfied with all my friends'

detained at Dover six hours, was afterwards twelve hours upon the sea, and yet arrived here the third night, having been no longer than forty-eight hours in making the land journey. He called at my door this morning,[2] but I was at the Palais this forenoon to hear a pleading there. He gives an extraordinary account of the election at Cambridge in telling us that in so great a body of electors the numbers should be equal.[3] I hear it likewise reported from him that the Parliamentary business of this session is over,[4] and that Mr Pitt has lately taken an opportunity of abusing Mr Neville excessively.[5] Pray tell me on what occasion; as he was my predecessor[5a] here, I am curious to know.

The Court of France is hurt as you may easily conceive with the shameful and unprecedented behaviour of Deon.[6] How far the laws of England will permit the King to make use of his power in satisfying what he certainly owes in justice to the law of nations, I cannot determine; but I hope some method may be found to give him up, and to reconcile his Majesty's regard to the laws and privileges of his people with what he owes, as far as he is at liberty, to the security of his own affairs and those of the other powers in Europe with whom he is in connection.

If these enormities can be committed with impunity, every foreign minister dissatisfied with his own Court has it in his power to take vengeance on his sovereign, to betray the secrets of his Court and do infinite mischief to his country.[7] I am a friend to the liberty of the press, though I am a little sore perhaps at the unprovoked treatment I have lately met with; however I think I am still unprejudiced enough to decide fairly and impartially that it was never so much abused as it has been lately. In your father's time resemblances from history were thought sufficient to describe the man you wished to offend; nothing less is now sufficient than the name at length, and

reception of me' (Tavistock to Bedford 6 April, *Bedford Corr.* iii. 260).

2. 'I have not yet seen my Lord [Hertford], but found my Lady at home last night, who talked a great deal of their obligations to you for the part you took in the affair of the printers. They seem to be very well liked here' (ibid.).

3. See *post* 5 April 1764 *bis*.

4. Parliament was not prorogued until 19 April (*Journals of the House of Commons* xxix. 1059).

5. HW says in reply, *post* 12 April, that he knows nothing of this incident, nor has any other reference to it been found.

5a. As minister.

6. Praslin and Choiseul had complained to Hertford about d'Éon at Versailles, 3 April (Hertford to Halifax, 6 April, S.P. 78/261, ff. 19, 20).

7. Hertford is repeating part of the complaint made to him by Praslin and Choiseul (above, n. 6).

it is a tribute every private character seems likely to pay for any real or supposed weakness. In short, it is abominable and will be productive of every evil, since no man's character, which is his most valuable possession, is safe under these circumstances of abuse.

General Barrington[8] died on Tuesday night of an abscess in his head.

I hope in a fortnight or three weeks' time to get into my new house; the garden and situation are so fine that the season of the year makes it very desirable. Do not believe the papers about me;[9] I do not seem in favour with them. It will cost me more than six hundred a year, and I shall pay well in furniture etc. for the goodness of the house, but I am quite contented and happy about it provided I have justice done me. I remain, dear Horry, with the best compliments of the family,

Most affectionately yours,

HERTFORD

I will write to Rouen about Lady Harvey's *bibliothèque,* etc.

To HERTFORD, Thursday 5 April 1764

Printed from *Works* ix. 100–4.

Arlington Street, April 5, 1764.

YOUR idea, my dear Lord, of the abusive paragraph on you being conceived at Paris, and transmitted hither, tallies exactly with mine. I guessed that a satire on your whole establishment must come from thence: I said so immediately to two or three persons; but, I did not tell you I thought so, because I did not choose to fill you with suggestions for which I had no ground, but in my own reasoning. Your arguments convince me I was in the right. Yet, were you master of proofs, the wisest thing you can do, is to act as if you

---

8. Maj.-Gen. the Hon. John Barrington, d. 2 April 1764 (GM 1764, xxxiv. 198; *London Chronicle* 7–10 April, xv. 342).

9. The rest of this paragraph implies that Hertford is replying to some allusion made by HW to the item in the *London Chronicle* 22–4 March, xv. 288, stating that Hertford was paying £500 rent for the Hôtel de Brancas. It is possible that some such allusion was omitted from the last sentence in the printed text of HW's letter of 27 March.

had no suspicion; that is, to act as you have done, civilly, but coolly. There are men whom one would, I think, no more acknowledge for enemies than friends. One's resentment distinguishes them, and the only gratitude they can pay for that distinction is, to double the abuse. Wilkes's mind, you see, is sufficiently volatile, when he can already forget Lord Sandwich and the Scotch, and can employ himself on you. He will soon flit to other prey, when you disregard him. It is my way; I never publish a sheet, but buzz! out fly a swarm of hornets, insects that never settle upon you, if you don't strike at them; and whose venom is diverted to the next object that presents itself.

We have divine weather. The Bishop of Carlisle has been with me two days at Strawberry, where we saw the eclipse[1] to perfection:—not that there was much sight in it. The air was very chill at the time, and the light singular; but there was not a blackbird that left off singing for it. In the evening, the Duke of Devonshire came with the Straffords from t'other end of Twickenham,[2] and drank tea with us: they had none of them seen the Gallery since it was finished; even the Chapel was new to the Duke, and he was so struck with it, that he desired to offer at the shrine an incense pot of silver filigrain.

The election at Cambridge has ended, for the present, in strange confusion. The proctors,[3] who were of different sides,[4] assumed each a majority: the votes, however, appear to have been equal.[5] The learned in university decisions say, an equality is a negative: if so, Lord Hardwicke is excluded. Yet the novelty of the case, it not having been very customary to *solicit* such a trifling honour, and the antiquated forms of proceeding retained in colleges,[6] leave the matter wide open for further contention,[7] an advantage Lord

1. A partial eclipse of the sun, 1 April; see GM 1764, xxxiv. 193.

2. For the Strafford's house at Twickenham, see R. S. Cobbett, *Memorials of Twickenham*, 1872, p. 249.

3. Daniel Longmire (ca 1729–89), proctor 1763–4; vicar of Sawston, Cambs, 1755–7, of Linton 1759, of Norton, Suffolk, 1775–89; and Ralph Forster (ca 1732–1804), proctor 1763–4; curate of Horningsea, Cambs, 1766–73, rector of Great Warley, Essex, 1772–1804 (Venn, *Alumni Cantab.*).

4. Longmire was for Hardwicke, Forster for Sandwich (MANN vi. 219, n. 22).

5. See ibid.

6. See Thomas Gray, *Correspondence*, ed. Toynbee and Whibley, Oxford, 1935, iii. 1238, and D. A. Winstanley, *The University of Cambridge in the Eighteenth Century*, Cambridge, 1922, p. 105.

7. The Court of King's Bench declared Hardwicke elected 25 April 1765 (MANN, loc. cit.).

Sandwich cherishes as much as success. The grave are highly scandalized:—popularity was still warmer. The undergraduates, who, having no votes, had, consequently, been left to their *real* opinions, were very near expressing their opinions against Lord Sandwich's friends in the most outrageous manner: hissed they were; and after the election, the juniors burst into the Senate House, elected a fictitious Lord Hardwicke, and chaired him.[8] The indecent arts and applications which had been used by the *Twitcherites* (as they are called, from Lord Sandwich's nickname, *Jemmy Twitcher*) had provoked this rage. I will give you but one instance: a voter, who was blooded on purpose that morning, was brought out of a mad-house with his keeper. This is the great and wise nation, which the philosopher Helvétius is come to study! When he says of us, *C'est un furieux pays!* he does not know that the literal translation is the true description of us.[9]

I don't know whether I did not tell you some lies in my last—very likely—I tell you what I *hear,* and do not answer for truth but when I tell you what I *know.* How should I *know* anything? I am in no confidence: I think of both sides alike: I care for neither: I ask few questions. The King's journey to Hanover is contradicted.[10] The return of Lord Bute is still a mystery. The zealous say, he declares for the administration; but some of the latter do not trust too much to that security; and, perhaps, they are in the right: I know what I think and why I think it: yet some, who do not go on ill grounds, have a middle opinion, that is not very reconcilable to mine. You will not wonder that there is a mystery, doubt, or irresolution. The scene will be opened further before I get to Paris.

8. A correspondent in the *St James's Chronicle,* 10–12 April, complained that though 'a great deal of pains has been taken to set the world right about *placets* and *non-placets,* and other matters transacted within doors on our late former election for High Steward,' he did not 'remember to have seen any proper notice taken of the very splendid conduct of our young men on the occasion.' He therefore sent in an elaborate narrative of the conduct of the undergraduates, containing all the details mentioned by HW except for the chairing of the fictitious Lord Hardwicke (though he does relate that after the election, carried with only three dissentient voices, the undergraduates left in evidence of their act 'an instrument in due form, signifying what they had done, in the V.C.'s chair').

9. Figuratively and familiarly, *furieux* means 'impetuous, given to excess'; literally, it means 'violently mad.'

10. 'The several paragraphs that have appeared in newspapers, relative to his Majesty's journey to Hanover this season, were wholly groundless, no such thing having been ever intended' (*London Chronicle* 31 March – 3 April, xv. 320).

Lord Lyttelton and Lord Temple have dined with each other, and the reconciliation of the former with Mr Pitt is concluded.[11]—It is well that enmities are as frail as friendships.

The Archbishop and bishops, who are so eager against Dr Pearse's[12] divorce from his see,[13] not as illegal, but improper, and of bad example, have determined the King, who left it to them, not to consent to it, though the Bishop himself still insists on it. As this decision disappoints Bishop Newton,[14] Lord Bath has obtained a consolatory promise for him of the mitre of London,[15] to the great

11. Lyttelton's latest biographer has been unable to find any more details of either reconciliation; see Rose Mary Davis, *The Good Lord Lyttelton*, Bethlehem, Pennsylvania, 1939, p. 281. Lyttelton's relations with Temple and Pitt had begun to cool in 1754, after he had, without their authorization, pledged their support for Newcastle's administration (Namier and Brooke iii. 74).

12. Zachary Pearce, Bp of Rochester.

13. Pearce, sometime late in 1763, had asked the King's permission to resign his bishopric and the deanery of Westminster because of old age and after some delay had received the King's consent to do so. 'But unfortunately for the Bishop, Lord Bath, as soon as he heard of the King's consent being given, requested him to give the bishopric and deanery, which were to be resigned, to Doctor Newton, then Bishop of Bristol. This alarmed the ministry, who thought, as other ministers had done before them, that no dignities in the Church should be obtained from the Crown, but through their hands. They therefore resolved to oppose the resignation, as the shortest way of keeping the bishopric from being disposed of otherwise than they liked; and the lawyer [Lord Northington], who had been doubtful, and who soon after had been clear, was employed to inform his Majesty that he was then again doubtful, and that the bishops generally disliked the design. His Majesty upon this sent again, but at some distance of time, to the Bishop of Rochester, and at a third audience in his closet told him, that he must think no more about resigning the bishopric, but that he would have all the merit of having done it. The Bishop

replied, "Sire, I am all duty and submission," and then withdrew' (Pearce's autobiographical sketch in *The Lives of Dr Edward Pocock . . . Dr Zachary Pearce . . . Dr Thomas Newton*, 1816, i. 406–7). Reports of the intended resignation had appeared in the newspapers in mid-January, but were promptly denied (*St James's Chronicle* 17–19, 19–21 Jan.; *London Chronicle* 14–17, 28–31 Jan., xv. 49, 102 quoting the *Gazetteer*).

14. Thomas Newton (1704–82), Bp of Bristol 1761–82. Pearce and Lord Bath had intended that Newton, who had once been Bath's chaplain, should succeed the former in his bishopric and deanery (n. 13, above).

15. Newton, in his autobiography, gives a rather different account of the promises he had received. He writes that he 'was rather indifferent about the proposal' to succeed Pearce 'from the first, and afterwards was more so, when Mr Grenville advised him by no means to think of it, and assured him that better things were intended for him. . . . Upon the death of Bishop Osbaldeston in the spring of 1764 Mr Grenville, the Duke of Bedford, and others of the ministers agreed on the Bishop of Bristol as a proper person to fill the vacant see of London, and Mr Grenville in a particular manner recommended him to the King for the preferment. His Majesty [however] . . . had given some kind of promise for Bishop Terrick in Lord Bute's administration, which he thought himself now obliged to fulfill; and afterwards the Princess of Wales had the goodness at one time, and Lord Bute condescended at another, to speak to him concerning this matter, and in some measure apolo-

discomfort of Terrick[16] and Warburton.[17] You see Lord Bath does not hobble up the back stairs for nothing. Oh, he is an excellent courtier! The Prince of Wales shoots him with plaything arrows; he falls down dead; and the child kisses him to life again. Melancholy ambition! I heard him, t'other night, propose himself to Lady Townshend as a rich widow. Such spirits at fourscore are pleasing; but when one has lost all one's children,[18] to be flattering those of Kings!

The Bishop of Carlisle told me, that t'other day in the House of Lords, Warburton said to another of the Bench, 'I was invited by my Lord Mansfeld to dine with that Helvétius, but he is a professed patron of atheism, a rascal, and a scoundrel, and I would not countenance him; besides, I should have worked him, and that Lord Mansfeld would not have liked.'—No, in good truth: who can like such vulgarism! His French, too, I suppose, is equal to his wit and his piety.

I dined, on Tuesday, with the Imperial Minister;[19] we were two and twenty, collected from the four corners of the earth. Since it is become the fashion to banquet whole kingdoms, by turns, I should pray, if I was minister, to be sent to Lucca. Have you received D'Éon's very curious book, which I sent by Colonel Keith? I do not find that the administration can discover any method of attacking him.[20] Monsieur de Guerchy very properly determines to take no

gized for it' (*The Lives of Dr Edward Pocock*, [etc.], ii. 149, 152). Later in the year Newton was offered the primacy of Ireland, but declined it.

16. Richard Terrick (1710–77), Bp of Peterborough 1757–64, of London 1764–77. Grenville subsequently (8 May) informed Warburton that when he had first approached the King about a successor to the bishopric of London, he found that the King had destined Terrick to the see 'even so early as when the present Bishop of London was appointed to it,' and that he 'considered himself as too strongly engaged to depart from it upon the present occasion' (*Grenville Papers* ii. 314).

17. He was not yet openly a candidate for the see, but a month later, on a report of Bishop Osbaldeston's death, he asked Grenville for the translation, only to be informed of the prior promise to Terrick (ibid. ii. 313–15, 316).

18. His only son, William Pulteney (b. ca 1731), styled Vct Pulteney, had died in 1763, while his only daughter, Anna Maria (b. 1727), had died in 1742.

19. Seilern.

20. The Duke of Bedford had the day before suggested the seizing of d'Éon's papers by Sir John Fielding's warrant; but Grenville had opposed such a step which would, he feared, 'in the present situation, contribute very little to put a stop to what is complained of, and would, if the legality of the proceedings should be even questionable, be the subject of much clamour and uneasiness' (ibid. ii. 286). The two secretaries of state and the legal officers had also planned a meeting on 3 April on the steps that could be taken, but nothing was finally done until the 9th (ibid.; *post* 12 April 1764, n. 25).

notice of it. In the meantime, the wit of it gains ground, and palliates the abomination, though it ought not.

Princess Amelia asked me again about her trees. I gave her your message. She does not blame you, but Madame de Boufflers, for sending them so large. Mr Legge is in a very bad way; but not without hopes: his last night was better.[21]

Adieu! my dear Lords and Ladies!

Yours, ever,

H. W.

To HERTFORD, Thursday 12 April 1764

Printed from *Works* ix. 105–9.

Arlington Street, April 12th 1764.

MAKE yourself perfectly easy, my dear Lord, about newspapers and their tattle; they are not worth a moment's regard. In times of party it is impossible to avoid abuse. If attached to one side, one is pelted by the other; if to neither, by both. One can place oneself above deserving invectives; and then it signifies little, whether they are escaped or not. But when one is conscious that they are unmerited, it is noblest to scorn them—perhaps, I even think, that such a situation is not ineligible. Character is the most precious of all blessings; but, pray allow that it is too sacred to be hurt by anything but itself: does it depend on others, or on its own existence? That character must be fictitious, and formed for man, which man can take away. Your reputation does not depend on Mr Wilkes, like his own. It is delightful to deserve popularity, and to despise it.

You will have heard of the sad misfortune that has happened to Lord Ilchester by his daughter's marriage with O'Brien the actor.[1] But, perhaps, you do not know the circumstances, and how much his grief must be aggravated by reflection on his own credulity and negli-

---

21. He died 23 Aug. (*post* 27 Aug. 1764).

———

1. Lady Susan Sarah Louisa Fox-Strangways (1743–1827), m. (7 April 1764) William O'Brien (d. 1815), actor. For further details see Lord Ilchester, *Henry Fox*, 1920, ii. 278–9, and Lady Sarah Bunbury's letter to Lady Susan in *The Life and Letters of Lady Sarah Lennox*, ed. Lady Ilchester and Lord Stavordale, 1902, i. 137ff.

gence. The affair has been in train for eighteen months. The swain had learned to counterfeit Lady Sarah Bunbury's hand so well, that in the country Lord Ilchester has himself delivered several of O'Brien's letters to Lady Susan; but it was not till about a week before the catastrophe that the family was apprised of the intrigue. Lord Cathcart went to Miss Reade's,[2] the paintress—she said softly to him—'My Lord, there is a couple in next room that I am sure ought not to be together, I wish your Lordship would look in.' He did, shut the door again, and went directly and informed Lord Ilchester. Lady Susan was examined, flung herself at her father's feet, confessed all, vowed to break off—but—what a *but!*—desired to see the loved object, and take a last leave. You will be amazed—even this was granted. The parting scene happened the beginning of the week. On Friday she came of age, and on Saturday morning—instead of being under lock and key in the country—walked downstairs, took her footman, said she was going to breakfast with Lady Sarah,[3] but would call at Miss Reade's; in the street, pretended to recollect a particular cap in which she was to be drawn, sent the footman back for it, whipped into a hackney chair, was married at Covent Garden Church, and set out for Mr O'Brien's villa at Dunstable. My Lady— my Lady Hertford! what say *you* to permitting young ladies to act plays,[4] and go to painters by themselves?

Poor Lord Ilchester is almost distracted; indeed, it is the completion of disgrace—even a footman were preferable; the publicity of the hero's profession perpetuates the mortification. *Il ne sera pas milord, tout comme un autre.* I could not have believed that Lady Susan would have stooped so low. She may, however, still keep good company, and say, 'Nos numeri sumus'[5]—Lady Mary Duncan,[6] Lady Caroline Adair,[7] Lady Betty Gallini[8]—the shopkeepers of next age

2. Catherine Read (d. 1778), portrait painter. An engraving of her portrait of Lady Susan is ibid. ii. facing p. 136.

3. Lady Sarah Bunbury.

4. HW mentions to Montagu, 22 Jan. 1761, Lady Susan's acting in a play at Holland House (MONTAGU i. 335); presumably she had met O'Brien at one of these amateur performances.

5. HW's variation of 'Nos numerus sumus' (Horace, *Epistles* I. ii. 27): 'We are mere ciphers.'

6. Lady Mary Tufton (1723–1806), daughter of 7th E. of Thanet, m. (1763)

William Duncan, M.D., cr. (1764) Bt (Collins, *Peerage,* 1812, iii. 446).

7. Lady Caroline Keppel (1737–69), daughter of the 2d E. of Albemarle, m. (1759) Robert Adair, surgeon (ibid. iii. 741).

8. Lady Elizabeth Bertie (ca 1724–1804), daughter of 3d E. of Abingdon, m. (at an unknown date) Giovanni Andrea Battista (called John) Gallini, cr. a papal Kt; dancing master and later manager of the Italian opera in London (DNB *sub* Gallini; GM 1804, lxxiv pt ii. 795).

will be mighty well born. If our genealogies had been so confused four hundred years ago, Norbo[r]ne Berkeley would have had still more difficulty with his obsolete barony of Bottetourt, which the House of Lords at last has granted him.[9] I have never attended the hearings, though it has been much the fashion, but nobody cares less than I about what they don't care for. I have been as indifferent about other points, of which all the world is talking, as the restriction of franking,[10] and the great cause of Hamilton and Douglas.[11] I am almost as tired of what is still more in vogue, our East India affairs. Mir Jaffeir and Cossim Aly Cawn, and their deputies Clive and Sullivan,[12] or rather their principals, employ the public attention, instead of Mogul Pitt and Nabob Bute, the former of whom remains shut in Asiatic dignity at Hayes,[13] while the other is again mounting his elephant and levying troops. What Lord Tavistock meaned of his

9. 10 April (*Journals of the House of Lords* xxx. 561). 'You know to be sure that Berkeley has carried his great cause and is now the happiest lord in England. I hear he has said he did not think it was in human nature to be so happy' (Conway to Hertford 12 April, MS now WSL).

10. A committee of the House of Commons had been sitting since 1 March 'to inquire into the several frauds and abuses in relation to the sending of letters and parcels free from the duty of postage; and to consider the most proper methods of preventing the same,' following complaints about the forging of franks. A bill (eventually 4 Geo. III, c. 24) was presented 3 April, passed the Commons on the 11th, the Lords on the 16th, and received the royal assent the 19th (*Journals of the House of Commons* xxix. 893, 1027, 1047, 1056; *Journals of the House of Lords* xxx. 578). The principal change it required was that the whole superscription be in the hand of the franker, not merely his signature. Part of the controversy over the bill centred on repeated Opposition attempts to include a clause prohibiting the opening of enclosed letters (*Journals of the House of Commons* xxix. 908, 1027; *Grenville Papers* ii. 493–4).

11. The *cause célèbre* between the guardians of James George Hamilton (1755–69), 7th D. of Hamilton, and those of Archibald James Edward Douglas (before 1761 Stewart) (1748–1827), cr. (1790) Bn Douglas, over the succession to the Lanarkshire estates of the 1st D. of Douglas (d. 1761). Young Douglas's guardians had claimed them for him as heir by entail (nephew) of the Duke while Hamilton's disputed the claim for their ward (the Duke's cousin and heir male of the family), charging that Douglas was a supposititious child. The case had been in the Scottish courts since 1762; both parties had recently filed cross appeals to the House of Lords on certain details in the proceedings, on which the Lords had heard counsel 10, 11 and 12 April, giving judgment 13 April (*Journals of the House of Lords* xxx. 563, 566, 568–9, 573). The case was not settled until 1769 when the House of Lords, on appeal, decided in favour of Douglas, reversing the 1767 decision of the Scottish Court of Session.

12. Laurence Sulivan (ca 1713–86), deputy chairman of the East India Company 1763–4, 1772–3, 1780–1; chairman 1758–9, 1760–2, 1781–2; M.P Taunton 1762–8, Ashburton 1768–74. Clive and Sulivan were personal enemies, and Clive had refused to return to India as long as Sulivan remained in control of the Company (A. M. Davies, *Clive of Plassey*, 1939, p. 359).

13. Where he was suffering from the gout.

invisible Haughtiness's invective on Mr Neville, I do not know. He has not been in the House of Commons since the war of privilege. It must have been something he dropped in private.

I was diverted just now with some old rhymes that Mr Wilkes would have been glad to have North-Britonized for our little Bishop of Osnaburgh.[14]

> Eligimus puerum, puerorum festa colentes,
> Non nostrum morem, sed Regis jussa sequentes.[15]

They were literally composed on the election of a juvenile bishop.

Young Dundas[16] marries Lady Charlotte Fitzwilliam. Sir Lawrence[17] settles four thousand per annum in present, and six more in future—compare these riches got in two years and a half,[18] with D'Éon's account of French economy![19] Lord Garlies remarries[20] himself with the Duchess of Manchester's[21] next sister, Miss Dashwood.[22] The youngest is to have Mr Knightley[23]—apropos to D'Éon, the

14. Frederick Augustus (1763–1827), 2d son of George III, cr. (1784) D. of York, had been elected Bp of Osnaburgh in Feb. (GM 1764, xxxiv. 143).

15. 'We elect a boy, celebrating the feast of boys, following not our custom, but the orders of the King.' The lines were composed and handed about on the occasion of the election of the youthful Jean, archdeacon of Orléans, to the bishopric of that see in 1096. He had been nominated for the position by Philippe I of France as a favour to Raoul II, archbishop of Tours, whose *mignon* Jean had reputedly been, and the lines were quoted by Yves, bishop of Chartres, at the end of a letter he wrote to Pope Urban II (*Patrologiæ cursus completus . . . series* [*latina*], ed. J.-P. Migne, 1844–65, clxii. 85–7) protesting the nomination and election on the grounds of Jean's youth and moral turpitude. The phrase, *puerorum festa colentes*, refers sarcastically to the fact that the election had taken place on the 28th of Dec., the day of the *festa puerorum* or feast of the innocents, held in commemoration of the slaughter of the innocents by Herod, at which a boy 'bishop' was traditionally elected to preside over the celebration (P. B. Gams, *Series episcoporum*, Ratisbon, 1873, p. 593; M. J. Rigollot d'Amiens, *Monnaies*

inconnues des évêques des innocens, des fous, [*etc.*], 1837, pp. 143–6). For a full account of the 'boy bishop,' see E. K. Chambers, *Medieval Stage*, 1903, i. 336–71.

16. Thomas Dundas (1741–1820), 2d Bt, 1781; cr. (1794) Bn Dundas, m. (14 May 1764) Lady Charlotte Fitzwilliam.

17. Sir Lawrence Dundas (ca 1710–81), cr. (1762) Bt; M.P. Linlithgow burghs 1747–8, Newcastle-under-Lyme 1762–8, Edinburgh 1768–80, 1781, Richmond 1780–1; commissary general and contractor to the army 1748–59; father of Thomas Dundas.

18. Probably a reference to Dundas's profits on his offices during the early years of the Seven Years' War; at his death he left an estate of £16,000 a year and 'a fortune of £900,000 in personalities and landed property' (GEC, *Baronetage*).

19. See *ante* 27 March 1764, n. 13.

20. His first wife (m. 1762) was Lady Charlotte Mary Greville (1745–63), 3d daughter of the 1st E. Brooke of Warwick Castle.

21. Elizabeth Dashwood (ca 1741–1832), eldest daughter of Sir James Dashwood, 2d Bt, m. (1762) George Montagu, 4th D. of Manchester.

22. Anne Dashwood (ca 1743–1830). The wedding took place 13 June.

23. Catherine Dashwood (d. 1809), m.

foreign ministers had a meeting yesterday morning at the Imperial Minister's[24] and Monsieur de Guerchy went from thence to the King, but on what result I do not know, nor can I find that the lawyers agree, that anything can be done against him.[25] There has been a plan of some changes among the *dii minores,* your Lord Norths, and Carysforts,[26] and Ellises, and Frederick Campbells, and such like; but the supposition that Lord Holland would be willing to accommodate the present ministers with the paymaster's place, being the axle on which this project turned, and his Lordship not being in the accommodating humour, there are half a dozen abortions of new lords of the Treasury and Admiralty[27]—excuse me if I do not send you this list of embryos; I do not load my head with such fry. I am little more *au fait* of the confusion that happened

(14 April 1764) Lucy Knightley (1742–91), of Fawsley, Northants, M.P. Northampton borough 1763–8, Northamptonshire 1773–84 (GM 1809, lxxix pt ii. 683).

24. Seilern's. Selwyn, writing to Lord Holland 17 April, mentions that 'the *corps diplomatique* have had one or two meetings to consider what satisfaction should be demanded, but all I can learn from them is that it is a *cause commune*' (*Letters to Henry Fox,* ed. Lord Ilchester, Roxburghe Club, 1915, pp. 193–4, where the letter is erroneously dated ?18 Oct. 1763).

25. On 9 April, Halifax had informed the Attorney-General that 'his (the Attorney-General's) opinion, and that of the Advocate and Solicitor-General, that the book supposed to be written and published by M. d'Éon . . . and complained of by the Count de Guerchy . . . is a libel, and as such punishable by indictment or information' had been laid before the King, and that he having 'at the same time informed his Majesty of the doubts which were suggested on his, the Attorney's part, with respect to a different way of proceeding against the author, it is his Majesty's pleasure that a prosecution be immediately commenced against the author, printers, and publishers, and that he should file an information against them in the King's Bench' (*Calendar of Home Office Papers, 1760–1765,* ed. J. Redington, 1878, p. 402).

26. John Proby (1720–72), cr. (1752) Bn

Carysfort; a lord of the Admiralty 1757, 1763–5.

27. Similar reports were still abroad five days later, when the postscript to the *London Chronicle* 14–17 April reported: 'We hear that the Right Hon. Mr Stanley will be made secretary at war, in the room of Mr Ellis; and that Lord North and Mr Ellis will be appointed joint paymasters-general of the army in the room of the Right Hon. Henry Fox, Lord Holland, who will be raised to the dignity of an earl' (xv. 368). The reports reached Holland in Paris, who informed a correspondent, 15 April, that 'I have not had a hint directly or indirectly about my place. So that these rumours spring from those who wish me removed, and not from those who can remove me' (Lord Ilchester, *Henry Fox,* 1920, ii. 277). Selwyn, writing to Holland 17 April, observes that a mention about his place in a letter from him 'tallies exactly with what I heard Lord Thomond say today, in contradiction to a report that a proposal had been sent to you from Bedford House to quit it. The report added that you had mentioned the privy seal as an alternative' (idem, *Letters to Henry Fox,* p. 194). Conway also mentions, 12 April, 'a strong report here that Lord Holland is out of the pay office or to be so immediately, and the office is to be divided between Ellis and either Stanley or Lord North and the other to be secretary at war. This is all mystery to me' (Conway to Hertford 12 April).

yesterday at the East India House;[28] I only know it was exactly like the jumble at Cambridge. Sullivan's list was chosen,[29] all but himself—his own election turns on one disputed vote.[30] Everything is intricate—a presumption that we have few heads very clear. Good night, for I am tired; since dinner I have been at an auction of prints,[31] at the Antiquarian Society in Chancery Lane,[32] at Lady Dalkeith's in Grosvenor Square, and at loo at my niece's[33] in Pall Mall; I left them going to supper, that I might come home and finish this letter; it is half an hour after twelve, and now I am going to supper myself. I suppose all this sounds very sober to you!

Yours ever,

H. Walpole

28. At the election of directors for the coming year.

29. There were a total of 36 candidates for 24 positions on the board of directors; of these, 12 were on the House (Sulivan's) list only, 12 on the Proprietors' (Clive's) list only, and 12 were double-listed (meaning they were acceptable to both sides). The 12 double-listed were of course all elected, while 8 of Sulivan's list, to 4 of Clive's, were chosen (*London Chronicle* 12–14 April, xv. 353; Lucy S. Sutherland, *The East India Company in Eighteenth-Century Politics*, Oxford, 1952, pp. 109, 129).

30. Sulivan's election turned in part on the validity of the vote of Mrs Drummond, wife of the Archbishop of York, it being in question whether she could be considered an owner of stock in her own right. After investigation, her ballot was not admitted. 'Upon this very nice circumstance did the certainty of Mr Sulivan's being elected into the direction depend. For it is remarkable, that the numbers of the last three gentlemen [Cummings, Smith, and Sulivan] were equal, being 604 each; and if Mrs Drummond's ballot had been admitted (which was for the Proprietor's list) it would have given Mr Cummings 605, and put Mr Cruttenden upon an equality with Mr Smith and Mr Sulivan. Mr Cummings would consequently have been elected by a clear majority; and it must have been determined by casting lots (agreeable to the charter) which two out of Messrs Smith, Sulivan, and Cruttenden, should come into the direction' (*London Chronicle*, loc. cit.; *St James's Chronicle* 12–14 April).

31. Presumably to view the 'collection of prints, books of prints and fine drawings, of the late Mr Alexander Waddes . . . amongst which are the capital of M. Antonio, Rembrandt, Rubens, etc.'; the actual sale began 13 April (*Daily Adv.* 12 April).

32. Of which HW had been a member since 1753. He later (1772) struck his name from their book (Gray i. 28, n. 188; 47).

33. Lady Waldegrave's; she was presumably living in her father's house in Pall Mall.

From HERTFORD, Sunday 15 April 1764

Printed for the first time from a photostat of BM Add. MSS 23218, ff. 141–2.

Paris, April 15th 1764.

Dear Horry,

MADAME Pompadour is at last dying.[1] She has made her will,[2] received extreme unction, knows her own danger, enjoys her senses perfectly, and meets death with great firmness and resignation. Who her successor will be I cannot yet tell you. Madame de Grammont,[3] the Duke de Choiseuil's sister, will be a candidate, but her beauty cannot decide for her. The King, it is said, must have a woman, but it is not yet clear what perfections are to determine the choice. I shall divert myself with the competition; it may be an entertaining one.

I am glad you had fine weather in England for the eclipse; it is some credit to our climate. We had here the darkest of days with a great deal of rain; consequently the only apparent symptoms of eclipse were an additional darkness for some minutes and the sinking of the thermometer about two degrees. The fine ladies of Paris were assembled at the observatory early in the morning for this sight, but were so much disappointed that perhaps the eclipse may not be generally believed here.

I am much obliged to you for Déon's book; everybody is curious to read it,[4] but as my brother ambassador and the minister here with whom we negotiate[5] are so roughly treated, I am very prudent about it. I think there is parts with some knowledge in it, but there is much more malice with a great deal of passion and madness. The Court of France, the foreign ministers, and all ranks of people here are much offended at it. You will not be surprised if they are unwilling to be persuaded that the laws of England can protect him for

1. She died the same day; see post-script.

2. Rather she added a second codicil to her will of 15 Nov. 1757 (with first codicil of 30 March 1761); her will is printed in full in Edmond and Jules de Goncourt, *Madame de Pompadour,* 1888, pp. 306–12.

3. Béatrix de Choiseul-Stainville (1730–99), m. (1759) Antoine-Antonin, Duc de Gramont. For her unsuccessful 'candidacy'

to succeed Mme de Pomadour, see Comte Fleury, *Louis XV intime et les petites maîtresses,* 1909, pp. 288–9.

4. The demand for the book was so great in Paris that Lord Holland lent his copy 'about by the hour' (Robert Digby to Selwyn 19 April, J. H. Jesse, *George Selwyn and his Contemporaries,* 1882, i. 276).

5. Praslin.

such a breach of trust in a public character.[6] I talk however like an Englishman, and they hear as Frenchmen who have no such ideas.

The Princess's trees and Lady Harvey's *bibliothèque* must surely be at the custom-house in London. They were shipped at Rouen months ago and must be arrived long since in London; be so good to send there and inquire. It makes me uneasy that anything which passes through my hands should be so long delayed, but I am innocent in having done what I could to forward them; be so good to tell the Princess that if these trees should have suffered, she will command from me any number of any kind which may be sent in a more expeditious way.

We go on Tuesday to our new house, but we shall not be magnificent there for some time; the furniture for the best apartment may require some time and consideration, but in the meantime we shall be well and most pleasantly lodged.

Adieu, my dear Horry, we have a thousand thanks to return you for all your entertaining letters.

Lord Holland leaves us next week; he goes directly to England.[7] Lord and Lady Holdernesse go in the beginning of May, but pass through Holland, where I hear Lady Yarmouth is to meet them. Does Lady Mary Coke meet them or does she visit Paris?

I remain, dear Horry, with the best compliments of the family,

Ever affectionately yours,

HERTFORD

Since I wrote my letter Madame Pompadour is dead.[8]

---

6. Praslin and Choiseul, complaining to Hertford of d'Éon's behaviour (*ante* 5 April 1764, n. 6), had observed that if d'Éon 'met with protection, England could never, in any similar case, require her ministers to be delivered to her, and that this practice was directly contrary to the laws of nations, which always supposed a minister, though residing in a foreign country, to be directly under the command of his own sovereign' (Hertford to Halifax 6 April, S.P. 78/261, f.

20). Hertford, in return, pleaded 'the strictness of the English law, which admitted of no topics but what arose from itself, and did not commonly hearken to any pleadings derived from the law of nations' (ibid. f. 21).

7. He and Lady Holland arrived at Holland House 2 May (*London Chronicle* 1–3 May, xv. 421).

8. 'About 7 o'clock' (Hertford to Halifax, 16 April, S.P. 78/261, f. 89).

From HERTFORD, Monday 16 April 1764

Printed for the first time from a photostat of BM Add. MSS 23218, ff. 143–4.

Paris, April 16th 1764.

Dear Horry,

I KNOW you had curiosity about Madame de Pompadour. I must therefore add to the account I have given you in another letter of her death, by informing you that upon opening her will and examining her circumstances she is found, much to the astonishment of the generality of people here, to have died rather poor than rich, considering her situation for so many years past.[1] Her personal estate, consisting chiefly in diamonds, is pretty considerable.[2] The chief part of it she has left to her brother,[3] with an estate of thirty thousand livres a year, an expensive place which always cost her more than it produced. This, with two considerable annuities that cease with her life,[4] were all the fortune she seems to have possessed. She was extremely charitable[5] and therefore you will be the less surprised that she has left a million of livres debt. Her very fine house at Paris[6] she has left to the King; his Majesty is not yet resolved whether he shall accept it. If he does he proposes to give the value of it to her brother. She has likewise left some few legacies which are inconsiderable. The King seemed today affected with her death, but you will not be surprised if you hear his Majesty should take comfort in Mademoiselle Romance,[7] by whom he has had a son, and whose

1. Hertford wrote to Halifax, 19 April, that Mme de Pompadour 'has died poor which wipes off the imputation of rapacity, that popular clamour had thrown upon her' (S.P. 78/261, f. 89).

2. In an inventory of her expenses during nineteen years drawn up shortly before her death, Mme de Pompadour valued 'une . . . cassette contenant tous mes diamants' at 1,783,000 livres (J.-A. le Roi, 'Relevé des dépenses de Madame de Pompadour,' in his Curiosités historiques, 1864, p. 216). Other items in the inventory indicate a considerable investment in gold and silver plate, gems, porcelain, and land.

3. The Marquis de Marigny. She had made him her 'legataire universel' in her original will, and had added 'ma terre du marquisat-pairie de Menars et ses dépendances' in the codicil of 30 March 1761

(Edmond and Jules de Goncourt, Madame de Pompadour, 1888, pp. 308, 310–11).

4. The Goncourts mention only a pension, originally 24,000 livres per month, which declined to not more than 4,000 livres a month (ibid. 303).

5. Mme de Pompadour estimated that she had 'donné aux pauvres pendant toute ma règne' 150,000 livres (le Roi, op. cit. 218); another of her accounts lists a large number of pensions, gifts, and acts of charity (ibid. 222–8).

6. The Hôtel d'Évreux, which had cost her 650,000 livres. 'Je supplie le Roi d'accepter le don que je lui fais de mon hôtel de Paris, étant susceptible de faire le palais d'un de ses petits-fils. Je désire que ce soit pour monseigneur le comte de Provence' (Goncourt, op. cit. 307, 310n.).

7. Mademoiselle de Romans (ante 22 March 1764, n. 2).

conduct in leading a most prudent retired life is said to have recommended her very strongly. Perhaps, as we love to flatter ourselves, his Majesty may think it is pure passion for him that has been the cause of so much retirement.

I am sorry for Lord Ilchester, but I have no idea of his imprudence in trusting the young lady's passions so far. I believe you may conclude Lady Hertford does not intend to commit that mistake with her daughters, nor will her Lord recommend it from any ideas he has conceived of that kind of disposition in nature. I remain, dear Horry,

Most sincerely and affectionately yours,

HERTFORD

To CONWAY, Thursday 19 April 1764

Printed from *Works* v. 105.

Arlington Street, April 19, 1764.

I AM just come from the Duchess of Argyll's,[1] where I dined. General Warburton[2] was there, and said it was the report at the House of Lords, that you are turned out[3]—he imagined, of your regiment— but that I suppose is a mistake for the Bedchamber. I shall hear more tonight, and Lady Strafford, who brings you this, will tell you; though to be sure you will know earlier by the post tomorrow. My only reason for writing is, to repeat to you, that whatever you do I shall act with you. I resent anything done to you as to myself. My fortunes shall never be separated from yours—except that sometime or other I hope yours will be great, and I am content with mine.

The Manns go on with the business[4]—the letter you received[5] was

1. Widow of John Campbell, Duke of Argyll. She was sister to General Warburton, and had been maid of honour to Queen Anne (HW).

2. Hugh Warburton (d. 1771); Lt-Gen. 1758; Col. of the 27th Ft 1761 (Coke, *Journals*, i, p. xvi; *Army Lists* 1765, p. 80; GM 1771, xli. 426).

3. See *post* 20 April 1764.

4. Of army clothiers. James Mann, who had been in charge of the business after

the death of his brother Galfridus in 1756, had died a few days earlier; presumably his surviving brother in England, Edward Louisa Mann (1702–75), and his nephew, Horace Mann the younger (1744– 1814), continued the business together (see MONTAGU i. 204 and nn. 2, 3; MANN v. 50 and n. 2; vi. 225–6).

5. Presumably notifying Conway of James Mann's death.

from Mr Edward Mann,[6] not from Gal's widow.[7] Adieu! I was going
to say, my *disgraced* friend—how delightful to have a character so
unspotted, that the word *disgrace* recoils on those who displace you!

Yours unalterably,

HOR. WALPOLE

To HERTFORD, Friday 20 April 1764

Printed from *Works* ix. 110–13.

Arlington Street, April 20th 1764.

THERE has been a strong report about town for these two days
that your brother is dismissed, not only from the Bedchamber,
but from his regiment,[1] and that the latter is given to Lord Pembroke.[2] I do not believe it. Your brother went to Park Place but
yesterday morning at ten;[3] he certainly knew nothing of it the night
before[4] when we parted, after one, at Grafton House; nor would he
have passed my door yesterday without stopping to tell me of it: no
letter has been sent to his house since, nor were any orders arrived
at the War Office at half an hour after three yesterday;—nay, though
I can give the ministry credit for much folly, and some of them
credit for even violence and folly, I do not believe they are so rash
as this would amount to. For the Bedchamber, you know, your
brother never liked it, and would be glad to get rid of it. I should
be sorry for his sake, and for yours too, if it went farther:—gentle
and indifferent as his nature is, his resentment, if his profession were
touched, would be as serious as such spirit and such abilities could
make it. I would not be the man that advised provoking him; and

6. Edward Louisa Mann (n. 4 above).

7. Sarah Gregory (ca 1716–1804), m.
Galfridus Mann.

———

1. The report was true: 'His Majesty
has been pleased to appoint the Right
Hon. the Earl of Pembroke to the regiment late General Conway's who has resigned' (*St James's Chronicle* 19–21 April,
sub 20 April).

2. Henry Herbert (1734–94), 10th E.
of Pembroke. He succeeded Conway as
Col. of the 1st Dragoons.

3. Accompanied by the Duke of Devonshire (*Grenville Papers* ii. 300).

4. Conway did not learn of his dismissal until 22 April (Conway to Hertford 23 April, MS now WSL, printed in
Works ix. 114–17).

one man[5] has put himself woefully in his power! In my own opinion, this is one of the lies of which the time is so fruitful; I would not even swear that it has not the same parent with the legend I sent you last week, relating to an intended disposition in consequence of Lord Holland's resignation. The Court confidently deny the whole plan, and ascribe it to the fertility of Charles Townshend's brain. However, as they have their Charles Townshends too, I do not totally disbelieve it.

The Parliament rose yesterday—no new peers, not even Irish: Lord Northumberland's list is sent back ungranted.[6] The Duke of Mecklenburgh and Lord Halifax are to have the Garters.[7] Bridgman[8] is turned out of the Green Cloth, which is given to Dick Vernon,[9] and his place of surveyor of the Gardens, which young Dickinson[10] held for him, is bestowed on Cadogan.[11] Dyson[12] is made a lord of Trade. These are all the changes I have heard—not of a complexion that indicates the removal of your brother.

The foreign ministers agreed, as to be sure you have been told, to make Monsieur de Guerchy's *cause commune;* and the Attorney-

5. Presumably Grenville, in his conversation of 4 Dec. (*ante* 9 Dec. 1764).

6. According to Croker (*Works* ix. 111, n. 2) the list consisted of Sir Ralph Gore, Sir [Edward] King, and Mr Stephen Moore, who were created peers during the year as [Gore], Kingston, and Kilworth.

7. 'In the room of the Earls Granville and Waldegrave, deceased' (*Daily Adv.* 24 April). They were elected by the King at a chapter of the Garter held at St James's, 23 April (ibid.). See also MANN vi. 227, n. 10.

8. Henry Bridgeman (1725–1800), 5th Bt, cr. (1794) Bn Bradford; M.P. Ludlow 1748–68, Wenlock 1768–94; clerk comptroller of the Board of Green Cloth 1761–4. He was turned out for voting against the government on the general warrants.

9. Richard Vernon (1726–1800), 'father of the turf'; M.P. Tavistock 1754–61, Bedford 1761–74, Okehampton 1774–84, Newcastle-under-Lyme 1784–90; brother-in-law of the Ds of Bedford. He remained clerk comptroller until 1765.

10. John Marshe Dickinson (d. 1771), son of Alderman Marshe Dickinson, M.P. for Brackley (GM 1771, xli. 335). This

change was not accomplished without friction. George III wrote to Bute ca 18 April that 'the D. of Bedford came to me full of anger at [the elder] Dickenson for having declared his son should not accept the pension, I said the whole transaction was his own to provide for Vernon, therefore that he must make his friends agree as they could, for that I had no part in this dispute.' The next day he informed Bute that Grenville had 'made out the arrangement as well as it could at present; Dyson comes into the Board of Trade, Dickenson resigns the Gardens to Cadogan and Vernon gets the Green Cloth' (*Letters from George III to Lord Bute 1756–1766*, ed. Sedgwick, 1939, pp. 237–8; see also Namier and Brooke ii. 321).

11. Hon. Charles Sloane Cadogan (1728–1807), 3d Bn Cadogan, 1776; cr. (1800) E. Cadogan; surveyor of the Gardens 1764–9. He subsequently (1777) married, as his second wife, HW's niece Mary Churchill.

12. Jeremiah Dyson (1722–76), politician and civil servant. He remained at the Board of Trade until 1768.

General has filed an information against D'Éon:[13] that poor lunatic was at the opera on Saturday, looking like Bedlam. He goes armed, and threatens, what I dare say he would perform, to kill or be killed, if any attempt is made to seize him.

The East Indian affairs have taken a new turn. Sullivan had twelve votes to ten:[14] Lord Clive bribed off one. When they came to the election of chairman, Sullivan desired to be placed in the chair without the disgrace of a ballot; but it was denied.[15] On the scrutiny, the votes appeared eleven and eleven. Sullivan understood the blow, and with three others left the room.[16] Rous,[17] his great enemy, was placed in the chair; since that, I think matters are a little compromised, and Sullivan does not abdicate the direction;[18] but Lord Clive, it is supposed, will go to Bengal[19] in the stead of Colonel Barré, as Sullivan and Lord Shelburne had intended.[20]

13. The *London Chronicle* 14–17 April mentions the filing of the information *sub* 16 April (xv. 361). The writ had been served on him before the 19th (*Grenville Papers* ii. 299).

14. For the election to the chairmanship of the East India Company, 13 April.

15. 'The important question, whether Mr Sullivan should or should not continue in the lead of the company's affairs . . . depended upon the choice that the directors should make of their chairman. Upon holding up hands, it was said, a majority appeared for Mr Sullivan; but a ballot being demanded, the issue was, that Mr Rous took the chair in his stead' (GM 1764, xxxiv. 192).

16. 'Yesterday [13 April] was held a court of directors of the East India Company, when Thomas Rous, Esq. was elected chairman, and Henry Crab Boulton, Esq. deputy chairman; upon which Messrs Sulivan, Thornton, Smith, Rooke, and Boyd, withdrew from the court, with an intention (as it is supposed) to disqualify themselves from acting in the direction' (*London Chronicle* 12–14 April, xv. 360).

17. Thomas Rous (d. 1771) of Piercefield, Monmouth (GM 1771, xli. 378; Namier and Brooke iii. 379).

18. 'Yesterday [18 April] a court of directors was held at the India House in Leadenhall Street, in order to settle the

committee, etc. for the ensuing year, when the following gentlemen, viz. John Boyd, Esq. Giles Rook, Esq. Richard Smith, Esq. Laurence Sullivan, Esq. and William Thornton, Esq. who at the court on Friday last, it was said, would disqualify themselves, were, at the intercession of several proprietors, prevailed on to receive their places; after which the different committees were settled, and all things amicably adjusted' (*St James's Chronicle* 17–19 April).

19. 'Lord Clive was at the India House several hours, and we hear everything is settled to the satisfaction of all parties; but no time is yet fixed on for Lord Clive's departure for the East Indies' (*London Chronicle* 17–19 April, xv. 373). It was agreed upon at another meeting, on the 19th, that the time of his departure would be set at a meeting on the 27th (ibid. 19–21 April, xv. 377). According to another report, at the same meeting Clive informed the directors 'on what conditions he chose to go abroad in the Company's service' and a general meeting was set for 'next Wednesday sennight [2 May] to bring the proposal before them' (*St James's Chronicle* 19–21 April).

20. HW gives a similar account in *Mem. Geo. III* of Shelburne's support of Sulivan (i. 316), but Shelburne's biographer states that his support arose not from a desire to help Barré, but merely 'from a strong distrust of the policy of territorial con-

Mr Pitt is worse than ever with the gout.[21] Legge's case is thought very dangerous:—thus stand our politics, and probably will not fluctuate much for some months. At least—I expect to have little more to tell before I see you at Paris, except balls, weddings, and follies, of which, thank the moon! we never have a dearth: for one of the latter class, we are obliged to the Archbishop,[22] who, in remembrance, I suppose, of his original profession of midwifery,[23] has ordered some decent alterations to be made in King Henry's figure in the Tower.[24] Poor Lady Susan is in the most deplorable situation, for her Adonis is a Roman Catholic, and cannot be provided for out of his calling. Sir Francis Delaval being touched with her calamity, has made her a present—of what do you think?—of a rich gold stuff! The delightful charity! O'Brien comforts himself, and says it will make a shining passage in his little history.

I will tell you but one more folly, and hasten to my signature. Lady Beaulieu was complaining of being waked by a noise in the night: my Lord replied, 'Oh, for my part, there is no disturbing me; if they don't wake me before I go to sleep, there is no waking me afterwards.'[25]

Lady Hervey's table is at last arrived, and the Princess's trees, which I sent her last night; but she wants nothing, for Lady Barrymore[26] is arrived.

quest represented by Lord Clive' (Lord Fitzmaurice, *Life of . . . Shelburne*, 1912, i. 221). See also, for Shelburne's connection with Sulivan and his interests in the East India Company, Lucy S. Sutherland's 'Lord Shelburne and East India Company Politics, 1766–9,' *English Historical Review*, 1934, xlix. 450–86.

21. Selwyn wrote to Lord Holland, 17 April, that 'Pitt's gout is so bad that his particular friends are of opinion that he cannot last long; his thighs are swelled to an enormous size' (*Letters to Henry Fox*, ed. Lord Ilchester, Roxburghe Club, 1915, p. 194, misdated ?18 Oct. 1763). However, Pitt informed Newcastle on the 19th that, though he had been confined for the past week 'most part of the time to my bed,' he was now better (BM Add. MSS 32958, f. 170).

22. Secker.

23. See *ante* 28 Sept. 1762, n. 36.

24. For this figure see Montagu i. 70,

n. 22. HW, in his notes to Maty's *Memoires . . . of Lord Chesterfield* (Hazen, *Cat. of HW's Lib.*, No. 3915), writes: 'It was very indecent: young women used to stick a pin into a certain part as a good omen for getting husbands. George Augustus Selwyn, to laugh at the Archbishop, wrote a letter to Archbishop Secker in the person of a pious young nobleman, who pretended to have been shocked on going to the Tower with his sisters. The Archbishop took it seriously, and desired Lord Granby, Master of the Ordnance, to see the stone of offence taken away, which was done' (printed at the end of Philobiblon Society, *Miscellanies*, 1867–8, xi. 51).

25. Lord Beaulieu was an Irishman, and presumably this is intended as an example of an 'Irish bull,' 'an expression . . . involving a ludicrous inconsistency unperceived by the speaker' (OED).

26. Hon. Margaret Davys (d. 1788), m.

I smiled when I read your account of Lord Tavistock's expedition. Do you remember that I made seven days from Calais to Paris, by laying out my journeys at the rate of travelling in England thirty miles a day; and did not find but that I could have gone in a third of the time![27] I shall not be such a snail the next time.[28] It is said that at Lord Tavistock's return, he is to decide whom he will marry.

Is it true that the Choiseuls totter, and that the Broglios are to succeed;[29] or is there a Charles Townshend at Versailles?

Adieu! my dear Lord.

Yours ever,

H. W.

To Conway, Saturday 21 April 1764

Printed from *Works* v. 106–7.

Strawberry Hill, Saturday night, eight o'clock, April 21, 1764.

I WRITE to you with a very bad headache; I have passed a night, for which George Grenville[1] and the Duke of Bedford shall pass many an uneasy one! Notwithstanding I heard from everybody I met, that your regiment, as well as Bedchamber, were taken away, I would not believe it, till last night the Duchess of Grafton told me, that the night before the Duchess of Bedford said to her, 'Are not

(1738) James Barry, 5th E. of Barrymore. She was a lifelong friend of Princess Amelia; see Ossory ii. 517, 534.

27. 'This vehicle [the post-chaise] will, upon occasion, go fourscore miles a day, but Mr Walpole, being in no hurry, chooses to make easy journeys of it, and they are easy ones indeed.' 'Six days have we been coming hither [to Paris], which other people do in two' (Gray to Mrs Gray 1 April 1739 NS, to West 12 April 1739 NS, in his *Correspondence*, ed. Toynbee and Whibley, Oxford, 1935, i. 99–100, 101). 'Directions for Mr Walpole's Journey,' drawn up by Bowman and enclosed by Conway to HW *ante* 24 March 1739, had suggested three, or at most four days for the trip.

28. In Sept. 1765 HW spent three days

on the road between Boulogne and Paris ('Paris Journals,' du Deffand v. 259–60).

29. HW mentions this report also to Mann, 20 April 1764 (Mann vi. 227); the *St James's Chronicle* 12–14 April had reported that 'the following change in the ministry at Versailles has lately taken place: The Duke de Praslin and his son have resigned; and the Duke de Broglio and his brother, with Cardinal Bernis, are to be employed.' However, both Praslin and his cousin Choiseul continued in office as secretaries of state until 1770 (du Deffand ii. 497, iii. 5).

1. Deleted in *Works;* the deleted names in this letter were first restored in Wright.

you very sorry for poor Mr Conway? He has lost everything.' When the Witch of Endor pities, one knows she has raised the devil.

I am come hither alone to put my thoughts into some order, and to avoid showing the first sallies of my resentment, which I know you would disapprove; nor does it become your friend to rail.[2] My anger shall be a little more manly, and the plan of my revenge a little deeper laid than in peevish bons mots. You shall judge of my indignation by its duration.

In the meantime, let me beg you, in the most earnest and most sincere of all professions, to suffer me to make your loss as light as it is in my power to make it:[3] I have six thousand pounds in the funds; accept all, or what part you want. Do not imagine I will be put off with a refusal. The retrenchment of my expenses, which I shall from this hour commence, will convince you that I mean to replace your fortune as far as I can. When I thought you did not want it, I had made another disposition. You have ever been the dearest person to me in the world. You have shown that you deserve to be so.—You suffer for your spotless integrity.—Can I hesitate a moment to show that there is at least one man who knows how to value you? The new will, which I am going to make, will be a testimonial of my own sense of virtue.[4]

One circumstance has heightened my resentment. If it was *not* an accident, it deserves to heighten it. The very day on which your dismission was notified, I received an order from the Treasury for the payment of what money was due to me there.[5] Is it possible that they could mean to make any distinction between us? Have I separated

2. 'Yet for the first time in my life I acted with a phlegm of which I did not know myself capable. I shut myself up in the country for three days, till I had conquered the first ebullitions of my rage' (*Mem. Geo. III* i. 325).

3. Conway was offered financial assistance also by Hertford, the Duke of Devonshire, and Lord Strafford; Devonshire offered him a thousand pounds a year 'as long as this situation lasted' (Conway to Hertford, 11 May, MS now WSL). At first Conway was rather worried about the sudden and sharp reduction in his income, which came 'unluckily at the end of two German campaigns which I felt the expense of with a much larger income, and have not yet recovered' (idem to idem, 23 April, MS now WSL, printed

Works ix. 116); however, though by his dismissals and the loss of one thousand pounds of Lady Ailesbury's jointure his income was now reduced from £6000 to £2600 per annum, he eventually decided that through economy he would be able to make his present income suffice without becoming indebted to his friends (idem to idem, 11 May).

4. 'I altered my will, giving him almost my whole fortune unless his regiment should be restored to him' (*Mem. Geo. III* i. 324–5).

5. 'Grenville, the very day before the dismission of Mr Conway, whether to detach me from him, or fearing I should make use of the indiscretion he had been guilty of, ordered the payment of my bills at the Treasury' (ibid. 325).

myself from you? Is there that spot on earth where I can be suspected of having paid court? Have I even left my name at a minister's door, since you took your part? If they have dared to hint this, the pen that is now writing to you will bitterly undeceive them.

I am impatient to see the letters you have received, and the answers you have sent. Do you come to town? If you do not, I will come to you tomorrow sennight, that is, the 29th. I give no advice on anything, because you are cooler than I am—not so cool, I hope, as to be insensible to this outrage, this villainy, this injustice![6] You owe it to your country to labour the extermination of such ministers!

I am so bad a hypocrite, that I am afraid of showing how deeply I feel this. Yet last night I received the account from the Duchess of Grafton with more temper than you believe me capable of: but the agitation of the night disordered me so much, that Lord John Cavendish, who was with me two hours this morning, does not, I believe, take me for a hero. As there are some who I know would enjoy my mortification, and who probably designed I should feel my share of it, I wish to command myself—but that struggle shall be added to their bill. I saw nobody else before I came away but Legge, who sent for me and wrote the enclosed[7] for you. He would have said more both to you and Lady A., but I would not let him, as he is so ill: however, he thinks himself that he shall live. I hope he will! I would not lose a shadow that can haunt these ministers.

I feel for Lady A., because I know she feels just as I do—and it is not a pleasant sensation. I will say no more, though I could write volumes. Adieu!

Yours, as I ever have been and ever will be,

HOR. WALPOLE

From CONWAY, ca Monday 23 April 1764

Missing; answered *post* 24 April 1764.

---

6. Conway wrote to Hertford, 23 April: 'It requires all the philosophy one can muster, not to show the strongest resentment. I think I have as much as my neighbours, and I shall endeavour to use it, yet not so as to betray quite an unmanly insensibility to such extraordinary provocation.'

7. Missing.

To Conway, Tuesday 24 April 1764

Printed from *Works* v. 108.

Arlington Street, April 24, 1764.

I REJOICE that you feel your loss so little: that you act with dignity and propriety does not surprise me. To have you behave in character and with character, is my first of all wishes; for then it will not be in the power of man to make you unhappy. Ask yourself —is there a man in England with whom you would change character?—is there a man in England who would not change with you? Then think how little they have taken away!

For me, I shall certainly conduct myself as you prescribe. *Your* friend shall say and do nothing unworthy of *your* friend. You govern me in everything but one: I mean the disposition I have told you I shall make. Nothing can alter that, but a great change in your fortune. In another point you partly misunderstood me. That I shall explain hereafter.

I shall certainly meet you here on Sunday, and very cheerfully. We may laugh at a world in which nothing of us will remain long but our characters. Adieu! the dear family!

Yours eternally,

Hor. Walpole

From Henrietta Seymour Conway, Friday 27 April 1764

Printed for the first time from a photostat of BM Add. MSS 23218, f. 145.

Chichester, 27th April 1764.

Good Mr Walpole,

I HAD the pleasure and favour of yours, dated the 23d of February,[1] and methinks I am very sorry now that I gave you so much unnecessary trouble (though I am sure you have no reason to be so) as the privilege of franking is over; or at least as it is settled on such

1. Missing.

a footing that no reasonable body, I think, can presume or desire to ask such a favour.[2]

But still I am going to trespass upon your good nature (which has ever been indulgent to me) to beg the favour of you when you write to my brother Hertford, as you tell me you often correspond with, to convey the enclosed[3] in your packet to him, as I have no proper direction to him, and having no answer to my letter I wrote him soon after he got to Paris, makes me doubt that he never received it. I am very glad he gives such a general satisfaction, and is so well received, and it likewise makes me very happy to hear my brother the General has made so fine a figure in Parliament, though I am sorry his health has suffered by it, and I doubt his pocket will too if it be true what the papers say, that he has resigned his regiment.

Our beautiful Duchess of Richmond has been in our neighbourhood and was got much better.[4] I hear now she is gone or going to Bath. She brought me over a sweet pretty snuff-box from France.

Believe me, good Sir, your much obliged friend and humble servant,

H. SEYMOUR CONWAY

From HERTFORD, Monday 30 April 1764

Printed for the first time from a photostat of BM Add. MSS 23218, ff. 146–9.

Paris, April 30th 1764.

Dear Horry,

I AM greatly hurt and offended at the conduct of the administration towards my brother. You know I have not approved the part he has taken this winter; I foresaw with some concern that he would incur the King's displeasure, and I saw, I will confess with more anxiety, that by the part he took he had politically detached himself from me. I did not pretend to remonstrate because he had a good right to choose for himself; but I felt unhappy that we must be supposed to be separated in our political views and connections. I had accepted the embassy to this Court and was executing the com-

2. See *ante* 12 April 1764, n. 10.
3. Missing.

4. See *ante* 24 Feb. 1764.

mands of his Majesty and the present ministers. My brother had
given me notice in one of his letters that his obligations to his other
friends were of such a nature as to determine the conduct he was
pursuing.¹ I felt unhappy to see myself thus separated from my
friends and I secretly cursed the politics of our country which from
their uncertainty produce nothing but division and uneasiness in
private connections.² I was afraid the consequences might be unpleasant to us both, and I wish I had foreseen with more³ judgment
the disagreeable⁴ situation in which it has involved me.⁵

I have received from Mr Grenville by a courier who arrived before the post a long letter,⁶ wrote as you will suppose such an one to
be, expressing great uneasiness at the part my brother had taken this
winter and informing me, as he thought he owed it to me, before I
could hear it from other hands, that his Majesty's displeasure had at
last determined him though very unwillingly to part with him from
the employment he held in his Bedchamber and from the command
of his regiment of dragoons. He declares that he did all he could
with propriety to avert his Majesty's displeasure, by recommending
to my brother a more moderate conduct, and ascribes the determined part my brother had taken to an unbounded attachment to
some of his friends. He then professes to feel very sincerely for me
the unpleasing situation in which I was thereby involved, but says he
flatters himself I shall have too much candour and too just a judg-

1. Unless Hertford is referring to a
statement in some letter from Conway
which has not survived, he is misrepre-
senting what Conway wrote in his letter of
5 Dec. 1763 (MS now WSL). While Hertford
makes it seem as if Conway had declared
that he felt himself bound by his obligations to his friends to act politically according to their wishes, actually Conway
had asserted, somewhat unclearly, perhaps, his complete independence from
others, including his friends in Opposition, adding only that if he should at
some juncture differ from them, he felt
honour-bound not to allow himself to
profit by it. He had informed Hertford
of his telling Grenville that he was 'determined to take the part I should choose
hereafter without making myself responsible for it to any person whatever, and
should only add that my obligations to
some particular persons, and I named the

Dukes of Devonshire and Grafton, who
were understood to be in Opposition,
were such that if hereafter I should happen in any degree to differ from them,
I should steer my conduct so as not to be
in any shape the better for it; thus far
I thought my honour engaged.'
2. 'In private connections' written over
'amongst friends' in the MS.
3. 'Less' in the MS, presumably a slip;
see post 17 May 1764.
4. 'Disagreeable' written over 'unpleasant' in the MS.
5. Lord Albemarle wrote to Newcastle,
29 April: 'My Lord at Paris will be
greatly concerned at it (not angry) and
much more upon his own account than
his brother's' (BM Add. MSS 32958, f. 242).
6. Dated 18 April, printed Grenville
Papers ii. 296–9. Hertford's paraphrase
follows the text closely.

ment not to see it as it is, or to suffer my affection to carry me beyond the bounds of reason and justice, and what I owe to myself, my King and my country.

That they were all deeply concerned upon this occasion, and he was persuaded from my temper and character would have their due weight in not permitting private inclination to get the better of a public duty which I had exercised with so much reputation to myself, so much approbation from his Majesty, and with so much benefit to his kingdoms. That these were the earnest wishes and expectations of many as well as himself, who should think his best endeavours well employed whenever they could prevent anything disagreeable to me or that could contribute to make my situation more pleasing and honourable.

To this I have answered[7] that I have seldom felt a more sensible uneasiness than I received from the perusal of his letter, though wrote with delicacy, and that the disagreeableness of the subject could not be overcome by his manner of treating it. That my brother's conduct in Parliament this winter I had never approved and that I had often represented to him my sentiments on that head; that I foresaw he would incur his Majesty's displeasure, but that I had never imagined or foreseen that the offence would be followed with such consequences or that the merits of his military character could ever be obliterated by his Parliamentary behaviour; that civil offices were supposed to be conferred from favour or to be purchased by civil services, and it was natural to imagine they might be forfeited by opposite causes, but that employments in the army were thought to lie out of the reach of ministerial influence; that few instances had occurred to the contrary in our time, and those had always been considered as violent and extraordinary; that it was particularly grievous to me that my brother, for an offence so usual in our government, should be treated with such unusual severity; and that, I might add, the weight of this punishment fell the heavier on account of the public employment with which his Majesty had at present been pleased to honour me. That nothing could give me greater consolation than his assurances that my conduct at this Court had been so happy

---

7. 26 April, printed ibid. ii. 307–9. Hertford here paraphrases closely all but the last paragraph of his letter. He concluded: 'It must be contrary to his Majesty's interest to lessen in any degree my credit with the Court where I reside, and if my situation contains any disagreeable circumstances which is of a public nature, and cannot be concealed, it ought, in my humble opinion, in sound policy, to be corrected' (ibid. ii. 309).

as to obtain his Majesty's approbation, and that those assurances were the more agreeable on this head, as I should have been otherways inclined from this and other instances to have had very melancholy apprehensions to the contrary. That though no personal displeasure would relax my zeal in his Majesty's service, yet I was afraid I might henceforth have less influence in promoting it, and that the French Court, seeing my family at home distinguished by such particular marks of resentment, might on occasion pay less regard to my sentiments and remonstrances. This is the chief substance of both letters, which I will beg you to communicate to my brother. I intend writing to him myself, but I was unwilling to copy the extract of these letters twice unnecessarily, having always a great deal to write. I had likewise a very short letter from Lord Halifax, saying no more than that he was sorry it fell to his lot to communicate to me so disagreeable an event, which I answered as shortly and civilly.[8]

Pray tell me who is the author or suspected to be such of this very bad counsel in dismissing officers, and particularly *one* of the best connections, the fairest character and most acknowledged abilities. I am hurt to the greatest degree at this dismission from the army, and so vexed with English politics that I detest the name and idea of them. You know the state and circumstances of my family which brought me to Paris and has so far settled me here. If I was a *garçon*[9] I could retire to my woods in Warwickshire and be indifferent to the folly and madness of English ministers. I have lately met with an accident[10] in returning from Versailles which might easily have put an end to all my difficulties in this world. The fault was entirely that of my own postilions, but notwithstanding the risk I am, thank God, very well and have suffered no other hurt than in two cuts upon the forehead and the loss of some blood, which is easily repaired.

The hôtel which I have taken here is charming. I hope you will see it soon. The best compliments of the family attend you. I am, dear Horry,

Always most affectionately yours,

Hertford

---

8. These letters are not with Hertford's diplomatic correspondence in S.P. 78.

9. In the sense of bachelor.

10. 'Mylord Comte d'Hertfort, ambassadeur d'Angleterre, versa dernièrement en revenant de Versailles; les glaces de sa chaise de poste se trouvant levées, elles lui ont fracassé le visage, et tout le monde prend beaucoup de part à cet accident' (*Mercure historique*, 1764, clvi. 534).

To HERTFORD, ca Friday 11 May 1764

Missing; answered *post* 17 May 1764. In it HW disapproved of Hertford's continuing as ambassador.

From HERTFORD, Thursday 17 May 1764

Printed for the first time from a photostat of BM Add. MSS 23218, ff. 150–1. *Memoranda* (by HW):
Robinson[1]
Lady Bel Finch[2]

Paris, May 17th 1764.

Dear Horry,

I AM very sorry to find you disapprove my continuing at Paris, especially as that opinion arises from affection to a person whom I love as well as you can love him.

My brother's dismission I think as weak and unwarrantable an act as ever I remember on the part of government, and I am fully sensible of the unpleasant circumstances in which it has involved me. At the same time, before your private judgment condemns me for not quitting the King's service, I must entreat you to consider that I am so circumstanced as to have many duties to fulfil. I have that of a husband and a father as well as that of a brother to take into my judgment, and I will conscientiously act to the best of my opinion by them all. My family is now settled in France and my children scattered about for their education without any expectation of such an event; the removing therefore would be attended with all the difficulties imaginable to me and them. My honour I cannot conceive requires it from me; my passion and affections would too naturally prompt me to it; but in the circumstances [in] which I stand, my brother is, I am persuaded, too reasonable to wish me to take a step so full of inconvenience and difficulty. My attachment to the

1. Possibly Sir Septimus Robinson (*ante* 22 Jan. 1764, n. 90); HW had in his possession a 'copy of Lady Waldegrave's letter [actually composed by HW] to Prince William, sent by Sir Septimus Robinson

May 3d, 1764' (HW's endorsement; MS now WSL; see *Mem. Geo. III* iii. 268).
2. HW mentions her in his letter to Conway *post* 5 June 1764.

present ministry would, I confess, be an insufficient motive to determine my conduct. You know I believe that I owe them personally nothing that I enjoy, and the dismission of my brother is certainly no instance of their tenderness for me. The politics of last winter have given me an indifference I never felt before, and when I leave Paris either from my own inclination or that of any present or future minister, I can retire here or in England with the contempt that a man easy in his circumstances should feel for any Court disappointment. My single concern is to appear separated from my friends whom I both love and esteem, but in this respect I cannot charge my own conduct; my judgment, weak as my abilities are, would have prevented all the difficulties which now surround us. I do not love parties enough to have any of them alleviated by that kind of spirit. I have long considered the whole system as a mere game which has been too often played to deceive a child. I see the impracticability of satisfying my own mind, and I have taken the part of remaining at Paris, as the one least liable to just censure, not as a step free from objection. I feel fully for my brother the very heavy punishment he has suffered, and I am aware of the delicacy of my own situation in consequence of it; I shall therefore be prepared for every political event that may happen, and I can comfort myself as far as my own importance is concerned, by having learnt a good lesson of political indifference.

We hear nothing here of Guerchy's leaving the Court of London. He comes over to review his regiment,[3] but it is supposed will return to England.[4]

The King of France has begun his summer parties with the Duchess of Grammont, Madame de Mirepoix and a Madame d'Aiguilly,[5] but I do not believe his Majesty's inclinations will be engaged

3. Guerchy had been named 'colonel-lieutenant et inspecteur du régiment du Roi, infanterie,' in 1745 (La Chenaye-Desbois, xvi. 925; *Répertoire . . . de la Gazette de France*, ed. de Granges de Surgères, 1902–6, iv. 27).

4. He set out for Paris in late July, and returned to England 15 Oct. (Mann vi. 248, n. 10; *London Chronicle* 16–18 Oct., xvi. 369). gm 1764, xxxiv. 347 alludes to the rumour of Guerchy's leaving the English Court: 'Count de Guerchy, the French ambassador, set out for Paris, to be present, as is given out, at the review of the regiment of which he is colonel; others assign a very different motive for his journey.'

5. Probably either Anne-Charlotte de Crussol de Florensac (1700–72), m. (1718) Armand-Louis Vignerot du Plessis de Richelieu, cr. (1731) Duc d'Aiguillon; or, more likely, her daughter-in-law, Louise-Félicité de Bréhan de Plélo (1726–96), a favourite of Marie Leszczyńska, m. (1740) Emmanuel-Armand du Plessis de Richelieu, Duc d'Aiguillon (1750) (*Dictionnaire*

by any one of these ladies. If the women are to be changed, as it is now said, in the different parties, perhaps some woman with art or beauty may contrive in the course of the summer to succeed Madame de Pompadour.

I write to you as a friend and you will treat me as such; if private motives are not sufficient to determine in any political question, you will conceal mine where I wish them to remain, entirely to yourself.

I am, dear Horry, with the best compliments of the family,

Most sincerely and affectionately yours,

HERTFORD

To HERTFORD, Sunday 27 May 1764

Printed from *Works* ix. 121–5.

Arlington Street, May 27th 1764, very late.

My dear Lord,

I AM just come home, and find a letter from you, which gives me too much pain to let me resist answering it directly (though past one in the morning), as I go out of town early tomorrow.

I must begin with telling you, let me feel what I will from it, how much I admire it. It is equal to the difficulty of your situation, and expressed with all the feeling which must possess you. I will show it your brother, as there is nothing I would not and will not do to preserve the harmony and friendship which has so much distinguished your whole lives.

You have guessed, give me leave to say, at my wishes, rather than answered to anything I have really expressed. The truth was, I had no right to deliver any opinion on so important a step as you have taken, without being asked. Had you consulted me, which certainly

de biographie française, 1933– , i. 909–12, 916–20). La Noue wrote to the Chevalier de Fontette, 29 Sept. 1767, about the younger Duchess: 'Mme d'Aiguillon, qui est la favorite de la Reine, est appelée chez sa maîtresse, dans les moments les plus particuliers, et . . . le Roi vient causer avec Mme d'Aiguillon qui le guide sur toutes les affaires de l'état' (*La Chalotais et le Duc d'Aiguillon. Correspondance du Chevalier de Fontette*, ed. H. Carré, 1893, p. 498).

was not proper for you to do, it would have been with the utmost reluctance that I should have brought myself to utter my sentiments, and only then, if I had been persuaded that friendship exacted it from me; for it would have been a great deal for me to have taken upon myself: it would have been a step, either way, liable to subject me to reproach from you in your own mind, though you would have been too generous to have blamed me in any other way. Now, my dear Lord, do me the justice to say, that the part I have acted was the most proper and most honourable one I could take. Did I, have I dropped a syllable, endeavouring to bias your judgment one way or the other? My constant language has been, that I could not think, when a younger brother had taken a part disagreeable to his elder, and totally opposite, even without consulting him, that the elder was under any obligation to relinquish his own opinion, and adopt the younger's. In my heart I undoubtedly wished, that even in party your union should not be dissolved; for that union would be the strength of both.

This is the summary of a text on which I have infinitely more to say; but the post is so far from being a proper conveyance, that I think the most private letter transmitted in the most secure manner is scarcely to be trusted. Should I resolve, if you require it, to be more explicit (and I certainly shall not think of saying a word more, unless I know that it is strongly your desire I should) it must only be upon the most positive assurance on your honour (and on their honour as strictly given too) that not a syllable of what I shall say shall be communicated to any person living. I except *nobody*, except my Lady and Lord Beauchamp. What I should say now is now of no consequence, but for your information. It can tend to nothing else. It therefore does not signify, whether said now, or at any distant time hereafter, or when we meet. If, as perhaps you may at first suppose, it had the least view towards making you quit your embassy, you should not know it at all; for I think that would be the idlest and most unwise step you could take; and believe me, my affection for your brother will never make me sacrifice your honour to his interest. I have loved you both unalterably, and without the smallest cloud between us, from children. It is true, as you observe, that party, with many other mischiefs, produces dissensions in families. I can by no means agree with you, that all party is founded in interest—surely, you cannot think that your brother's conduct was not the result of the most unshaken honour and conscience, and as surely the result of no interested motive? You are not less mistaken, if you believe that the present state of party in this country is not of a most serious nature, and not a mere contention for power and employments. That topic, however, I shall pass over; the discussion, perhaps, would end where it began. As you know I never tried to bring you to my opinion before, I am very unlikely to aim at it now. Let this and the rest of this subject sleep for the present. I trust I have convinced you that my behaviour has been both honourable and respectful towards you; and that, though I think with your brother and am naturally very warm, I have acted in the most dispassionate manner, and had recourse to nothing but silence, when I was not so happy as to meet you in opinion.

This subject has kept me so long, and it is so very late, that you will forgive me if I only skim over the gazette part of my letter—my next shall be more in my old gossiping style.

Dr Terrick and Dr Lambe[1] are made Bishops of London and Peterborough, without the nomination or approbation of the ministers.[2] The Duke of Bedford declared this warmly, for you know his own administration always allow him to declare his genuine opinion, that they may have the credit of making him alter it. He was still more surprised at the Chancellor's being made an earl[3] without his knowledge, after he had gone out of town, blaming the Chancellor's coldness on D'Éon's affair,[4] which is now dropped.[5] Three marquisates going to be given to Lords Cardigan, Northumberland, and Townshend,[6] may not please his Grace more, though

1. Robert Lamb (ca 1703–69), LL.D. 1728; Dean of Peterborough 1744–64; Bp of Peterborough 1764–9 (Venn, *Alumni Cantab.*). They kissed hands for their bishoprics 18 May (*London Chronicle* 17–19 May, xv. 478).

2. The King had promised the bishopric of London to Terrick 'so early as when the present Bishop of London [Osbaldeston] was appointed to it,' but Grenville and the ministry apparently approved the choice (*Grenville Papers* ii. 312–15).

3. The Chancellor's patent as Earl of Northington is dated 19 May 1764 (GEC), but he kissed hands for the promotion 16 May (*London Chronicle* 15–17 May, xv. 469). The matter, much pressed by Grenville, had initially met with the King's opposition (*Grenville Papers* ii.

502; *Letters from George III to Lord Bute 1756–1766*, ed. Sedgwick, 1939, p. 237). Bedford was informed of the promotion by Lord Sandwich only after it had occurred (*Bedford Corr.* iii. 259, where the letter is misdated 16 March).

4. Bedford had suggested, at a Cabinet meeting 30 March, a short act of Parliament to remedy the defects in the law of extradition to enable the Crown to send d'Éon out of the kingdom, but the Chancellor had seen 'a thousand difficulties' in such a proceeding, a view which received Grenville's support; see *Grenville Papers* ii. 280–3.

5. However, d'Éon was tried and convicted for libel in early July; see MANN vi. 247–8 and n. 9.

6. None of these creations took place at

they may his minister,[7] who may be glad his master is angry, as it may produce a good quieting draught for himself.

The Northumberlands are returned;[8] Hamilton is dismissed,[9] and the Earl of Drogheda[10] made secretary in his room.

Mechell[11] is recalled by desire of this Court, who requested to have it done without giving their reasons,[12] as Sir Charles Williams had been sent from Berlin in the same manner.[13]

Colonel Johnson is also recalled from Minorca.[14] He had been

this time; Cardigan and Northumberland received dukedoms in 1766, Townshend a marquisate in 1787. Hertford had already heard a report that the King had 'thoughts of making a promotion from the Earl's bench,' since he wrote to Grenville, 29 May, requesting to be included in the list (*Grenville Papers* ii. 331). Grenville, replying 12 June, informed him for the King that there was no intention of promoting any earls at the time (ibid. ii. 352–3).

7. Presumably Richard Rigby.

8. From Ireland, where Northumberland was lord lieutenant 1763–5; they arrived in London 17 May (*London Chronicle* 17–19 May, xv. 473).

9. William Gerard Hamilton was reported to have 'resigned' as chief secretary the day Northumberland left the kingdom (ibid. 22–4 May, xv. 493). Montagu had written to HW, 15 Nov. 1763, that 'Hamilton always treated the great people of Ireland with contempt and the Primate . . . could never endure him' (Montagu ii. 110), while Northumberland complained to Bedford, 15 March 1764, 'of the uneasiness that Mr Hamilton's conduct brought upon me, on the first opening of the session here, and of my entire disappointment in the hopes I had conceived from his assistance to me' (Bedford MSS 49, f. 78, quoted Namier and Brooke ii. 573).

10. Charles Moore (1730–1822), 6th E. of Drogheda, cr. (1791) M. of Drogheda; army officer; chief secretary 1764–5; m. (1766) Anne Seymour-Conway, Hertford's eldest daughter.

11. Andreas Ludwig Michell, Prussian chargé d'affaires in London 1747–64 (*ante* 22 Jan. 1756).

12. The ostensible reason for Michell's recall, that which sufficed for George III and Grenville, was his fraternization with the Opposition, 'avec une faction qui ne s'occupait qu'à mettre des entraves dans les resolutions du gouvernement' (Michell to Newcastle, 21 May, BM Add. MSS 32959, f. 1); other reasons were Michell's intrigues with Alexander Vorontsov, the Russian minister at London, to prevent the conclusion of an Anglo-Russian alliance, and Sandwich's desire to bring England closer to Austria by producing a breach with Prussia (see Lord Sandwich, *Diplomatic Correspondence 1763–1765*, ed. Frank Spencer, Manchester, 1961, p. 53 *et passim*). Michell had his last audience 15 Aug. (*Repertorium der diplomatischen Vertreter aller Länder*, Vol. II, ed. F. Hausmann, Zurich, 1950, p. 297).

13. In the winter of 1751; for a full treatment of the affair, see D. B. Horn, *Sir Charles Hanbury Williams and European Diplomacy (1747–1758)*, 1930, pp. 51–67.

14. See *ante* 6 Feb. 1764. Johnston was apparently court-martialled but acquitted, since Lyttelton wrote to Grenville, 15 Oct., that 'the decision of the Board of General Officers, to the astonishment of mankind, appears by their report to have acquitted Colonel Johnston of some of the accusations referred to their consideration, whilst other articles of charge of disobedience or neglect have been passed over by them unnoticed, such seems to have been the weight of Court influence and power exerted in his favour.' He goes on to complain of the neglect of petitions forwarded by him to the King in Council, and of a notification to Johnston 'that he may forthwith return to Minorca, and re-assume the government of that island,' and concludes by asking to resign (*Grenville Papers* ii. 449–50). He was offered, and accepted, the governorship of Guernsey instead of Minorca in 1766, while Johnston continued as Lt-Gov. of

very wrong-headed with his governor, Sir Richard;[15] that wound was scarce closed, when the judicious deputy chose to turn out a brother-in-law of Lord Bute.[16]

Lady Falkener's[17] daughter[18] is to be married to a young rich Mr Crewe,[19] a Maccarone, and of our loo. Mr Skreene[20] has married Miss Sumner,[21] and her brother[22] gives her £10,000. Good night.

Yours most sincerely,

H. W.

The watchman cries three!

Minorca until 1774 (Namier and Brooke iii. 75; *Record of Old Westminsters*, ed. G. F. Russell Barker and A. H. Stenning, 1928, i. 521).

15. Lyttelton.

16. Perhaps the reference is to Capt. William Courtenay, Commissary of Stores and Provisions, at this time also Capt. in the 72d Ft, Invalids (*Army Lists*, to Nov. 1763, pp. 127, 135; 1765, pp. 127, 135); one of Bute's sisters, Lady Jean Stuart, married a William Courtenay (*Scots Peerage* ii. 301). Capt. Courtenay, however, remained commissary until Minorca was retaken by the Spanish in 1782 (*Army Lists, passim*). The anonymous author of *An Account of the Deplorable State of the Island of Minorca . . . Under the Command of Lieutenant-Governor Johnston*, complains about Johnston's dismissal of 'an English officer greatly beloved,' who had been 'captain of the port of Mahon' (appendix to Rev. Edward Clarke, *A Defence of the Conduct of the Lieutenant-Governor of the Island of Minorca, in Reply to a Printed Libel*, 1767, p. 66); this officer, apparently no relation of Bute's, may have been confused by rumour with Courtenay.

17. Harriet Churchill (1726–77), m. 1 (1747) Sir Everard Fawkener (1684–1758); m. 2 (1765) Hon. Thomas Pownall (*ante* 31 Oct. 1741 OS).

18. Henrietta (Harriet) Fawkener (ca 1751–1825), m. 1 (30 June 1764) Hon. Edward Bouverie (1738–1810); m. 2 (1811) Lord Robert Spencer (OSSORY ii. 348, n. 19; *St James's Chronicle* 28–30 June, *sub* 30 June; Namier and Brooke ii. 105).

19. John Crewe (1742–1829), cr. (1806) Bn Crewe; M.P. Stafford 1765–8, Cheshire

1768–1802. The *Daily Adv.* 19 May, and the *St James's Chronicle* 17–19 May and *London Chronicle* 17–19 May, xv. 474, all carried a false report that Miss Fawkener had been married 17 May to 'the Hon. William Bouverie, Esq.,' who is mis-styled, having succeeded his father as 2d Vct Folkestone in 1761, and who in fact was presumably in mourning at this time for his second wife, Rebecca, who had died 4 May. The *St James's Chronicle* 19–22 May, *sub* 21 May, repudiated this report, asserting, again in error, that it was 'John Crew, Esq.,' whom Miss Fawkener had married 17 May; this second report was repeated by the GM for May (1764, xxxiv. 250). Actually, no wedding had taken place 17 May, it having perhaps been planned for that day but postponed because of the death of Lord Folkestone's wife, and it was Lord Folkestone's younger brother, the Hon. Edward Bouverie (see preceding note), whom Miss Fawkener finally married 30 June. John Crewe was a friend of John Hinchliffe, afterwards Bishop of Peterborough, who performed the ceremony (*St James's Chronicle* 28–30 June, *sub* 30 June), and may have been a suitor of Miss Fawkener's; two years later he married the latter's friend, Frances Greville.

20. William Skrine (?1721–83), M.P. Callington 1771–80 (Warren H. Smith, *Originals Abroad*, 2d edn, New Haven, 1952, pp. 3–9, 179).

21. Jane Sumner (d. 1766), m. (21 May 1764) William Skrine; she was a discarded mistress of Lord Sandwich. See ibid. 7–8, 179.

22. William Brightwell Sumner (b. ca 1730), later of Hatchlands, Surrey; a

To Conway, Tuesday 5 June 1764

Printed from *Works* v. 108–9.

Arlington Street, June 5, 1764.

YOU will wonder that I have been so long without giving you any signs of life; yet, though not writing *to* you, I have been employed *about* you, as I have ever since the 21st of April;[1] a day your enemies shall have some cause to remember. I had writ nine or ten sheets of an answer to the *Address to the Public,*[2] when I received the enclosed *mandate.*[3] You will see *my masters* order me, as a

nabob (ibid. 7; J. M. Holzman, *Nabobs in England,* New York, 1926, pp. 10, 120, 129, 164; Sir Bernard Burke, *Landed Gentry,* 1868, p. 1457).

———

1. In late April HW drew up an address praising Conway's disinterestedness and approving his stand against general warrants; this he submitted to the Duke of Grafton, who had recommended Conway's being chosen for the borough of Thetford. The Duke approved it, and with the concurrence of the Dukes of Cumberland and Devonshire, prevailed upon the mayor and 25 aldermen of the borough to sign it and transmit it to Conway as coming from themselves. The address, dated 28 April (printed Appendix 6), and Conway's reply, dated 30 April, were, through HW's efforts, 'circulated in all the newspapers' (HW's account in his MS 'foul copy' of *Mem. Geo. III,* p. 157; *Lloyd's Evening Post* 30 April – 2 May, xiv. 417; *St James's Chronicle* 1–3 May; *London Chronicle* 3–5 May, xv. 427). HW also attempted, unsuccessfully, 'to form a little junto of the most considerable part of our friends in the House of Commons, who should plan our future measures and conduct them' (*Mem. Geo. III* i. 326–7), and afterwards to 'inflame' the 'factions of the Court' (ibid. i. 328).

2. *An Address to the Public on the Late Dismission of a General Officer,* by William Guthrie (1708–70), a hack-writer for the government; it was published 24 May ('Short Notes,' GRAY i. 40 and n. 267). HW on 29 May began his answer (printed *Works* ii. 549–76), which was in reply not only to Guthrie's *Address* but

also to a letter printed in the *Gazetteer* for 9 May (ibid. ii. 550); it was finished 12 June, but not published till 2 Aug., under the title of *A Counter Address to the Public, on the Late Dismission of a General Officer* ('Short Notes,' GRAY i. 40 and n. 268); a condensed version appeared in GM Aug. 1764, xxxiv. 362–9. One of HW's copies of the pamphlet is now WSL. See Hazen, *Cat. of HW's Lib.,* No. 1609:8:6; idem, *Bibl. of HW* 50–2.

3. Thomas Pitt to HW 25 May 1764 (printed in *Additional Grenville Papers, 1763–1765,* ed. J. Tomlinson, Manchester, 1962, p. 130). George Grenville had written Pitt 15 May (*Grenville Papers* ii. 320–4) complaining of a report being spread that in his meeting with HW held at Pitt's house 3 Dec. (*ante* 9 Dec. 1763), he had said that 'if General Conway voted in Parliament according to his conscience he was unfit to have any command in the King's army.' Grenville also observed that 'it has been said that this absurd and monstrous falsehood has not been discouraged by Mr Walpole himself,' gave his version of the meeting, and asked Pitt to write him word 'whether you have heard anything of this honourable report, what part of this transaction you remember, and what you think of the whole of it.' In his reply of 25 May (*Grenville Papers* ii. 324–7) Pitt wrote that 'the facts are, I believe, precisely as you represent them,' giving his own version of the meeting, which agreed substantially with Grenville's, and assuring Grenville that HW 'will make it his business to state the direct contrary when he knows of the report'; the same day he wrote to HW,

subaltern of the Exchequer, to drop you and defend them—but you will see too, that, instead of obeying, *I have given warning*.[4] I would not communicate any part of this transaction to you, till it was out of my hands, because I knew your affection for me would not approve my going so far—but it was necessary. My honour required that I should declare my adherence to you in the most authentic manner. I found that some persons had dared to doubt whether I would risk everything for you. You see by these letters that Mr Grenville himself had presumed so. Even a change in the administration, however unlikely, might happen before I had any opportunity of declaring myself; and then those who should choose to put the worst construction, either on my actions or my silence, might say what they pleased. I was waiting for some opportunity: they have put it into my hands, and I took care not to let it slip. Indeed they have put more into my hands, which I have not let slip neither. Could I expect they would give me so absurd an account of Mr Grenville's conduct, and give it me in writing?[5] They can only add to this obligation that of provocation to print my letter,[6] which, however strong in facts, I have taken care to make very decent in terms, because it imports us to have the candid (that is, I fear, the mercenary) on our side.—No, that we must not expect, but at least disarmed.

Lord Tavistock has flung his handkerchief to Lady Elizabeth Keppel. They all go to Woburn on Thursday, and the ceremony is to be performed as soon as her brother, the Bishop, can arrive from Exeter.[7] I am heartily glad the Duchess of Bedford does not set her heart on marrying me to anybody; I am sure she would bring it

enclosing a copy of his reply to Grenville, and asking him to refute the report.

4. HW, in his long reply to Pitt's letter, 5 June 1764, conceded that Grenville had not made the statement attributed to him in just those words, but contended that 'the report may easily have arisen from what he assuredly did say.' Towards the end of the letter he proclaims that 'it is high time for the administration to discountenance and disclaim the language held by all the writers on their side, particularly by the author of the *Address to the Public, that officers are to be dismissed for their behaviour in Parliament.*'

5. In his reply to Grenville 25 May, Pitt wrote that 'I am ready to testify that in that conversation' with HW 'there appeared in you every mark of kindness and friendly disposition to General Conway' (ibid. ii. 325).

6. In his letter to Pitt, HW wrote that 'Mr Grenville is welcome to publish this letter; it will be the fullest answer to anything that is said against him without foundation.'

7. See *post* 8 June 1764, and Lord Tavistock's letter to Sir Charles Bunbury 8 June on his approaching marriage (*Bedford Corr.* iii. 262–3).

about. She has some small intention of coupling my niece[8] and Dick Vernon,[9] but I have forbidden the banns.

The Birthday, I hear, was lamentably empty. We had a funereal loo last night in the great chamber at Lady Bel Finch's: the Duke, Princess Emily, and the Duchess of Bedford were there. The Princess entertained her Grace with the joy the Duke of Bedford will have in being a grandfather; in which reflection, I believe, the grandmotherhood was not forgotten. Adieu!

From Hertford, Wednesday 6 June 1764

Printed for the first time from a photostat of BM Add. MSS 23218, ff. 152–3.

Paris, June 6th 1764.

Dear Horry,

I HAVE some right to that friendship you are so good to express and show for me in every instance, because no man loves or esteems you more than myself. Had I been in England or within reach of your opinion, I should have given you a disagreeable proof of my regard upon this occasion, by desiring your sentiments before I returned any answer to the letters I had received. I do not say those sentiments might have absolutely determined the conduct I was to pursue, because I had a thousand difficulties in my view into which no man could see so well as myself. Upon comparing every circumstance and every one of those difficulties, I have told you that I did not intend to quit the embassy, because it seemed upon the whole to be the best part I could take in a very disagreeable situation. I do not tell you I have determined rightly; my poor judgment is far from being infallible, and I will blame no impartial dispassionate man who differs with me in opinion upon that judgment. It must upon the whole be the rule of my actions, though it may be freest from error when I have the assistance of my friends to form it justly.

In all my letters except to yourself and my brother, as well as in what I have had occasion to say upon this unpleasant subject, except

8. Lady Waldegrave.
9. Deleted in *Works*, restored in Wright, iv. 425. He was the Duchess's brother-in-law; his wife had died in 1763 (*ante* ca 15 Feb. 1752, n. 9; 20 April 1764, n. 9).

in one instance, out of my own family, I have never spoke of any resolution I had formed about it. I have mentioned, what everybody would naturally suppose, how grievous it must be to me, and I have satisfied their curiosity no farther. It was more respectful by my brother and more prudent by myself than in declaring what those present intentions were, and indeed the subject is of too delicate and too complicated a nature to tempt me to express any other sentiments upon it than such as relate to my brother or my own public situation. I shall receive with friendship the freest of your thoughts upon any occasion where you are so good to give them, and I beg you will treat this subject without any reserve. You may rest assured it shall not be communicated, even to the two persons you have excepted, without it is your desire.

On Monday the 4th, being the King's Birthday, I thought it my duty to entertain his Majesty's subjects at Paris, and I hope you will hear that I did it in a manner suitable to the rank of an English ambassador. We were ninety and nine in company, and I believe they were all satisfied.[1] We had a band of music to entertain us during the time of dinner, which was pretty long, and when we retired to drink tea and coffee we had a faro table ready to employ those who did not choose whist or to walk and enjoy our fine prospect. I do not know if you are acquainted upon what a[2] footing faro is at Paris. No gentleman deals; the employment is not esteemed *trop honnête*. You send to the *lieutenant de police* for a banker, and he sends you a very civil man, who is under the rod of the police of Paris if he offends.

The King and his Court continue to treat me with the greatest respect and attention; one of his Majesty's principal ministers has taken this occasion to tell me how concerned he should be as well as

1. 'Lord Hertford gave yesterday a grand dinner to all the English here except *one*, and to the true Irish Whigs; nor, like a good courtier, did he omit the new converts, the Scots. He did not, however, observe the distinction which is so much in fashion on your side of the water; for the true friends of the Hanover family were received as well, at least, as their known enemies. My lot is particular, and droll enough. I am the single Englishman not invited by the ambassador of my country, on the only day I can at Paris show my attachment to my sovereign, as if I was disaffected to the present establishment. . . . You may believe me when I assure you, it was not the slightest mortification to me that I did not receive an invitation to the Hôtel de Brancas. When I was asked how it could happen that so staunch a Whig as Mr Wilkes was not invited on the 4th of June, I laughed, like the old Roman. I had rather you should ask, why I was *not* invited, than why I was invited?' (Wilkes to Almon 5 June in his *Correspondence*, ed. Almon, 1805, iii. 124–6).

2. 'A what' in MS.

everyone here if anything should induce me to quit Paris. It has, I dare say, arisen from Guerchi's representation of what has passed in England about my brother, but I do not desire you to mention this compliment to anyone.

Shall we not see you at Paris? You know how happy we shall be to make it agreeable to you. About the 26th of this month I must go to Compiègne with the Court for six or seven weeks; in the middle of August we expect to return to Paris. If you like the Compiègne life, it is nearer England and in your road to this place.

I remain, with the best compliments of the family, dear Horry,

Most sincerely and affectionately yours,

Hertford

To Hertford, Friday 8 June 1764

Printed from *Works* ix. 126–9.

Strawberry Hill, June 8th 1764.

TO be sure, you have heard the event of this last week? Lord Tavistock has flung his hankerchief, and, except a few jealous *sultanas,* and some *sultana valides*[1] who had marketable daughters, everybody is pleased that the lot is fallen on Lady Elizabeth Keppel.

The House of Bedford came to town last Friday. I supped with them that night at the Spanish Ambassador's,[2] who has made Powis House magnificent.[3] Lady Elizabeth was not there, nor mentioned.

1. *Sic* in *Works;* probably HW meant *sultanas invalides.*

2. The Prince de Masserano. 'On Friday night last [1 June] his Excellency the Spanish Ambassador gave an elegant cold collation at Powis House to the Duke and Duchess of Bedford, the Duke and Duchess of Marlborough, and many others of the principal nobility. It is said there was served up at the said supper the most noble salad that has been seen this season' (*London Chronicle* 2–5 June, xv. 534).

3. 'His Excellency the Spanish Ambassador maintains his household, we hear, with great splendour, paying ready money for everything that is brought to his house. It is said that the Princess, spouse to his Excellency, is every day expected, together with their young son, and that the house has been for some time furnishing, with great elegance and magnificence in the Spanish manner for her reception. The Prince keeps six footmen and a coachman in livery, and four gentlemen to wait on his person, and usher the ladies; these gentlemen, on days of ceremony, are dressed in uniforms, light blue with a rich silver arras lace' (ibid. 7–9 June, xv. 549).

On the contrary, by the Duchess's conversation, which turned on Lady Betty Montague, there were suspicions in her favour. The next morning Lady Elizabeth received a note from the Duchess of Marlborough,[4] insisting on seeing her that evening. When she arrived at Marlborough House, she found nobody but the Duchess and Lord Tavistock. The Duchess cried, 'Lord! They have left the window open in [the] next room!'—went to shut it, and shut the lovers in too, where they remained for three hours. The same night all the town was at the Duchess of Richmond's.[5] Lady Albemarle[6] was at tredille;[7] the Duke of Bedford came up to the table, and told her he must speak to her as soon as the pool was over. You may guess whether she knew a card more that she played. When she had finished, the Duke told her he should wait on her the next morning, to make the demand in form. She told it directly to me and my niece Waldegrave, who was in such transport for her friend,[8] that she promised the Duke of Bedford to kiss him, and hurried home directly to write to her sisters.[9] The Duke asked no questions about fortune, but has since slipped a bit of paper in Lady Elizabeth's hand, telling her, he hoped his son would live, but if he did not, there was something for her; it was a jointure of £3000 a year, and £600 pin money. I dined with her the next day at Monsieur de Guerchy's,[10] and as I hindered the company from wishing her joy, and yet joked with her myself, Madame de Guerchy said, she perceived I would let nobody else tease her, that I might have all the teasing to myself. She has behaved in the prettiest manner in the world, and would not appear at a vast assembly at Northumberland House on Tuesday,[11] nor at a great haymaking at Mrs Pitt's on

4. Lord Tavistock's sister. The Marlboroughs are mentioned as being at the Spanish Ambassador's on the Friday (above, n. 2), but another item in the papers reports them as coming to town only on Saturday, 2 June (ibid. 2–5 June, xv. 530).

5. 'Yesterday [sic] there was a very grand entertainment at his Grace the Duke of Richmond's in Privy Garden, Whitehall' (ibid. 31 May – 2 June, xv. 525, sub 2 June).

6. Aunt of the Duke of Richmond and mother of Lady Elizabeth Keppel.

7. Tredrille or tredille, 'a card-game

played by three persons, usually with thirty cards' (OED).

8. And connection by marriage, Lady Waldegrave's sister Laura having married Lady Elizabeth's brother Frederick, Bishop of Exeter.

9. Mrs Keppel and Charlotte Walpole (1738–89), m. (1760) Lionel Tollemache, styled Vct Huntingtower, 5th E. of Dysart, 1770.

10. Presumably on the King's Birthday, 4 June, when, according to the London Chronicle, 'the French Ambassador's house in Soho Square was illuminated in a very splendid manner' (2–5 June, xv. 536).

11. See below, next paragraph.

Wednesday.[12] Yesterday they all went to Woburn, and tomorrow the ceremony is to be performed, for the Duke has not a moment's patience till she is breeding.

You would have been diverted at Northumberland House; besides the sumptuous liveries, the illuminations in the garden,[13] the pages, the two chaplains in waiting in their gowns and scarves, *à l'ir-landaise,* and Dr Hill and his wife,[14] there was a most delightful Countess,[15] who has just imported herself from Mecklenburgh. She is an absolute Princess of Monomotapa;[16] but I fancy you have seen her, for her hideousness and frantic accoutrements are so extraordinary, that they tell us she was hissed in the Tuileries. She crossed the Drawing-Room on the Birthday to speak to the Queen *en amie,* after standing with her back to Princess Amalie. The Queen was so ashamed of her, that she said cleverly, 'This is not the dress at Strelitz; but this woman always dressed herself as capriciously there, as your Duchess of Queensberry does here.'

The haymaking at Wandsworth Hill did not succeed, from the excessive cold of the night; I proposed to bring one of the cocks into the great room, and make a bonfire. All the beauties were disappointed, and all the macaronies afraid of getting the toothache.

The Guerchys are gone to Goodwood, and were to have been carried to Portsmouth, but Lord Egmont[17] refused to let the Ambassador see the place. The Duke of Richmond was in a rage, and I do not know how it has ended, for the Duke of Bedford defends

12. At Mrs George Pitt's (MANN vi. 572).

13. 'Lady Northumberland being under a necessity of leaving town on Monday . . . the grand illuminations designed as a compliment to his Majesty's birthday, were postponed till her Ladyship's return, which was on Tuesday evening; when everything was conducted with a decorum and magnificence peculiar to the Countess of Northumberland: 1500 persons of distinction were invited and the garden was decorated with 10,000 lamps, 400 of which being fixed to the balustrades descending by the steps, had a most beautiful effect. Two bands of music were provided, one in the house (where the great gallery was illuminated to an astonishing degree of splendour) and the other in the garden, which answered alternately, and upon Lord Granby's entrance struck up, "See the Conquering Hero Comes," a mark of

respect to the extraordinary merit of that illustrious officer, which was instantly returned by a general huzza from the whole company. The company departed at half an hour after twelve, and at seven o'clock yesterday morning her Ladyship set out for Sion House' (*London Chronicle* 5–7 June, xv. 544).

14. Presumably 'Dr' John Hill, miscellaneous writer and quack (*ante* 28 Sept. 1758), and his second wife Wilhelmina or Henrietta Jones, sister of 4th Vct Ranelagh (DNB; M. Archdall and J. Lodge, *The Peerage of Ireland,* 1789, iv. 304).

15. A Madame de Yertzin (see postscript); not further identified.

16. A native empire in the Mozambique-Zambezi region of Eastern Africa. HW couples it with Mecklenburg in MASON i. 448.

17. First Lord of the Admiralty.

the refusal, and says, they certainly would not let you see Brest. The Comte d'Ayen[18] is going a longer tour. He is liked here. The three great ambassadors[19] danced at Court—the Prince of Masserano they say well; he is extremely in fashion, and is a sensible very good-humoured man, though his appearance is so deceitful. They have given me the honour of a bon mot, which, I assure you, does not belong to me, that I never saw a man so full of *orders* and *disorders*. He and his suite, and the Guerchys and theirs, are to dine here next week.[20] Poor little Strawberry never thought of such fêtes. I did invite them to breakfast, but they confounded it, and understood that they were asked to dinner, so I must do as well as I can. Both the ambassadors are in love with my niece, therefore, I trust they will not have unsentimental stomachs.

Shall I trouble you with a little commission? It is to send me a book that I cannot get here, nor am I quite sure of the exact title, but it is called *Origine des mœurs*,[21] or something to that import. It is in three volumes, and has not been written above two or three years.

Adieu, my dear Lord, from my fireside,

Yours ever,

H. W.

PS. Do you know that Madame de Yertzin, the Mecklenburgh Countess, has had the honour of giving the King of Prussia a box of the ear?—I am sure he deserved it, if he could take liberties with such a chimpanzee.

Colonel Elliot[22] died on Thursday.

---

18. Presumably Jean-Louis-François-Paul de Noailles (1739–1824), Comte d'Ayen; Duc d'Ayen, 1766; Duc de No-ailles, 1793 (*La Grande encyclopédie*, 1886–1902, xxiv. 1153; La Chenaye-Desbois xiv. 990).

19. Of France, Spain, and the Empire.

20. See MONTAGU ii. 126–7.

21. Presumably HW is referring to one or both of two volumes by F. V. Toussaint: *Les Mœurs*, Amsterdam, 1763 (in 3 parts), and *Éclaircissement sur les mœurs*, Amsterdam, 1762 (Hazen, *Cat. of HW's Lib.*, No. 2050:23); HW later refers to the work or works in question as *Essais sur les mœurs* and *Les Considéra-tions sur les mœurs* (post 5 Oct., 3 Dec. 1764).

22. William Elliot (d. 7 June 1764), Capt. 1723, Maj. 1737, Lt-Col. 1741, ret. 1745; m. (1737) HW's friend Lady Frances Nassau d'Auverquerque, dau. of E. of Grantham (GM 1764, xxxiv. 302; MANN vii. 416, n. 18).

From HERTFORD, Friday 22 June 1764

Printed for the first time from a photostat of BM Add. MSS 23218, ff. 154–5.

Paris, June 22d 1764.

Dear Horry,

I ADMIRE the suddenness of Lord Tavistock's passion and wedding. It has the air of an intrigue and I dare say was much easier than I can suppose the generality of such parties. It was so right to consent that Lady Elisabeth had not a pretense for doubting, and I think the Duchess[1] determined with great sensibility when she left her to accept Lord Tavistock's proposal. From the little I have seen and all that I have heard of the young lady, he could not have chose better for his own happiness. Is she so likely to bear children? In that respect I think he might have decided with a greater probability of answering the Duke's wishes.

Is your niece going to be married? I hear she is besieged so closely that the bets at White's are made,[2] and that one man is taken against the field.[3]

I am glad the ambassadors are to dine with you. Strawberry is a great curiosity; I know how well you can do the honours of it, and Guerchi will return satisfied with that instance of attention to him.

If you have the same weather in England that we have at Paris, it must be charming. The hot dry weather is now making us great amends for all the rain and all the cold that the winter and spring afforded us. In our country habitation[4] at Paris we are less sensible of it; if there is any air, we can enjoy it, and those who have not the

1. Of Marlborough.
2. None is recorded in its betting book in *The History of Whites*, [1892], Vol. II, pt 1.
3. HW writes in *Mem. Geo. III* that at this time Prince William Henry, the future Duke of Gloucester, 'openly' showed himself 'her admirer' (iii. 268). Lady Waldegrave consented ca 3 May to copy and send to the Prince the following letter composed by HW (MS now WSL): 'Sir, your Royal Highness commanded me not to give you a direct answer till you should be of age [Prince William would be 21, 14 Nov.]; but my duty, my character, and every reason of honour and prudence oblige me to put an immediate end to a correspondence which would bring disgrace either on your R. H. or on me. . . . Let me therefore with all humility entreat your R. H. never to think of me more, and at the same time to be persuaded that there is no art or coquetry in this entreaty,' etc. After 'a short fortnight . . . the Prince renewed his visits with more assiduity . . . , and Lady Waldegrave received him without disguise' (*Mem. Geo. III*, loc. cit.).
4. Hertford called his house at Paris 'town and country' *ante* 22 March 1764; it was on the river, and had a large garden.

same advantages have little houses at small distances from the town where they can find it. I did not know till I came into this country that the French lived so much there. They do not in general go so far into the country as we do, nor wish entirely for the same degree of retirement, but they are often there. They can leave Paris without regret, and they begin to talk of improving there with some pleasure. Next week I am going to Compiègne for great part of two months I fear; our return is to depend upon the size of the partridges; when they are fit to be killed, the political scene changes and the King returns to Versailles.[5] I think I shall wish for that moment; I have no great idea that the pleasures of the Court will make me amends for the inconvenience of removing into a very moderate house in a very indifferent town. We have still numbers of English here; as fast as one set goes they are succeeded by another. The sights and young ladies of Paris employ most of them. We have a kind of Vauxhall Gardens where there[6] are balls in the environs of the town.[7] I have not yet been at them, but they are said to be pretty, and that some of the oldest of my countrymen make a considerable figure in the gayest part of the amusement. I must not mention names for fear of disturbing some worthy citizen's family.

The Duke of Berwick carries this letter, who is going with his wife and son[8] for six weeks or two months into England. He is a relation as you know of Lady Hertford's, and a good-tempered man. She has given him some letters of recommendation to her friends in England, and you will oblige us by showing him any civility that will not be attended with inconvenience to yourself at this season of the year.

Adieu, my dear Horry. I have an appointment this morning with a black prince who calls himself son of the King of Angola, and has desired a conference with the English ambassador. I dare to say he

5. For the King's stay at Compiègne, 20 June – 16 August, see A. Demarsy, 'Le Séjour de Louis XV à Compiègne en 1764,' Société Historique de Compiègne, Bulletin, 1869–72, i. 159–68.

6. 'They' in the MS.

7. The various public places in and around Paris of the kind Hertford describes were called *vauxhalls* after the English Vauxhall (see P.-T.-N. Hurtaut

and —— Magny, *Dictionnaire historique de . . . Paris*, 1779, iv. 778, *sub* 'Vauxhall'). HW went 'to the Opera and Vauxhall with Duke and Duchess of Richmond' in 1769 ('Paris Journals,' DU DEFFAND v. 328).

8. Charles-Bernard-Pascal-Janvier Fitzjames (1751–87), Marquis de la Jamaïque; 4th D. of Berwick (attainted), 1785 (MANN vii. 402, n. 14).

is an[9] impostor[10] and I am curious to know in what manner he proposes to impose upon me. I remain, with the best compliments of the family,

Ever sincerely and affectionately yours,

Hertford

To Hertford, ca July 1764

Two letters, missing, answered *post* 17 and 28 July 1764. The one answered 28 July was probably written before the one answered 17 July; see *post* 28 July 1764, n. 1.

To Conway, Monday 2 July 1764

Printed from a photostat of the MS in the Pierpont Morgan Library; first printed Toynbee vi. 86–8. For the history of the MS, see *ante* 31 Oct. 1741 OS. *Endorsed:* Mr W. 2 July 1764.

Strawberry Hill, Monday night.

IF my Lady Ailesbury does not think the little bull as handsome as Jupiter himself, I shall resent it. He is accompanied by seven bantams for the Infanta.

As Lord Frederic and Lord John[1] are gone to you this evening, I can tell you no politics but what they know. The Bedfords are certainly jealous of some negotiation being on foot between Lord Bute and Pitt, but I cannot find it is with any reason, though I do not desire to have them undeceived.[2]

9. 'He is an' written over 'however that' in the MS.

10. He was. 'The pretended Prince of Angola, at Paris, proves to be an impostor, and was therefore lately taken up, having, under that false title, contracted debts to a large amount, to support his brilliant appearance. He had been a servant to an Irish merchant, who was very active in the late rebellion in Scotland in the year 1745, and is since settled at Nantz. This *chevalier d'industrie* had very proper talents for that profession, having a fine address, etc. However, he has got a lodging, with his attendants, in the Bicêtre of Paris [a prominent insane asylum]' (*London Chronicle* 11–14 Aug., xvi. 145).

1. Cavendish.

2. Lord Sandwich wrote to Grenville, 3 July: 'I am . . . inclined to think Mr Pitt has hopes of coming into employment from some division among ourselves; and I understand, from those who talk his language, that they lay great stress upon differences they believe have hap-

I sent your papers to Mr Matthews[3] the moment I got to town; he said he was very ill, but would transcribe them if he could.

Lord Bath has been dying, but is out of danger;[4] and what I like more, Legge mends again.[5]

Your brother has sent me the Duke and Duchess of Berwick, and what upon earth to do with them I don't know. They have the grace to call themselves Lirias[6] here, yet they do not go to Court,[7] and say they are only come to see their relations. He looks like a cook, but does not seem to have parts enough for one.[8] He had never heard that his great-grandmother[9] married Mr Godfrey: he told me today that she called herself Churchill, but that her family name was Marlborough. The Duchess of Liria, who is sister of the Duc of Alva,[10] is a rational civil being, not at all handsome, but easy and genteel. They have more debts than dukedoms, though he is Duke of Veraguez[11] too, and have crowded all their rich blood into *la rue de* Suffolk Street.[12]

They talk of a match between Lord Middlesex and Lady Jane Stuart: in the meantime Mr Ellis[13] is dying for her, and Lord Holland's young Maccartney[14] very desirous of living by her.

The fashionable diversion in town is a conjurer:[15] we had him last

pened between the Duke of Bedford and Lord Bute. To what this report can owe its rise I am at a loss to guess, as I am convinced it is utterly void of foundation. . . . Lord Gower . . . assures me . . . that though he [Bedford] is jealous of Lord Bute, and naturally adverse to him, he . . . is of opinion that the report is utterly groundless' (*Grenville Papers* ii. 376–7).

3. Not identified.

4. He died 8 July.

5. 'Mr Legge is said to be wonderfully better, in consequence of his drinking some waters upon Blackheath; but I pay little credit to this, which seems to be an old woman's story' (Charles Jenkinson to Grenville 5 July, ibid. ii. 383).

6. Berwick was also the 3d D. of Liria and Xerica in Spain.

7. However, 'the Duke of Berwick . . . was introduced to his Majesty at St James's' 5 July (*Daily Adv.* 6 July).

8. HW wrote to Montagu, 16 July 1764, that Berwick 'has just the sort of capacity which you would expect in a Stuart en-

grafted on a Spaniard' (MONTAGU ii. 129).

9. Arabella Churchill (1648–1730), sister of the 1st D. of Marlborough, m. Col. Charles Godfrey (ca 1648–1714); mistress of James II (*Political State of Great Britain*, 1715, ix. 155; John Le Neve, *Monumenta Anglicana*, 1717–19, iv. 279–80).

10. Fernando de Silva Álvarez de Toledo (1714–76), 12th D. of Alba or Alva (CHATTERTON 169, n. 11).

11. 10th Duke of Veragua and La Vega.

12. Noted for its poor accommodations; see *ante* 9 Sept. 1762.

13. Perhaps Welbore Ellis.

14. George Macartney (1737–1806), cr. (1776) Bn, (1792) Vct, and (1794) E. Macartney; M.P.; diplomatist. He was an intimate friend of the Holland family, and had travelled on the Continent as companion and mentor to Stephen Fox (Lord Ilchester, *Henry Fox, First Lord Holland*, 1920, ii. 262–3; see also *Leinster Corr.* i. 106). He married Lady Jane Stuart in 1768.

15. Not identified.

night at my Lady Harrington's. His tricks are ten times more dexterous than Sandwich's.

There was last night at Guerchy's a daughter[16] of Lord Dillon, just come out of a convent, who is to be the future Duchess of Norfolk;[17] she has a fine person, and not at all a disagreeable face.

The Mecklemburgh-Countess was there too, ten times more dirty, frowzy, extravagant and mad than ever. Prince William has said, 'This is the worst sample we have had yet.' I begin to think he will not command the army.[18]

My Lord Townshend and Charles had quarrelled lately. My Lady[19] made a reconciling dinner for them, and all was made up. As soon as they parted, George wrote the most abusive letter in the world to Charles, and they are rather ill together again.[20] Adieu!

Yours ever,

H. W.

16. Presumably Frances Dillon (1747–1825), eldest daughter of Henry Dillon (d. 1787), 11th Vct Dillon, 1741; m. (1767) William Jerningham (1736–1809), 6th Bt, 1774, of Cossey, Norfolk (GEC, Baronetage).

17. Presumably a match was being rumoured at this time between Frances Dillon and Edward Howard (1744–67), nephew and heir presumptive of the 9th D. of Norfolk (MANN vi. 483, n. 4).

18. HW wrote, post 27 Aug. 1764, that 'no household is to be established for Prince William, who accedes nearer to the malcontents every day.'

19. The Dowager Lady Townshend, their mother.

20. The brothers had been estranged since Charles's refusal to follow George into the Grenville administration in 1763, and his going into Opposition with Pitt and Newcastle. However, after the death of their father in March, their differences began to be made up, and Charles wrote to his mother about George, 17 July 1764: 'Lady Dalkeith has told your Lady-

ship how frequently I have received letters from Raynham written in a temper not excusable, in a language quite ill-bred, and continually alluding to circumstances and reports which have not the least foundation. At last, and after a long neglect, I answered the indifferent parts of one of these letters, and in a very plain and free manner gave my reasons for declining all correspondence upon other subjects. This resistance, not to say resentment, has produced by the last post a letter as remarkably affectionate, filled with apology, commendation, and confidence, with a very slight mixture of complaint, and even that rather meant to express concern than complaint' (Townshend MSS at Raynham, quoted by Sir Lewis Namier and John Brooke, Charles Townshend, 1964, p. 103). In the following year, Charles, partly through his brother's efforts, took office in the Grenville administration, and their rapprochement was complete. See also Namier and Brooke iii. 552.

From Hertford, Wednesday 4 July 1764

Printed for the first time from a photostat of BM Add. MSS 23218, ff. 156–7.

Compiègne, July 4th 1764.

Dear Horry,

YOU must know what becomes of me though my motions are of ever so little consequence, and you must submit to hear from me though I have little to say. By the date of my letter you will see where I am settled for a month or six weeks to come. I left Paris with regret. We have there many conveniences we want here. The first week I have passed alone; yesterday Lady Hertford and my son arrived, but I believe not with an intention of staying here very long. The life of this place is rather calculated for ministers and sportsmen than for ladies who are not attached to the Court. The company is not numerous. It consists chiefly of those whose duty and services oblige them to residence. It is not entertaining enough for such as can choose where they will pass their time. There is but one public entertainment, which is a comedy, and that I am told is not well acted. The great amusement is whist; you have no idea what a passion the French have for it and how ill they play. The dinners and suppers are very constant, but a man may make his excuse when he wishes to be quiet; business is a very just plea against which there can be no remonstrance.

The King hunts five or six times a week. As it is not a bad way of paying court, I have attended him, and had the good fortune to be near him when he shot a boar with great dexterity.[1] I could with truth take the opportunity of making him a compliment upon it.

I was flattered the other day with a letter I received from Princess Amelia wherein she tells me I am to expect you soon. I hope her information is good. You know how much we all esteem and love you. That you may choose the time and place which will please you most in case you intend us a visit this summer: I shall probably stay here till the 7th of next month, and afterwards be settled at Paris till

1. 'Le 2 [juillet], le roi va à la chasse au carrefour des Routes. . . . Il chasse deux sangliers dont un est pris près de Longpont' (A. Demarsy, 'Le Séjour de Louis XV à Compiègne en 1764,' Société Historique de Compiègne, *Bulletin*, 1869–72, i. 164–5).

the beginning of October, when the Court goes to Fontainbleau; during that interval I have nothing but little shooting-parties to take me from my fine house at Paris, and those will not interfere with the pleasure I shall have in seeing you. You will always command me wherever I am, but perhaps Paris may be most agreeable to you.

I hear little or nothing from England. Possibly there may not be much to hear; it is a dull time of year and politics make no figure without a House of Commons to show them.

I intend writing to my brother very soon; what has happened to him has given and still gives me much concern. I was brought into a situation where I could not act to satisfy my mind.

Lady Hertford and my son desire their best compliments. I remain, dear Horry,

Most truly and affectionately yours,

HERTFORD

From HERTFORD, Tuesday 17 July 1764

Printed for the first time from a photostat of BM Add. MSS 23218, ff. 158–9.

Compiègne, July 17th 1764.

Dear Horry,

I HAVE just time to acknowledge your short letter[1] and to say with what impatience I wait the arrival of the one you give me reason to expect.

I have been at Paris for a couple of days.[2] In the hurry of my business there I saw for a minute Mr Selwyn,[2a] who told me he should pass two months in this country. I likewise saw Mr Churchill, who arrived from the provinces just as I was obliged to leave it. I was much disappointed in not being able to see Lady Mary,[3] but Lady

---

1. Missing.

2. Hertford wrote to Halifax from Paris, 14 July: 'As I foresaw no immediate appearance of business at Compiègne I have taken the opportunity of coming here for two or three days to settle some family affairs and I propose returning there on Monday [16 July]' (S.P. 78/262, f. 165).

2a. George Selwyn.

3. Lady Mary Churchill, HW's sister.

Hertford promised to entertain her today at dinner before she returned to Compiègne.[4] Mr Churchill seems very uncertain where he shall dispose of himself and his children.[5] His first intention upon leaving Caen seems to have been for Nancy or some town in Lorraine, but I think at present he is rather inclined to go to some old château in the neighbourhood of Paris which the proprietor does not inhabit.

We are now in the gayest minutes of Compiègne. The camp is formed.[6] I saw today *deux hommes de paille* shot again and again with cannon bullets. We had likewise a number of bombs well thrown into a work prepared to receive them, and there was a little redoubt attacked and taken which we did not see. The sun was hot and the ladies' faces could not withstand it. The King and all the royal family except the Queen attended.[7] These amusements are to continue till the 24th;[8] on the 8th of next month or about that time we shall return to Paris to settle. Why will not you come sooner than September?[9] We shall be ready to receive you.

The Spanish courier[10] for whom I intend this letter is in a hurry

4. Selwyn wrote to Lord Holland, 19 July, that the Churchills 'were at Lady Hertford's the other day' (*Letters to Henry Fox*, ed. Lord Ilchester, Roxburghe Club, 1915, pp. 195, 196).

5. Charles Churchill (ca 1747–85); Robert Churchill (b. 1748); George Churchill (d. 1808), army officer; Henry Churchill; Horatio (Horace) Churchill (1759–1817), army officer; Mary Churchill (*ante* 6 July 1754, n. 5); and Sophia Churchill (before 1759–1797), m. (1781) Hon. Horatio Walpole, later 2d E. of Orford, n.c. (HW's 'Pedigree of Walpole,' 1776, in his annotated *Description of . . . Strawberry Hill*, 1784, now WSL; MANN iii. 465, n. 18, v. 279, nn. 10, 11; BERRY ii. 212, n. 6; *Notes and Queries*, 1864, 3d ser., vi. 318).

6. 'Du 12 au 25 de ce mois, nous avons eu 4 camps dans nos environs; et ils étaient formés, le 1er par le régiment de la Marine infanterie, le 2me par le régiment de Royal Normandie, cavalerie, le 3me par le régiment de la Reine, aussi cavalerie, et le 4me par la brigade de Desmaris, artillerie. . . . Sa Maj. a paru extrême-

ment contente de ces corps; Elle se propose de faire venir successivement et chaque année les autres corps de ses troupes afin de juger par Elle-même si ses ordonnances sont bien executées' ('Lettre de Compiègne . . . 28 juillet,' *Mercure historique*, 1764, clvii. 161–2).

7. 'Le Roi et la famille royale ont vu, le 15, dans le camp de l'artillerie, le jeu des bombes, des obus et du canon, ils y ont eu encore le cheminement de la sape le 17' (ibid. 162).

8. 'Le Roi et la famille royale . . . le 22 . . . ont été présents aux évolutions du régiment de la Marine . . . [Les] 4 corps sont partis de leurs camps . . . savoir, le régiment de Royal Normandie le 23, celui de la Reine le 24, celui de la Marine le même jour, et la brigade d'artillerie le 25' (ibid.).

9. HW wrote to Montagu, 16 July 1764, that 'my mind is pretty fixed on going to Paris the beginning of September' (MONTAGU ii. 128–9), but he did not go until Sept. 1765, after Hertford had left.

10. Not identified.

to leave Paris, and will be gone if I do not finish before he receives it. I must therefore conclude with assuring you that I am, dear Horry,

Always very sincerely and affectionately yours,

HERTFORD

Lady Mary Coke has wrote Lady Hertford word that we have a chance of seeing her at Paris.[11]

From HERTFORD, Saturday 28 July 1764

Printed for the first time from a photostat of BM Add. MSS 23218, ff. 160–2.

Compiègne, July 28th 1764.

Dear Horry,

I HAVE ten thousand thanks to return you for your very long and very friendly letter.[1] You may with the utmost freedom deliver your sentiments to me upon any occasion, and I will make that return which I owe you in justice and friendship by feeling the strongest obligation.

The politics of last winter have, you know, disgusted me. The being separated from my friends and obliged to take a part in the divisions of the country during my absence from it have given me an indifference I never felt before, and that I think to a great degree I shall ever retain even in the present state of my own family. I will not look back to judge how by different means I am brought into this disagreeable situation, but I know I did all I could to prevent a separation in politics from that person whom I shall ever esteem and love with the most tender affection. That I did not determine to resign the commission with which I am now invested upon his dismis-

11. She had left London for the Continent 19 June, and was at Spa 19 July (Coke, *Journals* i. 7, 8).

———

1. Missing. Presumably this was the letter Hertford gave HW leave to write, *ante* 6 June 1764, 'without any reserve' on the subject of Conway's dismissal; it was heralded by HW in his missing letter to Hertford, received ca 17 July (*ante* 17 July 1764), and delayed presumably because of the lack of a trustworthy messenger (see *post* 3 Aug. 1764).

sion, might perhaps be ill-judged. After weighing every circumstance of my own behaviour, what I owed to those with whom I am nearly connected, and what others owed to me, I thought it least wrong to continue here. I will not trouble you with a detail of all my motives and reasons. I am heartily punished in this instance for my political ambition, but my conduct shall be that of an honest man whilst I am employed for the public, and my mind shall be prepared for any political disappointment which may happen from parties or the ill will of private enemies.

That my brother's dismission might be owing in a peculiar manner to Lord Holland, and that his Lordship might thereby mean to involve me in a most unpleasant situation, I can very readily suppose.[2] You know I have long thought he wished to do me all the political prejudice he could,[3] and I am very sorry he had arms to act so powerfully against me, for I should be concerned[4] to acquaint him that he had succeeded so completely. My own conduct shall neither give him nor any other man room to attack me justly. I will act as I have hitherto done with that spirit, firmness and regard to my country that I owe it as a minister. I feel perfectly the delicacy of my situation and shall always acknowledge your friendship in placing it so justly before me. I have done nothing, I have said nothing that can hurt me in the opinion of any honest man. If my letters and behaviour are ever examined, I trust you will agree with the world in being of that opinion. I shall preserve that caution which you so wisely recommend to me, and you may be assured without my judgment fails me strangely that I will do right.

The case you suppose in your letter of bending to this country does to my knowledge not exist, and I assure you from what has passed through my hands to this time I must do the ministers justice

2. HW wrote to Hertford, *post* 3 Aug. 1764, that 'the Duke [of Newcastle] mentioned to me his having heard Lord Holland's inclination to your Embassy.' Apparently HW had suggested in the missing letter which is answered here that Holland had encouraged Conway's dismissal in order to place Hertford in a position where he would feel himself obliged to resign in protest against his brother's dismissal or be forced to resign because of his lowered credit in the eyes of the world, either way leaving the embassy vacant for Holland to fill.

3. Holland had, without Hertford's knowledge or consent, arranged for his wife's brother-in-law, Thomas Charles Bunbury, to be appointed secretary to the embassy in April 1763 (see *ante* 18 Oct. 1763, n. 11), and HW regarded Holland as being, 'on all occasions' and for reasons he 'never knew . . . the personal enemy' of Hertford and Conway (*Mem. Geo. III* i. 209).

4. 'Concerned' written over 'sorry' in the MS.

to say that I should suppose nothing of that sort could have happened by means of others. The negotiations are clear and to be justified in every instance on the part of England to this time, as far as they have passed through my hands. I will preserve that caution you so wisely recommend to me, and you may be assured when I am examined, if ever the day comes, that I will appear free from intentional error either on my own part or in subserviency to others. Hitherto I have been untried. If ever it should be my lot, I think in this instance I can easily resist temptation, and have no great merit in taking your friendly advice. I will not allow you, when you write with so much friendship and goodness to me, to suppose that I can suspect you of any passionate design to mislead me. I know the pureness of your heart and intentions; I am persuaded that you are the most disinterested of all men I ever knew. You love my brother and you love me (if I am allowed to say it), and you can in no instance prove it more strongly to me than in expressing your concern for what has passed, and in endeavouring to heal a wound that I flatter myself from mere affection could never happen, and that politics should not have given if I could have foreseen before I engaged in them that the price was to be so dear to my mind. I have showed your letter to no person whatever. If I have the pleasure of seeing you in September I can say more to you than I can possibly write.

Lord March, Mr Selwyn and Mr Elliot[5] are arrived here. They propose going to Paris on Monday, but from the civilities shown and proposed to be shown to them till Tuesday night, they do not go till Wednesday. The two first stay at Paris, the latter talks of going into the country for his health and amusement, and has some thoughts, he says, of settling his son[6] and tutor[7] at Reims or some other town in France for the sake of the language. Barré is likewise at Paris; his view is understood to be political, and I have heard he proposes to view the sea-coasts, etc., to form observations. You may therefore in the course of next winter, I think, expect to hear something very material about this country. Mr E[lliot] I do not suspect from anything I can yet see.

5. Gilbert Elliot (1722–77), 3d Bt, 1766.

6. Gilbert Elliot (1751–1814), 4th Bt, 1777; cr. (1797) Bn and (1813) E. of Minto. He and his younger brother Hugh were educated at La Pension Militaire, Fontainebleau, 1764–6, the school chosen for them by David Hume, a close friend of their father's; see Hume's letters to their father, 22 Sept. – 17 Nov. 1764, in his *Letters*, ed. Greig, Oxford, 1932, i. 467–74, 480–2.

7. Robert Liston (1742–1836), K.B. 1816, diplomatist.

When I mentioned Lord Holland I should have said that he was very attentive and civil to us at Paris,[8] and that he often invited my Lady and us to his house, though I did not so often accept the parties. I suppose I was therefore politically speaking of his Lordship to think he intended me the deeper cut, but I really ascribed it in part to intelligence he might hope to procure about the Canada bills[9] in which he was then said to be dealing largely. I remain, dear Horry, with the truest friendship and regard,

Ever yours,

HERTFORD

This letter is not to go the post, and you will burn it when you have read it.

From CONWAY, ca August 1764

Missing; received 7 Aug. (*post* 3 Aug. 1764, *sub* 7 Aug.).

To HERTFORD, Friday 3 August 1764

Printed from *Works* ix. 130–40.

Strawberry Hill, August 3d 1764.

AS my letters are seldom proper for the post now, I begin them at any time, and am forced to trust to chance for a conveyance. This difficulty renders my news very stale; but what can I do? There does not happen enough at this season of the year to fill a mere gazette. I should be more sorry to have you think me silent too long. You must be so good as to recollect, when there is a large interval between my letters, that I have certainly one ready in my writing-box, and only wait for a messenger. I hope to send this by Lord

8. In his letter to Selwyn of 29 July, Holland asks him to convey his 'best compliments to Lord and Lady Hertford' and Lord Beauchamp (J. H. Jesse, *George*

Selwyn and his Contemporaries, 1882, i. 288).

9. See *post* 27 Aug. 1764, n. 27.

Coventry.[1] For the next three weeks, indeed, I shall not be able to write, as I go in a few days with your brother to Chatsworth[2] and Wentworth Castle.[3]

I am under more distress about my visit to you—but I will tell you the truth. As I think the Parliament will not meet before Christmas, though they now talk of it for November,[4] I would quit our politics for a few weeks; but the expense frightens me, which did not use to be one of my fears. I cannot but expect, knowing the enemies I have, that the Treasury may distress me. I had laid by a little sum which I intended to bauble away at Paris; but I may have very serious occasion for it. The recent example of Lord Holderness, who has had every rag seized at the custom-house,[5] alarms my present prudence. I cannot afford to buy even clothes which I may lose in six weeks. These considerations dispose me to wait till I see a little farther into this chaos. You know enough of the present actors in the political drama, to believe that the present system is not a permanent one— nor likely to roll on till Christmas without some change. The first moment that I can quit party with honour, I shall seize. It neither suits my inclination nor the years I have lived in the world, for though I am not old, I have been in the world so long, and seen so much of those who figure in it, that I am heartily sick of its commerce. My attachment to your brother, and the apprehension that fear of my own interest would be thought the cause if I took no part for him, determined me to risk everything rather than abandon him. I have done it, and cannot repent whatever distresses may follow. One's good name is of more consequence than all the rest.—My dear

1. He sent it by Robert Strange, the engraver (post 27 Aug. 1764).

2. In Derbyshire, the Duke of Devonshire's seat.

3. In Yorkshire, the Earl of Strafford's seat. The journey was called off; see below, sub 'Arlington Street, Tuesday night.'

4. Parliament did not meet until 10 Jan. 1765, after successive prorogations on 19 April, 21 June, 23 Aug., and 30 Oct. (Journals of the House of Commons xxix. 1059, xxx. 3).

5. 'We hear that a great seizure was lately made at the custom-house, of vast quantities of French embroidery, French silks, French ruffles, and French everything, the property of a certain great Earl'

(London Chronicle 24–6 July, xvi. 88). A list of the items is ibid. 4–7 Aug., xvi. 122. Lady Mary Coke wrote to Lady Strafford, 14 Sept., that 'since the seizure of Lord and Lady Holdernesse's baggage everything that can is taken from everybody' (Coke, Journals, i. 15), and Lady Holland wrote to Lady Kildare, 8 Sept., that 'the custom-house people are most immensely strict just now on account of the infinite quantity of French goods imported,' and 10 Oct. that 'Lady Holdernesse has done us all great mischief—indeed the officers are so exceeding strict just now, 'tis a bad time to attempt getting anything from abroad' (Leinster Corr. i. 409, 417).

Lord, do not think I say this with the least disrespect to you—it is only to convince you that I did not recommend anything to you that I would avoid myself, nor engaged myself, nor wished to engage you, in party from pique, resentment, caprice, or choice. I am dipped in it much against my inclination. I can suffer by it infinitely more than you could.[5a] But there are moments when one must take one's part like a man. This I speak solely with regard to myself. I allow fairly and honestly, that you was not circumstanced as I was. You had not voted with your brother as I did; the world knew your inclinations were different. All this certainly composed serious reasons for you not to follow him, if you did not choose it. My motives for thinking you had better have espoused his cause, were for your own sake: I detailed those motives to you in my last long letter: that opinion is as strong with me as ever.

The affront to you, the malice that aimed that affront, the importance that it gives one, upon the long run, to act steadily and uniformly with one's friends, the enemies you make in the Opposition, composed of so many great families, and of your own principal allies,[6] and the little merit you gain with the Ministry by the contrary conduct, all these were, to me, unanswerable reasons, and remain so for what I advised; yet as I told you before, I think the season is passed, and that you must wait for an opportunity of disengaging yourself with credit. I am persuaded that occasion will be given you, from one or other of the causes I mentioned in my last; and if the fairest is, I entreat you by the good wishes which I am sure you know from my soul I bear you, to seize it.—Excuse me:—I know I go too far, but my heart is set on your making a great figure, and your letters are so kind, that they encourage me to speak with a friendship which I am sensible is not discreet;—but you know you and your brother have ever been the objects of my warmest affection; and, however partial you may think me to him, I must labour to have the world think as highly of you, and to unite you firmly for your lives. If this was not my motive, you must be sure I should not be so earnest. It is not one vote in the House of Lords that imports us. Party is grown so serious, and will, I doubt, become every day more

5a. Because most of his income came from places under the government, while most of Hertford's came from his rent-rolls in England and Ireland.

6. Lady Hertford was aunt of the Duke of Grafton, one of the Opposition leaders.

so, that one must make one's option; and it will go to my soul to see you embarked against all your friends—against the Whig principles you have ever professed, and with men, amongst whom you have not one well-wisher, and with whom you will not ever be able to remain upon tolerable terms, unless you take a vigorous part against all you love and esteem.

In warm times lukewarmness is a crime with those on whose side you are ranged. Your good sense and experience will judge whether what I say is not strictly the case. It is not your brother or I that have occasioned these circumstances. Lord Bute has thrown this country into a confusion which will not easily be dissipated without serious hours. Changes may, and as I said in the beginning of my letter, will probably happen; but the seeds that have been sown will not be rooted up by one or two revolutions in the Cabinet. It had taken an hundred and fifty years[7] to quiet the animosities of Whig and Tory—that contest is again set on foot, and though a struggle for places may be now as has often been, the secret purpose of principals, the Court and the nation are engaging on much deeper springs of action. I wish I could elucidate this truth, as I have the rest, but that is not fit for paper, nor to be comprised within the compass of a letter;—I have said enough to furnish you with ample reflections. I submit all to your own judgment:—I have even acted rightly by you, in laying before you what it was not easy for you, my dear Lord, to see or know at a distance. I trust all to your indulgence, and your acquaintance with my character, which surely is not artful or mysterious, and which, to you, has ever been, as it ever shall be, most cordial and well intentioned. I come to my gazette.

There is nothing new, but the resignation of Lord Carnarvon,[8]

7. Perhaps a slip for 'an hundred revolutions and fifty years.' As Croker, who questions the MS, points out, the struggle between Whig and Tory had reached a peak of violence just fifty years before.

8. James Brydges (1731–89), styled Marquess of Carnarvon; 3d Duke of Chandos 1771; M.P. Winchester 1754–61, Radnorshire 1761–8; lord of the Bedchamber 1760–4; lord lieutenant of Hampshire 1763–4, 1771–80; lord steward of the Household 1783–9. He had applied to Grenville 26 June to succeed the dying Lord Holmes as governor of the Isle of Wight, Hampshire (*Additional Grenville Papers 1763–1765*, ed. J. Tomlinson, Manchester, 1962, pp. 142–3), but upon being informed by Grenville 17 July that Hans Stanley was to be appointed instead (ibid. 158), he resigned the lieutenancy of Hampshire and the Bedchamber, protesting that 'as Mr Stanley's connexions and mine are very different in the county, it will be impossible for me or my friends to cooperate with him, or to give him that assistance we should wish to any person employed by his Majesty' (Carnarvon to Grenville 21 July, *Grenville Papers* ii. 399–401), and that he could 'never consent to be placed at the head of a county,

who has thrown up the Bedchamber; and they say, the lieutenancy of Hampshire, on Stanley[9] being made governor of the Isle of Wight.

I have been much distressed this morning:—the royal family reside chiefly at Richmond, whither scarce necessary servants attend them, and no mortal else but Lord Bute. The King and Queen have taken to going about to see places; they have been at Oatlands[10] and Wanstead.[11] A quarter before ten today, I heard the bell at the gate ring—truth is, I was not up, for my hours are not reformed, either at night or in the morning,[12]—I inquired who it was? the Prince of Mecklenburgh[13] and De Witz[14] had called to know if they could see the house; my two Swiss, Favre and Louis, told them I was in bed, but if they would call again in an hour they might see it. I shuddered at this report,—and would it were the worst part! The Queen herself was behind, in a coach: I am shocked to death, and know not what to do! It is ten times worse just now than ever at any other time: it will certainly be said, that I refused to let the Queen see my house.—See what it is to have republican servants! When I made a tempest about it, Favre said, with the utmost sang-froid, 'Why could not he tell me he was the Prince of Mecklenburgh?' I shall go this evening and consult my oracle, Lady Suffolk—if she approves it, I will write to De Witz,[15] and pretend I know nothing of anybody but the Prince, and beg a thousand pardons, and assure him how proud I should be to have his master visit my castle of Thundertentronk.[16]

August 4th.

I have dined today at Claremont, where I little thought I should dine, but whither *our* affairs have pretty naturally conducted me.[17]

when the power is put into other hands' (idem to idem 22 July, Tomlinson, op. cit. 161). See Namier and Brooke ii. 126–7.

9. Hans Stanley; see n. 8 above. He was appointed 18 July (*Daily Adv.* 20 July).

10. Seat of the Earl of Lincoln.

11. Seat of Earl Tylney of Castlemaine.

12. HW had been ill the previous week; in a note to Newcastle of ca 28 July, he had deferred his visit to Claremont (see below) because of his being 'confined with a rash and fever.'

13. Prince Georg August (1748–85), youngest brother of Queen Charlotte (Isenburg, *Stammtafeln* i. taf. 124). He had reached London from the Continent 20

April (*London Chronicle* 19–21 April, xv. 384), and returned 11 Aug. (ibid. 11–14 Aug., xvi. 150).

14. Presumably Freiherr von Dewitz, envoy extraordinary from Mecklenburg-Strelitz and Mecklenburg-Schwerin to Great Britain 1763–5; not further identified (*Daily Adv.* 5 Sept. 1763, 25 May 1765; *Repertorium der diplomatischen Vertreter aller Länder*, Vol. II, ed. F. Hausmann, Zurich, 1950, p. 221).

15. No letters between HW and Dewitz are known.

16. Thunder-ten-tronckh, Candide's childhood home.

17. See G. L. Lam, 'Walpole and the

It turned out a very melancholy day. Before I got into the house, I heard that letters were just arrived there, with accounts of the Duke of Devonshire having had two more fits. When I came to see Lord John's[18] and Lord Frederick's[19] letters, I found these two fits had been but one,[20] and that very slight, much less than the former, and certainly nervous by all the symptoms, as Sir Edward Wilmot,[21] who has been at Chatsworth, pronounces it. The Duke perceived it coming, and directed what to have done, and it was over in four minutes. The next event was much more real. I had been half round the garden with the Duke[22] in his one-horse chair; we were passing to the other side of the house, when George Onslow[23] met us, arrived on purpose to advertise the Duke of the sudden death of the Duchess of Leeds,[24] who expired yesterday at dinner in a moment:[25] he called it apoplectic; but as the Bishop of Oxford,[26] who is at Claremont, concluded, it was the gout flown up into the head. The Duke received the news as men do at seventy-one; but the terrible part was to break it to the Duchess, who is ill. George Onslow would have taken me away to dinner with him, but the Duke thought that would alarm the Duchess too abruptly, and she is not to know it yet: with her very low spirits it is likely to make a deep

Duke of Newcastle,' *Horace Walpole: Writer, Politician, and Connoisseur,* ed. Warren H. Smith, New Haven, 1967, pp. 80–1.

18. Lord John Cavendish. His letter to Newcastle is not in the Newcastle Papers, though mentioned by Newcastle BM Add. MSS 32961, f. 52.

19. Lord Frederick Cavendish. Lord Frederick's letter to the Duke of Newcastle, 3 Aug., received 4 Aug., is in BM Add. MSS 32961, f. 36; in it he summarizes two letters from Lord John to himself about the Duke of Devonshire's condition.

20. According to Lord Frederick's letter, the Duke had suffered two fits. 'My brother had . . . another fit on last Monday evening [30 July], though very short in comparison of that he had at Lord Strafford's. He went to bed and was restless the beginning of the night but slept very well from one till eight in the morning. He got up to breakfast (Tuesday morning) and was pretty well. After breakfast he walked out in the garden and

in his walk he was seized with a numbness in his hand and presently after fainted again but recovered very soon, was sick and by the help of camomile tea brought out a great deal of foul stuff.' Judging by Newcastle's reply, 4 Aug., to Lord Frederick's letter (BM Add. MSS 32961, f. 36), Lord John did not mention the second fit in his letter to Newcastle.

21. (1693–1786), Bt, 1759; physician.

22. Of Newcastle.

23. Nephew by marriage to Newcastle.

24. Sister of the Duchess of Newcastle.

25. 'Her Grace was taken with a fit, at dinner . . . and died, soon after 9 o'clock last night' (John Hughes to Newcastle, 4 Aug., BM Add. MSS 32961, f. 56). 'The poor little Duchess went off shocking sudden. . . . She was taken at four of noon and died that night at nine' (letter of Lady Dalkeith, quoted GEC vii. 514, n. 'd').

26. John Hume (ca 1706–82), Bp of Bristol 1756–8, of Oxford 1758–66, and of Salisbury 1766–82 (OSSORY ii. 338, n. 12; SELWYN 1, n. 7).

impression. It is a heavy stroke too for her father, poor old Lord Godolphin,[27] who is eighty-six. For the Duke, his spirits, under so many mortifications and calamities, are surprising: the only effect they and his years seem to have made on him is to have abated his ridicules. Our first meeting to be sure was awkward, yet I never saw a man conduct anything with more sense than he did. There were no notices of what is passed; nothing fulsome, no ceremony, civility enough, confidence enough, and the greatest ease. You would only have thought that I had been long abroad, and was treated like an old friend's son with whom he might make free. In truth, I never saw more rational behaviour: I expected a great deal of flattery, but we had nothing but business while we were alone, and common conversation while the Bishop and the Chaplain[28] were present. The Duke mentioned to me his having heard Lord Holland's inclination to your Embassy. He spoke very obligingly of you, and said that next to his own children, he believed there was nobody the late Lord Hardwicke loved so much as you. I cannot say the Duke spoke very affectionately of Sir Joseph Yorke, who has never written a single line to him since he was out.[29] I told him that did not surprise me, for Sir Joseph has treated your brother in the same manner, though the latter has written two letters to him since his dismission.[30]

Arlington Street, Tuesday night, 10 o'clock.

I am here alone in the most desolate of all towns. I came today to visit my Sovereign Duchess[31] in her lying-in,[32] and have been there

27. Francis Godolphin (1678–1766), 2d E. of Godolphin, 1712. He would be 86 on 3 Sept.

28. Rev. Thomas Hurdis (ca 1707–84), D.D. 1766; prebendary of York 1750–84, of Chichester 1755–84; canon of Windsor 1766–84 (Venn, *Alumni Cantab.*). 'He was forty years private secretary and domestic chaplain to the late Duke of Newcastle' (GM 1784, liv pt i. 316).

29. This was not true; as recently as 30 April Newcastle had received a long letter from Yorke thanking him for his letter of 30 March, in which he expressed his condolences on the death of Lord Hardwicke (BM Add. MSS 32958, f. 198). However, Yorke's letters to Newcastle had been dwindling steadily since Newcastle's resignation (BM Add. MSS 32939–32961), and his previous letter, that of 3 Jan., had

been the first in over seven months (BM Add. MSS 32948, f. 367, 32955, f. 25).

30. Conway wrote to Hertford, 9 Sept., that since his last trip through Holland, when Yorke had renewed their old acquaintance with great warmth, till the past winter, Yorke had 'kept up punctually on his part' a correspondence with him, but that since the time his behaviour had displeased the Court, Yorke 'then left me off short, a first letter of mine remained unanswered, a second I had occasion to write and even a third, for I was resolved to know it was not mere accident, had the same fate' (MS now WSL).

31. Of Grafton.

32. Her second son, Lord Charles Fitzroy, was born 14 July (Namier and Brooke ii. 435).

till this moment, not a soul else but Lady Jane Scott. Lady Waldegrave came from Tunbridge yesterday *en passant,* and reported a
new woeful history of a *fracas* there—don't my Lady Hertford's
ears tingle? but she will not be surprised. A footman—a very comely
footman, to a Mrs Craster,[33] had been most extremely impertinent to
Lord Clanbrazil,[34] Frederick Vane, and a son[35] of Lady Anne Hope;[36]
they threatened to have him turned away—he replied, if he was, he
knew where he should be protected. Tunbridge is a quiet private
place, where one does not imagine that everything one does in
one's private family will be known:—yet so it happened that the
morning after the fellow's dismission, it was reported that he was
hired by another Lady, the Lord knows who.[37] At night, that Lady
was playing at loo in the rooms. Lord Clanbrazil told her of the
report, and hoped she would contradict it: she grew as angry as a
fine lady could grow, told him it was no business of his, and—and I
am afraid, still more. *Vane* whispered her—one should have thought
that name would have had some weight[38]—oh! worse and worse! the
poor English language was ransacked for terms that came up to her
resentment:—the party broke up, and, I suppose, nobody went home
to write an account of what happened to their acquaintance.

O'Brien and Lady Susan are to be transported to the Ohio,[39] and
have a grant of forty thousand acres.[40] The Duchess says sixty thou-

33. Possibly Catherine Villiers (d. 1772),
daughter of Col. Henry Villiers, Gov. of
Tynemouth Castle, m. (1727) John Craster
(?1697–1763), M.P. (Edward Bateson, *A
History of Northumberland,* Vol. II, New-
castle-upon-Tyne, 1895, p. 178).

34. Hon. James Hamilton (1730–98), 2d
E. of Clanbrassil, 1758.

35. Either Henry Hope (d. 1789). Capt.
27th Ft, 14 March 1764, Lt-Col. 44th Ft
1777, Col. 1782, Brig.-Gen. 1784, Lt-Gov.
of Quebec 1785–9; or Charles Hope (d.
1808), Capt. R.N. 1777 (J. P. Wood,
Parish of Cramond, Edinburgh, 1794, p.
150; *Army Lists, passim;* L. M. Le Jeune,
Dictionnaire général . . . du Canada, Ot-
tawa, 1931, i. 761; John Hardy, *List of
the Captains of his Majesty's Royal Navy,*
1779, p. 56; GM 1808, lxxviii pt ii. 860).

36. Lady Anne Vane, sister of Frederick
Vane, m. 1 (1746) Hon. Charles Hope
Weir (divorced 1757) (*ante* 30 March 1746
OS, n. 2).

37. Doubtless Lady Harrington, who
had protected another impertinent footman in 1756; see *ante* 24 Jan. 1756.

38. An allusion to Lady Harrington's
affair in 1750 with Henry Vane, 2d E. of
Darlington, 1758; see MANN iv. 140,
MONTAGU i. 104, 107.

39. They left for New York in September (*Life and Letters of Lady Sarah
Lennox,* ed. Lady Ilchester and Lord
Stavordale, 1902, i. 146; *Leinster Corr.* i.
405, 408, 410).

40. On 20 July grants of twenty
thousand acres each in New York were
approved for Lord Holland and Lord
Ilchester, land which they apparently intended to turn over to O'Brien and Lady
Susan; at the same time another twenty
thousand acres, also in New York, was
approved for Clotworthy Upton (1721–85),
cr. (1776) Bn Templetown, an intimate
friend of the Hollands (*Acts of the Privy
Council . . . Colonial Series,* 1908–12, iv.

sand were bestowed, but a friend of yours, and a relation of Lady Susan,[41] nibbled away twenty thousand for a Mr Upton.[42]

By a letter from your brother today,[43] I find our northern journey is laid aside; the Duke of Devonshire is coming to town; the physicians want him to go to Spa. This derangement makes me turn my eyes eagerly towards Paris; though I shall be ashamed to come thither after the wise reasons I have given you against it in the beginning of this letter: *nous verrons*—the temptation is strong, but patriots must resist temptations; it is not the etiquette to yield to them till a change happens.

I enclose a letter, which your brother has sent me to convey you, and two pamphlets.[44] The former is said to be written by Shebbeare,[45] under George Grenville's direction:[46] the latter, which makes rather more noise, is certainly composed by somebody who does not hate your brother—I even fancy you will guess the same person for the author that everybody else does. I shall be able to send you soon another pamphlet, written by Charles Townshend,[47] on the subject of the warrants:—you see, at least, *we* do not ransack Newgate and the pillory for writers.[48] We leave those to the Administration.

818; *Journals of the Commissioners for Trade and Plantations . . . 1764 to . . . 1767*, 1936, p. 98). The three, however, during the next several years encountered 'difficulties and obstructions . . . in locating the lands ordered by his Majesty to be granted to them in New York' (ibid. 156), and a suit was instituted by them to locate the grants on land claimed by a Col. John Van Rensselaer (ibid. 218; *Acts* iv. 700); eventually they gave up the suit, Upton agreeing to have his twenty thousand acres located elsewhere and Holland and Ilchester completely relinquishing their grants (*Journals . . . 1768 to . . . 1775*, 1937, p. 92; Ilchester and Stavordale, op. cit. i. 221). O'Brien and Lady Susan returned to England in 1770 (ibid. i. 224). See also Lord Ilchester, *Henry Fox, First Lord Holland*, 1920, ii. 278–9.

41. Lord Holland, Lady Susan's uncle.
42. See above, n. 40.
43. Missing.
44. Guthrie's *Address to the Public on the Late Dismission*, and HW's *Counter Address* (see *ante* 5 June 1764).

45. John Shebbeare, political writer (*ante* 19 Sept. 1758).
46. In February a memorial 'in favour of Dr Shebbeare' had been presented to Grenville by 14 members of Parliament, asking that he be granted an annual pension (*Grenville Papers* ii. 270–1); presumably the pension was granted, leading to the rumour that Shebbeare, now subsidized by the government, was the author of the *Address to the Public*.
47. *A Defence of the Minority in the House of Commons, on the Question Relating to General Warrants*, published anonymously 15 Aug. (Hazen, *Cat. of HW's Lib.*, No. 1609:8:8); a truncated version is in GM 1764, xxxiv. 355–9. See Sir Lewis Namier and John Brooke, *Charles Townshend*, 1964, pp. 121–2, for the pamphlet's reception.
48. Shebbeare had been sentenced to Newgate and the pillory in 1758 for treasonable expressions in his *Sixth Letter to the People of England* (*Mem. Geo. II*, iii. 152).

I wish you would be so kind as to tell me, what is become of my sister and Mr Churchill. I received a letter[49] from Lady Mary today, telling me she was that instant setting out from Paris, but does not say whither.[50]

The first storm that is likely to burst in politics, seems to be threatened from the Bedford quarter. The Duke and Duchess have been in town but for two days the whole summer, and are now going to Trentham, whither Lord Gower, *qui se donnait pour favori*, is retired for three months. This is very unlike the declaration in spring, that the Duke must reside at Streatham, because the King could not spare him for a day.

The memorial left by Guerchy at his departure,[51] and the late *arrêts* in France on our American histories,[52] make much noise, and seem to say that I have not been a false prophet! If our ministers can stand so many difficulties from abroad, and so much odium at home, they are abler men than I take them for.

Adieu! the whole Hôtel de Lassay![53] I verily think I shall see it soon.

Yours, ever,

H. WALPOLE

---

49. Missing.

50. The Churchills went to Champagne (*post* 21 Aug. 1764).

51. At a conference with Grenville 16 July, Guerchy presented a memorial (S.P. 78/262, ff. 186–9) claiming that France owed England a balance of only fifteen million livres (about £670,000) for the maintenance of prisoners of war after deducting what the English owed the French and certain other items; at the same time he verbally proposed that the balance be paid over a period of fifteen years (Grenville to Sandwich 16 July, *Grenville Papers* ii. 390–1; Halifax to Hertford 20 July, S.P. 78/262, f. 169). Grenville objected particularly to France's striking off the expenses for prisoners taken before war was declared, and insisted that England 'had a right to have whatever was due paid at farthest in a year or two' (Grenville to Sandwich 16 July, op. cit. ii. 391). By the time of Guerchy's departure 20 July (S.P. 78/262, f. 169), Grenville had indicated that some of the large deductions might be agreed to, but only upon condition that France make 'a speedy payment' of the balance; Guerchy, however, would not agree to a period of less than 'four or five years,' urging 'the great difficulty of their finding the money' (Grenville to Hertford 20 July, *Grenville Papers* ii. 396–7; see also Halifax to Hertford 20 July, op. cit. ff. 170–2). The following January, Parliament agreed to a French proposal to pay £670,000 in three years (*post* 20 Jan. 1765).

52. See *post* 27 Aug. 1764, n. 27.

53. HW means the Hôtel de Lauraguais (or Brancas), Hertford's house in Paris, formerly known as the Hôtel de Lassay (*ante* 22 March 1764, n. 5).

From HERTFORD, Tuesday 21 August 1764

Printed for the first time from a photostat of BM Add. MSS 23218, ff. 163–6.

Paris,[1] August 21st 1764.

My dear Horry,

YOU are very good to give up so much of your time to the amusement of an absent friend. I have received your long letter with
the two pamphlets[2] and a letter from my brother. You will be perhaps surprised to hear that the one wrote by yourself in his justification had been before sent to me by a friend[3] in London. You will
not want to be informed that I read it with singular satisfaction and
approbation; the other pamphlet which I should have read first I
have not yet had time to look into.

The part of your letter which regards myself and that you have
treated with so much openness and friendship is in great measure
answered as well as I can recollect by the last I wrote you.[4] The
present state of parties in England is become a very necessary but
a very disagreeable consideration to my mind. If I could have foreseen the inconveniences, my ambition would hardly have placed me
where I am; not that I have anything to reproach myself with since
I have undertaken my present commission, but the chain of party is
endless, and a man may be involved in difficulties, as I now feel too
sensibly, without any just reproach upon his own conduct. In short
I am divided from my friends because they have separated themselves from me, and a very unpleasant situation I shall readily confess it even under those circumstances. But what could I do? Should
I have resigned[5] when the Duke of Devonshire broke his Stick?[6] You
know that neither his Grace nor the Duke of Newcastle have ever
treated me with political friendship, and yet that was the moment to
obtain party merit, for from that instant I lost some of my friends,
and the most material to me was in effect detached. I could not be

1. Hertford had returned to Paris from
Compiègne 11 Aug. (Hertford to Halifax
12 Aug., S.P. 78/263, f. 31); the King left
Compiègne on his return to Versailles 16
Aug. (ante 22 June 1764, n. 5).

2. Guthrie's *Address to the Public on
the Late Dismission*, and HW's *Counter
Address* (ante 3 Aug. 1764, n. 44).

3. Presumably either Dr William

Hunter (see *post* 27 Aug., 3 Dec. 1764),
or a Mr Wilson, mentioned by Conway to
Hertford 9 Sept. as sending 'what comes
out to you' (MS now WSL), not further
identified.

4. *Ante* 28 July 1764.

5. As lord of the Bedchamber.

6. See *ante* 30 Oct. 1762.

called upon to resign at that time; it would have been deemed folly where I personally owed so little. I continued to act with Government as I have hitherto always done upon the same principles, and you know the motives that induced me chiefly to accept this Embassy. Those reasons were family ones as you are already well acquainted; indeed it was a peculiar satisfaction to me when I was appointed, to think that my absence from England might in some measure excuse me from taking part in those party broils where my friends were unhappily engaged on different sides. I proposed to myself a very strict discharge of my duty here, and was in hopes under those circumstances I might be excused on all sides by promoting the education of my children here. Unhappily I was mistaken, for I seem to be considered as much a party man as if I had been acting amongst them all the last winter, when in truth the only part I have taken was doing the duty of an English minister at this Court. In the course of last winter you may have heard from my brother that I at different times represented to him the uneasiness I felt from his taking so strong a part against a set of men with whom I was supposed to be in some measure connected, because I received his Majesty's commands at this Court through their hands, and I said this from a strong desire to remain politically connected with him, and for fear his behaviour should at last involve us both in disagreeable circumstances. Not that I foresaw or could imagine they would have taken his military commission; the robbing him of his civil one was sufficient to convince the world of the little political connection that subsisted between the two brothers. My arguments had no weight; I dare say they deserved none, because I am perfectly persuaded of his just way of thinking. He owed more to others, and he told me in one of his letters he could not give up the Duke of Devonshire and men to whom he had obligations.[7] He thought, upon the best reflection he could give it, that this was the fairest and justest conduct he could pursue. I therefore ceased to remonstrate, and was in hopes that time and political changes, which are so frequent in England, might remove all difficulties and all appearance of difference between us, when the most unwelcome news of his dismission arrived. Then indeed I felt all sorts of difficulties. I had received no personal disobligation from Government except on his removal; for him I had all the affection I have and shall ever pro-

7. See *ante* 30 April 1764, n. 1.

fess. He had brought the difficulty upon himself (though he did not deserve the punishment inflicted on him) by acting in opposition to my sentiments and wishes. Thus I stood circumstanced with regard to him when my family and children were just settled and established at Paris. To remove them and to return to England at that moment would have been attended with all sorts of distress and perplexity to my own mind and to those with whom I live in the most intimate connection. Upon the whole therefore I determined not to resign, because I did not think my honour concerned to do it, and that it was the least of the evils between which I had my option. Had interest been the sole consideration, had passion directed, or had I been a single man, I will agree with you that the balance should have leaned the other way. In the resolution formed I see plainly all the objections you have so justly pointed out. I am separated from my friends, because the taking no part is not allowable in parties, and I am supposed to be connected with men with whom I have no other connection than a public correspondence. I am not wild enough to suppose I shall acquire their friendship by the part I act, or weak enough to imagine I do not lose ground with the Opposition in receiving my orders from men with whom they differ in politics. I am fully sensible of all the difficulties your friendly hand has pointed out. In answer I can only say that my refuge, whatever the consequences may be, must be found in acting an honest, a guarded, and a becoming part in the employment I have undertaken. Your friendship will contribute to strengthen the resolution I took upon that subject when I entered into it even before these difficulties occurred. I am not sensible that I have yet erred in any one instance, and when my correspondence comes into the hands of the public, if that moment should ever happen, I flatter myself they will think I have acted with that zeal which I owe to them and with that dignity and firmness which I owe to my own character.

Thus I must stand till some circumstance or some new event shall change the scene. My ambition, I flatter myself, will not mislead me, and as my principles are those which they have ever been, I hope I shall live to be politically reunited with those who profess the same, at least with that part of them whom I love and esteem.

I shall be very happy to see you at Paris and to contribute everything in my power to your satisfaction. If the part you have so nobly taken in defence of your friend will permit it, come and see us; and do not in this instance allow your patriotism to be so singular as to prevent the attainment of any little purchases you have proposed in France. I know you love to do acts of friendship and to avoid even an appearance of return; I am therefore afraid to speak, but you know my circumstances are easy or rather affluent with regard to myself. I have learned to conquer all desire of amassing except in that degree that may become the father of a numerous family; and to them it can be no prejudice to offer the use of any money which your opposition may prevent your receiving from your own funds in its usual course. You see I offer very cautiously, but it is to satisfy your delicacy. I am truly sensible of your friendship and shall be very happy with any occasion of proving my title to it.

I admire the Duke of Newcastle's reception of you and am much flattered with the late Lord Hardwicke's good opinion of me. Elliot and Stanley are at Paris,[8] and Rigby is gone through it in his way to the south with the Provost of Dublin,[9] but I believe you may be assured that none of these gentlemen have any political commission to execute. Stanley is a great deal with the Duke de Choiseuil, from his connection with Madame de Grammont,[10] but I am far from having any reason to suspect him. Rigby is gone, and Elliot leads a very different life, knows nothing hardly of French, sees still less of the ministers and gives no cause of suspicion whatever. If anything of that sort was attempted I could not long be a stranger to it. The correspondence and conversation of ministers would soon discover it.

Lady Hertford, my son and oldest daughter[11] are now all out of

8. 'Very happy . . . with his new government [of the Isle of Wight],' Stanley, together with Rigby and Lord Farnham, had 'set out for Paris . . . on a mere jaunt of pleasure' (Selwyn to Lord Holland, 13 Aug., George Macartney to Lord Holland, 7 Aug., *Letters to Henry Fox*, ed. Lord Ilchester, Roxburghe Club, 1915, pp. 198–9).

9. Francis Andrews (ca 1719–74), provost of the University of Dublin, 1758; it was largely through Rigby's interest that Andrews had secured the provostship (Constantia Maxwell, *A History of Trinity College, Dublin, 1591–1892*, Dublin, 1946, pp. 115–22). Selwyn wrote to Lord Holland 13 Aug., loc. cit., that 'Rigby and his provost scour the provinces next Wednesday for two months.'

10. Sister of the Duke. Stanley had been envoy to Paris 1761 and 1762–3 during the peace negotiations, and prior to that had been 'several times in France, and once resided two years at Paris,' where he had had 'opportunities of . . . cultivating useful acquaintance' (Stanley to Pitt, 18 April 1761, *Chatham Corr.* ii. 117–18). He was 'literally at home at the Duc de Choiseul's,' having an apartment at his house at Compiègne (Bedford MSS 50, f. 58, cited Namier and Brooke iii. 470), and Gibbon wrote from Paris the previous year that 'his character is indeed at Paris beyond anything you can conceive' (to Dorothea Gibbon, 12 Feb. 1763, in Gibbon, *Letters*, ed. J. E. Norton, New York, 1956, i. 133).

11. Lady Anne Seymour-Conway.

Paris. I expect the two last tomorrow and my son next week. I remain, dear Horry, with the truest regard,

Most faithfully yours,

HERTFORD

Mr Churchill and Lady Mary are gone into Champagne, but I do not find they are yet settled at any place.

To HERTFORD, Monday 27 August 1764

Printed from *Works* ix. 140–9.

Strawberry Hill, August 27th 1764.

I HOPE you received safe a parcel and a very long letter that I sent you, above a fortnight ago, by Mr Strange[1] the engraver. Scarce anything has happened since worth repeating, but what you know already, the death of poor Legge,[2] and the seizure of Turk Island:[3] the latter event very consonant to all my ideas. It makes much noise here, especially in the City, where the Ministry grow every day more and more unpopular.[4] Indeed, I think there is not much probability of their standing their ground, even till Christmas.

1. Robert Strange (1721–92), Kt 1787.

2. Who died 23 Aug. (*London Chronicle* 23–5 Aug., xvi. 190).

3. 110 miles north of San Domingo. A French squadron commanded by the Comte de Guichen, under orders from the Comte d'Estaing (S.P. 78/263, f. 100), had seized the island 1 June; the troops 'burned and destroyed all the houses erected thereon, and carried away a number of British vessels (said to be fourteen) with their crews, to Cape François, where they were set at liberty' (Halifax to Hertford, 20 Aug., S.P. 78/263, f. 48). At a conference with Hertford 28 Aug., the Duc de Praslin promised 'that satisfaction should be given for any act of violence which had been committed against England, and that full reparation of damages should be made' (Hertford to Halifax 28

Aug., S.P. 78/263, f. 83); an order to that effect was dispatched to d'Estaing 2 Sept., commanding him to restore the island to England (copy of order ibid., ff. 92–4). See also *post* 20 Sept. 1764; *Journal of the Commissioners for Trade and Plantations from . . . 1764 to . . . 1767*, 1936, pp. 108–9; MANN vi. 252, n. 1.

4. 'If Mr Pitt had been suffered to remain in the ministry, the perfidious French durst not have treated us thus. . . . But Mr Pitt was discarded, and Lord —— has ever since been sole minister. This has discovered our weakness; and while our helmsmen are attending to nothing but persecutions of the press at home, it furnishes a fine opportunity to the enemy for stealing our possessions abroad' (*London Chronicle* 18–21 Aug., xvi. 169).

Several defections are already known, and others are ripe which they do not apprehend.[5]

Doctor Hunter,[6] I conclude, has sent you Charles Townshend's pamphlet:[7] it is well written, but does not sell much, as a notion prevails that it has been much altered and softened.

The Duke of Devonshire is gone to Spa;[8] he was stopped for a week by a rash, which those who wished it so, called a miliary fever, but was so far from it, that if he does not find immediate benefit from Spa, he is to go to Aix-la-Chapelle, in hopes that the warm baths will supple his skin, and promote another eruption.

I have been this evening to Sion,[9] which is becoming another Mount Palatine. Adam has displayed great taste, and the Earl matches it with magnificence. The gallery is converting into a museum in the style of a columbarium, according to an idea that I proposed to my Lord Northumberland.[10] Mr Bowlby[11] and Lady Mary[12] are there, and the Primate,[13] who looks old and broken enough to aspire to the papacy. Lord Holland, I hear, advises what Lord Bute much wishes, the removal of George Grenville, to make room for Lord Northumberland at the head of the Treasury.

The Duchess of Grafton is gone to her father.[14] I wish you may hear no more of this journey! If you should, this time, the complaints will come from her side.[15]

5. Attacking such reports, one writer in the *London Chronicle* observed: 'We can but smile at the little arts which are made use of to keep up the spirit of party during the intervals of Parliament. One while we are told, that the minority is strengthened by an addition of twelve members. At another, that a certain Duke has acceded to the number,' etc. (6–8 Sept., xvi. 239).

6. Dr William Hunter (*ante* 22 Oct. 1760).

7. *A Defence of the Minority in the House of Commons, on the Question Relating to General Warrants (ante 3 Aug. 1764, n. 47).*

8. He set out from London 24 Aug. (*London Chronicle* 23–5 Aug., xvi. 190).

9. Sion or Syon House, not far from SH, seat of the Earl of Northumberland; the interior was redone ca 1761–9 by Robert Adam (Montagu i. 169, n. 7; Arthur T. Bolton, *The Architecture of Robert and James Adam (1758–1794)*, 1922, i. 246–73, ii. index of Adam drawings p. 28).

10. In Bentley's 'Designs for SH' are drawings for a 'Gothic Columbarium' at the Vyne as well as at SH; neither was executed; see Mann v. 157. Bolton, op. cit. i. 269 dismisses HW's claim of having influenced the gallery.

11. Thomas Bowlby (1721–95), commissioner of excise 1762–76; M.P. Launceston 1780–3 (Namier and Brooke ii. 108).

12. Lady Mary Brudenell, m. 2 (1754) Thomas Bowlby.

13. Of Ireland, George Stone.

14. Lord Ravensworth; see below, *sub* 9 Sept., for HW's account of the dissensions between the Duke and Duchess which he assigns as the reason for her visit.

15. In the past the Duke had complained often of the Duchess's passion for gambling (see Montagu i. 363, n. 9), but

You have got the *sposo*[16] Coventry with you, have not you?[17] And you are going to have the Duke of York.[18] You will not want such a nobody as me. When I have a good opportunity, I will tell you some very sensible advice that has been given me on that head,[19] which I am sure you will approve.

It is well for me I am not a Russian. I should certainly be knouted. The murder of the young Czar Ivan[20] has sluiced again all my abhorrence of the Czarina. What a Devil in a Diadem! I wonder they can spare such a principal performer from hell!

September 9th.

I had left this letter unfinished, from want of common materials, if I should send it by the post; and from want of private conveyance, if I said more than was fit for the post. But being just returned from Park Place, where I have been for three days, I not only find your extremely kind letter of August 21st, but a card[21] from Madame de Chabot,[22] who tells me she sets out for Paris in a day or two, and offers to carry a letter to you, which gives me the opportunity I wished for.

I must begin with what you conclude—your most friendly offer, if I should be distressed by the Treasury. I can never thank you enough for this, nor the tender manner in which you clothe it, though, believe me, my dear Lord, I could never blush to be obliged to you. In truth, though I do not doubt their disposition to hurt me, I have had prudence enough to make it much longer than their reign can

now he was neglecting the Duchess during her lying-in (*ante* 3 Aug. 1764) and openly living with his mistress, Anne ('Nancy') Parsons.

16. An allusion to the Earl's approaching marriage (his second) to Barbara St John (d. 1804), daughter of the 11th Baron St John of Bletso; the wedding took place 27 Sept.

17. He arrived in Paris ca 20 Aug. (Selwyn to Lord Holland 9 Sept., *Letters to Henry Fox*, ed. Lord Ilchester, Roxburghe Club, 1915, p. 201).

18. 'Paris, *Aug. 17*. The Earl of Hertford . . . was commissioned by the Duke of York to provide a hotel for him . . . which is now furnishing for the reception of his Royal Highness' ('Brussels Gazette,' quoted *London Chronicle* 23–5 Aug., xvi.

189). He was summoned home before he had a chance to move into the house, which was being prepared for him by his banker, not Hertford; see below, *sub* 9 Sept., and *post* 20 Sept. 1764.

19. By Lady Suffolk; see below, *sub* 9 Sept.

20. Ivan VI (1740 – 16 July 1764), Czar of Russia 1740–1; HW later wrote that 'it is very doubtful whether the Czarina could be privy to his death' (MANN vi. 253, n. 10). See ibid. for various accounts of the murder.

21. Missing.

22. Probably Lady Mary Apolonia Scolastica Stafford-Howard (1721–69), m. (1744) Guy-Auguste de Rohan-Chabot, Comte de Chabot. See MORE 29 and MONTAGU ii. 172.

Drawn by J. Swan, Esq.　　　　Engraved by W. Leake.

PARK PLACE, HENLEY

last, before it could be in their power to make me feel want. With all my extravagance, I am much beforehand, and having perfected and paid for what I wished to do here, my common expenses are trifling, and nobody can live more frugally than I, when I have a mind to it. What I said of fearing temptations at Paris, was barely serious: I thought it imprudent, just now, to throw away my money; but that consideration, singly, would not keep me here. I am eager to be with you, and my chief reason for delaying is, that I wish to make a longer stay than I could just now. The advice I hinted at, in the former part of this letter, was Lady Suffolk's, and I am sure you will think it very sensible. She told me, should I now go to Paris, all the world would say I went to try to persuade *you* to resign; that even the report would be impertinent to you, to whom she knew and saw I wished so well; and that when I should return, it would be said I had failed in my errand. Added to this, which was surely very prudent and friendly advice, I will own to you fairly, that I think I shall soon have it in my power to come to you on the foot I wish, I mean, having done with politics, which I have told you all along, and with great truth, are as much my abhorrence as yours. I think this Administration cannot last till Christmas, and I believe they themselves think so. I am cautious when I say this, because I promise you faithfully, the last thing I will do shall be to give you any false lights knowingly. I am clear, I repeat it, against your resigning now; and there is no meaning in all I have taken the liberty to say to you, and which you receive with so much goodness and sense, but to put you on your guard in such ticklish times, and to pave imperceptibly to the world the way to your reunion with your friends. In your brother, I am persuaded, you will never find any alteration; and whenever you find an opportunity proper, his credit with particular persons will remove any coldness that may have happened. I admire the force and reasoning with which you have stated your own situation; and I think there are but two points in which we differ at all. I do not see how your brother could avoid the part he chose. It was the Administration that made it decisive—no inclination of his. The other is a trifle; it regards Elliot, nor is it my opinion alone that he is at Paris on business: everybody believes it, and considering his abilities, and the present difficulties of Lord Bute,[23] Elliot's absence

23. See below.

would be very extraordinary,[24] if merely occasioned by idleness or amusement, or even to place his children, when it lasts so long.[25]

The affair of Turk Island, and the late promotion of Colonel Fletcher[26] over thirty-seven older officers, are the chief causes, added to the Canada bills,[27] logwood[28] and the Manilla affairs,[29] which have

24. Elliot had long been an adherent of Bute.

25. Nevertheless, Hertford in his reply to this letter, written after Elliot's departure, declares that 'if he came on business here, as you suppose, he had not the appearance of it, nor can I discover that anything passed between him and any French Minister' (*post* 20 Sept. 1764).

26. Henry Fletcher (d. 1803), Lt-Col. 35th Ft 1758, Col. 1762, Col. 35th Ft 10 Aug. 1764, Maj.-Gen. 1772, Lt-Gen. 1777, Gen. 1793 (GM 1803, lxxiii pt i. 292; *Army Lists*, 1759, pp. 8, 82, 1803, pp. 2, 149). He succeeded as Col. of the 35th upon the death of Gen. Charles Otway (GM 1764, xxxiv. 398). John Roberts wrote to Newcastle 5 Sept. that 'the Army in general are much disgusted at the advancement of Col. Fletcher. . . . The finger of Lord Bute appeared but too plainly in it' (BM Add. MSS 32962, f. 29). See *Mem. Geo. III* ii. 14.

27. In his 'separate and private instructions,' 29 Sept. 1763, Hertford had been told 'to find means of informing yourself if possible whether the French ministers have any real intention of paying the bills due to their . . . late subjects of Canada, according to the declaration signed by the Duc de Praslin the 10th February last' (*British Diplomatic Instructions*, Vol. VII, France, Pt IV, 1745–1789, ed. L. G. Wickham Legg, 1934, p. 90). In this declaration the French had agreed that the bills and letters of exchange 'which had been delivered to the Canadians for the necessaries furnished to the French troops . . . shall be punctually paid, agreeably to a liquidation made in a convenient time' (*A Collection of All the Treaties . . . between Great Britain and Other Powers*, 1772, ii. 291). By *arrêts* of 29 June and 2 July 1764, however, they stipulated that they would pay only a fraction of the face value of these bills and letters (copies of the *arrêts* in S.P. 78/262, ff. 194–200). The dispute

continued until the Duc de Choiseul unexpectedly agreed to almost total compensation in Jan. 1766 (see SELWYN 213, n. 2; MORE 97, n. 11).

28. By Article XVII of the definitive treaty of peace, Charles III of Spain had guaranteed that he would 'not permit his Britannic Majesty's subjects, or their workmen, to be disturbed, or molested, under any pretence whatsoever, in the [Bay of Honduras] . . . in their occupation of cutting, loading, and carrying away logwood' (*Journals of the House of Commons* xxix. 579). However, in June there was published in the London newspapers a petition from 'the principal settlers on the Bay of Honduras' to Lyttelton, the governor of Jamaica, complaining that on 4 Feb. they had received a letter from the Governor of Yucatan, ordering them to desist from cutting logwood until they produced a schedule from Charles III or orders from George III authorizing them to do so (*Daily Adv.* 15 June; *London Chronicle* 14–16 June, xv. 572). At the time of the present letter the situation of the logwood cutters was still in doubt, despite repeated remonstrances from the British to the Spanish ministry, and on 13 Sept. Rochford, the British ambassador to Madrid, warned Grimaldi, the Spanish foreign minister, that, failing satisfaction over the cutters, George III 'would be obliged to take his measures for reinstating his injured subjects,' which 'would be the same thing as to *sonner le tocsin de la guerre*' (Rochford to Sandwich 17 Sept., S.P. 94/168, quoted in Lord Sandwich, *Diplomatic Correspondence 1763–1765*, ed. Frank Spencer, Manchester, 1961, p. 221). On 16 Sept. Grimaldi drew up satisfactory orders for the Governor, instructing him to allow the cutters to return, and not to disturb them under any pretence (ibid.).

29. Another current point of dispute between Great Britain and Spain was the refusal of Spain to pay the bills accepted

ripened our heats to such a height. Lord Mansfield's violence against the press[30] has contributed much—but the great distress of all to the Ministers, is the behaviour of the Duke of Bedford, who has twice or thrice peremptorily refused to attend Council.[31] He has been at Trentham,[32] and crossed the country back to Woburn, without coming to town. Lord Gower has been in town but one day. Many causes are assigned for all this; the refusal of making Lord Waldegrave of the Bedchamber;[33] Lord Tavistock's inclination to the minority; and above all, a reversion, which it is believed Lord Bute has been so weak as to obtain, of Ampthill, a royal grant, in which the Duke has

in lieu of pillage by the British forces under Col. William Draper and Rear-Adm. Samuel Cornish upon the taking of Manila in Oct. 1762. Though the conquest was made before the preliminary peace had been signed, news of it did not reach Europe until after the signing of the definitive treaty; consequently Manila, not mentioned in the treaty, had to be restored without equivalent, and the ransom bills were never paid (J. S. Corbett, *England in the Seven Years' War*, 1907, ii. 365; conditions of surrender printed *London Gazette Extraordinary* 19 April 1763, reprinted GM 1763, xxxiii. 176–7). See *post* 10 Jan. 1765.

30. 'Yesterday morning [26 July] came on at Guildhall, before Lord Mansfield and a special jury, the trial of Mr John Williams, for republishing No. 45 of the *North Briton*, in volumes; and after a hearing of three hours, the jury (being out near two hours) . . . [brought] in their verdict, guilty. . . . Immediately after this trial came on that of Mr Kearsly, for originally publishing the same number of the *North Briton;* and he was likewise found guilty' (*London Chronicle* 26–8 July, xvi. 89–90). Almon wrote to Temple, 14 Aug., that 'the violence and partiality of the Chief Justice in those causes was not only astonishing, but is shocking to think of. . . . The carrying this favourite point of convicting the *North Briton* in the City, has struck such a panic into the printers, etc., that I am afraid I now stand alone in the resolution to publish with spirit' (*Grenville Papers* ii. 428–31).

31. In a conference with Grenville 3

Sept. the King observed that Bedford 'had absented himself very much this summer, and had not attended the Cabinet Councils. Mr Grenville touched upon that subject in his letter to the Duke, who . . . in regard to his absence, pleaded his health in some instances, and his having received no summons to the last Cabinet Council; he said his health had been so bad that he must be under a necessity of asking his Majesty's leave to go to Bath this autumn' (Grenville's diary, ibid. ii. 513). A possible cause of Bedford's absence was his dispute with Grenville over the stand Britain should take towards France with regard to the expense of prisoners of war (see *ante* 3 Aug. 1764, n. 51): he was for being more 'indulgent to the French in point of time,' and Grenville complained that he 'had not kept up his language high enough' in talking with Guerchy about the matter (Bedford to Sandwich 18 July, in Sandwich, op. cit. 181; Grenville's diary, *Grenville Papers* ii. 506–7; see also ibid. ii. 510). Bedford came to town 21 Sept. and attended a Council meeting the same evening (ibid. ii. 513).

32. Seat of Lord Gower.

33. Married to a sister of the Duchess of Bedford, he had been groom of the Bedchamber 1747–63. John Roberts wrote to Newcastle 5 Sept. that 'the difference between the two great men in Bedfordshire [Bute and Bedford] turned chiefly . . . upon a refusal being given to his Grace's application for Lord Waldegrave to be appointed a lord of the Bedchamber' (BM Add. MSS 32962, f. 29).

but sixteen years to come.[34] You know enough of that court, to know that, in the article of Bedfordshire, no influence has any weight with his Grace. At present, indeed, I believe little is tried. The Duchess and Lady Bute are as hostile as possible. Rigby's journey convinces me of what I have long suspected, that his reign[35] is at an end. I have even heard, though I am far from trusting to the quarter from which I had my intelligence, that the Duke has been making overtures to Mr Pitt, which have not been received unfavourably;[36] I shall know more of this soon, as I am to go to Stowe[37] in three or four days. Mr Pitt is exceedingly well disposed to your brother, talks highly of him, and of the injustice done to him,[38] and they are to meet on the first convenient opportunity. Thus much for politics, which, however, I cannot quit, without again telling you how sensible I am of all your goodness and friendly offers.

The Court, independent of politics, makes a strange figure. The recluse life led here at Richmond, which is carried to such an excess of privacy and economy, that the Queen's *friseur* waits on them at dinner, and that four pounds only of beef are allowed for their soup, disgusts all sorts of people. The drawing-rooms are abandoned: Lady Buckingham was the only woman there on Sunday sennight. The Duke of York was commanded home.[39] They stopped his remit-

34. 'It is said, by the late grant procured by a great Lord, he can deprive a noble Duke of a manor, which has been in his family some hundred years; and by which he can so incommode his Grace, as to render his manor very disagreeable, even while his Grace possesses the lease, which, it is said, is only for thirteen years. Almost the whole county is now in the possession of these two powerful noblemen' (*London Chronicle* 9–11 Aug., xvi. 140). The manor of Ampthill had been leased by Charles II to the 1st E. of Ailesbury in 1677 for ninety-nine years; the lease was sold by the 2d Earl in 1730 to the 3d Duke of Bedford. Despite rumours, the manor remained in the possession of the Dukes of Bedford until 1800, when it became the property of the Earl of Upper Ossory (*Vict. Co. Hist. Beds* iii. 271–2; OSSORY i. 44, n. 5).

35. Over the Duke of Bedford.

36. However, Newcastle, reporting to Rockingham in his letter of 8 Sept. the substance of the remarks made by Pitt in

a recent conversation with 'young Tommy Townshend,' wrote that Pitt 'thinks nothing can be done, by way of Opposition, and seems not disposed to take any active part' (BM Add. MSS 32962, f. 52); and Pitt himself, in a letter to Newcastle written in Oct., declared that 'I have no disposition to quit the free condition of a man standing *single,* and daring to appeal to his country at large, upon the soundness of his principles and the rectitude of his conduct' (*Chatham Corr.* ii. 297).

37. Seat of Earl Temple.

38. 'I hear . . . that he [Pitt] is very violent upon the dismission of the officers, Conway, etc.' (Newcastle to Rockingham, 8 Sept., loc. cit., f. 53).

39. 'Very abruptly' (HW to Mann, 13 Sept. 1764, MANN vi. 252); he arrived in London 1 Sept. (*London Chronicle* 1–4 Sept., xvi. 217). The Duke seems to have been called home for two reasons: the possibility of a rupture with France over the Turk Island affair (see MANN loc. cit. n. 3), and the extravagance of the Duke's

tances, and then were alarmed on finding he still was somehow or other supplied with money. The two next Princes are at the Pavilions at Hampton Court, in very private circumstances indeed; no household is to be established for Prince William,[40] who accedes nearer to the malcontents every day. In short, one hears of nothing but dissatisfaction, which in the City rises almost to treason.

Mrs Cornwallis has found that her husband[41] has been dismissed from the Bedchamber this twelvemonth with no notice; his appointments were even[42] paid; but on this discovery they are stopped.

You ask about what I had mentioned in the beginning of my letter, the dissensions in the house of Grafton. The world says they are actually parted:[43] I do not believe that; but I will tell you exactly all I know. His Grace, it seems, for many months has kept one Nancy Parsons,[44] one of the commonest creatures in London, once much liked, but out of date. He is certainly grown uncommonly attached to her, so much, that it has put an end to all his decorum. She was publicly with him at Ascot races, and is now in the Forest;[45] I do not know if actually in the house.[46] At first, I concluded this was merely stratagem to pique the Duchess; but it certainly goes further. Before the Duchess laid in, she had a little house on Richmond Hill, whither the Duke sometimes, though seldom, came to dine. During her month of confinement, he was scarcely in town at all, nor did he even come up to see the Duke of Devonshire. The Duchess is certainly gone to her father. She affected to talk of the Duke familiarly, and said she should call in the Forest as she went to Lord Ravensworth's. I suspect she is gone thither to recriminate

expenditures while abroad ('the largeness of his H.'s drafts,' Conway to Hertford, 9 Sept., MS now wsl).

40. He was created Duke of Gloucester and a household established for him in Nov., upon his coming of age.

41. Lt-Gen. Hon. Edward Cornwallis (ante 1 July 1744 NS, n. 16), groom of the Bedchamber 1747–63. Grenville wrote to Lord Townshend, a nephew of Mrs Cornwallis, 4 July, that by some arrangement made before he became first lord of the Treasury, Cornwallis was removed—'I own I do not perfectly understand upon what foundation' (Grenville letter-book, quoted Namier and Brooke ii. 257). Apparently George III disliked Cornwallis; in 1762

he had suggested removing him from his post as governor of Gibraltar (Letters from George III to Lord Bute 1756–1766, ed. Sedgwick, 1939, p. 166).

42. 'Ever' in Works; Wright emends to 'even,' which seems correct.

43. For their separation, see post 3 Dec. 1764.

44. Anne ('Nancy') Parsons (ca 1735 – ca 1814), m. 1 — Horton; m. 2 (1776) Charles, 2d Vct Maynard (Ossory i. 293, n. 2).

45. Whittlebury Forest in Northamptonshire; the Duke was Ranger of it (Montagu i. 122).

46. Wakefield Lodge (ibid.; du Deffand v. 367).

and complain. She did not talk of returning till October. It was said the Duke was going to France, but I hear no more of it. Thus the affair stands, as far as I or your brother, or the Cavendishes, know; nor have we heard one word from either Duke or Duchess of any rupture. I hope she will not be so weak as to part, and that her father and mother[47] will prevent it. It is not unlucky that she has seen none of the Bedfords lately, who would be glad to blow the coals.[48] Lady Waldegrave was with her one day, but I believe not alone.[49]

There was nobody at Park Place but Lord and Lady William Campbell.[50] Old Sir John Barnard[51] is dead; for other news I have none. I beg you will always say a great deal for me to my Lady. As I trouble you with such long letters, it would be unreasonable to overwhelm her too. You know my attachment to everything that is yours. My warmest wish is to see an end of the present unhappy posture of public affairs, which operate so shockingly even on our private. If I can once get quit of them, it will be no easy matter to involve me in them again, however difficult it may be, as you have found, to escape them. Nobody is more criminal in my eyes than George Grenville, who had it in his power to prevent what has happened to your brother. Nothing could be more repugnant to all the principles he has ever most avowedly and publicly professed—but he has opened my eyes—such a mixture of vanity and meanness, of falsehood and hypocrisy, is not common even in *this* country![52] It is a ridiculous *embarras* after all the rest, and yet you may conceive the distress I am under about my Lady Blanford, and the negotiations I am forced to employ to avoid meeting him there,[53] which I am determined not to do.

I shall be able, when I see you, to divert you with some excellent

47. Anne Delmé (1712–94), m. (1735) Henry Liddell, cr. (1747) Bn Ravensworth.

48. Lady Holland wrote to Lady Kildare in December about the separation: 'Her good friends the Bedford clique, I believe, she may thank for having contributed to make her bring things to this *éclat;* had she fallen into better company I do believe she would have behaved more wisely' (*Leinster Corr.* i. 423).

49. Presumably she was accompanied by Prince William; see *ante* 22 June 1764, n. 3.

50. Sarah Izard (d. 1784) of Charleston, South Carolina, m. (1763) Lord William Campbell (ca 1732–78), M.P. Argyllshire 1764–6; Capt. R.N. 1762; Gov. of Nova Scotia 1766–73, South Carolina 1773–6; Lady Ailesbury's brother (OSSORY ii. 50, nn. 8, 9).

51. (ca 1685 – 29 Aug. 1764), Kt 1732; M.P. London 1722–61; lord mayor of London 1737–8.

52. 'County' in *Works.*

53. Lady Blandford's second husband, Sir William Wyndham, Bt, was father (by his first wife) of Mrs Grenville.

stories of a principal figure on our side, but they are too long and too many for a letter, especially of a letter so prolix as this.

Adieu! my dear Lord,

Yours most devotedly,

H. Walpole

To Conway, Saturday 1 September 1764

Printed from *Works* v. 110–11.

September 1, 1764.

I SEND you the reply to the Counter-Address;[1] it is the lowest of all Grub Street,[2] and I hear is treated so. They have nothing better to say, than that I am in love with you,[3] have been so these twenty years,[4] and am no giant.[5] I am a very constant old swain: they might have made the years above thirty; it is so long I have had the same unalterable friendship for you, independent of being near relations and bred up together. For arguments, so far from any new ones, the man gives up or denies most of the former. I own I am rejoiced not only to see how little they can defend themselves, but to know the extent of their malice and revenge! They must be sorely hurt, when reduced to such scurrility. Yet there is one paragraph, however, which I think is of George Grenville's own inditing. It says,

1. *A Reply to the Counter Address,* by William Guthrie, author of *An Address to the Public (ante* 5 June 1764). It is dated 'Aug. 30th' by HW in his copy, now WSL (Hazen, *Cat. of HW's Lib.,* No. 1609:8:10).

2. For example, at one point Guthrie suggests that HW is a hermaphrodite, 'a being . . . whom, if naturalists were to decide on, they would most likely class him by himself; by nature maleish, by disposition female, so halting between the two, that it would very much puzzle a common observer to assign to him his true sex' (p. 7).

3. 'The complexion of the malice, the feeble tone of the expression, and the passionate fondness with which the *personal* qualities of the officer in question are continually dwelt on [in the *Counter Address*], would almost tempt one to imagine, that this arrow came forth from a female quiver' (p. 6).

4. 'One of the beaux esprits of the present times, has christened this regard [of HW for Conway], calling it, with a feigned concern, "an unsuccessful passion, during the course of twenty years"' (p. 12).

5. 'As to the apology he [HW] is pleased to make for undertaking the defence of his friend, viz. the clumsiness of his antagonist, I own fairly and freely, I have no such excuse in my behalf. My antagonist, the author of the *Counter Address* . . . is not liable to that objection. Whoever has seen the delicate structure of his frame, will never choose out the epithet, *clumsy,* to apply to it' (p. 7).

I flattered, solicited, and then basely deserted him.[6] I no more expected to hear myself accused of flattery, than of being in love with
you; but I shall not laugh at the former as I do at the latter. Nothing
but his own consummate vanity could suppose I had ever stooped
to flatter *him!* or that any man was connected with him, but who
was low enough to be paid for it. Where has he one such attachment?

You have your share too—the miscarriage at Rochfort[7] now
directly laid at your door:[8] repeated insinuations against your
courage:[9]—but I trust you will mind them no more than I do, ex-
cepting the *flattery,* which I shall not forget, I promise them.

I came to town yesterday on some business, and found a case.—
When I opened it, what was there but my Lady A.'s most beautiful
of all pictures![10] Don't imagine I can think it intended for me, or
that, if it could be so, I would hear of such a thing. It is far above
what can be parted with, or accepted. I am serious—there is no
letting such a picture, when one has accomplished it, go from where
one can see it every day. I should take the thought equally kind
and friendly, but she must let me bring it back, if I am not to do
anything else with it, and it came by mistake. I am not so selfish to
deprive her of what she must have such pleasure in seeing. I shall
have more satisfaction in seeing it at Park Place; where, in spite of
the worst kind of malice, I shall persist in saying my heart is fixed.
They may ruin me, but no calumny shall make me desert you. Indeed your case would be completely cruel, if it was more honourable

6. 'But who are my patrons? Why are
his shafts directed against their blameless
bosoms? Does he suspect them to be
those whom he has flattered, solicited, and
shamefully deserted?' (p. 40). See *Mem.
Geo. III* ii. 4–5 for HW's refutation of
this charge.

7. See *ante* 4 Aug.–24 Nov. 1757 *passim*
for the expedition against Rochefort, the
failure of which resulted in the court
martial of the commander, Lt-Gen. Sir
John Mordaunt.

8. 'But our favourite general, it seems,
must be brought off at all events. He did
not *command* at Rochefort. True; but the
success of that attempt depended on the
second in command' (p. 40). See *ante* 13
Oct. 1757 for the public's reaction to Conway after the Rochefort expedition.

9. For example, Guthrie observes that
Conway 'did *not,* tired of the routine

of picket duty, and the parade of lucrative
German campaigns, leave his friends and
family and fly to a new scene of action,
where . . . the service was sharp and
painful, dangers frequent and unavoidable, and the very climate an alarming
enemy' (p. 14).

10. A landscape executed in worsteds by
Lady Ailesbury. It is now at Strawberry
Hill (HW). It was 'after Van Uden' ('Des.
of SH,' *Works* ii. 428). See *ante* 16 Sept.
1757 and *post* 3 Oct. 1773 for Lady Ailesbury's worsted-work pictures. In 1768 she
exhibited 'a piece of fowls in needlework'
at the exhibition of the Society of Artists;
HW wrote in the margin of his copy of
the catalogue (now wsl), 'very fine,' while
the commentator in the 'Critical Observations' of the exhibition remarked, 'This
elegant performance does honour to the
class to which it belongs.'

for your relations and friends to abandon you than to stick to you. My option is made, and I scorn their abuse as much as I despise their power.

I think of coming to you on Thursday next for a day or two, unless your house is full, or you hear from me to the contrary.[11] Adieu!

Yours ever,

HOR. WALPOLE

From HERTFORD, Thursday 20 September 1764

Printed for the first time from a photostat of BM Add. MSS 23218, ff. 167–8.

Paris, September 20th 1764.

Dear Horry,

YOU will allow me to feel some disappointment in not seeing you at Paris as you gave us hopes, though you promised us in return a much longer stay than you could now have made; and I must in gratitude and friendship feel more concern, as it is regard for me and my character which prevents it. I am sorry to be in a situation where seeing you can be supposed in any light to be a prejudice to either. You know my feelings and sentiments upon this subject, therefore I need not repeat them. It is your prudence, not mine, which shall prevent it; I am ambitious of expressing my friendship for you, and it is superior to every dirty interested consideration.

I received the letter[1] and parcel[2] safe which you sent by Mr Strange, and if I have not already said it, will now assure you that I was vastly pleased with the spirited, sensible answer given by your pamphlet to the most unjust attack upon my brother's character. He tells me there is another wrote to abuse you.[3] The press must be at liberty, to avoid a greater evil, but I abhor the abuses of it and despise those who encourage it. Surely it is not prudence to attack the fairest characters when there are so many who offer their reputa-

---

11. HW was at Park Place 6–9 Sept. (*ante* 27 Aug. 1764, *sub* 9 Sept.).

1. *Ante* 3 Aug. 1764.
2. Containing a letter from Conway to

Hertford, Guthrie's *Address to the Public,* and HW's *Counter Address* (ibid., n. 44).
3. Guthrie's *Reply to the Counter Address* (*ante* 1 Sept. 1764).

tions wantonly. I am obliged to you for the account you give me of parties in England, and it agrees in substance with what I hear, though not so particularly, from other hands. If the Duke of Bedford is dissatisfied, the revolution must soon follow. I have no idea, as things now stand, of filling such a gap without having recourse to some in Opposition.

What you tell me of the court of Richmond gives me concern. It hurts the King, and you know for his personal goodness to me[4] I am attached to him by inclination. The Duke of York has an hôtel at Paris to pay for six months; his banker took it for him; I was not concerned. His Royal Highness ordered Mr St John[5] to acquaint me from Genoa how much he was mortified in finding himself obliged to return to England, and desired I would take an opportunity of expressing his concern and his intention of returning to Paris when his affairs would allow him. Lord Coventry is gone home to be married;[6] I understand he is not out of practice by his Paris expedition.[7] Lord March and Mr Selwyn return for Newmarket.[8] Lord Farnham[9] I think will carry this letter, though he seems of all men the most uncertain in his resolutions.[10] Elliot is gone home; if he came on business here, as you suppose, he had not the appearance of it, nor can I discover that anything passed between him and any French Minister. His life here was very different. It would not be easy to conceal it from the person who does the business of the English Court here, and we saw and knew too much of him whilst he was here to be easily mistaken.

4. About this time Halifax expressed to the King and Grenville his dissatisfaction with Hertford on the grounds that he was 'cold and insufficient'; but the King personally took up Hertford's defence, observing 'that there are not among his servants too many people of decent and orderly characters; that Lord Hertford is respectable in that light, and therefore not lightly to be cast aside' (Grenville diary *sub* 22 Sept., *Grenville Papers* ii. 514).

5. Hon. Henry St John (1738–1818), army officer; M.P.; groom of the Bedchamber to the Duke of York.

6. Selwyn wrote to Holland from Paris 9 Sept. that 'Lord Coventry . . . sets out on Tuesday [11 Sept.] for England, to prepare for his nuptials' (*Letters to Henry Fox*, ed. Lord Ilchester, Roxburghe Club, 1915, p. 201). The wedding took place 27 Sept.; see *ante* 27 Aug. 1764, n. 16.

7. 'His preparation here has been the most extraordinary that ever was made for any sacrament whatever' (Selwyn to Holland 9 Sept., loc. cit.).

8. March and Selwyn did not return to England until the following April (*post* 7 April 1765).

9. Robert Maxwell (ca 1720–79), 2d Bn Farnham, 1759, cr. (1760) Vct Farnham and (1763) E. of Farnham.

10. Hertford wrote *post* 12 Oct. 1764 from Fontainebleau that he left Lord Farnham at Paris still 'uncertain whether he would go to England for business or stay at Paris for diversion.'

I have heard lately from the Duke of Grafton in that friendly style and manner with which he has always treated me, but he did [not] mention the Duchess's name or give any intimation of difficulties in that house. If the Duchess is well advised, she will not leave Bond Street.

You will see by the *Gazette* that my representations upon the outrage committed at Turk's Island have produced a very full and satisfactory answer from this Court.[11] I wish I could promise myself as much success in every point of business committed to my care, but I will do my duty whilst I am employed here, and I flatter myself leave no room for censure on my conduct in the part I act, even in these ticklish times, of which I am fully sensible.

My son proposes setting out for Italy the beginning of next month; about the same time I intend removing to Fontainbleau for a six weeks' expedition.

Lady Hertford and my family desire their best compliments. I remain, dear Horry,

Always very affectionately and sincerely yours,

HERTFORD

To Hertford, Monday 1 October 1764

Missing; mentioned by HW *post* 5 Oct. 1764.

---

11. 'The Court of France has disavowed the said proceedings, has disclaimed all intention or desire of acquiring or conquering the Turks Islands; and has given orders to the Comte d'Estaing, Governor of St Domingo, to cause the said islands to be immediately abandoned on the part of the French, to restore everything therein to the condition in which it was on the 1st of June last, and to make reparation of the damages which any of his Majesty's subjects shall be found to have sustained in consequence of the said proceedings' (*London Gazette* No. 10451, 8–11 Sept., *sub* St James's, 11 Sept.).

To Hertford, Friday 5 October 1764

Printed from *Works* ix. 149–52.

Strawberry Hill, Oct. 5th 1764.

My dear Lord,

THOUGH I wrote to you but a few days ago,[1] I must trouble you
with another line now. Dr Blanchard,[2] a Cambridge divine, and
who has a good paternal estate in Yorkshire,[3] is on his travels, which
he performs as a gentleman; and, therefore, wishes not to have his
profession noticed.[4] He is very desirous of paying his respects to you,
and of being countenanced by you, while he stays at Paris. It will
much oblige a particular friend of mine,[5] and consequently me, if
you will favour him with your attention. Everybody experiences
your goodness, but in the present case I wish to attribute it a little to
my request.

I asked you about two books, ascribed to Madame de Boufflers.[6] If
they are hers, I should be glad to know where she found, that Oliver
Cromwell took orders,[7] and went over to Holland to fight the Dutch.[8]
As she has been on the spot where he reigned (which is generally
very strong evidence), her countrymen will believe her in spite of
our teeth; and Voltaire, who loves all anecdotes that never happened,

1. 1 Oct.; missing. HW mentions in his
letter to Newcastle 2 Oct. 1764 his 'having
written to Lord Hertford but yesterday.'
2. Wilkinson Blanshard (1734–70), who
was, however, a physician, not a divine;
M.D. (Cambridge) 1761; F.R.C.P. 1762
(Venn, *Alumni Cantab.*).
3. His father was Wilkinson Blanshard
of York, an attorney (*Yorkshire Pedigrees*,
ed. J. W. Walker, 1942, Pt I, p. 61
[Harleian Society Publications, Vol.
XCIV]).
4. 'The Doctor desires that his profession may be sunk, and that he may be
recommended as a gentleman of fortune
in Yorkshire, as he really is' (Dr Richard
Warren to Ds of Newcastle, 30 Sept., BM
Add. MSS 32962, f. 181).
5. The Duke of Newcastle. Dr Warren,
the Ds of Newcastle's physician and a
friend of Blanshard, had written the
Duchess (n. 4 above) prompting her to
remind the Duke of the request he had

made earlier on behalf of Blanshard for
a letter of recommendation to Hertford.
The Duke then, in a missing letter acknowledged by HW in his reply 2 Oct.
1764, asked HW to write the recommendation.
6. Presumably *Des Passions* and *De
l'Amitié*. '4 septembre. Il paraît un livre,
intitulé *Des Passions*, qu'on attribue à
Madame de Boufflers' (Louis Petit de
Bachaumont, *Mémoires secrets*, 1780–9, ii.
88). The author of *Des Passions. Par l'auteur de traité de l'Amitié*, was later identified as Marie-Geneviève-Charlotte Dar-
lus (1720–1805), m. —— Thiroux d'Ar-
conville. A second edition of *De l'Amitié*,
first published in 1761, came out in 1764
(NBG; Bibl. Nat. Cat.; BM Cat.). See also
Grimm, *Correspondance*, ed. Tourneux,
1877–82, vi. 98–9.
7. *Des Passions*, p. 151.
8. Ibid. 165.

because they prove the manners of the times, will hurry it into the first history he publishes. I, therefore, enter my caveat against it, not as interested for Oliver's character, but to save the world from one more fable. I know Madame de Boufflers will attribute this scruple to my partiality to Cromwell (and, to be sure, if we must be ridden, there is some satisfaction when the man knows how to ride). I remember one night at the Duke of Grafton's, a bust of Cromwell[9] was produced: Madame de Boufflers, without uttering a syllable, gave me the most speaking look imaginable, as much as to say, is it possible you can admire this man!—Apropos—I am sorry to say the reports do not cease about the separation, and yet I have heard nothing that confirms it.

I once begged you to send me a book in three volumes, called *Essais sur les mœurs;*[10] forgive me if I put you in mind of it, and request you to send me that, or any other new book. I am woefully in want of reading, and sick to death of all our political stuff, which, as the Parliament is happily at the distance of three months, I would fain forget till I cannot help hearing of it. I am reduced to Guicciardin,[11] and though the evenings are so long, I cannot get through one of his periods between dinner and supper.[11a] They tell me Mr Hume has had sight of King James's journal;[12] I wish I could see all the trifling passages that he will not deign to admit into history.[13] I do

9. Engraved by J. K. Sherwin as a frontispiece to the second volume of Mark Noble's *Memoirs of the Protectoral-House of Cromwell*, Birmingham, 1787.

10. See *ante* 8 June 1764.

11. Francesco Guicciardini (1482–1540), author of *Della istoria d'Italia*, of which HW owned an edition published at Venice 1738–40 (Hazen, *Cat. of HW's Lib.*, No. 877).

11a. Guicciardini is notorious for his remarkably involved sentences, some of them extending for hundreds of words. For discussions of his style, see the sources cited in Roberto Ridolfi, *Life of Francesco Guicciardini*, trans. C. Grayson, 1967, p. 328, n. 14.

12. 'Doctor Robertson tells me that David Hume has got a sight of James II's journal' (Dalrymple to HW, 26 Sept. 1764, DALRYMPLE 103). Hume had written to Robertson, 1 Dec. 1763: 'I have here met with a prodigious historical curiosity, the

memoirs of King James II in fourteen volumes, all wrote with his own hand, and kept in the Scots College' (Hume, *Letters*, ed. Greig, Oxford, 1932, i. 417). Actually, only three of the volumes were in the King's hand (Thomas Inese to James Edgar, 17 Oct. 1740, in Winston Churchill, *Marlborough: His Life and Times*, New York, 1933–8, ii. 61). James II's autograph memoirs had in 1701 been entrusted by James's own warrant to the Principal of the Scots College in Paris and his successors; they remained at the College until about 1793, when they were destroyed (ibid. ii. 54; see also *Memoirs of James II*, trans. A. Lytton Sells, Bloomington, Ind., 1962, pp. 19–20, 25–6 *et passim;* DALRYMPLE 103, n. 4).

13. Hume made several extracts from the memoirs, which he used in revising his *History* (post 7 Dec. 1764; Hume, op. cit. i. 426; *History of England*, 1770, vii. 385, 386, 431).

not love great folks till they have pulled off their buskins and put on their slippers, because I do not care sixpence for what they would be thought, but for what they are.

Mr Elliot brings us woeful accounts of the French ladies, of the decency of their conversation, and the nastiness of their behaviour.[14]

Nobody is dead, married, or gone mad, since my last. Adieu!

Yours, ever,

Walpole

PS. I enclose an epitaph[15] on Lord Waldegrave, written by my brother, which I think you will like, both for the composition and the strict truth of it.

Arlington Street, Friday evening.

I was getting into my post-chaise this morning with this letter in my pocket, and coming to town for a day or two, when I heard the Duke of Cumberland was dead:[16] I find it is not so.[17] He had two fits yesterday at Newmarket, whither he would go. The Princess Amelia, who had observed great alteration in his speech, entreated him against it. He has had too some touches of the gout, but they were gone off, or might have prevented this attack. I hear since the fits yesterday, which are said to have been but slight, that his leg is broken out, and they hope will save him. Still, I think, one cannot but expect the worst.

The letters yesterday, from Spa, give a melancholy account of the poor Duke of Devonshire: as he cannot drink the waters, they think of removing him;—I suppose, to the baths at Aix-la-Chapelle;[18] but

14. A passage has been deleted here by Croker, indicated by asterisks.

15. 'Oct. 3. Printed 100 copies of my brother's epitaph on Lord Waldegrave' (*Journal of the Printing Office at Strawberry Hill*, ed. Toynbee, 1923, p. 13). The epitaph, on the first two Earls Waldegrave but devoted primarily to the second, is reprinted Hazen, *SH Bibl.* 192.

16. See *post* 5 Oct. 1764 *bis*.

17. 'The report of the death of . . . the Duke of Cumberland, at Newmarket, which universally prevailed on Thursday evening [4 Oct.] and yesterday morning, is happily without foundation' (*London Chronicle*, 4–6 Oct., xvi. 334, *sub* 6 Oct.). He died 31 Oct. 1765.

18. Newcastle wrote to Lincoln, 4 Oct., that 'Lord Frederick [Cavendish] wrote me word . . . that he had seen a gentleman, who came from thence [Spa] the 24th, who said it was reported, that the D. of Devonshire would soon leave Spa, as the waters do not agree with him. If so, I suppose, it is to go to Aix-la-Chapelle, and perhaps bathe there' (BM Add. MSS 32962, f. 199).

I look on his case as a lost one![19] There's a chapter for moralizing! but five-and forty, with forty thousand pounds a year, and happiness wherever he turned him! My reflection is, that it is folly to be unhappy at anything, when felicity itself is such a phantom!

To Conway, Friday 5 October 1764

Printed from *Works* v. 111–12.

Strawberry Hill, October 5, 1764.

IT is over with us!—If I did not know your firmness, I would have prepared you by degrees; but you are a man, and can hear the worst at once. The Duke of Cumberland[1] is dead. I have heard it but this instant. The Duke of Newcastle was come to breakfast with me, and had pulled out a letter from Lord Frederick, with a hopeless account of the poor Duke of Devonshire.[2] Ere I could read it, Colonel Schutz[3] called at the door and told my servant this fatal news! I know no more—it must be at Newmarket, and very sudden; for the Duke of Newcastle had a letter from Hodgson,[4] dated on Monday, which said the Duke was perfectly well, and his gout gone:[5] —yes, to be sure, into his head. Princess Amelia had endeavoured to prevent his going to Newmarket, having perceived great alteration in his speech, as the Duke of Newcastle had.—Well! it will not be.— Everything fights against this country! Mr Pitt must save it himself —or, what I do not know whether he will not like as well, share in overturning its liberty—if they will admit him; which I question now if they will be fools enough to do.[6]

---

19. He died 2 Oct., aged 44.

---

1. William Duke of Cumberland, son of George II (HW). It was a false report; see *ante* 5 Oct. 1764 to Hertford.

2. See ibid., n. 19.

3. Armand Johann Schutz (d. 1773), formerly an officer in the Guards, and sometime warden of the Stannaries (MONTAGU i. 112, n. 4).

4. Studholme Hodgson (1708–98), army officer; Master of the Horse to the Duke of Cumberland (*Court and City Register*, 1764, p. 102).

5. In his letter to Hodgson of 29 Sept., Newcastle had expressed his hope that 'his Royal Highness's little touch of the gout is gone off' (BM Add. MSS 32962, f. 173).

6. Gilly Williams wrote to Selwyn, 29 Sept., after a two-day stay at SH, 'The Duke of Devonshire's illness seems to have sunk Horry's spirits prodigiously. He expects the resurrection of Mr Pitt, as the Jews do the coming of the Messiah, and, for all I can see, with as much reason' (J. H. Jesse, *George Selwyn and his Contemporaries*, 1882, i. 301).

You see I write in despair. I am for the whole, but perfectly tranquil. We have acted with honour, and have nothing to reproach ourselves with. We cannot combat fate. We shall be left almost alone; but I think you will no more go with the torrent than I will. Could I have foreseen this tide of ill fortune, I would have done just as I have done; and my conduct shall show I am satisfied I have done right. For the rest, come what come may, I am perfectly prepared! and while there is a free spot of earth upon the globe, that shall be my country. I am sorry it will not be this, but tomorrow I shall be able to laugh as usual. What signifies what happens when one is seven-and-forty, as I am today?

'They tell me 'tis my birthday'—but I will not go on with Antony, and say

                   _____ and I'll keep it
    With double pomp of sadness.—[7]

No; when they can smile, who ruin a great country, sure those who would have saved it may indulge themselves in that cheerfulness which conscious integrity bestows. I think I shall come to you next week; and since we have no longer any plan of operations to settle, we will look over the map of Europe, and fix upon a pleasant corner for our exile—for take notice, I do not design to fall upon my dagger, in hopes that some Mr Addison a thousand years hence may write a dull tragedy about me. I will write my own story a little more cheerfully than he would; but I fear now I must not print it at my own press.[8] Adieu! You was a philosopher before you had any occasion to be so: pray continue so; you have ample occasion!

Yours ever,

Hor. Walpole

7. Dryden, *All for Love*, Act I.
8. An allusion to the current repressive measures of the government against printers of anti-government material; see *ante* 27 Aug. 1764.

From Hertford, Friday 12 October 1764

Printed for the first time from a photostat of BM Add. MSS 23218, ff. 169–70.

Fontainebleau, October 12th 1764.

Dear Horry,

A THOUSAND thanks for your constant attention to me. If it was not for your correspondence I should remain in perfect darkness, and hear of nothing but expense of prisoners, Canada bills and Turk's Island.[1] Dr Blanchard shall be received by me as you wish him, that is, when I have an opportunity of receiving him at all, for I am now settled here for some time, and perhaps the Doctor's curiosity may not lead him to Fontainebleau. In the meantime I will write him a note expressing my concern that I am not at Paris to receive a person for whose entertainment you are so much interested. The two books ascribed to Madame Boufflers are not hers; Mr Hume, who is or wishes to be in all her secrets,[2] assures me she denies them positively and sincerely. I am ashamed to have forgot that you desired me to send you *Essais sur les mœurs;* I have not the least recollection of it, but you shall have it by the first opportunity with any other book I can find that may give you a few moments' amusement.

The Duke of Cumberland I suppose will not live, and by the accounts you give me and those we receive at Paris of the Duke of Devonshire, I am very sorry to think his life is so uncertain. There is a physician here who saw him at Spa that thinks it will not be even a tedious case, and Mrs Pointz[3] and the Spencers found him much changed. I agree with you in thinking this poor Duke an excellent subject of morality. If happiness was of this world, he had the fairest pretensions to it. The emptiness of such an idea cannot be better proved, and the gentlemen of this country seem the best philosophers who do not hunt the shadow, but embrace the substance in amusement. I admire the epitaph on Lord Waldegrave; is it not your own?

I am now settled here with the Court for a month or five weeks.[4]

1. See *ante* 3 Aug. 1764, n. 51; 27 Aug. 1764, n. 27; 20 Sept. 1764.

2. For Hume's affair with Madame de Boufflers, see J. Y. T. Greig, *David Hume,* New York, 1931, pp. 305–17.

3. Anna Maria Mordaunt (d. 1771), m.

(1733) Stephen Poyntz; mother of Lady Spencer (Mann iv. 208, n. 11).

4. Hertford wrote to Halifax 12 Oct. of his 'removal with the Court to Fontainebleau where I shall remain till the middle of next month' (S.P. 78/263, f. 157).

Lord and Lady Spencer are here, and I flatter myself will be satisfied with the success I have had in getting them entertained and
well received. There is a difficulty about English ladies that are not
presented which nothing but favour and pains can remove. We have
once a week an opera, once a play, and once an Italian comedy.
These entertainments are magnificent and very showy. Lady Hertford is here and I think will continue at Fontainbleau, as my son
leaves us next week for Turin. I shoot, hunt, and play a great deal at
whist when I have not the business of my Court to do.

Lord March and George Selwyn are still at Paris. I hear the former
is distressed and much concerned for the Duke of Cumberland, because he had a bet with him which may become doubtful in case of
death.

Lord Farnham I left uncertain whether he would go to England
for business or stay at Paris for diversion.

Adieu, my dear Horry; my courier must set out for Paris.[5] Mr
Rigby will, I believe, carry this letter to England.[6] I remain with
the best compliments of the family,

Most sincerely and affectionately yours,

HERTFORD

To HERTFORD, ca Saturday 13 October 1764

Missing; acknowledged *post* 21 Oct. 1764. Presumably written about the same
time as HW's letter to Conway 13 Oct. on the same subject (Devonshire's
legacy to Conway).

5. Presumably with Hertford's dispatch
of 12 Oct. to Halifax, cited in the preceding note.

6. Rigby reached London 18 Oct. (*London Chronicle* 18–20 Oct., xvi. 378).

To Conway, Saturday 13 October 1764

Printed from *Works* v. 113.

Strawberry Hill, October 13, 1764.

LORD John Cavendish has been so kind as to send me word[1] of the Duke of Devonshire's[2] legacy to you.[3] You cannot doubt of the great joy this gives me; and yet it serves to aggravate the loss of so worthy a man! And when I feel it thus, I am sensible how much more it will add to your concern, instead of diminishing it. Yet do not wholly reflect on your misfortune. You might despise the acquisition of five thousand pounds simply; but when that sum is a public testimonial to your virtue, and bequeathed by a man so virtuous, it is a million! Measure it with the riches of those who have basely injured you, and it is still more! Why, it is glory, it is conscious innocence, it is satisfaction—it is affluence without guilt.—Oh! the comfortable sound! It is a good name in the history of these corrupt days. There it will exist, when the wealth of your and their country's enemies will be wasted, or will be an indelible blemish on their descendants.

My heart is full, and yet I will say no more. My best loves to all your opulent family. Who says virtue is not rewarded in this world? It is rewarded by virtue, and it is persecuted by the bad: can greater honour be paid to it?

Yours ever,

Hor. Walpole

1. Missing.
2. William, fourth Duke of Devonshire. During his administration in Ireland Mr Conway had been secretary of state there (HW).
3. 'Thursday night [11 Oct.] the Duke of Devonshire's will was opened, when the following codicil appeared in his Grace's own handwriting, dated July 23: "I give to General Conway five thousand pounds, as a testimony of my friendship for him; and of my sense of his honourable conduct, and friendship for me"' (*London Chronicle* 13–16 Oct., xvi. 363).

From HERTFORD, Sunday 21 October 1764

Printed for the first time from a photostat of BM Add. MSS 23218, ff. 171–2.

Fontainebleau, October 21st 1764.

Dear Horry,

YOU have been the first to communicate to me[1] the legacy the late Duke of Devonshire has so generously left my brother. It gives me great pleasure on all accounts. My brother's delicacy in not accepting the offers of his friends[2] makes it convenient to his circumstances, and it proves to the world the justness of my brother's sentiments in his attachment to the Duke. I am sincerely concerned for the loss my brother has sustained in the death of so good a friend,[3] and it is a poor consolation to think that nothing could have saved him. He had a swelling in his head, a glandular one I think they call it, which no medicines could reach;[4] his inside was perfect and might have supported him to the age of a hundred.

Lord and Lady Spencer, who have been with us for some time at Fontainebleau, received an early account of his death. The two persons I have just named have been extremely well received here. Lady Spencer has been much admired for her very amiable behaviour; his Lordship is thought silent and of little use to society except in having contributed so properly to it by introducing Lady Spencer to the world. We have many other English here, which you will allow me to say are very troublesome to their ambassador. Some of them seem to expect everything. I am not sure they do not think he is to blame that the French do not always admire and solicit their company. We have them of all ages, of all sorts and of all tempers. They must therefore wish to hunt, to shoot and to partake of every forbidden fruit. It

1. The letter is missing.
2. See *ante* 21 April 1764 and n. 5.
3. Conway wrote to Hertford 17 Oct. of the grief he felt over the death of his 'much honoured, loved and lamented friend. . . . I need say nothing on his qualities or my loss, which I must think is irreparable' (MS now WSL).
4. Lady Mary Coke wrote to Lady Strafford, 26 Oct., that 'Sir William Duncan [physician to George III] was with me this morning, and told me he had

seen the accounts that were come over from the doctors who were present when the poor Duke of Devonshire was opened, and that they had found upon the brain a spongy substance as big as a walnut, and that when he had his fit at Wentworth Castle [seat of Lord Strafford] it was occasioned by that substance pressing the brain, and as that pressure increased he lost the use of his limbs and at last [it] deprived him of his life' (Coke, *Journals* i. 16).

is not in my power to provide so largely for such extensive wishes, and I wish in some instances the disappointment may not be charged to my account. It is not always sufficient to be innocent. I do what I can with propriety even for their amusement; I think they will not blame me for not entertaining them at my table, and if you hear of any complaints I beg you will answer for me that I do all I can and that I am not made by nature to be indifferent to any part of my duty. We have sent Monsieur de Guerchy back,[5] who seems a good-natured well-meaning man. I must in justice say that he declares the strongest partiality for you; perhaps you will think he is French enough to know how to pay his court to me.

My son is set out for Italy; Lady Hertford bears it tolerably well, but wishes, I believe, most anxiously, that the next months of her life may pass quickly till his return.[6]

Fontainebleau is not so gay as I found it last year. We have no balls, and consequently not so much company; perhaps this alteration may be owing to the present Lord of the Bedchamber in waiting,[7] who is brother to the Bailli de Fleuri[8] that you saw in England,[9] and a much graver man than the Lord who waited last year.[10] To prove his power in this instance I must tell you that the Lord in waiting for the year acts here as the Chamberlain does in England, and consequently provides for the King's *menus plaisirs*. We have however three *spectacles* in the week: French tragedy on Tuesdays, operas on Thursdays, and Italian comedies on Saturdays, which with hunting, shooting, business and company fill up the time sufficiently.

I am in search of some books for your amusement, but cannot yet find any worth your reading; the *Essai sur les mœurs* you shall receive by the first courier or opportunity I can find, with any other books I think worthy of you.[11] You are very good to let me hear from

---

5. He reached London 16 and waited on the King 17 Oct. (*Daily Adv.* 18 Oct.).

6. On this head Conway wrote to Hertford, 2 Nov.: 'I can easily imagine what Lady Hertford feels on the prospect of so long a parting from Lord Beauchamp; but for his sake must rather regret the necessity of this thing than the thing itself; with his understanding and disposition he cannot fail of making the proper advantage of his travels' (MS now WSL).

7. André-Hercule de Rosset (1715–88), Duc de Fleury (DU DEFFAND ii. 197).

8. Pons-François de Rosset de Fleury (1727–74), Bailli de Fleury (ibid. i. 76).

9. Presumably the Bailli was one of the 'Messieurs de Fleury' whom HW mentions to Montagu 17 May 1763 as having visited SH that day (MONTAGU ii. 70).

10. Emmanuel-Félicité de Durfort (1715–89), Duc de Duras (DU DEFFAND ii. 153; *Almanach royal*, 1763, p. 133).

11. Along with the *Essai*, Hertford sent HW a new edition of the *Testament politique* of Cardinal Richelieu (*post* 3, 7 Dec. 1764).

you so often; it is a great comfort to a man who is out of his country to know what passes where he is so much interested.

Lord March is here; G. Selwyn is at the Prince of Conti's but expected every day. Stanley set out this morning but stops at Paris. Adieu, dear Horry, believe me

Always sincerely and affectionately yours,

HERTFORD

To HERTFORD, ca Tuesday 23 October 1764

Missing; mentioned by HW to Hertford *post* 1 Nov. 1764 ('My last told you of my sister's promotion [to housekeeper at Windsor Castle]'). Dated conjecturally by the former housekeeper's having died 22 Oct. (GM 1764, xxxiv. 499) and by Montagu's thanking HW 25 Oct. 1764 for notifying him of Lady Mary's promotion (MONTAGU ii. 136).

From CONWAY, ca Saturday 27 October 1764

Missing; answered *post* 29 Oct. 1764. Dated conjecturally by the urgency of HW's reply, and the fact that letters from Park Place to SH should not have taken more than a day or two to arrive.

To CONWAY, Monday 29 October 1764

Printed from *Works* v. 113–15.

Strawberry Hill, October 29, 1764.

I AM glad you mentioned it:[1] I would not have had you appear without your close mourning[2] for the Duke of Devonshire upon any account. I was once going to tell you of it, knowing your inaccuracy in such matters; but thought it still impossible you should be ignorant how necessary it is. Lord Strafford, who has a legacy of only

1. Conway's letter is missing.   2. 'Mourning such as worn by the nearest relatives; deep mourning' (OED).

£200, wrote to consult Lady Suffolk. She told him, for such a sum, which only implies a ring, it was sometimes not done; but yet advised him to mourn. In your case it is indispensable; nor can you see any of his family without it. Besides, it is much better on such an occasion to over-, than underdo. I answer this paragraph first, because I am so earnest not to have you blamed.

Besides wishing to see you all, I have wanted exceedingly to come to you, having much to say to you; but I am confined here, that is, Mr Chute[3] is: he was seized with the gout last Wednesday sennight, the day he came hither to meet George Montagu,[4] and this is the first day he has been out of his bedchamber. I must therefore put off our meeting till Saturday, when you shall certainly find me in town.

We have a report here, but the authority bitter bad, that Lord March is going to be married to Lady Anne Conway.[5] I don't believe it the less for our knowing nothing of it; for unless their daughter were breeding, and it were to save her character, neither your brother nor Lady Hertford would disclose a tittle about it. Yet in charity they should advertise it, that parents and relations, if it is so, may lock up all knives, ropes, laudanum, and rivers, lest it should occasion a violent mortality among his fair admirers.

I am charmed with an answer I have just read in the papers of a poor man in Bedlam, who was ill used by an apprentice because he would not tell him why he was confined there. The unhappy creature said at last, 'Because God has deprived me of a blessing which you never enjoyed.'[6] There never was anything finer or more moving! Your sensibility will not be quite so much affected by a story I heard

3. John Chute, Esq. of the Vine in Hampshire (HW).

4. See MONTAGU ii. 135, 136; MANN vi. 257.

5. Gilly Williams wrote to Selwyn, 13 Nov.: 'Whom do you think they have married Lord March to?—no less a person than Lady Anne Conway' (J. H. Jesse, George Selwyn and his Contemporaries, 1882, i. 321). However, Hertford declared emphatically, post 18 Jan. 1765, that March had never shown 'the most distant regard for my daughter.'

6. 'Worcester, Oct. 25 . . . A young fellow of the city of Bristol, being in London lately, was, out of curiosity, led to see the lunatics confined in Bedlam. His first approach was to the cell of a poor man, to whom he addressed himself thus: "Soho! What brings thee here?" The miserable object remaining silent, he repeated his question, and was answered only by a languishing look, which so enraged the visitant, that he immediately spit in his face through the grate; this caused him to gently wipe his face with a whisp of straw, and raising his drooping head, he made him this calm, sage, and sensible reply: "Because God, Sir, deprived me of that blessing which you never enjoyed"' (Public Adv. 29 Oct.; St James's Chronicle 27–30 Oct., sub 29 Oct.).

t'other day of Sir Fletcher Norton. He has a mother[7]—yes, a mother: perhaps you thought, that, like that tender urchin Love,

> —————————— duris in cotibus *illum*
> Ismarus, aut Rhodope, aut extremi Garamantes,
> Nec nostri generis puerum nec sanguinis edunt.[8]

Well, Mrs Rhodope lives in a mighty shabby hovel at Preston, which the dutiful and affectionate Sir Fletcher began to think not suitable to the dignity of one who has the honour of being his parent. He cheapened a better, in which were two pictures which the proprietor valued at threescore pounds. The *attorney*[9] insisted on having them for nothing, as fixtures—the landlord refused, the bargain was broken off, and the dowager Madam Norton remains in her original hut. I could tell you another story which you would not dislike; but as it might hurt the person concerned, if it was known, I shall not send it by the post; but will tell it you when I see you. Adieu!

Yours most cordially,

Hor. Walpole

To Hertford, Thursday 1 November 1764

Printed from *Works* ix. 153–7.

Strawberry Hill, Nov. 1st 1764.

I AM not only pleased, my dear Lord, to have been the first to announce your brother's legacy to you, but I am glad whenever my news reach you without being quite stale. I see but few persons here. I begin my letters without knowing when I shall be able to fill them, and then am to winnow a little what I hear, that I may not

---

7. Elizabeth Serjeantson (d. 1774), m. Thomas Norton (ca 1683–1719) of Grantley, York (GM 1774, xliv. 446; Collins, *Peerage*, 1812, vii. 551).

8. '——————duris in cotibus illum
    aut Tmaros aut Rhodope aut extremi Garamantes
    nec generis nostri puerum nec sanguinis edunt'

('On hard stones Tmarus bore him, or Rhodope, or most distant Garamantes, a child not of our race or blood') (Virgil, *Eclogue VIII*, ll. 43–5).

9. Norton had been appointed attorney-general in Dec. 1763 (*ante* 22 Jan. 1764, n. 21).

send you absolute second-hand fables; for though I cannot warrant all I tell you, I hate to send you every improbable tale that is vented. You like, as one always does in absence, to hear the common occurrences of your own country, and you see I am very glad to be your gazetteer, provided you do not rank my letters upon any higher foot. I should be ashamed of such gossiping, if I did not consider it as chatting with you *en famille,* as we used to do at supper in Grosvenor Street.

The Duke of Devonshire has made splendid provision for his younger children; to Lady Dorothy,[1] £30,000; Lord Richard[2] and Lord George[3] will have about £4,000 a year apiece; for, besides landed estates, he has left them his whole personal estate without exception, only obliging the present Duke[4] to redeem Devonshire House, and the entire collection in it[5] for £20,000: he gives £500 to each of his brothers,[6] and £200 to Lord Strafford, with some other inconsiderable legacies. Lord Frederick carried the Garter, and was treated with very gracious speeches of concern.[7]

The Duke of Cumberland is quite recovered, after an incision of

1. Lady Dorothy Cavendish (1750–94), m. (1766) William Henry Cavendish Bentinck, 3d D. of Portland.

2. Lord Richard Cavendish (1752–81), M.P. Lancester 1773–80, Derbyshire 1780–1.

3. Lord George Augustus Henry Cavendish (1754–1834), cr. (1831) E. of Burlington; M.P. Knaresborough 1775–80, Derby 1780–96, Derbyshire 1797–1831.

4. William Cavendish (1748–1811), 5th D. of Devonshire, 1764; K.G. 1782.

5. 'The collection of pictures with which this house is adorned is surpassed by very few either at home or abroad' (*London and its Environs Described*, 1761, ii. 225). A partial list of the pictures, including works by Rembrandt, Vandyke, Rubens, Titian, da Vinci, etc., is ibid. ii. 225–32, and in [Thomas Martyn], *The English Connoisseur*, 1766, i. 41–50. There was also a valuable collection of gems and medals; see CHATTERTON 189, n. 4, 204, 208–10, 301, n. 19.

6. Lords George Augustus, Frederick and John Cavendish.

7. 'On Friday last [26 Oct.] . . . Lord George [Frederick] Cavendish brother to

. . . the [late] Duke of Devonshire, waited on his Majesty at St James's with the ensigns of the Order of the Garter with which his late Grace was invested' (*London Chronicle* 27–30 Oct., xvi. 413). Lord Frederick wrote to Newcastle, 30 Oct., that 'the affair of the Closet went off as well as could possibly be; after I had delivered the George [the jewel of the Order] his Majesty said (a little disconcerted) that he must express the greatest concern on this occasion, that notwithstanding an unpleasant circumstance that had happened [Devonshire's forced resignation as Lord Chamberlain and dismissal from the Privy Council in 1762] his regard was not altered for a man that he knew was most sincerely attached to him and his family, and whose character and way of thinking he should always admire, and that he felt the greatest concern for the loss of him. This or words to this effect he repeated two or three times over and added that he knew how steadily our family had always been attached to his, and should always esteem them, and had the greatest opinion of us all' (BM Add. MSS 32963, f. 106).

many inches in his knee.[8] Ranby[9] did not dare to propose that a hero should be tied, but was frightened out of his senses when the hero would hold the candle himself, which none of his generals could bear to do: in the middle of the operation, the Duke said, 'Hold!' Ranby said, 'For God's sake, Sir, let me proceed now—it will be worse to renew it.' The Duke repeated, 'I say, hold!' and then calmly bade them give Ranby a clean waistcoat and cap, 'for,' said he, 'the poor man has sweat through these.'—It was true; but the Duke did not utter a groan.

Have you heard that Lady Susan O'Brien's is not the last romance of the sort? Lord Rockingham's youngest sister, Lady Harriot,[10] has stooped even lower than a theatric swain, and married her footman; but still it is you Irish that commit all the havoc. Lady Harriot, however, has mixed a wonderful degree of prudence with her potion, and considering how plain she is, has not, I think, sweetened the draught too much for her lover: she settles a single hundred pound a year upon him for his life, entails her whole fortune on their children, if they have any;[11] and, if not, on her own family;—nay, in the height of the novel, provides for a separation, and ensures the same pin-money to Damon, in case they part. This deed she has vested out of her power, by sending it to Lord Mansfield,[12] whom she makes her trustee; it is drawn up in her own hand, and Lord Mansfield says is as binding as any lawyer could make it. Did one ever hear of more reflection in a delirium! Well, but hear more: she has given

8. 'I had this morning a letter from Newmarket to tell me that the inflammation on his Royal Highness's leg (. . . the outside of his right leg just below the knee) is come to a gathering and was opened yesterday in the afternoon, and above a pint of matter let out' (Lord Frederick Cavendish to Newcastle, 8 Oct., BM Add. MSS 32962, f. 232). The *London Chronicle* 27–30 Oct., *sub* 29 Oct., reported that 'the Duke of Cumberland is so well recovered as to have appeared in his coach upon the course at Newmarket every day last week' (xvi. 409).

9. John Ranby (1703–73), sergeant-surgeon to the King.

10. Lady Henrietta Alicia Watson Wentworth (b. 1737), m. (21 Oct. 1764) William Sturgeon (1741–1831) (Joseph Foster, *Pedigrees of . . . Yorkshire*, 1874, Vol. II *sub* Wentworth). Gilly Williams

wrote to Selwyn, 10 Nov., that 'it is supposed she is with child by him, for they used to pass many hours together, which she called teaching John [*sic*] the mathematics' (J. H. Jesse, *George Selwyn and his Contemporaries*, 1882, i. 315). Lady Louisa Stuart's observations on this marriage have been printed in Coke, *Journals* i. 249 and in *Notes by Lady Louisa Stuart on George Selwyn and his Contemporaries by John Heneage Jesse*, ed. W. S. Lewis, New York, 1928, p. 20.

11. Their children were: Thomas William Sturgeon (d. 1823), naval officer; Charles Alexander Sturgeon (d. 1845); Henry Robert Sturgeon (d. 1814), army officer; Charlotte Sturgeon, m. (1789) Capt. James Edwards; and Agnes Sturgeon, m. Pierre Jacques La Chesnay (Foster, loc. cit.).

12. Her uncle by marriage.

away all her clothes, nay, and her Ladyship, and says linen gowns are properest for a footman's wife, and is gone to his family in Ireland, plain Mrs Henrietta Sturgeon. I think it is not clear that she is mad, but I have no doubt but Lady Bel will be so,[13] who could not digest Dr Duncan,[14] nor even Mr Milbank.[15]

My last[16] told you of my sister's promotion.[17] I hear she is to be succeeded at Kensington by Miss Floyd,[18] who lives with Lady Bolingbroke; but I beg you not to report this till you see it in a *Gazette* of better authority than mine, who have it only from fame and Mrs A[nne] Pitt.[19]

I have not seen Monsieur de Guerchy yet, having been in town but one night since his return. You are very kind in accepting, on your own account, his obliging expressions about me: I know no foundation on which I should like better to receive them: the truth is, he has distinguished me extremely, and when a person in his situation shows much attention to a person so very insignificant as I am, one is apt to believe it exceeds common compliment: at least, I attribute it to the esteem which he could not but see I conceived for him. His civility is so natural, and his good nature so strongly marked, that I connected much more with him than I am apt to do with new acquaintances. I pitied the various disgusts he received,[20]

13. 'Lady Mansfield went with a doctor and surgeon to acquaint poor Lady Bell Finch with her favourite niece having run away with her footman; they blooded her; but everybody is apprehensive it will go near to kill her, as she was not well at the time' (Lady Mary Coke to Lady Strafford, 26 Oct., Coke, op. cit. i. 16).

14. William Duncan, M.D., m. (1763) Lady Mary Tufton, Lady Bel Finch's great-niece; see *ante* 12 April 1764.

15. John Milbanke (ca 1725–1806), son of Sir Ralph Milbanke, 4th Bt; m. (31 May 1764) Lady Mary Watson Wentworth, daughter of the 1st M. of Rockingham and niece of Lady Bel Finch (G. F. Russell Barker and A. H. Stenning, *Record of Old Westminsters*, 1928, ii. 645; GM 1764, xxxiv. 302, 1806, lxxvi pt i. 481).

16. Missing.

17. To housekeeper at Windsor Castle. Lady Mary Coke wrote to Lady Strafford, 26 Oct., that 'Lord Gower has a fine place to dispose of by the death of Mrs Handy-side [22 Oct.] . . . 'tis certainly worth six hundred a year, besides one of the prettiest apartments I ever saw' (Coke, op. cit. i. 16–17; GM 1764, xxxiv. 499). See MONTAGU ii. 136.

18. Rachel Lloyd (ca 1720–1803) (ibid. ii. 305, n. 8).

19. The *London Gazette* No. 10479, 15–18 Dec., *sub* St James's, 18 Dec., reported that 'the King has been pleased to grant unto Rachel Lloyd the office of housekeeper and wardrobe-keeper of his Majesty's palace of Kensington.'

20. For instance, d'Éon's attack on him in his *Lettres, mémoires et négociations particulières*, published in March (*ante* 27 March 1764). Also, the previous year Guerchy had had a dispute with Grenville over the quantity of wine he should be allowed to bring into the country duty-free, and earlier in the present year had been angered by the attempted arrest of one of his servants for breach of the peace, and by the confiscation by Customs

and I believe he saw I did. If I felt for him, you may judge how much I am concerned that you have your share. I foresaw it was unavoidable, from the swarms of your countrymen that flock to Paris, and generally the worst part; boys and governors are woeful exports. I saw a good deal of it when I lived with poor Sir Horace Mann at Florence—but you have the whole market. We are a wonderful people—I would not be our King, our minister, or our ambassador, for the Indies. One comfort, however, I can truly give you; I have heard their complaints, if they have any, from nobody but yourself. Jesus! if they are not content now, I wish they knew how the English were received at Paris twenty years ago[21]—Why, you and I know they were not received at all. Ay, and when the fashion of admiring English is past, it will be just so again; and very reasonably—Who would open their house to every staring booby from another country?

Arlington Street, November 3d.

I came to town today to meet your brother, who is going to Euston[22] and Thetford,[23] and hope he will bring back a good account of the domestic history,[24] of which we can learn nothing authentic. Fitzroy[25] knows nothing. The town says the Duchess is going thither.

We have been this evening with Duchess Hamilton, who is arrived from Scotland, visibly promising another Lord Campbell.[26] I shall take this opportunity of seeing Monsieur de Guerchy, and that opportunity of sending this letter, and one from your brother. Our politics are all at a stand. The Duke of Devonshire's death, I concluded, would make the ministry all-powerful, all-triumphant, and all-insolent. It does not appear to have done so. They are, I believe,

of an *habit de gala* he had sent for to wear on the King's Birthday (*Grenville Papers* ii. 188, 259–60, 334, 360–1, 503–4).

21. When diplomatic relations were broken off between the two countries; HW is apparently referring further back to when he was at Paris in 1739 and 1741; James, 1st E. Waldegrave was ambassador 1730–40 and Anthony Thompson chargé d'affaires 1740–4, during which time relations between France and England progressively worsened (D. B. Horn, *British Diplomatic Representatives 1689–1789*, 1932, pp. 19–20).

22. Seat of the Duke of Grafton.

23. Conway's Parliamentary borough, four miles from Euston. Conway wrote to Hertford 2 Nov., 'I set out for Euston tomorrow for a day or two only, and to visit my friends at Thetford' (MS now WSL).

24. The rumoured estrangement of the Duke and Duchess of Grafton.

25. Charles Fitzroy, later Bn Southampton.

26. Presumably this pregnancy ended in a miscarriage; the Duchess's next child of record was the future 6th Duke of Argyll, born in 1768. Her first son by her present husband (the future 5th Duke), George John Campbell, styled Lord Campbell, b. 17 Feb. 1763, had died 12 July 1764 (GM 1764, xxxiv. 350).

extremely ill among themselves, and not better in their affairs foreign or domestic. The cider counties[27] have instructed their members to join the minority.[28] The *House of Yorke* seems to have laid aside their coldness and irresolution, and to look towards Opposition.[29] The unpopularity of the Court is very great indeed—still I shall not be surprised if they maintain their ground a little longer. There is nothing new in the way of publication: the town itself is still a desert. I have twice passed by Arthur's today, and not seen a chariot.

Hogarth is dead,[30] and Mrs Spence,[31] who lived with the Duchess of Newcastle. She had saved £20,000, which she leaves to her sister[32] for life, and after her, to Tommy Pelham. Ned Finch[33] has got an

27. In this case, Devonshire and Cornwall.

28. At a general meeting of the High Sheriff, gentlemen, clergy, and freeholders of Devonshire, held 4 Oct. at Exeter, it was resolved that the county's representatives in Parliament, Sir Richard Warwick Bampfylde and John Parker, be instructed to 'unite' themselves 'with all such persons . . . as shall be ready to join their endeavours' with theirs towards obtaining relief from the new excise duty on cider (see *ante* 22 Jan. 1764, n. 86), 'and who shall, on every other occasion, oppose all exorbitant stretches of power, everything that may tend towards an encroachment on our happy constitution' (*Public Adv.* 16 Oct., *sub* Exeter, 4 Oct.). Sir George Yonge, representing 'the gentlemen who composed the prevailing interest' at the meeting, wrote Newcastle 17 Oct. for his advice on what further course to pursue, claiming that 'Cornwall acts in entire concert with Devonshire,' and proposing a coalition of all the M.P.'s from both counties with the minority (BM Add. MSS 32962, ff. 329–30). Newcastle, in letters of 19 Oct., referred the matter to Pitt and Cumberland (through Albemarle) (ibid. ff. 351–2, 360–3; the letter to Pitt is printed *Chatham Corr.* ii. 293–5). Pitt, in his reply, restated his intention of 'continuing . . . not to mix myself, nor to suffer others to mix me, in any bargains or stipulations whatever' (Pitt to Newcastle 19 Oct., BM Add. MSS 32962, ff. 347–50, printed *Chatham Corr.* ii. 296–8), while Cumberland, after 'examining the list of members for . . . Devon and Cornwall,' decided that 'the acquisition of the few, not already determined, would not be

equal to the risque of disobliging many friends by a coalition with the Tories' (Albemarle to Newcastle 24 Oct., BM Add. MSS 32963, f. 19). See *Mem. Geo. III* ii. 28–9.

29. However, see *post* 25 Nov., 3 Dec. 1764.

30. 'On Friday night [26 Oct.] died suddenly . . . at his house in Leicester Fields, the celebrated William Hogarth, Esq.' (*London Chronicle* 27–30 Oct., xvi. 409–10).

31. Elizabeth Spence (ca 1694 – 15 Oct. 1764) (William Berry, *Pedigrees of . . . Sussex*, 1830, p. 27; John Comber, *Sussex Genealogies*, Cambridge, 1931–3, iii. 278). 'Last week died, at . . . the Duke of Newcastle's at Claremont, Mrs Elizabeth Spence' (*London Chronicle* 25–7 Oct., xvi. 402, *sub* 26 Oct.). Newcastle wrote to Lord Albemarle, 16 Oct.: 'Your Lordship, I am sure, will be very sorry to hear of the loss of your old acquaintance, Mrs Spence, which happened yesterday about five in the afternoon. You may imagine how much the poor Duchess of Newcastle is affected with the loss of so good a friend, who has lived with us above 45 years' (BM Add. MSS 32962, f. 319).

32. Probably Ruth Spence (d. 1767), to whom Elizabeth Spence 'by her will devised all her manors, etc. (charged with an annuity subsequently released) . . . for life' (Ronald Morris, 'Manor of Houndean,' in *Sussex Notes and Queries*, 1931, iii. 192; Berry, loc. cit.; Comber, op. cit. iii. 277). Another sister, Mary, died in 1764 (Berry, loc. cit.; Comber, loc. cit.).

33. Hon. Edward Finch (afterwards Finch Hatton) (?1697–1771); M.P. Cambridge University 1727–68; diplomatist.

estate from an old Mrs Hatton[34] of £1500 a year, and takes her name. Adieu! my Lord and Lady, and your whole *et cetera*.

Yours, most faithfully,

Hor. Walpole

To Hertford, Friday 9 November 1764

Printed from *Works* ix. 158–61.

Strawberry Hill, Nov. 9th 1764.

I DON'T know whether this letter will not reach you, my dear Lord, before one[1] that I sent to you last week by a private hand, along with one from your brother. I write this by my Lord Chamberlain's[2] order—you may interpret it as you please, either as by some new connection of the Bedford squadron with the Opposition, or as a commission to you, my Lord Ambassador. As yet, I believe you had better take it upon the latter foundation, though the Duke of Bedford has crossed the country from Bath to Woburn, without coming to town. Be that as it may, here is the negotiation entrusted to you. You are desired by my Lord Gower, to apply to the Gentilhomme de la Chambre[3] for leave for Doberval[4] the dancer, who was here last year,[5] to return and dance at our opera forthwith.[6] If the Court of France will comply with this request, we will send them a discharge in full, for the Canada bills[7] and the ransom of their prisoners,[8] and we will permit Monsieur D'Estain[9] to command in the

34. Hon. Anne Hatton (d. 5 Oct. 1764) (*London Chronicle* 6–9 Oct., xvi. 338), daughter of the 1st Vct Hatton and Finch's aunt (Collins, *Peerage*, 1812, iii. 403; GEC xii pt ii. 784). By her death Finch became sole heir of the Hatton estates (ibid. 788).

1. *Ante* 1 Nov. 1764.
2. Lord Gower.
3. The Duc de Fleury (*ante* 21 Oct. 1764).
4. Jean Bercher (1742–1806), called Dauberval, French dancer and chore-

ographer (*Enciclopedia dello spettacolo*, Rome, 1954–62, iv. 206–7).

5. Dauberval was one of the dancers at the Opera for the 1763–4 season (*London Stage* Pt IV, ii. 1007).

6. The permission was not granted; see *post* 7, 20 Dec. 1764.

7. See *ante* 27 Aug. 1764, n. 27.
8. See *ante* 3 Aug. 1764, n. 51.
9. Jean-Baptiste-Charles d'Estaing (1729–94), Comte d'Estaing; naval officer (*La Grande Encyclopédie*, [1886–1902], xvi. 398). As governor-general of San Domingo (La Chenaye-Desbois vii. 472; *Almanach*

West Indies, whether we will or not. The City of London must not know a word of this treaty, for they hate any mortal should be diverted but themselves, especially by anything relative to *harmony*. It is, I own, betraying my country and my patriotism to be concerned in a job of this kind. I am sensible that there is not a weaver in Spitalfields but can dance better than the first performer in the French Opera; and yet, how could I refuse this commission? Mrs George Pitt delivered it to me just now, at Lord Holderness's at Sion, and as my virtue has not yet been able to root out all my good-breeding—though I trust it will in time—I could not help promising that I would write to you—nay, and engaged that you would undertake it. When I venture, sure you may, who are out of the reach of a mob!

I believe this letter will go by Monsieur Beaumont.[10] He breakfasted here t'other morning, and pleased me exceedingly: he has great spirit and good humour. It is incredible what pains he has taken to *see*. He has *seen* Oxford, Bath, Blenheim, Stowe, Jews, Quakers, Mr Pitt, the Royal Society, the Robinhood,[11] Lord Chief Justice Pratt, the Arts and Sciences,[12] has dined at Wildman's,[13] and, I think, with my Lord Mayor,[14] or is to do. Monsieur de Guerchy is full of your praises; I am to go to Park Place with him next week, to make your brother a visit.[15]

royal, 1765, p. 111), he had ordered the attack upon Turk Island, made 1 June (see *ante* 27 Aug. 1764, n. 3). However, though Hertford was instructed by Halifax in the latter's dispatch of 20 Aug. to insist that 'the several French officers concerned either in the direction, or in the execution of this unjustifiable proceeding, be forthwith disavowed and punished' (S.P. 78/263, f. 49), Hertford reported back, 5 Sept., that on this point 'the Court of France may not be found to come up entirely to his Majesty's just expectations' (ibid. ff. 89–90): the action was disavowed, but d'Estaing not punished.

10. Jean-Baptiste-Jacques Élie de Beaumont (1732–86), jurist. Gilly Williams wrote to Selwyn, 13 Nov., that 'de Beaumont has breakfast with him [HW] at Strawberry. He is now as much a curiosity to all foreigners as the tombs [in the Abbey] and lions [at the Tower]' (J. H. Jesse, *George Selwyn and his Contemporaries*, 1882, i. 322).

11. The Robin Hood Society, an oratorical club in Essex Street (*Mem. Geo. II* i. 42 and n. 1). See H. B. Wheatley and Peter Cunningham, *London Past and Present*, 1891, ii. 18.

12. I.e., the Society for the Encouragement of Arts, Manufactures, and Commerce (see GRAY i. 37, n. 250).

13. The Opposition club in Albemarle Street; see *ante* 22 Jan. 1764, n. 98.

14. Sir William Stephenson (d. 1774), Kt 1759; alderman of Bridge Within 1754–74; lord mayor 1764–5, elected 29 Sept. and sworn in 8 Nov. as successor to William Bridgen (A. B. Beaven, *Aldermen of . . . London*, 1908–13, ii. 131; GM 1764, xxxiv. 449, 1774, xliv. 495; W. A. Shaw, *Knights of England*, 1906, ii. 289; *Court and City Register* 1754–1774 *passim*; *London Chronicle* 6–8 Nov., xvi. 448).

15. HW mentions the visit to Mann, 15 Nov. 1764, *sub* 25 Nov. (MANN vi. 263).

You know how I hate telling you false news: all I can do, is to retract as fast as I can. I fear I was too hasty in an article I sent you in my last, though I then mentioned it only as a report.[16] I doubt, what we wish in a private family[17] will not be exactly the event.

The Duke of Cumberland has had a dangerous sore throat;[18] but is recovered.[19] In one of the bitterest days that could be felt, he would go upon the course at Newmarket with the windows of his landau down. Newmarket heath, at no time of the year, is placed under the torrid zone.[20] I can conceive a hero welcoming death, or at least despising it; but if I was covered with more laurels than a boar's head at Christmas, I should hate pain, and Ranby, and an operation. His nephew of York has been at Blenheim, where they gave him a ball, but did not put themselves to much expense in dancers; the *figurantes* were the maid-servants. You will not doubt my authority, when I tell you my Lady Bute was my intelligence. I heard today, at Sion, of some bitter verses made at Bath, on both their Graces of Bedford. I have not seen them, nor if I had them, would I send them to you before they are in print, which I conclude they will be, for I am sorry to say, scandalous abuse is not the commodity which either side is sparing of. You can conceive nothing beyond the epigrams which have been in the papers, on a pair of doves and a parrot that Lord Bute has sent to the Princess.[21]

I hear—but this is another of my paragraphs that I am far from

16. 'The town says the Duchess [of Grafton] is going thither [to Euston, seat of the Duke]' (*ante* 1 Nov. 1764).

17. The reconciliation of the Duke and Duchess.

18. 'I own, your letter of this day gives me great concern, that H.R.H.'s throat continues sore and inflamed' (Newcastle to Albemarle, 1 Nov., BM Add. MSS 32963, f. 159).

19. 'I most sincerely congratulate your Lordship upon H.R.H.'s safe arrival at Cumberland House and in perfect good health' (idem to idem, 9 Nov., ibid. f. 324).

20. 'I always dreaded last Friday's north-east wind upon the course. I have felt it more, on the Warren Hill, than on any other part of Europe, where I may have been. . . . Indeed H.R.H. owes it to his own royal family, to his country,

and to his faithful servants, and well-wishers . . . to take more care of himself than he does' (idem to idem, 1 Nov., ibid. f. 159).

21. The Princess Dowager. Presumably the epigrams equated the parrot with Bute, and the doves with the Princess and a Miss Vansittart, maid of honour to the Princess, whose sedan chair Bute made use of in his visits to the Princess, and who was also alleged to be Bute's mistress: 'The Earl for several years visited her regularly every evening at seven for at least two hours' (HW's foul copy of *Mem. Geo. III*, p. 16; *Court and City Register*, 1764, p. 101; *The Historical and the Post-humous Memoirs of Sir Nathaniel William Wraxall*, ed. H. B. Wheatley, 1884, i. 327-8).

giving you for sterling—that Lord Sandwich is to have the Duke of Devonshire's Garter;[22] Lord Northumberland[23] stands against Lord Morton[24] for President of the Royal Society, in the room of Lord Macclesfield.[25] As this latter article will have no bad consequences if it should prove true, you may believe it.

Earl Poulet[26] is dead, and Soame,[27] who married Mrs Naylor's[28] sister.[29]

You will wonder more at what I am going to tell you in the last place: I am preparing, in earnest, to make you a visit—not next week, but seriously in February. After postponing it for seven idle months, you will stare at my thinking of it just after the meeting of the Parliament. Why, that is just one of my principal reasons. I will stay and see the opening, and one or two divisions; the minority will be able to be the majority, or they will not: if they can, they will not want me, who want nothing of them: if they cannot, I am sure I can do them no good, and shall take my leave of them;—I mean always, to be sure, if things do not turn on a few votes: they shall not call me a deserter. In every other case, I am so sick of politics, which I have long detested, that I must bid adieu to them. I have acted the part by your brother that I thought right. He approves what I have done, and what I mean to do; so do the few I esteem, for I have notified my intention;[30] and for the rest of the world, they may think what they please. In truth, I have a better reason, which would prescribe my setting out directly, if it was consistent with my honour. I have a return of those nightly fevers and pains in my breast, which

22. Sandwich never had the Garter; the Prince of Wales (the future George IV) was elected in place of Devonshire 26 Dec. 1765 (Shaw, op. cit. i. 46).

23. Fellow of the Royal Society since 1736.

24. F.R.S. since 1733, he was chosen by a special council to be the new president, which choice was confirmed by the Society at its anniversary meeting 30 Nov. (C. R. Weld, History of the Royal Society, 1848, ii. 22; London Chronicle 29 Nov.–1 Dec., xvi. 526).

25. Died 17 March (ante 18 March 1764); President of the Royal Society 1752–64.

26. John Poulett (1708–3 Nov. 1764), 2d E. Poulett 1743 (GM 1764, xxxiv. 545).

Gilly Williams wrote to Selwyn, 10 Nov., that 'he made an end like Falstaffe, "babbling of green fields"' (Jesse, op. cit. i. 314).

27. Stephen Soame (ca 1709–3 Nov. 1764), of Little Thurlow, Suffolk (COLE i. 377; DALRYMPLE 309; London Chronicle 6–8 Nov., xvi. 442).

28. Carlotta or Charlotte, daughter of Joseph Alston of Edwardstone, Suffolk; m. (1743) Francis Hare Naylor (MANN ii. 268, n. 13).

29. Anne Alston (Venn, Alumni Cantab., sub Stephen Soame).

30. For example, to Cole, in his letter of 8 Nov., and, later, to Gilly Williams (COLE i. 82; Jesse, op. cit. i. 321).

have come for the three last years at this season: change of air and a better climate are certainly necessary to me in winter.[31] I shall thus indulge my inclinations every way. I long to see you and my Lady Hertford, and am woefully sick of the follies and distractions of this country, to which I see no end, come what changes will! Now, do you wonder any longer at my resolution? In the meantime adieu! for the present,

Yours ever,

H. W.

From Hertford, Saturday 10 November 1764

Printed for the first time from a photostat of BM Add. MSS 23218, ff. 173–4.

Fontainebleau, November 10th 1764.

Dear Horry,

I SENT the letter you enclosed to me for Lady Mary Churchill the first moment I could. Mr Foley,[1] who is Mr Churchill's banker, was fortunately here and undertook to forward it. They are I believe at Nancy, at least in some part of Lorrain. I am very glad Lord Gower has made so good a choice.[2] I should not have doubted your wishes for Lady Mary, but I can easily conceive from what I know of you that you would not, at this moment particularly, owe an obligation there.

I shall remove from hence to Paris after tomorrow,[3] and shall then be the only ambassador except the Imperial one[4] with this Court. Do not imagine this attention is entirely policy. I like the life of this place. It is a mixture of hunting and shooting, of exercise and society, that suits my health and taste, and when I have the business of my

---

31. HW gives the same excuse for his trip in his letter to Cole of 8 Nov. (n. 30 above).

———

1. Robert Ralph Foley (ca 1727–82), cr. (1767) Bt.
2. Of Lady Mary as housekeeper at Windsor Castle (*ante* 1 Nov. 1764, n. 17).
3. Hertford was back at Paris by the 13th (Hertford to Halifax 13 Nov., S.P. 78/264, f. 31).

4. George Adam Starhemberg (1724–1807), Graf (Fürst, 1765) von Starhemberg, minister plenipotentiary from Austria to France 1754–7, ambassador 1757–66 (*Allgemeine deutsche Biographie*, Berlin, 1967–71, xxxv. 471–3; *Repertorium der diplomatischen Vertreter aller Länder*, Vol. II, ed. F. Hausmann, Zurich, 1950, pp. 63, 675).

Court to do I never wait long to see the minister of my department.[5]

As soon as I get to Paris I shall endeavour to find Dr Blanchard[6] and show him all the civility in my power. Do not spare me upon such occasions; I shall always be glad to be of any use to you. Mr Selwyn dined here today, and has just left us in very good spirits. He talks of staying in France till near the meeting of Parliament, not because he seems to be particularly diverted here, but because Lord March cannot leave it.[7] He has made the Queen's party at Court different times, but is now disgusted from being cheated at it by an old Polish Princess Talmond,[8] who seems to make a trade of her Majesty's cavagnole. Lady Hertford has likewise subscribed to this Polish bank; the poor good Queen does what she can to prevent it, but the Princess with a saint upon her breast[9] is not to be diverted from her purpose.

If you hear of my losses at whist, do not be surprised nor think them of any consequence to my circumstances. I have played for some time with ill luck and astonished the French with being able to lose; their idea of my superiority had made them hardly conceive the possibility, and it has been a subject of conversation, but I have lately reconciled all difficulties of this kind by a turn of luck which has proved the equal hand of fortune.

The next winter or rather the next year is to be gay at Versailles, if the King will consent to it. The Duke de Richlieu is to be in waiting, and has asked his Majesty's leave to give balls and entertainments there.

I thank you for the fable.[10] You are very good by every means to

5. The Duc de Praslin, secretary of state for foreign affairs.

6. See *ante* 5 Oct. 1764.

7. Presumably because of some romantic entanglement; see *post* 7 Dec. 1764. It appears from a letter written by March to Selwyn the following summer (ca 30 June) that during their Paris stay and after, Selwyn was dependent upon March for paying his gambling debts: 'So you have lost a thousand pounds. . . . [However] there will be no bankruptcy without we are both ruined at the same time. You may be very sure all this will soon be known here [in London], since everybody knows it at Paris' (J. H. Jesse, *George Selwyn and his Contemporaries*, 1882, i. 375–6).

8. Marie-Louise Jablonowska (1701–73), m. (1730) Antoine-Charles-Frédéric de la Trémoïlle, Prince de Talmond.

9. Or rather, her wrist; she wore a bracelet with a portrait of the Young Pretender on one side, and Christ on the other (DU DEFFAND vi. 58). HW, in his account of Madame du Deffand's 'portraits,' writes that 'to please the good Queen she [Madame de Talmond] acted devotion in her latter days, as in her earlier she had been gallant to please herself' (ibid. vi. 57). She had been the Young Pretender's mistress (MANN iv. 44, n. 11).

10. *The Magpie and Her Brood, A Fable, from the Tales of Bonaventure des Periers*. HW wrote the fable 15 Oct.,

contribute to the entertainment of your friends. Lady Hertford desires me to make her best compliments, and you will do me the justice to believe me, with the sincerest affection, dear Horry,

Always yours,

HERTFORD

To HERTFORD, Sunday 25 November 1764

Printed from *Works* ix. 162–6.

Strawberry Hill, Nov. 25th 1764.

HOW could you be so kind, my dear Lord, as to recollect Dr Blanchard, after so long an interval? It will make me still more cautious of giving recommendations to you, instead of drawing upon the credit you give me. I saw Mr Stanley[1] last night at the opera, who made his court extremely to me by what he said of you. It was our first opera,[2] and I went to town to hear Manzoli,[3] who did not quite answer my expectation,[4] though a very fine singer, but his voice *has been* younger, and wants the touching tones of Elisi.[5] However, the audience was not so nice, but applauded him immoderately,[6] and encored three of his songs.[7] The first woman[8] was advertised for a perfect beauty, with no voice; but her beauty and voice are by no means unequally balanced: she has a pretty little small

and printed 200 copies of it at SH 17 Oct. (COLE i. 80; GRAY i. 41).

1. 'On Thursday night [22 Nov.] the Hon. Hans Stanley arrived in town from Paris, where he has been for some time' (*Daily Adv.* 24 Nov.).

2. *Ezio*, a pasticcio, which opened the season at the Haymarket (MANN vi. 264, n. 24; *London Stage* Pt IV, ii. 1085).

3. Giovanni Manzuoli (b. ca 1725, d. after 1780), first male singer at the opera for the 1764–5 season (MANN v. 128, n. 16).

4. Manzuoli had been touted by Mann to HW, 27 Aug. 1757, as 'the best singer at present in Italy' (MANN v. 128).

5. Filippo Elisi, first male singer at the opera for the 1760–1 and 1761–2 seasons

(*ante* 13 June 1761; *London Stage* Pt IV, ii. 810, 884).

6. 'The applause was hearty, unequivocal, and free from all suspicion of artificial zeal; it was a universal thunder' (Charles Burney, *General History of Music*, ed. F. Mercer, 1935, ii. 868).

7. Manzuoli sang three arias by Pescetti: '*Recagli quell' acciaro*, an animated *aria parlante*; *Caro mio bene addio*, an adagio in a grand style of cantabile; and *Mi dona mi rende*, of a graceful kind' (ibid.).

8. Isabella Young (d. 1791), m. (1757) Hon. John Scott; billed as 'Signora Scotti' (GM 1791, lxi pt ii. 782; *London Stage* Pt IV, ii. 1085).

pipe, and only a pretty little small person, and share of beauty, and does not act ill.[9] There is Tenducci,[10] a moderate tenor, and all the rest intolerable. If you don't make haste and send us Doberval, I don't know what we shall do. The dances were not only hissed, as truly they deserved to be, but the gallery, *à la Drury Lane,* cried out, 'Off! off!' The boxes were empty, for so is the town, to a degree. The person[11] who ordered me to write to you for Doberval, was reduced to languish in the Duchess of Hamilton's box. My Duchess[12] does not appear yet—I fear!

Shall I tell you anything about D'Éon? it is sending coals to Paris: you must know his story better than me; so in two words: Vergy,[13] his antagonist,[14] is become his convert: has wrote for him,[15] and sworn for him,—nay, has made an affidavit[16] before Judge Wilmot,[17] that Monsieur de Guerchy had hired him to stab or poison D'Éon.[18] Did you ever see a man who had less of an assassin than your *pendant,* as Nivernois calls it! In short, the story is as clumsy as it is abominable. The King's Bench cited D'Éon to receive his sentence; he absconds:[19] that Court issued a warrant to search for him, and a house[20] in Scotland yard, where he lodged, was broken open, but in

9. 'Scotti, the first woman, with an elegant figure, a beautiful face, and a feeble voice, sang in a very good taste; and, though in want of power, she possessed great flexibility and expression' (Burney, loc. cit.).

10. Giusto Ferdinando Tenducci (ca 1736 – ca 1800), male soprano and composer, who had come to London in 1758 (*Enciclopedia dello spettacolo,* Rome, 1954–62, ix. 819). '[At Ranelagh] I heard the famous Tenducci, a thing from Italy – It looks for all the world like a man, though they say it is not. The voice, to be sure, is neither man's nor woman's; but it is more melodious than either; and it warbled so divinely, that, while I listened, I really thought myself in paradise' (Smollett, *Humphry Clinker,* 1771, i. 194).

11. Lord Gower (*ante* 9 Nov. 1764).

12. Of Grafton.

13. Pierre-Henri Treyssac de Vergy (d. 1774), adventurer (GM 1774, xliv. 494).

14. According to HW, the previous year d'Éon 'took it into his fancy' that Vergy had been brought over by Guerchy to assassinate him (*Mem. Geo. III* i. 242), and had 'threatened to put [his soul] . . .

into the chamber-pot and make him drink it' (HW to Mann, 12 Dec. 1763, MANN vi. 190). Vergy, in turn, had sworn the peace against d'Éon after the latter's arrest following a quarrel with Guerchy at Lord Halifax's (*Mem. Geo. III,* loc. cit.).

15. *Lettre à Monseigneur le Duc de Choiseul . . . par M. Treyssac de Vergy, avocat au Parlement de Bordeaux,* Liège, 1764, 12 pp., followed by a second *Lettre,* 30 pp. (MANN vi. 262, n. 10).

16. Sworn 11 Oct. before the Lord Mayor (Bridgen) and attested by George Schutz and Hodges, printed in the second *Lettre,* pp. 29–30.

17. Sir John Eardley Wilmot (1709–92), Kt, 1755; puisne judge of the Court of King's Bench, 1755; chief justice of the Court of Common Pleas 1766–71.

18. The price he was to pay for succeeding d'Éon as Guerchy's secretary of embassy; see MANN vi. 262, n. 11.

19. He was hiding in the house of an elderly French procuress named Dufour (Archives des Affaires Étrangères, cited by E. M. Vizetelly, *True Story of the Chevalier d'Éon,* 1895, p. 189).

20. The house of the Rev. Dr Eddowes

vain. If there is anything more, you know it yourself. This law transaction is buried in another. The Master of the Rolls[21] is dead, and Norton[22] succeeds. Who do you think succeeds him? his predecessor.[23] The House of York is returned to the House of Lancaster: they could not keep their white roses pure. I have not a little suspicion that disappointment has contributed to this *faux pas*. Sir Thomas made a new will the day before he died, and gave his vast fortune,[24] not to Mr Yorke, as was expected,[25] but to Lord Macclesfield,[26] to whom, it is come out, he was natural brother.[27] Norton, besides the Rolls, which are for life, and near £3,000 a year, has a pension of £1,200. Mrs Anne Pitt, too, has got a third pension:[28] so you see we are not quite such beggars as you imagined!

Prince William, you know, is Duke of Gloucester,[29] with the same *apanage* as the Duke of York.[30] Legrand[31] is his *Cadogan;*[32] Clinton[33] and Ligonier[34] his grooms.

Colonel Crawford[35] is dead at Minorca, and Colonel Burton[36] has

(ibid. 198). When it was broken open, 20 Nov., by a search party, Mrs Eddowes stated that d'Éon had been gone 'more than two months' (*London Chronicle* 22–4 Nov., xvi. 498).

21. Sir Thomas Clarke (1703–13 Nov. 1764), Kt, 1754; Master of the Rolls 1754–64; M.P. Mitchell 1747–54, Lostwithiel 1754–61.

22. Sir Fletcher Norton. He did not succeed Clarke, but continued as attorney-general; see *post* 3 Dec. 1764.

23. Charles Yorke; so reported in the *London Chronicle* 15–17 Nov., xvi. 479. See *post* 3 Dec. 1764.

24. Said to be £200,000 (Namier and Brooke ii. 217).

25. Clarke had been a protégé of Lord Hardwicke, Yorke's father (ibid.).

26. Thomas Parker (1723–95), 3d E. of Macclesfield 1764, grandson of Clarke's first patron, the 1st E. of Macclesfield (ibid.).

27. A false report; he was the second son of Thomas Clarke, carpenter of Holborn (ibid.).

28. See *post* 3 Dec. 1764.

29. Announced in the *London Gazette* No. 10470, 13–17 Nov., *sub* St James's, 17 Nov.

30. £12,000 a year, the same as the

Duke of York's initial allowance; see MANN vi. 264 and n. 26.

31. Edward Le Grand (d. 1781), treasurer to the Duke of Gloucester 1764–81; formerly his governor (*Court and City Register* 1764–81 *passim*; George III's *Corr.*, ed. Fortescue, v. 216–21).

32. The Hon. Charles Sloane Cadogan (*ante* 20 April 1764), treasurer to Prince Edward (subsequently Duke of York) 1756–67 (Namier and Brooke ii. 169).

33. Henry Clinton (1730–95), Col. 1762; K.B. 1777; Lt-Gen. 1777; commander-in-chief in America 1778–82; Gen. 1793; M.P.; groom of the Bedchamber to the Duke of Gloucester 1764–78.

34. Edward Ligonier (1740–82), 2d Vct Ligonier 1770, cr. (1776) E. Ligonier; Col. 1763; secretary of the Embassy at Madrid 1763–5; Lt-Gen. 1777; K.B. 1781; groom of the Bedchamber to the Duke of Gloucester 1764–70 (*Army Lists, passim*; *Court and City Register* 1766–70 *passim*; *Repertorium der diplomatischen Vertreter aller Länder*, Vol. II, ed. F. Hausmann, Zurich, 1950, p. 167).

35. John Craufurd (ca 1725–2 Aug. 1764), Col. 3d Ft 1763–4; Lt-Gov. Minorca June–Aug. 1764; M.P.

36. Ralph Burton (d. 1768), Col. 1760; Maj-Gen. 1762; appointed Col. of the 3d

his regiment; the Primate (Stone) is better, but I suppose, from his distemper, which is a dropsy in his breast, irrecoverable.[37] Your Irish Queen[38] exceeds the English Queen, and follows her with seven footmen before her chair—well! what trumperies I tell you! but I cannot help it—Wilkes is outlawed,[39] D'Éon run away, and Churchill dead[40]—till some new genius arises, you must take up with operas, and pensions, and seven footmen.—But patience! your country is seldom sterile long.

George Selwyn has written hither his lamentations about that Cossack Princess.[41] I am glad of it, for I did but hint it to my Lady Hervey (though I give you my word, without quoting you, which I never do upon the most trifling occurrences), and I was cut very short, and told it was impossible. *À la bonne heure!* Pray, who is Lord March going to marry? We hear so, but nobody named.[42] I had not heard of your losses at whisk; but if I had, should not have been terrified: you know whisk gives no fatal ideas to anybody that has been at Arthur's and seen hazard, *quinze,* and *trente-et-quarante.* I beg you will prevail on the King of France to let Monsieur de Richelieu give as many balls and fêtes as he pleases, if it is only for my diversion. This journey to Paris is the last colt's tooth I intend ever to cut, and I insist upon being prodigiously entertained like a *sposa monacha,*[43] whom they cram with this world for a twelve-month, before she bids adieu to it forever. I think, when I shut my-self up in my convent here, it will not be with the same regret. I have for some time been glutted with the world, and regret the friends that drop away every day; those, at least, with whom I came into the

Ft 22 Nov. 1764; M.P. (*Army Lists* 1765, pp. A4, 56).

37. He died 19 Dec. (Mann vi. 269).

38. The Countess of Northumberland.

39. 'On Thursday last, the 1st instant [Nov.], John Wilkes, Esq., had sentence of outlawry pronounced against him, at the Sheriff's county court in Holborn, by the Sheriff, Coroner, and other officers' (*London Chronicle* 6–8 Nov., xvi. 442). This was for failure to appear for sentencing after his having been found guilty 21 Feb. in the King's Bench of reprinting and publishing the *North Briton* No. 45 and of printing and publishing the *Essay on Woman (ante* 24 Feb. 1764, n. 8).

40. Charles Churchill, the poet, died 4 Nov. at Boulogne (Mann vi. 260, n. 1).

41. The Princesse de Talmond (*ante* 10 Nov. 1764).

42. HW is being disingenuous: he had mentioned Hertford's daughter Lady Anne Conway as March's rumoured bride in his letter to Conway, *ante* 29 Oct. 1764. Hertford wrote *post* 7 Dec. 1764 that 'I have never heard that Lord March was going to be married,' and *post* 18 Jan. 1765 that March had never 'shown the most distant regard for my daughter.'

43. A prospective nun (Alfred Hoare, *Italian Dictionary,* Cambridge, 1925, p. 394).

world, already begin to make it appear a great void. Lord Edge-cumbe, Lord Waldegrave, and the Duke of Devonshire leave a very perceptible chasm. At the opera last night, I felt almost ashamed to be there. Except Lady Townshend, Lady Schaub,[44] Lady Albemarle, and Lady Northumberland, I scarce saw a creature whose *début* there I could not remember—nay, the greater part were Maccaronies. You see I am not likely, like my brother Cholmondeley (who, by the way, was there too), to totter into a solitaire[45] at threescore. The Duke de Richelieu is one of the persons I am curious to see—oh! am I to find Madame de Boufflers, Princess of Conti?[46] Your brother and Lady Aylesbury are to be in town the day after tomorrow to hear Manzoli,[47] and on their way to Mrs Cornwallis, who is acting *l'ago-nisante;*[48] but that would be treason to Lady Aylesbury. I was at Park Place last week: the bridge is finished, and a noble object.[49]

I shall come to you as soon as ever I have my *congé,* which I trust will be early in February. I will let you know the moment I can fix my time, because I shall beg you to order a small lodging to be taken for me at no great distance from your palace, and only for a short time, because, if I should like France enough to stay some months, I can afterwards accommodate myself to my mind. I should like to be so near you that I could see you whenever it would not be incon-venient to you, and without being obliged to that intercourse with my countrymen, which I by no means design to cultivate. If I leave the best company here, it shall not be for the worst. I am getting out of the world, not coming into it, and shall therefore be most indif-ferent about their acquaintance, or what they think of my avoiding it. I come to see you and my Lady Hertford, to escape from politics, and to amuse myself with *seeing,* which I intend to do with all my

44. Marguerite de Ligonier du Buisson (d. 1793), m. 1 —— de Panne; m. 2 (ca 1740) Sir Luke Schaub, Kt (Ossory i. 49).

45. 'A loose neck-tie of black silk or broad ribbon worn by men in the 18th century' (OED); affected by the macaronies.

46. Madame de Bouffler's husband, the Marquis de Boufflers-Rouverel, had re-cently died, theoretically freeing her to marry the Prince, to whom she was mistress; however, the Prince was not will-ing. See *post* 7, 18 Dec. 1764.

47. Who was to sing that night in the second performance of *Ezio* at the Hay-market (*London Stage* Pt IV, ii. 1085; n.

3 above). Actually, however, Conway's principal reason for coming to town was to help adjust the terms of the separation of the Duke and Duchess of Grafton: 'I am called up to town just now for a few days on some business, the principal of which is . . . meeting [Gen. Ellison] . . . to set-tle the terms of the [Duchess's] . . . sep-arate maintenance' (Conway to Hertford 29 Nov., MS now WSL). See *post* 3 Dec. 1764.

48. Over her husband's dismissal from the Bedchamber. See *ante* 27 Aug. 1764.

49. See Montagu ii. 104–5 and n. 8; Ossory iii. 15 and n. 4.

eyes. I abhor show, am not passionately fond of literati, don't want to know people for a few months, and really think of nothing but some comfortable hours with you, and indulging my curiosity. Excuse almost a page about myself, but it was to tell you how little trouble I hope to give you.

Yours most sincerely,

H. W.

To Hertford, Monday 3 December 1764

Printed from *Works* ix. 167–72.

Arlington Street, Dec. 3d 1764.

I LOVE to contradict myself as fast as I can when I have told you a lie, lest you should take me for a chambermaid, or Charles Townshend. But how can I help it? Is this a consistent age? How should I know people's minds, if they don't know them themselves? In short, Charles Yorke is not attorney-general, nor Norton Master of the Rolls. A qualm came across the first,[1] and my Lord Chancellor[2] across the second, who would not have Norton in his Court.[3] I cannot imagine why; it is so gentle, amiable, honest a being! But I think the Chancellor says, Norton does not understand *equity,* so he remains prosecutor-general. Yorke would have taken the Rolls, if they would have made it much more considerable;[4] but as they would not, he has recollected that it will be clever for one Yorke to

1. For Yorke's characteristic irresolution in his negotiations for office at this time, which earned him the scorn of Court and Opposition alike, see MANN vi. 263, 268–9 and Namier and Brooke iii. 676.

2. Northington.

3. HW repeats this allegation in *Mem. Geo. III* ii. 26; the Master of the Rolls was subordinate to the Lord Chancellor in the Court of Chancery. After Yorke had turned down the office of attorney-general, which Norton had agreed to vacate in exchange for that of Master of the Rolls (MANN vi. 263, n. 21), Northington informed the latter 'that now it became material to Government that his abilities

should be employed in the office of Attorney' (Northington to Grenville 26 Nov., *Grenville Papers* ii. 468). Apparently Norton had agreed to become Master of the Rolls in hopes that that office would prove a stepping-stone to the next vacant chief justiceship (Namier and Brooke iii. 214).

4. Yorke had asked that the salary for the post, then just over £2000, be increased to £4000, and that he be given a peerage (Grenville's diary, *sub* 15 Nov., *Grenville Papers* ii. 525). These requests were turned down by George III on the 16th (ibid. ii. 526).

have the air of being disinterested, so he only disgraces himself, and takes a patent of precedence[5] over the solicitor-general[6]—but do not depend upon this—he was to have kissed hands on Friday, but has put it off till Wednesday next—between this and that, his virtue may have another fit.[7] The Court ridicule him even more than the Opposition.[8] What diverts me most, is, that the pious and dutiful House of Yorke, who cried and roared over their father's memory, now throw all the blame on him, and say, he forced them into Opposition[9]—but *amorem nummi expellas furca, licet usque recurret.*[10] Sewell[11] is Master of the Rolls.

Well! I may grow a little more explicit to you; besides, this letter goes to you by a private hand. I gave you little hints, to prepare you for the separation in the House of Grafton. It is so, and I am heartily sorry for it.[12] Your brother is chosen by the Duke, and General Ellison[13] by the Duchess, to adjust the terms, which are not yet settled.[14]

5. As a 'public mark of the King's favour' for his support of 'his Majesty's measures'; it was 'a patent of precedency for life between the attorney and solicitor-general' (ibid. ii. 469, 530).

6. William De Grey (1719–81) Kt, 1771; cr. (1780) Bn Walsingham; M.P. Newport 1761–70, Cambridge University 1770–1; solicitor-general, 1763; attorney-general, 1766; lord chief justice of the Common Pleas, 1771.

7. 'Friday, November 30th. Mr Yorke sent to Lord Chancellor to state some difficulties about the patent, and desired to consider farther upon it 'till the Wednesday following, probably not caring to kiss hands on so public a day as the Princess of Wales's birthday' (Grenville's diary, *Grenville Papers* ii. 531–2). Despite HW's doubts, Yorke did kiss hands on the Wednesday (5 Dec.) (ibid. ii. 532), and on 6 Dec. 'took his seat of precedency in the Court of Chancery' (*London Chronicle* 6–8 Dec., xvi. 545).

8. For example, Northington wrote to Grenville 19 Nov. that Yorke's behaviour 'makes one sick' (*Grenville Papers* ii. 464).

9. However, they had been protesting this more or less all along. For instance, at the time of his resignation as attorney-general in Nov. 1763, Charles Yorke, in an audience with the King, had 'expressed himself with the greatest duty and affec-

tion to the King, and put the step he had taken entirely upon his father, under the Duke of Newcastle's influence' (Grenville's diary, *Grenville Papers* ii. 218). See also the article on John Yorke in Namier and Brooke iii. 678, and *ante* 22 Jan. 1764, where HW himself notes that 'Charles Yorke resigned, against his own and Lord Royston's inclination,' despite Lord Hardwicke's being 'violent against the Court.'

10. 'Drive out the love of money with a pitchfork, it may always come back,' HW's adaptation of Horace's 'Naturam expellas furca, tamen usque recurret': 'Drive out Nature with a pitchfork, yet she will always come back' (*Epistles*, I. x. 24).

11. Sir Thomas Sewell (ca 1710–84), Kt 1764; M.P. Harwich 1758–61, Winchelsea 1761–8. He was knighted 30 Nov., and sworn in as Master of the Rolls 4 Dec. (*London Chronicle* 29 Nov.–1 Dec., 4–6 Dec., xvi. 526, 537).

12. The separation took place 11 Jan. 1765. The Duke divorced the Duchess 23 March 1769 after she had a child by Lord Ossory.

13. Gen. Cuthbert Ellison (*ante* 6 March 1746), first cousin of Lord Ravensworth, the Duchess's father (Ossory ii. 502, n. 7).

14. 'She [the Duchess] is to have £3000 annuity, which is her jointure; Lady Georgiana and the youngest son [Lord Charles] to remain for the present with

The Duke takes all on himself, and assigns no reason but disagreement of tempers.[15] He leaves Lady Georgiana[16] with her mother, who, he says, is the properest person to educate her, and Lord Charles,[17] till he is old enough to be taken from the women. This behaviour is noble and generous—still I wish they could have agreed!

This is not the only parting that makes a noise. His Grace of Kingston has taken a pretty milliner from Cranborn Alley, and carried her to Thoresby. Miss Chudleigh, at the Princess's[18] birthday on Friday, beat her side till she could not help having a real pain in it, that people might inquire what was the matter, on which she notified, a pleurisy, and that she is going to the baths of Carlsbad, in Bohemia.[19] I hope she will not meet with the *Bulgares* that demolished the Castle of Thunderten-tronck.[20] My Lady Harrington's robbery[21] is at last come to light, and was committed by the porter,[22] who is in Newgate.

Lady Northumberland[23] (who, by the way, has added an eighth footman since I wrote to you last) told me this morning that the Queen is very impatient to receive an answer from Lady Hertford,

her; and for their maintenance he allows £190 a year—he gives her all her jewels too and whatever else she may desire or think convenient out of his house' (Conway to Hertford, 1 Jan. 1765, MS now WSL).

15. 'His Grace treats this matter in the noblest and handsomest way, laying nothing at all to her charge but an unfortunate disagreement of temper, and confining her to no term or condition whatever, but that of doing what was suitable to his honour and her rank' (Conway to Hertford 29 Nov., MS now WSL).

16. Lady Georgiana Fitzroy (1757–99), m. (1778) John Smyth, of Heath, Yorks (OSSORY i. 2, n. 10).

17. Lord Charles Fitzroy (14 July 1764 – 1829); M.P. Bury St Edmunds 1787–96, 1802–18; Gen., 1814 (Namier and Brooke ii. 435–6).

18. Of Wales.

19. 'Miss Chudleigh is going to wash herself in the baths in Bohemia. They will be very famous if they can cleanse her from all her disorders. She sets out in February, and has, as the town says, left the Duke of Kingston a milliner that she found in Cranburn Alley to supply her

place during her absence; but others say they have quarrelled and that she leaves England on that account' (Lady Mary Coke to Lady Strafford, 5 Dec., Coke, *Journals* i. 18). See Charles E. Pearce, *The Amazing Duchess*, 1911, i. 297–8, and Elizabeth Mavor, *The Virgin Mistress*, 1964, pp. 81–2.

20. In Voltaire's *Candide* (Chapter VIII). During the attack of the Bulgarians on the Castle, Cunégonde is violated by a Bulgarian soldier and afterwards carried off by a captain.

21. See *ante* 9 Dec. 1763.

22. John Wesket (ibid. n. 47). 'Yesterday [30 Nov.] was found, on searching two houses frequented by John Bradley, alias Walker [Wesket's accomplice in the robbery], most of the valuable goods stolen out of the Earl of Harrington's in December last' (*London Chronicle* 29 Nov.–1 Dec., xvi. 527). At the Old Bailey 14 Dec. Wesket was capitally convicted for the crime, Bradley being admitted as a witness for the Crown (ibid. 13–15 Dec., xvi. 575), and he was executed 9 Jan. (*post* 10 Jan. 1765).

23. Lady of the Bedchamber to the Queen.

about Prince George's[24] letters coming through your hands, as she desired they might.

A correspondence between Legge and Lord Bute about the Hampshire election is published today,[25] by the express desire of the former, when he was dying. He showed the letters to me in the spring, and I then did not think them so strong or important as he did. I am very clear it does no honour to his memory to have them printed now. It implies want of resolution to publish them in his lifetime, and that he died with more resentment than I think one should care to own. I would send them to you, but I know Dr Hunter takes care of such things. I hope he will send you, too, the finest piece that I think has been written for liberty since Lord Somers'.[26] It is called *An Inquiry into the Late Doctrine on Libels*,[27] and is said to be written by one Dunning,[28] a lawyer lately started up, who makes a great noise. He is a sharp thorn in the sides of Lord Mansfield and Norton, and, in truth, this book is no plaster to their pain. It is bitter, has much unaffected wit, and is the only tract that ever made me understand law. If Dr Hunter does not send you these things, I suppose he will convey them himself, as I hear there will be a fourteenth occasion for him.[29] Charles Fitzroy[30] says, Lord

24. Prince Georg August, youngest brother of the Queen (*ante* 3 Aug. 1764, n. 13).

25. In *Some Account of the Character of the Late Right Honourable Henry Bilson Legge*, by John Butler, later Bishop of Hereford, a pamphleteer for the Opposition (Hazen, *Cat. of HW's Lib.*, No. 1609:56:5). On 3 Dec. 1759, exactly five years earlier, Legge had been returned for Hampshire against Simeon Stuart, who had been set up as a candidate by Lord Carnarvon and supported by the Prince of Wales and Bute. Legge, having successfully opposed the Prince in that election, was urged by Bute to make amends by supporting his nominees at the next general election, but he declined to do so, thus incurring the wrath of the Prince and Bute, who had hitherto looked upon him with favour (Butler, op. cit. 13–18; Namier and Brooke iii. 30–1). Turned out of office in 1761 after the accession of George III, he wished, by the publication of his correspondence with Bute, to vindicate his honour in the public eye (Butler, op. cit. 12).

26. John Somers (1651–1716), cr. (1697) Bn Somers; lord chancellor 1697–1700. He was the author of several political tracts; see HW's *Catalogue of the Royal and Noble Authors*, 1758, ii. 110–13.

27. *An Inquiry into the Doctrine, Lately Propagated, Concerning Libels, Warrants, and the Seizure of Papers;* dated 'November 29th' by HW in his copy, now WSL (Hazen, op. cit. No. 1609:9:2).

28. John Dunning (1731–83), cr. (1782) Bn Ashburton. HW adds in *Mem. Geo. III* ii. 27 that Dunning was supposed to have been 'assisted by the Lord Chief Justice Pratt, and one or two others.' Other authors have been suggested, including Lord Temple and John Almon (GRAY ii. 137, n. 5; Hazen, loc. cit.).

29. Meaning that Lady Hertford was pregnant again, a false rumour (*post* 18 Dec. 1764). She was to have no more children; a pregnancy in 1767 ended in a miscarriage (Coke, op. cit. ii. 42).

30. Later Bn Southampton, grandson of Mrs Cosby.

Halifax told Mrs Cosby[31] that you are to go to Ireland.[32] I said he knows you are not the most communicative person in the world, and that you had not mentioned it—nor do I now, by way of asking impertinent questions; but I thought you would like to know what was said.[33]

I return to Strawberry Hill tomorrow, but must return on Thursday, as there is to be something at the Duke of York's that evening, for which I have received a card.[34] He and his brother are most exceedingly civil and good-humoured—but I assure you every place is like one of Shakspeare's plays:—Flourish, enter the Duke of York, Gloucester, and attendants. Lady Irwin[35] died yesterday.

Past eleven.

I am just come from a little impromptu ball at Mrs Ann Pitt's. I told you she had a new pension,[36] but did I tell you it was £500 a year?[37] It was entertaining to see the Duchess of Bedford and Lady Bute with their respective forces, drawn up on different sides of the room: the latter's were most numerous. My Lord Gower seemed very willing to promote a parley between the two armies. It would have made you shrug up your shoulders at dirty humanity, to see the two Miss Pelhams[38] sit neglected, without being asked to dance. You may imagine this could not escape me, who have passed through the

31. Grace Montagu (ca 1687–1767), m. Brig.-Gen. William Cosby (MONTAGU i. 134, n. 14); aunt of Lord Halifax.

32. Halifax in September had expressed to the King and Grenville his dissatisfaction with Hertford on the grounds that he was 'cold and insufficient,' and had asked that he be recalled; Grenville noted in his diary that he had 'great difficulty in combatting Lord Halifax's eagerness upon this subject' (Grenville's diary, *Grenville Papers* ii. 514). However, the King was 'by no means disposed to recall him,' observing that Hertford was of a 'decent and orderly' character, and 'therefore not lightly to be cast aside' (ibid.). Presumably the transferral of Hertford to the lord lieutenancy of Ireland was suggested as a compromise. However, when Hertford did finally go to Ireland (the following autumn; see *post* 10 Oct. 1765), it was after the changeover to the first Rockingham administration, and since Halifax

was no longer secretary of state for the south, his influence was no longer a factor.

33. Hertford replied, *post* 20 Dec. 1764, that no 'such alteration had been proposed' to him.

34. See below.

35. Lady Anne Howard (ca 1696–2 Dec. 1764), m. 1 (1717) Rich Ingram, 5th Vct Irvine; m. 2 (1737) Col. William Douglas; lady of the Bedchamber to the Princess Dowager of Wales. 'Poor Lady Irwin had a party at cards on Friday and died on Sunday morning' (Lady Mary Coke to Lady Strafford, 5 Dec., Coke, op. cit. i. 17).

36. *Ante* 25 Nov. 1764.

37. 'Young Tommy' Townshend cites the same figure in his letter to Selwyn of 11 Dec. (J. H. Jesse, *George Selwyn and his Contemporaries*, 1882, i. 329).

38. Frances and Mary.

several gradations[39] in which Lady Jane Stuart and Miss Pelham are and have been; but I fear poor Miss Pelham[40] feels hers a little more than ever I did. The Duke of York's is to be a dinner and ball for Princess Amelia.[41]

Lady Mary Bowlby gave me a commission, a genealogic one, from my Lady Hertford, which I will execute to the best of my power.[42] I am glad my part is not to prove eighteen generations of nobility for the Bruces. I fear they have made some *mésalliances* since the days of King Robert—at least, the present Scotch nobility are not less apt to go into Lombard Street[43] than the English.

My Lady Suffolk was at the ball; I asked the Prince of Masserano whom he thought the oldest woman in the room, as I concluded he would not guess she was. He did not know my reason for asking, and would not tell me. At last, he said very cleverly, his own wife.[44]

Mr Sarjent[45] has sent me this evening from you, *Les Considéra-tions sur les mœurs*, and *Le Testament politique*,[46] for which I give you, my dear Lord, a thousand thanks. Good night.

Yours most cordially,

H. Walpole

PS. Manzoli is come a little too late, or I think he would have as many diamond watches and snuff-boxes as Farinelli[47] had.

---

39. As the child of a minister in and out of power.

40. HW is presumably referring to the elder Miss Pelham, Frances.

41. Whose company at the dinner were to be 'the Duke of Gloucester, the Princess's lady, Lord and Lady Holder-nesse, myself [Lady Mary Coke], and Lord De La War' (Lady Mary Coke to Lady Strafford, 5 Dec., Coke, op. cit. i. 18).

42. See *post* 18 Dec. 1764.

43. The Wall Street of London.

44. Charlotte-Louise de Rohan-Guémé-née (1722–86), m. (1737) the Principe di Masserano (MORE 57, n. 22).

45. Not identified.

46. *Maximes d'état, ou testament poli-tique d'Armand du Plessis, cardinal duc de Richelieu*, ed. François-Louis-Claude Marin, Paris, 1764 (Hazen, op. cit. No. 3044; Bibl. Nat. Cat.).

47. Carlo Broschi (1705–82), called Farinelli; soprano; sang in England 1734–7 (*Enciclopedia dello spettacolo*, Rome, 1954–62, v. 21–8). Apparently the practice of showering expensive presents on favourite male sopranos was on the wane.

From Hertford, Friday 7 December 1764

Printed for the first time from a photostat of BM Add. MSS 23218, ff. 175–7.

Paris, December 7th 1764.

Dear Horry,

MY son's[1] apartment is unoccupied and will be ready for you whenever you arrive. I hope you will agree with me in thinking it one of the best in Paris. It is separated from the rest of the house by a long gallery, that you may be as quiet and unconnected with it as you please. If you do not like it, you may choose for yourself when you are here. February is a little too late for the showy entertainments of this place. The balls and masquerades are earlier this year, as the carnival will be short, but we must take you when you are to be had and when the horrid divisions of England will allow you to be absent.

I have spoke to the Lord of the Bedchamber[2] about Dauberval, and I have even mentioned my commission to the Duke de Praslin, not as minister of state, though you had given me instructions how to treat it; but as it is not in the department of either of these offices, I must wait the return of the Comte de St Florentin[3] to Paris, who is minister of state and has Paris and its amusements under his orders and inspection. I may however venture to tell you beforehand that I shall hardly obtain leave for him to go to England. He is a great favourite of the town, and the opera wants all sorts of support to keep it up; besides that, this dancer has little pretension to particular encouragement from having gone to England last year without leave, which is punishable in this country like a *crime d'état*.

I sent you the *Essai sur les mœurs* and the *Testament du Cardinal de Richlieu*, which I hope you have received.[4] Madame de Bouflers is not the author of the books of which she was some time suspected.[5] I cannot tell you with the same certainty whether she will be Princess of Conti.[6] The point is perhaps not yet determined. I rather think

1. That is, Lord Beauchamp's.
2. The Duc de Fleury; see *ante* 9 Nov. 1764.
3. Louis Phélypeaux (1705–77), Comte de Saint-Florentin, later (1770) Duc de la Vrillière; secretary of state, 1725, and minister of foreign affairs 1770–1 (Mann vi. 342, n. 10). See *post* 20 Dec. 1764.
4. See *ante* 3 Dec. 1764.
5. See *ante* 5 Oct. 1764.
6. See *ante* 25 Nov 1764.

she will. The present Countess of Toulouse[7] was Madame de Gondrin, sister to the Maréchal de Noailles, and yet she has always been treated by the King with as much respect as if he had made the choice himself. You will perhaps make some distinctions between the two cases from knowing private histories, and those may perhaps occasion the doubt, but what I mean to infer is that I fancy the Prince himself will determine it, and that if he resolves to make her his wife she will be received at Court.

I have never heard that Lord March was going to be married.[8] I have been told that he had a genteel passion here[9] which a hundred men have had before him. With this lady he will run no risk of a very serious attachment. She is a married woman, and has shown her indifference to persons by admitting many to some share of her favour.

Mr Hume has seen King James's journal,[10] and so may you when you come to Paris. It is in the Scotch College, from whence it is not permitted to remove it. I do not believe he has taken any extracts from it, but I will ask him when he returns to Paris.[11] Mr Hume is now too idle and too well received at Paris to write histories, and it is perhaps the best understood philosophy to be amused.

Guerchy professes the greatest regard and respect for my brother. I proposed to him the visit to Park Place[12] when he was at Paris, being very confident that my brother would approve it.

Garrick dined with me today; I believe he will pass the winter at Paris.[13] He has had an ague which has pulled him down, but he is getting better. Mrs Garrick[14] is much altered. If you hear that he is to act here, do not believe it. There was some inclination that he should, and it was even proposed to make a piece on purpose; but he

7. Marie-Victoire-Sophie de Noailles (1688–1766), m. 1 (1707) Louis de Pardaillan d'Antin, Marquis de Gondrin; m. 2 (1723) Louis-Alexandre de Bourbon, Comte de Toulouse (DU DEFFAND i. 92, n. 11).

8. See *ante* 25 Nov. 1764.

9. Presumably the Maréchale d'Estrées, identified as March's 'passion' in HW's letter to Thomas Brand, 19 Oct. 1765. This was Adélaïde-Félicité Brulart de Puisieulx de Sillery (1725–86), m. (1744) Louis-Charles-César le Tellier de Louvois, Maréchale-Duc d'Estrées.

10. See *ante* 5 Oct 1764. HW visited the Scots College and saw the journal 15 March 1766 (DU DEFFAND v. 358–9).

11. See below.

12. See *ante* 9 Nov. 1764.

13. For Garrick's stay at Paris the winter of 1764–5, see Frank A. Hedgcock, *A Cosmopolitan Actor, David Garrick and His French Friends,* 1912, pp. 214–37.

14. Eva Maria Veigel (1724–1822), called Violette, m. (1749) David Garrick; dancer.

has assured me today he will not be so great a fool as to act in a foreign language.

Adieu, my dear Horry,

Yours most affectionately and sincerely,

HERTFORD

Mr Hume is returned to Paris and tells me that he has taken extracts from King James's memoirs, and that there are some very curious anecdotes to illustrate the history of the two last Stewart reigns.[15]

To LADY HERTFORD, ca Monday 10 December 1764

Missing; answered *post* 18 Dec. 1764. Dated conjecturally by HW's promise to Hertford *ante* 3 Dec. 1764 that he will execute Lady Hertford's pedigree, which was presumably enclosed in this letter, and is acknowledged *post* 18 Dec. 1764 by Lady Hertford.

To HERTFORD, ca Tuesday 18 December 1764

Missing; answered *post* 28 Dec. 1764. It contained HW's rejection of Hertford's invitation, *ante* 7 Dec. 1764, to lodge him in his own house at Paris.

From LADY HERTFORD, Tuesday 18 December 1764

Printed for the first time from a photostat of BM Add. MSS 23218, ff. 178–9.

Paris, December the 18th 1764.

Dear Sir,

WAS any return ever so unequal? I received the most agreeable letter[1] that was possible from you, and I am reduced to write a very dull one in answer; but don't pronounce any judgment against

15. See *ante* 5 Oct. 1764, n. 13.   1. Missing.

me till you find by experience how difficult it is to write letters from a foreign country. I sup in company almost every night with twenty people, and yet there are scarcely any of them that you know anything about or that you would wish to be troubled with their history. I believe you did not adore Madame D'Usson while she was in England, and of course will have no curiosity about her.[2] Madame de Boufflers is in retirement because her husband[3] is lately dead, but the report of Paris is, that she will come out soon Princesse de Conti. She and the Prince both are at Madame D'Arthy's[4] (a sister of Madame de la Touches[5]) and the first mistress the Prince of Conti ever had; in any other country but this, this circumstance would prevent these ladies living together, but here it makes not the least difference, and Madame D'Arthy I am told has a great friendship for the other. Mr Hume is always with Madame de Boufflers,[6] and is certainly in the secret, but he won't divulge it yet;[7] and he is so much in love with her that I am convinced he will be grieved to see her married to anybody. Did my Lord ever tell you that Lord Holdernesse, who always must sigh for some lady, chose the same object?[8] In England, between thirty and forty is not just the age for women to have many admirers, but

2. HW had inquired sarcastically about Madame d'Usson's 'affection' for England in his letter to Hertford *ante* 18 Oct. 1763; Madame d'Usson, who had visited England and SH in the spring of 1763, was 'generally thought to love abuse' (Hertford to HW, *ante* 11 Nov. 1763). However, Hertford announced to HW, *post* 9 Feb. 1765, that Madame d'Usson was 'prepared to receive you,' and HW visited her and her husband 19 Sept., just six days after his arrival at Paris (DU DEFFAND v. 262).

3. Édouard de Boufflers-Rouverel, Comte (Marquis, 1751) de Boufflers-Rouverel, died Oct. 1764 (David Hume to Madame de Boufflers, 31 Oct., in his *Letters*, ed. Greig, Oxford, 1932, i. 476).

4. Marie-Anne-Guillaume (or Marie-Louise) de Fontaine (1710–65), m. (1724) Antoine-Alexis Pineau, Seigneur d'Arty, from whom she separated in 1725 (*Dictionnaire de biographie française*, 1933 – , iii. 1223; Élisabeth, Duchesse de Clermont-Tonnerre, *Histoire de Samuel Bernard et de ses enfants*, 1914, pp. 107, 116; Hume, op. cit. i. 495).

5. Françoise-Thérèse (or Françoise-Guillaume) de Fontaine (b. 1712), m. (1729) Nicolas Vallet, Seigneur de la Touche (Clermont-Tonnerre, loc. cit.; Henri Jougla de Morenas, *Grand Armorial de France*, 1934–49, vi. 395). She, Madame d'Arty, and a third sister, Madame Claude Dupin, the natural daughters of Samuel Bernard, financier, by Madame de Fontaine, actress, were known as 'les Trois Grâces' (*Dictionnaire*, loc. cit.).

6. For Hume's relationship with her, see J. Y. T. Greig, *David Hume*, New York, 1931, pp. 305–17 *et passim*.

7. Hume wrote to Madame de Boufflers 10 Dec., advising her to 'gradually diminish your connexion with the Prince,' suspecting, correctly, that the Prince would eventually 'fix his resolution on the side least favourable to you' (Hume, op. cit. i. 484–8).

8. Madame de Boufflers paid a visit to Lord and Lady Holdernesse in England the following June (Greig, op. cit. 320).

here you will find that they are much more fashionable than the very young women.[9]

You are so occupied with royalty in your letter that you don't bestow one line upon two curious anecdotes in my family, which I should have wished to have been informed of: that is, the separation,[10] and the extraordinary account of the robbery at Lord Harrington's.[11]

You must bring all the pamphlets[12] yourself, for there is certainly no occasion for Doctor Hunter's coming to Paris,[13] though all my letters from London have told me so. I supped in company with Madame la Maréchale de Mirepoix last night and told her you had promised to be here in February; but she says she has been so often disappointed that she is determined not to expect you till she hears you are landed at Calais. I am sure you are too faithful to your promises to forfeit them again about coming; and it will add vastly to the pleasure we shall have in your being here, if you accept my Lord's proposal to you[14] of inhabiting my son's apartment while he is absent. We would not offer it to you if you was a fat man, as it is so very small; but that is its only fault, and it has many advantages of warmth, quietness, prospect, etc.

We saw several French officers last night who laughed at themselves for being so credulous as to believe a foolish report, when they were in Germany, that the reason Lord Granby did not wear a wig was because the Duke of Rutland[15] had given him four and twenty thousand pounds upon condition he never would put on one. They don't know who spread it, but till three days ago they believed it. I am sure Lord Granby would be surprised to find that his bald head had been the subject of a falsity. Lord March and Mr Selwyn seem to intend to stay here till February, which I am glad of, for I see Mr S. often and I need not tell you that he is entertaining. He falls asleep now and then at the faro table, but it is not surprising, as we have

---

9. Madame de Boufflers was 39.

10. Of the Duke and Duchess of Grafton.

11. These subjects are dealt with in HW's letter to Hertford *ante* 3 Dec. 1764, which may have not yet reached the Hertfords, having been sent 'by a private hand'; it was answered by Hertford *post* 20 Dec. 1764.

12. *Some Account of the Character of . . . Henry Bilson Legge,* and *An Inquiry into the Doctrine . . . Concerning Libels (ante* 3 Dec. 1764 and nn. 25, 27).

13. To attend Lady Hertford in her alleged pregnancy; see *ante* 3 Dec. 1764.

14. In his letter *ante* 7 Dec. 1764. HW objected to it in a missing letter answered by Hertford *post* 28 Dec. 1764.

15. John Manners (1696–1779), 3d Duke of Rutland, 1721; Granby's father.

played sometimes till seven o'clock in the morning; and he tells me he has often slept as heartily at ten o'clock at Arthur's. I am not at all disgusted with my pedigree, though Rebecca[16] comes in rather abruptly; but you have the advantage of making everything you do appear agreeable to one, and I believe would almost be able to make your good old relation Lady Walpole[17] satisfied with hers. I believe it is thirty years since she was here, and yet they have not forgot her.[18]

I have seen very few of the sights in Paris and its environs, and I intend to reserve all the rest, that I may have the pleasure of going with you; for I am sure you will want to see everything that is worth seeing, and you are the best guide in the world. I am going to sup at the Duchesse de Duras',[19] and as it is late I have not time even to make a second excuse for sending you such a dull letter. I am dear Mr Walpole's

Most faithful and obedient servant,

I. HE.

I had a letter today from Turin from my son, who is perfectly well, and was to go to Genoa the beginning of this week. Lady Anne hopes you will approve of her drawing,[20] for it is in a different style and she thinks much better than what she drew in England. The Duc de Nivernois is impatient for your arrival.

16. Rebecca Child (d. 1712), daughter of Sir Josiah Child, Bt; m. 1 (1683) Charles Somerset, styled Marquess of Worcester; m. 2 (1703) John Granville, Lord Granville of Potheridge; Lady Hertford's maternal grandmother.

17. Mary Magdelaine Lombard (ca 1695–1783), m. (1720) Horatio Walpole, cr. (1756) Bn Walpole of Wolterton, HW's uncle. She was the daughter of Peter Lombard, tailor, described by HW to Lady Ossory 11 March 1783 as a 'French refugee staymaker' (OSSORY ii. 392 and nn. 5, 6).

18. Her husband had been envoy and ambassador to France 1723–30 (ibid., n. 7).

19. Louise-Françoise-Maclovie-Céleste de Coëtquen (d. 1802), m. (1736) Emmanuel-Félicité de Durfort, Duc de Duras (DU DEFFAND ii. 258, n. 20).

20. Possibly the drawing of a little shepherd girl with her sheep 'by Lady Anne Conway Countess of Drogheda' (HW's MS note) with the inscription 'Francis Londonir int et sculp 1750 A. Conway delint 1765' in HW's A Collection of Prints Engraved by Various Persons of Quality, now WSL (Hazen, Cat. of HW's Lib., No. 3588). There was also at SH a water-colour of 'a bunch of flowers' by Lady Anne ('Des. of SH,' Works, ii. 453).

From HERTFORD, Thursday 20 December 1764

Printed for the first time from a photostat of BM Add. MSS 23218, ff. 180–1.

Paris, December 20th 1764.

Dear Horry,

I HAVE executed your commission about Dauberval, but not succeeded. The Comte de St Florentin told me yesterday at Versailles they could not at present give him leave to quit Paris without doing great prejudice to the opera. Shall I not appear to have acted feebly if I acknowledge the truth of it, and tell you the opera here can hardly be supported with all the assistance they can give it? As the taste for music declines, the great expense of this *spectacle* makes it necessary to support it with dancing, which you know is essential to a French opera. Vestris,[1] the first dancer, is lately gone to Stutgard. These and the new dances the undertakers propose giving were the reasons for not granting the permission, which you will be so good to lay before the persons who gave the commission, as you think proper. Dauberval himself tells me the Duchess of Ancaster and Lady Rockingham are his great patronesses in England. If these ladies or any other persons should from this instance judge of my merit as a minister, I must beg you will answer for me that I have done my duty in everything that has been committed to my management.

I have not heard a word of what you tell me from Fitzroy and Mrs Cosby;[2] my brother seemed in one of his last letters to intimate the same thing, and to suspect me of mystery,[3] but I have none indeed, and should have acquainted you both with it, if any such alteration had been proposed to me.

We are told here that when Stanley returned to England,[4] his trunk was opened, according to the present rigour which prevails,[5]

1. Gaetano Appolino Baldassare Vestris (1729–1808), who became 'premier danseur des ballets du Roi' in 1751, and was a member of the Paris Opera 1749–82 (MANN ix. 134, n. 19).

2. See *ante* 3 Dec. 1764.

3. 'I have heard something strongly surmised of a change in your situation, which I heartily wish if desirable to you, and I am not quite discouraged in this thought by hearing nothing of it from you' (Conway to Hertford 29 Nov., MS now WSL).

4. See *ante* 25 Nov. 1764, n. 1.

5. See *ante* 3 Aug. 1764, n. 5.

and a parcel taken out by the custom-house officers which was suspected to be books; but that upon opening them in London where they were sent, they proved to be twelve copies of Mr Wilks's letters to his old constituents at Ailesbury,[6] which his servant,[7] who is a friend of Mr Stanley's servant, found means to place there for security. The English are the more diverted with it at Paris, because Wilks from being once in company with him when he was here, now drinks his health in a bumper. Wilks is[8] going to Italy[9] and proposes to employ himself there in writing; amongst other things it is said he intends writing the history of our present King, and beginning with the present moment to write backwards into the English history from the Revolution.[10] Garrick is likely to spend the winter here, and to pass it agreeably; I think it will be fashionable to see and admire him, though his language is very indifferent.

Lord Palmerston[11] is so good to undertake to carry this letter; I

6. Wilkes wrote to Lord Temple, 1 Nov.: 'I finished *a letter to the Electors of Aylesbury*, which I have read twice to Mr Dunning at Paris, and to my two friends at Boulogne [Humphrey Cotes and Charles Churchill]. I have profited by their lights, and therefore I shall now send it on the wings of the wind, as it has their full and entire approbation' (*Grenville Papers* ii. 456). According to a note in GM 1764, xxxiv. 580, Wilkes's 'Letter to the Worthy Electors of the Borough of Aylesbury,' dated 22 Oct. 1764, was 'said to have been printed at Paris, and copies of it sent to the principal persons in the administration, by the hands of a servant belonging to a gentleman, formerly employed by the government in certain preliminary negotiations in France, the man being ignorant of the importance of the dispatches with which he was charged.' It was later reprinted in various London newspapers and magazines (e.g., *London Chronicle* 20–22 Dec., xvi. 596–7; GM 1764, xxxiv. 580–4). In it Wilkes attempted to refute charges made against him in connection with the *North Briton* No. 45 and the *Essay on Woman*. Wilkes had been M.P. for Aylesbury from 1757 till his expulsion from the House on 20 Jan. 1764. See also

Horace Bleackley, *Life of John Wilkes*, 1917, p. 159; BM Cat.

7. Presumably one Matthew Brown; see Bleackley, op. cit. 142, 162, 170.

8. 'In' in the MS.

9. For Wilkes's trip to Italy at this time, see Bleackley, op. cit. 162–6, 168–70, 171–2.

10. 'I shall employ this active mind in an employment I am not totally, perhaps, unqualified for, I mean the History of my own Country since the Revolution. I will try to equal the dignity of the ancient historians, and as I shall try to bring it down to my own times, I shall have an opportunity of telling my own story, and of doing justice to the very few friends I love, and their country ought to adore' (Wilkes to Temple, 1 Nov., *Grenville Papers* ii. 455). 'I commission you . . . to contract in my name with any bookseller, for a History of England, from the Revolution; to be in two quarto volumes. . . . This is the work for my fame and purse' (Wilkes to Humphrey Cotes, 12 Dec., in his *Correspondence*, ed. Almon, 1805, ii. 101). Only an introduction was published (in 1768); HW's copy, now WSL, is Hazen, *Cat. of HW's Lib.*, No. 1609:57:1.

11. Henry Temple (1739–1802), 2d Vct Palmerston, 1757.

must therefore finish it before he comes to take it, by repeating the assurances of regard and esteem with which I am, dear Horry,

Always yours,

HERTFORD

From HERTFORD, Friday 28 December 1764

Printed for the first time from a photostat of BM Add. MSS 23218, ff. 182–3.

Paris, December 28th 1764.

Dear Horry,

I CAN lodge you nowhere so well as in my own house, and your apartment would be so far separated from the noisy and busy part of it as not to expose you to the inconveniences of it; but if you will positively have it otherways,[1] I will take the cleanest and most convenient lodging for you that I can, and as near as I can find one to the Hôtel de Brancas.

Our balls begin here in about a fortnight and will I suppose continue with intermissions till near Lent. The first part of the carnival should be the gayest, when the young people are all in health; the constant occupations of it generally affect some of them. You must not, if the business of Parliament is not very interesting, put off your journey till Lent. There is nothing during that season but little suppers. The English are diminishing every day; the charms of Parliament are irresistible. Lord March and Mr Selwyn propose staying some time longer here than the 10th January, and Mr Fox[2] intends passing the winter. What will arrive from the south I cannot answer, but I do not believe you will be much troubled with your countrymen from the present appearance.

Do you continue to love faro? We can give it you here in per-

1. Presumably HW voiced his objection in a missing letter.
2. The Hon. Stephen Fox, eldest son of Lord Holland. George Selwyn wrote to Holland, 13 Feb., that 'your son is very well, and indeed it is requisite to be so, if you are determined, as he seems to be, to lose no one diversion of the Carneval' (*Letters to Henry Fox*, ed. Lord Ilchester, Roxburghe Club, 1915, p. 209).

fection, and you may make your own game till next day. The marshals and great ladies of the place will keep you company as long as you will. We are all spoiled; there will not be a hint given to break up the party.

Pray tell me when you meet, what appearance there is of business in Parliament and what matters are likely to be agitated. We hear at present no more of Opposition than if it was unknown to England; on the contrary we have the intelligence from one of the King's messengers who is gone through Paris, that Mr Pitt is to come in. I have not heard it from any other person, and perhaps you do not know it.

I remain, dear Horry, with the best compliments of the family,

Very sincerely and affectionately yours,

Hertford

Lady Hertford has received from the Duchess of Grafton as proper a letter as can be written in her circumstances.

To Lady Hertford, Monday 7 January 1765

Missing; mentioned *post* 10 Jan. 1765.

To Hertford, Thursday 10 January 1765

Printed from *Works* ix. 173–7.

Arlington Street, January 10th 1765.

I SHOULD prove a miserable prophet or almanac maker, for my predictions are seldom verified. I thought the present session[1] likely to be a very supine one, but unless the evening varies extremely from the morning, it will be a tempestuous day—and yet it was a very southerly and calm wind that began the hurricane. The King's Speech[2] was so tame, that as George Montagu said of the

1. Which opened 10 Jan. (*Journals of the House of Commons* xxx. 3).   2. Printed ibid. xxx. 3–4.

earthquake, you might have stroked it.[3] Beckford (whom I certainly did not mean by the *gentle* gale) touched on Draper's[4] letter about the Manilla money.[5] George Grenville took up the defence of the Spaniards, though he said he only stated their arguments.[6] This roused your brother, who told Grenville he had adopted the reasoning of Spain; and showed the fallacy of their pretensions.[7] He exhorted everybody to support the King's government, 'which I,' said he, 'ill used as I have been, wish and mean to support—not that of ministers, when I see the laws and independence of Parliament struck at in the most *profligate* manner.'[8] You may guess how deeply this wounded. Grenville took it to himself, and asserted that his own life and character were as pure, uniform, and little profligate as your brother's.[9] The silence of the House did not seem to ratify this

3. HW quotes this, with acknowledgment to Montagu, to Montagu 26 May 1765; also to Sir William Hamilton 13 Aug. 1773; to Lady Ossory 17 Feb. 1779; and to Lord Strafford 1 Aug. 1783. Gray said the same of his gout to Thomas Wharton, 10 July 1764 and 28 Dec. 1767 (Gray, *Correspondence,* ed. Toynbee and Whibley, Oxford 1935, ii. 837, iii. 986).

4. Col. William Draper (1721–87), K.B. 1765; Maj.-Gen. 1772; Lt-Gen. 1777; Lt-Gov. of Minorca 1779–82 (*Army Lists, passim*).

5. See *ante* 27 Aug. 1764, n. 29. *Colonel Draper's Answer, to the Spanish Arguments, Claiming the Galeon, and Refusing Payment of the Ransom Bills, for Preserving Manila from Pillage and Destruction: In a Letter Addressed to the Earl of Halifax* was printed 24 Dec. (HW's MS note in his copy, now wsl, Hazen, *Cat. of HW's Lib.,* No. 1609:9:6). Presumably Beckford was led to touch on Draper's letter by the Speaker's mentioning to the House his receipt of Vice-Admiral Cornish's belated acknowledgment of the House's vote of thanks to him for his part in the reduction of Manila (*Journals of the House of Commons* xxx. 4).

6. Spain's principal arguments were that the promise of ransom had been 'signée par la voie de la violence et de la rigueur,' and that 'malgré cette honteuse capitulation . . . le Général Draper ordonna, ou permit, que la ville fut saccagée pendant 40 heures par 4000 An-

glais, qui en tirèrent plus d'un million de piastres' ('The Spanish Arguments for Refusing Payment,' Draper, op. cit. 12–15).

7. Draper, in his *Answer,* argued that 'the objection and pretence of force and violence may be made use of to evade any military agreements whatsoever, where the two parties do not treat upon an equality,' and that what pillaging did take place was mostly 'antecedent to our settling the terms of the capitulation,' adding that his forces totalled 'little more than two thousand,' and that the assertion that 'the place was pillaged for forty hours, and that pillage authorized and permitted by me, is . . . most false and infamous' (pp. 18, 21, 22).

8. 'Conway [was] passionate, but chiefly in his own cause, and called the removal of himself the most profligate measure that ever was attempted' (Gilly Williams to Selwyn, 11 Jan., in J. H. Jesse, *George Selwyn and his Contemporaries,* 1882, i. 351–2). See *Mem. Geo. III* ii. 31.

9. 'Mr Conway worked himself into a rage at his last year's dismission, which produced some repartees from Mr Grenville, not quite so warm, however, as the former' (Henry St John to Selwyn, 11 Jan., Jesse, op. cit. i. 346–7). 'Mr Conway made a hot, angry attack upon Mr Grenville, which he answered with spirit and with the approbation of all his friends' (Grenville's diary, *sub* 10 Jan., *Grenville Papers,* iii. 115).

declaration. Your brother replied with infinite spirit, that he certainly could not have meant Mr Grenville, for he did not take him for the minister[10]—(I do not believe this was the least mortifying part)—that he spoke of public acts that were in everybody's mouth, as the warrants, and the disgrace thrown on the Army by dismissions for Parliamentary reasons; that for himself he was an open enemy, and detested men who smiled in his face and stabbed him—(I do not believe he meant this personally, but unfortunately the whole House applied it to Mr Grenville's grimace); that for his own disgrace, he did not know where to impute it, for every minister had disavowed it. It was to the warrants, he said, he owed what had happened; he had fallen for voting against them, but had he had ten regiments, he would have parted with them all to obey his conscience; that he now could fall no lower, and would speak as he did then, and would not be hindered nor intimidated from speaking the language of Parliament. Grenville answered, that he had never avowed nor disavowed the measure of dismissing Mr Conway—(he disavowed it to Mr Harris[11])—that he himself had been turned out for voting against German connections;[12] that he had never approved inquiring into the King's prerogative, on that head—(I can name a person[13] who can repeat volumes of what he has said on the subject)—and that the King had as much right to dismiss military as civil officers, and then drew a ridiculous parallel betwixt the two, in which he seemed to give himself the rank of a civil lieutenant-general. This warmth was stopped by Augustus Hervey,[14] who spoke to order, and called for the question; but young T. Townshend confirmed, that the term *profligacy* was applied by all mankind to the conduct on the warrants. It was not the most agreeable circumstance to Grenville, that Lord Granby closed the debate, by declaring how much he disapproved the dismission of officers for civil reasons, and the more, as he was persuaded it would not prevent officers from acting according to their consciences; and he spoke of your brother with many encomiums. Sir W. Meredith then notified his intention of taking up the affair of the warrants on Monday sennight.[15] Mr Pitt was not there,

10. Meaning that Lord Bute really was.

11. John Harris, Conway's brother-in-law.

12. Grenville was dismissed from the treasurership of the Navy in Nov. 1755 for opposing treaties made with Russia and Hesse-Cassel to secure the German dominions of George II. See *ante* 15 Nov.

1755; Mann iv. 512; *Grenville Papers* i. 433–4.

13. Not identified.

14. Hon. Augustus John Hervey (1724–79), 3d E. of Bristol, 1775; naval officer; M.P. Bury St Edmunds 1757–63, 1768–75, Saltash 1763–8.

15. See postscript.

nor Lord Temple in the House of Lords; but the latter is ill.[16] I should have told you that Lord Warkworth[17] and T. Pitt[18] moved our addresses; as Lord Townshend and Lord Bottetourt did those of the Lords. Lord Townshend said, though it was grown unpopular to praise the King, yet he should, and he was violent against libels; forgetting that the most ill-natured branch of them, caricaturas, his own invention,[19] are left off. Nobody thought it worthwhile to answer him, at which he was much offended.

So much for the opening of the Parliament which does not promise serenity. Your brother is likely to make a very great figure: they have given him the warmth he wanted, and may thank themselves for it. Had Mr Grenville taken my advice, he had avoided an opponent that he will find a tough one, and must already repent having drawn upon him.

With regard to yourself, my dear Lord, you may be sure I did not intend to ask you any impertinent question.[20] You requested me to tell you whatever I heard said about you:[21] you was talked of for Ireland, and are still; and Lord Holland, within this week told me, that you had solicited it warmly.[22] Don't think yourself under any obligation to reply to me on these occasions. It is to comply with your desires that I repeat anything I hear of you, not to make use of them to draw any explanation from you, to which I have no title; nor have I, you know, any troublesome curiosity. I mentioned Ireland with the same indifference that I tell you that the town here has bestowed Lady Anne, first on Lord March,[23] and now on Stephen Fox—tattle not worth your answering.[24]

You have lost another of your lords justices, Lord Shannon, of whose death an account came yesterday.[25]

16. 'Lord Temple was ill and absent' (Gilly Williams to Selwyn, 11 Jan., Jesse, op. cit. i. 351).

17. Hugh Percy (1742–1817), styled Lord Warkworth 1750–66 and Lord Percy 1766–86; 2d D. of Northumberland 1786; army officer; K.G. 1788; M.P. Westminster 1763–76. On moving the Address, Warkworth, at this time a staunch government supporter, referred to the Peace as 'the most honourable, glorious, and advantageous, that ever was made' (James Harris's MS 'Debates,' quoted in Namier and Brooke iii. 269).

18. According to Harris, Pitt seconded the Address 'with uncommon propriety

and force' (ibid., quoted Namier and Brooke iii. 287).

19. In 1756 first appeared 'a new species of . . . ['satiric prints'], invented by George Townshend: they were caricatures on cards' (Mem. Geo. II ii. 228). See ante 4 March 1756, n. 9.

20. See ante 3, 20 Dec. 1764.

21. 'If you hear me abused at any time in London I desire to know it' (Hertford to HW ante 11 Nov. 1763).

22. See post 18 Jan. 1765.

23. See ante 29 Oct. 1764.

24. Hertford absolutely denies both rumours post 18 Jan. 1765.

25. 'By yesterday's Irish mails we have

Lady Harrington's porter[26] was executed yesterday,[27] and went to Tyburn with a white cockade in his hat, as an emblem of his innocence.[28]

All the rest of my news I exhausted in my letter to Lady Hertford three days ago.[29] The King's Speech, as I told her it was to do, announced the contract between Princess Caroline and the Prince Royal of Denmark.[30]

I don't think the tone the session has taken will expedite my visit to you; however, I shall be able to judge when a few of the great questions are over. The American affairs are expected to occasion much discussion, but as I understand them no more than Hebrew, they will throw no impediment in my way. Adieu! my dear Lord; you will probably hear no more politics these ten days.

Yours ever,

H. W.

Friday [11 Jan.].

The warrants are put off to the Tuesday;[31] therefore, as it will probably be so long a day, I shall not be able to give you an account of it till this day fortnight.

advice, that on the 28th ult. died . . . the Earl of Shannon' (*London Chronicle* 8–10 Jan., xvii. 38, *sub* 10 Jan.). '*Dublin Castle, Dec. 28, 1764*. This morning at eight o'clock . . . the . . . Earl of Shannon . . . one of the lords justices of this kingdom, departed this life' (*Daily Adv.* 10 Jan.). See also Mary Granville, Mrs Delany, *Autobiography and Correspondence*, ed. Lady Llanover, 1861–2, iv. 41; Jesse, op. cit. i. 344.

26. John Wesket.

27. See *ante* 9 Dec. 1763, 3 Dec. 1764.

28. This was also the interpretation of Gilly Williams (to Selwyn, 11 Jan., Jesse, op. cit. i. 354–5), who wrote that he 'died game,' and of Henry St John (to Selwyn, 11 Jan., ibid. i. 345), who added that he 'died with the same hardness as appeared through his whole trial.' According to the *Daily Adv.* 10 Jan., however, he and the other prisoners executed with him 'all behaved penitently,' and the Ordinary of Newgate reported that Wesket had told him that he was wear-

ing the white cockade because 'I believe I am come to an untimely end, in order that my soul might be saved; and I look upon this as my wedding day' (Joseph Moore, *The Ordinary of Newgate's Account of the Behaviour, Confession, and Dying Words, of . . . Seven Malefactors . . . Executed at Tyburn . . . Jan. 9, 1765*, 1765, p. 14).

29. Missing.

30. Christian VII (1749–1808), K. of Denmark 1766–1808, m. (1766) Princess Caroline Matilda (Isenburg, *Stammtafeln* ii. taf. 65, 73). 'I have agreed with my good brother the King of Denmark, to cement the union which has long subsisted between the two Crowns, by the marriage of the Prince Royal of Denmark with my sister the Princess Caroline Matilda, which is to be solemnized as soon as their respective ages will permit' (*Journals of the House of Commons* xxx. 3).

31. 'Sir W. Meredith gave notice that he had a motion to make on Tuesday

From HERTFORD, Friday 18 January 1765

Printed for the first time from a photostat of BM Add. MSS 23218, ff. 184–5.

Paris, January 18th 1765.

Dear Horry,

UPON the return of an English messenger from Spain who is just come into my house and just going to leave it on his way to England, I have left my dinner to thank you for the account you have given me of the debate on the opening of the session. I rejoice to hear my brother has gained so much honour, and it is confirmed to me from the City and on all hands. The warmth he now possesses will I hope entitle him, by making use of his abilities, to that praise and reputation which he might in any time have acquired by an exertion of them. He is from his character and talents equal to any employment, and I hope the injustice which has been done him may lead him into public business, where I have always wished to see him, because he must make so considerable a figure in it.

You are very good to tell me what you hear said of or about me; it is what I shall request you to continue. I asked for the government of Ireland when Lord Halifax got it;[1] that is now some years since, and the King was I dare say informed of my wishes, but I have not wrote nor said one word about it except in answer to yours and my brother's letters upon the present report since I have been in France. If it is offered to me upon proper terms, I shall accept it for the same reasons that induced me to come into this country, the convenience and advantage of my children, whose ages might now make my return to England advantageous to them. As to myself I am very easy here; I have moments of trouble and dissatisfaction which every man must expect who engages in public business, but I lay them not to heart because I am conscious I do my duty, and I am personally treated with all sorts of respect and civility. This intelligence I must beg you to keep entirely to yourself. Lord Holland is not my friend,[2] and whether he is well or ill informed I should be sorry he knew more. He might make use of any intelligence to my prejudice, and

sennight, so the old story of the warrants will be told over again' (Gilly Williams to Selwyn, 11 Jan., Jesse, op. cit. i. 352). See MANN vi. 274, n. 6; post 20 Jan. 1765.

1. Lord Halifax was lord lieutenant of Ireland from March 1761 to April 1763.
2. See ante 28 July 1764.

he hardly would use any for my service. I have acquired for what regards myself personally great indifference; perhaps I am indolently disposed. I feel at my ease and know the danger of all public and responsible situations, yet the advantage of my children might lead me where I could see a probable prospect of success. The government of Ireland in case of vacancy I shall therefore accept or refuse as it is offered to me, and I shall desire you to keep these sentiments which I communicate to you as my friend entirely to yourself; at the same time you will give me leave to ask why Lord Northumberland is supposed to quit,[3] and what is the nature of the Vice-Admiralty of all America for which I saw him named in all the papers?[4] Neither Lord March or Mr Fox have ever shown the most distant regard for my daughter. She is yet perfectly at liberty (I think because she is not known); I am partial to her from thinking her the best girl in the world; still it is my duty to settle her in it, and when a proper opportunity offers I must rojoice in it; in the meantime I have the satisfaction of living with the best of daughters.

Mr Selwyn tells me he was invited to partake of the diversions of Parliament,[5] but that he has refused till next month; this perhaps you should not say. Adieu, dear Horry, I must conclude in haste,

Ever yours,

HERTFORD

3. See *post* 20 Jan. 1765, postscript.

4. 'His Majesty has . . . been pleased to appoint the . . . Earl of Northumberland (lord lieutenant of Ireland) to be Vice-Admiral of all America' (*Daily Adv.* 26 Dec. 1764; *London Chronicle* 25–7 Dec. 1764, xvi. 609). See *post* 20 Jan. 1765, postscript.

5. 'It is not I alone, but all your friends, nay, the King himself, who have expressed themselves with some concern that you still continue to run after gewgaws and hunt butterflies, when your presence is absolutely wanted at Westminster. I have authority for mentioning the surprise of the Royal Personage, and Lord Gower desires me to acquaint you with it' (Gilly Williams to Selwyn, 11 Jan., J. H. Jesse, *George Selwyn and his Contemporaries*, 1882, i. 351).

To Hertford, Sunday 20 January 1765

Printed from *Works* ix. 177–82.

Sunday, Jan. 20th 1765.

DO you forgive me, if I write to you two or three days sooner than I said I would.[1] Our important day on the warrants is put off for a week, in compliment to Mr Pitt's gout[2]—can it resist such attention?[3] I shall expect it in a prodigious quantity of black ribands. You have heard, to be sure, of the great fortune that is bequeathed to him by a Sir William Pynsent,[4] an old man of near ninety, who quitted the world on the peace of Utrecht; and, luckily for Mr Pitt, lived to be as angry with its *pendant*, the treaty of Paris. I did not send you the first report, which mounted it to an enormous sum:[5] I think the medium account is £2000 a year, and £30,000 in money. This Sir William Pynsent, whose fame, like an aloe, did not blow till near an hundred,[6] was a singularity. The scandalous chronicle of Somersetshire talks terribly of his morals. . . .[7]

Lady North[8] was nearly related to Lady Pynsent,[9] which encouraged Lord North to flatter himself that Sir William's extreme propensity to him would recommend even his wife's parentage for heirs; but the uncomeliness of Lady North, and a vote my Lord gave against the Cider Bill, offended the old gentleman so much, that he

---

1. See *ante* 10 Jan. 1765, postscript.

2. See MANN vi. 274, n. 6. The debate took place 29 Jan.; see *post* 9 Feb. 1765.

3. Pitt was not able to attend the debate (MANN vi. 283–4; *post* 12 Feb. 1765).

4. (ca 1679 – 8 Jan. 1765), 2d Bt 1719, M.P. Taunton 1715–22 (Sedgwick ii. 377).

5. £200,000, according to HW to Mann 13 Jan. 1765 (MANN vi. 276). For various other estimates of the legacy, see ibid. n. 22.

6. A popular superstition, repeated by HW to Lady Ossory 9 June 1778 (OSSORY ii. 18); see OED, *sub* 'aloe.'

7. A passage has been deleted here by Croker, indicated by asterisks, with the explanatory note: 'The original contains an imputation against Sir W. Pynsent,

which, if true, would induce us to suspect him of a disordered mind' (*Works* ix. 178). HW, in a passage in the fair copy of his MS of *Mem. Geo. III* deleted by Russell Barker, wrote that he was said to have been 'living to her death with his own only daughter in pretty notorious incest' (ff. 180–1).

8. Anne Speke (ca 1740–97), m. (1756) Frederick North, styled Lord North, 2d E. of Guilford 1790.

9. Mary Jennings, m. 1 Edmund Star; m. 2 Sir William Pynsent (Sedgwick, loc. cit.). She and Lady North were first cousins, once removed, her mother being Lady North's great-aunt (Burke, *Landed Gentry*, 1836–8, iv. 538).

burnt his would-be heir in effigy.[10] How will all these strange histories sound at Paris!

This post, I suppose, will rain letters to my Lady Hertford, on her death and revival.[11] I was dreadfully alarmed at it for a moment;[12] my servant was so absurd as to wake me, and bid me not be frightened—an excellent precaution! Of all moments, that between sleeping and waking is the most subject to terror.—I started up, and my first thought was to send for Dr Hunter; but, in two minutes, I recollected that it was impossible to be true, as your porter had the very day before been with me to tell me a courier was arrived from you, and was to return that evening.[13] Your poor son Henry, whom you will dote upon for it, was not tranquillized so soon. He instantly sent away a courier to your brother; who arrived in the middle of the night. Lady Milton, Lady George Sackville,[14] and I, agreed this evening to tell my Lady Hertford, that we ought to have believed the news, and to have imputed it to the gaming rakehelly life my Lady leads at Paris, which scandalizes all us prudes, her old friends. In truth, I have not much right to rail at anybody for living in a hurricane. I found myself with a violent cold on Wednesday, and till then had not once reflected on all the hot and cold climates I had passed through the day before: I had been at the Duke of Cumberland's levee,[15] then at Princess Amalie's drawing-room, from thence to a crowded House of Commons,—to dinner at your brother's,—to the opera,[16]—to Madame Seillern's,[17]—to Arthur's,—and to supper at

---

10. According to Lady Chatham, Pynsent struck North out of his will upon hearing that he had voted for the 'inadequate' Peace of Paris (Basil Williams, *Life of . . . Pitt*, 1913, ii. 169–70).

11. 'Yesterday [16 Jan.] an express arrived in town, with advice of the death of the lady of the . . . Earl of Hertford at Paris' (*London Chronicle* 15–17 Jan., xvii. 61). 'The report of the death of Lady Hertford is without the least foundation' (ibid. 19–22 Jan., xvii. 74, *sub* 21 Jan.).

12. HW was apparently notified of the rumour between midnight and the morning of 17 Jan.

13. Halifax wrote to Hertford, 15 Jan., that 'I received yesterday, by Bullock, your Excellency's letters of the 8th and

10th inst.,' concluding that 'as your Excellency desires that Bullock may return to you as soon as possible, I redispatch him' (S.P. 78/265, f. 31). Bullock apparently left London the evening of the 16th.

14. Diana Sambrooke (ca 1731–78), m. (1754) Lord George Sackville.

15. 'Yesterday [15 Jan.] . . . the Duke of Cumberland had a very numerous levee at his house in Upper Grosvenor Street' (*London Chronicle* 15–17 Jan., xvii. 58).

16. To see another performance of *Ezio* (*London Stage* Pt IV, ii. 1093); see *ante* 25 Nov. 1764.

17. Charlotte von Solms-Sonnewalde (1725–83), m. (1741) Christian August, Graf von Seilern (Ossory i. 19, n. 15).

Mrs George Pitt's,—it is scandalous; but, who does less? The Duke looked much better than I expected; is gone to Windsor, and mends daily.

It was Lady Harcourt's[18] death that occasioned the confusion, and our dismay: she died at a Colonel Oughton's;[19] such a small house, that Lord Harcourt has been forced to take their family into his own house. Poor Lady Digby[20] is dead too, of a fever, and was with child. They were extremely happy, and her own family adored her.[21] My sister[22] has begged me to ask a favour, that will put you to a little trouble, though only for a moment. It is, if you will be so good to order one of your servants when you have done with the English newspapers, to put them in a cover, and send them to Mr Churchill, au Château de Nubecourt, près de Clermont, en Argone; they cannot get a gazette that does not cost them six livres.

Monday evening [21 Jan.].

We have had a sort of day in the House of Commons: the proposition for accepting the £670,000 for the French prisoners passed

18. Rebecca Le Bas (d. 16 Jan. 1765), m. (1735) Simon Harcourt, 2d Vct Harcourt, cr. (1749) E. Harcourt (*London Chronicle* 17–19 Jan., xvii. 65).

19. James Adolphus Dickenson Oughton (1720–80); Maj.-Gen. 1761; Col. 31st Ft 1762; Lt-Gen. 1770; K.B., 1773 (DNB; W. A. Shaw, *Knights of England*, 1906, i. 172). Lady Harcourt's second son, the Hon. William Harcourt, later 3d E. Harcourt, had been appointed Lt-Col. of Oughton's regiment 28 Nov. 1764 (*Army Lists* 1765, p. 84). She died 'suddenly, on a visit at tea, at the Hon. Col. Houghton's [*sic*]' (GM 1765, xxxv. 47). However, since the *London Chronicle* loc. cit. reports that she died 'Wednesday night [16 Jan.] . . . at . . . [Harcourt's] house in Cavendish Square,' she may have been taken ill at Col. Oughton's, but carried to Harcourt's house, where she died.

20. Elizabeth Feilding (ca 1742–19 Jan. 1765), m. (4 Sept. 1763) Henry Digby, 7th Bn Digby (*ante* 9 Aug. 1763, n. 5). 'On Saturday morning [19 Jan.] died the lady of the Hon. Lord Digby . . . at his house in Dover Street' (*London Chronicle*

19–22 Jan., xvii. 74). 'Poor Lady Digby is dead; she came to town a fortnight ago with child, and was so tired with her journey and so feverish, she went to bed but got no sleep; her fever went off, but she was so nervous that she had fits of convulsions so strong and so frequent that she died in a fortnight' (Lady Sarah Bunbury to Lady Susan O'Brien, 23 Jan., *Life and Letters of Lady Sarah Lennox*, ed. Lady Ilchester and Lord Stavordale, 1902, i. 157). Her only child, Edward, b. 20 June 1764, died an infant (Collins, *Peerage*, 1812, v. 384).

21. 'I hear poor Lord Digby is more melancholy than you can conceive; he is at his mother's, and very wretched indeed. It is quite shocking to have the comfort of a whole family so suddenly lost, for they seem all vastly miserable' (Lady Sarah Bunbury to Lady Susan O'Brien, 23 Jan., loc. cit.).

22. Lady Mary Churchill, who had been sojourning in France with her husband and children (see *ante* 17 July 1764), had returned temporarily to England (see postscript), presumably in con-

easily.[23] Then came the Navy:[24] Dowdeswell, in a long and very sensible speech, proposed to reduce the number of sailors to 10,000.[25] He was answered by—Charles Townshend—oh! yes!—are you surprised? nobody here was: no, not even at his assertion, that he had always applauded the Peace, though the whole House and the whole town knew that, on the preliminaries, he came down prepared to speak *against* them; but that on Pitt's retiring, he plucked up courage, and spoke *for* them.[26] Well, you want to know what place he is to have—so does he too.[27] I don't want to know *what* place, but that he has some one; for I am sure he will always do most hurt to the side on which he professes to be; consequently, I wish him with the Administration, and I wish so well to both sides, that I would have him more decried, if that be possible, than he is. Colonel Barré spoke against Dowdeswell's proposal, though not setting himself up at auction, like Charles, nor friendly to the Ministry, but temperately and sensibly. There was no division. You know my opinion of Charles Townshend is neither new nor singular.[28] When Charles Yorke left us,[29] I hoped for this event, and my wish then slid into this couplet:

nection with her promotion to housekeeper at Windsor Castle (*ante* 1 Nov. 1764).

23. See *ante* 3 Aug. 1764, n. 51. On 5 Jan. Guerchy, the French ambassador to London, had presented a memorial proclaiming that Louis XV 'a ordonné au . . . son ambassadeur à la Cour de Londres, de déclarer qu'elle est prête de payer au Roi de la Grande Bretagne la somme de £670,000 sterling pour l'acquit et extinction totale de toutes les prétensions et demandes de la part de la Grande Bretagne pour subsistance, entretien, et autres dépenses quelconques faites pour les prisonniers français,' and to make the payment in full by the end of 1767; an additional sum was to be paid after 1767 for the expense of prisoners incurred after 11 Nov. 1762, and for the expense of French prisoners in India (copy in S.P. 78/265, ff. 7-10). After the King had referred the proposal to both Houses 15 Jan., both Houses voted unanimously to accept it 21 Jan. (*Journals*

of the House of Commons xxx. 16, 36-7; *Journals of the House of Lords* xxxi. 9, 14; *Mem. Geo. III* ii. 31-2).

24. 'An Estimate of the Charge of What May Be Necessary for the Buildings, Rebuildings, and Repairs of Ships of War,' etc. 'for the Year, 1765,' presented to the House 21 Jan., is printed *Journals of the House of Commons* xxx. 34-5.

25. From 16,000 (*Mem. Geo. III* ii. 33). The most constant theme of Dowdeswell's speeches in Parliament was the need to reduce government expenditures and lower taxation (Namier and Brooke ii. 333; see *ante* 22 Jan. 1764, n. 85).

26. On 9 Dec. 1762. See *Mem. Geo. III* i. 183; Sir Lewis Namier and John Brooke, *Charles Townshend*, 1964, pp. 76-83.

27. He became paymaster-general in May (*post* 20 May 1765).

28. See *ante* 22 Jan., 20 April 1764.

29. See *ante* 3 Dec. 1764.

To the Administration.

One Charles, who ne'er was ours, you've got—'tis true:
To make the grace complete, take t'other too.

The favours I ask of them, are not difficult to grant.
Adieu! my dear Lord,

Yours, ever,

H. Walpole

Tuesday, 4 o'clock.

I had sealed my letter and given it to my sister, who sets out tomorrow, and will put it into the post at Calais; but having received yours[30] by the courier from Spain, I must add a few words. You may be sure I shall not mention a tittle of what you say to me. Indeed, if you think it necessary to explain to me, I shall be more cautious of telling you what I hear. If I had any curiosity, I should have nothing to do, but to pretend I had heard some report, and so draw from you what you might not have a mind to mention: I do tell you when I hear any, for your information, but insist on your not replying. The Vice-Admiral of America is a mere feather;[31] but there is more substance in the notion of the Viceroy's[32] quitting Ireland. Lord Bute and George Grenville are so ill together, that decency is scarce observed between their adherents; and the moment the former has an opportunity or resolution enough, he will remove the latter, and place his son-in-law[33] in the Treasury.[34] This goes so far, that Charles Townshend, who is openly dedicated to Grenville, may possibly find himself disappointed, and get no place at last. However, I rejoice that we have got rid of him. It will tear up all connection between him and your brother, root and branch: a circumstance you will not be more sorry for than I am. In the meantime, the Opposition is so staunch that, I think, after the three questions on warrants, dismission of officers, and the Manilla money, I shall be at liberty to come

30. *Ante* 18 Jan. 1765.
31. See ibid., n. 4.
32. Northumberland.
33. A slip for 'son-in-law's father.' Northumberland's son, Lord Warkworth (*ante* 10 Jan. 1765), had married Bute's daughter, Lady Anne Stuart, 2 July 1764.

34. See *Mem. Geo. III* ii. 118. After the King's unsuccessful attempt to replace his ministry in May, his ministers, in retaliation, succeeded in having Northumberland dismissed from the viceroyalty. See *post* 20 May 1765.

to you, when I shall have a great deal to tell you. If Ch. T. gets a place, Lord G. Sackville expects another, by the same channel, interest, and connection;[35] but if Charles may be disappointed himself, what may a man be who trusts to him? Adieu!

To Hertford, Sunday 27 January 1765

Printed from *Works* ix. 182–8, where it is misdated.

Arlington Street, Jan. 27th, 1764[5].

THE brother[1] of your brother's neighbour, Mr Freeman,[2] who is going to Paris, and I believe will not be sorry to be introduced to you, gives me an opportunity which I cannot resist, of sending you a private line or two,[3] though I wrote you a long letter,[4] which my sister was to put into the post at Calais two or three days ago.

We had a very remarkable day on Wednesday[5] in the House of Commons,—very glorious for us, and very mortifying to the Administration, especially to the principal performer,[6] who was severely galled by our troops, and abandoned by his own. The business of the day was the army,[7] and, as nothing was expected, the House was not full. The very circumstance of nothing being expected, had encouraged Charles Townshend to soften a little what had passed on Monday;[8] he grew profuse of his whispers and promises to us, and offered your brother to move the question on the dismission of

35. '[Charles Townshend] was now influenced by Lord George Sackville, who, dissatisfied with Lord Bute for not supporting him, had joined the Opposition. . . . But the declining state of the Opposition, by deaths and other causes . . . had alarmed Lord George, and he began to look towards Grenville, who would want all manner of strength to support himself against the Favourite' (*Mem. Geo. III*, ii. 33–4). Townshend appears to have been Sackville's sole political connection at this time (Namier and Brooke iii. 393); see Hist. MSS Comm., *Stopford-Sackville MSS*, 1904–10, i. 60–2.

1. John Freeman (ca 1722–94), attorney (Foster, *Alumni Oxon.;* John S. Burn,

History of Henley-on-Thames, 1861, facing p. 254; GM 1794, lxiv pt ii. 870). Another brother, Jeremiah (listed Burn, loc. cit.), died in 1759 (GM 1759, xxix. 293).

2. Sambrooke Freeman (*ante* 21 Oct. 1756).

3. Conway also sent a letter to Hertford by Freeman (dated 31 Jan., MS now WSL).

4. *Ante* 20 Jan. 1765.

5. 23 Jan.

6. Grenville.

7. The business was to vote the army for the year (*Journals of the House of Commons* xxx. 54–5). See HW's account of the debate in *Mem. Geo. III* ii. 34–7.

8. See *ante* 20 Jan. 1765, *sub* 'Monday evening.'

officers: the debate began; Beckford fell foul on the dismissions,[9] and dropped some words on America.[10] Charles, who had placed himself again under the wing of Grenville, replied on American affairs;[11] but totally *forgot* your brother. Beckford, in his boisterous Indian style, told Charles, that on a single idea he had poured forth a *diarrhœa* of words.[12] He[13] could not stand it, and in two minutes fairly stole out of the House. This battery being dismounted, the whole attack fell on Grenville, and would have put you in mind of former days. You never heard any minister worse treated than he was for two hours together, by Tommy Townshend, Sir George Saville, and George Onslow,—and what was worse, no soul stepped forth in his defence, but Rigby and Lord Strange, the latter of whom was almost as much abashed as Charles Townshend; conscience flew in his black face,[14] and almost turned it red:[15] T. Townshend was still more bitter on Sandwich, whom he called a profligate fellow,[16]—hoped he was present, and added, 'if he is not, I am ready to call him so to his face in any private company': even Rigby, his accomplice,[17] said not a word in behalf of his brother culprit. You will wonder how all this ended—what would be the most ridiculous conclusion to such a

9. 'Beckford began [the debate] . . . by declaring that if any man would second him, he would oppose so large a number as sixteen thousand men [for the army], because we were in no danger of being attacked by surprise; and because he apprehended there was an intention of modelling the army, which he concluded from the dismission of General Conway' (*Mem. Geo. III* ii. 34).

10. 'He mentioned . . . an expression dropped by Charles Townshend, which he said had made his ears tingle; it was that *the Colonies were not to be emancipated.* The Colonies, said Beckford, are more free than Ireland, for America had not been conquered; on the contrary, it was inhabited by the conquerors' (ibid.).

11. 'Townshend ridiculed Beckford's alarm, affirming he had only meant that the Colonies were not to be emancipated from their dependence on the supremacy of this country' (ibid.).

12. 'Beckford told him he had expressed a single idea by a multitude of circumlocutions, and was troubled with a *diarrhœa of words*—an expression with

which Townshend was much hurt' (ibid.).

13. Townshend.

14. HW wrote, in a note to his 'Patapan,' that Strange was 'remarkable for his ugliness' (Selwyn 302, n. 51).

15. 'Lord Strange, attempting to defend [the ministers] . . . was so roughly handled on his own tergiversations by Onslow, Sir George Saville, and Thomas Townshend, that he who was wont to be all spirit, quickness, and fire, was quite abashed, and showed at least the sensibility of virtue' (*Mem. Geo. III* ii. 35).

16. Upon mentioning 'a list of sixteen officers, carried into the Closet for dismission by Lord Sandwich' (ibid.).

17. Rigby was at this time a prominent defender of unpopular government measures, among them the dismission of officers and the prosecution of Wilkes. The latter affair had earned Sandwich the sobriquet of 'Jemmy Twitcher' for his betrayal of Wilkes, and Rigby, like Sandwich, had betrayed a friend (Fox) for political expediency. See Namier and Brooke iii. 356–7.

scene? as you cannot imagine, I will tell you: Lord Harry Paulet[18] telling Grenville, that if Lord Cobham[19] was to rise from the dead, he would,—if he could be ashamed of anything, be ashamed of him;[20]— by the way, everybody believes he meant the apostrophe stronger than he expressed it:[21] Grenville rose in a rage, like a basket-woman, and told Lord Harry that if he chose to use such language, he knew where to find him. Did you ever hear of a prime minister, even *soi-disant tel,* challenging an opponent, when he could not answer him? Poor Lord Harry, too, was an unfortunate subject to exercise his valour upon![22] The House interposed; Lord Harry declared he should have expected Grenville to breakfast with him next morning; Grenville explained off and on two or three times,[23] the Scotch laughed, the Opposition roared, and the Treasury bench sat as mute as fishes. Thus ended that wise Hudibrastic encounter.

Grenville however, attended by every bad omen, provoked your brother, who had not intended to speak, by saying that some people have a good opinion of the dismissed officers, others had not. Your brother rose, and surpassed himself: he was very warm, though less so than on the first day; very decent in terms, but most severe in effect; he more than hinted at the threats that had been used to him, —said he would not reveal what was improper; yet left no mortal in the dark on that head.[24] He called on the officers to assert their own freedom and independence. In short, made such a speech as silenced all his adversaries, but has filled the whole town with his praises: I

18. Lord Harry Powlett (1720–94), 6th Duke of Bolton 1765; M.P. Christchurch 1751–4, Lymington 1755–61, Winchester 1761–5; naval officer.

19. Grenville's uncle.

20. Both Cobham and Powlett's uncle, the 3d Duke of Bolton, had been dismissed from their regiments by Sir Robert Walpole in 1733 for opposing his measures (see J. H. Plumb, *Sir Robert Walpole: The King's Minister,* 1960, pp. 267–81). During the debate Rigby, in defence of Grenville, had quoted Sir Robert as saying that 'it must be a pitiful minister that would not dare to turn out a man that voted against him' (*Mem. Geo. III* loc. cit.).

21. Powlett was apparently an awkward speaker; see Namier and Brooke iii. 314.

22. HW wrote in *Last Journals* that Powlett's 'valour was . . . problematic' (ii. 229). He had twice been court-martialled, in 1752 and 1755; the first time he was acquitted, and the second time admonished (DNB). He is said to be the 'Captain Whiffle' of Smollett's *Roderick Random,* and the 'Admiral Sternpost' of *Town and Country Magazine,* 1778, x. 289 (GEC *sub* Bolton; John Charnock, *Biographia navalis,* 1794–8, v. 5–12).

23. 'Grenville acknowledged he had thrown out a challenge; but at last explained it away' (*Mem. Geo. III* loc. cit.).

24. 'He himself had received intimations to take care what he did—Grenville started!—yet he should not say from what quarter' (ibid. ii. 36).

believe as soon as his speech reaches Hayes, it will contribute extremely to expel the gout, and bring Mr Pitt to town, lest his presence should be no longer missed. Princess Amalie told me the next night, that if she had heard nothing of Mr Conway's speech, she should have known how well he had done by my spirits. I was not sorry she made this reflection, as I knew she would repeat it to Lady (Betty)[25] Waldegrave;[26] and as I was willing that the Duchess of Bedford,[27] who, when your brother was dismissed, asked the Duchess of Grafton if she was not sorry for *poor Mr Conway,* who had lost everything,[28] should recollect that it is they who have cause to lament that dismission, not we.

There was a paragraph in Rigby's speech, and taken up, and adopted by Goody Grenville, which makes much noise, and, I suppose, has not given less offence; they talked of 'arbitrary *Stuart* principles,' which are supposed to have been aimed at the *Stuart* favourite; that breach is wider than ever:—not one of Lord Bute's adherents have opened their lips this session. I conclude a few of them will be ordered to speak on Friday; but unless we go on too triumphantly and reconcile them, I think this session will terminate Mr Grenville's reign, and that of the Bedfords too, unless they make great submissions.

Do you know that Sir W. Pynsent had your brother in his eye! He said to his lawyer, 'I know Mr Pitt is much younger than I am, but he has very bad health: as you will hear it before me, if he dies first, draw up another will with Mr Conway's name instead of Mr Pitt's, and bring it down to me directly.'[29] I beg Britannia's pardon, but I fear I could have supported the loss on these grounds.

A very unhappy affair happened last night at the Star and Garter;[30] Lord Byron[31] killed a Mr Chaworth[32] there in a duel. I know none of the particulars,[33] and never believe the first reports.

25. Possibly inserted by Croker.
26. Lady Elizabeth Leveson Gower, m. (1751) Col. John Waldegrave, 3d E. Waldegrave, 1763; lady of the Bedchamber to Princess Amelia 1749–63 (*ante* 1 Aug. 1758, n. 28).
27. Lady Waldegrave's sister.
28. The Duchess of Bedford's remark was mentioned by HW to Conway, *ante* 21 April 1764.
29. However, in *Mem. Geo. III* HW writes that 'immediately before his

death, [Pynsent] had indubitably given orders to his lawyer to draw a new will entirely in favour of General Conway; but it was not prepared in time' (ii. 32).
30. A tavern in Pall Mall (MANN vi. 284 and n. 9).
31. William Byron (1722–98), 5th Baron Byron, 1736.
32. William Chaworth (d. 27 Jan. 1765), of Annesley, Notts, a relative of Lord Byron's (ibid., n. 8).
33. See below.

My Lady Townshend was arrested two days ago in the street[34] at the suit of a house-painter,[35] who, having brought her a bill double of the estimate he had given in, she would not pay it. As this is a breach of privilege, I should think the man would hear of it.[36]

There is no day yet fixed for our intended motion on the dismission of officers;[37] but, I believe, Lord John Cavendish and Fitzroy[38] will be the movers and seconders. Charles Townshend, we conclude, will be very ill that day; if one could pity the poor toad, one should: there is jealousy of your brother,—fear of your brother,—fear of Mr Pitt,—influence of his own brother,—connections entered into both with Lord Bute and Mr Grenville, and a trimming plan concerted with Lord George Sackville and Charles Yorke, all tearing him or impelling him a thousand ways, with the addition of his own vanity and irresolution, and the contempt of everybody else. I dined with him yesterday at Mr Mackinsy's,[39] where his whole discourse was in ridicule of George Grenville.

The enclosed novel[40] is much in vogue; the author is not known,[41] but if you should not happen to like it, I could give you a reason why you need not say so. There is nothing else new, but a play called *The Platonic Wife*,[42] written by an Irish Mrs Griffiths,[43] which in charity to her was suffered to run three nights.

34. In 'Vigoe Lane, opposite the Duke of Queensberry's house' (testimony of John Osborne, Lady Townshend's coachman, *Journals of the House of Lords* xxxi. 25).

35. See next note.

36. On 5 Feb., in the House of Lords, complaint was made by Lord Winchelsea on behalf of Lady Townshend, 'That the Lady . . . Townshend was, on Friday the 25th day of January last, arrested upon a common writ of capias, taken out against her . . . by Edmund Coombe [or Combe] an attorney, at the suit of Henry Horth and Robert Winter painters, upon the oath of the said Henry Horth, directed to Peter King bailiff . . . in breach of the privilege of peerage' (ibid. xxxi. 25; J. H. Jesse, *George Selwyn and his Contemporaries*, 1882, i. 357–8, 373). As a result of this complaint, it was ordered that Horth, Coombe, and King be taken into custody (*Journals of the House of Lords* xxxi. 26). After pleading that they had acted through ignorance, on 11 Feb.

the three were reprimanded and discharged, Horth and Coombe being ordered to pay their respective fees and also the fees of King (ibid. xxxi. 30, 34–5).

37. See *post* 12 Feb., 18 April 1765.

38. Charles Fitzroy, later Bn Southampton.

39. The Hon. James Stuart Mackenzie, Lord Bute's brother (*ante* 14 Aug. 1759).

40. *The Castle of Otranto*, published 24 Dec. (500 copies). HW had started writing it the beginning of June and finished it 6 Aug. ('Short Notes,' Gray i. 41; Cole i. 88).

41. HW did not acknowledge his authorship until the book had succeeded. See *post* 26 March 1765.

42. Opened 24 Jan. at Drury Lane; closed 31 Jan. after six performances (*London Stage* Pt IV, ii. 1095–6).

43. Elizabeth Griffith (ca 1720–93), m. (1751) Richard Griffith (Mason i. 447, n. 21).

CONWAY'S BOOKPLATE

Since I wrote my letter, the following is the account nearest the truth that I can learn of the fatal duel last night: a club of Nottinghamshire gentlemen had dined at the Star and Garter, and there had been a dispute between the combatants, whether Lord Byron, who took no care of his game, or Mr Chaworth, who was active in the association,[44] had most game on their manor. The company, however, had apprehended no consequences, and parted at eight o'clock; but Lord Byron stepping into an empty chamber, and sending the drawer for Mr Chaworth, or calling him thither himself, took the candle from the waiter,[45] and bidding Mr Chaworth defend himself, drew his sword. Mr Chaworth, who was an excellent fencer, ran Lord Byron through the sleeve of his coat,[46] and then received a wound fourteen inches deep into his body. He was carried to his house in Berkeley Street,—made his will with the greatest composure, and dictated a paper, which they say, allows it was a fair duel,[47] and died at nine this morning. Lord Byron is not gone off, but says he will take his trial, which, if the coroner brings in a verdict of manslaughter, may, according to precedent, be in the House of Lords, and without the ceremonial of Westminster Hall.[48] George Selwyn is much missed on this occasion, but we conclude it will bring him over.[49] I feel for both families, though I know none of either, but poor Lady Carlisle,[50] whom I am sure you will pity.

Our last three Saturdays at the opera have been prodigious,[51] and

44. The Association for the Preservation of the Game All Over England, a meeting of which is advertised in the *Daily Adv.* 11 Feb. Chaworth had been active in prosecuting poachers of game on his property, while Byron advocated leniency ('Trial of William Lord Byron . . . for the Murder of William Chaworth,' in T. B. Howell, *Complete Collection of State Trials*, 1816–26, xix. 1203 *et passim*).

45. One John Edwards (ibid. xix. 1211–13). Byron and Chaworth apparently met on the landing-place of the stairs, and called the waiter, who showed them into an empty chamber, set the candle on the table, and withdrew (ibid. xix. 1212, 1229).

46. Chaworth's sword 'cut my waistcoat and shirt' (statement of Lord Byron, ibid. xix. 1230).

47. 'Sunday morning, the 27th of January, about three of the clock, Mr Chaworth said, that my Lord's sword was half-drawn, and that he, knowing the man, immediately, or as quick as he could, whipt out his sword, and had the first thrust; that then my Lord wounded him, and he disarmed my Lord' (statement of Chaworth taken down by Thomas Walley Partington, ibid. xix. 1220).

48. However, the grand jury of Middlesex returned an indictment for murder (printed ibid. xix. 1180–1), and Byron was tried on that charge in Westminster Hall 16–17 April. See *post* 18 April 1765.

49. An allusion to Selwyn's morbid interest in trials and executions.

50. Lord Byron's sister (*ante* 27 Aug. 1758).

51. *Berenice*, a pasticcio, had been performed 12 and 19 Jan. (*London Stage* Pt IV, ii. 1093–4).

a new opera by Bach[52] last night was so crowded, that there were ladies standing behind the scenes during the whole performance.[53]

Adieu! my dear Lord: as this goes by a private hand, you may possibly receive its successor before it.

Yours, ever,

H. Walpole

To Hertford, ca Wednesday 30 January 1765

Missing; answered *post* 9 Feb. 1764. Dated conjecturally by the Commons debate of 29 Jan., described in the letter, ending the morning of 30 Jan. (*Mem. Geo. III* ii. 45).

From Hertford, Saturday 9 February 1765

Printed for the first time from a photostat of BM Add. MSS 23218, ff. 186–8.

Paris, February 9th 1765.

Dear Horry,

I PERCEIVE you will not come to Paris till balls and all our fine shows are over. There is no tempting you from the House of Commons though you hate and despise it. In Lent you can only see sights, play at faro and partake of small suppers. Great feasts are not usual; the fine ladies are supposed to do penance at that time. I have announced you to Madame de Mirepoix and she longs to see you; Madame de Boufflers and Madame d'Usson are prepared to receive you. How can you resist this and all the new acquaintances you will

52. Johann Christian Bach (1735–82). His *Adriano in Siria,* composed to the libretto of Metastasio, opened 26 Jan. 'by command of their Majesties' (ibid. 1095; C. S. Terry, *John Christian Bach,* 1929, pp. 83–4). It closed 23 Feb. after seven performances (*London Stage* Pt IV, ii. 1095–1100).

53. 'The expectations of the public the first night . . . this drama was performed, occasioned such a crowd at the King's theatre as had been seldom seen

there before. It was impossible for a third part of the company collected together on this occasion to obtain places. But whether from heat or inconvenience, the unreasonableness of expectation, the composer being out of fancy, or too anxious to please, the opera failed. Everyone seemed to come out of the theatre disappointed' (Charles Burney, *General History of Music,* ed. Mercer, 1935, ii. 869).

make here? The Duke de Chartres'[1] balls once a week, Madame d'Egmont's at Versailles, the opera, masked balls which you once loved—I must repeat it, all this will be over whilst you are staying in England to attend a question[2] of which you know the fate must be before decided.[3]

The event of the last day[4] has however surprised me. The amendment[5] proposed to the motion[6] is, I think, the worst piece of language I ever read and the least intelligible,[7] and it puts the opposition to the resolution proposed on the weakest foundation it can stand.[8] You tell me a great many particulars which entertain me much, and help to raise that good opinion I had before formed of the most considerable performers in the drama. My brother is on all hands allowed to make a very considerable figure; I hope therefore the promoters or advisers of his dismission are by this time severely punished by their own reflection.

1. Louis-Philippe-Joseph de Bourbon (1747–93), Duc de Chartres; Duc d'Orléans 1785; 'Philippe Égalité' (DU DEFFAND i. 159).

2. On the dismission of officers.

3. Meaning that the Administration was certain of winning the division.

4. 29 Jan., when the question of general warrants was again renewed. HW evidently wrote Hertford a missing letter on this debate, which he recounts at length in *Mem. Geo. III* ii. 37–45 and to Mann 11 Feb. 1765, MANN vi. 283–4; see *post* 12 Feb. 1765, where he mentions that he sent to Hertford 'two packets together by Mr Freeman,' one of which contained his extant letter *ante* 27 Jan. 1765.

5. 'An amendment . . . [was] proposed [by Dr George Hay] to be made to the question, by prefixing thereto these words, 'That in the particular case of libels, and of no other crime, it is proper and necessary to fix, by a vote of this House only, what ought to be deemed a law in respect of general warrants; and for that purpose, at the time when the determination of the legality of such warrants, in the instance of a most seditious and treasonable libel, is actually depending before the courts of law, for this House to declare' (*Journals of the House of Commons* xxx. 70); the House subse-

quently agreed that the words 'and of no other crime' be left out of the proposed amendment (ibid.).

6. 'A motion was made [by Sir William Meredith], and the question . . . proposed, That a general warrant for apprehending the authors, printers, or publishers, of a libel, together with their papers, is not warranted by law and is an high violation of the liberty of the subject' (ibid.).

7. A 'strange and scarce intelligible sentence' (*Mem. Geo. III* ii. 39).

8. However, HW, in *Mem. Geo. III*, states that the ministry actually mitigated the unpopularity of their opposition to the resolution by forcing the amendment upon its proponents. 'The ministry, to load Sir William Meredith's question with absurdity, made use of their power, as the majority, thus to amend the question, and forced the opponents to debate it thus hampered, or withdraw it; and even the latter could not be done without leave of the House, that is, of the majority, who probably would not have granted that permission, that they might give a negative to the question thus loaded, instead of rejecting Sir W. Meredith's plain question, which it would have been more unpopular to do' (ii. 40). The amendment was prefixed to the question by a vote of 224 to

I wish Sir W. Pynsent had lived longer, and I think his memory would have been as respected by his having chosen my brother for his heir. We know his principles and may be allowed to be partial to his character and virtues.

I can tell you no news but about the parliament of Brittany,[9] and I think you have had enough of your own not to wish for a long history of that sort. I have endeavoured to give my brother so abstracted a state of it that I fear it will hardly be intelligible, but if he requires a longer I will give it him though my time is much employed here.

G. Selwyn is still at Paris and I think likely to be here. He waits for and upon Lord March, who does not seem disposed to leave it. Mr Selwyn told me yesterday he began to fear the consequences of his absence as he should be very sorry to offend the King,[10] but I think without his Lordship he cannot return, and must necessarily run every risk.

The English play here a good deal, but it is chiefly amongst themselves and in a particular society, so that no great harm is likely to arise from it.

You will be surprised when you come to Paris to hear how well Lady Hertford talks French. It is not only in England that they fight duels; Lady Hertford, Mr Hume and myself were melancholy eyewitnesses to one last week between two French soldiers in which we saw one killed before our window as we sat at dinner.

I remain, dear Horry, with the best compliments of the family,

Very sincerely and affectionately yours,

HERTFORD

185, and then the question, so amended, passed in the negative (*Journals of the House of Commons*, loc. cit.).

9. The current phase of the long-simmering crisis between the parliament of Rennes and the central administration had begun 16 Oct. 1764 with the handing down by the Chambre des Vacations of an *arrêt* prohibiting the collection of a levy of two sols per livre authorized by a royal declaration of 21 Nov. 1763; after a series of measures and counter-measures, the King at the beginning of February ordered that a deputation from the parliament attend him at Versailles 20 Feb. to hear his intentions (Abbé Eugène Bossard, *Le Parlement de Bretagne et la royauté 1765–1769*, 1882, pp. 12–16; A. Le Moy, *Le Parlement de Bretagne et le pouvoir royal au xviiie siècle*, 1909, pp. 298–315; Marcel Marion, *La Bretagne et le duc d'Aiguillon 1753–1770*, 1898, pp. 260–319). See *post* 22 March, 5 Dec. 1765 for subsequent developments.

10. See *ante* 18 Jan. 1765, n. 5.

I could tell you a good story of an Irish gentleman here if it was not too indecent for a modest man to relate very circumstantially.[11] Mr Richards[12] is the name of the gentleman; the lady[13] is Italian, a woman of fashion and said to be very homely. To go from the Prince of Conti's she imprudently accepted a place in his coach. He did not lose an instant in endeavouring to improve the opportunity. He drew upon her before the coach was out of the yard. She defended herself by saying there were then strong reasons against it, to get rid of him; but that was not sufficient for Irish ardour. He was determined as he said to pass *outre,* upon which she was reduced to cry out for protection, and the story as you may imagine is well told amongst the ladies who can relate decently.

I have been soliciting to obtain for a person of my acquaintance here the last papers which d'Éon has published,[14] by which I suppose is meant all that he has published since his first large work;[15] what it is I do not know. Be so good to inform me what they are and to obtain them for me if it is easy. Pray who is the Chevalier Stapleton[16] that is minister from some German court in London?

11. HW describes Hertford to Montagu, 16 May 1759, as 'a little of the prude' (MONTAGU i. 235).

12. Presumably the Mr Richards mentioned in HW's 'Paris Journals' for Sept. 1765, DU DEFFAND v. 261–3. Known as 'the Beau Richard,' he subsequently kept up his acquaintance with Hertford (see *post* 20 Jan. 1766, ca 20 Aug. 1767, 8 Sept. 1775 *bis,* 25 Sept. 1775), and was presumably the Fitzherbert Richards (?b. ca 1729) who succeeded the Hon. Robert Seymour Conway as M.P. for Lisburn borough, county Antrim, Ireland, in 1776 ([Great Britain, Parliament, House of Commons], *Members of Parliament,* 1878, pt ii. 668, 673; see also *Alumni Dublinenses,* ed. G. D. Burtchaell and T. U. Sadleir, Dublin, 1935, p. 700; J. H. Jesse, *George Selwyn and his Contemporaries,* 1882, i. 410; Hist. MSS Comm., 15th Report, App. pt vi, *Carlisle MSS,* 1897, p. 294 *et passim*).

13. Not identified.

14. Various writings by d'Éon were collected in *Pièces relatives aux lettres, mémoires, et négociations particulières du chevalier d'Éon,* 1764 (Yale Cat.), and the *London Chronicle* 11–14 Aug. 1764, xvi. 147–8, printed four letters allegedly by d'Éon written to Mansfield, Bute, Temple, and Pitt, which had been 'handed about at some of the coffee-houses in town, under the title of *Nouvelles Lettres du Chevalier d'Éon.*' See also MANN vi. 272 and n. 3 for a possible collaboration by d'Éon.

15. Presumably Hertford means d'Éon's *Lettres, mémoires, et négociations particulières (ante* 27 March 1764), though d'Éon had previously published an *Essai historique sur les différentes situations de la France par rapport aux finances sous le règne de Louis XIV et la régence du duc d'Orléans* (one volume, 1753), and *Mémoires pour servir à l'histoire générale des finances* (two volumes, 1758) (Yale Cat.; BM Cat.; Bibl. Nat. Cat.).

16. A Chevalier de Stapleton is listed as minister plenipotentiary from Württemberg in the *Court and City Register,* 1765, p. 109; see also *Court and City Calendar,* 1766, p. 122. He has not been further identified.

To Hertford, Tuesday 12 February 1765

Printed from *Works* ix. 188–93.

Arlington Street, Feb. 12th 1765.

A GREAT many letters pass between us, my dear Lord, but I think they are almost all of my writing. I have not heard from you this age. I sent you two packets together by Mr Freeman,[1] with an account of our chief debates. Since the long day,[2] I have been much out of order with a cold and cough, that turned to a fever:[3] I am now taking James's powder, not without apprehensions of the gout, which it gave me two or three years ago.[4]

There has been nothing of note in Parliament but one slight day on the American taxes,[5] which, Charles Townshend supporting,[6] received a pretty heavy thump from Barré,[7] who is the present Pitt, and the dread of all the vociferous Norths and Rigbys, on whose lungs depended so much of Mr Grenville's power. Do you never hear them to Paris?

The operations of the Opposition are suspended in compliment

1. Containing HW's letter of 27 Jan. 1765, and presumably also a missing letter of ca 30 Jan. 1765 (see *ante* 9 Feb. 1765, n. 4).

2. 29 Jan. (ibid.).

3. HW wrote to Montagu, 19 Feb. 1765: 'I have been dying of the worst and longest cold I ever had in my days, and have been blooded and taken James's powders to no purpose' (MONTAGU ii. 147). See *post* 9, 26 March 1765.

4. In 1762; see *ante* 15 March 1762, MONTAGU ii. 29.

5. 6 Feb., when Grenville introduced the American Stamp Bill (*Journals of the House of Commons* xxx. 90; *Mem. Geo. III* ii. 49; Jared Ingersoll to Thomas Fitch, 11 Feb., *Fitch Papers*, ed. A. C. Bates, Hartford, Conn., 1918–20, ii. 321 [*Collections of the Connecticut Historical Society*, Vols. XVII, XVIII]). The 55 resolutions which formed the basis of the bill are printed *Journals of the House of Commons* xxx. 98–101. It was enacted as 5 Geo. III c. 12 on 22 March (ibid. xxx. 293; Owen Ruffhead, *Statutes at Large*, 1763–1800, x. 18–31).

6. James Harris in his MS 'Debates' described Townshend's speech as 'lively and eloquent' (Sir Lewis Namier and John Brooke, *Charles Townshend*, 1964, p. 129). Townshend concluded 'with the following or like words:—And now will these Americans, children planted by our care, nourished up by our indulgence until they are grown to a degree of strength and opulence, and protected by our arms, will they grudge to contribute their mite to relieve us from the heavy weight of that burden which we lie under?' (Ingersoll to Fitch 11 Feb., op. cit. ii. 322).

7. Barré's oft-quoted rejoinder—'They planted by your care? No! your oppressions planted them in America,' etc. is given at length in Ingersoll's letter, ibid. 322–3. Ingersoll goes on to say that 'these sentiments were thrown out so entirely without premeditation, so forceably and so firmly, and the breaking off so beautifully abrupt, that the whole House sat awhile as amazed, intently looking and without answering a word' (ibid. 323).

to Mr Pitt,[8] who has declared himself so warmly for the question on the dismission of officers, that that motion waits for his recovery.[9] A call of the House is appointed for next Wednesday,[10] but as he has had a relapse, the motion will probably be deferred. I should be very glad if it was to be dropped entirely for this session,[11] but the young men are warm and not easily bridled.

If it was not too long to transcribe, I would send you an entertaining petition of the periwig-makers to the King, in which they complain that men will wear their own hair.[12] Should one almost wonder if carpenters were to remonstrate, that since the Peace their trade decays, and that there is no demand for wooden legs?[13] Apropos, my Lady Hertford's friend, Lady Harriot Vernon, has quarrelled with me for smiling at the enormous headgear of her daughter, Lady Grosvenor.[14] She came one night to Northumberland House with

8. Who was suffering from the gout (*ante* 20 Jan. 1765).

9. This is what HW wanted the ministry and the public at large to believe. However, in *Mem. Geo. III* he reveals that Pitt, still obstinately aloof from the Opposition, was by no means so warm for the question as he would have Hertford believe here—Pitt 'feared too many negatives on that question would authorise the Court to dismiss officers' (ii. 48). Pitt's luke-warmness on the question underscored HW's own reservations; consequently, HW advised Lord John Cavendish that he delay the motion and 'give out that it was in compliment to Mr Pitt, which would do credit to our cause,' while his primary purpose in advising the delay was ultimately to avoid the question altogether (ibid.; see n. 11 below). Later on Pitt was even less eager for the question, which was dropped; see *Mem. Geo. III* ii. 61 and *post* 18 April 1765.

10. 20 Feb.

11. The various objections of HW and others to the question are summarized in *Mem. Geo. III* ii. 47. Conway wrote to Hertford 31 Jan.: 'There is so much fear and caution and indeed I think very poor timidity in so many quarters, that a vast number of those who think the . . . [dismission of officers] wrong are afraid to take any manly part in declaring so for fear of future consequences which goes so far that I now question if the thing will

be moved at all. *Personally* I am much better pleased than if it was; *politically* I think it shameful' (MS now WSL). HW wrote in *Mem. Geo. III*, loc. cit., that 'Conway himself, aware that he should be deserted by his brethren, the officers, was by no means eager for bringing on the question'; the officers 'were . . . little desirous of seeing a topic agitated, which would have obliged them to approve the practice, or exposed them to the resentment of the Crown.'

12. 'Monday 11 [Feb.] . . . A petition of the master peruke-makers was presented to his Majesty, setting forth the distresses of themselves, and an incredible number of others dependent upon them from the almost universal decline of the trade, occasioned by the present mode of men in all stations wearing their own hair' (GM 1765, xxxv. 95). The petition is printed in the *London Chronicle* 12–14 Feb., xvii. 154.

13. 'In ridicule of the barbers, a petition from the company of body carpenters, as they are called, was ludicrously framed, imploring his Majesty to wear a wooden leg himself, and to enjoin his servants to appear in the royal presence with the same badge of honour, etc.' (GM loc. cit.). Croker suggests that 'this *jeu d'esprit* was from the pen of Mr Walpole' (*Works* ix. 189); see Hazen, *Bibl. of HW* 178.

14. Henrietta Vernon (d. 1828), m. 1

such display of friz, that it literally spread beyond her shoulders. I happened to say it looked as if her parents had stinted her in hair before marriage, and that she was determined to indulge her fancy now. This, among ten thousand things said by all the world, was reported to Lady Harriot, and has occasioned my disgrace. As she never found fault with anybody herself, I excuse her! You will be less surprised to hear that the Duchess of Queensberry has not yet done dressing herself marvellously: she was at Court on Sunday in a gown and petticoat of red flannel. The same day the Guerchys made a dinner for her, and invited Lord and Lady Hyde,[15] the Forbeses,[16] and her other particular friends: in the morning she sent word she was to go out of town, but as soon as dinner was over, arrived at Madame de Guerchy's, and said she had been at Court.

Poor Madame de Seillern, the imperial ambassadress, has lost her only daughter[17] and favourite child, a young widow of twenty-two, whom she was expecting from Vienna. The news came but this day sennight, and the Ambassador, who is as brutal as she is gentle and amiable, has insisted on her having company at dinner today, and her assembly as usual.

The town says that Lord and Lady Abergavenny[18] are parted, and that he has not been much milder than Monsieur de Seillern on the chapter of a mistress he has taken.[19] I don't know the truth of this;

(1764) Richard Grosvenor, cr. (1761) Bn Grosvenor and (1784) E. Grosvenor (separated 1770); m. 2 (1802) Lt-Gen. George Porter (after 1819, de Hochepied), Baron de Hochepied of Hungary.

15. Thomas Villiers (1709–86), cr. (1756) Bn Hyde of Hindon and (1776) E. of Clarendon, n.c., m. (1752) Lady Charlotte Capel (afterwards Hyde) (1721–90).

16. Adm. the Hon. John Forbes (1714–96), m. (1758) Lady Mary Capel or Capell (1722–82) (Collins, *Peerage*, 1812, iii. 484; GM 1782, lii. 206). Lady Hyde and Lady Mary Forbes were sisters, and the Duchess's nieces.

17. Maria Anna von Seilern (1743–19 Jan. 1765), m. (1761) Raimund, Graf von Vilana Perlas (ca 1732–64) (Constant von Wurzbach, *Biographisches Lexikon des Kaiserthums Oesterreich*, Vienna, 1856–91, xxxiv. genealogical table facing p. 20; *Genealog. hist. Nachrichten*, 1765–6, 1766–7, 3d ser. iv. 694, v. 174). 'On Sunday [3 Feb.] Count de Seilern, the imperial am-

bassador, received dispatches from his Court, together with an account of the death of his daughter, a young lady but lately married' (*London Chronicle* 2–5 Feb., xvii. 126, *sub* 5 Feb.).

18. George Nevill (1727–85), 17th Bn Abergavenny, cr. (1784) E. of Abergavenny, m. (1753) Henrietta Pelham (1730–68), widow of the Hon. Richard Temple (*ante* 14 July 1761, n. 22).

19. 'He has been making love to my lady's maid, I believe, and her Ladyship is gone out of town sulky, but I do not find they are parted' (Richard Rigby to Selwyn, 12 March, J. H. Jesse, *George Selwyn and his Contemporaries*, 1882, i. 365). 'What say you to your friend Abergavenny? Did you think those turtles, that were always on the same perch, would have ever fought? I think he might have made love to his nursery-maid anywhere else, and his wife need not have run away from him to have told the whole town of it. In short they have both acted like a

but his Lordship's heart, I believe, is more inflammable than tender.

Lady Sophia Thomas[20] has begged me to trouble you with a small commission. It is to send me for her twelve little bottles of *le Baume de Vie, composé par le Sieur Lievre, apothicaire distillateur du Roi*.[21] If George Selwyn or Lord March are not set out, they would bring it with pleasure, especially as she lives at the Duke of Queensberry's.[22]

We have not a new book, play, intrigue, marriage, elopement, or quarrel; in short, we are very dull. For politics, unless the ministers wantonly thrust their hands into some fire, I think there will not even be a smoke. I am glad of it, for my heart is set on my journey to Paris, and I hate everything that stops me. Lord Byron's foolish trial is likely to protract the session a little;[23] but unless there is any particular business, I shall not stay for a puppet-show. Indeed, I can defend my staying here by nothing but my ties to your brother. My health, I am sure, would be better in another climate in winter. Long days in the House kill me, and weary me into the bargain. The individuals of each party are alike indifferent to me; nor can I at this time of day grow to love men whom I have laughed at all my lifetime —no, I cannot alter;—Charles Yorke, or a Charles Townshend are alike to me, whether ministers or patriots. Men do not change in my eyes, because they quit a black livery for a white one. When one has seen the whole scene shifted round and round so often, one only smiles, whoever is the present Polonius or the grave-digger, whether they jeer the Prince, or flatter his frenzy.

Thursday night, 14th.

The new assembly-room at Almack's was opened the night before last, and they say is very magnificent, but it was empty;[24] half the

couple of fools' (Gilly Williams to Selwyn, March, ibid. i. 368–9). A later mistress to Abergavenny was a 'Mrs P——,' mentioned in *Town and Country Magazine*, 1774, vi. 457–9.

20. Lady Sophia Keppel (1711–73), m. Gen. John Thomas (*ante* 6 Oct. 1748).

21. 'A new, excellent, and efficacious stomachic medicine, first discovered by Mr Le Lievre, the King's apothecary at Paris' (advertisement in *Lloyd's Evening Post*, 23–5 Oct. 1765, xvii. 403). It was later marketed in England (ibid.).

22. March was the Duke's cousin and heir. See *post* 20 Feb., 22 March 1765.

23. For Byron's trial, see *post* 18 April 1765.

24. 'Last night [12 Feb.] the grand assembly room, which has for some time been building for the nobility and gentry, adjoining to Almack's in Pall Mall, was opened for the first time, when a great number of nobility were present' (*Daily Adv.* 13 Feb.). 'There is now opened at Almack's, in three very elegant new-built rooms, a ten guinea subscription, for

town is ill with colds, and many were afraid to go, as the house is scarcely built yet. Almack[25] advertised that it was built with hot bricks and boiling water—think what a rage there must be for public places, if this notice, instead of terrifying, could draw anybody thither. They tell me the ceilings were dropping with wet—but can you believe me, when I assure you the Duke of Cumberland was there?—Nay, had had a levee in the morning, and went to the opera[26] before the assembly! There is a vast flight of steps, and he was forced to rest two or three times. If he dies of it,—and how should he not?— it will sound very silly when Hercules or Theseus ask him what he died of, to reply, 'I caught my death on a damp staircase at a new club-room.'

Williams,[27] the reprinter of the *North Briton*, stood in the pillory today in Palace Yard. He went in a hackney-coach, the number of which was 45. The mob erected a gallows opposite to him, on which they hung a boot with a bonnet of straw. Then a collection was made for Williams, which amounted to near £200.[28] In short, every public

which you have a ball and supper once a week for twelve weeks. You may imagine, by the sum, the company is chosen' (Gilly Williams to Selwyn, 22 Feb., Jesse, op. cit. i. 360). 'Our female Almack's flourishes beyond description. If you had such a thing at Paris, you would fill half a quire of flourished paper with the description of it. Almack's Scotch face, in a bagwig, waiting at supper, would divert you, as would his lady in a sack, making tea and curtseying to the duchesses' (idem to idem, March, ibid. i. 369). See H. B. Wheatley and Peter Cunningham, *London Past and Present*, 1891, i. 37–8.

25. William Almack (d. 1781) (GM 1781, li. 46).

26. For a performance of *Ezio* (*London Stage* Pt IV, ii. 1098; *ante* 25 Nov. 1764).

27. John Williams (d. after 1774) (H. R. Plomer *et al., Dictionary of the Printers and Booksellers . . . from 1726 to 1775*, Oxford, 1932, pp. 264–5).

28. 'Yesterday morning [14 Feb.] Mr Williams, bookseller in Fleet Street, was brought from the King's Bench prison, to stand in the pillory in New Palace Yard, Westminster, for republishing the *North Briton*, No. 45, in volumes. The coach which carried him there was No. 45. A few minutes after twelve he mounted,

amidst the repeated acclamations of a prodigious concourse of people. Opposite to the pillory were erected four ladders with cords running from each other, on which were hung a jack boot, an axe, and a Scotch bonnet. The latter, after remaining there some time, was burnt, and the top of the boot chopped off. During his standing also, a purple purse, ornamented with ribbons of an orange colour, was produced by a gentleman, who began a collection in favour of the culprit, by putting a guinea into it himself, after which the purse being carried round, many contributed, to the amount in the whole, as supposed, of about 200 guineas. Mr Williams, at going into pillory, and getting out, bowed to the spectators. He held a sprig of laurel in his hand all the time' (*London Chronicle* 14–16 Feb., xvii. 161). See *ante* 27 Aug. 1764, n. 30, for Williams' trial. He had been sentenced 23 Jan. 'to pay a fine of £100, six months imprisonment in the King's Bench, to stand once on the pillory in old Palace Yard, and to give security in the sum of £1000 for his good behaviour for seven years' (*London Chronicle* 22–4 Jan., xvii. 85). The jack-boot was hung as a pun on the Christian name and title of Lord Bute (John Stuart, Earl of Bute), while the event informs the Administration how thoroughly they are detested, and that they have not a friend whom they do not buy. Who can wonder, when every man of virtue is proscribed, and they have neither parts nor characters to impose even upon the mob! Think to what a government is sunk, when a secretary of state is called in Parliament to his face, *the most profligate sad dog in the kingdom,* and not a man can open his lips in his defence.[29] Sure power must have some strange unknown charm, when it can compensate for such contempt! I see many who triumph in these bitter pills which the ministry are so often forced to swallow; I own I do not; it is more mortifying to me to reflect how great and respectable we were three years ago, than satisfactory to see those insulted who have brought such shame upon us. 'Tis poor amends to national honour to know, that if a printer is set in the pillory, his country wishes it was my Lord This, or Mr That. They will be gathered to the Oxfords, and Bolingbrokes, and ignominious of former days;[30] but the wound they have inflicted is perhaps indelible. That goes to *my* heart, who had felt all the Roman pride of being one of the first nation upon earth! —Good night!—I will go to bed, and dream of Kings drawn in triumph; and then I will go to Paris, and dream I am proconsul there: pray, take care not to let me be wakened with an account of an invasion having taken place from Dunkirk!

Yours ever,

H. W.

From HERTFORD, Wednesday 20 February 1765

Printed for the first time from a photostat of BM Add. MSS 23218, ff. 189–90.

Paris, February 20th 1765.

Dear Horry,

THE post or the secretary's office have done me great injustice if you have been long without hearing from me. I have wrote constantly and am surprised you have not received my letters. The

purple purse ornamented with orange ribbons was meant to suggest the Glorious Revolution, which had ousted the Stuarts.

29. See MANN vi. 283–4; Barré applied the expression to Sandwich in the debate of 29 Jan.

30. Robert Harley, afterwards 1st E. of Oxford and Mortimer, had dismissed Sir

least I can do is to acknowledge your indulgence to me in writing so often, and it is not my fault if I am not so entertaining in my answers as I could wish.

I am very sorry you are out of order and wish you to come to Paris—the air of this place can do wonders—when the political system in which friendship has involved you will permit it. I will in the meantime execute the commission you have given me for Lady Sophia Thomas by the first opportunity I can take. I do not think it will be either by Lord March or Mr Selwyn, for they seem so much settled at Paris that you may possibly find them here.

I have received the genteelest and most obliging letter from Sir Horace Mann upon the acquaintance he has made with my son at Florence.[1] He did not give me time to finish the acknowledgments I was preparing for him at my son's desire, before he added this mark of his particular friendship and attention for me to all the civilities he had shown Conway.[2] I beg you will assure him how much I feel obliged. I have not said half so much as I could wish.

The masked balls ended last night with the carnival. Lady Ecklin[3] whom perhaps you did not suppose at Paris was near bringing a countryman of mine into a difficulty at it, but he has extricated himself with great good sense and propriety. Lord Anglesea[4] was walking in the ball-room without a mask when he was desired by a person in mask to put his on and to give her assistance to go through the crowd into another room. The masked person was dressed in man's clothes unknown to his Lordship, but proved to be Lady Ecklin. In passing

Robert Walpole in Jan. 1711 for opposing his administration while Henry St John, afterwards 1st Vct Bolingbroke, had been the main instigator of the attack on Sir Robert which resulted in his being expelled from the House and sent to the Tower in Jan. 1712 for alleged corrupt practices as secretary at war; see J. H. Plumb, *Sir Robert Walpole: The Making of a Statesman*, Boston, 1956, pp. 165, 178–81.

———

1. 'As Lady Hertford has lately honoured me with a most obliging note in your Lordship['s] as well as her own name, I with eagerness seize the opportunity to express my thanks to both for that honour and for the opportunity with which by that means she has been pleased

to furnish me of being in any degree useful to my Lord Beauchamp, the most accomplished young nobleman who has passed here for many years' (Mann to Hertford, 1 Feb., S.P. 105/294, f. 118; see also Mann to HW, 9 Feb. 1765, MANN vi. 282).

2. Lord and Lady Hertford called Beauchamp familiarly 'Con' or 'Conway'; see *post* 10 Oct. 1765.

3. Elizabeth Bellingham (ca 1711–83), m. (1725) Sir Robert Echlin, 2d Bt (GEC, *Baronetage* v. 343).

4. Arthur Annesley (1744–1816), 8th Vct Valentia, 1761, cr. (1793) E. of Mountnorris; titular E. of Anglesey. His claim to the latter earldom was disallowed in 1771.

through the crowd a young gentleman[5] who is nearly related to Madame de Mirepoix is[6] unluckily pushed against her so violently that Lady Ecklin felt it sensibly and with so much resentment that she struck him two blows, upon which he attacks the mask and is informed it is a woman. The honorary laws of this country, you must be informed, for I believe nobody would guess it without being told, make a man under any circumstance strictly answerable for the behaviour of a lady with whom he is in company, and Lord Anglesea might if he chose it have very regularly cut this young gentleman's throat; but upon his saying with great propriety and at the same time with very becoming spirit that he was far from intending any insult by the blows given by Lady Ecklin, her Ladyship will not have the credit of having any blood spilt for her upon this occasion.

We have a new tragedy here with which the town is charmed. The subject is the siege of Calais,[7] a very heroic piece; when it is printed I will send it to you.[8] Though my letter is in a sort of cipher,[9] I will say nothing political from this country that you may receive it.

I remain, dear Horry,

Very affectionately yours,

HERTFORD

To HERTFORD, ca Tuesday 5 March 1765

Missing. 'Three weeks are a great while, my dear Lord, for me to have been without writing to you' (HW to Hertford, *post* 26 March 1765).

---

5. Not identified.

6. *Sic* in MS.

7. *Le Siège de Calais,* by Pierre-Laurent Buirette de Belloy (1727–75); it dealt with the siege by Edward III in 1347 (MONTAGU ii. 150, n. 3, 4; *Dictionnaire de biographie française,* 1933– , vii. 641–2). '*13 février.* Enfin a paru aujourd'hui *Le Siège de Calais,* cette tragédie tant annoncée. La fureur avait rédoublé, et l'on a peu vu de foule aussi considérable' (Louis Petit de Bachaumont, *Mémoires secrets,* 1780–9, ii. 156). The play's singular success was due

more to its patriotic fervour than to its artistic merit: '*19 février* . . . Le fanatisme gagne au point que les connoisseurs n'osent plus dire leur avis. On est réputé mauvais patriote pour oser élever la voix' (ibid. ii. 158). 'On convient généralement qu'elle est barbarement écrite' (ibid. ii. 171). See Erich Zimmerman, *Pierre-Laurent Buirette de Belloy, sein Leben und seine Tragödien,* Leipzig, 1911, pp. 71–102.

8. See *post* 22 March 1765.

9. Hertford's handwriting is difficult to read.

From HERTFORD, Saturday 9 March 1765

Printed for the first time from a photostat of BM Add. MSS 23218, ff. 191–3. *Memoranda* (very faint, by HW, for his reply to Hertford, *post* 26 March 1765):

Baume de Vie
Fréron[1]
Garrick
L [?]
Ly [?]
Gevaudan

Paris, March 9th 1765.

Dear Horry,

I AM extremely sorry you have been and still continue out of order.[2] You neglect the true remedy which is a better climate. The air of Paris can do wonders upon a person who is sick of the smoke of London, but I must wait with patience till the Parliament rises; I see you will not leave England sooner.

George Selwyn talks of returning to you next week; I do not know whether he can drag Lord March so soon away.[3] They seem much divided in inclination, and hitherto my Lord's has prevailed. They cannot part. There will go from hence a very pretty sort of man with them; the Comte de Schualoff.[4] He is a Russian and was the favourite of the late Empress; since her death he has lived chiefly out of his own country, whether for private reasons or from choice I cannot tell.[5] He talks of returning there again.

The English gentlemen supped with us last night; I do not mean all, but the cream of our young men at Paris. The company was pretty large and it was necessary to have faro for Madame de

1. Élie-Catherine Fréron (1718–76), critic (OSSORY i. 40, n. 26). See below, nn. 17, 18.

2. Hertford is presumably replying to a missing letter of ca 5 March 1765. HW had gone to SH 'to try change of air' for his cold (HW to Cole, 28 Feb. 1765, COLE i. 85). See *post* 26 March 1765.

3. HW announced their return *post* 7 April 1765.

4. Count Ivan Ivanovitch Shuvalov (1727–97), favourite of the Empress Elizabeth (MANN vi. 59, n. 56).

5. Catherine II wrote of him in 1762 as 'le plus bas et le plus lâche des hommes' (ibid.), and in 1763 'suggested' that he go abroad; he did not return to Russia until 1777 (*Bol'shaia sovetskaia entsiklopediia*, Moscow, 1949–58, Vol. XLVIII, ed. Vvedenskiĭ, p. 221; Shuvalov to Mme du Deffand, 10 Oct. 1777, DU DEFFAND vi. 205; see also *Dispatches and Correspondence of . . . Earl of Buckinghamshire*, ed. A. D'Arcy Collyer, 1900–2, ii. 37–8; *Sbornik imperatorskago russkago istoricheskago obshchestva*, 1885, xlvi. 448).

Mirepoix and the Duchess of Praslin. Do not add to Lord Holland's disorder[6] by telling him his son[7] lost five hundred louis; perhaps he may know or love me so little as to think I had a share in the bank.[8] The Comtesse d'Egmont and Madame de Mirepoix took their leave of Lady Hertford the next morning at eleven o'clock. Young Fox is a very good lad without guile or design, and he will probably, I think, spend money[9] as fast as his father has collected it.[10] Lord Ossory[11] likewise loves play much, but is more prudent. They will be good recruits for Almack's.

Garrick stays with us some time longer. I do not think he seems impatient to adventure himself in England; his health is indifferent. He has no mind[12] to return upon the theatre and he may be called for when he is in London.[13] He is much admired at Paris, even by those who do not know him; it is a fashion to think him excellent. He is to dine here next week with some French ladies of great distinction who have solicited this favour. Mademoiselle Clairon[14] will likewise be invited, whom Garrick admires with great reason. I do not know that he has any other favourite at the French comedy except Préville,[15] a very celebrated comedian here, whom Garrick has endeavoured to improve by his lessons and example. They met

6. 'Lord Holland has been very near death for these three days, with his old suffocation' (Gilly Williams to Selwyn, 22 Feb., J. H. Jesse, *George Selwyn and his Contemporaries*, 1882, i. 359). 'He is extremely weak and feeble in his limbs, but looks better, and breathes easier, than before his last plunge' (idem to idem, 19 March, ibid. i. 372).

7. Stephen Fox. His gambling at this time got him into difficulties with a banking firm at Paris; see Lord Ilchester, *Henry Fox, First Lord Holland*, 1920, ii. 284.

8. For Holland's antipathy towards Hertford, see *ante* 28 July 1764. However, Hertford had a general reputation for avarice; see *ante* 11 Nov. 1763, n. 1.

9. By 1769 Fox had accrued debts of over £20,000, and by 1773, of over £100,000 (Namier and Brooke ii. 466).

10. Holland had made a large fortune as paymaster.

11. John Fitzpatrick (1745–1818), 2d E. of Upper Ossory, 1758, m. (1769) Anne

Liddell, formerly Duchess of Grafton, HW's correspondent.

12. 'Mind' is written over 'plan' in the MS.

13. Garrick wrote to George Colman, 10 March: 'Do the town in general *really* wish to see me on the stage? Or are they (which I rather think the truth) as cool about it as their humble servant?—I have no maw for it at all . . . . the physicians here . . . advise me, to a man, against appearing again' (Garrick, *Letters,* ed. D. M. Little and G. M. Kahrl, Cambridge, Mass., 1963, ii. 449).

14. Claire-Joseph Léris (1723–1803), called Mlle Clairon, of the Comédie-Française 1743–66 (*Dictionnaire de biographie française*, 1933– , viii. 1342–3; *Enciclopedia dello spettacolo*, Rome, 1954–62, iii. 921–4). This note corrects the earlier identifying notes in DU DEFFAND, MONTAGU, and GRAY.

15. Pierre-Louis Dubus or Du Bus (1721–99), called Préville, of the Comédie-Française 1753–86 (*Enciclopedia dello spettacolo* viii. 456–7).

the other day upon a public walk here, and in conversing upon their profession Garrick told Préville he acted the drunken man well, but he would act it still better if he did it more nobly, and that his *jambes n'étaient pas assez enivrés.* To persuade him perfectly he showed him how to act the part by playing it himself; the other was tempted to improve upon so good a model, and they both performed so naturally that they assembled a crowd around them to see what would be the end of the drunken frolic.[16]

Mademoiselle Clairon has threatened to quit the stage but is again reconciled to it; her reason was that she was ill-used in a sort of monthly magazine that comes out here.[17] She even complained to the Duke de Choiseuil, who told her that if she would compare her situation with his, she could be at no loss for his opinion that it was her fate, though this instance was indeed an exception, to be praised and applauded every day; that his lot was widely different: that he was as constantly hissed and abused and yet he continued to act.[18]

16. A rather different account of this famous 'frolic,' recalled to Préville by Garrick in a letter of 7 Jan. 1775 (Garrick, op. cit. iii. 978), is given in Grimm, *Correspondance,* ed. Tourneux, 1877–82, vi. 320, *sub* 'juillet 1765': 'Un jour, en revenant avec Préville, à cheval, du bois de Boulogne, il lui dit: "Je m'en vais faire l'homme ivre; faites-en autant." Ils traversèrent ainsi le village de Passy, sans dire un mot, et, en un clin d'œil, tout le village fut assemblé pour les voir passer. Les jeunes gens se moquèrent d'eux, les femmes crièrent de peur de les voir tomber de cheval, les vieillards haussèrent les épaules et en eurent pitié, ou, suivant leur humeur, pouffèrent de rire. En sortant du village, Préville dit à Garrick: "Ai-je bien fait, mon maître?— Bien, fort bien, en vérité, lui dit Garrick; mais vous n'étiez pas ivre des jambes." '

17. The critic Fréron (n. 1 above), in Lettre V (17 Jan.) of his *Année littéraire* for 1765, had attacked the loose morals of actresses, asserting that 'c'est en vain qu'après avoir acquis une honteuse célébrité par le vice, on affecte un maintien grave et réservé. Cette honnêteté tardive et fausse ne sert qu'à former un contraste révoltant avec l'histoire connue d'une jeunesse infâme' (i. 120). His words were interpreted as being directed against Mlle

Clairon, the favourite actress of Voltaire and the philosophes, of whom Fréron was the arch-enemy: 'Le journaliste, sans la nommer, la peint avec des couleurs si fortes et si caracterisées, qu'on ne peut la méconnaître, pour peu qu'on soit au fait de ses anecdotes et de sa célébrité' (Louis Petit de Bachaumont, *Mémoires secrets,* 1780–9, ii. 146, *sub* 24 Jan. 1765). Consequently, Mlle Clairon threatened to quit the stage if she were not given satisfaction, and an order was solicited from the King for Fréron's incarceration in the For l'Évêque. It was delayed by Fréron's being confined with the gout (ibid. ii. 157, *sub* 14 Feb.). Later the Queen herself intervened in his behalf, and Mlle Clairon carried her complaint to the Duc de Choiseul (ibid. ii. 161, *sub* 21 Feb.). See next note.

18. 'Mademoiselle, nous sommes, vous et moi, chacun sur un théâtre; mais avec la différence que vous choississez les rôles qui vous conviennent, et que vous êtes toujours sûre des applaudissements du public. Il n'y a que quelque gens de mauvais goût, comme ce malheureux Fréron, qui vous refusent leurs suffrages. Moi, au contraire, j'ai ma tâche souvent très désagréable; j'ai beau faire de mon mieux, on me critique, on me condamne, on me hue, on me bafoue et cependant je ne donne

I have seen the new piece, the *Siege of Calais,* which is excessively admired, but it did not quite answer my expectation; there is too great and too general an uniformity in every part of it.[19] We have likewise a little musical new piece taken from a chapter of *Tom Jones* and carries the name of the *Romance.*[20] It was condemned the first night, but is revived with great applause by the countenance and protection of the Duke of Nivernois.[21]

point ma démission. Immolons, vous et moi, nos ressentiments à la Patrie; et servons-la de notre mieux, chacun dans notre genre. D'ailleurs la Reine ayant fait grâce, vous pouvez, sans compromettre votre dignité, imiter la clémence de S. M.' (ibid.). Still not satisfied, Mlle Clairon persuaded the rest of the troupe of the Comédie-Française to threaten to quit with her if nothing were done (ibid. ii. 161–2). She was finally appeased by the argument that the giving of the order for Fréron's incarceration was satisfaction enough (C. S. Favart to the Comte de Durazzo, 5 March, in Favart, *Mémoires et correspondance littéraires, dramatiques et anecdotiques,* ed. A. P. C. Favart, 1808, ii. 220–1; see also Fréron to the Duc de Richelieu, 2 March, the Comte de St-Florentin to Richelieu, 9 March, and Richelieu to 'MM. les Comédiens français,' 10 March, in *Révue retrospective,* 1837, 2d ser. x. 143–5). The following month Mlle Clairon and several of her fellow *comédiens* were arrested for refusing to go on stage with an actor named Dubois; see *post* 29 April 1765.

19. 'Jamais je n'en ai vu de cette longueur; elle dura une heure de plus qu'une tragédie ordinaire. Des conversations sans fin, des descriptions épiques pleines d'enflure et de faiblesse, un bavardage continuel, les mêmes idées à tout instant fastidieusement répétées sous d'autres tournures, nulle véritable chaleur, nul pathétique, nulle trace des mœurs du siècle, pas un moment de terreur sur le sort de ces généreux citoyens: ah! Monsieur de Belloy! je crains que, malgré votre succès, malgré quelques beaux vers et quelques détails heureux, vous ne soyez un homme sans ressource' (Grimm, op. cit. vi. 201–2). HW wrote to Montagu, 5 April 1765: 'I have read *The Siege of Calais,* and dislike it extremely,

though there are fine lines, but the conduct is woeful' (Montagu ii. 150), and Conway wrote to Hertford, 13 April, 'I can't so much admire your famous *Siege of Calais,* and can attribute the astonishing success of it to nothing but that eternal repetition of superb sentiments of honour and valour and patriotism; and their superiority to the English; and commendations of their countrymen,' etc. (MS now wsl).

20. *Tom Jones, comédie lyrique en trois actes, imitée du roman anglais de M. Fielding,* by Antoine-Alexandre-Henri Poinsinet (1735–69), the music by François-André Danican (1726–95), called Philidor; it was 'représentée pour la première fois par les comédiens italiens ordinaires du roi, le 27 février 1765' (Yale Cat.; Selwyn 215, n. 32; Sir George Grove, *Dictionary of Music and Musicians,* 5th edn, ed. Blom, 1954–61, vi. 708; *Enciclopedia dello spettacolo* viii. 84). Critics praised the music, but condemned the libretto; see Bachaumont, op. cit. ii. 163, and Grimm op. cit. vi. 218–19.

21. 'Les Enfants de France, pour qui Poinsinet a fait un divertissement assez mauvais, ayant su sa disgrâce au théâtre italien, en ont été si touchés que les gentilshommes de la Chambre, pour faire leur cour, ont éxigé des comédiens de jouer *Tom Jones* une seconde fois. On a distribué beaucoup de billets *gratis,* et par une révolution assez extraordinaire, cette pièce, huée, bafouée la veille, hier [28 Feb.] est montée aux noues' (Bachaumont, loc. cit.). 'Mais le coup était porté, et ce pauvre *Tom Jones* n'a jamais pu se relever de son premier malheur' (Grimm, op. cit. vi. 219). It was revived the following year with great success, thanks to the revision of the libretto by Michel-Jean Sedaine (ibid. vi. 491; Bachaumont, op. cit. ii. 291). HW saw this revised version performed on 2

We are going to send you another Frenchman from hence, of whom I will beg you to take some notice. It is the Comte de Caraman,[22] who perhaps may carry this letter,[23] for he is going very soon. He married a relation of Madame de Mirepoix's. He is a very well-behaved man and has been learning English for this journey. If he is not one of the first families, he is as well received and upon as good a footing as any man in Paris. He lives extremely well here and has a good fortune to support it.

The Comte de Lillebonne,[24] a relation of Monsieur de Guerchy's, was likewise going, but I hear within these few days has put it off to visit a dying relation at Genoa.[25]

Lady Hertford and the family desire their best compliments. I remain, dear Horry,

Very sincerely and affectionately yours,

HERTFORD

From HERTFORD, Friday 22 March 1765

Printed for the first time from a photostat of BM Add. MSS 23218, ff. 194–5. Sent with Hertford's dispatches to Halifax of 20 and 22 March, received 27 March (S.P. 78/265, ff. 302, 303, 312, 316). There are three enclosures (see below), copies of Voltaire's letter to Buirette de Belloy and of Louis XV's two speeches to the parliament of Brittany.

Paris, March 22d 1765.

Dear Horry,

I HAVE not heard from you for an age, if I calculate upon the goodness of your correspondence, but I will not suffer myself to be spoiled and to abuse your favour; I will promise to be perfectly satisfied if I can hear you are well in health.

March 1766 and again on 12 Sept. 1767 ('Paris Journals,' DU DEFFAND v. 305, 319). See Carl Waldschmidt, *Die Dramatisierungen von Fielding's Tom Jones*, Wetzlar, 1906, pp. 29–46; Eric Blom, '"Tom Jones" on the French Stage,' in his *Stepchildren of Music*, [1925], pp. 45–54.

22. Victor-Maurice de Riquet (1727–1807), Comte de Caraman, m. (1750) Marie-Anne-Gabrielle-Josèphe-Françoise-Xavière d'Alsace-Hénin-Liétard (1728–

1810), niece of Madame de Mirepoix (DU DEFFAND *passim;* La Chenaye-Desbois i. 388, ii. 740–1).

23. See *post* 26 March 1765.

24. François-Henri d'Harcourt (1726–1804), Comte de Lillebonne; Duc d'Harcourt 1783; cousin of Madame de Guerchy (DU DEFFAND i. 42, n. 10; La Chenaye-Desbois x. 318–22).

25. He went the following year (*post* ca 6 March 1766).

I am going to send a messenger[1] to England sooner than I intended, and I am much hurried in preparing for him;[2] therefore you will excuse me for not saying more at present than that I mean to accompany this with the new play,[3] which you may wish to read, with a letter of Voltaire's to the author,[4] and the King of France['s] two speeches[5] to his parliament of Brittany upon their attending him at Versailles.[6]

G. Selwyn hopes to leave Paris in two or three days, but he is tied to a noble Lord who seems to want resolution, and he can answer for nothing where his friend governs. I remain, dear Horry,

Always most affectionately yours,

Hertford

[Enclosures]

Lettre de Voltaire à Monsieur du Belloy [6 March]

Je suis presque entièrement aveugle, Monsieur, mais j'ai encore des oreilles; et les cris de la renommée m'ont appris vos grands succès. J'ai un cœur qui s'y intéresse. Je joins mes acclamations à celles de tout Paris. Jouissez de votre bonheur et de votre mérite; il ne vous manque que d'être dénigré par Fréron, pour mettre le comble

1. Bullock (S.P. 78/265, ff. 303, 316).

2. 'Since I wrote the enclosed dispatch [of 20 March], I have received a certain, and complete account, of the state of the French colony at Cayenne [in Guiana]. I shall have the honour of communicating it to your Lordship, as it will be sufficient to remove every alarm which may come from that part of the world' (Hertford to Halifax, 22 March, ibid. ff. 302, 312). The English ministry had feared an invasion from French Guiana of the neighbouring English and Portuguese settlements (ibid. f. 313).

3. *Le Siège de Calais* (ante 20 Feb., 9 March 1765); it had been printed by 18 March (Emmanuel, Duc de Croÿ, *Journal inédit*, ed. Grouchy and Cottin, 1906–7, ii. 190). HW read it by 5 April (Montagu ii. 150).

4. Voltaire to Buirette de Belloy, 6 March, printed below; cf. Voltaire's *Correspondence*, ed. T. Besterman, Geneva,

1953–65, lvii. 171. Buirette de Belloy's reply, ca 12 March, is printed ibid. lvii. 187–8. Voltaire later wrote pejoratively of the play in his *Essai sur les mœurs et l'esprit des nations*, 1756–75 (*Œuvres complètes*, ed. Moland, 1877–85, xii. 21).

5. Printed below; cf. A. Le Moy, *Le Parlement de Bretagne et le pouvoir royal au xviiie siècle*, 1909, p. 318; *Mercure historique* 1765, clviii. 422–3.

6. The King had ordered a deputation to attend him 20 Feb. (ante 9 Feb. 1765, n. 9), but after the parliament asked for a delay, ordered the whole parliament to attend, which they did 18 March (Le Moy, op. cit. 315–18; Marcel Marion, *La Bretagne et le duc d'Aiguillon 1753–1770*, 1898, pp. 319–20; Abbé Eugène Bossard, *Le Parlement de Bretagne et la royauté 1765–1769*, 1882, pp. 16–18). The first of the King's two speeches was delivered that day, and the second 20 March. See *post* 5 Dec. 1765.

à votre gloire. Je vous embrasse sans cérémonies. Il n'en faut pas entre confrères.

Première Réponse du Roi au Parlement de Bretagne [18 March]

Vous avez violé ma confiance en révélant le secret que j'avais confié à trois de vos membres.

Vous avez renvoyé mes lettres patentes par la poste.

Vous avez eu la hardiesse de déchirer les affiches des arrêts de mon conseil.

Vous avez achevé de ruiner ma province de Bretagne par la cessation du service.

Jugez de ma bonté à les [the remonstrances of the parliament] bien recevoir.

Je vous ferai ma réponse mercredi.

Seconde Réponse du Roi au Parlement de Bretagne [20 March]

J'ai lu vos remonstrances. J'y ai trouvé une chaleur que je désapprouve; je défends qu'elles soient imprimées. On m'a rendu un compte exact de tout ce qui s'est passé à mon parlement de Bretagne; et j'ai vu tous les ordres qui y ont été envoyés de ma part.

Repartez sur le champ pour Rennes, et reprenez vos fonctions dans l'instant que vous y serez arrivés; votre prompte obéissance est le seul moyen de ramener ma bienveillance. Je ferai réponse aux autres articles de vos remonstrances quand vous aurez repris vos fonctions.

To HERTFORD, Tuesday 26 March 1765

Printed from *Works* ix. 194–8.

Arlington Street, March 26th 1765.

THREE weeks are a great while, my dear Lord, for me to have been without writing to you;[1] but besides that I have passed many days at Strawberry, to cure my cold (which it has done), there has nothing happened worth sending cross the sea. Politics have dozed, and common events been fast asleep. Of Guerchy's affair,[2]

1. HW's earlier letter is missing.
2. See *ante* 25 Nov. 1764. 'On Friday [1 March] a bill of indictment was found by the grand jury of Middlesex, at Hick's Hall, against a foreigner, for a conspiracy against the life of the Chevalier

you probably know more than I do;[3] it is now forgotten. I told him
I had absolute proof of his innocence, for I was sure, that if he had
offered money for assassination, the men who swear against him[4]
would have taken it.

The King has been very seriously ill, and in great danger.[5] I would
not alarm you, as there were hopes when he was at the worst. I doubt
he is not free yet from his complaint, as the humour fallen on his
breast still oppresses him.[6] They talk of his having a levee next week,[7]
but he has not appeared in public, and the bills are passed by commission;[8] but he rides out. The Royal Family have suffered like us
mortals; the Duke of Gloucester has had a fever, but I believe his
chief complaint is of a youthful kind. Prince Frederick is thought to
be in a deep consumption;[9] and for the Duke of Cumberland, next
post will probably certify you of his death, as he is relapsed, and there
are no hopes of him.[10] He fell into his lethargy again, and when they
waked him, he said he did not know whether he could call himself
obliged to them.

I dined two days ago at Monsieur de Guerchy's, with the Count de
Caraman, who brought me your letter.[11] He seems a very agreeable
man, and you may be sure, for your sake, and Madame de Mirepoix's,

d'Éon' (*London Chronicle* 2–5 March, xvii.
218); a translation of the bill is printed
in *Mémoires du Chevalier d'Éon*, ed. F.
Gaillardet, 1836, ii. 60–3. Guerchy re-
sponded by applying for a *nolle prosequi*,
which was disallowed by the Attorney-
General, Sir Fletcher Norton, at Lincoln's
Inn 30 April; however, the case was not
further prosecuted (ibid. ii. 63–7; J. B.
Telfer, *The Strange Career of the Chevalier d'Éon de Beaumont*, 1885, p. 181;
E. A. Vizetelly, *The True Story of the
Chevalier d'Éon*, 1895, pp. 204–10).

3. Conway wrote to Hertford 15 March
about the indictment against Guerchy (MS
now WSL).

4. Depositions were laid before the
grand jury by d'Éon, Pierre-Henri Treyssac de Vergy (*ante* 25 Nov. 1764), Jacques
Dupré, Richard Kirwan, Jacques Braillard,
and Louis Lapeyre (Vizetelly, op. cit. 204);
Vergy, Dupré, Kirwan, and Braillard witnessed the indictment (Gaillardet, op. cit.
ii. 62).

5. See HW to Mann 26 March 1765,
MANN vi. 288. This was sometimes considered to be the first major attack of the

King's 'madness,' which has recently been
diagnosed as acute intermittent porphy-
ria; see ibid. ix. 679, n. 2, and Ida Macal-
pine and Richard Hunter, *George III
and the Mad-Business*, 1969, pp. 177–91.

6. See MANN vi. 288, n. 2. 'I should
have sent for you today had I not been
forced to fresh discipline from some little
additional cough and pain in the breast'
(George III to Grenville, 22 March, *Grenville Papers* iii. 15).

7. See *post* 7 April 1765.

8. 22 March; the commission is dated
20 March (*Journals of the House of Commons* xxx. 293–4; *Journals of the House of
Lords* xxxi. 91–3).

9. He died 29 Dec., 'après une longue
maladie' (George III to Louis XV, 31 Dec.,
Hist. MSS Comm., *Bathurst MSS*, 1923, p.
690).

10. However, Knowles wrote, 27 March,
that the Duke was 'better' (to Newcastle, BM Add. MSS 32966, f. 113), and
Albemarle, 30 March, that he was 'upon
the whole much better' (to Newcastle,
ibid. f. 117); he did not die until 31 Oct.

11. *Ante* 9 March 1765.

no civilities in my power shall be wanting. I have not yet seen Schou-valoff,[12] about whom one has more curiosity—it is an opportunity of gratifying that passion which one can so seldom do in personages of his historic nature, especially remote foreigners. I wish M. de Cara-man had brought the *Siege of Calais,* which he tells me is printed, though your account has a little abated my impatience. They tell us the French comedians are to act at Calais this summer[13]—is it pos-sible they can be so absurd, or think us so absurd as to go thither, if we would not go further? I remember, at Rheims,[14] they believed that English ladies went to Calais to drink champagne—is this the suite of that belief? I was mightily pleased with the Duc de Choiseul's an-swer to the Clairon; but when I hear of the French admiration of Garrick, it takes off something of my wonder at the prodigious adora-tion of him at home. I never could conceive the marvellous merit of repeating the works of others in one's own language with propriety, however well delivered. Shakspeare is not more admired for writing his plays, than Garrick for acting them. I think him a very good and very various player—but several have pleased me more, though I al-low not in so many parts. Quin,[15] in Falstaffe, was as excellent as Gar-rick in Lear. Old Johnson[16] far more natural in everything he at-tempted. Mrs Porter[17] and your Dumesnil[18] surpassed him in pas-sionate tragedy; Cibber and O'Brien[19] were what Garrick could never reach, coxcombs, and men of fashion.[20] Mrs Clive is at least as per-fect in low comedy—and yet to me, Ranger[21] was the part that suited Garrick the best of all he ever performed. He was a poor Lothario,[22]

12. See *post* 7 April 1765.

13. A false rumour; see Louis Petit de Bachaumont, *Mémoires secrets,* 1780–9, ii. 184–239 *passim;* H. Carrington Lancaster, *The Comédie Française 1701–1774,* Phila-delphia, 1951, pp. 813–15 (*Transactions of the American Philosophical Society,* 2d Ser., Vol. XLI, Pt IV).

14. HW stayed at Rheims for three months in 1739 with Gray and Conway; see connecting note between letters of *ante* 24 March and ca 8 Nov. 1739.

15. James Quin (1693–1766) (*ante* 4 Sept. 1751, n. 8). See Ossory ii. 87, n. 10.

16. Benjamin Johnson (?1665–1742).

17. Mary Porter (d. 24 Feb. 1765) (GM 1765, xxxv. 146).

18. Marie-Françoise Marchand (1713–

1803), called Mlle Du Mesnil, of the Comédie-Française 1737–76 (GRAY ii. 145, n. 12; *Dictionnaire de biographie fran-çaise,* 1933– , xii. 174–5). This note corrects the identifying notes in DU DEFFAND, MONTAGU, and OSSORY.

19. William O'Brien (*ante* 12 April 1764).

20. 'Garrick acted every part admirably except a common man of fashion' (*Letters of Lady Louisa Stuart to Miss Louisa Clinton,* 1st ser., ed. Hon. James Home, Edinburgh, 1901, p. 343, *sub* Dec. 1823).

21. In *The Suspicious Husband,* 1747, by Benjamin Hoadly (1706–57) and his brother John Hoadly (1711–76).

22. In Rowe's *Fair Penitent,* 1703.

a ridiculous Othello, inferior to Quin in Sir John Brute[23] and Macbeth, and to Cibber in Bayes,[24] and a woeful Lord Hastings[25] and Lord Townley.[26] Indeed, his Bayes was original, but not the true part: Cibber was the burlesque of a great poet, as the part was designed, but Garrick made it a garreteer. The town did not like him in Hotspur, and yet I don't know whether he did not succeed in it beyond all the rest.[27] Sir Charles Williams and Lord Holland thought so too, and they were no bad judges. I am impatient to see the Clairon, and certainly will, as I have promised, though I have not fixed my day.[28] But do you know you alarm me! There was a time when I was a match for Madame de Mirepoix at pharaoh, to any hour of the night, and I believe did play with her five nights in a week till three and four in the morning[29]—but till eleven o'clock tomorrow morning—Oh! that is a little too much even at loo. Besides, I shall not go to Paris for pharaoh—if I play all night, how shall I see everything all day?

Lady Sophia Thomas has received the *Baume de Vie*,[30] for which she gives you a thousand thanks, and I ten thousand.

We are extremely amused with the wonderful histories of your hyena in the Gévaudan;[31] but our fox-hunters despise you: it is exactly the enchanted monster of old romances. If I had known its history a few months ago, I believe it would have appeared in the *Castle of Otranto*,—the success of which has, at last, brought me to own it, though the wildness of it made me terribly afraid; but it was comfortable to have it please so much, before any mortal suspected the author: indeed, it met with too much honour far, for at last[32] it was universally believed to be Mr Gray's. As all the first impression is

23. In Vanbrugh's *Provok'd Wife*, 1697.
24. In Buckingham's *Rehearsal*, 1672.
25. In Rowe's *Jane Shore*.
26. Lord Townly in Vanbrugh's and Cibber's *Provok'd Husband*, 1728.
27. Garrick played Hotspur five times in Dec. 1746 and 'never resumed the part' (John Genest, *Some Account of the English Stage*, Bath, 1832, iv. 212); see Ossory ii. 87, n. 15.
28. The Clairon retired from the stage the following year (DU DEFFAND i. 146); HW first saw her act at Mme du Deffand's in Aug. 1767 ('Paris Journals,' ibid. v. 316).

29. During her husband's embassy to England 1749–55 (*ante* 18 Oct., 21 Dec. 1763).
30. See *ante* 12, 20 Feb. 1765.
31. 'Prodigious was the noise made about that beast, which was believed to be really some famished or mad wolves' (note by HW to his letter to Mann, 26 March 1765, MANN vi. 289, n. 12). See MORE 52–3, 56; *London Chronicle* 21–3 March, xvii. 288; *Année littéraire* 1765, i. 311–29; *post* 2 Oct. 1765.
32. 'Least' in *Works* ix. 198, presumably a misreading by Croker.

sold, I am hurrying out another, with a new preface, which I will send you.[33]

There is not so much delicacy of wit, as in M. de Choiseul's speech to the *Clairon,* but I think the story I am going to tell you in return, will divert you as much: there was a vast assembly at Marlborough House, and a throng in the doorway. My Lady Talbot[34] said, 'Bless me! I think this is like the *Straits* of Thermopylæ!' my Lady Northumberland replied, 'I don't know what *Street* that is, but I wish I could get my —— through.' I hope you admire the contrast.

Adieu! my dear Lord.

Yours, ever,

H. W.

To Hertford, Sunday 7 April 1765

Printed from *Works* ix. 199–203.

Strawberry Hill, Easter Sunday, April 7th 1765.

YOUR first wish will be to know how the King does: he came to Richmond last Monday for a week;[1] but appeared suddenly and unexpected at his levee at St James's last Wednesday;[2] this was managed to prevent a crowd.[3] Next day he was at the Drawing-Room,[4] and at chapel on Good Friday.[5] They say he looks pale; but it is the

---

33. A second edition of 500 copies was printed 11 April ('Short Notes,' GRAY i. 41).

34. Mary de Cardonnel (d. 1787), m. (1734) William Talbot, 2d Bn Talbot, 1737; cr. (1761) E. Talbot.

---

1. 'Yesterday [1 April] at noon their Majesties removed from the Queen's Palace to Richmond, where it is said they will continue some time' (*London Chronicle* 30 March – 2 April, xvii. 318, *sub* 2 April).

2. 'The levee days which used to be at St James's on Mondays, Wednesdays, and Fridays, are to be discontinued during their Majesties' residence at Richmond' (ibid.). 'Yesterday [3 April] his Majesty came from Richmond to St James's, after

which there was a cabinet council' (ibid. 2–4 April, xvii. 326, *sub* 4 April).

3. HW wrote in *Mem. Geo. III* ii. 62 that 'this sudden appearance was at that time supposed calculated to prevent any notion of his being ill; and consequently to avoid any proposal for a Bill of Regency, in case he should fail.' See *post* 18 April, 5, 12 May 1765.

4. 'When his Majesty received the compliments of the nobility and gentry on his recovery from his late indisposition' (*London Chronicle* 4–6 April, xvii. 330). See also *Grenville Papers* iii. 125–6.

5. 'Yesterday [5 April] the Bishop of Rochester preached before their Majesties at the Chapel Royal' (*London Chronicle* 4–6 April, xvii. 335, *sub* 6 April).

fashion to call him very well;—I wish it may be true. The Duke of Cumberland is actually set out for Newmarket today:[6] he too is called much better;[7] but it is often as true of the health of princes as of their prisons, that there is little distance between each and their graves. There has been a fire at Gunnersbury,[8] which burned four rooms; her servants announced it to Princess Amalie with that wise precaution of 'Madame, don't be frightened—' accordingly, she was terrified,—when they told her the truth, she said, 'I am very glad; I had concluded my brother was dead.'—So much for royalties!

Lord March and George Selwyn are arrived,[9] after being wind-bound for nine days at Calais. George is so charmed with my Lady Hertford, that I believe it was she detained him at Paris, not Lord March. I am full as much transported with Schouvaloff; I never saw so amiable a man! so much good breeding, humility, and modesty, with sense and dignity! an air of melancholy, without anything abject. Monsieur de Caraman is agreeable too, informed and intelligent; he supped at your brother's t'other night, after being at Mrs Anne Pitt's. As the first curiosity of foreigners is to see Mr Pitt, and as that curiosity is one of the most difficult points in the world to satisfy, he asked me if Mr Pitt was like his sister? I told him, *Qu'ils se resemblaient comme deux gouttes de* feu.

The Parliament is adjourned till after the holidays, and the trial.[10] There have been two very long days[11] in our own House, on a complaint from Newfoundland merchants, on French encroachments.[12] The Ministry made a woeful piece of work of it the first day,[13] and

6. 'Yesterday [7 April] at noon . . . the Duke of Cumberland paid a visit to their Majesties at the Queen's House; and afterwards, accompanied by several of the nobility, set out for Newmarket' (ibid. 6–9 April, xvii. 338, *sub* 8 April).

7. See ante 26 March 1765, n. 10.

8. 'Saturday night [30 March]' (*London Chronicle* 30 March – 2 April, xvii. 319, *sub* 2 April).

9. 'Yesterday [5 April] the Earl of March, and Mr Selwyn . . . arrived in town from Paris' (ibid. 4–6 April, xvii. 335, *sub* 6 April).

10. Of Lord Byron (see *post* 18 April 1765). The Lords adjourned 4 April till the 15th, holding the trial of Lord Byron 16 and 17 April (*Journals of the House of Lords* xxxi. 124–35), while the Com-

mons adjourned 4 April till the 19th (*Journals of the House of Commons* xxx. 344).

11. April 3–4 (ibid. xxx. 336, 344); on the second day the House 'sat till eleven o'clock at night' (*Grenville Papers* iii. 127).

12. 'A petition of several merchants and traders . . . concerned in the cod and seal fishery, and fur trade . . . of Newfoundland . . . setting forth, that since the conclusion of the late Treaty of Peace, the subjects of his Most Christian Majesty have interrupted the British subjects in their fishery,' etc. (*Journals of the House of Commons* xxx. 338). The petition was presented by Humphry Sturt and John Pitt (Namier and Brooke iii. 284, 507; *Mem. Geo. III* ii. 63).

13. 'The ministers had the assurance to

we the second. Your brother, Sir George Savile, and Barré shone; but on the second night, they popped a sudden division upon us about nothing;[14] some went out, and some stayed in; they were 161, we but 44, and then they flung pillows upon the question, and stifled it,[15]—and *so* the French have *not* encroached.

There has been more serious work in the Lords, upon much less important matter; a bill for regulating the poor,[16]—(don't ask me how, for you know I am a perfect goose about details of business), formed by one Gilbert,[17] a member, and steward to the Duke of Bridgewater, or Lord Gower, or both,[18]—had passed pacifically through the Commons,[19] but Lord Egmont set fire to it in the Lords.[20] On the second reading,[21] he opposed it again, and made a most admired speech; however it passed on. But again, last Tuesday,[22] when it was to be in the Committee, such forces were mustered against the Bill, that behold all the world regarded it as a pitched battle between Lord Bute and Lord Holland on one side, and the Bedfords and Grenville on the other. You may guess if it grew a day of expectation. When it arrived, Lord Bute was not present,

oppose the reception of the petition, but managed as awkwardly as indecently; and at last moved to examine Commodore Palliser, who commanded on the station in question' (ibid. ii. 63–4). Capt. Hugh Palliser was then governor of Newfoundland (Namier and Brooke iii. 245–6).

14. 'Late at night a sudden dispute arising whether Palliser should be asked his opinion on an Act of Parliament relating to the fisheries, the ministers, who sought to evade further examination, opposed the question being put to him. Some warm men in the Opposition supporting that motion (though the wisest did not concur with them), divided the House, to the great joy of the ministers' (*Mem. Geo. III* ii. 64); the motion was defeated 161-44 (*Journals of the House of Commons* xxx. 344). According to Bamber Gascoyne, the examination of Palliser on 4 April lasted 'six hours, when the House was so thoroughly satisfied with the governor's conduct, and he being very lame by a wound in his thigh, it was determined to trouble him no more' (to John Strutt, 7 April, Strutt MSS, quoted in Namier and Brooke iii. 246).

15. 'The ministers . . . at once determined to stifle any further inquiry, Rose Fuller moving to adjourn the considera-

tion for three months; and Nugent to thank Palliser for his account of his own conduct. . . . So eager were the pacific ministers to justify France, and wink at her encroachments' (*Mem. Geo. III* ii. 64).

16. 'For the better relief and employment of the poor, within that part of Great Britain called England' (*Journals of the House of Commons* xxx. 76 *et passim*); the bill proposed grouping parishes together in large districts, such as hundreds, for the administration of the poor laws (Thomas Gilbert, *A Scheme for the Better Relief and Employment of the Poor*, 1764, pp. 1–2).

17. Thomas Gilbert (?1719–98), M.P. Newcastle-under-Lyme 1763–8, Lichfield 1768–94.

18. He was land agent to Lord Gower; his brother, John Gilbert, was land agent to the Duke of Bridgwater, Gower's brother-in-law (DNB).

19. Presented and read for the first time 1 Feb., it was passed by the Commons 18 March (*Journals of the House of Commons* xxx. 76, 260).

20. On the first reading, 19 March (*Journals of the House of Lords* xxxi. 85).

21. 28 March (ibid. xxxi. 107).

22. 2 April.

Lord Northumberland voted *for* the bill, and Lord Holland went away. Still politicians do not give up the mystery. Lord Denbigh[23] and Lord Pomfret, especially the latter, were the most personal against his Grace of Bedford.[24] He and his friends, they say (for I was not there, as you will find presently), kept their temper well. At ten at night, the House divided,[25] and, to be sure, the minority was dignified; it consisted of the Dukes of York and Gloucester, the Chancellor,[26] Chief Justice,[27] Lord President,[28] Privy Seal,[29] Lord Chamberlain,[30] Chamberlain to the Queen,[31] Lord Lieutenant of Ireland,[32] and a Secretary of State.[33] Lord Halifax, the other Secretary, was ill.[34] The numbers were 44 to 58. Lord Pomfret then moved to put off the Bill for four months;[35] but the Cabinet rallied, and rejected the motion by a majority of one.[36] So it is to come on again after the holidays.[37] The Duke of Newcastle, Lord Temple, and the Opposition, had once more the pleasure, which, I believe, they don't dislike, of being in a majority.

Now, for my disaster; you will laugh at it, though it was woeful to me. I was to dine at Northumberland House, and went a little after four:[38] there I found the Countess, Lady Betty Mekinsy, Lady Strafford, my Lady Finlater,[39] who was never out of Scotland before, a tall lad of fifteen, her son,[40] Lord Drogheda, and Mr Worseley.[41] At five, arrived Mr Mitchell,[42] who said the Lords had begun to read the Poor Bill, which would take at least two hours, and perhaps

23. Basil Feilding (1719–1800), 6th E. of Denbigh 1755.

24. HW wrote in his memoirs in 1769 that 'to disguise his opposition, Lord Bute absented himself, and the Earl of Northumberland voted for . . . [the bill]; but as his creatures, the Earls of Denbigh and Pomfret, as well as Lord Egmont, conducted the party against the bill, the Bedford faction were not the dupes of such flimsy arts' (HW's MS draft, now WSL, f. 195; *Mem. Geo. III* ii. 62–3).

25. On recommitting the bill (ibid. ii. 63).

26. Lord Northington.

27. Lord Mansfield.

28. The Duke of Bedford.

29. The Duke of Marlborough.

30. Lord Gower.

31. Lord Harcourt.

32. Lord Northumberland.

33. Lord Sandwich.

34. 'Yesterday [12 April] . . . the Earl of Halifax, who has been for some time indisposed, attended his Majesty's levee at St James's, for the first time since his recovery' (*London Chronicle* 11–13 April, xvii. 358, *sub* 13 April).

35. Two months (ibid.; *Journals of the House of Lords* xxxi. 118).

36. 50-49 (ibid.; *Mem. Geo. III* loc. cit.); with the proxies figured in, the count was 66-59 (BM Add. MSS 32966, f. 157).

37. See *post* 18 April 1765.

38. 'Hour' in *Works* ix. 201, doubtless a misreading by Croker.

39. Lady Mary Murray (1720–95), m. (1749) James Ogilvy, 6th E. of Findlater, 1764.

40. James Ogilvy (1750–1811), styled Lord Deskford 1764–70; 7th E. of Findlater, 1770.

41. Thomas Worsley (1710–78), M.P.; surveyor-general of the Office of Works 1760–78.

42. Andrew Mitchell (1708–71), M.P.; envoy to Prussia 1756–65, 1765–71; K.B. 13 Dec. 1765.

would debate it afterwards. We concluded dinner would be called for, it not being very precedented for ladies to wait for gentlemen:—no such thing. Six o'clock came,—seven o'clock came,—our coaches came,—well! we sent them away, and excuses were we were engaged. Still the Countess's heart did not relent, nor uttered a syllable of apology. We wore out the wind and the weather, the opera and the play, Mrs Cornelys's[43] and Almack's, and every topic that would do in a formal circle. We hinted, represented—in vain. The clock struck eight: my Lady, at last, said, she would go and order dinner; but it was a good half hour before it appeared. We then set down to a table for fourteen covers; but instead of substantials, there was nothing but a profusion of plates striped red green and yellow, gilt plate, blacks and uniforms! My Lady Finlater, who had never seen these embroidered dinners, nor dined after three, was famished. The first course stayed as long as possible, in hopes of the Lords: so did the second. The dessert at last arrived, and the middle dish was actually set on when Lord Finlater and Mr Mackay[44] arrived!—would you believe it?—the dessert was remanded, and the whole first course brought back again!—Stay, I have not done:—just as this second first course had done its duty, Lord Northumberland, Lord Strafford, and Mekinsy came in, and the whole began a third time! Then the second course, and the dessert! I thought we should have dropped from our chairs with fatigue and fumes! When the clock struck eleven, we were asked to return to the drawing-room, and drink tea and coffee, but I said I was engaged to supper, and came home to bed. My dear Lord, think of four hours and a half in a circle of mixed company, and three great dinners, one after another, without interruption;—no, it exceeded our day at Lord Archer's![45]

Mrs Amiger,[46] and Mrs Southwell,[47] Lady Gower's niece, are dead, and old Dr Young, the poet.[48] Good night!

Yours, ever,

H. W.

43. The assembly-rooms of Theresa Cornelys (1723–97).

44. Probably John Ross Mackye (1707–97), M.P.; treasurer of the Ordnance 1763–80.

45. Perhaps in 1751; see *ante* 14 Aug. 1760 and n. 1.

46. Elizabeth Bunbury (1711 – 30 March 1765), m. Lt-Gen. Robert Armiger (George Ormerod, *History of . . . Cheshire*, 1882, ii. 396; *London Chronicle* 4–6 April, xvii. 330; *Army Lists*, 1766, p. 94).

47. Hon. Catherine Watson (d. 5 April 1765), m. (1729) Edward Southwell (GRAY ii. 119, n. 1; *London Chronicle* 9–11 April, xvii. 346).

48. Died 5 April (ibid. 6–9 April, xvii. 344).

From Hertford, Wednesday 10 April 1765

Printed for the first time from a photostat of BM Add. MSS 23218, ff. 196–7.

Paris, April 10th 1765.

Dear Horry,

I HAVE just received a packet of medals from Geneva with a note from Lady Stanhope[1] to tell me they are sent by your order. You will therefore acquaint me what use I am to make of them; whether they are to remain at Paris till your arrival, or that I am to send them by the first opportunity to London.[2]

We have lately remitted you another cargo of French gentlemen. To the Comte de Lauragais, who is the proprietor of the house I inhabit, and to the Vicomte de Choiseuil,[3] who is the Duke of Praslin's son, I would wish you to show some attention on my account. The first has behaved very handsomely and generously by me. He is a man of parts and some reading, but is thought not to have an equal share of prudence and judgment.[4] The other is a very good-tempered polite man without pretensions. The first you will find at Lord Pembroke's, the latter at the Comte de Guerchi's where he is to be lodged. They are gone for the trial,[5] and will be glad to see as much as they can of the London life by being introduced to the best assemblies.

My son is still at Florence.[6] He has found the place so much to his taste that by remaining there so long he has not left time to see Rome and Naples before the heats. He therefore proposes to go to Venise for the Ascension,[7] and to see the northern parts of Italy which he has not yet visited,[8] to return from thence to Rome when he can do it safely.[9] This alteration of plan will probably make his stay something longer in Italy, but Lady Hertford is very reasonably reconciled to it from the danger of travelling about Rome in the midst of summer.

1. Grisel Hamilton (ca 1719–1811), m. (1745) Philip Stanhope, 2d E. Stanhope.

2. See *post* 18 April, 20 May, 20 June 1765.

3. Renaud-César-Louis de Choiseul (1735–91), Vicomte de Choiseul; Duc de Praslin, 1785; ambassador to Naples 1766–72 (see *post* 8 April 1766).

4. See *ante* 22 March 1764.

5. Of Lord Byron.

6. See *ante* 20 Feb. 1765.

7. 16 May.

8. He was at Milan by 18 June, staying there till about the end of July (MANN vi. 319 and n. 14).

9. He apparently did not visit Rome, returning from Milan to Florence, where he stayed till the middle of September (ibid. vi. 319, 327, 336, 338). See *post* 10 Oct. 1765.

The beast in the Gévaudan[10] still continues to eat women and children, not allegorically but very seriously; it is computed that he has already destroyed eighty persons.[11]

I hope the King is well. My government letter says all danger is over.[12] If the reports of Paris were to be credited he would be far from it, but this may be one of the thousand mistakes that circulate here. I mentioned it yesterday to the King of France at his levee when he asked me after my master, and he very properly replied there were no men so soon killed by public conversation as Kings.

I am very sorry for the fire which has happened at Gunnersbury, which I desire you will take an opportunity of saying for me to the Princess Amelia.

We have company tonight at supper, which makes it necessary for me to dress and be prepared for them. The post leaves Paris tomorrow morning; I must therefore conclude by assuring you that I am, dear Horry,

Very sincerely and affectionately yours,

HERTFORD

To HERTFORD, Thursday 11 April 1765

Missing; mentioned *post* 20 May 1765.

10. See *ante* 26 March, *post* 2 Oct. 1765.
11. The *Mercure historique* for Feb. 1765, clviii. 162, reported that 'on fait monter à 70 personnes, parmi lesquelles 42 filles ou femmes, les tristes victimes da sa fureur.'

12. 'I have the pleasure to acquaint your Excellency that his Majesty is so well recovered, that he removed yesterday to Richmond for a week for the benefit of the air' (Halifax to Hertford, 2 April, S.P. 78/266, f. 4).

To Hertford, Thursday 18 April 1765

Printed from *Works* ix. 204–8.

Arlington Street, April 18th 1765.

LADY Holland carries this,[1] which enables me to write a little more explicitly than I have been able to do lately. The King has been in the utmost danger; the humour in his face having fallen upon his breast. He now appears constantly; yet, I fear, his life is very precarious, and that there is even apprehension of a consumption. After many difficulties from different quarters, a Regency Bill is determined;[2] the King named it first to the ministers,[3] who said, they intended to mention it to him as soon as he was well: yet they are not thought to be fond of it. The King is to come to the House on Tuesday,[4] and recommend the provision to the Parliament. Yet, if what is whispered proves true, that the nomination of the Regent is to be reserved to the King's will,[5] it is likely to cause great uneasiness. If the ministers propose such a clause, it is strong evidence of their own instability, and, I should think, would not save them, at least, some of them. The world expects changes soon, though not a thorough alteration; yet, if any takes place shortly, I should think it would be a material one than not. The enmity between Lord Bute and Mr Grenville is not denied on either side. There is a notion, and I am inclined to think not ill-founded, that the former and Mr Pitt are treating. It is certain that the last has expressed wishes that the Opposition may lie still for the remainder of the Session. This, at least, puts an end to the question on your brother,[6] of which I am glad for the present. The common town-talk is, that Lord Northumberland does not care to return to Ireland,—that

1. She was visiting Paris with her two sisters, Lady Louisa Conolly and Lady Sarah Bunbury, and her two eldest sons, Stephen and Charles James Fox. See *post* 29 April 1765.

2. For a detailed history of the Regency Bill, see *Mem. Geo. III* ii. 67–100, and also John Brooke, *King George III*, New York, 1972, pp. 110–13.

3. 4 April when 'he had given to his four ministers an order for preparing a Bill of Regency, in case any accident happened to him' (D. of Cumberland's 'Ac-

count,' in Lord Albemarle, *Memoirs of . . . Rockingham*, 1852, i. 186–7).

4. 23 April; he came on Wednesday, 24 April (*Journals of the House of Lords* xxxi. 151).

5. The minutes of the Cabinet Council of 5 April mention 'his Majesty's idea of reserving to himself the power of appointing a regent' (George III's *Corr.*, ed. Fortescue, i. 73).

6. I.e., on the dismission of officers; see *ante* 12 Feb. 1765.

you are to succeed him there,[7] Lord Rochford[8] you,[9] and that Sandwich is to go to Spain.[10] My belief is that there will be no change, except, perhaps, a single one for Lord Northumberland, unless there are capital removals indeed.

The Chancellor,[11] Grenville, the Bedfords, and the two Secretaries,[12] are one body; at least, they pass for such: yet it is very lately if one of them[13] has dropped his prudent management with Lord Bute. There seems an unwillingness to discard the Bedfords, though their Graces themselves keep little terms of civility to Lord Bute, none to the Princess (Dowager).[14] Lord Gower is a better courtier, and Rigby would do anything to save his place.

This is the present state, which every day may alter: even tomorrow is a day of expectation, as the last struggle of the Poor Bill.[15] If the Bedfords carry it, either by force or sufferance (though Lord Bute has constantly denied being the author of the opposition to it), I shall less expect any great change soon. In those less important, I shall not wonder to find the Duke of Richmond come upon the scene, perhaps for Ireland, though he is not talked of.[16]

Your brother is out of town, not troubling himself, though the time seems so critical.[17] I am not so philosophic,[18] as I almost wish for anything that may put an end to my being concerned in the *mêlée*—for any end to a most gloomy prospect for the country: alas! I see it not.

Lord Byron's trial lasted two days,[19] and he was acquitted totally

7. Northumberland was succeeded by Lord Weymouth 29 May (*post* 20 May 1765, n. 53), and Hertford succeeded Weymouth 1 Aug. (*post* 12 Aug. 1765, n. 4).
8. William Henry Nassau de Zuylestein (1717–81), 4th E. of Rochford, 1738; ambassador to Madrid 1763–6, to Paris 1766–8.
9. The *London Chronicle* 11–13 April, xvii. 360, reported a rumour that Lord Temple was to succeed him. See below, n. 16.
10. Sandwich was dismissed in July as part of the changeover to the first Rockingham administration; he had been appointed ambassador to Spain in 1763, but did not proceed.
11. Northington.
12. Halifax and Sandwich.
13. Probably Northington.
14. Presumably an emendation by Croker.

15. See below, *sub* 20 April.
16. He succeeded Hertford as ambassador to Paris; see *post* 2 Oct. 1765, n. 58.
17. Conway wrote to Hertford from Park Place, 13 April, that 'upon reflexion I am afraid I have been very idle lately. . . . I am just come to pass the holidays where my time is almost as much employed and a great deal more agreeably than in London. . . . I shall not be in town till the end of this week [the Commons met again 19 April]' (MS now WSL).
18. In the same letter Conway expressed his 'contempt for most of the grand trifles for which men fly from east to west and toil and trouble themselves and torment one another to so little purpose.'
19. 16–17 April; he had been indicted for the murder of William Chaworth (*ante* 27 Jan. 1765 and n. 48).

by four Lords, Beaulieu, Falmouth, Despenser, and Orford, and found guilty of manslaughter by one hundred and twenty.[20] The Dukes of York and Gloucester were present in their places. The prisoner behaved with great decorum, and seemed thoroughly shocked and mortified. Indeed, the bitterness of the world against him has been great, and the stories they have revived or invented to load him, very grievous.[21] The Chancellor[22] behaved with his usual, or, rather greater vulgarness and blunders.[23] Lord Pomfret kept away decently, from the similitude of his own story.[24]

I have been to wait on Messrs Choiseul and de Lauragais, as you desired, but have not seen them yet. The former is lodged with my Lord Pembroke, and the Guerchys are in terrible apprehensions of his exhibiting some scene.[25]

The Duke of Cumberland bore the journey to Newmarket extremely well,[26] but has been lethargic since; yet they have found out that Daffy's Elixir agrees with, and does him good. Prince Frederick is very bad. There is no private news at all. As I shall not deliver this till the day after tomorrow, I shall be able to give you an account of the fate of the Poor Bill.

The medals that came for me from Geneva, I forgot to mention to you, and to beg you to be troubled with them till I see you. I had desired Lord Stanhope to send them; and will beg you too, if any bill is sent, to pay it for me, and I will repay it you. I say nothing of my journey, which the unsettled state of affairs makes it impossible for me to fix. I long for every reason upon earth to be with you.

20. 119 (*Journals of the House of Lords* xxxi. 134; T. B. Howell, *Complete Collection of State Trials*, 1816–26, xix. 1233–5).

21. He encumbered his estate, sold his property at Rochdale, Lancs, as well as the family pictures, and dismantled the house at Newstead; he was known as 'the wicked Lord' (GEC ii. 456, n. 'd').

22. Northington, who acted as Lord High Steward at the trial; he had also (as Bn Henley) been Lord High Steward at Lord Ferrers's trial in 1760 (GEC; DNB).

23. HW wrote to Montagu, 19 April 1760, that at Lord Ferrers's trial Northington 'neither had any dignity, nor affected any' (MONTAGU i. 279). 'He despised form, even where he had little to do but to be formal . . . he could not, or would not,

stoop to . . . ceremonial' (*Mem. Geo. II* iii. 277).

24. He had been convicted of manslaughter at the Old Bailey in 1752 for killing Capt. Thomas Grey in a duel (MANN iv. 303 and nn. 15, 16).

25. HW is describing Lauraguais, not Choiseul; see *ante* 10 April 1765.

26. See *ante* 7 April 1765. 'The Duke of Cumberland . . . arrived on Sunday evening [14 April] from Newmarket in perfect health' (*London Chronicle* 13–16 April, xvii. 365, *sub* 16 April). However, Lord Albemarle wrote to Newcastle from Newmarket, 12 April, that 'H. R. H. is not so well as he was when he came down. . . . The drowsiness is returned, and his speech at that time is very bad' (BM Add. MSS 32966, f. 192).

May [April] 20th, Saturday.

The Poor Bill[27] is put off till Monday;[28] is then to be amended,[29] and then dropped:[30] a confession of weakness, in a set of people[31] not famous for being moderate!

I was assured, last night, that Ireland had been twice offered to you, and that it hung on their insisting upon giving you a secretary, either Wood[32] or Bunbury.[33] I replied very truly that I knew nothing of it, that you had never mentioned it to me, and I believed not even to your brother. The answer was, Oh! his particular friends are always the last that know anything about him. Princess Amalie loves this topic, and is forever teasing us about your mystery. I defend myself by pleading that I have desired you never to tell me anything till it was in the *Gazette*.

They say there is to be a new alliance in the House of Montagu; that Lord Hinchinbrook[34] is to marry the sole remaining daughter of Lord Halifax; that her fortune is to be divided into three shares, of which each father is to take one, and the third is to be the provision for the victims. I don't think this the most unlikely part of the story.

Adieu! my dear Lord,

Yours, ever,

H. W.

27. See *ante* 7 April 1765.

28. 22 April; so ordered 19 April, the day originally appointed (2 April) for recommitting the bill (*Journals of the House of Lords* xxxi. 118, 141).

29. No amendment is mentioned in the *Lords Journals*.

30. 'Ordered, That the House be put into a committee again upon the said bill, on this day two months' (ibid. xxxi. 146, *sub* 22 April). Lord Hardwicke wrote to Newcastle, 19 April, that 'the billeting clause in the American Mutiny Bill is dropped, which together with the not pushing on the Poor Bill looks like quieting the waves before the great business [of the Regency Bill] comes on' (BM Add. MSS 32966, f. 215).

31. The Bedfords.

32. Robert Wood (*ante* 9 Dec. 1763). He was never secretary in Ireland.

33. Officially Hertford's secretary at Paris but ignored by Hertford in favour of Hume (see *ante* 18 Oct. 1763, n. 11), he was named in May as secretary to Lord Weymouth in Ireland (*post* 30 May 1765); however, both Weymouth and Bunbury were removed from their offices in July (*post* 1 July 1765).

34. John Montagu (1744–1814), styled Vct Hinchingbrooke, eldest surviving son of the 4th E. of Sandwich; 5th E. of Sandwich 1792; m. 1 (1766) Lady Elizabeth Montagu-Dunk (1745–68), the only legitimate surviving child of the 2d E. of Halifax (MONTAGU i. 396, n. 3). The *London Chronicle* 4–6 April, xvii. 336, *sub* 6 April, announced that 'next week . . . [has been] appointed by the . . . Earl of Sandwich for celebrating Lord Hinchingbrook's coming of age,' at which time presumably the announcement was made of his forthcoming marriage.

From Hertford, Monday 29 April 1765

Printed for the first time from a photostat of BM Add. MSS 23218, ff. 198–9.

Paris, April 29th 1765.

Dear Horry,

ENCLOSED herewith I send you a small book[1] of d'Alembert's[2] which has just appeared in print upon the fall of the Jesuits. It may amuse you whilst your hair is dressing.

Lady Holland has just now sent me the letter[3] she brought from England, for which I am much obliged. You need not tell the person[3a] so, who thinks I am particularly mysterious to my friends, but you may be assured yourself that I know no more of the government of Ireland than when I wrote last.[4] It has neither been offered or refused.

The three sisters[5] are, I hear, all arrived;[6] they have sent to Lady Hertford to say they would wait upon her as soon as the present Court mourning ended, which is I think the day after tomorrow,[7] to which she has answered that that need be no objection whenever they wish to do it.[8] The two Messrs Foxes[9] were with me yesterday.

1. *Sur la destruction des Jésuites en France, par un auteur désintéressé*, Geneva, 1765 (Grimm, *Correspondance*, ed. Tourneux, 1877–82, vi. 254). It does not appear in the records of the SH library.

2. Jean le Rond d'Alembert (1717–83), 'philosophe.'

3. *Ante* 18 April 1765.

3a. Princess Amelia.

4. Hertford wrote last about Ireland *ante* 18 Jan. 1765.

5. Lady Holland, Lady Sarah Bunbury, and Lady Louisa Augusta Lennox (1743–1821), who m. (1758) Rt Hon. Thomas Conolly (*Life and Letters of Lady Sarah Lennox*, ed. Lady Ilchester and Lord Stavordale, 1902, i. 161).

6. Lady Sarah wrote to Lady Susan O'Brien from Paris, 5 May, that 'I arrived here this day sevennight [28 April]' (ibid.).

7. The Court went into mourning 20 April for Élisabeth-Alexandrine de Bourbon (1705 – 15 April 1765), Mlle de Sens, daughter of Louis, Duc de Bourbon (1668–1710) by his wife Louise-Françoise de

Bourbon (1673–1743), Mlle de Nantes, natural daughter of Louis XIV. This mourning was supposed to have lasted through 1 May but was discontinued 30 April, when the Court took up mourning for Marie Luise, Princess Dowager of Orange (1688 – 9 April 1765), grandmother of Willem V (1748–1806), stadtholder of the Netherlands (*Gazette de Leyde* 26 April, *sub* Paris, 19 April; ibid. 10 May, 'Supplément,' *sub* Paris 3 May; *Mercure historique*, 1765, clviii. 556–7; La Chenaye-Desbois iii. 761–2; Isenburg, *Stammtafeln* ii. taf. 1; *Genealog. hist. Nachrichten*, 1766–7, 3d ser. v. 246–7).

8. They had presumably all visited the Hertfords by 5 May, when Lady Sarah Bunbury wrote to Lady Susan O'Brien that 'Lord and Lady Hertford are very civil to me, there was never anything so beautiful as their house is, it is quite a palace, even here where the style of houses in general are charming in my opinion' (Lady Ilchester and Lord Stavordale, op. cit. i. 162).

9. Stephen and Charles James.

The eldest[10] is much altered by a fever he has had lately; the second seems much more like his father than his brother. He tells me that my own son Henry has six feet three inches in height, but I hope he has not measured him and may be mistaken.[11]

The French theatre here is all in confusion; the actors quarrelled amongst themselves and many of the principal ones refused to act with one of them named Dubois.[12] There was in consequence of this dispute no representation when the house was filled to hear the *Siege of Calais*. The public was of course disappointed, and the actors were immediately ordered into confinement.[13] They come from thence to act and return when the play is over.[14] Mademoiselle Clairon, whose bad state of health required it, is *aux arrêts* in her own house,[15] but perhaps may be so offended at the treatment she has met with as not to act again,[16] at least during the Duke of Richlieu's year, who is now in waiting. The theatre is under his orders at present, and the other Lords his brethren[17] differ with him. He is a protector of a handsome actress[18] who is daughter to Dubois; the other Lords are for Mademoiselle Clairon.[19] It serves to amuse

10. Stephen.

11. Henry's brothers Robert, Edward, and George all reached heights of well over six feet (*post* 3 June 1781).

12. Louis Blouin (1706 or 1710–ca 1775), called Dubois, of the Comédie-Française 1736–65 (*Enciclopedia dello spettacolo*, Rome, 1954–62, iv. 1047). He had been ostracized by the troupe for refusing to acknowledge a debt he allegedly owed to a surgeon for treatment of 'une maladie honteuse.' However, through the efforts of his daughter (see n. 18 below), an *ordre du Roi* had been obtained commanding the troupe to take him back. In defiance of this order, Mlle Clairon and the actors Molé, Dauberval, Lekain, and Brizard (see *Enciclopedia dello spettacolo, passim,* and *Dictionnaire de biographie française,* 1933– , *passim*) on 15 April refused to go on stage with him for a performance of *Le Siège de Calais* (Louis Petit de Bachaumont, *Mémoires secrets,* 1780–9, ii. 176, 178–80; see also Grimm, op. cit. vi. 257–9).

13. In the For l'Évêque; they were all sent there at various times between 15 and 18 April (Bachaumont, op. cit. ii. 181, 184; Grimm, op. cit. vi. 260).

14. '25 avril . . . On fait sortir journellement les prisonniers pour jouer et l'on les reconduit au For l'Évêque' (Bachaumont, op. cit. ii. 187).

15. '22 avril . . . Mlle Clairon est sortie hier au soir du For l'Évêque, sur la représentation de son chirurgien, qui a déclaré que sa santé était en danger. . . . Elle s'est rendue chez elle. Elle y est aux arrêts' (ibid.).

16. She quit the Comédie-Française the following year.

17. The other gentilshommes de la Chambre were the Ducs d'Aumont, de Fleury, and de Duras (*Almanach royal,* 1765, p. 135).

18. Marie-Madeleine Blouin (1746–79), called Mlle Aînée Dubois, of the Comédie-Française 1759–73 (*Enciclopedia dello spettacolo,* iv. 1047). Bachaumont intimates that she was mistress to the Duc de Fronsac, Richelieu's son, and that she exerted her charms on him to obtain the order reinstating her father (op. cit. ii. 176, 178–9; see also Grimm, op. cit. vi. 282).

19. Mlle Clairon, in her *Mémoires,* 1822, ed. Andrieux *et al.,* p. 45, credits only Aumont with taking her part: 'Au moment où l'on me permit de quitter mes

the town here as much as a dispute between Mr Pitt and Mr Fox would formerly have entertained London.

There was on Friday last[20] an assembly of the parliament of Paris.[21] I do not know that you will think it worth hearing. It was upon a motion[22] of the Prince of Conti's, who is the leader here upon such occasions.[23] The affair was not new or very extraordinary; it is the assertion of a claim which they made 15 months ago[24] that the parliament of Paris is the sole House of Peers.[25] The other provincial parliaments were then offended at this pretension and passed votes and printed remonstrances against it.[26] It is not probable they will be now more disposed to acquiesce,[27] and it will furnish new matter

arrêts, je fus remercier M. le duc d'Aumont, qui seul s'était dignement conduit dans cette ridicule bagarre.' The affair ended with the freeing of the prisoners 9 May and the retiring of Dubois from the Comédie on a pension of 1500 livres (Bachaumont, op. cit. ii. 191).

20. 26 April.

21. Hertford wrote about this assembly also to Halifax, 28 April (S.P. 78/266, f. 76).

22. An *écrit* (*Mercure historique*, 1765, clviii. 548).

23. Conti was the 'porteur de l'écrit,' which was signed by himself and the Comte de Clermont (ibid.).

24. 'Displeased with some violent proceedings of the parliament of Toulouse against the Duke of Fitzjames' (Hertford to Halifax, 28 April, loc. cit.). For these proceedings, see *ante* 28 Dec. 1763, 23 Jan. 1764.

25. On 30 Dec. 1763 the parliament of Paris annulled a decree passed by the parliament of Toulouse against the Duke of Fitzjames on the grounds that they alone were his legal judges (*ante* 23 Jan. 1764 and n. 38). The present *écrit* of 26 April contained 'une protestation formelle contre tout arrêt ou acte portant préjudice aux droits et aux prérogatives de la pairie'; an *arrêt* was then passed and the *écrit* annexed to the minute of the *arrêt*, 'par lequel sont déclarés nuls et de nulle valeur, tous actes contraires à la dignité des princes et pairs, et tendant à les soustraire à la jurisdiction de la cour de parlement [of Paris] comme unique cour des pairs' (*Mercure historique*, 1765, clviii. 548-9). The

écrit was apparently presented in response to a *mémoire* signed by 20 peers asserting that 'les pairs forment une cour séparée et indépendente du parlement' (ibid. 424, 548-9).

26. Hertford is telescoping events considerably. In response to further assertions of the parliament of Paris that it was the sole court of peers (see its *arrêts* of 29 May and 7 June 1764, *Mercure historique*, 1764, clvi. 634-5, clvii. 33-4), the parliament of Rouen issued an *arrêt* 10 Aug. 1764 denying this claim and asserting the right of any parliament in France to fulfil that rôle (É. Glasson, *Le Parlement de Paris*, 1901, ii. 292-3; A. Floquet, *Histoire du Parlement de Normandie*, 1840-2, vi. 519-21; *Mercure historique*, 1764, clvii. 407-9). The parliaments of Toulouse, Bordeaux and Grenoble issued *arrêts* to the same effect 23 Aug. and 7 Sept. 1764, and 22 March 1765 (Vicomte de Bastard-d'Estang, *Les Parlements de France*, 1857, ii. 363; J. Egret, *Le Parlement de Dauphiné et les affaires publiques*, Grenoble, 1942, i. 253; *Mercure historique*, 1765, clviii. 423).

27. The parliament of Rouen issued a new *arrêt* 19 Aug. in which they charged that the parliament of Paris, in annulling the decree of the parliament of Toulouse against the Duke of Fitzjames (n. 25 above), 's'est abusivement arrogé un droit de correction et de révision,' and reaffirmed the right of any parliament to judge peers; pursuant to this *arrêt*, the parliament forbad that any peer within its jurisdiction avail himself of the *écrit* and *arrêt* of 26 April of the parliament of Paris, presumably to claim judgment by

of contestation; but all questions that regard the constitution of this country are yet vague and uncertain. Nothing is determined by the authority of laws and very little by clear and undoubted precedents. There is a spirit of liberty in this country which is daily seeking occasions to show itself, but it may require a century of dispute and contention to clear up all these controversies before any new system of government or reformation would prevail.

I am curious to know the state of the proposed regency in case of an event which I hope far removed; I shall likewise wish to hear if the close of the session produces no alteration amongst the ministers; by your account there is a bomb which may burst.

I remain, dear Horry,

Most affectionately yours,

HERTFORD

To HERTFORD, Sunday 5 May 1765

Printed from *Works* ix. 209–14.

Arlington Street, May 5th 1765.

THE plot thickens; at least, it does not clear up. I don't know how to tell you in the compass of a letter, what is matter for a history, and it is the more difficult, as we are but just in the middle.

During the recess, the King acquainted the Ministry that he would have a Bill of Regency, and told them the particulars of his intention.[1] The town gives Lord Holland the honour of the measure;[2] certain it is, the Ministry, who are not the Court, did not taste some

that assembly alone or escape judgment altogether ('Extrait d'une lettre de Paris, du 2 Septembre,' *Mercure historique*, 1765, clix. 296–7; Floquet, op. cit. vi. 523–5).

1. The King gave to his ministers an order for preparing a Bill of Regency 4 April, and the Cabinet Council met on the order 5 April, the first day of the recess (*ante* 7 April 1765, n. 10, 18 April 1765, n. 3; MANN vi. 295, n. 10).

2. 'I have the happy consciousness of having had a great hand in bringing about a Regency. Not in the mode it appears. I only was anxious for a bill, no matter what' (Lord Holland to J. Campbell, 29 May, in Lord Ilchester, *Henry Fox, First Lord Holland*, 1920, ii. 288). He had pressed it on Lord Bute and Lord Mansfield, but once the bill was launched, had no further hand in the matter (ibid. ii. 288–90; *Mem. Geo. III* ii. 69–71).

of the items: such as the Regent to be *in petto*,[3] the Princes[4] to be omitted,[5] and four secret nominations to which the Princes *might* be applied.[6] However, thinking it was better to lose their share of future power than their present places, the Ministers gave a gulp and swallowed the whole potion; still it lay so heavy at their stomachs, that they brought up part of it again, and obtained the Queen's name to be placed as one that might be Regent.[7] Mankind laughed, and proclaimed their Wisdoms bit. Upon this, their Wisdoms beat up four opponents, and set fire to the old stubble of the Princess and Lord Bute. Everybody took the alarm; and such uneasiness was raised, that after the King had notified the Bill to both Houses,[8] a new message was sent,[9] and instead of four secret nominations, the five Princes were named, with power to the Crown of supplying their places if they died off.[10]

Last Tuesday[11] the bill was read a second time in the Lords. Lord Lyttelton opposed an unknown Regent,[12] Lord Temple, the whole bill,[13] seconded by Lord Shelburn.[14] The first division came on

3. 'In reserve'; i.e., the choice of the regent was to be reserved to the King's will (*ante* 18 April 1765, n. 5).

4. The King's uncle and four brothers.

5. 'The King was averse to having the Princes of the Blood in the Council of Regency, and said he thought it would create jealousy and uneasiness' (Grenville's diary, 3 April, *Grenville Papers* iii. 126), and it was settled that the names would appear neither in the new Regency Bill nor in the King's speech, 24 April; see MANN vi. 295, n. 15.

6. Sect. iii of the Regency Act (24 Geo. II, c. 24) of 1751, which was to be followed exactly by the present bill except for the *in petto* provision (*Grenville Papers* iii. 17), empowered George II to 'nominate and add,' 'by three instruments under his sign manual,' to the Council of Regency 'such and so many other persons (being natural-born subjects of this realm) not exceeding the number of four' (Owen Ruffhead, *Statutes at Large*, 1763–1800, vii. 356).

7. The minutes of 5 April conclude: 'That they [the lords of the Council] understand his Majesty's idea of reserving to himself the power of appointing a regent, is meant to be restrained to the

Queen or any other person of the royal family, usually resident in Great Britain' (Geo. III's *Corr.*, ed. Fortescue, i. 73).

8. 24 April (*ante* 18 April 1765, n. 4).

9. To the Lords, 29 April, when the bill was read for the first time (*Journals of the House of Lords* xxxi. 162).

10. The King told Halifax 'that this thought came into his mind' 25 April; 'that he heard there would be a great deal of opposition to the Regency Bill, and that it would be very disagreeable if they should move to name the Princes, his brothers, and the Duke of Cumberland, to be of the Council, and for his ministers to put a negative to them: that he thought it might therefore be better to name them' (*Grenville Papers* iii. 131; Fortescue, op. cit. i. 76–7).

11. 30 April.

12. 'Lord Lyttelton made a fine speech against giving unconstitutional powers, such as that of appointing an unknown person regent' (*Mem. Geo. III* ii. 79).

13. 'Lord Temple said he . . . was, and had been, against all regency bills' (ibid. ii. 80).

14. For notes and a summary of Shelburne's speech, see Lord Fitzmaurice, *Life of . . . Shelburne*, 1912, i. 226–8.

the commitment of the whole bill. The Duke of Newcastle and almost all the Opposition were with the majority, for his Grace could not decently oppose so great a likeness of his own child, the former bill,[15] and so they were one hundred and twenty. Lord Temple, Lord Shelburne, the Duke of Grafton, and six more[16] composed the minority;[17] the slenderness of which so enraged Lord Temple, though he had declared himself of no party, and connected with no party, that he and the Duke of Bolton came no more to the House.[18] Next day Lord Lyttelton moved an address to the King, to name the person he would recommend for Regent.[19] In the midst of this debate, the Duke of Richmond started two questions; whether the Queen was naturalized, and if not, whether capable of being Regent;[20] and he added a third much more puzzling; who are the Royal Family?[21] Lord Denbigh answered flippantly, all who are prayed for: the Duke of Bedford, more significantly, those *only* who are in the order of succession—*a direct exclusion of the Princess;*[22] for the Queen is named in the Bill. The Duke of Richmond moved to consult the Judges;[23] Lord Mansfield[24] fought this off, declared he had his opinion, but would not tell it[25]—and stayed away next day![26] They then proceeded on Lord Lyttelton's motion,[27] which was re-

15. Of 1751, which Newcastle had presented to the House of Lords (*Journals of the House of Lords* xxvii. 542, 553). HW, in *Mem. Geo. III* ii. 79, writes that Newcastle's sole voiced objection was to the *in petto* provision.

16. The Duke of Bolton, the Earls of Thanet, Ferrers, and Cornwallis, Viscount Torrington, and Lord Fortescue (ibid. ii. 82).

17. Totalling 129 votes, the number of lords listed as present in the *Journals of the House of Lords* xxxi. 165. Although HW gives the same vote count in *Mem. Geo. III* ii. 81, he there writes that Newcastle and his followers retired rather than actually cast their votes.

18. They are last listed as present, 30 April (*Journals of the House of Lords,* loc. cit.).

19. Lyttelton made his motion 30 April, but upon the Duke of Bedford's motion, consideration of it was adjourned till the next day, 1 May (ibid. xxxi. 168, 170–1; *Mem. Geo. III* ii. 82).

20. See below.

21. 'Was the Princess Dowager of the

royal family? Were the Princess Amalie, and the Princess of Hesse and her children? Were the Hereditary Prince [of Brunswick] and the King of Prussia?' (ibid. ii. 82–3).

22. 'That the Princess Dowager of Wales *was of his Majesty's royal family* . . . [is] directly contrary to what the Duke of Bedford declared yesterday [1 May], in the House, and confirmed to me afterwards in private' (Newcastle to Albemarle, 2 May, BM Add. MSS 32966, f. 300).

23. Of the King's Bench and Common Pleas.

24. Lord Chief Justice of the King's Bench.

25. HW, in *Mem. Geo. III* ii. 84, asserts that both Mansfield and Lord Northington had 'told the King that neither the Queen nor the Princess Dowager were of the royal family.'

26. See *Journals of the House of Lords* xxxi. 171.

27. The speakers for and against the motion are listed in Fortescue, op. cit. i. 80,

jected by eighty-nine to thirty-one;[28] after which, the Duke of New-castle came no more; and Grafton, Rockingham, and many others, went to Newmarket;[29] for that rage is so strong, that I cease to wonder at the gentleman[30] who was going out to hunt as the battle of Edgehill began.[31]

The third day[32] was a scene of folly and confusion, for when Lord Mansfield is absent,

> Lost is the nation's sense, nor can be found.[33]

The Duke of Richmond moved an amendment, that the persons capable of the Regency should be the Queen, the Princess Dowager, and all the descendants of the late King usually resident in England.[34] Lord Halifax endeavoured to jockey this, by a previous amendment of *now* for *usually*. The Duke persisted with great firmness and cleverness; Lord Halifax, with as much peevishness and absurdity; in truth, he made a woeful figure. The Duke of Bedford supported t'other Duke against the Secretary, but would not yield to name the Princess, though the Chancellor declared her of the Royal Family.[35] This droll personage is exactly what Woodward[36] would be, if there

28. 'Newcastle and his friends, and the bishops attached to him, chiefly forming the minority' (*Mem. Geo. III* ii. 85).

29. Newcastle, last listed as present in the House 1 May (*Journals of the House of Lords* xxxi. 168), wrote to Albemarle 2 May, loc. cit., that 'I was much solicited to go to the House; but after what I conceived to be his Royal Highness's [The Duke of Cumberland's] opinion, after what was agreed with your Lordship, the Marquess [of Rockingham], the Duke of Grafton, and many of our friends, I should not have gone to the House, to divide with the Duke of Richmond and seven or eight more; as my Lord Temple did, the other day.' 'The Duke of Grafton, my Lord Rockingham, and my Lord Albemarle set out yesterday morning [2 May] early for Newmarket. . . . I am setting out this morning for Claremont' (Newcastle to Earl of Jersey, 3 May, BM Add. MSS 32966, f. 308). 'I do not intend to go any more upon this bill' (Newcastle to Albemarle 2 May, loc. cit.). However, he did attend 13 May, the day the bill was returned from the Commons (*Journals of the House of Lords* xxxi. 199).

30. Sir Richard Shuckburgh (1596–1656).

31. This was one of HW's favourite anecdotes. See *post* 22 Jan. 1775; COLE ii. 75; MONTAGU ii. 277; and MASON ii. 147.

32. 2 May; the speakers in the debate are listed in Fortescue, op. cit. i. 81–2.

33. *Dunciad* iv. 611.

34. He 'persisted . . . in naming the Princess Dowager of Wales, as well as the Queen, with the Princes of the Blood, capable of being appointed regents' (Newcastle to Albemarle 2 May, loc. cit.). HW relates in *Mem. Geo. III* loc. cit. that he personally persuaded the Duke to insert the name of the Princess in the motion (which the Duke had originally not intended), so as not to risk unintentionally offending her.

35. Northington 'declared his opinion that he had not the least doubt, but that the Princess Dowager of Wales *was of his Majesty's royal family*' (Newcastle to Albemarle 2 May, loc. cit.). 'He thought she was naturalized by her marriage, and incorporated one of the royal family, the Christian religion having been adopted into the common law' (*Mem. Geo. III* ii. 86).

36. Henry Woodward (1714–77), actor.

was such a farce as Trappolin[37] Chancellor. You will want a key to all this, but who has a key to chaos? After puzzling on for two hours how to adjust these motions, while the spectators stood laughing around, Lord Folkstone[38] rose, and said, why not say *now and usually?* They adopted this amendment at once,[39] and then rejected the Duke of Richmond's motion,[40] but ordered the Judges to attend next day on the questions of naturalization.[41]

Now comes the marvellous transaction, and I defy Mr Hume, all historian as he is, to parallel it. The Judges had decided for the Queen's capability,[42] when Lord Halifax rose, by the King's permission, desired to have the Bill recommitted, and then moved the Duke of Richmond's own words, with the single omission of the Princess Dowager's name, and thus she alone is rendered incapable of the Regency—and stigmatized by Act of Parliament![43] The astonishment of the world is not to be described. Lord Bute's friends are thunderstruck. The Duke of Bedford almost danced about the House for joy. Comments there are, various; and some palliate it, by saying it was done at the Princess's desire; but the most inquisitive say, the King was taken by surprise, that Lord Halifax proposed the amend-

---

37. Hero of *A Duke and No Duke*, a farce by Nahum Tate (1652–1715), adapted from Sir Aston Cokayne's *Trappolin creduto principe* (BM Cat.). Woodward had played the rôle many times in London, most recently in Oct. 1757 (*London Stage* Pt IV, i. 622).

38. William Bouverie (1725–76), 2d Vct Folkestone, 1761; cr. (31 Oct. 1765) Earl of Radnor.

39. Halifax wrote to George III 2 May that he 'moved that the word *usually* residing in Great Britain, might be left out, and the word *now* (with the words *and usually* which were added) to take the place in the room of it. . . . Lord Halifax's motion . . . passed in the affirmative without a division' (Fortescue, op. cit. i. 81).

40. 'Without a division' (ibid.).

41. 'Ordered, That the Judges do attend this House tomorrow [3 May], to deliver their opinions upon the two following questions; "1. Whether an alien, married to a King of Great Britain, is, by operation of the common law, naturalized to all intents and purposes?" "2. Whether,

if she be so naturalized by the common law, such person would be disabled, by the Act of the Twelfth of King William the Third [c. 2], entitled, 'An Act for the further limitation of the Crown, and better securing the rights and liberties of the subject,' or by any other act, from holding and enjoying any office or place of trust, or from having any grant of lands, tenements, or hereditaments, from the Crown"' (*Journals of the House of Lords* xxxi. 173; Ruffhead, op. cit. iv. 61–3).

42. 'The Lord Chief Justice [Pratt] of the Court of Common Pleas delivered the unanimous opinion of the judges . . . "That an alien, married to a King of Great Britain, is, by operation of the law of the Crown (which is part of the common law), to be deemed as a natural-born person from the time of such marriage, so as not to be disabled, by the Act of the Twelfth of King William the Third . . . or by any other act"' (*Journals of the House of Lords* xxxi. 174).

43. See HW to Mann, 14 May 1765, Mann vi. 297–8 and nn. 32–3.

ment to him, and hurried with it to the House of Lords, before it could be recalled; and they even surmise that he did not observe to the King the omission of his mother's name.[44] Be that as it may, open war seems to be declared between the Court and the Administration, and men are gazing to see which side will be victorious.

Tomorrow[45] the Bill comes to us, and Mr Pitt, too, violent against the whole Bill, unless this wonderful event has altered his tone.[46] For my part I shall not be surprised, if he affects to be in astonishment at missing *a great and most respectable name!*[47] This is the sum total—but what a sum total? It is the worst of *North Britons* published by Act of Parliament!

I took the liberty, in my last,[48] of telling you what I heard about your going to Ireland. It was from one you know very well, and one I thought well informed, or I should not have mentioned it. Positive as the information was, I find nothing to confirm it. On the contrary, Lord Harcourt seems the most probable,[49] if anything is probable at this strange juncture. You will scarce believe me when I tell you, what I know is true, that the Bedfords pressed strongly for Lord Weymouth[50]—yes, for Lord Weymouth. Is anything extraordinary in them?

Will it be presuming too much upon your friendship and indulgence, if I hint another point to you, which, I own, seems to me right to mention to you? You know how eagerly the Ministry have laboured to deprive Mr Thomas Walpole[51] of the French commerce of tobacco. His correspondent sends him word, that you was so persuaded it was taken away, that you had recommended another per-

44. See ibid., n. 34; John Brooke, *King George III*, New York, 1972, p. 112.

45. 6 May.

46. He did not attend; see *post* 12 May 1765.

47. Upon coming into power in 1757 Pitt had expressed surprise over omission of 'a very respectable name'—Lord Anson's—from the ministerial list (*Mem. Geo. II* iii. 32). HW's allusion is a sarcastic one, as he had a low opinion of Anson.

48. *Ante* 18 April 1765.

49. Not appointed this time, he was lord lieutenant of Ireland 1772–7.

50. Thomas Thynne (1734–96), 3d Vct Weymouth; 1751; cr. (1789) Marquess of Bath; lord lieutenant of Ireland 29 May – ca 12 July 1765 (*post* 20 May 1765, n. 53;

MANN vi. 311). HW describes him in *Mem. Geo. III* ii. 126–7 as 'an inconsiderable, debauched young man.' His appointment as lord lieutenant was extremely unpopular with the Irish, and he never set foot in that country.

51. (1727–1803), merchant and banker; HW's cousin and correspondent. He was at this time politically allied with Newcastle and Pitt, and had been deprived of his government contracts in 1762 upon following the former into Opposition. He and Sir Joshua Vanneck (see below) had possession of the lucrative contract with the French *fermiers généraux* to purchase tobacco for them in London (Namier and Brooke iii. 598–600).

son[52]—You know enough, my dear Lord, of the little connection I have with that part of my family,[53] though we do visit again,[54] and therefore will, I hope, be convinced, that it is for your sake that I principally mention it. If Mr Walpole loses this vast branch of trade, he and Sir Joshua Vanneck[55] must shut up shop. Judge the noise that would make in the City! Mr Walpole's alliance with the Cavendishes[56] (for I will say nothing of our family) would interest them deeply in his cause, and I think you would be sorry to have them think you instrumental to his ruin. Your brother knows of my writing to you and giving you this information, and we are both solicitous that your name should not appear in this transaction. This letter goes to you by a private hand, or I would not have spoken so plainly throughout. Whenever you please to recall your positive order, that I should always tell you whatever I hear that relates to you, I shall willingly forbear, for I am sensible this is not the most agreeable province of friendship; yet, as it is certainly due when demanded, I don't consider myself, but sacrifice the more agreeable task of pleasing you, to that of serving you, that I may show myself

Yours most sincerely,

H. W.

52. A false rumour; see Hertford's reply, *post* 17 May 1765. However, Thomas Walpole, who in 1767 took over full responsibility for the contract, was deprived of it in 1774 by Sir Robert Herries, a business rival (Namier and Brooke ii. 615, iii. 600).

53. Due to his enmity towards his uncle, 'old Horace' Walpole, 1st Bn Walpole of Wolterton, Thomas Walpole's father, stemming from old Horace's conduct in the 'Nicoll affair' of 1751; see Gray ii. 193–233.

54. Old Horace had died in 1757.

55. (d. 1777), cr. (1751) Bt; 'a mighty international financier of Dutch extraction, who had interests in every part of western Europe and America' (L. B. Namier, 'Brice Fisher, M.P.: A Mid-Eighteenth Century Merchant and his Connections,' *English Historical Review*, 1927, xlii. 525). Thomas and Richard Walpole both married daughters of Sir Joshua.

56. Thomas Walpole's elder brother, another Horace, who succeeded his father as 2d Bn Walpole, had married (1748) Rachel, the youngest daughter of William Cavendish, 3d Duke of Devonshire.

To Hertford, Sunday 12 May 1765

Printed from *Works* ix. 215-22.

Arlington Street, Sunday, May 12th 1765.

THE clouds and mists that I raised by my last letter will not be dispersed by this; nor will the Bill of Regency, as long as it has a day's breath left (and it has but one to come),[1] cease, I suppose, to produce extraordinary events. For agreeable events, it has not produced one to any set or side, except in gratifying malice; every other passion has received, or probably will receive, a box on the ear.

In my last I left the Princess Dowager in the mire. The next incident was of a negative kind. Mr Pitt, who, if he had been wise, would have come to help her out, chose to wait to see if she was to be left there, and gave himself a terrible fit of the gout. As nobody was ready *to read his part to the audience* (though, I assure you, we do not want a genius or two who think themselves born to dictate), the first day in our House[2] did not last two minutes. The next,[3] which was Tuesday, we rallied our understandings (mine, indeed, did not go beyond being quiet, when the Administration had done for us what we could not do for ourselves), and combatted the bill till nine at night.[4] Barré, who will very soon be our first orator, especially as some[5] are a little *afraid* to dispute with him, attacked it admirably,[6] and your brother ridiculed the House of Lords delight-

1. The bill was returned by the Commons to the Lords 13 May and passed by the latter House the same day (*Journals of the House of Lords* xxxi. 200).

2. 6 May, when the bill was read for the first time (*Journals of the House of Commons* xxx. 403).

3. For accounts of the debates of 7 May see *Mem. Geo. III* ii. 92–5 and Grenville to George III 7 May, printed in *Grenville Papers* iii. 23–5 and also in Geo. III's *Corr.*, ed. Fortescue, i. 82–3. For a list of speakers see ibid. i. 58–9 where the list, an enclosure to Grenville's letter, is incorrectly printed as an enclosure to his letter to the King of 16 Nov. 1763 (see L. B. Namier, *Additions and Corrections to Sir John Fortescue's Edition of the Correspondence of King George the*

Third (Vol. I), Manchester, 1937, pp. 19–20).

4. There were two principal debates during the day; the first, on Lord John Cavendish's motion for an address to the King desiring him to name the regent, lasted 'till near 6 o'clock,' when the motion was defeated without a division. Following this the bill was read for the second time, after it was moved that the bill be committed; the ensuing debate lasted 'till past 9 o'clock,' when the motion was carried, also without a division (Grenville to George III 7 May, loc. cit.; *Journals of the House of Commons* xxx. 407).

5. Charles Townshend presumably being one of them (see below).

6. In the debate on committing the bill

fully, who, he said, *had deliberated without concluding, and concluded without deliberating.* However, we broke up without a division.⁷

Can you devise what happened next? A buzz spread itself, that the Tories would move to reinstate the Princess. You will perhaps be so absurd as to think with me, that when the Administration had excluded her, it was our business to pay her a compliment. Alas! that was my opinion, but I was soon given to understand, that patriots must be men of virtue, must be Pharisees, and not countenance naughty women; and that when the Duchess of Bedford had thrown the first stone, we had nothing to do but continue pelting. Unluckily I was not convinced; I could neither see the morality nor prudence of branding the King's mother upon no other authority than public fame: yet, willing to get something when I could not get all, I endeavoured to obtain that we should stay away.⁸ Even this was warmly contested with me, and, though I persuaded several, particularly the two oldest Cavendishes,⁹ the Townshends,¹⁰ and your nephew Fitzroy,¹¹ whom I trust you will thank me for saving, I could not convince Lord John, who, I am sorry to say, is the most obstinate, conceited young man I ever saw; George Onslow, and that old simpleton the Duke of Newcastle, who had the impudence to talk to me of *character,* and that we should be ruined with the public, if we did not divide against the Princess.¹² You will be impatient, and wonder I do not name your brother. You know how

(Fortescue, op. cit. i. 59); see HW's summary of Barré's remarks in *Mem. Geo. III* ii. 94.

7. Though Conway 'spoke very strongly' against 'the particular provisions and clauses in the present bill,' he 'declared that he would vote for committing the bill' (Grenville to George III 7 May, loc. cit.) 'out of respect, and in order to try to amend it' (*Mem. Geo. III* ii. 95). After the motion to commit the bill had been carried and the day appointed (9 May) for the committee, most of the House went away, those remaining dividing 117–18 against a motion to print the bill; this remainder broke up 'near ten o'clock' (Grenville to George III 7 May, loc. cit.; *Journals of the House of Commons* xxx. 407–8).

8. HW proposed this 7 May (*Mem. Geo. III* loc. cit.).

9. Lord George and Lord Frederick.

10. Presumably the Hon. Thomas Townshend (1701–80), his son Thomas Townshend (1733–1800), and his nephew Charles Townshend of Honingham (1728–1810).

11. Charles Fitzroy, afterwards Bn Southampton.

12. HW met with Newcastle 8 May (*Mem. Geo. III* loc. cit.). The same day Newcastle wrote to Albemarle: 'I think, I see, some of our best friends are for absenting, and not being in the House. I think that most unadvisable. . . . It will be most unpopular; and will give room to the nation to think that we desert them in the great point which they have at heart, viz. the excluding the P—— and my Lord Bute' (BM Add. MSS 32966, f. 353).

much he respects virtue and honour, even in their names; Lord John, who, I really believe, respects them too, has got cunning enough to see their empire over your brother, and had fascinated him to agree to this outrageous, provoking, and most unjustifiable of all acts.[13] Still Mr Conway was so good as to yield to my earnest and vehement entreaties, and it was at last agreed to propose to name the Queen; and when we did not carry it, as we did not expect to do, to retire before the question came on the Princess. But even this measure was not strictly observed. We divided[14] 67 for the nomination of the Queen,[15] against 157.[16] Then Morton[17] moved to reinstate the Princess.[18] Martin,[19] her treasurer, made a most indiscreet[20] and offensive speech in her behalf; said she had been stigmatized by the House of Lords, and had lived long enough in this country to know the hearts and falsehood of those who had professed the most to her.[21] Grenville vows publicly he will never forgive this, and was not more discreet, declaring, though he agreed to the restoration of her name, that he thought the omission would have been universally *acceptable*.[22] George Onslow and all the Cavendishes, gained over by Lord

13. For HW's heated conversation with Conway to dissuade him from 'so ungentleman-like, outrageous, provoking and unjustifiable an act, as stigmatizing the King's mother,' see *Mem. Geo. III* ii. 91–2, 96–8.

14. 9 May.

15. Moved by Rose Fuller.

16. Evidently the latter figure is a slip; according to Grenville's various accounts to George III of 9 May (*Grenville Papers* iii. 29–30; Fortescue, op. cit. i. 84, 86) and *Mem. Geo. III* ii. 102, the division was 67 against 258.

17. John Morton (?1714–80), chief justice of Chester 1762–80; M.P. Abingdon 1747–70, New Romney 1770–4, Wigan 1775–80.

18. 'Had this Bill come down from the other House agreeable to his Majesty's speech, it would have met with an almost general concurrence; but altered as it now is, I think it necessary to propose an amendment. His Majesty's speech comprehended all his royal family. One is now excluded, and if that exclusion is with her own consent it is an instance of magnanimity which makes the propriety of inserting her name the greater' (Mor-

ton's speech in Grenville's 'Report to the King,' 9 May, *Grenville Papers* iii. 29). 'This is entirely a measure of my Lord Bute and the Tories, in direct defiance of the Duke of Bedford, and in opposition to a contrary motion made by a secretary of state [Halifax], and more than insinuated to be by order of the King, or with his Majesty's approbation, and directly contrary to the language held in both Houses, and particularly by Mr George Grenville' (Newcastle to Albemarle 9 May, BM Add. MSS 32966, f. 363).

19. Samuel Martin (*ante* 15 Nov. 1755), treasurer to the Princess Dowager of Wales 1757–72.

20. 'Very injudicious' (Lord Temple to Lady Chatham, 10 May, *Chatham Corr.* ii. 309).

21. 'I might almost call this a Parliamentary brand upon her. . . . She has, in twenty-eight years' experience in this country, had reason enough to know how little encomiums are to be relied on' (Martin's speech in Grenville's 'Report,' *Grenville Papers* iii. 30).

22. 'Grenville replied, that the words moved by Lord Halifax [3 May, omitting the Princess's name] were inserted to pre-

John, and the most attached of the Newcastle band, opposed the motion;[23] but your brother, Sir William Meredith, and I, and others, came away,[24] which reduced the numbers so much, that there was no division. But now to unfold all this black scene; it comes out as I had guessed, and very plainly told them, that the Bedfords had stirred up our fools to do what they did not dare to do themselves. Old Newcastle had even told me, that unless we opposed the Princess, the Duke of Bedford would not.[25] It was sedulously given out, that Forrester,[26] the latter Duke's lawyer, would speak against her; and after the question had passed, he told our people, that we had given up the game when it was in our hands, for there had been many more noes than ayes. It was very true, many did not wish well enough to the Princess to roar for her; and many will say *no,* when the question is put, who will vote *ay,* if it comes to a division, and of this I do not doubt but the Bedfords had taken care—well! duped by these gross arts, the Cavendishes and Pelhams determined to divide the next day[27] on the report.[28] I did not learn this mad

vent doubt: himself had thought they would not be disagreeable to her Royal Highness—hoped they were not—thought they would be universally acceptable—thought there had been authority for the omission, but found there was not; would concur in any compliment to the mother of his sovereign' (*Mem. Geo. III* ii. 104). 'George Grenville seemed to convey, that the alteration made in the Lords was not without the King's knowledge; but that, to be sure, in his opinion, such a testimony of zeal and affection which now manifested itself in the House of Commons, in favour of his royal mother, could not but prove agreeable to his Majesty, and that therefore he should concur in it' (Lord Temple to Lady Chatham, 10 May, loc. cit.). 'This cold, half-owning, half-denying speech, completed Grenville's ruin with the Princess' (*Mem. Geo. III* loc. cit.).

23. The Cavendishes wrote to Newcastle 8 May that 'they will . . . be very happy to concur in any opposition to this *damnable* design' (BM Add. MSS 32966, f. 355).

24. 'While the House was expecting Morton's motion, Mr Conway came to me and said he would go away with me, as

would Sir William Meredith and others. . . . I immediately went out, but found nobody followed me. I did not like to be single, and returned, but at last carried Mr Conway away' (*Mem. Geo. III* ii. 102).

25. 'Some of our best friends . . . not being in the House . . . will give the justest reason to the Duke of Bedford and his friends to let . . . go' 'the great point . . . [of] excluding the P—— and my Lord Bute' (Newcastle to Albemarle 8 May, loc. cit.).

26. Alexander Forrester (*ante* 6 Feb. 1764).

27. 10 May; for an account of the debates and a list of the speakers see Grenville to George III 11 May and his enclosure (Fortescue, op. cit. i. 87–91; *Grenville Papers* iii. 34–7).

28. HW writes in *Mem. Geo. III* ii. 106 that 'Newcastle's people . . . insisted on a division, driven on by John White, an old republican, who governed both Newcastle and Lord John Cavendish, and who hoped this vote would divide the Opposition from Mr Pitt, whom White hated, and who he certainly knew would never personally affront the Court.'

resolution till four o'clock, when it was too late, and your brother in the House, and the report actually made; so I turned back and came away, learning afterwards to my great mortification, that he had voted with them.[29] If anything could comfort me, it would be, that even so early as last night, and this only[30] happened on Friday night, it was generally allowed how much I had been in the right, and foretold exactly all that had happened. They had vaunted to me how strong they should be. I had replied, 'When you were but 76[31] on the most inoffensive question, do you think you will be half that number on the most personal and indecent that can be devised?' Accordingly, they were but 37 to 167;[32] and to show how much the Bedfords were at the bottom of all, Rigby, Forrester, and Lord Charles Spencer, went up into the Speaker's chamber, and would not vote for the Princess! At first I was not quite so well treated. Sir William Meredith, who, by the way, voted in the second question against his opinion,[33] told me Onslow had said that he, Sir William, your brother, and Lord Townshend,[34] had stayed away from conscience, but all the others from interest. I replied, 'Then I am included in the latter predicament: but you may tell Mr Onslow that he will take a place before I shall, and that I had rather be suspected of being mercenary, than stand up in my place and call God to witness that I meant nothing personal, when I was doing the most personal thing

29. 'When the question came on, he had the weakness, though he tried to prevent a division, to vote with the Cavendishes against her. They pretended to desire he would not, but knew how much the fear of their silent reproaches would operate on him' (*Mem. Geo. III* ii. 105–6). Conway wrote to Hertford, 16 May, that 'on one single point I was in opinion against appearing or dividing, as thinking it too personal. I had even stopped it one day but the rest, some very particular friends, with whom I have lately acted having declared they thought themselves under a necessity of doing it, I, who thought the point ill judged, could not bring myself to separate in a case which of all others was liable to the worst interpretation. I never mean to be so bound to any men as not to differ when I find it right to do so; but nothing less than a very strong conviction indeed shall make me do it in any case where they may see personal interest in doing it' (MS now WSL).

30. 'Only this' in *Works*.

31. *Sic* in *Works*; presumably a slip for 67, the Opposition vote in favour of nominating the Queen.

32. By which vote the Princess Dowager's name was inserted in the bill (*Journals of the House of Commons* xxx. 418).

33. He was a teller for the yeas when the House divided on a motion to recommit the bill, on the grounds that 'no provision was made in case any of the females who were enabled to be appointed regent should marry a papist or subject' (Grenville's enclosure in his letter to George III, 11 May, Fortescue, op. cit. i. 89; *Journals of the House of Commons*, loc. cit.). Since HW describes Meredith in *Mem. Geo. III* i. 279 as 'a convert from Jacobitism,' he may be alluding here to a lingering tolerance toward papists on the part of Meredith.

34. A slip for Thomas Townshend; see *Mem. Geo. III* ii. 105.

in the world.'—I beg your pardon, my dear Lord, for talking so much about myself, but the detail was necessary and important to you, who I wish should see that I can act with a little common sense, and will not be governed by all the frenzy of party.

The rest of the bill was contested inch by inch, and by division on division,[35] till eleven at night,[36] after our wise leaders had whittled down the minority to 24.[37] Charles Townshend, they say, surpassed all he had ever done, in a wrangle with Onslow,[38] and was so lucky as to have Barré absent, who has long laid in wait for him. When they told me how well Charles had spoken *on himself,* I replied, 'That is conformable to what I always thought of his parts, that he speaks best on what he understands the least.'[39]

We have done with the bill, and tomorrow[40] our correction goes to the Lords. It will be a day of wonderful expectation, to see in what manner they will swallow their vomit. The Duke of Bedford, it is conjectured, will stay away:[41]—but what will that scape-goose, Lord Halifax, do, who is already convicted of having told the King a most notorious lie, that if the Princess was not given up by the Lords, she would be unanimously excluded by the Commons?[42] The Duke of Bedford, who had broke the ground, is little less blameable; but Sandwich, who was present, has, with his usual address, contrived not to be talked of, since the first hour.[43]

35. The *Journals of the House of Commons* xxx. 418–19 lists four divisions.

36. 'Till half an hour past eleven' (Grenville to George III 11 May, Fortescue, op. cit. i. 87; *Grenville Papers* iii. 35).

37. After a motion was made to read the bill for the third time, a countermotion to adjourn the House was defeated 150-24 (*Journals of the House of Commons* xxx. 419).

38. 'The two Onslows [George Onslow and his cousin Col. George Onslow of Ockham] . . . fell on Charles Townshend . . . lamenting the loss of their old friend, and commenting in particular on his late silence, for he spoke but little for some time past. This fired him, he rose and with the greatest vivacity and wit vindicated himself, and chastised his antagonists, to the no small entertainment, I may say relish, of the House' (James Harris's MS 'Debates,' quoted in Sir Lewis Namier and John Brooke, *Charles Townshend,* 1964, p. 131; see Fortescue, op.

cit. i. 88, 90). Townshend afterwards told Harris that Onslow had been sent to him five times by Newcastle 'to persuade him . . . to oppose the Regency Bill, and that he had always refused it' (ibid.).

39. HW writes in *Mem. Geo. III* ii. 107 that 'Townshend replied in one of his best speeches, but, with his usual want of judgment, boasted of his own steadiness for sixteen years; saying, "Surely in these times, with a little common sense, I might have been dependent if I had pleased." The answer was obvious—"With a little common sense you might." '

40. 13 May.

41. A wrong conjecture; see *Journals of the House of Lords* xxxi. 199.

42. Halifax's alleged argument for persuading the King to agree to the exclusion of his mother's name from the Regency Bill; see *ante* 5 May 1765 and nn. 43–4.

43. Sandwich's rôle in this affair is doubtful; see MANN vi. 297, n. 32.

When the bill shall be passed, the eyes of mankind will turn to see what will be the consequence. The Princess, and Lord Bute, and the Scotch, do not affect to conceal their indignation. If Lord Halifax is even reprieved, the King is more enslaved to a cabal than ever his grandfather was: yet how replace them? Newcastle and the most desirable of the Opposition have rendered themselves more obnoxious than ever, and even seem, or must seem to Lord Bute, in league with those he wishes to remove. The want of a proper person for chancellor of the Exchequer is another difficulty, though I think easily removable by clapping a tied wig on Ellis,[44] Barrington,[45] or any other block, and calling it George Grenville.[46] One remedy is obvious, and at which, after such insults and provocations, were I Lord Bute, I should not stick; I would deliver myself up, bound hand and foot, to Mr Pitt, rather than not punish such traitors and wretches, who murmur, submit, affront, and swallow in the most ignominious manner,—*oh il faudra qu'il y vienne,*—as Léonor says in the *Marquis de Roselle*,[47]—*il y viendra.*[48] For myself, I have another little comfort, which is seeing, that when the Ministry encourage the Opposition, they do but lessen our numbers.

You may be easy about this letter, for Monsieur de Guerchy sends it for me by a private hand, as I did the last. I wish, by some such conveyance, you would tell me a little of your mind on all this embroil, and whether you approve or disapprove my conduct. After the liberties you have permitted me to take with you, my dear Lord, and without them, as you know my openness, and how much I am accustomed to hear of my faults, I think you cannot hesitate. Indeed, I trust, I have done, or tried to do, just what you would have wished. Could I, who have at least some experience and knowledge

44. Welbore Ellis, currently secretary at war.

45. William Wildman Barrington, 2d Vct Barrington, currently treasurer of the Navy; he had been chancellor of the Exchequer 1761–2.

46. Grenville had been chancellor of the Exchequer as well as first lord of the Treasury since 1763. He was succeeded in July by William Dowdeswell, whom HW described in *Mem. Geo. III* ii. 139 as 'suited to the drudgery of the office.'

47. *Lettres du Marquis de Roselle*, a novel by Anne-Louise Molin-Dumesnil (1729–83), m. (1750) Jean-Baptiste-Jacques

Élie de Beaumont. It was published in London and Paris, 1764; HW's copy of the Paris edition is now in the Bodleian (Hazen, *Cat. of HW's Lib.*, No. 938; MANN vi. 271 and nn. 17, 18; MASON i. 7, n. 3).

48. Vol. I, Lettre 47. Léonor, a designing opera singer who has artfully seduced the young and inexperienced Marquis de Roselle, banishes the Marquis after he has become too ardent in his advances. Her exclamation comes upon her receiving a letter from the Marquis imploring her to let him see her again, and is an expression of avarice, not affection.

of the world, have directed, our party had not been in the contempt-ible and ridiculous situation it is. Had I had more weight, things still more agreeable to you had happened. Now, I could almost despair; but I have still perseverance, and some resources left. When-ever I can get to you, I will unfold a great deal; but in this critical situation, I cannot trust what I can leave to no management but my own.

Your brother would have writ, if I had not: he is gone to Park Place today, with his usual phlegm, but returns tomorrow. What would I give you were here yourself; perhaps you do not thank me for the wish.

Do not wonder if, except thanking you for D'Alembert's book,[49] I say not a word of anything but politics. I have not had a single other thought these three weeks. Though in all the bloom of my passion, lilac-tide, I have not been at Strawberry this fortnight.[50] I saw things arrived at the point I wished,[51] and to which I had singularly contributed to bring them,[52] as you shall know hereafter, and then I saw all my work kicked down by two or three frantic boys,[53] and I see what I most dread,[54] likely to happen, unless I can prevent it,—but I have said enough for you to understand me. I think we agree. However, this is for no ear or breast but your own. Remember Monsieur de Nivernois, and take care of the letters you receive.[55] Adieu!

To Hertford, Thursday 16 May 1765

Missing; mentioned *post* 20 May 1765.

49. *Sur la destruction des Jésuites en France* (*ante* 29 April 1765).

50. HW wrote to Mann from SH 14 May (Mann vi. 293).

51. I.e., the division between Lord Bute and the ministers (*Mem. Geo. III* ii. 97).

52. 'I . . . divided the ministry by sug-gesting to the Duke of Richmond to name the Princess' (ibid.; see *ante* 5 May 1765, n. 34).

53. HW, in *Mem. Geo. III* loc. cit., focuses the blame on Lord John Caven-dish.

54. The reintrenchment of the minis-ters.

55. Nivernais's private letters had been published without his consent by d'Éon (*ante* 27 March 1764; Mann vi. 217).

From Hertford, Thursday 16 May 1765

Printed for the first time from a photostat of BM Add. MSS 23218, ff. 200–1.
Memoranda (by HW):

[? list of letters to be written]

    Ld Digby
    D. of Grafton
    Chute
    Ly Hervey[1]
    Ly Northum[berland]
    Mr Gray
    Mr Taylor[2]

[? subject matter for letters]

    Ireland[3]
    Lady Cornwallis[4]
    [?Lo. Villers]
    D. of Richmond[5]
    D. of Manchester[6]

Paris, May 16th 1765.

Dear Horry,

EXCUSE me for troubling you with the enclosed memorial;[7] it is put into my hands by a person whom I should be happy to oblige. You are curious and well-informed in the histories of great and noble families. I do not know where else to apply. I believe the Herald's office, which is conducted by land-jobbers and men of all other trades, know everything better than the business to which they are appointed. You see the memorialist[8] will receive benefit or at least great satisfaction if you can connect him in blood with the Arundels and Percys.[9]

1. HW's next extant letter to her is the letter of 11 June 1765, in which he apologizes for his 'neglect' of her (MORE 35).

2. Not identified.

3. Mentioned after the receipt of this letter in HW's letter to Hertford *post* 20 May 1765, *sub* [24 May].

4. Hon. Elizabeth Townshend (d. 1785), m. (1722) Charles Cornwallis, 5th Bn Cornwallis, cr. (1753) E. Cornwallis.

5. Like 'Ireland' (n. 3 above), mentioned after the receipt of this letter in HW to Hertford *post* 20 May 1765.

6. Mentioned in HW's letter to Lord Holland, 29 May 1765 (SELWYN 187).

7. Of the family of Brébeuf (*post* 20 May 1765), an ancient and noble family of Normandy (La Chenaye-Desbois iv. 38; Henri Jougla de Morenas, *Grand Armorial de France*, 1934–49, ii. 248). Its most fa-

mous members were Jean de Brébeuf (1593–1649), Jesuit missionary and martyr, and Georges de Brébeuf (?1617–61), poet (*Dictionnaire de biographie française*, 1933– , vii. 187–8).

8. Perhaps the Seigneur de Brébeuf mentioned in the *Gazette de France*, 24 March 1759, as having been named 'inspecteur général des côtes maritimes' (*Répertoire . . . de la Gazette de France*, ed. de Granges de Surgères, 1902–6, i. 528).

9. Both English families with roots in Normandy. A Seigneur de Brébeuf was in the sixteenth century 'allié' to Marie, daughter of Gilles, Seigneur de la Luzerne by his wife Bernardine de Percy, daughter of Nicolas, Seigneur de Percy and de Soulles, possibly a distant cousin of the English Percys (La Chenaye-Desbois xii. 626). Through the Percys the Brébeufs may have been connected with the Arun-

I have not heard from you or any of my friends this month almost, and yet we are very curious to be particularly informed about the motives or truth of what we have heard relating to the Regency Bill. It is a singular transaction in the way it is reported here.

Lady Holland and her two sisters have been some days at Paris, in the course of which they have both dined and supped with us.[10] They are now going to the Prince of Conti's in the country.[11] Lady Hertford tells me Lady Louisa and Lady Sarah talk of returning to England in eight or ten days;[12] Lady Holland will stay longer.[13]

Accept the best compliments of the family and believe me, dear Horry,

Always truly and affectionately yours,

HERTFORD

From HERTFORD, Friday 17 May 1765

Printed for the first time from a photostat of BM Add. MSS 23218, f. 218.

Paris, May 17th 1765.

Dear Horry,

I HAVE just now received your letter of the 5th from Monsieur de Guerchy, and have but a moment to acknowledge it before the departure of a gentleman who has promised to carry this to London.

I am excessively obliged to you for the information you have given me about Mr Thomas Walpole. It is the first notice I have had about it and is absolutely void of all foundation on my part, which I beg you will say to any who are interested for him. I have wrote myself to Mr Walpole to assure him that I am incapable knowingly of doing anything that may prejudice him or his house, for which I have justly so much consideration, and to which I am

dels; see GEC i. 250, x. 458 and n. 'k.' For the Anglo-Norman Brébeufs, see Lewis C. Loyd, *The Origins of Some Anglo-Norman Families*, ed. C. T. Clay and D. C. Douglas, Leeds, 1951, p. 19 (Harleian Society Publications, Vol. CIII).

10. See *ante* 29 April 1765 and nn. 5, 6, 8.

11. Lady Holland wrote to Lady Kil-

dare from L'Isle Adam, 20 May: 'Here we are at the Prince of Conti's house in the country, about twenty-five miles from Paris, since Saturday evening [18 May]' (*Leinster Corr.* i. 426).

12. They left Paris 3 June (idem to idem, 16 July, ibid. i. 430).

13. She left 1 July (ibid.).

particularly invited by my connection with his name and family.[1]
The history of the Regency is a curious one. I need not tell you
what is said and thought of it here; there can be but one opinion
upon the conduct of it.

Be assured, my dear Horry, that I am perfectly sensible of your
friendship in telling me all that is said of or about me; it is the
kindest thing you can do and I always wish to hear. You may believe
me upon this subject, as well as that I am and always shall be

Most sincerely and faithfully yours,

HERTFORD

Lord Weymouth is a curious candidate;[2] I should not have
guessed it.

To HERTFORD, Monday 20 May 1765

Printed from *Works* ix. 222–33.

Arlington Street, Monday evening, May 20th 1765.

I SCARCE know where to begin, and I am sure not[1] where I shall
end. I had comforted myself with getting over all my difficulties:
my friends opened their eyes, and were ready, nay, some of
them eager, to list under Mr Pitt; for I must tell you, that by a
fatal precipitation, the King—when his ministers went to him last
Thursday, 16th, to receive his commands for his speech, at the end
of the session, which was to have been the day after tomorrow, the
22d—forbade the Parliament to be prorogued, which he said he
would only have adjourned; they were thunderstruck, and asked if
he intended to make any change in his administration? he replied,
certainly; he could not bear it as it was.[2] His uncle[3] was sent for,
was ordered to form a new administration, and treat with Mr Pitt.[4]

1. That is, through HW, who was their mutual first cousin.
2. For lord lieutenant of Ireland.

1. *Sic* in *Works*.
2. The King's conversation with his ministers took place on two separate days, the 16th and 19th; see *Grenville Papers* iii. 165–6, 170–2.

3. The Duke of Cumberland.
4. On 13 May, 'very late in the evening,' Lord Northumberland, who was intended by the King to be first lord of the Treasury in the new administration, 'sent in to desire to speak to me, acquainting me that he came to me by his Majesty's orders, that I should endeavour to see whether Mr Pitt and Lord Tem-

This negotiation proceeded for four days, and got wind in two.⁵ The town, more accommodating than Mr Pitt, settled the whole list of employments. The facilities, however, were so few, that yesterday the Hero of Culloden went down in person to the Conqueror of America, at Hayes, and though tendering almost *carte blanche,—blanchissime* for the Constitution, and little short of it for the whole red book of places,—brought back nothing but a flat refusal.⁶ Words cannot paint the confusion into which everything is thrown. The four ministers, I mean the Duke of Bedford, Grenville, and the two secretaries,⁷ acquainted their master yesterday, that they adhere to one another, and shall all resign tomorrow,⁸ and, perhaps, must be recalled on Wednesday,—must have a *carte noire*, not *blanche*, and will certainly not expect any stipulations to be offered for the Constitution, by no means the object of their care!

You are not likely to tell in Gath, nor publish in Ascalon,⁹ the alternative of humiliation to which the Crown is reduced. But, alas! this is far from being the lightest evil to which we are at the eve of being exposed. I mentioned¹⁰ the mob of weavers which had besieged the Parliament, and attacked the Duke of Bedford,¹¹ and I

ple, with the other great Whig families, could not be brought to form him a strong and a lasting administration, which might empower him to form systems at home and abroad, such as the dangers of the times might require; desiring withal that this negotiation might be carried on with the utmost secrecy and celerity, as its magnitude would allow of' (D. of Cumberland's misdated 'Account,' in Lord Albemarle, *Memoirs of . . . Rockingham*, 1852, i. 191–2).

5. The Duke of Bedford wrote to the Duke of Marlborough, 19 May, that it 'transpired on Thursday night [16 May] that a negotiation was actually then carrying on, through the channel of the Duke of Cumberland, with Mr Pitt, Lord Temple,' etc. (*Bedford Corr.* iii. 279).

6. For Pitt's terms, see Albemarle, op. cit. i. 193, 196–8.

7. Halifax and Sandwich.

8. Sandwich wrote to Grenville, 19 May, that 'the Duke of Bedford, Lord Halifax, and Lord Chancellor [Northington], will be at my house this morning at 12 o'clock, to consider what language we shall hold to the King . . . we shall be much obliged to you if you will be at

this meeting' (*Grenville Papers* iii. 38). In his interview with the King, Grenville asserted that the adjournment of Parliament should be moved by his successor (Grenville's 'Diary,' ibid. iii. 171); Bedford had, 16 May, 'entreated' the King, 'for his own sake, the public's, our own, and his future ministers, to fix our successors immediately' (Bedford to Marlborough, 19 May, *Bedford Corr.* iii. 280). However, Grenville's account of the ministers' interviews with the King does not mention a specific date for their resignation (*Grenville Papers* iii. 170–2).

9. 'Tell it not in Gath, publish it not in the streets of Askelon; lest the daughters of the Philistines rejoice, lest the daughters of the uncircumcised triumph' (2 Samuel 1. 20).

10. Presumably in his missing letter to Hertford, *ante* 16 May 1765.

11. 'On a bill for their relief being thrown out of the House of Lords by the Duke' (HW to Mann, 25 May 1765, MANN vi. 301). The Wrought Silks and Velvets Bill, 'for laying several additional duties upon the importation of wrought silks and velvets; for the encouragement of the silk manufacturers,' etc., which had

thought no more of it; but on Friday,[12] a well disciplined, and, I fear, too well conducted a multitude,[13] repaired again to Westminster, with red and black flags;[14] the House of Lords, where not thirty were present,[15] acted with no spirit;—examined Justice Fielding, and the magistrates, and adjourned till today.[16] At seven that evening, a prodigious multitude assaulted Bedford House, and began to pull down the walls, and another party surrounded the garden, where there were but fifty men on guard, and had forced their way, if another party of guards that had been sent for had arrived five minutes later.[17] At last, after reading the proclamation,[17a] the gates of the court were thrown open, and sixty foot soldiers marched out; the mob fled, but being met by a party of horse, were much cut and trampled, but no lives lost.[18] Lady Tavistock,[19] and everything valuable in the house, have been sent out of town. On Saturday, all

passed the Commons 6 May (*Journals of the House of Commons* xxx. 403), came to the Lords the same day, and was ordered to 'be rejected' on its second reading 13 May (*Journals of the House of Lords* xxxi. 180, 200). 'Bedford alone spoke against it; nobody said a word for it, and it was thrown out' (*Mem. Geo. III* ii. 110–11). The House of Lords was 'besieged' 15 May, and the same day the Duke of Bedford narrowly escaped serious injury when a stone thrown into his chariot bruised him on the temple (ibid. ii. 111; *Grenville Papers* iii. 164). See also George F. Rudé, *The Crowd in History; a Study of Popular Disturbances in France and England, 1730–1848*, New York, 1964, p. 72.

12. 17 May.

13. HW, in *Mem. Geo. III* ii. 113, writes that 'in my own opinion, the mob was blown up by Humphrey Cotes, and the friends of Wilkes. Almond [*sic*], the friend and printer of the latter, owned to me, that they were directed by four or five gentlemen in disguise.'

14. The *London Chronicle* 14–16 May, xvii. 465 mentions 'a black flag carried before them . . . to represent to his Majesty their distressed condition for want of work.'

15. 43 are listed, *Journals of the House of Lords* xxxi. 208.

16. Ibid. 210.

17. 'While I am now writing two Messengers are arrived to inform me that Bed-

ford House is actually attacked by many thousands. I have given orders to Lt-Col. Warrender to march with his squadron immediately; and a troop of grenadier guards and one of horse guards to proceed as speedily thither as is possible. Two officers and fifty men of the foot guards have orders to take post at Bedford House and to continue there all night, and a patrol of horse to be maintained all night in the fields at the back of Bedford House' (Welbore Ellis to George III, 'half past six,' 17 May, Geo. III's *Corr.* ed. Fortescue, i. 95).

17a. I.e., the Riot Act.

18. 'Justice Walsh read the proclamation and the mob not dispersing thereupon, the Justice ordered his troop to charge upon them; which it accordingly did, but with orders to his men not to cut with their swords nor to draw a pistol. This charge broke the mob and threw many down and the rest ran into courts and the openings of the streets, where, there being some houses rebuilding, the mob with the bricks pelted the guards very severely and hurt several men and horses . . . No one of the mob was materially hurt as had been heard of. . . . There remained one hundred and seventy of the foot guards at Bedford House and the remainder of the night passed quietly' (idem to idem, 18 May, ibid. i. 100–1). See also Halifax to George III, 17 May, ibid. i. 97 and *Grenville Papers* iii. 168.

19. The Duke's daughter-in-law.

was pretty quiet; the Duchess was blooded,[20] and everybody went to visit them. I hesitated, being afraid of an air of triumph; however, lest it should be construed the other way, I went last night at eight o'clock; in the square I found a great multitude, not of weavers, but seemingly of Sunday passengers. At the gate guarded by grenadiers, I found so large a throng, that I had not only difficulty to make my way, though in my chariot, but was hissed and pelted, and in two minutes after, the glass of Lady Grosvenor's coach was broken, as those of Lady Cork's[21] chair were entirely demolished afterwards. I found Bedford House a perfect garrison,[22] sustaining a siege, the Court full of horse-guards, constables, and gentlemen. I told the Duke that however I might happen to differ with him in politics, this was a common cause, and that everybody must feel equal indignation at it. In the meantime the mob grew so riotous, that they were forced to make both horse and foot parade the square before the tumult was dispersed.[23]

Tomorrow we expect much worse. The weavers have declared they will come down to the House of Lords for redress, which they say they have been promised.[24] A body of 500 sailors were on the road from Portsmouth to join them, but luckily the Admiralty had notice of their intention, and stopped them. A large body of weavers are on the road from Norwich, and it is said have been joined by numbers in Essex; guards are posted to prevent, if possible, their approaching the city.[25] Another troop of manufacturers are coming from Manchester, and what is worst of all, there is such a general spirit of mutiny and dissatisfaction in the lower people, that I think

20. See *Grenville Papers* iii. 169.

21. Anne Courtenay (ca 1742–85), m. (1764) Edmund Boyle, 7th E. of Corke.

22. Bedford wrote to Marlborough, 19 May, that 'I am yet obliged to keep garrison here with 100 infantry and 36 cavalry' (*Bedford Corr.* iii. 279).

23. 'Monday, May 20th.—Lord Halifax came early in the morning to Mr Grenville, to show him a letter from the Duke of Bedford, giving an account of the mob having gathered again before Bedford House the night before, where they had been very outrageous, and the Guards were again obliged to disperse them' (Grenville's 'Diary,' *Grenville Papers* iii. 172).

24. The King, addressing 'three or four thousand' weavers who had come to petition him 14 May, 'told them he would do all that lay in his power to relieve them, and they returned pleased and orderly' (*Mem. Geo. III* ii. 111).

25. 'Notice having been received that many thousands of weavers were coming from Norwich to join those in London, orders were timely dispatched to the officers of several regiments, to take their quarters on the London road; which had the desired effect, for the country weavers, on finding their junction with their town brethren prevented, returned home again' (*London Chronicle* 21–3 May, xvii. 489, *sub* 22 May).

we are in danger of a rebellion in the heart of the capital in a week. In the meantime, there is neither administration nor government. The King is out of town,[26] and this is the crisis in which Mr Pitt, who could stop every evil, chooses to be more unreasonable than ever.[27]

Mr Craufurd,[28] whom you have seen at the Duchess of Grafton's, carries this, or I should not venture being so explicit. Wherever the storm may break out at first, I think Lord Bute cannot escape his share of it. The Bedfords may triumph over him, the Princess, and still higher, if they are fortunate enough to avoid the present ugly appearances; and yet how the load of odium will be increased, if they return to power! One can name many in whose situation one would not be,—not one, who is not situated unpleasantly.

Adieu! my dear Lord; you shall hear as often as I can find a conveyance; but these are not topics for the post!

Poor Mrs Fitzroy[29] has lost her eldest girl.[30] I forgot to tell you that the young Duke of Devonshire goes to Court tomorrow.

Yours, ever,

H. W.

Wednesday evening [22 May].

I am forced to send you journals rather than letters. Mr Craufurd, who was to carry this, has put off his journey till Saturday, and I choose rather to defer my dispatch than trust it to Guerchy's courier, though he offered me that conveyance yesterday, but it is too serious to venture to their inspection.

---

26. He was at Richmond, but returned the next day (Fortescue, op. cit. i. 102, 105, 107).

27. Edmund Burke wrote to Henry Flood, 18 May: 'Nothing but an intractable temper in your friend Pitt can prevent a most admirable and lasting system from being put together; and this crisis will show whether pride or patriotism be predominant in his character; for you may be assured, that he has it now in his power to come into the service of his country upon any plan of politics he may choose to dictate; with great and honourable terms to himself and to every friend he has in the world; and with such a stretch of power as will be equal to every thing but absolute despotism over the King and kingdom. A few days will show whether he will take this part or that of continuing on his back at Hayes talking fustian' (Burke, *Correspondence*, Vol. I, ed. T. W. Copeland, Cambridge, 1958, p. 194).

28. John Craufurd (?1742–1814), HW's correspondent (OSSORY i. 24, n. 28).

29. The wife of Charles Fitzroy, later Bn Southampton (*ante* 15 Feb. 1764).

30. Anne Caroline Fitzroy (b. 1759) (Collins, *Peerage*, 1812, vii. 540).

Such precautions have been taken, and so many troops brought into town, that there has been no rising, though the sheriffs of London acquainted the Lords on Monday that a very formidable one was preparing for five o'clock the next morning.[31] There was another tumult, indeed, at three o'clock yesterday, at Bedford House, but it was dispersed by reading the Riot Act. In the meantime, the revolution has turned round again. The Ministers desired the King to commission Lord Granby, the Duke of Richmond, and Lord Waldegrave, to suppress the riots,[32] which, in truth, was little short of asking for the power of the sword against himself. On this, his Majesty determined to name the Duke of Cumberland captain-general;[33] but the tranquillity of the rioters happily gave H. R. H. occasion to persuade the King to suspend that resolution.[34] Thank God! From eleven o'clock yesterday, when I heard it, till nine at night, when I learned that the resolution had dropped, I think I never passed such anxious hours! nay, I heard it was done, and looked upon the civil war as commenced. During these events, the Duke was endeavouring to form a ministry, but, luckily, nobody would undertake it when Mr Pitt had refused; so the King is reduced to the mortification, and it is extreme, of taking his old ministers again. They are insolent enough, you may believe: Grenville has treated his master in the most impertinent manner, and they are now actually digesting the terms that they mean to impose on their captive, and Lord Bute is the chief object of their rage; though I think Lord Holland will not escape, nor Lord Northumberland,[35] whom they treat as an encourager of the rioters. Both he

31. 'The sheriffs said they had received certain information that the weavers were to rise in arms at five in the morning, were to be joined by the butchers and watermen, and destroy Bedford House' (*Mem. Geo. III* ii. 120).

32. 'His Majesty will determine whether it may not be proper to appoint the Marquis of Granby to the chief command of the troops tomorrow, with the Earl of Waldegrave (who offers himself, as well as the Duke of Richmond, for the service), or any other general his Majesty shall please to appoint. Lord Granby is a very popular man, and might save the lives of these deluded wretches, which may be exposed and sacrificed by another commander, equally well-intentioned, but

less a favourite of the people' (Lord Halifax to George III 20 May, Fortescue, op. cit. i. 105; L. B. Namier, *Additions and Corrections to Sir John Fortescue's Edition of the Correspondence of King George the Third (Vol. I)*, Manchester, 1937, p. 28).

33. 'I little thought I should be so troublesome to you as the conduct of the men I have employed forces me . . . but now I must desire you to take the command tomorrow morning as captain general' (George III to Cumberland 20 May, Fortescue, op. cit. i. 106).

34. See *Mem. Geo. III* ii. 121–2.

35. Both were removed from their offices (see below), though apparently only Northumberland was involved in the

and my Lady went on Monday night to Bedford House, and were received with every mark of insult. The Duke turned his back on the Earl, without speaking to him, and he was kept standing an hour exposed to all their raillery.[36] Still I have a more extraordinary event to tell you than all I have related. Lord Temple and George Grenville were reconciled yesterday morning, by the intervention of Augustus Hervey;[37] and, perhaps, the next thing you will hear, may be, that Lord Temple is sent by this ministry to Ireland, though Lord Weymouth is again much talked of for it.

The report of Norwich and Manchester weavers on the road is now doubted. If Lord Bute is banished, I suppose the Duke of Bedford will become the hero of this very mob, and every act of power which they have executed, let who will have been the adviser, will be forgotten. It will be entertaining to see Lord Temple supporting Lord Halifax on general warrants!

You have more than once seen your old master[38] reduced to surrender up his closet to a cabal[39]—but never with such circumstances of insult, indignity, and humiliation! For our little party, it is more humbled than ever. Still I prefer that state to what I dread; I mean, seeing your brother embarked in a desperate administration. It was proposed first to make him secretary at war, then secretary of state,[40] but he declined both. Yet I trembled, lest he should think himself bound in honour to obey the commands of the King and Duke of Cumberland; but, to my great joy, that alarm is over, unless the triumphant faction exact more than the King can possibly suffer. It will rejoice you, however, my dear Lord, to hear that Mr Conway is perfectly restored to the King's favour, and that if he continues in Opposition, it will not be against the King, but a most

negotiation for a new ministry (n. 4 above).

36. 'Lord and Lady Northumberland made a visit at Bedford House while Mr Grenville was there. Lord Northumberland had a very cold reception, and the language which passed before him could not be very pleasing' (Grenville's 'Diary,' 20 May, *Grenville Papers* iii. 176).

37. HW's report of the reconciliation is a trifle premature; though 'Mr Grenville waited upon Lord T[emple] at twelve o'clock [21 May] . . . many difficulties arising in the course of the conversation upon past matters, they parted without

agreeing' (Grenville's MS memorandum, 21 May, *Grenville Papers* iii. 43). Their reconciliation, encouraged by Halifax, Sandwich, and Bedford, was effected the next day (ibid. iii. 42–3, 174, 176, 183).

38. George II.

39. For instance, in 1746 George II dismissed Newcastle and Harrington and then had to take them back when Granville was unable to form a government.

40. In Newcastle's list of 'persons who should be immediately considered' 17 May, Conway is noted with William Dowdeswell as 'regiment, government, or Treasury' (BM Add. MSS 32966, f. 424).

abominable faction, who having raged against the Constitution and their country to pay court to Lord Bute, have even thrown off that paltry mask, and avowedly hoisted the standard of their own power. Till the King has signed their demands, one cannot look upon this scene as closed.

Friday evening [24 May].

You will think, my dear Lord, and it is natural you should, that I write my letters at once, and compose one part with my prophecies, and the other with the completion of them; but you must recollect that I understand this country pretty well,—attend closely to what passes,—have very good intelligence,—and know the characters of the actors thoroughly. A little sagacity added to such foundation, easily carries one's sight a good way; but you will care for my narrative more than my reflections, so I proceed.

On Wednesday, the Ministers dictated their terms; you will not expect much moderation, and, accordingly, there was not a grain: they demanded a royal promise of never consulting Lord Bute;[41] secondly, the dismission of Mr Mekinsy[42] from the direction of Scotland;[43] thirdly, and lastly,[44] for they could go no further, the Crown itself—or, in their words, the immediate nomination of Lord Granby to be captain-general.[45] You may figure the King's indignation—for himself, for his favourite, for his uncle. In my own opinion, the proposal of grounds for taxing his Majesty himself hereafter with breaking his word, was the bitterest affront of all.[46] He expressed his anger and astonishment, and bade them return at

41. 'That the King's ministers should be authorized to declare that Lord Bute is to have nothing to do in his Majesty's councils or government, in any manner or shape whatever' (minutes of the ministers' meeting 'at Mr Grenville's,' 22 May, *Grenville Papers* iii. 41).

42. James Stuart Mackenzie, Bute's brother.

43. 'That Mr Stewart Mackenzie be removed from his office of lord privy seal of Scotland, and from the authority and influence which has been given to him in that kingdom' (ibid.).

44. There were two more terms; see below, nn. 52–3.

45. 'That Lord Granby be appointed

commander-in-chief of the army' (*Grenville Papers* loc. cit.).

46. Mackenzie's office of privy seal had in effect been promised to him for life (George III to Lord Egmont, 23 May, Fortescue, op. cit. i. 113). He reported the King as saying to Grenville that 'if you force me . . . to violate my royal word, remember you are responsible for it, not I!' (to William Mure, 4 June, *Selections from the Family Papers Preserved at Caldwell*, ed. William Mure, Glasgow, 1854, Pt II, ii. 37). The King also told Granby and the ministers that he had promised the command of the army to the Duke of Cumberland (n. 50 below).

ten at night for his answer;[47] but, before that, he sent the Chancellor
to the junto, consenting to displace Mekinsy,[48] refusing to promise
not to consult Lord Bute,[49] though acquiescing to his not interfering
in business, but with a peremptory refusal to the article of Lord
Granby.[50] The rebels took till next morning to advise on their answer, when they gave up the point of Lord Granby, and contented
themselves with the modification on the chapter of Lord Bute. However, not to be too complimentary, they demanded Mekinsy's place
for Lord Lorn,[51] and the instant removal of Lord Holland;[52] both
which have been granted. Charles Townshend is paymaster, and
Lord Weymouth viceroy of Ireland;[53] so Lord Northumberland remains on the *pavé*, which, as there is no place vacant for him, it was
not necessary to stipulate. The Duchess of Bedford, with colours
flying, issued out of her garrison yesterday, and took possession of
the Drawing-Room. Today their *Majesty-Graces* are gone to Woburn;
but as the Duchess is a perfect Methodist against all suspicious characters, it is said, today, that Lord Talbot is to be added to the list

47. 'The King said he would consider
. . . and give Mr Grenville his answer in
the evening' (*Grenville Papers* iii. 184).
'I sent for Grenville at twelve last night
and answered his questions' (George III to
Egmont, loc. cit.).

48. He consented 'that they might make
use of other persons in the management
of Scotch affairs than Mr Mackenzie,' but
did not yield on the point of dismissing
him as privy seal until the following day
(George III to Egmont, 23 May, loc. cit.;
Grenville Papers iii. 185-7).

49. The King agreed 'that Lord Bute
should not be consulted by me in public
affairs'; see George III to Egmont, 23
May, loc. cit.; *Grenville Papers* iii. 185.
This promise was relatively easy to make
since the King was no longer so influenced by Bute as was generally supposed;
in fact, according to a memorandum by
Gilbert Elliot, the King claimed that 'he
had talked no politics with Lord Bute
since he retired to his house at Luton,
August 1763' (*Jenkinson Papers 1760–
1766*, ed. N. S. Jucker, 1949, p. 371). See
also John Brooke, *King George III*, New
York, 1972, p. 125.

50. The King had in an interview with
Granby earlier that day found him willing to decline the command of the army,
and explained to Grenville 'that after
what had passed with the D. of Cumberland I was engaged to put him alone at
the head of the army, that the Duke had
again reminded me of my promise, that I
had seen Lord Granby who declared I
could not in honour do otherwise' (George
III to Lord Egmont, 23 May, loc. cit.;
Grenville Papers iii. 184–5). See also Egmont's notes written on the King's letter,
Fortescue, op. cit. i. 113–15 and *Grenville
Papers* iii. 186–7.

51. See below.

52. From the post of paymaster general.
This was one of the original terms out-
lined by the ministers 22 May, and was
agreed to by the King the same evening
(*Grenville Papers* iii. 41; George III to
Egmont, 23 May, loc. cit.).

53. His appointment was announced
in the *London Gazette* No. 10526, 28 May–
1 June, *sub* 29 May. Another of the original terms outlined by the ministers 22
May, also agreed to by the King the same
evening, was 'that the King would be
pleased to settle the government of Ireland with his ministers' (*Grenville Papers*
iii. 41, 186; George III to Egmont, 23
May, loc. cit.).

of proscriptions,[54] and now they think themselves established for-ever.—Do they so?

Lord Temple declares himself the warmest friend of the present Administration;—there is a mystery still to be cleared up,—and perhaps, a little to the mortification of Bedford House.—We shall see.

The Duke of Cumberland is retired to Windsor: your brother gone to Park Place: I go to Strawberry tomorrow,[55] lest people should not think me a great man too. I don't know whether I shall not even think it necessary to order myself a fit of the gout.

I have received your short letter of the 16th, with the memorial of the family of Brébeuf;—now my head will have a little leisure, I will examine it, and see if I can do anything in the affair. In that letter you say, you have been a month without hearing from any of your friends. I little expected to be taxed on that head: I have written you volumes almost every day; my last dates have been of April 11th,[56] 20th,[57] May 5th, 12th, and 16th.[58] I beg you will look over them, and send me word exactly, and I beg you not to omit it, whether any of these are missing.[59] Three of them[60] I trusted to Guerchy, but took care they should contain nothing which it signi-fied whether seen or not on t'other side of the water, though I did not care they should be perused on this. I had the caution not to let him have this, though; by the eagerness with which he proffered both today and yesterday, to send anything by his couriers, I sus-pected he wished to help them to better intelligence than he could give them himself. He even told me he should have another courier depart on Tuesday next; but I excused myself, on pretence of hav-ing too much to write at once, and shall send this and a letter your brother has left me by Mr Craufurd, though he does not set out till Sunday; but you had better wait for it from him, than from the Duc de Choiseul. Pray commend my discretion—you see I grow a consummate politician; but don't approve of it too much, lest I only send you letters as prudent as your own.

You may acquaint Lady Holland with the dismission of her Lord,

54. HW wrote to Hertford, *ante* 22 Jan. 1764, that Lord Talbot was 'greatly dis-satisfied' with the administration. He continued as lord steward of the House-hold till his death in 1782.

55. HW wrote to Montagu from SH 26 May (MONTAGU ii. 152).

56. Missing.

57. *Ante* 18–20 April 1765.

58. Missing.

59. Hertford announced that he had received all of them, *post* 30 May 1765.

60. The last three.

if she has not heard it, he being at Kingsgate.[60a] Your secretary[61] is likely to be prime minister in Ireland.[62] Two months ago the new Viceroy himself was going to France for debt, leaving his wife and children[63] to be maintained by her mother.[64]

I will be much obliged to you, my dear Lord, if you will contrive to pay Lady Stanhope for the medals;[65] they cost, I think, but £ 4 7s., or thereabout—but I have lost the note.

Adieu! here ends volume the first. *Omnia mutantur, sed non mutamur in illis.*[66] Princess Amelia, who has a little veered round to northwest, and by Bedford, does not speak tenderly of her brother[67]—but if some families are reconciled, others are disunited. The Keppels are at open war with the Keppels,[68] and Lady Mary Coke weeps with one eye over Lady Betty Mackinsy,[69] and smiles with t'other on Lady Dalkeith;[70] but the first eye is the sincerest.[71] The Duke of Richmond, in exactly the same proportion, is divided between his sisters, Holland and Bunbury.

Thank you much for your kindness about Mr T. Walpole—I have not had a moment's time to see him, but will do full justice to your goodness.

Yours ever,

H. W.

60a. His seat on the coast of Kent near the North Foreland; see Lord Ilchester, *Henry Fox, First Lord Holland,* 1920, ii. 168, 279–80, 294–5.

61. Bunbury.

62. He was named secretary to Weymouth in Ireland, but was dismissed along with his chief in July; see below, and *post* 30 May, 1 July 1765.

63. Louisa Thynne (1760–1832), m. (1781) Heneage Finch, 4th E. of Aylesford; Henrietta Thynne (1762–1813), m. (1799) Philip Stanhope, 5th E. of Chesterfield; Sophia Thynne (1763–91), m. (1784) George Ashburnham, styled Vct St Asaph; and Thomas Thynne (25 Jan. 1765 – 1837), 2d Marquess of Bath, 1796 (Collins, *Peerage,* 1812, ii. 510–11; GEC).

64. Margaret Cavendish Harley (1715–85), m. (1734) William Bentinck (1709–62), 2d Duke of Portland.

65. See *ante* 10, 18 April 1765.

66. 'All things change, but we do not change with them,' HW's adaptation of 'Omnia mutantur, nos et mutamur in

illis' ('All things change, and we change with them'), a motto designed by Matthias Borbonius (1566–1629) for the emperor Lotharius I (795–855) (*Delitiæ poetarum germanorum,* ed. Janus Gruterus, Frankfurt, 1612, i. 685). HW owned copies of the *Epigrammata* of John Owen (?1560–1622), Amsterdam, 1632, and a translation of these by Thomas Harvey, entitled *Latine Epigrams,* London, 1677 (Hazen, *Cat. of HW's Lib.,* Nos 2022, 2250); Epigram 58 of Book 8 is Owen's adaptation of Borbonius's motto: 'Tempora mutantur, nos et mutamur in illis.'

67. The Duke of Cumberland.

68. The alleged feud perhaps bore some relation to the fact that Lady Elizabeth Keppel was married to the Duke of Bedford's son, while her brother, Lord Albemarle, was the Duke of Cumberland's chief adherent.

69. Her sister, wife of Stuart Mackenzie.

70. Another sister, wife of Charles Townshend.

71. Lady Mary was an avid courtier.

Pray remember the dates of my letters—you will be strangely puzzled for a clue, if one of them has miscarried. Sir Charles Bunbury is not to be secretary for Ireland, but Thurloe,[72] the lawyer: they are to stay five years without returning. Lord Lorn has declined, and Lord Frederic Campbell[73] is to be Lord Privy Seal for Scotland.[74] Lord Waldegrave, they say, chamberlain to the Queen.[75]

From HERTFORD, Tuesday 21 May 1765

Printed for the first time from a photostat of BM Add. MSS 23218, ff. 203–4.

Paris, May 21st 1765.

Dear Horry,

I OWE it to your friendship to say everything I think when you ask it,[1] and not to be silent if I could be vain enough to think my opinion of any use, even when you did not require it. In the present case I may speak without difficulty to you because I entirely approve your conduct. The management of the Regency Bill has been in my humble opinion a very weak and most singular transaction. I shall always blame a minister who does not well consider any public act he proposes, and when it is well weighed and undertaken I shall think he wants spirit or judgment if he has not resolution enough to carry it. I do not tell you my system would have been an exclusion to the Princess; I have not penetration enough to perceive the prudence of such an attempt in the ministers, and I have

72. Edward Thurlow (1731–1806), cr. (1778) Bn Thurlow. He was never chief secretary for Ireland; Weymouth, his protector, intended him for that position, but was forced to yield to the wishes of the Duke of Bedford, who wanted Bunbury for the post. See Namier and Brooke ii. 138, iii. 530; *Life and Letters of Lady Sarah Lennox*, ed. Lady Ilchester and Lord Stavordale, 1902, i. 170.

73. Lorne's brother.

74. He was nominated to the post by Grenville 23 May, after Lord Lorne had turned it down in his favour, being also entrusted with the management of Scotland, 'under certain limitations . . . but without access to the Closet' (Gilbert

Elliot's memorandum, in Jucker, op. cit. 373; *Grenville Papers* iii. 187). He resigned his post 23 July after the dismissal of the Grenville administration, and followed Grenville and Bedford into Opposition (Namier and Brooke ii. 182).

75. He was never chamberlain to the Queen, but was appointed master of the Horse to the Queen in 1770. HW writes in *Mem. Geo. III* ii. 129 that at this time 'the ministers proposed to make Lord Waldegrave or Lord Suffolk master of the Horse to the Queen. Her Majesty said no minister should interfere in *her* family, and named the Duke of Ancaster.'

1. *Ante* 12 May 1765.

still less to perceive the wisdom of those in Opposition to adopt it at their desire. As a man unconnected with any party I should think myself ill justified from common fame in stigmatizing by Parliament the King's mother. The most moderate disapprobation I should have showed to such a measure would have been by staying away, but if I could have persuaded my friends and was so far connected with a party in Opposition, I should have proposed reinstating her Royal Highness. It is therefore contrary to all ideas of mine that my brother should be led by old men and boys[2] to lend his name to so outra-geous and so provoking a reflection. When I have said that, I can only repeat my constant wishes and inclination to serve him. I am very sorry to have been so long politically separated from him. I think of it with pain because we both suffer from it, I suppose, in the opinion of mankind; but that matter is now over, and as we are formed by nature I suppose it was unavoidable. Whenever we meet again it will make me happy. I think the division of families a mis-fortune even in a political light, but I hope we love one another too well to let it proceed farther. I am grieved for everything I think an imprudence in him; perhaps he has a different way of condemning me. I have done remonstrating, it does not now become me; but I shall always take the same warm though silent part in promoting his interest to the utmost of my power, and I am con-cerned he should listen to such politicians as you name in preference to your friendly advice, which in my poor opinion would conduct him much better. I have not the same ambition I once had in poli-tics; my separation from my friends has made me more indifferent. I do my duty at the Court where I reside in a manner I think and hope not to be reproved by any party, and if any set of men dislike me and even recall me before my own term shall be elapsed without doing anything to mark the King's approbation of my conduct, I can retire with great resignation to the care of my family and af-fairs, and philosophize on politics, ambition, etc., etc., etc.

I long to see you and converse with you. It is impossible to say everything in a letter. You are acquainted with most of my senti-ments; I have acquired few or no new ones since I have been here. My private affairs may make it necessary for me to ask leave to return to England for a fortnight, and I propose it, but there is always some-thing which makes me defer it. I intend it however when business

2. The D. of Newcastle and the Cavendishes.

and the circumstances of my own family will properly admit of it, and it will be a great inducement to see you in England since you are not hasty in coming to Paris.

Adieu, my dear Horry; this goes by a messenger,[3] as you will imagine. It would ill become me in prudence to say so much to anyone but yourself; and I write in great haste.

Yours ever,

HERTFORD

From HERTFORD, Thursday 30 May 1765

Printed for the first time from a photostat of BM Add. MSS 23218, ff. 205–7.

Paris, May 30th 1765.

My dear Horry,

WHEN I complained[1] of not having heard from my friends in England, I did not admit a suspicion that you had not wrote, perhaps often, within the time I had named. I meant rather to inform you that the means of conveyance were not always certain in point of time. However, as soon as my letter was finished, many of those whose dates you mention[2] arrived. I have since examined my papers, and you may now rest assured that they are all safe in my hands. I have no letter of the 20th April, but I have one of the 18th, so I suppose that that may be the letter which you thought of the 20th, as there is so little difference in time.[3]

Your letter of the 20th,[4] which I received last night, I waited for with impatience, as I knew there had been a strange scene in London and that you would be so good to inform me with the particulars. The first notice I had of the re-establishment of the ancient and

3. It appears that in his haste Hertford has left out a word before 'messenger,' perhaps 'trustworthy.' The same day he wrote a letter to Halifax which he dispatched by William Pollock, a King's messenger (S.P. 78/266, f. 45; *ante* 22 March 1764, n. 11); presumably either Pollock could be trusted not to show to Halifax Hertford's letter to HW, or Hertford sent his letter to HW by another messenger.

1. *Ante* 16 May 1765.
2. *Ante* 20 May 1765.
3. HW's letter *ante* 18 April 1765 was concluded 20 April.
4. May.

present administration was from the Duke of Praslin, who received his letter from Guerchy whilst I was at Versailles, with the chief facts and changes, but without any reasoning, and indeed, I believe happily for our credit, foreigners are not easily acquainted with the dirty and disgraceful intrigues that are used upon such occasions. The reconciliation of Lord Temple, Mr Pitt and Mr Grenville[5] was not forgot. The eyes of all foreigners and politicians are upon one of those gentlemen; Pitt and war are esteemed almost synonymous terms. The Broglios[6] who intend to shine in the next troubles of Europe are curious to know if Mr Pitt is to be employed in the Cabinet; and the Comte[7] who supped with me last night has already got on his gala coat.

I have often told them they concluded too fast about our politics, and that we had often changed names and preserved the same system; but I believe when we talk pleasantly or seriously we do not often convince each other.

Monsieur de Guerchy's first servant has always brought me your letters very exactly upon their arrival at Paris, and he wrote me himself a very handsome note with one of the last packets to say how happy he was to find himself of any use in facilitating the correspondence between me and my friend. This I owe to him to say, though it will not induce you to send any letters by that means when you think any possible inconvenience can arise.

What can I say upon all this wonderful scene of the last month? There is no part of it that I approve except what you have told me of yourself, and in your last letter of my brother. It is a disgraceful scene for his Majesty, and has I think been miserably conducted from the opening to the conclusion. If I was to enter into particulars I should tire you with my poor observations. You may reason for me

5. Grenville's reconciliation with Lord Temple (*ante* 20 May 1765) did not extend to Pitt, at least not politically; though the three dined together at Hayes 30 May, it was agreed that 'their intercourse might be of a friendly domestic nature, without entering upon political topics' (Grenville's 'Diary,' *Grenville Papers* iii. 191). HW, in *Mem. Geo. III* ii. 124, suggests that Temple's reconciliation with Grenville was a function of his growing hostility to Pitt, whose greater political pre-eminence he resented; consequently, Pitt is to be viewed at this point as being politically separate not only from Grenville, but increasingly from Temple as well.

6. The Duc and Comte de Broglie. Hertford uses a variation of the original Piedmontese 'Broglia' formerly used by the family.

7. Charles-François de Broglie (1719–81), Comte de Broglie.

upon this occasion. I cannot however help confirming what you have so justly concluded, that I am made happy with knowing that my brother is restored to the King's favour. He is every way qualified to serve his Majesty and his country, but as much as I wish it, I should be sorry to see him embark upon a desperate foundation and without a stronger bottom than I can conceive at present without Mr Pitt. I am entirely of his and your opinion that he did wisely in refusing any of the great employments. Lord Weymouth is extremely welcome to go to Ireland. I will not dispute it with his *valet-de-chambre* at this moment. I am quiet here and it still answers the service of my family; when I think otherways I can retire to an easy fortune, and the day may come when the employment will be desirable for me on many accounts. If it never does, I am very easy. His Lordship goes at a very critical moment, and he must be very able or very fortunate if he succeeds in that kingdom; at this time I dare say you do not wish me to have it. When the King pleases to oblige me he may do it by placing me about his own person. I love my ease, and my chief or only ambition is to have credit or importance enough to serve my children.

Lady Holland supped here last night. Lady Hertford tells me she can perceive through all her coolness that she is stung with the sacrifice made of her husband to Mr Townshend. Lady Sarah seems as happy in proportion with the news she has received of Sir Charles Bunbury's promotion in Ireland.[8] Will you believe it, I cannot persuade a Frenchman to think her handsome, though she was in beauty last night.[9] They astonish me by answering that Lady Louisa has more beauty.[10] I beg you will not mention anything which I have said in this letter. I have a particular reason for it at present, which I will tell you if my suspicion appears hereafter to have any foundation. Adieu, dear Horry; let me hear from you now and then, though you have not always such histories to relate. This goes by

8. She wrote to Lady Susan O'Brien, 22 June, that the Bedfords 'making Lord Weymouth name Sir Charles his secretary to Ireland' made her 'vastly obliged to the Duke of Bedford' (*Life and Letters of Lady Sarah Lennox*, ed. Lady Ilchester and Lord Stavordale, 1902, i. 170).

9. 'If I don't tell you that I am *vastly* admired you will say I am mortified, and it's very certain I cannot say it, but I assure you I bear my misfortune very well' (Lady Sarah Bunbury to Lord Holland, May, ibid. i. 163).

10. Lady Holland wrote to Lady Kildare, 31 May, that Lady Louisa's 'being thought handsomer than Sarah, I own, does amaze me; but it's very general, even some who admire Sarah and know her, all say *Miladi Lousia est sans doute la plus belle*' (*Leinster Corr.* i. 429).

Sir John Lambert,[11] who has promised to carry it very safely. I re-main,

Most truly and affectionately yours,

Hertford

To Hertford, ca Saturday 1 June 1765

Missing; answered *post* 11 June 1765.

From Hertford, Tuesday 11 June 1765

Printed for the first time from a photostat of BM Add. MSS 23218, ff. 208–9.

Paris, June 11th 1765.

Dear Horry,

I HAVE just time to say by a messenger[1] whom I am going to send to England, that I am by no means determined upon my journey to London. My business will necessarily carry me there for a few days, but I do not know exactly when. I have put it off from time to time, and now the Court is going to Compiègne,[2] which though it is no objection, it still throws more difficulties in my way. If this is your only reason for deferring your journey to Paris,[3] I beg you will come, and I will promise you not to go to England till your return. I long to see you and you cannot take a better moment to see this place than at present. The town is now more easy, more empty and more quiet, which perhaps may answer your intentions better, and it is always full enough for the purposes of society.

---

11. English banker in Paris (*ante* 18 Aug. 1762).

---

1. Perhaps Thomas Sansom (d. 1772), King's messenger ca 1762–72, by whom Hertford sent his dispatch to Halifax of 12 June (*London Magazine* 1772, 1st ser. xli. 501; *Court and City Register* 1762–72 *passim;* S.P. 78/266, ff. 217–19).

2. At the beginning of July; see *post* 4 July 1765.

3. Presumably HW gave this reason in a missing letter to Hertford answering Hertford's letter, *ante* 21 May 1765. Another reason for deferring the journey is given in his letter to Montagu, 26 May 1765: 'I am thinking of my journey to France, but as Mr Conway has a mind I should wait for him, I don't know whether it will take place before the autumn' (Montagu ii. 154).

Operas and plays never cease, and we have a new actor[4] and a good one to entertain you. In the meantime I beg you will continue to write; your letters are a great comfort to a man at a distance from his friends, and I will determine upon no motion to England without giving you full and sufficient notice. Perhaps if my affairs do not require it I may defer it for some months; it is quite uncertain, therefore I must insist upon it that in friendship for Lady Hertford and myself you do not think about it. Does my brother not intend to make us a visit whilst we are in France?[5]

I am not surprised at the news you tell me from St James's.[6] If I was King I should certainly serve you and every friend who I thought most capable of doing my business or most deserving of my favour; I would lose my crown sooner than my power. I wish, as his Majesty begins to dispose of offices, that he would take this opportunity of restoring my brother. I see by the papers[7] there is a vacancy by Sir R. Rich's death;[8] and I will love him for it.

Ireland I fancy will be troublesome enough. I should not be jealous, because I do not at this moment desire it; the circumstances in general are not favourable to my mind; but still I will not con-

---

4. Jean Rival (1728–1804), called Aufresne; Swiss actor. He made his début 30 May at the Comédie-Française in the role of Auguste in Corneille's *Cinna*. His style was notable for its simplicity and naturalness, in contrast to the prevailing mode at the Comédie. Though received as a *sociétaire* 29 June, he left the troupe before the end of the year and spent the rest of his career performing successfully throughout Europe (*Enciclopedia dello spettacolo*, Rome, 1954–62, i. 1126–7; *Dictionnaire de biographie française*, 1933–, iv. 483; Grimm, *Correspondance*, ed. Tourneux, 1877–82, vi. 298–300, 316–17, 415–16).

5. See n. 3 above.

6. HW wrote to Mann, 26 June 1765, that after being 'obliged to take back his old ministers,' the King 'not only smiled on the Opposition, but bestowed every employment that fell on the Duke of Cumberland's or Lord Bute's friends' (MANN vi. 306–7). On 29 May the Duke of Ancaster had been named master of the Horse to the Queen, contrary to the wishes of the ministers, who wanted Lord

Waldegrave or Lord Suffolk for the post (*ante* 20 May 1765, n. 75; SELWYN 186–7; *Grenville Papers* iii. 190–1); and on 31 May Gen. William Keppel, brother of Lord Albemarle, chief follower of Cumberland, was named colonel of the 14th Foot, a post left vacant by the death of Gen. Charles Jefferyes (*Army Lists* 1765, p. 67; 1766, p. 68; *Mem. Geo. III* ii. 129; MS cited in Sir William Musgrave, *Obituary*, ed. Armytage, 1899–1901, iii. 318).

7. E.g., the *Daily Adv.* 7 June and the *London Chronicle* 4–6 June, xvii. 541, *sub* 6 June.

8. A false report; Sir Robert Rich, 4th Bt, field marshal, governor of Chelsea Hospital, and colonel of the 4th Dragoons (*ante* 28 Jan. 1759 bis; *Army Lists* 1765, p. 28; *Court and City Register* 1765, p. 193), did not die until 1768. However, he was apparently near death; on 5 June Grenville had recommended Gen. John Mostyn to succeed Rich as governor of Chelsea Hospital, and on 7 June he recommended Lord Robert Manners for his Dragoons, 'in case they became vacant' (*Grenville Papers* iii. 193).

ceal from you that I do not think Lord Weymouth a proper person for it. The moment may perhaps be a delicate one, and I do not think his Lordship has age, dignity, experience or any other peculiar advantage to remove prejudices and impose upon a people who are disposed to be troublesome and to find fault.

Lady Hertford and the family desire their best compliments. I remain, dear Horry,

Most truly and affectionately yours,

Hertford

Pray make my best compliments to Lady Harrington,[9] and tell her I heartily wish Lady Caroline all sort of happiness.

From Hertford, Thursday 20 June 1765

Printed for the first time from a photostat of BM Add. MSS 23218, ff. 210–13.

Paris, June 20th 1765.

Dear Horry,

YOUR friendship will readily excuse me for desiring your opinion and advice upon a family occasion; it is an interesting one to me, as it regards the happiness of a child[1] whose merit and good qualities have particularly recommended her to my affection. There is at present in this place a Mr Forbes,[2] with whom you may possibly have some little acquaintance, though it is more likely you will know him only by name; his life as an officer has thrown him out of your way, and he still serves his Majesty in the Foot Guards.[3] He is son to Lord Forbes,[4] only son I should say to be precise, and grandson to Lord Granard.[5] He married one of the Miss Bailies[6] without the

9. On the engagement of her eldest daughter, Lady Caroline Stanhope, to Kenneth Mackenzie, styled Vct Fortrose (ante 5 May 1753, n. 25). They were married 7 Oct.

1. His eldest daughter, Lady Anne Seymour-Conway.
2. George Forbes (1740–80), styled Vct Forbes as of the day before this letter was written (19 June) due to the death of his

grandfather, Lord Granard (see below and post 4 July 1765); 5th E. of Granard 1769.
3. He held the rank of lieutenant and captain in the 3d Foot Guards (Army Lists, 1765, p. 49).
4. George Forbes (1710–69), styled Vct Forbes 1734–65; now 4th E. of Granard.
5. George Forbes (1685 – 19 June 1765), styled Vct Forbes 1704–34; 3d E. of Granard 1734.
6. Dorothea Bayly (1738–64), sister of

consent of his family, for which he has never been forgiven by the old Earl. He had three children by that lady before [s]he died, one of whom, a boy,[7] is still living. This gentleman has, by means of an acquaintance[8] of his at Paris who is known to Lady Hertford, proposed for my eldest daughter, saying he had not or should ever name it to any person without I approved it; that his grandfather had acquainted him he wished him to settle, either by marrying a great fortune or allying himself with some good family, and that in order to satisfy his own inclination as well as to please his family he wished it could be with my daughter. My answer was that he did me and my daughter great honour in making choice of her under such circumstances, but that I could not at present see any probability of such a proposal being accepted by her friends; that my ideas with respect to the marriage of my daughters did not allow me to aspire to Dukes and the first persons only of my country, but that I could still never consent to the marriage of my daughter without seeing a certainty of ease in point of fortune for her and her children; that my own circumstances enabled me to give her moderate satisfaction in that respect whilst she was single, and that therefore, with the pleasure I should have in making her happy, I could never consent to a prospect of her being otherways. That he had a son born by another woman, who if he lived must enjoy his title, and that I could never be tempted to contribute towards the prejudice of that child. His answer was that Lord Granard would never forgive his first marriage nor give his estates to the child which proceeded from it;[9] that Lord Granard had six or seven thousand pounds a year in present and in future, had fifty or sixty thousand pounds in the funds, and that I should be quite satisfied I did nothing to the prejudice to that boy if he lived, and that if I had no objection to his character or personal qualities he did not doubt but he could satisfy me in point of fortune. I told him I had not the honour of a sufficient acquaintance with either to determine my opinion; that from his behaviour I was

Henry, 1st E. of Uxbridge, and 2d daughter of Sir Nicholas Bayly, 2d Bt; m. (1759) George Forbes, afterwards 5th E. of Granard. Her sisters were Mary Bayly (d. 1790); Caroline Bayly (d. 1786); Gertrude Bayly (d. 1761); and Louisa Augusta Bayly (b. 1750) (Collins, *Peerage*, 1812, v. 198).

7. George Forbes (1760–1837), styled Vct

Forbes 1769–80; 6th E. of Granard 1780. The 5th Earl's other children by Dorothea Bayly are not mentioned ibid. ix. 324, where the 6th Earl is called his 'only . . . son' by her.

8. Not identified.

9. However, he could not prevent this child from succeeding as the 6th E. of Granard (n. 7 above).

inclined to think partially of both, but that in a case of such moment as this he would excuse me that I did my duty in the strictest manner by inquiring, and giving her the advice of a father; and that as things now stood I thought there was but little appearance of its succeeding. He desired he might have leave to write to his parents.[10] I told him, provided my name was no otherways used than as father to my girl, I could not reasonably object, and he sent me the letter to show me it was wrote according to my instructions.

My daughter knows nothing of it. He perhaps never spoke to her, nor has she the least suspicion of his wishes or intention. His behaviour has been very respectful and proper. He comes no otherways than as a formal visitor to Lady Hertford, nor has he a young acquaintance that knows his inclinations.

Thus it stands, and that I may be prepared to answer properly and to act under any circumstances in which this proposal may be made to me by the consent or commands of his parents, I must beg you to learn in England his behaviour and character to this time.[11] I have every sort of refusal in my power, and my daughter [is] always reasonable and obedient, but it is my duty to neglect nothing by which her happiness can be advanced when I see a prospect of it. What he proposed by his friend, who is an elderly sober man, was to leave the Army in case he married and settle as I should direct; but before I consent to take that direction, I must be well informed in all particulars.

If it does not succeed, we mean never to name it, and he it seems goes into Italy. I will beg you therefore to communicate this matter to none but my brother, and to avoid the trouble of writing so long a letter a second time, I will beg he may know it from you.

I will pay Lady Stanhope for your medals[12] the first moment that I can. Excuse all this trouble; you love to do generous acts, and I have the greatest dependence on your friendship.

Yours ever,

HERTFORD

10. His mother was Letitia Davys (d. 1778), m. (1736) George Forbes, 4th E. of Granard.

11. The following year he eloped with his second wife, Georgiana Augusta Berkeley, eldest daughter of the 4th E.

of Berkeley, who, according to her sister, the Margravine of Anspach, fell in love with and proposed to him (GEC vi. 57 and n. 'a').

12. See *ante* 20 May 1765.

Mr Hume is at last made secretary to this Embassy.[13] I believe you will think I did right in expressing myself plainly upon this occasion, when Sir C. Bunbury was removed;[14] it would not have become me to be disappointed a second time,[15] and I have no reason to think myself a favourite at present.

13. His commission as secretary is dated 3 July; he was chargé d'affaires between Hertford's departure in July and the arrival of the new ambassador, the Duke of Richmond, in November (see *post* 29 Nov. 1765, n. 7; D. B. Horn, *British Diplomatic Representatives 1689–1789*, 1932, p. 22). The commission of his successor as secretary, Lord George Henry Lennox, is dated 16 Aug. 1765 (ibid. 23).

14. To become secretary to Lord Weymouth in Ireland (*ante* 20, 30 May 1765).

15. The first time being in 1763 when he had failed to have Hume named in place of Bunbury, who had been appointed without his knowledge or approval (*ante* 18 Oct. 1763, n. 11).